Down a Country Lane

Dennis G. Raible

A Camden County Historical Society Publication

Camden, N.J.

The scriptwork above was derived from Haddon Township's first book of Town Meeting minutes.

Substantial contributions for publication were received from two sources:

In recognition of the 135th anniversary of incorporation of Haddon Township (February 23rd, 1865), the citizens proudly lend their support towards publication of *Down a Country Lane.*

William J. Park, Jr., Mayor
Nicholas J. Laurito, Commissioner
Charles V. DiPietropolo, Commissioner

With the publication of *Down a Country Lane,* the Camden County Historical Society commemorates its 100th anniversary. Funding has been made possible, in part, through a grant from the Society's William G. Rohrer Publication Fund and the generosity of the members, contributors, employees, past and present trustees and our volunteers, who continue to support the work of the Society into its second century.

Paul W. Schopp, Executive Director

Camden, NJ. Camden County Historical Society, 1999

ISBN 0-916101-31-2

Preface

In 1865, the New Jersey Legislature created the Township of Haddon from the eastern portion of Newton Township. The newly formed municipality reached its largest geographical size some six years later, when yet more land was annexed by the township. In 1871, Haddon Township included all of what is now Audubon, Audubon Park, Collingswood, Haddon Township, Oaklyn, Woodlynne, most of what is now Haddonfield and portions of Haddon Heights, Camden and Gloucester City.

The majority of the township in the nineteenth century was occupied by farms; however, few signs of the bygone physical features have survived. The modern day communities that evolved from "old" Haddon Township have developed to a point where, today, it is difficult to tell where one leaves off and another begins. The farms, barns, hot-houses, corn-cribs, apple-orchards, gristmills and blacksmith shops no longer exist. It is the intent of this project to view the past through the scattered pieces of evidence that remain.

The geographical sphere of the work encompasses the land now within the ten modern day municipalities that unfolded from the 1870s Haddon Township. The project's focus is on the people, places, physical geography, agriculture, industry, commerce, events, institutions, life styles, and issues of the era.

The span of years covered begins with the Civil War and continues through the 1870s, a period when the nation experienced dramatic changes that permanently altered the economic, political and social landscape of America. New technologies evolved in transportation, communication, manufacturing and farming. The country was in transition. Agriculture began to decline, while industrialization began to expand. Overall, the population was shifting from the farms and small villages to the cities. To a lesser extent, reverse migration from the cities to newly-built suburbs was just starting.

In many ways, life in old Haddon Township mirrored that of the rest of the country. Across the nation, the vast majority of the population was white in 1870. The bulk of the white population, mostly Protestants, were of northern European extraction. Three-quarters of the nation's people were living on farms or in towns of less than 2,500 people. There were about 2.6 million farms at that time.

African-Americans did not fare as well as whites. Even though the Civil War had resolved the issue of slavery, African-Americans still had not achieved equality. They often resided in substandard housing and the life expectancy of African-Americans was substantially less than that of whites.

America's industrial economy grew remarkably during the period, changing cities, suburbs, factories, transportation, farms and family life-styles. In many instances, mass-produced goods were now marketed on a national scale. The need for material items became more commonplace, due in part to the emergence of marketing. Increasingly, new demands of consumers for goods were now satisfied with mass-produced commodities such as food products, construction components, farming implements, clothing and even horse-drawn vehicles. For most citizens, the standard of living steadily improved over the last quarter of the 1800s.

A number of disparate topics are offered in Part I of this study, including the progression and development of events leading to formation of Newton and Haddon Townships. The text charts the progress of the township's commercial, political and cultural hub, the village of Haddonfield. The villages of Rowandtown, now known as Westmont, Collingswood and Stonetown are also studied.

Suburbia eventually unfolded along two railroad right-of-ways that connected Camden and Atlantic City. The railroad companies encouraged city dwellers to relocate to planned communities that were growing near the railroad stations. Most of the present-day communities fashioned from old Haddon Township grew around nearby railroad depots. The railroad's extraordinary impact in shaping the region, and how nineteenth century commuters and farmers took to it, are examined in this work.

The other themes scrutinized in the project are the township's roadways and their significance to the region; usefulness of Cooper's Creek and the three branches of Newton Creek; use of Camden's ferries; and the types of horse-drawn vehicles that traveled on the roadways. Education, the public school system, private schools, churches and meeting houses about the township are also explored.

Important events and issues of the day are analyzed from a local perspective. The subjects include the Civil War; treatment of African-Americans and the controversy over civil rights laws; the ban on the sale of liquor; women's causes; choice of currency; the deplorable condition of the local fire company; the heated issue of whether to incorporate Haddonfield; improper burials at the township's public graveyard; and the debate about a bridge that many did not bargain for. This book also examines nineteenth century instruments of communication—newspapers, telegraph and telephone. Leisure activities; the fanfare created by the Philadelphia Centennial Exhibition; the routine of a young township farmer; the interplay of the neighboring villages; and the overall importance of Camden and Philadelphia are also weighed.

Farmers laboring in the fields were familiar sights to a nineteenth century observer in old Haddon Township. Farm families lived by the rhythm of agriculture. Time was measured by the changing seasons and crop planting and harvest cycles. Farmers and their helpers dominated the employment scene. Even the non-farm jobs, for the most part, serviced the agricultural community. Because of the overriding importance of agriculture, Part II of this book charts husbandry related matters such as the nearby markets, crops and farm products grown by local farmers, livestock, farm labor, farming tools and the various supporting outbuildings around the township.

Besides agricultural products, many nineteenth century necessities were manufactured within the township. Part II of this study also examines the township's commercial facets. Water- and steam-powered mills once ground wheat into flour and cut lumber for local inhabitants; clay bricks were made at two brickyards; drainage tiles for diverting water away from the fields were fashioned locally; wagons, carriages and carts were assembled at a handful of wheelwright shops; plows and farming implements were repaired at blacksmith shops; and paint and varnish products were manufactured at two paint works. A Haddonfield tanner purchased hides and skins from nearby farmers and turned them into leather for use by local shoemakers in making boots and shoes; the harnessmaker cut and stitched leather into saddles and harnesses; a tinsmith punched-out small metallic items for households and installed metal roofs; a handful of tailors made men's vests, pants and coats; clay was molded into earthenware at a pottery; and a master weaver made rag carpets on his looms. The local barrelmaker made containers from oak staves and filled them with vinegar, wine and apple cider. "Applejack," a controversial alcoholic beverage that was made in a still, was another favorite South Jersey beverage. One township entrepreneur processed paper for photographic use, and sold it in Philadelphia. Inhabitants could even expect to be buried in a coffin or a burial box assembled by one of several Haddonfield cabinetmakers.

This work reconstructs the history of commerce in the 1870s, even though the industry or occupations have long vanished. A description of the types of goods manufactured, as well as nineteenth century techniques of manufacturing or applying a trade, have been researched and recounted.

More than half of old Haddon Township's residents lived in the village of Haddonfield in the mid-1870s. The village, with its beautiful tree-lined Main Street (Kings Highway), was also the center of commerce in the township. Merchants and service-oriented professionals worked among shoemakers, blacksmiths and wheelwrights. The 1870s village was the site of a number of general and hardware stores, butcher shops, bakeries, confectioneries, dressmakers and drug stores. Travelers could find food and shelter at any of the four hotels along Main Street. A scattering of professionals such as physicians, surveyors, conveyancers, real estate and insurance agents and postmasters worked in Haddonfield. These nineteenth century merchants, tradesmen and professionals, as well as others, are presented in this work to better enable readers to comprehend the era under study.

The ten modern-day communities that evolved from old Haddon Township are presented in separate chapters in Part III. A reader interested in studying the 1870s landholders, farmers and topography of the area, can focus on the appropriate chapter. One can relate today's landscape to the 1870s geography by the property boundaries of the one-time farms presented in terms of today's topography. The sites where former dwellings and outbuildings were once found, and other geographic features are pinpointed. Being acquainted with nineteenth century landscape, one can assess what has transpired in the area over time. Anecdotes and portraits of the landowners and tenants are also provided to help readers connect with the experiences of ordinary people who were the lifeblood of old Haddon Township.

Although the period of analysis concludes at a time when old Haddon Township was still a farming community in the early 1880s, many components were in place that soon caused transformation of the landscape into the residential communities that exist today. The 1880s was a decade in which the township's long-time economic mainstay, agriculture, began to recede. This writing attempts to document the impact of some changes on the inhabitants of old Haddon Township.

During the last fifteen years of the nineteenth century, more and more old farms were lost to residential development. As new housing began to arise across the township, the evolving communities required municipal improvements, police and fire protection that the Haddon Township was unwilling or unable to provide. In 1875, Haddonfield took its first step toward political independence to raise monies to build suitable sidewalks and streets. After the Borough of Haddonfield was carved from Haddon Township in 1875, the boroughs of Collingswood (1888), Woodlynne (1901), Haddon Heights (1904), Oaklyn (1905) and Audubon (including what later became Audubon Park [1905]) withdrew from the township. As Haddonfield's population continued to grow in the 1900s, the borough's governing body obtained other lands from the township. Along the western edge of the township, several former farms were ceded to Camden (1918) and Gloucester City (1927). Land that was not ceded or sold to the new communities, now makes up the modern-day Haddon Township.

It is the author's desire to depict places, events, occupations and inhabitants of old Haddon Township in a manner that portrayed things in the context of the times. Primary- and secondary-source documents are freely quoted to present a colloquial voice and to furnish background to the text. To this end, contemporaneous books, newspaper reports and advertisements, diaries, journals, account ledgers, tax ledgers, census data, surveys, maps and public documents were heavily utilized in researching and writing the book.

Hopefully, readers will enjoy a better understanding of how the one-time agricultural region once looked and grasp what nineteenth century life in old Haddon Township was like.

Dennis G. Raible
Haddon Township, NJ
February, 1999

Acknowledgments

During the long period devoted to research and writing this work, I have had the help from many people and institutions. I am especially grateful to Paul W. Schopp, Executive Director and Librarian at the Camden County Historical Society, and Katherine Tassini, Librarian for the Historical Society of Haddonfield. Throughout the years of research, they gave me their assistance in locating source documents and tracking down information for the project. A group of local historians (the West Jersey History Roundtable) have given me the benefit of their knowledge and insight into the history of the region. The members include William Farr, Edward Fox, Peter Hamilton, William Leap, David Munn and Paul Schopp. Dr. Randall Miller of Saint Joseph's University was kind enough to review, make substantive suggestions and edit the chapters on the Civil War and African-Americans. I am indebted to him for his assistance.

I would like to extend special thanks to the following: Kathy Tassini, Historical Society of Haddonfield; Marguritte Bennett, Haddon Township; Peter Childs, Collingswood Library; Linda Freedman, William G. Rohrer Memorial Library, Camden County Library System; Joseph Nicholson Hartell, Haddonfield; Historical Society of Pennsylvania; Edith Hoelle, Gloucester County Historical Society; Robert Hunter, Haddon Heights Historical Society; Rita Masters, Haddon Township, and Douglas Rauschenberger, Haddonfield Library; James Reilly, Rochester, NY; Rutgers University Libraries and Joanne Diogo, Camden County Historical Society. I interviewed three individuals that had first hand recollections of people discussed in this publication. I would like to thank Joseph Nicholson Hartell, Haddonfield; Marie Miller, Haddon Township; and Charles Whiley, Collingswood for sharing their stories with me.

I am grateful to John Stanton of MogoArt in Dallas, Texas for conceiving and designing the artwork on the cover. I wish to thank my cartographer, Denise Fox, for her excellent maps.

Further, I offer my thanks to Dominic M. Roberti for converting the typed manuscript into its present form. Carole Roberti was generous with her editorial advice.

I am grateful to Paul W. Schopp for his help outside his official duties at the Camden County Historical Society. He rounded up many of the sources and provided his insight in many areas of the manuscript. Paul also made editorial suggestions and helped prepare the manuscript for final publication. He supported me throughout the project and was always there to hear and respond to my questions and thoughts.

To my editor, David Munn I am greatly indebted for encouragement and support. Dave did a magnificent job of editing the book. He patiently read the manuscript, making many corrections and suggestions. He was very diligent ensuring the text of the manuscript had a sound historical prospective.

Finally, I would like to thank my wife Sharon and our children Eric, Jeffery and Kevin for their patience and unfailing support.

Abbreviations, Terminology and Notes

Abbreviations used in Citing Sources

The abbreviations that follow are used throughout the book.

Newspapers:

CD—*Camden Democrat*

CDP–*Camden Daily Post*

CP—*Courier-Post*

HB—*Haddonfield Basket*

LBGA—*Letter Basket and General Advertiser*

NR—*New Republic*

WJP—*West Jersey Press*

Other Sources:

ARSPS—*Annual Report of the Superintendent of Public Schools*

Boyer—Charles Boyer's *Annals of Camden*

HSP—Historical Society of Pennsylvania

Inv.—Inventory of Personal Property filed with the Camden County Surrogate's Office

MPWNJ—"Market Products of West New Jersey" *Report of the Commissioner of Agriculture for the Year 1865*

Prowell—George Prowell's *The History of Camden County, New Jersey*

Rowand—Jacob Rowand's Fire Insurance Surveys–Historical Society of Haddonfield

TC—Minutes of Township Committee meetings–Haddon Township

TM—Minutes of Town Meetings–Haddon Township

Will—Wills filed with the Camden County Surrogate's Office

Nineteenth Century Terminology

Throughout the text, the names of nineteenth century roads, creeks and place names are utilized. The following are nineteenth century names referenced to their respective modern day names.

Roadways & Creeks:

Atmore's Road–Lees Lane

Brick Kiln Road–Hopkins Road

Blackwoodtown Turnpike–Black Horse Pike/Mt. Ephraim Avenue

Clement's Bridge Road–Chews Landing Road

Coles Landing Road–Locust Street/Coles Mill Road

Collings Road–Collings Avenue

Cooper's Creek–Cooper River

Crystal Lake Road–Crystal Lake Avenue

Dobbs Road–Lees Lane

Gloucester Road–Collings Avenue

Haddonfield Road–Haddon Avenue

Haddonfield Turnpike–Haddon Avenue

Haddonfield & Camden Turnpike–Haddon Avenue

Haddonfield & Mt. Ephraim Road–Kings Highway (outside the village of Haddonfield)

Hopkins Avenue–Hopkins Road

Hopkins Mill Road–Maple Avenue (Haddon Township & Haddonfield)

Main Street–Kings Highway (downtown Haddonfield)

Mill Road–Cuthbert Road, Cuthbert Boulevard

Mt. Ephraim & Haddonfield Road–Kings Highway (outside the village of Haddonfield)

Mt. Ephraim Turnpike–Black Horse Pike/Mt. Ephraim Avenue

Snow Hill Road–Warwick Road

Stoy's Landing Road–Grove Street (outside the village of Haddonfield)

Stoy's Mill Road–Crystal Lake Avenue

Stoy's Road–Crystal Lake Avenue

White Horse Road (Turnpike)–White Horse Pike

Willis Lane–Cooper Street (Haddon Township)

Municipalities:

"Old" Haddon Township—The author's general designation for 1870s Haddon Township including what is now now Audubon, Audubon Park, Collingswood, Haddon Township, Oaklyn, Woodlynne, most of Haddonfield and portions of Camden, Gloucester City and Haddon Heights.

Snow Hill—Lawnside

Village of Haddonfield—The area within several blocks to each side of Kings Highway and between Chews Landing Road and Cooper River.

Village of Rowandtown—The area along Haddon Avenue, between Maple Avenue and Cuthbert Road, in Westmont.

Other Text Notes

In order to assist readers in locating related topics or additional discussion of individuals elsewhere in the text, page references are inserted throughout the book noting the location of the addition information.

In most instances, quotes from newspapers and other sources were not edited. Nineteenth century spelling remains unchanged. In some instances, parenthetical notes were inserted within quotes to clarify the newspaper text.

Numerical references are utilized in Part III to correlate nineteenth century landholders, an 1877 map of the township and the property's whereabouts on a modern-day map.

Contents

I

Old Haddon Township

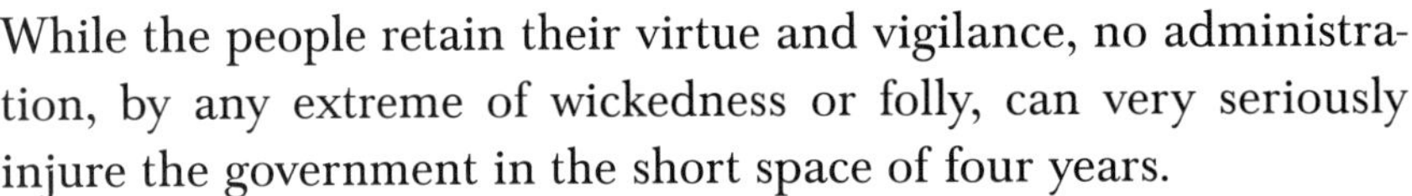

While the people retain their virtue and vigilance, no administration, by any extreme of wickedness or folly, can very seriously injure the government in the short space of four years.

Abraham Lincoln,
First Inaugural Address, March 4, 1861

1

The Municipal Landscape

A group of Quakers left Dublin, Ireland in 1681, sailed to America and landed near what is now Salem, New Jersey. After waiting out most of the winter, the assemblage of future Newton landholders once again boarded a boat for the comparatively short journey up the Delaware River and into Newton Creek. They had chosen plots of land in what was known as West Jersey. The names of these settlers were Thomas Sharp, Thomas Thackara, William Bates, George Goldsmith, and Mark Newbie. Many of the first settlers built their homes along creeks to be near the main transportation routes. Another early inhabitant arrived in 1701 to oversee her father's land. Still in her early twenties, Elizabeth Haddon settled near Cooper's Creek in an area that became known as Haddonfield.

As more and more settlers came to New Jersey, it became necessary to delineate boundaries within the region. Representatives of the settlers met in Gloucester Town (Gloucester City) in 1686 and organized a county named Gloucester. The new county included what is now Atlantic, Camden and Gloucester Counties. Gloucester Town was chosen as the county seat. By 1700, a jail and courthouse were erected to facilitate the needs of the new county. In 1694, the county was divided into townships, one being Newton Township. The township's borders were the Delaware River to what is now Haddonfield and between the South Branch of Newton Creek and Cooper River.

In 1682, the Quaker community of Philadelphia was laid out directly across the Delaware River from Newton Township. During the late 1680s, ferries were established for passage across the river between West Jersey and the "City of Brotherly Love." By the mid-eighteenth century a network of roads branched out from the ferry landings to the interior regions of West Jersey. One road was an early Indian trail that ran between Haddonfield and the ferry at Cooper's Point. It is now known as Haddon Avenue.

Early in the eighteenth century, a small village formed near where Elizabeth Haddon had settled. By the middle of the century a marketplace came about and a number of tradesmen had established themselves in the village of Haddonfield. The town stood near the head of navigation of Cooper's Creek, where the creek was shallow enough to wade across. The tidal creek was used to ship cordwood, lumber, logs and farm goods out to the Delaware River, and over to Philadelphia.

Newton Township's population grew slowly in the decades following the Revolutionary War. It was not until the early 1800s that the town of Camden began to unfold along the Delaware River. In 1828, the City of Camden was incorporated, although it remained within Newton Township. One of the reasons for setting up the new municipal status was to escape Haddonfield's domination of the governmental affairs within Newton Township. The new boundaries of the city were Little

Newton Creek (south of what is now Kaighns Avenue), the Delaware River, Cooper's Creek, and today's Federal Street, Newton Avenue and Broadway. Three years later, an act of the Legislature created a separate township out of the City of Camden, thereby all ties to Newton Township were finally severed.

By the late 1700s, Gloucester Town's fortunes had declined. After fire destroyed the county courthouse and jail, inhabitants of Gloucester County voted to move the seat of government to Woodbury. In 1844, the northern portion of Gloucester County was set off and called Camden County. The new county included Newton Township. A number of influential Camden politicians and businessmen pushed to bring Camden County's seat of government to their city. To the surprise of many citizens of the county, a vote on the issue brought the county government to Longacoming, now called Berlin. The political heavyweights of Camden were not satisfied with the outcome. In the late 1840s, Camden officials successfully convinced state legislators to place the issue on the whereabouts of the county seat on the ballot once again. When the results from the voters were tallied, Camden had wrestled the county seat away from Longacoming.

When Camden became a separate township, Newton Township's seat of government became Haddonfield. By the mid-1860s, Newton Township began to unravel.

Haddon Township

Just months before the end of the Civil War on February 23, 1865, the eastern portion of Newton Township was split off by an act of the New Jersey Legislature and the Township of Haddon was created. The area of the newly created township, comprised of 5,286 acres, included all land to the south and east of Collings Road (Collings Avenue), that had formerly been Newton Township. The new township included land that is within today's Oaklyn, Audubon, Audubon Park, Haddon Township and portions of Collingswood, Gloucester City, Fairview, Camden, Haddon Heights, and Haddonfield.

Changes in the way elections were held may have been part of the reason for splitting Newton Township. In the mid-1840s, the New Jersey Legislature enacted election reform legislation which changed the practice of holding general elections on two days each at different locations within the state's townships. The purpose of the new statute was to reduce costs and the likelihood of fraud by providing for a single voting place in each township. Over a period of years, the law forced many townships to divide into smaller political units. From 1798 to 1843 the number of townships in the state increased by 43. During the 1850s, 37 townships were created, with 58 more erected during the 1860s. (*County Governing Bodies in New Jersey*, p. 43)

Another reason for dividing Newton Township was residents of the eastern part of the township desired a greater degree of control over governing their affairs. The western district of Newton Township, with about 1,000 more residents, potentially had more political clout then the eastern section.

Many municipal housekeeping matters were addressed when Haddon Township was created. The act creating the township provided that any money on hand, property and indebtedness of Newton Township were to be apportioned between the new and old townships based upon the 1864 taxable valuations of property in each township. Although the area that remained in Newton Township had about a thousand more people than Haddon Township, its property values were only 44 percent of the combined townships' assessed values. (TC 4/10/1865)

Edward Bettle presided over the new township's first Town Meeting, held a few weeks after the incorporation. Bettle, an influential politician, may have had a hand in forming the new township. In 1866, he was elected to the State Senate. Several years later, he became President of the New Jersey State Senate. [See Edward Bettle, page 267]

Citizens enfranchised to vote in general elections and having resided in township for at least five months were qualified to vote for the township's governing body at the Annual Town Meetings. Five citizens were elected annually to serve on the Township Committee. The Township Committee oversaw the expenditures of all monies raised through taxation as well as any monies raised by the township's officers. The elected officers were Justice of the Peace, Judge of Election, Township Clerk, Assessor, Collector, Chosen Freeholder, Surveyor of Highway, Commissioners of Appeal, Constable, Overseer of the Poor, Poundkeeper, Township Physician, Overseer of Highways, and School Superintendent.

Upon formation, Haddon Township officials formed a committee to work with Newton Township representatives on matters such as collecting delinquent taxes and repayment of "old" Newton Township bonds. Representatives from the townships met periodically for several years to resolve issues such as maintenance of Collings Road, the boundary line between the two townships. The townships agreed to share maintenance costs on the road. Another logistical matter was establishing a border between Haddonfield Road (Haddon Avenue), at Collings Road, and Cooper's Creek.

Although the Civil War would be over in a matter of months, Haddon Township's officials spoke of the need to supply recruits and substitutes for President Lincoln's call for 300,000 men across the Union in 1865. Over most of South Jersey and throughout the Union states, governing officials attempted to raise money for new recruits. Of all the issues that were considered by newly elected township officials, top priority was given to fulfilling an obligation to provide men for the army.

Another issue of priority contained in township minutes was raising the necessary funds to pay the township's expenditures. The township's 1865 tax assessment records reveal about $17,000 was raised from real and personal property taxes. The township's assessment was at a rate of $1.25 per $100 of property value in 1865. Residents were also taxed on the value of their portfolio of stocks and bonds. An additional $10.00 poll tax was assessed on most township men. The largest tax bill in the new township was on the Estate of Samuel C. Champion. The heirs of the 300-acre tract on Collings Road paid $469.50 in taxes.

Following their election at the first town meeting, the township's officers began performing their duties. The majority of monies raised for township purposes came from a tax on property. The Tax Assessor's duty was to determine the value of real and personal property subject to taxation. The Commissioners of Appeal held hearings on unjust tax assessments.

In addition to a tax on real estate and personal property in 1869, the township raised money with a special school tax, fees on tavern owners and users of rooms in Town Hall. A tax on dogs was instituted to reimburse the owners of sheep killed by roaming canines. The Tax Collector, in addition to collecting township tax receipts, also collected taxes on behalf of the county. On average, about 70 percent of the funds collected by the township's Tax Collector during the 1870s went to the state and county. What was left over paid the day-to-day expenditures of the township such as road repairs and contributions to the public school system.

The Township Clerk kept the minutes of Town Meetings. Among the duties of the Clerk were notifying residents of town meetings, keeping ballot records, and swearing in officers. The Judge of Election challenged every voter they suspected or knew was not qualified to vote. The Overseer of Highways hired laborers, horses, wagons, etc. to keep the township's roadways in good order. The Surveyor of Highways assessed damages to owners' land or buildings when roadways were altered or repaired. The Superintendent of Schools monitored the public school system.

Records reveal township officials were often benevolent towards less fortunate residents. The Overseer of the Poor determined which residents qualified for an allowance from the township. They had the authority to build, purchase or rent a poor house. They approved hand-outs of medicine to the poor and paid for coffins to bury paupers. In one year, the community reimbursed a resident for the cost of nursing a non-resident "colored man" who had suffered from smallpox. (TC 5/20/1865) During the 1870s, the township donated $1.50 annually to the mother of a "deformed person" so she could maintain and support her son. (TM 3/12/1873)

Even though it was only part-time, the Justice of the Peace held many responsibilities. He might be compared to a modern-day municipal judge. He was charged with conserving the peace that included powers to enforce, imprison and punish lawbreakers. The Constable was the nineteenth century policeman. The township's first Constable, James Middleton, received $25 a year as compensation for his part-time services.

Unlike today's method of electing County Freeholders at large, nineteenth century Chosen Freeholders were elected by each township to represent their constituents in county matters. Some responsibilities of the county were caring for the poor and insane and overseeing the county's prisons, court system and public roads.

The township's Poundkeeper was in charge of impounding stray dogs and livestock wandering unattended along the roadways. Laws against stray animals existed throughout New Jersey going back to the mid-eighteenth century. Livestock that roamed freely caused crop damage and was a sure way to anger a neighbor. Any citizen could take horses, cattle, sheep or swine found running at large on public highways to the poundkeeper. In 1874, the reward paid to anyone that rounded up stray livestock amounted to twelve cents for each horse or cattle, five cents for each sheep and twenty-five cents for swine. Before an owner recovered his animals, he had to reimburse the poundkeeper for impounding, boarding and feeding. If an owner did not claim his animals within four days, the poundkeeper could sell the livestock.

Local statutes, however, did not address problems of fowl running at large. Unattended fowl could also cause damage:

> Some persons let their fowls run at large in the streets; thence they pass into the neighboring yards and gardens, and may destroy several dollars' worth in a short time. *(HB 7/23/1874)*

Township residents were also fearful of stray dogs roaming the area. In 1869, a local proclamation was passed at the annual Town Meeting in hope of ending the problem:

> Proclamation for destruction of all dogs male and female found running at large within the township except such as properly muzzled with wire muzzle about the nose securely fastened. *(TM 3/15/1869)*

Newton Township 1865 to 1871

Following the formation of Haddon Township, the surviving portion of Newton Township, comprised of 3,725 acres, carried on as a separate political entity. By the late 1860s, new homes were being built along Newton Township's western border with the City of Camden. The city was growing and expanding beyond its boundaries and spilling over into Newton Township:

> The portion of Newton Township bordering the city line, exhibits remarkable progress this season...buildings are going up, and the sound of saws and hammers ring out in every direction–presenting a busy scene. The township is being rapidly peopled by the most solid portion of society–mechanics and workingmen. (CD 7/9/1870)

Camden's elected officials were anxious to expand their borders so that the city could continue to grow, as well as increase tax ratables. Although many citizens in Camden had their eyes fixed on the neighboring community's land, not all Newton Township residents were in favor of joining Camden:

> The proposition of extending the city's limits so as to include a part of Newton Township is again under discussion. It is strenuously opposed as ever by those living beyond the line. *(WJP 1/5/1870)*

When the City of Camden fixed its sights on Newton Township's undeveloped farmland, the political clout wielded by its politicians ultimately rendered Newton Township's name to the history books. On March 7, 1871, the State Legislature approved an act whereby a part of Newton Township joined Camden. The remaining part of Newton Township was annexed to Haddon Township.

The newly acquired land which came under Haddon Township's jurisdiction included the area between present-day Ferry and Collings Avenues. The location on today's map would include Woodlynne and portions of Collingswood, Fairview and Camden. After the last remnants of Newton Township dissolved into Haddon Township, the surviving township was at its largest geographical area. The predominately rural township was comprised of 81 farms in 1875. Over 2,500 residents lived in the township, of which 1,400 were within the village of Haddonfield. Thirty-three manufacturing establishments were operating in Haddon Township, encompassing seventeen types of industries.

Village of Haddonfield

The streams and early roadways were vital to the existence of early European settlement in the region. The village of Haddonfield prospered at its location due to the proximity of Cooper's Creek and two overland routes. The Haddonfield Road (Haddon Avenue), once a Native-American route, ran west from the village to the Delaware River. Towards the east, the road met a highway that went to Longacoming (Berlin) and towards the shore. Another early roadway provided access to other eighteenth century villages including Woodbury, Salem, Moorestown, Mt. Holly and Burlington. The roadway later evolved into Kings Highway.

The area's importance, at least to the substantial Quaker community of the region, was heightened in 1721 when a Quaker meetinghouse was built along Haddonfield Road. Soon thereafter, a semblance of a village began to take shape. Clustered along Main Street, tradesmen and craftsmen bolstered the agricultural economy of the region. The village became more accessible because of improved roads, necessitated in part by stagecoach service, in the late 1700s.

For several brief periods during the Revolutionary War, British and Hessian soldiers occupied the village. Early in the war, the village became the unofficial capital of New Jersey. The Legislature took up refuge in the southern part of New Jersey for several months in order to avoid the British Army. The Assembly and Council enacted laws and the Governor issued proclamations in the tavern now known as *The Indian King.*

By the 1830s, some 100 homes dotted the village as well as two churches, two schools, two fire companies, a public library, seven stores, two taverns, two gristmills, two tanneries, and a woolen factory. (*A Gazetteer of the State of New Jersey*, p.154)

In the early 1850s, the Camden & Atlantic Railroad came to the village. The right-of-way went between Camden, through Newton Township, across the State to Absecon Inlet. The railroad had a considerable impact on growth in southern New Jersey. Following the Civil War, the residents of Haddonfield witnessed a "flood tide of progress and development" mostly attributable to the railroad. (WJP 4/22/1868) To a large extent, the rail line was the impetus for the transformation of Haddonfield and most of the remaining township, into

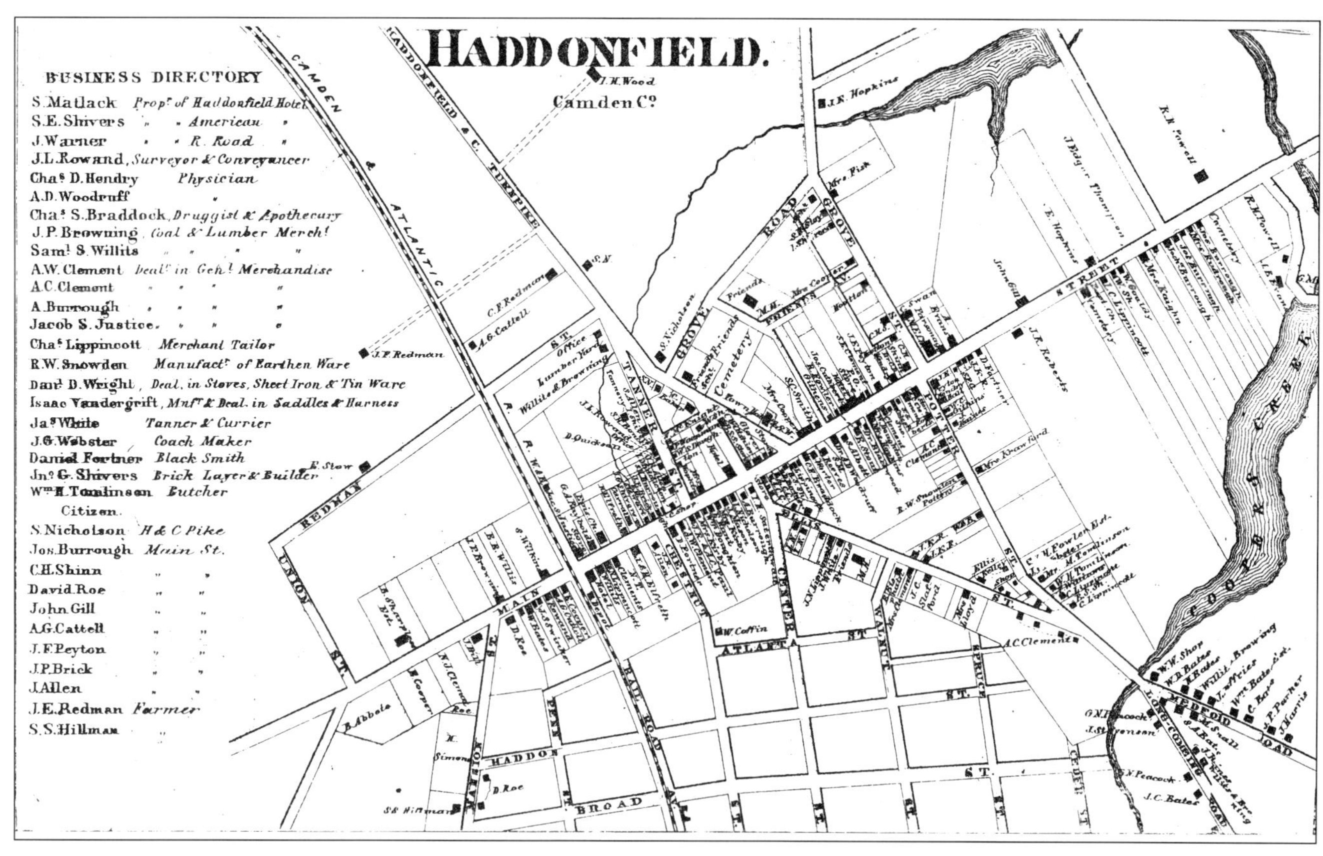

Village of Haddonfield and Business Directory. (A detail from *Map of the Vicinity of Philadelphia,* by D.I. Lake and S.N. Beers. Philadelphia, PA, 1860.)

the residential suburbs that exist today. The railroad offered workers a short commute to Camden and the ferries leading to Philadelphia. The old Camden & Atlantic's right-of-way is now used by PATCO.

By the 1870s, with over half of the township's population in Haddonfield, the community was the cultural, political, commercial and educational hub of old Haddon Township. The Camden newspapers often depicted the village in a favorable way. The 1870s village was not unlike other rural communities in the region at that time:

> Haddonfield, six miles from Camden is situated on the Camden & Atlantic Railroad. It is perhaps one of the prettiest villages in the State, and many denizens of Philadelphia, seek its invigorating breeze and cool shade during the summer months. Many business men in the city have made it their permanent residence, in consequence of the conveniences afforded by the railroad, and an excellent turnpike. Shade, shrubbery, water and products, unsurpassed. A large inland business is transacted here. *(WJP 6/3/1875)*

A variety of village shops, stores and small cottage industries served the region in the 1870s. Drug stores, bakeries, meat markets, grocery stores, barber shops, shoemakers, inns, taverns, stables and a post office stood along Main Street. Physicians, surveyors and conveyancers had offices in the village. Both merchants and professionals were neighbors to blacksmiths, wheelwrights, tinsmiths and cabinetmakers. A coal and lumberyard, tannery, earthenware manufacturer, paint works and flour mill were all within the Haddonfield 's borders.

In 1878, two fish and oyster stores and a "first class segar store" opened in town. (WJP 2/26/1879) The following year a Camden newspaper noted the "segar store's" proprietor retired. "Our old friend the Cuban, has sold out his segar store in the New Jersey Building." (WJP 3/5/1879) The "Cuban" returned to his native country to settle an estate.

One of a number of new commercial establishments commenced operations in the village in 1878:

> A.C. Bellows of Camden, who is a graduate of the Spencerian School of Penmanship opened a school for instruction in writing over the post office. Tuition was $2.00 for 13 lessons. (WJP 1/9/1878)

On the Sabbath, commercial activity was restricted in the nineteenth century community. The same municipal statutes existed until the late twentieth century. Some proprietors found it difficult to comply with the rules:

> The authority of Haddonfield has stopped the selling of segars and other articles on Sunday, within the limits of the borough. (WJP 7/24/1878)

> The action of Justice Fowler in his recent movement towards more strict enforcement of the Sunday law meets with much disapproval in certain quarters. It is said by some that if the barber shops, segar stores, etc. are closed, the proprietors will retaliate by taking action against milkmen and others. (WJP 5/8/1879)

> Saturday–Justice Fowler of Haddonfield, has given the barbers notice that if they shave tomorrow he will fine them, and it is understood that they will not shave. (CDP 5/17/1879)

During the 1870s, several energetic capitalists exploited building opportunities in the village. William Massey built "cottages" on his 40 acres of land on the southwest side of the village, along the railroad's right-of-way. It was no coincidence that William Massey, one of the village's largest landholders, was also a corporate officer of the Camden & Atlantic Railroad Company. It was common in this age for railroad executives to own land near their company's railroad route. The Camden & Atlantic Railroad's policy of encouraging workers to commute to and from Haddonfield was not only beneficial to the company, but also to Massey. As commuting caught on, Massey's land brought a greater price in the marketplace.

The Haddonfield Improvement Company was another owner and developer of vacant land in the village:

> Haddonfield Real Estate Improvement Company's large tract of land on the east side of town, laid out in lots with wide streets passing through them. (WJP 7/29/1874)

By 1875, some 297 homes stood in Haddonfield. (HB 1/14/1875) It was reported that 135 boarders lived in the community in 1875; many hailed from Philadelphia. (HB 8/16/1875) Some of the more affluent renters from the cities found the slow-paced country setting a welcomed relief. In 1879, the *Camden Daily Post* reported "there were quite a number of houses to rent in Haddonfield." (CDP 4/29/1879) The following year, the *West Jersey Press* reported the village was in need of additional rental properties:

> Good investment for some capitalist would be to build a number of cottages in Haddonfield at a cost of $1,000 to $1,200 each. Few houses for rent in Haddonfield. (WJP 6/23/1880)

Today, zoning laws regulate land use, although transformation of Haddonfield to a residential community did not occur without differing views:

> There is talk of a slaughter house being built in one of the most thickly settled portions of Haddonfield. It is hoped this will not be done. . . . (WJP 5/26/1880)

The smell emanating from refuse and runoff of a slaughter operation could be unbearable in a residential setting.

Despite its reputation as a tranquil county village, Haddonfield, like most villages had its share of problems. Local newspapers often reported incidents of crime and in some cases, a fitting punishment:

> Robbers in Haddonfield. The villains who have recently been infesting the locality, not content with entering houses, have commenced attacks on citizens, at night, upon the streets. Almost nightly, some outrage occurs. On Saturday night last Mr. Henry Plum was knocked down and beaten in the most atrocious manner. His pockets were rifled. . . . He was seriously injured. (WJP 11/10/1869)

> Chicken thieves have been depredating to a considerable extent in and around Haddonfield. Look out for them, you who still have your flocks intact, and if you have a chance, give these gentry "a warm reception and hospitable" quarters, by putting them in a chain gang and feeding them, but compelling them to work; or else revive the old whipping-post, and give them a dose of the whip when caught. This would probably reform them, or cause them to move to other quarters.
>
> Since writing the above, we understand that several of these marauders have been shot, and some of them seriously if not fatally wounded; and preparations are made and making to serve others in the same way, if circumstances should unfortunately make it necessary. (HB 1/1876)

Once in a while, politically partisan newspapers took aim at the village:

> A resident of Haddonfield says that everything is dull there, no one but doctors and undertakers having employment. (CDP 4/16/1879)

Although such reports were few, the village was large enough to have a "town drunk." The newspapers infrequently reported less than idyllic opinions of Haddonfield:

> "Alcoholic Jim" from Haddonfield admitted to us this morning that there were more "frauds" in that place for its size, than in any other town in New Jersey. (NR 2/9/1878)

In 1870, Haddonfield boasted of having the largest and finest public school in the county. A number of private schools also operated in the village including the Friends School and St. John's Military Academy, a private prep school operated by Episcopalian ministers. The community had several private kindergarten and primary schools for young students. African-American children attended a separate public school in the village. [See education, page 51.]

A discussion about Haddonfield would not be complete without mention of the Quaker influence. The village was founded in the early 1700s by English immigrants that belonged to the Society of Friends. Two Quaker meetinghouses stood in Haddonfield in the 1870s. One meeting was for Orthodox Friends and the other for Hicksite Friends. Other religious denominations including Baptists, Methodists, Episcopalians and Presbyterians, built their sanctuaries along Main Street. [See houses of worship, page 62.]

In 1869, a library and reading room, known as the Haddon Institute was located on Main Street. The books for the library first belonged to the Haddonfield Library Company, an organization founded by the Society of Friends in 1803.

The citizens obtained the news from a number of newspapers printed in Camden. In 1874, John Van Court, an enterprising publisher, began publishing a local newspaper, *The Haddonfield Basket.* Years later, several competitor newspapers followed Van Court's endeavor. [See newspapers, page 87.]

Bands and orchestras from Camden and Philadelphia traveled to Haddonfield and performed at concerts and parties. The Haddonfield Cornet Band entertained locals during the Civil War. The *West Jersey Press* observed that within the village, "Amusement consists of dancing, music and conversation. Able musicians rendered the recreation of dancing all the more delightful." (WJP 1/22/1868) A singing society was formed in the late 1870s. (WJP 11/27/78) Various fraternal societies and lodges held affairs and spearheaded charitable events in Haddonfield.

A baseball club, called "Old Haddon," played teams from other South Jersey communities and Philadelphia. (WJP 9/4/72) Other contests such as cricket, horse racing, and pigeon shooting were also held in the village.

During the era, picnics were a popular pastime. One popular site for these outings was Mann's grove. The tract is now next to Hopkins Lane, between Hopkins Pond and Kings Highway. On the Fourth of July, fireworks were launched from the site. [See leisure activities, page 93.]

Even before Haddonfield incorporated as a borough, inhabitants were desirous of improving the streets, sidewalks and street lighting. Kerosene lamps were installed along tree-lined Main Street in the 1860s. A portion of the sidewalks along the street were paved, other sections were covered with planks of wood. In March 1866, a law was enacted giving village residents the legal wherewithal to raise money so sidewalks and streets could be repaired. Residents of the village elected three Street Commissioners, an Assessor, a Collector of Taxes and three Commissioners of Appeals. The paving of the sidewalks was to be done with brick, wood or stone. It is likely that the improvements were carried out at an uneven pace.

Town Hall in Haddonfield

The Town Hall for Newton Township had been built in 1853 along the Haddonfield Road. Today, the site is the Haddonfield Fire Company building. Old fire insurance surveys provide a description of the building and how its rooms were utilized. The overall dimensions of the two-story frame, tin roof building was 30' x 45' in 1859. A two-story addition and belfry were attached to the main structure:

> The first story has 9 feet to ceiling and is divided as follows–2 Rooms, one on each side of the entrance hall 12 by 16 feet used as committee and recitation room–back room 29 feet by 28 feet used as a public school room. . .2nd floor is one room 29 by 44 feet, 14 feet to ceiling, used for Township and other public meetings–the whole building is well finished with wide cornice–lathed, plastered and well maintained throughout. (Rowand No. 122, 1859)

When Haddon Township separated from Newton Township in 1865, Town Hall continued to function as the hub for the new township's municipal, political and social affairs. Over the years many spirited meetings and debates were held in Town Hall. For instance, in 1875 the majority of voters in the township supported a referendum to keep the township "dry." [See local option, page 79.] When the results of the election to ban the sale of alcohol were announced, the partisan *Haddonfield Basket* correspondent wrote:

> . . .there went up from the crowded Town Hall, three very hearty cheers, when some one exclaimed, "Who'll take a drink on that?" This was followed by a fierce farewell yell to the rum-selling business in Haddonfield. (HB 4/1875)

Over the years, Town Hall served many needs of the community. For years, a room on the first floor served as a classroom for a private school. The township's officers voted against collecting rent from the private

Haddon Township's first Town Hall stood along the Haddonfield & Camden Turnpike in the village of Haddonfield. Built in 1853, the building was where the Haddonfield Fire Company is now located on Haddon Avenue.

(Historical Society of Haddonfield Collections)

school because the benefits associated with instructing the township's young children outweighed the need to earn rent. (TM 3/18/79) In the 1870s, a lower room became a library and reading room. Many local organizations held their functions in the building. For instance, the local farmers' organization set up exhibitions in Town Hall:

> Poultry Exhibition at Town Hall ... Admission 10 cents. Annual exhibition of the Farmers Mutual Benefit Association for display and exchange. (HB 12/1875)

Towards the later part of the 1860s, the building was in need of repair. A committee surveyed the condition of the building and reported its findings and recommendation to the township officials:

> ...leaking water has occasioned causing the lower rooms to be damp, unhealthy and most ultimately will produce decay and destruction to building. Recommend the Township Committee to have building weatherboarded in the usual manner and fully repaired before having said repainted. (TM 6/4/1868)

Surprisingly, smoke-free public buildings and an understanding of the harmful effect of second hand smoke were not a twentieth century phenomena:

> If ever we should have a respectable hall, we trust one of the regulations will be the prohibition of smoking in it, strictly, enforced. We can't help but think that it is a species of ill manners to go into a meeting and smoke, to the annoyance of those who do not smoke, and to whom the fumes of tobacco are offensive. At last election, one of the officers was taken ill and had to leave his post, attributable to being a long time enveloped in a cloud of tobacco smoke, and forced to inhale its poisonous perfumes. *(HB 11/1874)*

Twenty-seven feet to the south of the hall stood, "A small frame fire Engine and hook and ladder house." (Rowand No. 122, 1859) In 1874, the village fire department received permission to place a fire bell in the cupola of Town Hall and to dig a well on the premises. By the 1880s, the fire company had taken over the first floor of the building to shelter its fire fighting engines and accessaries.

Even after Haddonfield took its first step towards becoming an autonomous community in 1875, the Township Committee continued to meet in Town Hall. Sometime in the 1890s, the township's officials moved their meetings to Schnitzler Hall in Orston. Today, the building is at West Pine Street and East Atlantic Avenue in Audubon. The site took its name from a member of the Township Committee and real estate developer, Charles Schnitzler. Some years later, Schnitzler became the first mayor of Audubon.

After 98 years of continuous service, Haddon Township's first Town Hall was razed in 1951 to make way for the fire house that still stands today.

Borough of Haddonfield

Despite efforts in the 1860s, residents continued to complain into the following decade about the condition of sidewalks as well as the streets, lighting and public safety:

> Haddonfield is behind the age in its dark streets at night. There ought to be a movement of some kind to put the matter of lighting the streets on a permanent basis. This done, and the side-walks regulated so that there should be no uneven places, endangering the breaking of limbs or necks, or dislocating one's back, there would be much more satisfaction in passing from place to place, whether in going to church, places of amusement, on business, or visiting friends. *(HB 10/20/1874)*

Inhabitants knew that the Township Committee would not appropriate the funds necessary to fix the undesirable conditions. Many other villages throughout the State were also experiencing the same predicament. It was not unusual in New Jersey for residents of towns or villages to look for urban-type government services which townships either were unable or unwilling to provide. The answer to Haddonfield's residents' dilemma was to incorporate the village, thereby allowing residents to have more say over these local issues:

> ...ideas of incorporation was to obtain more powers over streets, and to provide lighting...there is not sufficient power under the law incorporating townships to permit the work to be done. *(WJP 1/27/1875)*

Incorporating the village of Haddonfield was not universally supported. The issue divided residents into two camps. One side, called "squatters," favored making improvements. (WJP 1/27/1875) They generally included citizens which had recently moved into the village. The other camp, made up of older residents and those firmly rooted in the area, were known as "anti-incorporators." Citizens that opposed incorporation feared their local taxes would increase to pay for unnecessary projects:

> Old residents of Haddonfield opposed any attempt at incorporating–holding that it was a useless expense and an effort to extract money from them. *(WJP 1/20/1875)*

The squatters out-flanked the anti-incorporators on the hotly debated issue. Many Haddonfield residents, including the editor of *The Haddonfield Basket*, were unaware that the New Jersey Legislature was contemplating a vote to incorporate the village. Upon learning about this action, the publisher of the local newspaper expressed surprise and printed his own version of legal notification:

> NOTICE "Is hereby given that application will be made to the Legislature of New Jersey at its next session, for an act to incorporate Haddonfield, Camden county, into a city or borough."
>
> We copy the above notice (gratis) in full from a Camden paper for the benefit of the Haddonfield people.... We do not known where it originated, or who authorized its publication, and have heard of no meeting of the inhabitants asking for this incorporation, although we have heard a few individuals speak of it ... We are told we will be informed all about the matter when it comes before the Legislature. It may be too late then for a thorough examination or remonstrance, if objectionable. We are not favorable to imposing any measures upon the people without their consent, after ample opportunity for examining such measures. Let whatever is done in the premises, be done openly, fairly and honestly. *(HB 12/1874)*

The squatters prevailed–the Borough of Haddonfield was created in March 1875 with powers to tax inhabitants for purposes of regulating and grading sidewalks and lighting the streets. The borough's citizens, however, remained under Haddon Township's jurisdiction for all other municipal aspects. They continued to pay taxes to the township for schools and general purposes. The township still maintained control and management of the village's roads.

One border of the new Borough was the vicinity of what is now Euclid Avenue. Another boundary line ran parallel to and about three modern-day blocks on the southeast side of Main Street. Much like today, the village's geographical center in 1875 was along Main Street. Along this street, the borough extended between Cooper's Creek and what is now Chews Landing Road. Over the ensuing years, adjoining farms were annexed into the borough, thereby increasing its size.

The month following passage of the incorporating act, the village elected five Commissioners of Streets and three Commissioners of Appeals. Residents voted on the sum of money to be assessed on the taxable property within the new borough. To appease those that feared large tax increases, the act limited the annual amount the Borough could raise to between $1,000 and $1,500 annually.

With new powers, the Commissioners of Streets set out to repair the streets, sidewalks and street lighting. It was reported, "a lamp lighter of Haddonfield travels his grand rounds in a carriage, carrying his ladder with him." (WJP 7/7/1875) A local surveyor/engineer was hired to fix the streets:

> J. Lewis Rowand, an experienced civil engineer, had been employed to make, and is now at work fixing the gravel of the street, sidewalks, etc. *(WJP 5/12/1875)*

Soon after receiving its designation as a borough, complaints were again registered on the deplorable condition of the main thoroughfare. Main Street was still under the jurisdiction of the township:

> The Main Street of Haddonfield, a short distance below the railroad, is a disgrace to the town. A regular mud road for considerable distance, utterly impassable for pedestrians without getting over shoe-tops. *(WJP 2/27/1878)*

The debate over adequate street lighting continued following incorporation:

> We happened to be out rather late on New Years' Eve, and when starting for home, found the streets of our town in utter darkness. We had supposed of course on this night, when so many towns and cities were vying with each other in illuminating and other demonstrations suitable to the ushering in of the Centennial year, that our street lamps at least would all be lighted up, especially as there is usually on such occasions quite a number of persons on the streets. But we were mistaken in this supposition, and are informed that they are frequently extinguished before the arrival of the night train from the city. As we have the lamps, and oil is cheap, we ought to have the full benefit of them, and think they should be kept burning during the whole night, when there is no moon on duty. It has been asserted that most of the thieving is done between twelve o'clock and daylight, and therefore the more necessity for the lamps to be burning during those hours, as a means of protection. And then in regard to being out late at night, although we are sometimes told that people had better be at home at such hours, still there are occasions when there seems to be no impropriety in doing so, and, indeed, there may be circumstances when there is a necessity for it. Therefore, Let us have lights, All the dark nights. *(HB 1/15/1876)*

The village maintained its semi-autonomous status for almost two decades. It was not until the 1890s, when State law allowed boroughs existing within the limits of townships to be independent of the parent township, that Haddonfield completely severed from Haddon Township.

Village of Rowandtown

Besides Haddonfield, the only other major village in old Haddon Township was Rowandtown, situated along the Haddonfield Turnpike (Haddon Avenue). Some two-dozen homes and shops were clustered along the turnpike in the area between what is now Maple Avenue and Cuthbert Road in Westmont. To a large extent, the village developed because of its proximity to the Camden & Atlantic Railroad. By 1871, local passenger trains to Camden stopped at Rowandtown seven times a day.

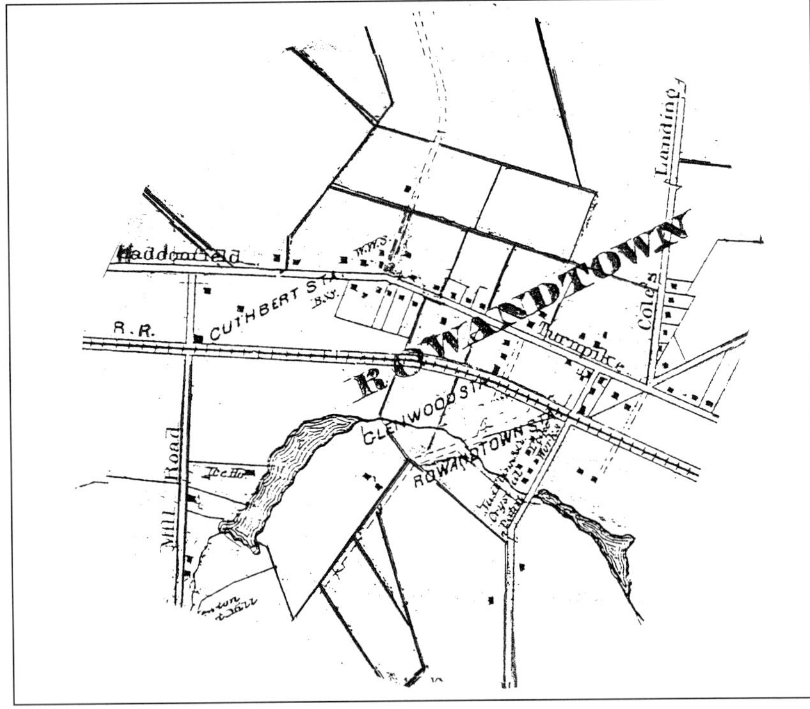

Rowandtown, now called Westmont, in 1877. The village's main thoroughfare was the Haddonfield & Camden Turnpike, now called Haddon Avenue.

(*Atlas of Philadelphia and its Environs.* G.M. Hopkins Company.)

A handful of commercial establishments were situated in Rowandtown. For a considerable part of the nineteenth century, blacksmith and wheelwright shops were located in the village. Workers shod horses, fabricated and repaired wagons, carts and farming implements for nearby farmers. The only sawmill in the township, located next to Crystal Lake, began operating in the early 1800s. A paint and varnish factory opened after the sawmill closed. A small grocery store along the Haddonfield Turnpike provided necessities for Rowandtown's citizens.

Children in the area attended a one-room schoolhouse built about 1825, at the site of what is now the Haddon Township Municipal Building. In 1872, a new two-story school replaced the antiquated one. Until the village's first church [Shiloh Baptist Church] was built in the 1880s, its likely most of those inclined to attend Sunday services did so in Haddonfield. The Rowandtown Fire Company's equipment was housed in a shed or barn of a fire company member or nearby village resident.

The village took its name from an early settler:

> Rowandtown is a small village about one mile from Haddonfield on the road to Philadelphia. It is an old place, and one of the earliest settlers was John Rowand. He was a blacksmith, and built his shop at the corner of a road, on the edge of what was then a sort of briar swamp. Here he prospered, and was a "happy" man, as he ought to have been, if true as reported of him, when he asserted that he had "the best horse, the best cow, and the best wife in the country." *(HB 8/20/1874)*

In 1874, residents of Rowandtown contemplated changing the village's name. After much discussion, a proposal was made to rename the town "Glenwood":

> Thus encouraged, and to be up with the times, a number of the inhabitants desiring to see old Rowandtown wake up, and shake off her Rip Van Winkleism, determined to call a meeting of the citizens, and if possible change the name of the town ... *(HB 9/20/1874)*

Not everyone agreed that a new name was necessary:

> Rowandtown has become Glenwood. Rowandtown was not perhaps a beautiful name; but it commemorated an old family of the county; it was established, it was distinctive, and probably stood by itself in the Post Office Directory. Glenwood is inappropriate ... *(WJP 7/1/1874)*

Four years after the new name was selected, residents were still carping. Some believed West Haddonfield was a better choice:

> I understand a portion of the inhabitants...are not yet satisfied with its name neither Rowandtown or Glenwood pleasing them; as it is now proposed to call it West Haddonfield. *(WJP 6/12/1878)*

According to a 1953 newspaper interview with Walter Stoy, the name Westmont came about in an unusual manner. Stoy, a life-long resident of Westmont, was 91 years old when the interview appeared in the *Courier-Post.* Walter recalled that the postmaster eventually rejected the name Glenwood because a town already existed in New Jersey with the same name. Inhabitants contemplated renaming the village "Fairton;" however, it, too, was rejected on the same grounds as Glenwood.

Walter Stoy recalled when the name "Westmont" first came up for discussion at a town meeting in 1884. The end result–the village took on a new designation:

> It seems the men [four young men at the meeting] had been to West Chester, Pa. where they had each won $100 bets on the failure of Westmont, a pacing horse belonging to a scouring soap magnate, to run under a certain time. *(CP 1/27/1953)*

Although Rowandtown was still a small community during the 1870s, like the neighboring village of Haddonfield, it, too, did not escape random acts of unlawful activities:

> A young man named Henry Grim was assaulted about midnight on Saturday night, near Glenwood station, on the Camden & Atlantic Railroad. He went out on the train that leaves Camden at 11:30. In going home, he met two colored men,who he says, struck him on the back of the head, and felled him to the ground. They then stripped him of his clothing except his shirt, drawers and stockings. His shirt studs, collar-button, watch and chain and money were all taken. Grim was quite exhausted from the loss of blood, but succeeded in getting as far as Mrs. Hobensack's where he received assistance, and was subsequently taken home. No clue as to the assailants have been found. *(WJP 8/1/1877)*

> Farmers near Rowandtown complain of numerous depredations from thieves. The blacksmith shop was broken open and robbed of nearly all the tools. (WJP 10/23/1878)

Collingswood and Two Sticks

During the 1870s, about a half-dozen dwellings stood on the south side of Haddonfield Road (Haddon Avenue) near today's Zane Avenue in Collingswood. In 1868, the area was called "Two Sticks." (WJP 8/19/1868) Some years later, the area was referred to as "Roseville." (WJP 2/3/1875) A Methodist Church sat along the turnpike near what years later became Narberth Terrace.

The present-day commercial center of the Borough of Collingswood is a three-quarter mile stretch along Haddon Avenue centered to each side of Collings Avenue between Madison and Stiles Avenues. In this vicinity, about ten dwellings stood during the 1870s. An inn/tavern known as the Half-Way House stood along the Haddonfield Road near today's Lincoln Avenue. The establishment was well-known to nearby inhabitants and teamsters that used the turnpike.

In 1871, the Camden & Atlantic Railroad Company added Collings Station to its stops on the rail line. When a telegraph station was placed there, the press reported:

> ...the railroad company has put one of the pilot houses of an old ferry boat here for a telegraph station. (WJP 7/7/1880)

In 1877, the vicinity was renamed Collingswood:

> At a town meeting...the station on the Camden & Atlantic Railroad, heretofore known as Collings' Road, was by a large majority changed to Collingswood. (WJP 1/24/1877)

Large-scale residential settlement first took place during the 1880s when Richard T. Collings divided 40 acres near the Camden & Atlantic Railroad's right-of-way at Collings Road, and began selling building lots. Soon, the community's first general store opened at the corner of Collings and Haddonfield roads. By the mid-1880s, residential growth and development accelerated and the Camden & Atlantic constructed a large railroad depot at Collings Road. In 1888, local citizens approved a referendum to incorporate the Borough of Collingswood.

Stonetown

In the early 1850s, Isaiah Stone, a builder, Emmons Mockridge and Richard Fetters, both Camden developers, combined to build some one dozen twin homes along the Haddonfield Road on a small tract of land originally owned by the Cooper Estate. The small cluster of rental properties took the name of one of the owners/builders, Stonetown. The location of former dwellings on today's map would be at the intersection of Haddon Avenue and Route 130. The later road, originally named Crescent Boulevard, was not built until the 1920s.

If, in the 1860s, one had to select a likely location for new residential development, Stonetown would have been a good guess. The area possessed all the essential ingredients: plenty of surrounding undeveloped land; an adjacent turnpike; and a nearby railroad right-of-way on which workers could commute to Camden.

As it turned out, Stonetown did not grow and residential development took place in other locations such as Collingswood. The Stonetown homes were razed when Crescent Boulevard was built.

Camden County

Compared to neighboring counties, Camden County is relatively new. Both Gloucester and Burlington counties were formed shortly after the first English settlers came to West Jersey. Camden County, on the other hand, was created in 1844 from the northern portion of Gloucester County. In 1875, almost 53,000 people inhabited Camden County. (NR 10/27/1877) The majority of the population lived in Camden, the industrial, commercial and political center of the county. Along with Haddon Township, other townships in the county included Centre, Delaware, Gloucester, Stockton, Waterford and Winslow townships as well as three incorporated municipalities: Camden and Gloucester City and the Borough of Merchantville.

Inhabitants of the county were taxed on the value of their real and personal property. The townships collected the county's taxes and remitted them to build and repair bridges; run the courts and pay judges' salaries; maintain the court house, vital records and prisons; support the administrative supervision of schools in the county; oversee elections and keep an almshouse and insane asylum.

Responsibility and oversight of the county's affairs was charged to the Board of Chosen Freeholders. In the nineteenth century, Freeholders were elected to represent individual townships. As newly formed boroughs in the county became entitled to elect a freeholder, the size of Camden County's Board of Chosen Freeholders grew. By the late 1930s, the board had an unwieldy 38 members. In 1939, the large board of Freeholders was abolished and replaced with a seven-member board. After the change, Camden County Freeholders were all elected at large.

Proposal—Haddon County

Almost three-quarters of Camden County's population lived in Camden during the mid-1870s. This allowed the city to flex its political muscle in the affairs of the county. On the other hand, the rural, outlying townships were desirous of gaining more control in matters affecting them. To achieve this, a movement was spearheaded whereby the county's seven townships were to sever ties with remaining incorporated cites in the county.

This proposal would have named the new area Haddon County. Local gossip, at least in Haddon Township, had the seat of anticipated government in Haddonfield, although residents of Berlin claimed their community was also worthy of consideration. Haddonfield's local newspaper, the *Haddonfield Basket,* reported on the movement, albeit with some bias:

> The division of Camden county, it is said, will be agitated again this winter before the Legislature, and an effort made to make a new county out of the townships of Stockton, Delaware, Haddon, Centre, Waterford, Winslow and Gloucester, to be called the County of Haddon, with the seat of Justice at Haddonfield. (HB 12/1874)

> Dividing the County of Camden had been up again before the Legislature, but has not been successful. When this does take place, we suppose the fight will then be as to the location of the new county capital. It is presumed Haddonfield will put in a strong claim, and Berlin is so expectant, that, as we understand, a site has already been selected there for the public building! What ambition! Or is it presumption? (HB 3/1875)

Proponents for a new county were unsuccessful in convincing the State Legislators to vote for the plan. The movement to create Haddon County was resurrected in the 1880s, but once again state lawmakers could not agree and the notion faded away.

Proposal—Camden's 8th Ward to Haddon Township

Many citizens in the western section of "old" Newton Township were irate after Camden annexed their land in 1871. For the most part, this section of Camden, known as the Eighth Ward, was largely farmland. The inhabitants' main objection was having to pay tax rates set to accommodate urban improvements in other areas of the city. The farmers asked the State Legislature to sever their connection with Camden and place them under Haddon Township's jurisdiction.

In April 1878, the New Jersey Legislature passed an act approving the annexation of the Eighth Ward of Camden to Haddon Township. The area of the Ward included portions of what is now Camden in the area of West Jersey Hospital, Morgan Village, Our Lady of Lourdes Medical Center, sections of Parkside and areas adjoining Woodlynne and Collingswood.

By the terms of the legislation, Camden was to receive compensation for the land it lost. The act became null and void after some three months if the municipalities could not agree on an amount. Although not completely free from doubt, its possible that the committees could not agree on a fair price for Camden's loss. The Eighth Ward remained within Camden's borders.

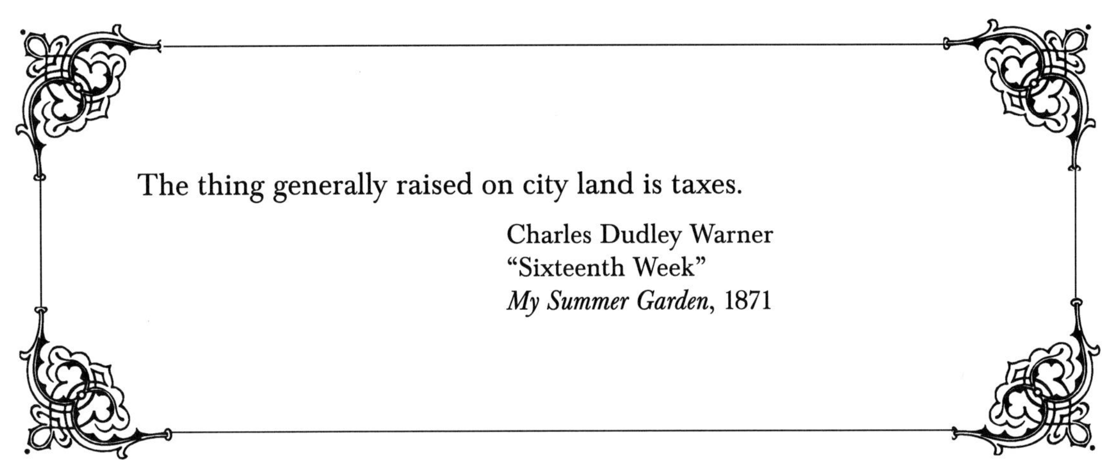

The thing generally raised on city land is taxes.

Charles Dudley Warner
"Sixteenth Week"
My Summer Garden, 1871

2

Nearby Cities and Villages

Most nineteenth century farmers were quite resourceful in providing for themselves, and, in many instances, were almost self-sufficient. They grew food for their families and raised crops to feed the livestock. Some farmers repaired their own wagons and farm implements and constructed dwellings and outbuildings on their land. Whatever they could not grow or make with their own hands, they often obtained by bartering.

On the other hand, the region's farmers could not operate without money. The money earned from the sale of agricultural products sustained farmers as well as the local economy of the region. Farmers, millers, dairymen and other producers obtained cash from the cities' marketplaces. The need for cash tied local inhabitants to the consumers living in Philadelphia, Camden and Gloucester City.

The small villages of Mt. Ephraim, Batesville, Snow Hill and Ellisburg were situated adjacent to or nearby old Haddon Township's borders. Because of the relative small number of people in the communities, the interplay and impact on the township's agricultural economy was minimal.

Philadelphia and Camden

During the 1700s, the natural deep-water port of Philadelphia emerged as the largest commercial center in the American Colonies. The city was home to wealthy merchants that utilized the port to bring in trade from all over the colonies and Europe. Philadelphia was the first great industrial city in the United States and was the leading urban manufacturing center until the era of the Civil War.

Dorothy Gondos Beers's *Philadelphia–A 300-Year History*, depicts Philadelphia's path to industrialization. To some extent, her analysis also portrays Camden's postwar economy:

> The United States in 1865 was on the path toward preeminence as an industrial giant. Returning soldiers, capital released from wartime investment, financing, manufacturing plants needing to be readjusted to peacetime activity, an influx of immigrants, new techniques in communication and transportation, fabulous new machinery, American inventiveness, and American enthusiasm—all contributed to industrialization. (p. 427)

During the 1870s, Philadelphia's wealth and prominence were sustained in manufacturing, commerce, banking, printing and transportation. In 1870, Philadelphia's population of about 674,000, was about thirty times the number of people in the neighboring city of Camden. (*Philadelphia–A 300 Year History*, p. 419)

During the early 1800s, the first residential building lots sold to investors in what became Camden were in the area along the Delaware River. Prior to this period, the area was known for its ferries that linked

Philadelphia with the system of roads leading to the interiors of New Jersey and New York City.

By the mid-1830s, Camden had become the terminus of the Camden & Amboy Railroad's highly profitable Philadelphia to New York right-of-way. The railroad brought an additional volume of freight and passengers to Camden's waterfront. Soon, other railroads built terminals in Camden and their right-of-ways traveled in all directions throughout New Jersey. The ferry facilities were improved to accommodate the new rail traffic. During the two decades preceding the Civil War, the City of Camden experienced remarkable industrial and population growth fueled predominately by the railroads and ferry service. In 1860, the census-taker counted 80 manufacturers in the city. Ten years later, there were 125 factories. The *Camden Democrat* summarized Camden's dominate industries:

> We have extensive lumber depots, large planing mills, sash, blind and door manufacturers, chemical works, nickel works, manufacturers of various kind, extensive shipyards, hay, calf and produce markets, machine shops, glass works, iron works, foundries. ... CD 1/28/1871)

Commerce on the Delaware River was vital to the region's economy. In Camden, dock workers were kept busy unloading coal boats and other vessels. Camden evolved into an industrial suburb of Philadelphia. A correspondent for the *Camden Daily Post* labeled Camden, "East Philadelphia." (CDP 10/5/1871) During one month in 1876, 138 vessels docked at Camden wharfs:

> Arrivals in Camden For month of November Schooners 102; Barks 6; Ship 1; Brigs 2; Steamer 2; Sloops 25; (CDP 12/2/1876)

> Camden's population grew rapidly in response to, and supported by, the concurrent nineteenth century labor needs. The city experienced an influx of immigration dominated by Germans, British, Irish, Italian and Eastern Europeans. In 1870, Camden's population was about 20,000, by 1875 it had grown to become the fourth-largest city in the state with about 34,000 people. (CDP 3/31/1877)

Camden, as well as other nineteenth century American cities, offered an array of unskilled jobs. The hard-working laborers from Camden built the city's infrastructure. Cheap immigrant laborers dug ditches, laid pipes and foundations, carried bricks, wood and iron to construct buildings and lay the railroads. New homes were built to accommodate the swelling population. The building trades employed many of the newcomers to the city in good paying skilled and unskilled jobs:

> Camden Wages Bricklayers $4.00 per day, a carpenter $3.00 a day, plasterer $4.50 a day, stone mason $3.50 a day, laborer $2.50 a day. (WJP 8/12/1868)

To most people's way of thinking, growth in population and a strong manufacturing-based economy were beneficial to everyone in the city:

> We confidently predict that the census of 1880 will show Camden at that time to have a population of 50,000 persons. The advantages of our city as a place of residence are more and more appreciated. Its schools and churches are first class. The rate of taxation and valuation taken together is low. Its streets are wide. It is one of the wealthiest cities in the United States. To these causes and the enterprise of its manufacturers we attribute the unexampled growth of our city. (WJP 8/29/1877)

With a growing population and a solid industrial base, some believed there was no end to Camden's expansion. A correspondent for the *Camden Daily Post* envisioned farmland between villages and cities eventually disappearing. In its place would be sprawling suburbs. "Ultimately the growth of Camden will reach Gloucester, Woodbury and Haddonfield." (CDP 3/31/1877) Although it didn't occur until decades later, for the most part the correspondent's prediction became reality.

Throughout the 1800s, Philadelphia's economy and the emergence of Camden and its expanding population fueled the dynamics of growth and development in old Haddon Township and, for that matter, the entire region.

When urban inhabitants consumed food products purchased at the local marketplaces, the city's economic prosperity spread to farmers of the area. Hay, straw, market garden vegetables, livestock and dairy products were sold directly to city inhabitants or to middlemen. For most farmers, the cities were the sole outlet for their cash crops.

Haddon Township farmers took advantage of the close proximity to the nearby centers of population to recruit farm laborers. Farmers often coaxed day labors from the city with better pay than their usual jobs during peak harvest periods. Farmers were not alone in taking advantage of the region's abundant labor pool. The Camden & Atlantic Railroad, Philadelphia & Atlantic City Railroad and Philadelphia, Marlton & Medford Railroad were built with muscle supplied by immigrant workers from Camden and Philadelphia. [See railroads, page 35.]

Some of the township's merchants and proprietors peddled their goods in Camden's neighborhoods. For

The Farmers & Butchers Market was built in 1876 on West Avenue in Camden. Farmers throughout the region leased stalls to sell their products to the public. Even though Camden's market place was readily accessible to area farmers, market houses in Philadelphia were the primary outlets for Camden County's farm products.

(Camden County Historical Society Collections)

instance, Isaac Prine delivered ice to customers in Camden; Joseph Hollingshead sold dairy products to customers along his Camden milk route; and flour, ground at Hiram Smith's Newton Gristmill, was sold to Camden's populace. [See Isaac Prine, page 257; Joseph Hollingshead, page 270; Hiram Smith, page 257.]

Workers commuted from their homes in Haddonfield and Rowandtown to jobs in Camden. Some passengers boarded ferries and crossed the Delaware River to get to their places of employment. Entrepreneurs, office workers, clerks, laborers and mechanics commuted into the city and returned in the evening to their dwellings in more rural parts.

Philadelphia had other attractions. Schools in the city allowed some township students to further their academic or technical training. The "City of Brotherly Love" was the nation's medical center, as well as the region's hub for artists, musicians, actors, publishers, and sporting events. Similar to modern-day suburbanites, at some point most nineteenth century township inhabitants visited Philadelphia's shops, stores and cultural activities.

To a lesser degree, urbanites sometimes traveled into the countryside. Pleasure seekers often escaped the crowded city streets to picnic or take a buggy ride in the rural country setting. Every so often a concert or event was held in Haddonfield where patrons from Camden would board the train and travel out to the village. Some affluent families from Philadelphia kept summer homes in the New Jersey countryside. One individual, John Whitall and his family found relief from the sweltering summer weather at their Haddon Township farm. [See John Whitall, page 248.]

Even though old Haddon Township inhabitants were the beneficiaries of Camden's industrialization, it came at a price. Many of those living outside the city were less tolerant of increasing urbanization. The local editor of the *Haddonfield Basket* concluded his report of a robbery with a comment that many rural inhabitants also shared. Whether the correspondent's perception of the city was realistic or imagined, rural residents were generally glad that a comfortable distance existed between Camden and their homes:

> Chas. Vennel, a young man in the employ of Hiram Smith, in passing out of Camden, on Saturday morning at 1 o'clock, when near the deep cut on the Camden and Atlantic Railroad, on his way to Rowandtown, was knocked down and robbed of clothing, watch, pocketbook, money & etc. by two colored men. Bad place, that Camden. (HB 12/1875)

Even Camden's own newspapers did not mince words when reporting or exposing less than acceptable circumstances.

> Who will say that Camden isn't a wicked city? We have but one church for every 1,101 of our population, while there is one drinking saloon to every 343. There is some consolation, however, to known that ours is not the wickedist city in Camden County, Gloucester City has one drinking saloon for every 258 of the inhabitants, though partly to make amends for this blot upon her good name, she has one church for every 1,032 people. (WJP 2/2/1876)

Despite these urban ills, Camden's industry sustained commercial and population growth well into the twentieth century.

Gloucester City

Gloucester City, once just one and one-half square miles, was situated between Haddon Township and the Delaware River. Today, the city still shares a border with a section of the township known as West Collingswood Heights.

The city is an old community, with its beginnings dating back to the late seventeenth century. At that time, the town was the first seat of government for old Gloucester County. When the county seat moved to Woodbury in 1786, the town lost all of its prominence. The city's main attribute became its geographical proximity to Philadelphia and Camden and its fisheries. Ferries linked Gloucester with Philadelphia. During the 1840s the town underwent a period of growth in population and emergence of new businesses. By the 1870s, Gloucester possessed many of the amenities found in larger cities. The handful of industrial establishments in the city employed a large number of its workers. The city had 3,700 residents in 1870.

In Prowell's *The History of Camden County, New Jersey*, his 1886 description of Gloucester City portrayed a community that offered almost everything:

> ...with the broad and fast-flowing river on the west, whence, in summer, cool breezes are wafted, joined to wide, clean streets abounding in shade, and the large yards and gardens in fruit-trees giving, at a distance, the appearance of an inhabited forest—to which add excellent water in abundance, good schools, numerous societies, full religious opportunities, with many industrial establishments, insuring work for those who will. (Prowell, p. 582)

Mt. Ephraim

Mt. Ephraim first developed at the intersection of what is now the Black Horse Pike and Kings Highway. The village's name, at least in part, originated from being 61 feet above tide water. Following the Civil War, the village was a cluster of homes and several shops. The *Camden Democrat* wrote the village offered a "first class hotel" and general store. (1/15/1870)

People with a financial interest in the village's development highlighted its location to lure city dwellers to take up residence here. In 1865, the village was described as follows:

> Mt. Ephraim...when not obstructed by intervening foliage, affords quite a perfect view of Philadelphia. The location is fanned by every breeze, and is considered healthy. No more eligible site could be selected by persons who desire quite country residence. It is within three miles of Gloucester City, and five of Camden. (WJP 6/3/1865)

In 1876, the Centre Township village became the terminus of the Camden, Gloucester & Mt. Ephraim Railway leading to Camden's Kaighn Point. Soon thereafter, the village's geographical location, nearby turnpike and inexpensive building lots, attracted residential development and new commerce. The village schoolhouse stood along the Blackwoodtown Turnpike. Beginning in the 1870s, some Haddon Township children began attending the school in the village.

Haddon Township had its share of wheelwrights and blacksmiths situated in Rowandtown and Haddonfield. If a farmer from the southeastern portion of old Haddon Township required the services of a blacksmith or wheelwright, it is likely they looked up mechanics in Mt. Ephraim.

Batesville

Haddonfield's Ellis Street crossed Cooper's Creek and into a community known as Batesville. Almost all the small building lots and homes were along Milford Road, now known as Kresson Road, and Berlin Road, present-day Haddonfield-Berlin Road. Being in close proximity to Haddonfield, many Batesville's residents found employment or frequented the shops and stores in the neighboring village located just several blocks away. In 1870, there were 86 residents in this Delaware Township village. The site is now in Cherry Hill.

When Haddon Township passed an ordinance in 1873 banning the sale of liquor, the most popular establishment in Batesville may have been the tavern known as the Blazing Rag. It stood at the intersection of what is now Brace and Haddonfield-Berlin roads.

Snow Hill

The village of Snow Hill was about two miles from Haddonfield along Snow Hill Road, now known as Warwick Road. The community was home to many African-Americans, many of which found employment as laborers on nearby farms. Today the community is known as Lawnside.

The *West Jersey Press* printed a letter in 1869 written by a traveler that described the community. Although Snow Hill was portrayed in the newspaper article in favorable way, the author also included a disparaging comment towards African-Americans. Remarks of this nature were common in newspapers at the period:

> Snow Hill—A beautiful village of Camden County.... The streets here are very straight and level and kept like a bar room floor, slightly sandier. The inhabitants are mostly black, though white in feelings. They are energetic people

A view towards Batesville from Haddonfield's Ellis Street where the tavern "The Blazing Rag" stood at the intersection of what is now Kresson and Haddonfield-Berlin Roads. It is likely patronage at the Delaware Township drinking establishment increased after Haddon Township voted to ban the sale of alcohol in 1873.

(Historical Society of Haddonfield Collections)

and infuse much of their activity into the neighborhood village of Haddonfield.

Snow Hill has two or three interesting churches, and at least one very autocratic pastor. (WJP 2/3/1869)

Ellisburg

Situated about a mile from Haddonfield, at the intersection of the Camden and Marlton Turnpike, now called Route 70, and the Moorestown-Haddonfield road, now known as Kings Highway, sat a group of homes and shops known as Ellisburg. This area is now part of Cherry Hill. In 1865, the *West Jersey Press* described the village as:

> ...very pleasant village, situated on the Marlton Turnpike. A hotel, and blacksmith shop, the usual essentials of a village, together with several neat and comfortable dwellings, make up the town... (WJP 6/3/1865)

The center of activity in this Delaware Township village was the Ellis family's Bush Tavern, also called the Waterford Hotel. Before newspapers were widely distributed, the tavern was where news and events of the day were discussed. In the era just before railroads, the inn/tavern offered drovers (a driver or dealer of animals) a place to meet and buy and sell cattle, horses and sheep. Sometime about 1872, a post office was established here. By the end of the 1870s, a schoolhouse had been constructed and a grocery store opened. In all, some one dozen buildings stood in the village.

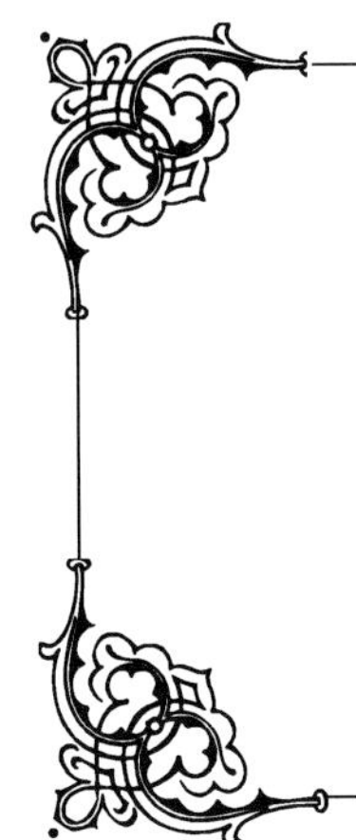

Over the river and through the wood,
To grandfather's house we go;
  The horse knows the way
  To carry the sleigh,
Through the white and drifted snow.

Lyndia Maria Child
Flowers for Children, 1844-1846
Thanksgiving Day, st. 1

3

Routes and Modes of Transportation

Creeks

The initial settlement of the region was along the navigable rivers and streams. Except for Indian trails which linked the interiors of West Jersey, the original colonists were totally dependent on rivers and creeks for transportation of produce, trade and commerce. The area's creeks played an important role in the transformation of Newton Township from wilderness to an agriculture settlement.

Cooper's Creek

The area's topography gradually rises from the Delaware River southeasterly until it reaches the highest area near Berlin. Many of Camden County's streams, running northwesterly toward the Delaware River, find their source from spring water surfacing near Berlin. One such waterway is the Cooper River, which flows through gently rolling landscape and low-lying flat lands, before emptying into the Delaware River.

The twisting creek served as the township's northern border with neighboring Delaware and Stockton townships. The tidal flow of Cooper's Creek, as it was known before they changed its name in 1911 to Cooper River, extended a distance of some seven miles from the Delaware River to Evans Pond, on the outskirts of Haddonfield. Officials changed the creek's name because they believed federal financial assistance earmarked for waterway improvements would be forthcoming if it was referred to as a river.

Until tidal gates were installed across Cooper's Creek near Kaighns Avenue in the 1930s, the waterway was navigable from the Delaware River to the vicinity of Grove Street, Haddonfield. In Camden, the creek was about 125 feet in width and sixteen feet in depth at mean low water. At Stoy's Landing, near Grove Street, the creek's width was about 40 feet and the depth of the water ten feet.

In the 1870s, a variety of industrial establishments in Camden stood along the creek including a nickel refinery, glassworks, woolen mills, manufacturer of textile machinery and chemical works. The owners of these businesses relied on the creek for delivery of raw materials and sometimes transportation of their finished goods.

When passage along the creek was interrupted, the local press was quick to report the incidents:

> The ice has almost completely closed the navigation of Cooper's Creek and much that was conveyed to the factories on the banks must be transported by truck. (WJP 12/20/1871)

> A sunken boat or hulk is obstructing the navigation Cooper's Creek... (WJP 12/17/1873)

Cooper's Creek was also beneficial to the agricultural community along its banks. Although the majority of farm goods were driven in market wagons, shipping records from the end of the nineteenth century reveal some farmers shipped farm produce on the creek. Some farmers that lived along or near the creek found it more economical to transport their products to Philadelphia by small boats rather then hauling their products by wagon.

A number of types of vessels traveled on the creek including flats, barges, canal boats, scows and yawls. Flats, scows and barges, common vessels on the creek, moved up and down the creek helped by the tide and by men with poles or oar-type rudders called sweep oars. The small vessels floated up the creek when the tide came in and returned to the Delaware River with the out-flowing current.

A commodity frequently shipped on the area's creeks was manure. Gathered from Philadelphia's streets and liveries, manure was loaded onto flats and shipped up Cooper's Creek to the various landings along the creek. Farm laborers spread it on fields to replenish nutrients in the soil. They frequently shipped manure to Joseph Stoy's landing, near what is now Grove Street. [See Joseph Stoy, page 229.]

Old Haddon Township resident James Lippincott gathered agricultural statistics for the United States Department of Agriculture. In Lippincott's 1865 treatise, "Market Products of West New Jersey," the benefits of manure were highlighted. It is plausible that Lippincott was writing about Stoy's Landing when he described shipping manure:

> Their [farmers] teams, also, have been busy during the winter in hauling stable manure from wharves or landings on the creek where it has been deposited, unloaded from the sloops and flat-boats which navigate these streams. The sloops carrying from 125 to 200 one-horse cart-loads of manure, are floated up on the tide and return by the current. Their services are invaluable to the farmers of the interior, bearing, as they do, a burden of heavy and bulky material which could not be economically conveyed by wagons to the same distance from the city. Districts situated in the vicinity of such streams and landings are, in consequence, more readily cultivated than those more distant, and agriculture in general declines in proportion to the remoteness from the facilities commanding a cheap supply of manure. The lands in the interior of New Jersey have not been in demand, mainly because they are distant from the source of supply of enriching agents, and can never compete with those more favored by proximity to creeks or the Delaware. (p. 269)

Lumber and coal were frequently shipped on Cooper's Creek to Coles Landing. The landing, owned by Samuel A. Willits & Company, was near what is now Coles Mill Road in Haddonfield. [See lumberyards, page 168.]

Boats that once journeyed up and down Cooper's Creek passed many landings and wharfs along both sides of the creek. Jutting out from the creek's bank were about a half dozen landings in old Haddon Township. One wharf was built by Samuel French on his "Creek Farm" in what is now Westmont. "He [French] has also, on this farm, built a large wharf, on

Cooper's Creek at Coles Landing. Today this area is near the Haddonfield/Haddon Township municipal boundary at Cooper River. During the second half of the nineteenth century, barges ferried coal and lumber up the tidal creek to the landing.

(Photo by Samuel Rhoads, 1909.) (Camden County Historical Society Collections)

which quantities of manure and different fertilizers for the use on his farms are landed." (WJP 9/19/1877) They unloaded fertilizers and manure at this site. [See Samuel French, page 258.]

All three bridges that crossed over Cooper's Creek in old Haddon Township were fixed bridges. Traveling northwest toward the Delaware River from Evans Pond, the creek passed under a stone bridge at Main Street (Kings Highway), then underneath a bridge at Stoy's Landing Road (Grove Street) and finally under a bridge at Browning Road. Bridges in Camden were all draws, allowing larger vessels to pass through. In Camden, they hired full-time operators to operate these swing bridges.

Although most boat-building in the region took place along the Delaware River, a number of boats were built farther up Cooper's Creek. In the 1830s, Josiah Coles built vessels at Coles Landing. Coles built the "Caroline," a vessel that carried up to 45 tons of coal.

In 1869, an ocean-going vessel was built on the creek at a site opposite old Haddon Township, near the present-day Cherry Hill/Pennsauken border. When the boat was completed, the bridge at Browning Road had to be cut to allow the vessel to pass into the Delaware River.

When settlers first came to America, they harnessed the waterpower of the small streams and creeks. They dammed several streams that emptied into Cooper's Creek and ponds were formed which provided waterpower for mills.

At the eastern most point of old Haddon Township, Cooper's Creek formed Evans Pond. A dam held back water some eleven feet above the creek. The pond created the waterpower to operate several mills that stood along its banks. [See gristmills, page 134.] Today, this body of water is still known as Evans Pond.

Hopkins Pond, just a short distance from Evans Pond, was formed by a stream called Hopkins's Mill Branch feeding into Cooper's Creek. The source of the stream that created the pond was a spring which surfaced south of Tanner Street. The run traveled under Tanner Street and Haddonfield Road (Haddon Avenue) and into Hopkins Pond. The pond was the source of waterpower for the Haddon (Hopkins) Mill, a gristmill situated below what is now the spillway. From the top of the pond, the water fell some 22 feet to the creek below, a substantial drop for a water-powered mill in South Jersey. The Haddon Mill ceased operations sometime in the 1850s.

While waterways were important sources of power, millponds around the region were also popular recreational spots. Evans and Hopkins ponds were known locations for boating, fishing, ice skating and swimming. In the late 1880s, a row of seven boat houses were built at the foot of Potter Street on Evans Pond. The second floor of the two-story high buildings were used as club houses. The clubs held boat and canoe races on the lake. (HB 6/22/1888)

Camden's newspapers frequently divulged the successes of local anglers fishing in the area's creeks and ponds. The West Jersey Game Protective Society reported, "50 black bass placed in Cooper's Creek in Haddonfield." (WJP 11/24/1875) Another popular nineteenth century sporting event was hunting. The woods and fields surrounding Cooper's Creek, and Newton Creek as well, were popular hunting areas. Camden's *West Jersey Press* often reported on hunting news.

When conditions were favorable in the winter, a pond was a desirable location for ice skaters. Jehu Wood, Jr. lived on his parent's farm near Hopkins Pond. As a teenager, Jehu wrote in his diary: "It was splendid skating on Hopkins Pond this evening and lots doing." (Jehu Wood Diary, 2/19/1864)

In the 1930s, a tidal gate was placed across the creek near Kaighns Avenue to halt the flow east of the gate. The marshland along much of the creek was dredged and the waterway was transformed into the body of water that exists today. Today, the banks of Cooper River are neatly manicured and in some areas, the onetime tidal creek now has the look of a lake.

The Three Branches of Newton Creek

The other waterways that traveled through old Haddon Township were the three branches of Newton Creek. The branches merged near Gloucester City and flowed into the Delaware River. The three branches of Newton Creek did not have shipbuilders or heavy industry along their banks as did Cooper's Creek. Unlike Cooper's Creek, Newton Creek was not known as a commercial watercourse, although people along the creek did use it for commercial purposes. Mill operators diverted water to operate their machinery and some township farmers joined to convert the creek's marshes into productive meadowland.

As early as the 1760s, farmers along Newton Creek wanted to stop the tide entering the stream from the Delaware River. During Colonial times, an earthen bank with a tidal sluice closed the mouth of Newton Creek to tides. This allowed many farmers to turn marshland into pastures for grazing or extra acreage to grow crops. Every so often, the tidal sluices near the mount of the creek were breached, causing flooding and havoc for the farmers:

A break in the dam at Newton Creek which has been washed out several times by high tide, is now permanently repaired. The farms in that locality have suffered considerable by those accidents. (WJP 3/2/1870)

Nineteenth century landowners along the creek formed an organization known as the Newton Creek Meadow Company to finance land reclamation projects. The company assessed its members an annual fee based on the number of acres of meadow, marsh and flats adjoining the creek. Meadow companies were common throughout New Jersey. Reclaiming land was possible because of the system of gates and sluices near the mouth of the creek that blocked the tidal effects of the Delaware River.

The meadow company hired a manager to maintain the waterway. Among his other duties, the manager hired workers to clean out the creek:

Managers of Newton Creek Meadow Company invite proposals for cleaning out the canal from the River to the bridge at the White Horse Turnpike. (WJP 6/15/1864)

In 1867, the New Jersey Legislature authorized the "deepening, clearing and cleaning out of Newton Creek." (Acts of the Ninety-First Legislature of State of New Jersey, 1867) The enabling legislation provided for steam mud and dredging machines to clear the creek. The state was not ready to absorb the cost of dredging. Expenses were passed onto the "owners and possessors [tenants]" along the waterway.

One member of the Newton Creek Meadow Company was George Lee, the owner of creek-front property along Lees Lane in Collingswood. [See George Lee, page 208.] In 1865, the meadow company assessed Lee about $94 for his eleven acres of meadow land. The same land was exempt from Haddon Township's tax on real property.

By the early 1870s, defects in the sluices and gates near the Delaware River prevented natural drainage of water that flowed from springs and rainfall. This impediment cause unhealthy conditions along the creeks and resulted in declining property values of adjoining farms. The state's Legislative body had to amend laws to correct the problem:

. . . the said [Newton] creek was stopped off at its mouth, and the natural flux and reflux of the tides therein were hindered and destroyed; and whereas, the said meadow have not only deteriorated in character, and become comparatively valueless in consequence of the lack of sufficient drainage, but also the waters have become stagnant, and the said meadows a nuisance highly injurious to the surrounding country. (Acts of the Ninety-Sixth Legislature of State of New Jersey, 1872)

After all legal hurdles were cleared, the meadow company removed the sluices and returned the creek to a natural tidal waterway. Without barriers to block the ebb and flow, water flooded the marshes of the three branches to a width of 500 to 1,000 feet at high tide, giving the waterway the appearance of a broad lake.

Even after they restored the creek to a tidal waterway, farmers could still convert marshland to useful fields by a process known as banking. Mud and sod were used to make a bank along the creek. Sometimes builders reinforced it with pilings and timber. Upon completion, they drained the marshland:

All owners of meadow on Newton Creek requested to meet at Parson's Hotel to consider the importance of banking in the meadows with a dredging machine. (WJP 9/22/1880)

When the tidal sluices were still in place, navigation on the creek was not practical because they precluded boats from entering the Delaware River. Even after the tidal gates were removed, commercial activity never developed because permanent bridges over the waterway prevented anything larger than a small flat or skiff from passing upstream.

Today, the upper portion of the creek's North Branch forms a natural border between Woodlynne and Camden. The origin of the North Branch of Newton Creek was in what is now Collingswood. A brickyard occupied a site on the southern bank, east of the Blackwoodtown Turnpike (Mt. Ephraim Avenue). In 1879, serious damage to the Stone & Deno brickyard resulted after the creek overflowed its banks. [See brickyards, page 128.] The branch flows along the northern edge of Fairview where it joins the Main Branch of Newton Creek.

Springs, surfacing near what is now the Camden County park in Haddon Heights formed the beginning of the South Branch of Newton Creek. The stream, at this location, was known as King's Run. For many years, two mill ponds existed on the eastern side of Kings Highway. A pond formed behind a dam built near today's intersection of Dallas and Sylvan Avenues. In the early part of the nineteenth century, the mill pond provided water power for Glover's fulling mill. A second pond was near the eastern edge of what is now Kings Highway. This pond, known at one time as Hugg's Mill Pond, provided water to operate a gristmill along the creek in what is now Audubon. The site of the mill is along Haddon Lake. [See gristmills, page 134.] The South Branch was the border separating Centre and Haddon townships. Its course took it under a bridge at the Blackwoodtown Turnpike, where it met the Main Branch of Newton Creek near Gloucester City.

The source of the Main Branch of Newton Creek was in what is now Haddonfield. The small stream pushed on through Haddon Township to a dam once located at present-day Crystal Lake Avenue. Here a pond was formed, known in the nineteenth century as Crystal Lake. This body of water still exists, although it is not as large as it was then.

For more than a half-century, Crystal Lake provided the power to run John Stoy's sawmill, on the north side of Crystal Lake Avenue. Soon after the sawmill closed in the mid-1870s, James Flinn opened the Crystal Lake Paint Works. Flinn's company used waterpower to grind paint. [See sawmill, page 143, paint works, page 140.]

Besides being a source of power, Crystal Lake was a swimming hole for Rowandtown residents. John Stoy's grove, situated next to the pond, was a popular place for outings and picnics. When Walt Whitman boarded the Camden & Atlantic Railroad for a journey to the rural countryside, he sometimes stopped at Rowandtown and walked to nearby Crystal Lake. [See John Stoy, page 251.]

Another millpond existed about a quarter-mile downstream from Crystal Lake. The pond's name changed with each new owner of the nearby gristmill; however, it was best known as Cuthbert Lake, named for the adjacent landowner, Joseph Cuthbert. The Newton Gristmill, once situated along what is now Cuthbert Road, pulled water from the pond to grind grain. [See gristmills, page 134.] An ice house once stood next to the pond near present-day Stokes Avenue in Haddon Township. Its owner, Isaac Prine, harvested ice from the pond. [See ice farmer, page 163.]

Just west of Cuthbert Road, the creek's route traveled by Dobbs Brick Yard and under the small bridge at Lees Lane, known as Boggy's Bridge. The origin of the bridge's name was not uncovered. Even today, some local residents still refer to the bridge at Lees Lane by its old name.

The creek's route to the Delaware River continued through what is now Collingswood and Oaklyn, where much of the surrounding land is now part of the Camden County Park system. The creek passed Kalium Springs where William Jones had commercial success in the 1880s selling spring water that surfaced near the creek. Jones's water was advertised as having medicinal qualities. [See William Jones, page 208.]

The path of the creek journeyed by some dozen larger farms in present-day West Collingswood Extension, Fairview, West Collingswood Heights and Gloucester Heights before passing through Gloucester City and discharging into the Delaware River.

All along the creek, springs and runs drained into the three branches of Newton Creek. Many of the runs and streams still exist today. One of the larger streams that emptied into the Main Branch of Newton Creek had its origin near today's Hopkins Avenue, Audubon. It traveled under a bridge at White Horse Pike at a point just west of Nicholson Road. The run, called Peter's Creek, is visible today. Peter's Creek flows west between Oaklyn and Audubon Park before merging with the Main Branch.

During the early 1890s, "Lake Newton" was planned along part of the Main Branch of Newton Creek. By 1906, a lake existed on the eastern side of tidal gates near the railroad trestle at West Collingswood and Oaklyn. In the twentieth century, tidal gates were placed across the Main and South branches of Newton Creek, at locations on the western side of the Black Horse Pike. In the 1930s, they dredged and reshaped much of the original tidal creek and surrounding marshland into what exist today.

Roads

After the first settlers of West Jersey established their farms along the rivers and creeks, new settlement spread eastward. As settlement pushed into the interiors of West Jersey, the old Indian trails were adopted for use. Eventually new roads came into being to facilitate travel, trade, agriculture and commerce. Following the colonial period, roads radiated out from Camden's ferries linking southern New Jersey with Philadelphia. Several of the heavily traveled routes went through New Jersey in a southwest, northeast direction between Philadelphia and New York.

Turnpikes

In the mid-1800s, many turnpike companies throughout New Jersey had received charters from the State Legislature to build or take ownership of and maintain certain roadways. Often, the managers and shareholders of the incorporated turnpikes were local farmers, shopkeepers and merchants that wanted to make money and improve the value of their properties and businesses with better transportation systems.

A turnpike company raised money initially from the sale of capital stock and, after the roadway was opened, from revenues generated by tolls. Three turnpikes crossed old Haddon Township: Haddonfield & Camden Turnpike (Haddon Avenue), White Horse Turnpike (White Horse Pike) and Camden & Blackwoodtown Turnpike (Black Horse

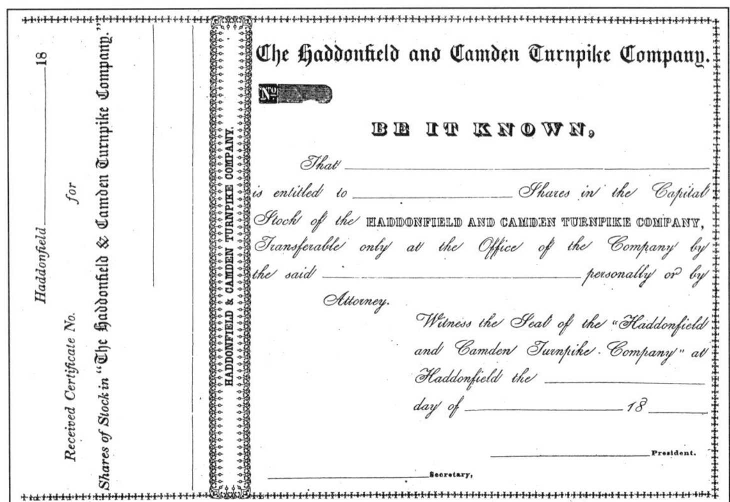

Haddonfield ______ 18

Received Certificate No. ______ for

Shares of Stock in "The Haddonfield & Camden Turnpike Company."

HADDONFIELD & CAMDEN TURNPIKE COMPANY.

The Haddonfield and Camden Turnpike Company.

No.

BE IT KNOWN,

That ______________________

is entitled to ______________ Shares in the Capital Stock of the HADDONFIELD AND CAMDEN TURNPIKE COMPANY, Transferable only at the Office of the Company by the said ______________ personally or by Attorney.

Witness the Seal of the "Haddonfield and Camden Turnpike Company" at Haddonfield the ______________ day of ______________ 18____

______________ President.

______________ Secretary,

Stock Certificate of the Haddonfield & Camden Turnpike Company. Incorporated in 1839, the company owned the road now known as Haddon Avenue. The county assumed ownership of the turnpike in 1893.
(Historical Society of Haddonfield Collections)

Pike). They all linked outlying farm districts to Camden and its ferries.

The first company to incorporate in Camden County was the Haddonfield & Camden Turnpike Company in 1839. Today the route is known as Haddon Avenue. The original incorporators and directors were influential citizens of Newton Township, several of whom resided in Haddonfield. The company did not commence operations until the late 1840s. At first, the road went from Main Street in Haddonfield to Line Street in Camden. In 1864, they extended the roadbed to Federal Street, Camden.

The company's charter gave them title to the existing public highway which, at one time, had been an Indian path. According to its incorporating charter, the highway was to be 32 feet in width, of which 20 feet was to be bedded with broken stone or gravel and crowned 15 inches from the middle to the side of the road. Ditches and underground drainage pipes were to carry water away from the road's surface.

They built two tollgates along the route, one near today's Euclid Avenue in Camden, the other tollhouse was at the southwestern corner of present-day Crystal Lake and Haddon avenues. In 1868, tolls were fixed at one and one-half cents per mile for a vehicle and a horse. Turnpikes in the state generally allowed free passage while traveling to and from public worship and while engaged in the business of farming. Stone markers were placed every mile along the highway. Each milestone was carved with the distance in each direction to Camden and/or Haddonfield.

The turnpike's patrons, as well as the local farmers, had a keen interest in the condition of the highway. Local newspapers often reported on the roadway's conditions:

> The portion of the Haddonfield Turnpike between the two toll gates is out of order and needs immediate attention. (WJP 10/4/1871)

> A superior quality of gravel now being put on the Haddonfield & Camden Turnpike, is from near Berlin. The turnpike is graveled the entire length, at a cost approximately $2,000. (WJP 12/31/1879)

The turnpike company employed nearby farmers to maintain the roadway. The Stoys of Rowandtown were hired to keep a stretch of the Haddonfield Turnpike in good condition. John Stoy and his son Walter used teams of horses to haul gravel to the toll road, then spread the material on the roadbed. During their tenure of working on the turnpike, Stoy's farmhouse was in clear view from the road, situated across a field from the tollgate. Today, the Stoys' dwelling stands at 330 Westmont Avenue. [See John Stoy, page 251.]

Upkeep of turnpikes included snow removal in the wintertime. Joseph Cuthbert resided on the southeastern corner of present-day Cuthbert Road and Haddon Avenue. [See Joseph Cuthbert, page 254.] On April 10, 1862, Joseph wrote his observations after a late-winter snowstorm:

> There has been a heavy N.E. storm for last three days the snow laying in drifts two feet or more in depth the snow plough has just passed down the turnpike. (Joseph O. Cuthbert–Book of Accounts)

It was common for nearby inhabitants to take advantage of the smooth roadway surface for their own enjoyment. Every so often, turnpike officials warned local inhabitants that the Haddonfield Road was a private roadway and not for the public's personal enjoyment and entertainment:

> Certain persons are in the habit of racing, by running and trotting their horses on and along the turnpike, whereby the persons and property of others peaceable travelling there on are greatly endangered. Printed hand bills will be posted up at the tollgates. Company will bring suit. . . . (WJP 3/23/1870)

Catherine Rhoads, the granddaughter of the turnpike's first president, Samuel Nicholson, wrote about her childhood memories. In *Memories of My Youth*, written in 1925, Catherine recalled traveling along the Haddonfield Turnpike between her home in Philadelphia and Haddonfield "in a large, two-horse carriage." She compared her childhood recollections to a later era:

> The good horses Charlie and Dick traveled well, and Grandfather pointed out to us the farms on either side of the graveled turnpike, with the cows and calves browsing in the fields. Mary and I were much delighted to drop the coins into the toll-gate keeper's hand, [now near Euclid Avenue in Camden] when we received the ticket which let us drive through the second gate. [Rowandtown tollgate] This turnpike between Camden and Haddonfield, after many repairs and paving has been made a macadamized thoroughfare free of tolls. Instead of farm wagons and pleasure vehicles, horse-drawn, we now see private and public autos traveling over it, and a double line of trolley cars. Instead of the forest-lined route that our Grandfather could remember, the Haddonfield road is bordered by an almost unbroken line of village residences, as he prophesied would be the result of citizens seeking the fresh air of a country home, and lower rents. (p. 15)

The White Horse Turnpike Company was granted power to take over and improve the existing road in its 1854 charter. Today, the route is the White Horse Pike. Most public roads then were in poor shape and local authorities were happy to have turnpikes companies assume roadway maintenance. After several years of existence, the roadway had been extended from the intersection of the Haddonfield Road, in Camden, to Longacoming, now called Berlin. A tollgate once stood on the roadway at Collings Avenue, Collingswood.

By the 1870s, the network of railroads carried most of the passenger and freight traffic in southern New Jersey. Turnpike fares collected at the tollgates could no longer cover operations, debt service and distributions to shareholders. Maintenance along many private roads, including the White Horse Turnpike, suffered when use declined:

> This so called turnpike is in worse condition than one-half of the county roads, and to extort toll for traveling on it is a wrong and an imposition the people should not be compelled to suffer. (WJP 4/13/1870)

The company known as the Camden & Blackwoodtown Turnpike Company, was granted a charter in 1855. They constructed the roadway between Blackwoodtown, now known as Blackwood, and Camden. Today, most of the route is known as the Black Horse Pike. Where the modern day route enters Camden, it is now called Mt. Ephraim Avenue.

A tollgate on the route stood at the intersection with Ferry Road, now Ferry Avenue. Every so often, turnpike patrons were treated to a reduction in toll rates. In one instance the tollgate keeper received an unexpected break in his duties when the turnpike officials decided not to charge tolls:

> Affairs of Blackwoodtown Turnpike Company are in such a flourishing condition that it has decided to reduce the rates of toll over the road under their control to one cent per mile. (WJP 1/14/1880)

> The late unpleasant weather has rendered the condition of the Camden and Blackwoodtown Turnpike very muddy, in consideration of which the company has decided to charge no toll for its use, until condition is bettered by dry weather. (WJP 1/28/1880)

Ongoing evolution in transportation technologies rendered turnpike companies obsolete, when railroad right-of-ways appeared throughout southern New Jersey. Just as the overland roads had replaced the rivers and streams as the major routes of transportation across the state, the railroads eclipsed the turnpikes. This phenomena was not unique to the region. In many locations throughout the country, well-traveled turnpikes were reduced to country roads after railroads took away most of the long-distance heavy transportation:

> Turnpike Roads. The multiplication of railroads in South Jersey has had the effect of destroying as a source of profit all turnpike roads except that which connect larger towns. (WJP 12/2/1868)

The value of many turnpike stocks plummeted because of the proliferation of railroad right-of-ways. Turnpike directors were reluctant to keep their roads in good condition, without foreseeable toll receipts. Eventually, conditions deteriorated to the point where local citizens demanded the county take control of the turnpikes to ensure the highways remained usable and in proper shape. The call for county ownership of the roadways came shortly after the Civil War. "The time is not far distance when all of these roads will revert to the county, and be kept in repair, as formerly, by direct taxation." (WJP 12/29/1869) However, it took many years from the time turnpike officials began neglecting their thoroughfares until the county took control of the private roads. Camden County officials purchased the Haddonfield Turnpike and White Horse Turnpike in 1893 and 1909, respectively. The State and county acquired the Blackwoodtown Turnpike, and made it into a toll-free road in 1903.

Tollgate Keeper

A turnpike company's incorporating charter gave them authority to charge fees for use of the highway. Turnpike companies hired tolltakers, or gatekeepers, to collect fees from travelers using the roadway. In 1849, the tolls on the Haddonfield Turnpike were fixed at one cent per mile for a carriage, sleigh or sled drawn by one beast and for every additional beast, one cent. The toll charged for a horse and rider, or lead horse or mule was five mills (one-half cent); for every dozen calves, sheep or hogs, five mills; for every dozen horses, mules or cattle, two cents. In 1868, they increased the basic tolls to one and one-half cents per mile for a vehicle and horse.

The turnpike's charter also placed limits on toll collections. The Haddonfield Turnpike Company was prohibited from collecting tolls from any person:

> . . . passing to or from public worship, on the Sabbath day, or to or from any mill to which he may usually resort, for the grinding of grain for his families' use, or horses, carriages, sleighs or sleds, carrying persons to or from a funeral, or any person passing to or from his common business on his farm, or any militia man passing to or from any training on a muster day appointed by law, or any other military officer or soldier passing or repassing, when called to duty by the laws of this state or of the United States. (Revised Statutes of the State of New Jersey 1839, p. 179)

Because vehicles could pass down the turnpike at any time of the day or evening, the gatekeepers were generally required to live in a house next to the road. Collecting tolls was a 24-hour, seven day a week job. In many instances, the turnpike company provided a small house for the keeper and his family.

Sometimes, tollgate keepers had to bid for their jobs. In 1863, the Blackwoodtown Turnpike Company accepted sealed bids for a position on the roadway. The job required "the Keeper to find his own fuel and light." (WJP 10/14/1863) One must keep in mind tolltakers had to go outside and collect tolls in the darkest of evenings.

In 1860, Isaac Albertson was one of two tollgate keepers on Haddonfield Turnpike. The gatekeeper's house was a small, one-story, frame dwelling on the turnpike near the southwest corner of what is now Crystal Lake Avenue. Isaac's wife, Martha, lived at the house with her husband. In 1870, Franklin Riley, age 50, was collecting tolls on the Haddonfield Turnpike.

As previously stated, a tollgate keeper's house stood at thc southcast corner of present-day White Horse Pike and Collings Avenue along the White Horse Turnpike. During the 1850s, Paul Laning, a gatekeeper, had an assistant tolltaker, Samuel Laning, working and living with him.

Tollgate on the Haddonfield & Camden Turnpike. The Rowandtown tollgate was located near the intersection of Crystal Lake and Haddon Avenues. The toll collector lived in a small dwelling on the turnpike. By the time this photograph was taken, two sets of trolley tracks ran down Haddon Avenue.

(Camden County Historical Society Collections)

When travelers came to the tollgate, they were greeted with a sign spelling out the various toll charges and other posted notices. For instance, signs displaying "keep to the right as the law directs" were posted at the Haddonfield Turnpike tollgates. When the tolltaker collected the proper fee, the long wooden gate or pike was opened so that travelers could pass through. The tollgate was similar to a present-day railroad crossing gate, although it was easily raised by hand. The gate was usually raised in the air. When the keeper went to bed, it was often lowered to ensure travelers stopped to pay their tolls.

Penalties or fines were assessed for violating the rules of the turnpike. They levied a $20 fine on anyone passing without paying the toll. If a person attempted to avoid the tollgate by entering private grounds next to the toll and reentering the turnpike farther down the road, the traveler was required to pay three times more than the legal toll.

Travelers had recourse to protect them against dishonest or overbearing gatekeepers. If a toll collector unnecessarily delayed or hindered any traveler at the gate, or collected more than the legal fee, the traveler could be reimbursed twenty dollars for his troubles.

A tollkeeper's job might seem quite routine and uneventful. Accidents at the tollgate were infrequent, although they were known to occur:

> Serious accident occurred on the Haddonfield Turnpike at the lower toll gate [Rowandtown]. . . . a pair of spirited colts . . . became frightened and unmanageable, running away and dashing through the toll gate at furious speed. Both men were thrown and injured. (WJP 12/29/1869)

Public Roads

Public roads were equally as important to local transportation needs as turnpikes in the nineteenth century. A portion of a local township's tax receipts for maintenance and road repairs of public roads within its borders. The counties were in charge of placing milestones along public roadways.

Local roadways were not always in ideal condition. In an age before smooth concrete and asphalt road surfaces, the weather, as well as frequent use, played havoc on a road's surface. Problems resulted when roads were too wet, rough, uneven or the soil was too sandy or loose. A road was considered in good condition if it were free from holes, ruts, mud, protruding stones and dusts. Loose stones on roadways could make traveling treacherous causing injury to horses and annoyance to travelers. Another problem was water traveling across the surface. In the winter months, sheets of ice were especially dangerous to teams of horses that could be seriously injured by slipping.

Each township in New Jersey appointed Overseers of the Highways to look after the public roads. An overseer, often a farmer or merchant, inspected public roads and hired crews to work on the highways in early spring or whenever repairs were necessary. Hired workmen filled ruts, cleaned out drainage courses, removed loose stones and scraped mud from the road surface.

They paid roadway work crews a standard rate of pay. In 1866, a team of four horses and two men that scraped a roadway cost the township $8 a day. A crew, comprising a horse, wagon and one man, was allotted $3.50 per day. State law required an overseer to ensure that a roadway was scraped and smoothed at least once before the arrival of each April:

> The public roads through the county are reported to be in fine condition. There has been quite an advance in road making, our farmers evidently concluding that taxes expended under their own supervision in road making, returns a good interest in the wear and tear of their teams. (WJP 9/8/1880)

In the wintertime, local citizens often pitched in and cleared snow from roads without any reimbursement from the township. This was the case in Haddonfield, when "John Gill and Benjamin Willis sent snow ploughs through town after each snow fall." (WJP 5/5/1871)

Poor conditions of local roads caused by harsh weather could upset a municipality's fiscal budget:

> Owing to heavy rains the past season the public roads have been greatly washed and gullied, and will require large outlays during the ensuing spring to place them in proper condition. Additional $800 is being raised for repair of public roads. (TC 3/6/1869)

Roadway hazards created by Mother Nature were not the only obstacle on public highways:

> Animals in the Highways. As the farmers in some parts of our county are seriously annoyed by cattle running at large, . . . (WJP 5/24/1865)

Another common road expenditure was for the purchase of lumber. In certain instances, poles and lumber were placed across muddy or soft road surfaces. During the 1870s, Joseph C. Stoy resided near Cooper's Creek along Stoy's Landing Road, now called Grove Street. As the appointed overseer of the route, Stoy often repaired the road's surface by placing lumber along the roadway. [See Joseph Stoy, page 229.]

Another township official was the Surveyor of Highways. When a public road or highway was laid across private property, any damage to the owner's land or real estate was calculated by Surveyors of Highways and reimbursement made.

Many public roadways around old Haddon Township are now main thoroughfares that link neighboring municipalities. Usually, nineteenth century roadway names were taken from a nearby mill, landing, landowner, or landmark. Some old roadway names have survived, while others took on new, generic names.

In the nineteenth century, what is now known as Collings Avenue was commonly called Collings Road, Gloucester Road, or Old Champion Road. The road, one of the first to be laid out by the original settlers, led to the Newton Cemetery and Meeting in what is now West Collingswood Extension. The *West Jersey Press* noted the thoroughfare was older than Kings Highway. (WJP 6/18/1879)

When Haddon Township was formed in 1865, Collings Road became the dividing line with Newton Township. Each township agreed to share maintenance chores along the roadway. Haddon Township maintained the roadbed between the Haddonfield Road and Blackwoodtown Turnpike and Newton Township assumed responsibility for the portion of Collings Road between the Blackwoodtown Turnpike and the bridge over Newton Creek, near Gloucester City.

Joseph Hollingshead, a dairy farmer along the White Horse Road, was caretaker for a portion of Collings Road. It is unclear whether Hollingshead was unaware of the roadway's deplorable state in 1869. It may have taken an article in the local press to grab Hollingshead's attention:

> A Dangerous Highway. The attention of the Overseers in Haddon Township is directed to the dangerous condition of the Collins [sic] road near the Haddonfield Turnpike. There is a breach at that point which extends nearby the middle of the road, and into which several people have fallen. The late rains have widened the breach making it dangerous to carriage, travelers as well as pedestrians. (WJP 5/5/1869)

Another township road steeped in history is Lees Lane. During the era covered in this project, the road was also known as Atmore's Road or Dobbs Road, both one-time owners of adjacent properties. The roadway existed in the eighteenth century and was a leg of the old stagecoach route known as the Philadelphia and Egg Harbor Road. Part of old Lees Lane still exists; however, the Zane-North School interrups its original path near the Haddonfield Road. The origin of its name was from George Lee, a nearby farmer who worked the land in Collingswood. [See George Lee, page 208.]

Present-day Browning Road, in what is now Collingswood, once led to a bridge that crossed Cooper's Creek. The roadway allowed passage from Haddonfield Road to Old Marlton Pike. Browning Road was named after the owner of farmland on the opposite side of Cooper's Creek. The roadway was also called Merchantville Road.

Cuthbert Road was known as Mill Road in the nineteenth century. The roadway took its name from the gristmill that once stood beside the highway near Newton Creek. By the beginning of the 1880s, they were referring to the roadway as Cuthbert Road, named after the Cuthbert family that resided along the Haddonfield Road. Mill Road did not extend north of the Haddonfield Road until the mid-twentieth century.

The incline on today's Cuthbert Road, between Newton Creek and Lees Lane, was once steeper. The hill, known as Dobbs' Hill, was named after the owner of an adjacent tract of land. In 1892, the township "cut down" the hill. They built and graded a new roadbed from Newton Creek to the White Horse Pike. (TC 4/1/1892) The roadbed was graded with gravel delivered at the Cuthbert Railroad Station by twelve cars on the Camden & Atlantic Railroad.

Nicholson Road received its name from the family that farmed land next to the road in Audubon. By the 1870s, the Nicholson family owned land on both sides of the road. For many years, the road went between the White Horse Turnpike and the Blackwoodtown Turnpike. In the early 1870s, the road was extended west of the Blackwood Turnpike to the South Branch of Newton Creek. After five years of controversy, a bridge to Gloucester City was finally completed in 1879. [See bridge to Gloucester City, page 85.]

For many years, the road that is now known as Hopkins Road was called Brick Kiln Road, named for Dobbs Brickyard that was along on Mill Road. In the 1830s, Brick Kiln Road was also called Hampton Road. The Hampton family resided on the route in today's Haddon Township. Brick Kiln Road, in the 1870s, intersected Cuthbert Road directly across from today's Lees Lane.

Citizens knew Crystal Lake Avenue as Stoy's Mill Road in the 1800s. Stoy's sawmill stood next to Crystal Lake. A survey drawn some three decades before the Civil War, noted the highway's name as Crystal Lake Road.

It is believed the roadbed for Coles Mill Road was first laid out in the 1820s. The route was once known as Coles Landing Road. Originally, the course ran in a straight line from Haddonfield Road to Cooper's Creek near Coles's Landing. The path traveled past Jacob

Cuthbert Road somewhere between Haddon Avenue and the White Horse Pike. The country road was also known as Mill Road. The road was named after Joseph O. Cuthbert, a farmer that resided at the intersection of Haddon Avenue and Cuthbert Road.

(Historical Society of Haddonfield Collections)

Coles's residence in today's Haddonfield. The original roadbed would include part of what is now Locust Avenue. Much like the present route, Coles Landing Road turned eastward at the creek and headed toward Grove Street.

The roadway now known as Maple Avenue in Westmont, was called Hopkins Mill Road in the 1870s. The old Hopkins Mill was once situated at Hopkins Pond.

An 1856 map, published by Barnes and Vanderveer, reveals Grove Street extended from Main Street in Haddonfield to an area near what is now Hopkins Avenue. Beyond this area, to Cooper's Creek and over into Delaware Township (Cherry Hill), as indicated before, the thoroughfare was called Stoy's Landing Road. Stoy's Landing, on Cooper's Creek, was named for the family that owned adjoining land.

Chews Landing Road was called Clement's Bridge Road during the period covered by this project. A bridge built outside Haddon Township on Clement's property gave rise to the name for both the road and bridge.

For many years, Warwick Road was called Snow Hill Road. The road took its former name from the "colored settlement," Snow Hill, later renamed Lawnside. When a new roadway was chosen in 1874, a reporter for the *Haddonfield Basket* wrote it was not universally agreed upon:

> "Snowhill Road," is not to be known any longer as Snowhill road, but as "Mansion Avenue." Ah! We will try to keep this in mind hereafter; but we confess that we do not like the constant desire that seems to be manifested to change old and well established names of places, roads and stations. But of course we must yield to "progress," and the "progressives," and it is best to do so as gracefully as possible. (HB 7/30/1874)

The main thoroughfare through the village of Haddonfield was called Main Street. Today we know it is as Kings Highway. Between the village's southwest border and the South Branch of Newton Creek, the highway was called Kings Highway or the Haddonfield and Mt. Ephraim Road. A road often took its name by the direction of travel. In Haddonfield, they called the highway the Haddonfield and Mt. Ephraim Road; in Mt. Ephraim, the same road would be known as the Mt. Ephraim and Haddonfield Road.

In the latter years of the 1860s, two prominent citizens of the village, Alfred Clement and Jacob Rowand, were placed in charge of maintenance along several roadways in the village. The entire length of Kings Highway, from the stone bridge over Cooper's Creek to the bridge over the South Branch Newton Creek near the village of Mt. Ephraim, was under their watchful eyes. The local citizenry often carped about the condition of Haddonfield's principal roadway:

Kings Highway, Haddonfield. During the nineteenth century, Haddonfield's main thoroughfare was known as "Main Street." Most of the village's commercial establishments were situated along the route.

(Paul W. Schopp Collections)

> The Main Street of Haddonfield, a short distance below the railroad, is a disgrace to the town—a regular mud road for considerable distance, utterly impassable for pedestrian without getting over shoe tops. (WJP 2/27/1878)

Between Haddonfield and the White Horse Pike, Kings Highway rose vertically some 110 feet. Stephen Collins, a nearby farmer helped with upkeep along this stretch of highway. In 1869, Collins presented a $32 bill to the township committee for his efforts fixing the road, including 150 loads of sand. [See Stephen Collins, page 236.]

A few sites in the township were preferred spots for racing horses. Main Street was one of those locations:

> Horse racing along main avenue of our town is out of place. Amusement occurs just at the dusk of evening. (WJP 8/23/1871)

Two other roadways in Haddonfield, Potter Street and Ellis Street, traveled from Main Street to a bridge over Cooper's Creek. Both streets were lined with homes and shops. Neither street has changed its name since the nineteenth century.

Private Lanes

When traveling to and from public highways or turnpikes, local inhabitants often used private lanes. In many instances, the nineteenth century lanes evolved into modern-day streets, while others have partially or completely disappeared and their existence is long forgotten.

Some private lanes were tree-lined passageways. One such path, on William H. Nicholson's farm, linked the White Horse Road to his dwelling in an area that is now Audubon. In 1897, Nicholson wrote a book entitled *My Ancestors*, in which he described the approach to the house as "shaded by an avenue of cherry-trees." (p. 82).

Of course there were many private lanes around the township; however, only three paths are discussed here. Other lanes are covered in Part III of this work.

Webster's Lane met the Haddonfield Turnpike where today's Glenwood Avenue intersects Haddon Avenue. The lane traveled from the turnpike, over a small run leading to the Main Branch of Newton Creek and onto a farm occupied by the Webster family. The former Webster homestead is now 205 Memorial Avenue. The lane continued past the dwelling toward two smaller lots of land. Part of the old lane is today's Glenwood Avenue; however, the remaining part of the path is no longer in existence. [See Hannah Webster, page 253.]

Willis Lane allowed Amos Willis, Jr. to pass from his homestead along Cooper's Creek to Haddonfield Road. The lane crossed over Samuel Reeve's lot and then between Thomas and David Albertson's lots before exiting at the Haddonfield Road. Over the years, they built homes along the lane. The lane evolved into present-day Cooper Street in Westmont.

During the 1870s, David Morgan's homestead was situated along Cooper's Creek at the end of Burr's Lane. Morgan's former house, now known as the Hopkins House, has survived the test of time and sits on South Park Drive in Haddon Township. The lane, named after the former owner Ann Burr, traveled from what is now Shady Lane to Haddonfield Road, intersecting the turnpike near today's Strawbridge Avenue.

During the twentieth century, the roadbed vanished into the residential properties along its former route. Although the lane has disappeared, the general location of the former lane is still apparent on any modern-day map as the boundary between Collingswood and Haddon Township.

Mickle's Trouble on Black Horse Pike

Traveling on rural roads during the nineteenth century could be a real adventure. One man's experience is documented in *The Diary of Isaac Mickle.* Isaac, a resident of Camden, was a lawyer, editor, politician and diarist. Although his account was written some three decades before the period covered by this project, it illustrates hazards encountered on country roads.

Isaac was eighteen in 1841 when he and a friend, Samuel Cowperthwait, were returning to Camden having spent the afternoon in Haddonfield. They returned home along the Haddonfield and Mt. Ephraim Road, now Kings Highway, and onto what is now the Black Horse Pike where Isaac and Sam encountered a hazard at the South Branch of Newton Creek:

> March 7, 1841. At about four o'clock we started, in a shower of rain, for home; coming, for the sake of variety, by way of Mount Ephraim. The road was good enough until we came to the causeway over the Newton Creek meadow, about a mile west of the Mount, which, owing to the breach in the dam at the mouth of the creek, was covered with water. The tide was running out with great swiftness, foaming and splashing over the road in a manner by no means pleasant to me, who am unable to swim, even in summer time when the water is warm. We had driven so far on the narrow isthmus, that we could not turn our wagon, without getting off into deep-water. After deliberating awhile, we espied to a house, not a great way off, upon our right; and began to cry "Murder! Murder" with all our lungs, hoping thereby to bring some one to the spot, of whom we might ascertain if there were any gullies in the causeway which it would be dangerous to attempt to pass. I remembered that Joseph Githens, my uncle's tenant, had nearly drowned himself and two women by passing such a place at Kaighn's Point after the freshet in January; and so thought it prudent not to try the invisible track.
>
> Finding our cries unanswered, Cowperthwait proposed to wait until the water ran off; but I objected to this, since it was already growing dark, and since the horse's patience might be exhausted by standing with his feet in water of a temperature of not more than forty degrees above zero. Should he become restive, we were certain to be backed off into the creek. It was agreed that one of us should wade across to the other shore, and try the depth of the water. We cast lots, and the business fell to Sam's share. He stripped, therefore, like a man of honor, jumped into the freezing cascade, and sounded across it. Then, coming back, he led the horse to the other shore, and jumped aboard, benumbed, and blue all over. The water was up to the wagon body two or three times, in places where the road had been carried away; and once the vehicle swam, rather than ran upon the earth.
>
> Sam had liked not to have got dressed again before we got to Camden; and the best of the joke was, we met a carriage load of girls, before he even had pulled his pantaloons on. He crept into the bottom of the wagon, of course, and lay there until the fair eyes were left astern. This was an adventurous ride, and I want no such again. At one time, I really expected never to see the morrow, but still I could not help laughing at Sam's ridiculous plight. (Vol. 1, p. 127)

Railroads

The rails upon which steam-powered locomotives traveled began to appear on the American landscape during the first-half of the nineteenth century. The geographic location of New Jersey, nestled between New York City and Philadelphia, assured the success of railroads. Passenger and freight service between the two cities along the Camden & Amboy Railroad's right-of-way was a commercial success. This railroad's contribution toward the industrialization of Camden was considerable. In southern New Jersey, the railroads opened the rural regions and allowed local industry to expand and prosper.

More than any other factor, the railroads contributed to the development of the residential communities outside Camden including Collingswood, Oaklyn, Audubon, and Haddon Heights. Even though the villages of Haddonfield and Rowandtown preceded the first railroads, the majority of residential building came about following the arrival of the "iron horse."

Camden & Atlantic Railroad Company

The first company to establish a right-of-way eastward across Newton Township was the Camden & Atlantic Railroad Company in the early 1850s. The PATCO High Speed Line and New Jersey Transit trains now use the Camden & Atlantic's roadbed.

A number of enterprising businessmen envisioned a profitable investment in a railroad that would carry Philadelphia's populace to a virtually uninhabited island named Absecon. While they were building the rail-line, the company's directors also laid out a town at the eastern terminus of the road. The planned community was incorporated in the 1850s as the City of Atlantic City. A popular resort town emerged and grew exponentially when riders were transported on the Camden & Atlantic.

In 1854, the 58.7 mile right-of-way was completed between Cooper's Point, in Camden, and Absecon Island. Ferryboats transported passengers across the Delaware River between the terminus in Camden, and Philadelphia.

Before the arrival of the Camden & Atlantic, Absecon Island was barren and unpopulated. By 1870, Atlantic City had 1,025 residents, 42 hotels, 50 boarding homes, and 278 dwellings. The city could easily accommodate 10,000 summer visitors. A boardwalk became the city's best-known attraction, invented by a Camden & Atlantic conductor to keep sand out of his cars. Atlantic City grew to become New Jersey's premier shore resort.

Much of the landscape changed along the Camden & Atlantic Railroad's right-of-way:

> A rapid development of wealth, and extended improvement, along the entire line of travel and an immense increase in population.
>
> They have encouraged settlement along the routes, by reducing the rates of fare and freight to actual settlers, and constantly offer inducements for travel to the sea shore by liberal deductions for excursions. (WJP 5/24/1865)

The hub of activity and starting point on the road was the Camden & Atlantic's facilities at its western terminus at Cooper's Point. The two hundred workers employed there built passenger and freight cars and repaired locomotives within a machine shop, smithery and other buildings. The Camden & Atlantic's wharfs extended into the Delaware River where coal and other commodities were received and loaded onto rail cars. The stockholders of the Camden & Atlantic also owned the ferry company that transported riders between Philadelphia and its Camden terminus.

Passenger service was the largest source of earnings for the company. Receipts from riders in 1877, were about four times the revenues earned from carrying freight. Sixty percent of the company's annual receipts were earned between June and September. Virtually the entire railroad's yearly operations were supported by four months worth of business. Transporting passengers to the shore was so popular, the Camden & Atlantic did not have enough passenger cars to accommodate the business. During the summer months, when the company needed the most passenger cars and locomotives, the Camden & Atlantic rented equipment to meet increased demand.

Patrons rode in first- second- or third-class passenger cars, while groups rented parlor cars. Bulky luggage was placed in a separate baggage car and once a day they attached a mailcar to a train returning from Atlantic City to Camden. In 1877, the Camden & Atlantic's rolling stock was composed of ten locomotives, nineteen first-class and 26 second-class passenger cars, five baggage cars, one smoking-car and five mailcars. The *Haddonfield Basket* noted the size of the excursion trains running through the village:

> The excursionists for Atlantic City on Wednesday last, occupied 38 cars, in two divisions, as they passed Haddonfield—one of 20 and the other 18 cars. Allowing 60 to a car, there must have been some 2,250 persons, or more. (HB 7/26/1875)

Many dignitaries traveled the railroad to Atlantic City. The *Haddonfield Basket* noted an unusual event in 1874, when a Civil War hero and sitting President of the United States, Ulysses S. Grant, was greeted at the Haddonfield Station by a group of residents:

> President Grant on his way to Atlantic City, on Saturday last, halted in Haddonfield where a large number of inhabitants had met to greet him. Among them was Captain Shinn. He acknowledged the attention paid to him by the people by stepping out and bowing to them. (HB (7/30/1874)

The popularity of excursion trips prompted the line to look for ways to encourage further use. In 1876, the Camden & Atlantic acquired land near Kirkwood Lake and built a picnic and recreation facility, known as Lake Side Park. The grounds had a large pavilion, ice cream saloon, kitchen, dining saloon and boat landing. The following year, 62 excursion trains, carrying 13,265 riders, visited the picnic grounds.

More important than the creation of Atlantic City was the agricultural and industrial development ushered in by the Camden & Atlantic. Before they constructed the railroad, New York City was the primary destination of products from New Jersey's coastal region. Small vessels carried their cargoes of iron, glass, charcoal, oysters and fish north to market. When the Camden & Atlantic began operations, the primary market for shore-produced goods became Philadelphia. The railroad also fostered development in South Jersey's glass and ceramic industries. One of the line's principal sources of freight revenue was lumber.

However, the region's agriculture benefited most. Farmers planted crops in areas of the pinelands that previously had not been profitable locations. The value of land appreciated significantly along the right-of-way. The Camden & Atlantic carried vegetables, fruit, cranberries to Philadelphia's market places.

Freight service was the company's second-largest source of revenue. Because there was more expense associated with loading and removing cargo on the cars, freight was not as profitable as passenger service. In 1876, it amounted to 21 percent of all receipts.

The company hauled more than 69,000 tons of freight in box, timber and gondola cars in 1872. The company owned 108 freight cars in 1877. By the late 1870s, refrigerated cars were in use along the line. Among other items, freight cars hauled ice, coal, stone, wood, lime, brick and marl. The Camden & Atlantic's 1878 annual report revealed a decline in freight from the previous year. Failure of the fruit crop was a reason for the decline.

On the whole, they moved most of the freight delivered on the roadway between industrial areas in Camden. However, the outlying stations also shipped and received freight. In 1873, 4,167 tons of coal, lumber, stone, lime, brick and fertilizer were deposited at Haddonfield's station. In that year, 308 tons of coal, lumber and fertilizer were loaded at Haddonfield and shipped to other points along the right-of-way. Some farmers along the right-of-way took advantage of reduced costs of bulk quantities of fertilizer delivered by rail. In the late 1870s, freight traffic at Haddonfield had increased to a point where they contemplated substantial improvements to the depot:

> Large improvements are contemplated at the railroad depot by the company in a short time for the purpose of increasing their facilities for the constant increase of merchandise landing here. (CDP 12/1/1879)

Although the majority of crops grown in Haddon Township were driven to market by wagon, the Camden & Atlantic's route became an expedient way for dairy farmers to ship their milk to market. The number of dairy farmers increased along the line:

> The farmers living within a radius of six to eight miles of Philadelphia enjoyed a monopoly until a few years ago. With the construction of railroads, . . . Milk is sent daily to this city [Camden] and places from every station within the grazing districts of South Jersey, over the Camden & Atlantic Railroad. Farmers wives find it much less troublesome and more profitable to dispose of their milk crop in that way than to manufacturer butter, and those contiguous to the railroad have nearly all embarked in the business. (WJP 9/11/1872)

In 1880, they built a new shelter to house milk cans on the freight platform at Haddonfield's depot. Before a new platform was constructed, the contents of freight cars were loaded and unloaded from wagons parked dangerously near the main tracks.

Although the most profitable segment of the railroad was whisking passengers to Atlantic City, commuter traffic also caught management's attention:

> If the people who live in West Philadelphia and in other suburbs of the great city . . . could be induced to cast their eyes towards the east. . . . They would see comfortable warmed ferry boats, leaving their docks every 10 minutes in the day. . . . By Camden & Atlantic Railroad any number of homes and small tracts of land can be found with a half hour ride of the business section of Philadelphia. . . . This is one of the things that has been brought about by intelligent railroad management. (WJP 12/1/1880)

To many township residents, the local trains that traveled between Haddonfield and Camden were the most important service offered by the railroad. In the years following the Civil War, the availability of rail transportation for Haddonfield commuters triggered a wave of development in Haddonfield. The seven-mile trip between Haddonfield and Camden took about seventeen minutes and cost 25 cents in 1874. The price included the nickel ferry charge to cross the Delaware

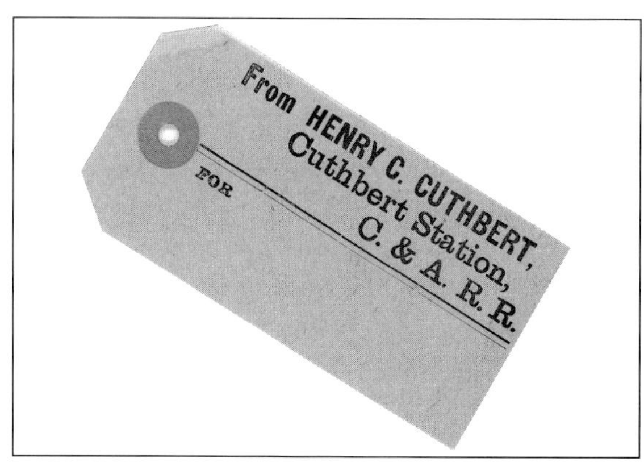

Shipping tag once affixed to Henry Cuthbert's farm products shipped from the Camden & Atlantic Railroad's station located at Cuthbert Road. Cuthbert's dwelling was situated along Haddon Avenue at Cuthbert Road.

(Historical Society of Haddonfield Collections)

CAMDEN & ATLANTIC R. R. CO.

677

20 COUPONS.

Each Coupon attached hereto WILL ENTITLE

M. Burrough

Or a member of his family to ONE PASSAGE in the cars of this Company, between

PHILADELPHIA AND HADDONFIELD.

The conditions upon which this Book and the Coupons attached hereto are sold by the Camden & Atlantic R. R. Co., and purchased and used by the holder, are as follows:—

1st. That the Coupons will be void if detached by any person but the Conductor.
2d. If this Book or any Coupons attached thereto are lost or destroyed, they will not be replaced by this Company.
3d. That wearing apparel only shall be taken as Baggage. If lost from any cause, this Company will be liable only to the extent of $100.

Treasurer.

ALLEN, LANE & SCOTT, PRS. PH'LA.

CAMDEN & ATLANTIC R.R. FERRY TICKET GOOD ONLY ON BOATS OF THIS COMPANY 677

CAMDEN & ATLANTIC R.R. FERRY TICKET GOOD ONLY ON BOATS OF THIS COMPANY 677

CAMDEN & ATLANTIC R.R. FERRY TICKET GOOD ONLY ON BOATS OF THIS COMPANY 677

CAMDEN & ATLANTIC R.R. FERRY TICKET GOOD ONLY ON BOATS OF THIS COMPANY 677

Coupons for passage between Philadelphia and Haddonfield aboard the Camden & Atlantic Railroad's passenger cars and ferries. Multiple coupons purchased in advance saved a patron passenger fare.

(Historical Society of Haddonfield Collections)

River. A yearly ticket was the most economical way to travel, costing $45, while a three-month pass was $15.

In 1876, ten trains traveled daily between Haddonfield and Camden. On Sundays, only one train was in service. For some Haddonfield inhabitants, that was one too many:

> Among the other matters discussed, as we understand, was the question of running a train on Sunday to the city in the morning and back in the evening–and several of those present favored the movement. It might be very pleasant and convenient for some of us to spend a portion of the Sabbath day occasionally in the city; but as the plea of necessity cannot in this case be urged, for thus further desecrating the day, we cannot understand how anyone professing to be guided by the laws and precepts of the Bible, can advocate such a measure. (HB 5/18/1876)

One wonders whether a notable difference existed in comforts on a PATCO High Speed Line train and a nineteenth century passenger car on the Camden & Atlantic. The answer certainly would be, yes! According to old newspaper accounts, riding a nineteenth century passenger train was often uncomfortable:

> The cars on the Camden and Atlantic Railroad are sometimes unnecessarily crowded. Such was the case especially on the four o'clock train on the 3d inst., on leaving Camden. The cars were full, and a number of persons, not being able to obtain seats, were standing out on the depot platform, expecting of course, that another car, which was standing in rear of the train, would be attached, when suddenly the train started, leaving those standing on the platform to scramble onto the steps of the cars and hold on the best way they could, or be left behind, and many persons had to stand till they reached Haddonfield. There certainly could be no necessity for this, as there are an abundance of idle cars standing about the depot. (HB 1/15/1876)

> The car left standing on the siding over night at Haddonfield, to carry passengers in the morning is perhaps one of the most antiquated and meanest on the road, with a stove away in one corner, and implacable wooded strips as ventilators, which stand from half way open to small apertures–not very agreeable these cold mornings. (HB 1/15/1876)

Even if nineteenth century patrons were fortunate enough to find a seat, they still encountered discomfort on many commuter trains. In the colder months, riders experienced chill and, during dry, summer months, dusty rides were common. During the 1870s improvements were made to rectify the annoyances:

> The forges of the machine shop of the Camden & Atlantic Railroad are in operation night and day. The machinists are at work placing "dusters" on passenger cars. They are

found greatly to increase the comfort of riding in dusty weather. (WJP 6/12/1872)

> Among the improvements in contemplation on the Camden & Atlantic Railroad for the coming season are cane seat car chairs. The old cushioned seats are dusty and decidedly uncomfortable in hot weather. (WJP 2/16/1876)

> . . . new desirable invention, designed to succeed the old method of heating cars by means of stoves . . . an entire train of cars is to be heated with steam generated in the engine. (WJP 10/31/1877)

> The patent steam heating apparatus is in successful operation upon the through trains on the Camden & Atlantic Railroad. The manner of heating is entirely new, having never been in use on any other road. (NR 12/1/1877)

Departing from Haddonfield's station, a westbound train could make as many as six stops before entering Camden. The first stop was Redman's Lane, just west of Haddonfield's station. The next stop was Rowandtown Station, situated on Stoy's Mill Road (Crystal Lake Avenue). By the end of the 1880s, the station was renamed the Westmont Station. About a quarter-mile down the line, on the north side of the tracks, sat the Glenwood Station platform, situated at what was Webster's Lane, now Glenwood Avenue. Due to the proximity to the Rowandtown Station, the company eliminated the station at Webster's Lane as a stop around 1880. The next westbound stop, Cuthbert Station, was a shelter on the northeast side of Cuthbert Road. Farther west along the tracks was Collings Road Station, situated on the northeast side of Collings Road. In 1877, they renamed the station:

> At a town meeting held on the 13th, the station on the Camden & Atlantic Railroad, heretofore known as Collings' Road, was by a large majority changed to Collingswood. (WJP 1/24/1877)

The last station before leaving the township was situated at the intersection of Ferry Road and the White Horse Road. They called it White Horse Station. The stop was next to John DaCosta's farm. DaCosta was an original director of the Camden & Atlantic in the early 1850s. [See John DaCosta, page 199.]

A locomotive engineer taking a train from Haddonfield Station to Camden had to be on the lookout for patrons waiting at nearby stops. Waiting passengers used flags to notify trainmen. For this reason, the stations were known as flag stops. Much to the surprise of the patrons, local trains did not always stop:

> The night train which leaves Haddonfield at 10 o'clock sometimes goes rushing by some of the stations without stopping when persons are waiting for it, and standing on the platform, with the moon so brightly shining that they could not help being seen if proper attention were given. One gentleman at Rowandtown informs us that he has been compelled more than once to hitch up his team and take people to Camden, who have been thus passed by. (HB 1/15/1876)

To better serve its riders, the Camden & Atlantic's entire roadway was upgraded in the 1870s with new T-shaped steel rails that replaced the old inverted

Locomotive "Curlew," Camden & Atlantic Railroad. The locomotive once traveled along the right-of-way now used by PATCO High Speed Line. The initial founders and directors of the railroad company also founded Atlantic City. The company's passenger trains transported passengers between Camden and Atlantic City.

(Camden County Historical Society Collections)

U-shaped iron rails. To accommodate local commuter traffic, an engine house and turntable were built at Haddonfield. By 1880, they widened the new roadbed to accommodate double tracking between Camden and Haddonfield, and a new platform was constructed at the Haddonfield station.

By 1878, a semaphore signal system had been installed on the Camden & Atlantic's roadway. The new system controlled train movement on the roadway by mechanical devices:

> Semaphore signal for the government of the trains, were erected at all telegraph stations last spring and proved to be great value in regulating train movement. (Camden & Atlantic Annual Report, 1878)

The press often portrayed the Camden & Atlantic as a benevolent employer. A number of local residents were employed by the company and worked at Haddonfield's station:

> The C&A R.R. Co. presented Mr. Evans, their flagman, with a handsome house, nicely painted and costly furnished, and now the tune is changed to be "I want to be a flagman, with a stick and flag in hand; To wave it o'er the car track, as a useful magic wand." (CDP 1/6/1877)

Working on the roadway could be hazardous, as some railroad employees learned:

> A son of Mr. Charles Shinn, of Haddonfield had his arm badly broken by being thrown from a hand car in the Camden & Atlantic Railroad the other day. His clothing caught in the wheels causing the accident. (WJP 5/17/1865)

In an era before automatic railroad crossing gates, accidents on the railroad were common. Engineers had to be alert for perils along the tracks. The *West Jersey Press* reported a wagon was destroyed by a passing train (10/16/1872). Livestock roaming to close to the tracks frequently became victims of the "iron-horse":

> Judge Tatem of this county was the loser of two cows struck by an express train on the Camden & Atlantic Railroad. The train was 20 minutes behind time, but the man who was driving the animals did not know it and it was while attempting to cross the track that the cows were killed. (WJP 9/22/1880)

Human fatalities on the line were also real possibilities:

> Thomas Bellinger of Rowandtown was walking on the side of the track, but not far enough to prevent the locomotive to pass without striking him. The accident occurred near Collings road. (WJP 12/22/1869)

> The railroad accident at Rowandtown, by which a man by the name of James Ewing (or Jack Wright), was run over by the night train from Camden. . . . He formerly belonged to Salem, and was in the employ of Edwin Willis. (HB 7/26/1875)

As important as the railway was to many inhabitants, others that lived near the right-of-way frequently carped about the railroad. One irritant was the constant blowing of the whistle as trains crossed lanes, roads or approached stations. The loud whistle was in stark contrast to an otherwise quiet countryside. Accounts taken from the *West Jersey Press* noted, "mothers of sick and nervous people are greatly disturbed" by the whistle. (WJP 7/28/1869) " . . . it [the whistle] is kept going all the time between Camden and Haddonfield." (WJP 10/30/1872) The summer excursion traffic was unsettling to many township residents. The local press furnished a glimpse of frustration experienced by some inhabitants:

> The farmers on the line of the railroad will be pleased to learn that the Sunday excursion train have been discontinued. (WJP 10/4/1871)

Not only were locomotives disquieting, they could be dangerous. Another concern to those farmers near the road was fire. Although the Camden & Atlantic took preventive measures to reduce the chance of this hazard by cutting weeds and brush, sparks emitted from locomotives' smokestacks still found their mark:

> A three acre field of wheat near Rowandtown belonging to Jehu Bates, of Haddonfield, was fired by a passing engine and about quarter an acre burned. It was put out by workers. (WJP 6/30/1880)

Philadelphia, Marlton & Medford Railroad Company

In the late 1870s, the directors of the Camden & Atlantic saw an opportunity to expand their rail service. In December 1879, they held a meeting at a hotel in Haddonfield for the purpose of selling stock in a proposed railroad between Camden and Medford, by way of Haddonfield and Marlton. A railroad to Medford had been in the planning for some seven years. As early as January 1873, work was to begin on the grading of a road, however; they delayed it.

The Camden & Atlantic had agreed to build the road and furnish the rolling stock if the public subscribed to $50,000 of stock in the new company. In return for its efforts, the Camden & Atlantic would become the majority shareholder in the company called the Philadelphia, Marlton & Medford Railroad Company.

The directors of the Camden & Atlantic had another motive for building a new line. They wanted a direct interchange with the Pennsylvania Railroad so that each company could exchange freight cars. They joined the new rail-line with the Pennsylvania Railroad's Mt. Holly, Marlton & Medford Railroad Company right-of-way at Medford.

The eleven and one-half mile road went through the agricultural district of Burlington County. The right-of-way split from the main line of the Camden & Atlantic near what is now Haddonfield's Reillywood Avenue, and headed to Cooper's Creek and on into Delaware Township (Cherry Hill). Haddonfield's J. Lewis Rowand was chief engineer for the new road.

During the construction phase, the *West Jersey Press* reported on the progress:

> The ravine near Riley's [sic] Academy . . . is nearly filled with dirt taken from near the Camden & Atlantic Railroad, where a deep cut has to be made. The field adjoining Cooper's Creek is already graded. A high trestle work bridge will cross the creek. (WJP 6/16/1880)

The Philadelphia Marlton & Medford hired a Philadelphia contractor named Ryan, and some 200 men and 100 teams of horses to work on the rail-line near Haddonfield. During construction, a labor dispute arose between the contractor and laborers over wages. A newspaper account reported on labor unrest and the ultimate resolution of the disagreement:

> Mr. Ryan, a contractor on the Haddonfield & Medford Railroad had some difficulty with his laborers on Thursday of last week. They struck for an increase of 10 cents per day in wages ($1.15 to $1.25). The advance was not allowed and the matter was settled by some going to work at old rates and others being paid off and leaving. (WJP 6/16/1880)

It seems railroad construction crews were a rough bunch and some village residents anticipated problems:

> The laborers employed on the Haddonfield & Medford Railroad by contractor Ryan have thus far been quiet and orderly, both while at work and in leisure hour, making no disturbances in or around Haddonfield. (WJP 6/30/1880)

Maybe local inhabitants were fortunate that workers employed along the line were able to buy goods from the contractor's store situated outside Haddonfield:

> Mr. Ryan, the Road contractor, has opened a store for his workmen, from which he supplies them with tobacco and a few other indispensable articles. (WJP 6/16/1880)

During the summer of 1880, the *West Jersey Press* reported that Ryan hired a "force of Italians from Philadelphia." (WJP 8/4/1880) By the following year, the completed railroad united one of New Jersey's choice agricultural regions, Burlington County, with Camden and Philadelphia, its principal outlet.

Railroads paid landowners damages when it was necessary to purchase land, move dwellings, outbuildings or orchards in the path of the right-of-way. It was common for landowners to seek damages caused by railroad laborers during the construction of roadbed. The *West Jersey Press* reported on damages claimed by area residents:

> Damages along route of new Railroad–Medford & Haddonfield. Reilly $1,000, Wm. Mann $38, Nathan Lippincott $96.60, Wm. Lippincott $88.50, Samuel Redman $2,545.50. (WJP 6/23/1880)

Sometimes disputes between citizens and railroads required legal intervention to resolve controversies:

> The company is laboring under an injunction being served at the insistence of Charles Redman, restraining them from working on his premise until $5,500 of damages awarded by the commission is paid. (WJP 7/28/1880)

Although the Philadelphia Marlton & Medford traveled predominantly through an agricultural region, surprisingly, the earnings generated from passenger service was more than sixty percent of combined earnings in 1888. The railroad to Medford was in existence until they abandoned it in the early 1930s.

Philadelphia & Atlantic City Railroad Company

In 1876, a dispute took place within Camden & Atlantic's management over lowering fares to the seashore for visitors to Philadelphia's Centennial Exhibition. Unable to convince the majority of directors that cut-rate fares could be beneficial and profitable, several directors, including Acting President, William Massey, resigned.

Shortly after the shake up, the former directors incorporated the Philadelphia & Atlantic City Railroad Company. Their objective in forming the new company was to lure Atlantic City-bound passengers from the Camden & Atlantic, thereby breaking the monopoly on shorebound rail traffic. The Camden & Atlantic had enjoyed exclusive rail service between Philadelphia and Atlantic City for twenty years.

Soon after incorporating, the company began to obtain the rights to build the route. The *Haddonfield Basket* reported:

> The Philadelphia and Atlantic city Narrow Gauge Railroad Co. is said to have paid $35,000 for the right of way through Camden county, and about $15,000 for the rest of the way, or about $50,000 for the whole way. It has

also been stated that the entire cost of the road will be some $70,000 less than the estimate, owing to the reduction in wages and the cost of materials. (LBGA 6/1877)

By May 1877, the entire 54.6 mile route had been graded and was awaiting tracks. The line's narrow gauge rails were 42 inches apart, instead of the standard gauge, which measured 56-1/2 inches. The company chose to build a narrow gauge road as a cost-saving measure. Also, building a smaller gauge railroad prevented a takeover by a standard gauge company. When the roadbed was completed, more than 900 laborers were hired and organized into track gangs. One gang started laying rails in Atlantic City, the other workers began in Camden. As odd as it may sound, the Philadelphia & Atlantic City's only competition, the Camden & Atlantic, hauled construction and roadway materials for the new railroad. Now, the right-of-way is still in use as a freight route running through West Collingswood, Oaklyn, Audubon, Haddon Heights and points east.

The Philadelphia & Atlantic City was not without it share of labor unrest during construction. Italian laborers went on strike while laying track in Camden. Unfortunately, the labor problems turned into a riot when Italian strikers battled with nearby African-American residents living in Camden's 8th Ward. Despite temporary labor unrest, track was in place along the entire line in just 96 days.

While they were building the railroad, the company purchased its rolling stock. Woodburning locomotives, twenty excursion cars, twenty first-class coaches, three passenger baggage combines, three baggage cars, twenty boxcars and thirty-one flatcars were obtained.

After Philadelphia's Centennial Exhibition closed, the railroad purchased rails and a number of buildings for use on their new route. In February 1877, the company obtained the Exhibition's Board of Finance Building, U.S. Commissioner Building and a shed. (CDP 2/13/1877) Several months prior, the company acquired the tracks from the railway temporarily laid throughout the fair grounds in Fairmount Park:

> The iron rails of the Centennial narrow gauge railway, amounting to over 190 tons, were sold at private sale to the Philadelphia & Atlantic City Narrow Gauge Railroad, to be used in making sidings and switches. (CDP 12/7/1876)

A station built on a wharf along Camden's waterfront at the foot of Bulson Street, became the line's western terminus. Ferries carried passengers to and from Philadelphia. At the eastern end of the line in Atlantic City, a passenger station stood at the intersection of Atlantic and Missouri avenues. One of the buildings from the Centennial was disassembled and taken to Atlantic City and erected as the station.

The company's directors were overly anxious to start excursions to Atlantic City. On July 14, 1877, sixteen cars filled with journalists, public officials and guests left Camden on the maiden inspection trip to Atlantic City. Upon reaching Tansboro, the fourth car of the train derailed. Ten passengers were seriously injured and a brakeman lost his life when a car rolled down an embankment.

A view looking west on Collings Road, now Collings Avenue. The former Philadelphia & Atlantic City Railroad Company's right-of-way intersected Collings Road at what is now Collingswood. The Champion School is situated to the right of the road.

(Collingswood Library Collections)

The first public excursion was just one week after the accident. The era of cutthroat competition between the Philadelphia & Atlantic City and the Camden & Atlantic had begun:

> The first public excursion of the Philadelphia and Atlantic City Railroad. ... A little excitement was created by the appearance of an individual offering a ticket for ninety cents by the "old reliable route" [Camden & Atlantic Railroad]. (NR 7/21/1877)

Despite a turbulent start, during the summer of 1877 four daily round trips to Atlantic City took as many as 2,300 passengers a day. The roadway's lure was its bargain fares, even though a trip to Atlantic City took an hour longer than its chief competitor. Extra time to travel the length was needed because the trains slowed at many locations such as the wobbly wooden trestle over the Main Branch of Newton Creek between what is now Collingswood and Oaklyn.

The company continued to acquire rolling stock after commencing business. In September 1877, the local press announced the Philadelphia & Atlantic City had entered several contracts:

> . . . contracts have been made with Bethlehem Iron Works for 3,500 tons of steel rails, Baldwin Locomotive Works for seven locomotives, Bailey & Co. for one locomotive; Bowers, Dure & Co. for eighty passenger and freight cars. (CDP 9/9/1877)

Although passenger cars were crowded during the railroad's first summer of operation, all was not well with the company's finances. In early 1878, the directors appointed a committee to investigate the company's accounts and report to its creditors. The *New Republic* noted there was "rumor of financial embarrassment." (NR 1/5/1878) The following month, having reviewed the company's financial affairs, creditors considered selling the rolling stock and personal property at a sheriff's sale. By mid-summer, the operations were placed in receivership. Patrons that prepaid their fares had reason for concern:

> The Philadelphia & Atlantic City Railroad having been placed in the hands of a receiver will fulfill all existing contracts with excursion parties. ... (WJP 7/17/1878)

The company's reputation was tarnished, at least in the opinion of the editor of the *West Jersey Press.* The paper referred to the Camden & Atlantic as the "Old Reliable," and the Philadelphia & Atlantic City as the "unreliable." (WJP 8/4/1878)

In January 1879, William Massey resigned as President and shortly afterwards, the company was unable to meet its payroll. When the summer excursion season arrived, the first-mortgage bondholders put in place a new management team to operate as trustees of the bankrupt company. Despite its financial problems, the trains continued to operate. The Philadelphia & Atlantic City was plagued with yet another disaster in the summer of 1879, when several people were killed in an accident near Clementon.

Undaunted, riders enticed by low fares, continued to fill passenger cars. To accommodate riders, boxcars were fitted with temporary seats. In 1880, reporters at the *West Jersey Press* wrote the roadway was "liberally supported." (WJP 8/4/1880)

There were no stops where the Philadelphia & Atlantic City's rail-line traveled through old Haddon Township in the late 1870s. A decade later, they established two stops in the township, both used for loading and unloading agricultural products. One stop was at William H. Nicholson's farm, called "Linden," in what is now Audubon. A second stop, known as "Oakland," was on Joseph Hollinghead's farm, in what is now Oaklyn.

In 1884, the Philadelphia & Reading Railroad acquired the Philadelphia & Atlantic City Railroad. In the late 1880s, the rail-line's management made policies that encouraged commuter service that ultimately led to development along the route. They converted the tracks to standard gauge in 1884 and double track was laid five years later. Concurrently, residential development began to take place along the route in the area outside Camden. Soon after that, passenger stations and platforms were built to satisfy the newly built residential communities of West Collingswood, Oaklyn, Audubon and Haddon Heights.

Other Railroad Matters

Officers and directors of railroads were once permitted to benefit personally from privileged information without violating laws. For instance, directors and officers informed about railroad construction plans, could purchase land from unknowing owners. They did not share the same information with the general public. The property could then be sold to the railroad company or held for future sale. In many instances, they turned a handsome profit. Today, these actions would be unethical if not unlawful.

Robert Fishman's *Bourgeois Utopias*, published in 1987, analyzed the development of the suburbs. The railroad executive's potential for personal gain was noted by Fishman:

> . . . the ultimate purpose of suburban transportation lines is not to move people; it is to increase the value of the land

> through which it passes. The best suburban land developer must also be a rail developer, so he can direct his lines through land he already owns, and retain the bulk of the increased value for himself. (p. 143)

William Coffin and John DaCosta, both township residents and influential board members of the Camden & Atlantic, purchased land along the right-of-way and resold it to the railroad company. Coffin lived in Haddonfield. DaCosta resided along the White Horse Road in what is now Collingswood. William Massey, President of the Camden & Atlantic in 1875, owned about 40 acres of land southwest of Haddonfield's depot. When the Camden & Atlantic began encouraging commuting between the village and Camden, the value of Massey's lots appreciated.

During the 1880s, Edward Knight obtained hundreds of acres of township farmland next to the Philadelphia & Atlantic City right-of-way. Knight founded the Collingswood Land Company to purchase and subdivide the land in the area now known as West Collingswood. Knight, while serving on the Board of Directors of the parent company of the local railroad, was able to exercise influence and control. The Philadelphia & Atlantic City's decision to build a passenger station at the site enhanced the value of Knight's lots. Knight's Collingswood Land Company subdivided its land into some 1,000 building lots.

Although tracks were never laid, plans were once in the works for other roadways through old Haddon Township. A common feature of the plans were that all the routes were to pass through Haddonfield.

In 1876, the Mt. Ephraim & Haddonfield Railway Company was incorporated. They formulated plans to build a three-mile branch connecting the existing three foot gauge Camden, Gloucester and Mt. Ephraim Railway with Haddonfield. The roadway was drawn to start in Mt. Ephraim, travel parallel and along the southern side of Kings Highway into Haddonfield. Once inside the village, the roadway was to parallel Cottage Avenue, cross the Camden & Atlantic's tracks, and end at the intersection of Centre Street and Cottage Avenue.

A branch of the Philadelphia & Atlantic City was once contemplated for Haddonfield as well. The terminus of the line was planned for somewhere on the western side of the village:

> Haddonfield is to be entered by a branch road, as we understand, on the west side, passing along the back of the town, near to Friends' Meeting House, and on through Wm. Mann's place, to we don't know where. (LBGA 6/1877)
>
> The contemplated branch from which is called "Baker's Corner," [White Horse Pike & Kings Highway] of the narrow Gauge railroad to this place [Haddonfield], when accomplished, will add another impetus to business.... (CD 9/18/1877)

A third right-of-way that did not come to fruition, was planned between Camden and Haddonfield. The *Camden Democrat* reported plans for the project:

> A project is on foot and is assuming definite shape, and that is to build a narrow gauge railroad between Haddonfield and Camden, to connect with the West Jersey Ferry Company, foot of Market street, the road to be run with dummy engines every hour of the day. ... The proposed road is to be along the Haddonfield turnpike, the stockholders of which, if we are credibly informed, are willing to give the right of way, provided a certain number of the shares of the stock of the turnpike company are taken for the privilege. ... The terminus of the proposed road, so far as we can ascertain, will be in the rear of the New Jersey Building, on Main street [Haddonfield]. (CD 12/22/1877)

Horse-Drawn Vehicles

When the original European settlers moved into the interior of West Jersey during the late seventeenth and early eighteenth centuries, roads laid on Indian trails became better and wider. New roads shortened distances between places by being made straighter. Improvements allowed carts and wagons to replace the packhorse. Where travel on the area's rivers and creeks was not possible, wagons carried commercial and agricultural products about the colony.

Before the railroads, stagecoach lines between New York and Philadelphia carried travelers and mail to and from these two commercial centers. In southern New Jersey, most stagecoach routes spread out to points east from the ferries in Camden. Stage routes could be found linking Philadelphia and Camden with Haddonfield, Burlington, Mt. Holly, Salem and occasionally to the seashore.

When the network of railroads was in place across southern New Jersey, the age of the stagecoaches, teamsters and long distance overland travel by wagon ended. Shipping goods by railroad was cheaper and safer than by wagons. Travel by wagon or stagecoach was also much slower.

Those inhabitants that lived during the era the railroad arrived, witnessed the end of long distance wagon and stage routes that once rolled through Haddonfield. In Sarah Hillman's work, entitled *Historical Sketch of Potter Street in Haddonfield, New Jersey,* she described the routine of the teamsters plying South Jersey's roadways:

> On the opposite side of Potter street, at this time, was a row of open sheds, for the accommodation of overland craft from the Seashore. The large white-covered Egg Harbor wagons, drawn by two horses, and freighted with clams, oysters, and fish came up the old road to Long-a-coming, now named Berlin, where they halted and fed. Then, they came by way of Cross Keys, the present Gibbsboro, and on to Haddonfield, which was their next and final stopping place, to rest and feed, before going on to Camden and Philadelphia with their cargo of sea-food. While the teams found shelter under the Potter street sheds, their drivers, no doubt refreshed themselves at the Old Tavern House.
>
> After supplying the trade in the village with such stock as they carried, these toilers pursued their journey along the King's Highway, and down the "Ferry Road," [Haddon Avenue] through sand or mud, to the Delaware [River].
>
> Returning, Potter street was again their harbor, where, after loading up with horse feed, pork, flour, and, undoubtedly, a supply of whisky, for all the stores then dealt in this commodity, they travelled back again to the shore, only to re-load, and repeat the same long, monotonous round; they usually made two or three trips a week. Some went by the way of Ellis street.
>
> But the above were not the only patrons of the well-known Potter St. sheds.
>
> The Glass-house wagons from Waterford, Winslow, and other points, drawn by six or eight mules, with a bell suspended from each side of the head, for protection in the darkness, also mingled with the Egg Harbor visitants, and the Charcoal teams of Long-a-coming and vicinity, as well as the Box Factory vehicles of Clementon.
>
> These various conveyances travelled, not in processions or trains, but at various intervals, through the day, and through the night, one, two, or more, coming or going, could be seen or heard, slowly winding their lonely way along the old pottery road to their destination.
>
> In the 50's, [1850s] however, conditions changed; turnpikes and railroads came to the rescue, and in the rapid march of progress and improvement, the former old methods of transportation so speedily passed out of existence, that it soon came to be a curiosity to see one of the "old-timers" on the road. (p. 7)

A variety of horse-drawn pleasure and general purpose vehicles once crisscrossed the roadways of South Jersey during the post Civil War era. There were a number of buggy type vehicles on the roadways and housed in carriage sheds of township residents. A buggy was a light, simply constructed, four wheel vehicle generally with a folding top. It was inexpensive and mass produced.

Jacob Collings, a resident of Haddonfield and Camden, owned a buggy wagon. (Inv. D-424, 1873) Another resident of the village, John Sheets of Audubon and later Haddonfield, drove a Syracuse buggy carriage. (Inv. I-61, 1888)

The more affluent citizens in the area drove comparatively more expensive coaches. Charles Bettle lived on a farm in what is now Audubon. He owned a popular style, an enclosed family vehicle known as a Rockaway carriage. (Assignment Book A-12, 1870) Two other stylish carriages once seen along the township roadways were York and Germantown carriages. John Sheets owned a two-seater phaeton. (Inv. I-61, 1888) These four-wheeled carriages had open sides and were named for a Greek god. There were a variety of carriages called phaetons.

Selecting the right carriage was somewhat similar in modern times to choosing an automobile. The owners of carriages looked at the practical or functional aspects of a vehicle, yet style was also important. The art of making carriages was to connect consumers' taste with the intended use of the vehicle. In the book, *19th Century American Carriages*, the essence of carriage design was stated:

> The principle of American carriage design was to express purpose to use. A carriage was a composite object, combining a variety of materials such as wood, paint, leather, metal and textiles; it was also a summation of diverse skills. From the most formal coach to the most lightweight, inexpensive buggy, a horse-drawn vehicle had to accommodate passengers and withstand the strain of horse-power drawing it and the impact of the various road surfaces it transversed, and combine all these requirements in such a way as to convey balance, harmony and proportion. . . . (p. 42)

Even in modern times, an antique or unusual model automobile often draws the attention of those nearby. The same could be said about quaint carriages of the nineteenth century. When William Mann's new carriage was spotted in his home village of Haddonfield, the local newspaper reported the event:

> Our attention was directed one morning recently to a new vehicle on our street, somewhat in the shape of a light omnibus drawn by two fine greys. On inquiry, we learned that it was a large family carriage, belonging to Mr. Wm. Mann, which he had provided for accommodations of his large family, in going to and from the railroad depot (from which his residence is a considerable distance,) and other purposes. It is convenient to get in and out, having a door at the rear end, and is capable of holding some eight or ten persons. It is quite a tasty looking affair, the body being of a dark color and the running gear yellow. (HB 3/1875)

When trains pulled into Haddonfield's depot, some arriving passengers were in need of transportation. A

Carriage and *Jenny Lynd* at William C. Nicholson's residence along Nicholson Road in what is now Audubon. Horse-drawn vehicles were necessities to farmers like William Nicholson that resided in the countryside.

(Courtesy of Joseph Hartel)

carriage for hire, or nineteenth century taxi, could be hailed outside the station:

> M.E. Farnsworth is now running the Haddonfield express for the accommodation of strangers and residents. The express meets all trains and conveys passengers to any part of the town for a nominal price. (WJP 2/10/1875)

Just as today, accidents were a part of the horse and carriage era, although certainly not as frequently as when automobiles began using the thoroughfares:

> Miss Hannah Webster and Miss Abbie Albertson of Haddonfield . . . [had a] collision with another carriage, their carriage was upset and both ladies received severe injuries. (WJP 11/14/1866)

> Mr. F.C. Lippincott had his carriage demolished a few days ago, while standing in front of Squire E. Clement's office, [Main Street, Haddonfield] by being run into by a two mule team heavy wagon, belonging to Levi Kimble. (HB 12/1875)

Traffic jams on country roads never really occurred. On the other hand, traffic slowed in Camden during harvest time:

> From twelve o'clock until four or later, there is almost a continual line of vehicles from the country conveying produce to the Philadelphia markets. Wagon after wagon, heavily loaded with truck, moves along in the direction of the West Jersey ferry, the drivers either asleep or close to the "land of nod." (WJP 8/15/1877)

While carrying out their daily chores, virtually all farmers in old Haddon Township relied on market wagons and carts. There were several style variations to the general-purpose farm wagon. Some were heavy, versatile box body vehicles used primarily for hauling freight. Other vehicles were light, standard utility wagons. For instance, Haddonfield's Charles Shinn owned a heavy spring wagon. (Inv. D-1, 1870) Shinn's square box wagon had moveable seatboards hung on elliptic springs. Dealers of goods and storekeepers relied on their delivery wagons to transport goods such as coal, lumber, meat, groceries and ice to customers. A cart was a two-wheeled vehicle utilized mainly for moving freight or bulk refuse.

Before the era of industrialization, wheelwrights, small carriage shops and blacksmiths like those in the township, dominated production of vehicles. These establishments used general-purpose machinery and hand tools to make vehicles. Work was usually carried out by a master carriagemaker, wheelwright or blacksmith, and often helped by one or more apprentices.

They assembled carts, wagons and carriages in the township's two villages. Charles Haines's shop in Rowandtown, and George Tule's shop in Haddonfield manufactured carriages, carts and wagons. Thomas Albertson's Rowandtown wheelwright shop also assembled carts and wagons. Albertson sold his wagons for about $125 a piece, and brought in on average, $40 a cart in 1860. Another Haddonfield wheelwright, William McKnight, assembled carts and wagons during his many years in the profession. [See wheelwrights, page 125.]

In the winter, when roadways were covered with ice and snow, horse-drawn sleighs replace carriages. A sliding vehicle on runners, a sleigh, was the only practical way of getting around when snow blanketed the land. Compared to a carriage, the sleigh had less intricate construction, thereby its cost was less and more families could afford them. Ownership of sleighs was common throughout the township.

The era of the horse-drawn vehicles gradually ended in Haddon Township after cheap, mass-produced automobiles became a reality.

Ferries

The ferries linking southern New Jersey and Philadelphia were important transportation facilities for travelers, agriculture, trade, and commerce for more than two and one-half centuries. The first ferry between West Jersey and Philadelphia began operating in the 1680s. As they built more roads, ferry demand also increased. By the early 1800s, a community evolved around the major ferries on the New Jersey side of the Delaware River. The City of Camden eventually unfolded.

There were about a half-dozen ferryboat companies operating during the 1870s between Camden and Philadelphia. Outside Camden's city limits, vessels owned by the Philadelphia Ferry Company traveled between Gloucester City and Philadelphia. Most of the area's turnpikes terminated at Camden's ferries where patrons, horses and wagons waited for the short trip to Philadelphia. The ferry wharfs in Camden were also terminals for the five railroads that radiated out from Camden. In most cases, each ferry company had an affiliation with a particular railroad.

Patrons traveling between Philadelphia and points north and east, generally rode the Federal Street Ferry, then transferred to the Camden & Amboy Railroad. By the end of the 1860s, the Federal Street Ferry had the largest annual passenger manifest among Camden's ferries:

> Federal Street Ferry 2,200,000 passengers; West Jersey Ferry Company 740,726 passengers; The Cooper's Point Ferry 202,262. . . . (WJP 1/6/1869)

The expense of transporting market wagons loaded with hay, straw or produce was a significant cost to the farmer. In 1864, the fare for a market wagon loaded with hay to cross the river was $1.25. Some farmers paid as much as $100 a year to ride across the Delaware River. Market wagons began lining up before midnight and continued to do so into the early morning hours to get to the Philadelphia market:

> Rush of wagons last couple of weeks that the ferry boats are compelled to commence their trip shortly after midnight, and run about every one-half hour until daylight. . . . (WJP 8/19/1874)

Many travelers relied on the ferries to transport them to Philadelphia. Most commuters that resided in old Haddon Township boarded Camden & Atlantic passenger trains at Haddonfield's station for the seven-mile ride to Camden's Cooper's Point. Some riders departed the train before reaching the Camden & Atlantic's terminal and boarded a ferry operated by a competitor of the Cooper's Point Ferry. A typical ferry ride took about fifteen minutes from the time the boat departed from the slip until the gates opened and the boat was secured to walk off into the ferryhouse on the opposite shore.

In 1880, the fare to cross the river between Camden and Philadelphia was three cents. Riders could purchase nine tickets for 25 cents. The ferry rates some fifteen years earlier, were actually more expensive:

> Each adult passenger 5 cents; children between 4 and 12 years of age, 2 cents; package tickets (34 rides) $1.00; six-month commutation tickets (day boats only) $5.00. (WJP 5/24/1865)

Ferry companies established regulations on the amount of baggage riders were allowed to carry onto a vessel. The Federal Street Ferry's rules were:

> Passengers were prohibited from taking anything excepting wearing apparel as "baggage," and all such baggage weighing over 50 pounds was charged for in addition to the regular rate of fare. (*The Span of a Century–The Chronicle History of the City of Camden 1828–1928*, p. 47)

In the early days of the ferry, accommodations such as waiting rooms for passengers were often nonexistent. Thirsty passengers visited several "commodious saloons" to quench their thirst. (Prowell, p. 368) As time went on, they built hotels near the ferry slips to accommodate waiting patrons. Passengers eagerly supported the hotel's bar room while waiting for their ferries. The

West Jersey Hotel, an affiliate of a ferry company, and the Parsons Hotel stood near ferry slips. During the 1870s and 1880s, ferry passenger patronage at the hotels was on the decline as ferry companies began building large stations.

The original ferry slips and houses in Camden were a block or two from today's river bank. In 1860, the land around the site of the original Market Street Ferry facility had "filled up to such an extent that a new ferry landing and ferry house were erected farther westward." (*Annals of Camden*, p. 18) In 1863, the owners of the Federal Street Ferry filled the river bank at the foot of Federal Street. Noted local author Charles Boyer wrote, "the street was extended four hundred feet westward. Upon the land so reclaimed, a new ferry house and slips were built. . . ." (*Annals of Camden*, p. 26)

Before renovations in the 1870s, Boyer described the Cooper's Point Ferry house:

> This ferry house . . . was a very primitive affair. In the center was an open driveway for teams and persons to get on and off the boats, while on the lower side of this driveway, or slip was a small waiting room, and on the upper side was a baggage room for use of the railroad. (p. 12)

The Cooper's Point Ferry, owned by the Camden & Atlantic Railroad Company, made substantial improvements to its facilities. In 1875, they completed a "commodious and showy ferry house at the foot of Vine Street in Philadelphia." (HB 6/1875) Five years later, the company made improvements on the Camden side of the river that included a new ferry house:

> Ferry building 40 feet by 60 feet waiting rooms. Two slips for boats with covered way leading to each so that passengers are fully protected from weather in passing to and from trains and boats of the Company. One shed 60 feet wide and 172 feet in length.
>
> Two train sheds 620 feet by 25 feet, the other 264 feet by 20 feet. (Camden & Atlantic Annual Report, 1880)

Another means by which passengers arrived at the Camden ferries was by horse and carriage. Often, the vehicle and horse remained in Camden while the owner went onto Philadelphia. Food and shelter for horses could be found at nearby livery stables. The Cooper's Point Ferry operated its own stables:

> In order to accommodate travel over the Boats of the Company, a hay shed 60 by 108 feet was erected near the Ferry in the stable yard, and the entire shedding around the yard. (Camden & Atlantic Annual Report, 1880)

In an attempt to attract riders, the Market Street Ferry made several innovative changes. The company inaugurated an all-night boat during the peak summer and fall months. To attract and hold the patronage of the New Jersey farmers, the ferry company opened a hay and straw market in Philadelphia in 1871. In 1876, the Market Street Ferry improved its facility to attract the anticipated Centennial crowd:

> This ferry house, which was the first one on this side of the river to have a cover over the entire slip, was used until 1876, when the new ferry house, . . . was rushed to completion in anticipation of the travel to the Centennial Exposition. One of the principal innovations in the new ferry house was the large clock on the cupola, which was the first large tower clock to be installed in Camden. (*Annals of Camden*, p.18)

At one time ferryboats were made of wood. By the 1870s, most of Camden's major ferryboats were fabricated with iron. Iron ferries were larger, stronger and more powerful than the old wooden boats. The *Baltic*, owned by the Market Street Ferry, was 157 feet long by 54 feet wide. The larger ferry boats of the era could transport some 1,500 to 2,000 passengers per trip.

Another advantage of larger and heavier iron boats was their ability to crush through ice on the river. Even with large iron vessels, when the ice became too thick, they halted ferry service:

> The boats at Vine Street ferry have ceased running on account of the ice in the river. . . . (CDP 1/5/1877)

> . . . the ice is getting heavy in the Delaware but does not as yet, much interfere with the crossing of the ferry boats between Camden and Philadelphia. (HB 1/14/1875)

After a ferry disaster in which 48 lives were loss when an on board fire caused the "*New Jersey*" to sink off the Camden shore in 1856, ferry owners were awakened to passenger safety. In years before 1856, boats were not fitted with lifesaving devices. After the "*New Jersey*" catastrophe, they outfitted ferryboats with life preservers, cork cushions and other life safety appliances. The Market Street Ferry's new vessel, "*Columbia*," had the distinction of being the first fireproof boat:

> . . . an iron boat, built in 1877, with iron wheel-houses, galleys, frames and engine-house, the first ferry-boat on the river so completely fire-proof. (Prowell, p. 375)

Competition among the ferry companies was fierce. In order to keep up with competitors, they installed the latest comforts in the boats. Some improvements however, were controversial:

> . . . the sub-dividing of the ferry seats by means of iron arms, to break up the habit which many of the passengers had of stretching out and taking comfortable naps on the

Cooper's Point Ferry, Cooper's Point, Camden. The ferry, owned by the Camden & Atlantic Railroad, transported passengers and freight to Philadelphia's Vine Street. Five ferry companies operated between Camden and Philadelphia in the 1870s.

(Camden County Historical Society Collections)

seats during the trip across the river, and in consequence of the number of seats occupied, compelling other passengers to stand. A woman correspondent in one of the "dailies" in 1858 censured the ferry company for installing these "iron bars" because it prevented those women who followed the fashion styles of the times from sitting down. (*Annals of Camden*, p. 19)

A newspaper article dated July 10, 1887, was clipped from an unidentified Camden publication and placed in a scrapbook entitled "Historical Clippings Relative to Camden, NJ." The article was titled "Crossing the Ferry—The Moving Panorama of Figures." The reporter spent the day on the Federal Street Ferry and made observations about the clientele on the boat:

> There [Federal Street Ferry] you will find all manner of men, from the lowest and most brutal to the most refined and gentle; from the maudlin drunkard to the straight-laced Prohibitionist; from the dull, plodding laborer, who travels o'er the even tenor of his way, unfired by any ambition other than to earn his weekly wage, to the astute and wily financier or politician, whose brain teems with schemes and plans emulating from an insatiable desire for personal aggrandizement.

Typically a day started with milk wagons pulling onto the ferry and laborers boarding for the journey across the Delaware River. The same reporter observed:

> The early morning is ushered in with the rattling of milk cans being conveyed from the railroads to the wagons in waiting, where their contents will soon be distributed among thousands of people. . . .
>
> The travelers on the early boats are mostly of the laboring classes. Then they are decked out in blue overalls and jumpers, ready for the toil of the day, and in their hands are their dinner pails filled with plain substantial food. . . . Most of them puff away at a short clay or wooden pipe. . . . And some who are less energetic than their fellows take advantage of the short trip across the river to drop into a faint doze, from which they are soon rudely awakened, either by the rude bumping of the boat into her slip or by the grasp of their companion's hand upon their shoulder and the ever-familiar words shouted in their ears, "The boat's in."

The newspaper account noted from six to eight o'clock the ferry house was crowded with:

> . . . pretty girls, ugly girls, homely girls . . . young men, old men and middle-aged men . . . all bound for the stores, shops and offices of the great city.

Everyone, from the poorest to the wealthiest individuals, rode on the ferry:

> About nine o'clock the portly, well dressed and wealthy businessmen began to make their appearance on the scene. . . . They push their way through the throng of hurrying humanity which at this hour is being rapidly dumped from long trains of cars from Atlantic and board the crowded boat. When the boat lands they make their way out and head down toward Chestnut street and the exchanges, or up into the dry goods and big commercial districts.

The reporter remarked that it was during the evening hours that the more interesting crowds boarded the ferry to cross over to Philadelphia. The same weary crowd later returned to the Camden ferry house:

> It is no longer the mixed crowd hurrying onward to business, but is the pleasure-seeking fraternity. All are happy and bright, and all thought of care and trouble is cast aside. 'Tis pleasure they are after, and they want none of the worry of toil to cling to them.
>
> Towards midnight these pleasure-seekers, now filled to overflowing, begin to return and the tide courses homeward till the first streaks of day appear and penetrate the mists of the busy river. The pleasures of the night are past ...

During most of the nineteenth century, Windmill Island stood between Camden's shore and Philadelphia. In earlier times, Windmill Island once caused ferry captains to take a circuitous route while crossing the river. The trip was shortened in the late 1830s, when they cut a canal through the piece of land in the Delaware River, making two islands. When Thomas Smith became owner of the northern island, it took the name Smith's Island. Much to the satisfaction of the ferry companies, in 1894, the United States Government removed both Windmill and Smith Islands from the river.

Bridges and Tunnels

Even though ferry service across the river was for the most part regular, there were times when travelers and local trade were inconvenienced. Time was lost while waiting for ferries to arrive and depart and, during the wintertime when ice was too thick, ferries remained tied in the slips. Throughout the 1800s, ideas and movements challenged the necessity for ferry service.

As early as 1818, an idea was conceived to build a bridge between Camden and Windmill Island. From the island, plans called for a ferry to carry patrons the remaining leg of the journey across the river to Philadelphia. The plans never materialized because investors were not as enthusiastic about the idea as its planners. Interest in a bridge was discussed again in the 1860s. Again, they did not put the idea into motion.

Thoughts of tunneling under the river were considered in the 1870s. These plans, too, did not come to fruition. Several editors of the Camden press supported the idea of a tunnel under the river:

> What happened to the Delaware River tunnel project? This winter has demonstrated the necessity for some means of crossing the Delaware from Philadelphia, in addition to the ferry boats. A bridge is impracticable. (CDP 1/13/1877)

When the first bridge spanned the Delaware River between Camden and Philadelphia in 1926, it marked the beginning of the demise of the local ferries. The bridge is now known as the Benjamin Franklin Bridge. The last ferry to steam across the Delaware River was almost thirty years after the bridge was completed.

4

Education and Houses of Worship

Education

Before the public began paying for childrens' education, often, schools prepared students vocationally for a life of farming or as a craftsman. Following the Civil War, the focus of Americans' educational system shifted and publicly supported education came into existence. Schools became a forum for the national transformation from an agrarian to an industrial-based society.

Changes in education in New Jersey began by addressing inherent problems. A magazine article entitled "The New School Law," from *The Northern Monthly*, was published by the New Jersey State Literacy Union in 1867. The article summarized several major problems facing New Jersey's schools:

> The defects of our common schools under the old system came under two heads–irregular attendance of the children, and incompetency of teachers. (Vol. No. 6, 1867)

During the late 1860s, New Jersey's Legislature addressed these concerns along with other education issues. New laws were enacted that provided for a system of taxation, plans for supervision, inspection of schools and teacher certification.

By the early 1870s, broad financial support from the state's coffers along with local school and poll taxes enabled school districts to build new facilities, modernize furniture and obtain new books. The Annual Report prepared in 1872, by New Jersey's Superintendent of Public Schools, noted public schools would no longer require students to pay tuition:

> Free schools and public schools, virtually are synonymous, but not until the passage of the free school act, by the Legislature of last winter, . . . The schools . . . established under the general law of the State have been pay schools, or virtually private schools with reduced tuition rates. Those who attended them were obliged to pay tuition fees–the State simply paid a part of the expenses of maintaining the schools, and thus reduced the amount to be paid by the patrons. By the passage of the free school act our whole school machinery is very much simplified, and the full benefits of a public school system is accorded to all the children of the State.
>
> Our schools will no longer depend for their support upon a fund which a mere majority at a town meeting may any year withhold. Heretofore the continuance of our schools every year depended upon the result of the vote at town meeting upon the question of school tax. If no money was voted, the schools were necessarily closed; if an insufficient amount was voted, the schools were supported in part by tuition fees; and even if enough was voted, the schools had only an assurance of one year's existence, for at the next town meeting all support might be withheld. (ARSPS 1872, p. 11)

Recognizing the importance of reworking the public educational system, Camden County became an early proponent for change. An important event that changed education in the county occurred in 1867, when a county agency assumed a good deal of the responsibility over the county's school districts. The county hired a school supervisor to implement new reforms that included coordinating and standardizing school curriculums and instruction. A board was formed to ensure the quality of teaching by qualifying instructors. The new system of education became a model for other counties throughout New Jersey.

The local press reported on the transformation of education in the county:

> There is a growing interest in the cause of education in all parts of our county, with the new school houses, competent teachers and standard text books are the order of the day. (WJP 4/27/1870)

Before reform was put into place, schools were purely local affairs. Trustees operated schools that suited the wants and needs of people living in the district. When the county superintendent came on board, there was a tendency to limit the powers of district trustees. Local trustees no longer selected textbooks, controlled the course of study, or certified teachers.

Beginning in 1872, they implemented the county-wide course of study. Several years later, standardized tests were given to students and diplomas awarded to those that demonstrated proficiency in the minimum standards:

> Teachers Association of Camden County met at the school building for the purpose of adopting measures for advancing the interest of schools. A systematic course of study was adapted. The people passing through the prescribed course satisfactory will be entitled to a county diploma. (NR 9/23/1876)

In 1874, teachers were required to pass an examination given by the State Board of Examiners to hold a teaching certificate. State laws provided rules for teachers' work-day. Teachers were not required to teach school on Christmas Day, New Year's Day, the Fourth of July and any day of "fasting or thanksgiving as may be appointed by the president of the United States or the governor." (Revised Statutes of the State of New Jersey, 1874)

With new educational reforms in place, local schools were using similar instructional content and textbooks for the first time. Teachers in the county used a standard register to accumulate information for the county supervisor. In 1870, local schools were keeping student data such as daily attendance, days tardy and number of children chastised, punished, suspended or expelled.

In 1870, the five schoolhouses in old Haddon Township were ungraded; that is, pupils of all ages were in the same classroom. It is amazing that teachers managed the students with the range of ages in one room. Students attended school for whatever period they wanted during the academic year. Attendance was not mandatory, so most students did not go to school for an entire academic year. In 1873, 37 percent of enrolled students in old Haddon Township's four school districts attended school for less than four months of the year. Only ten percent attended school more than ten months, twenty percent between eight and ten months and 35 percent between four and eight months. (ARSPS 1873, p.111)

The Camden County school superintendent, in an attempt to standardize the school program, adopted a model schedule to be followed by the local school districts. School opened at 9:00 A.M. During the first ten minutes, all students participated in opening exercises, followed by Bible reading; then, separate instruction was directed to various students of classes. The "little ones" were given oral instruction and each class received its appropriate share of the teacher's time.

A typical day in the classroom included reading, arithmetic, geography, spelling, grammar and writing. For older students, bookkeeping, reading and composition were substituted in the routine once or twice a week. The typical school day included a ten-minute recess at 10:30 A.M., noon recess from 12:00 to 1:30 P.M., another ten-minute recess at 2:56 P.M., and at 4:25 P.M., school ended.

During this era, the female teacher became the norm in the classroom. It was reasoned by some reformers that women possessed a "native tact" in the oversight of young. ("Governing the Young," p. 16) In 1877, Camden County's female teachers totaled 149, male teachers just 22. (CDP 3/18/1877)

Although females were dominate in the field of teaching, their salaries were much less that their male counterpart. Pay equity between men and women was unheard of in the nineteenth century. The average monthly salary for a male teacher was $77, where as a woman's average salary was just $44 a month. (CDP 3/18/1877).

Female teachers working in Haddonfield fared much better than other teachers in the county. This did not sit well with many taxpayers in Haddonfield. One citizen expressed outrage at having to pay female teachers more than the traditional family provider:

> I cannot see the propriety of paying young women salaries of a $1,000 or more per annum with long vacations, when there are figuratively speaking, an innumerable hosts of men with families to support throughout the land, with

$500 to $800 and who have to toil the year round. (WJP 3/8/1871)

Not only were women discriminated against in the salary they received, when compared to their male counterparts, but also there was a perception that female instructors were unable to adequately discipline incorrigible young men. The editor of the *Haddonfield Basket* wrote about misbehaving pupils in a "lady" teacher's class:

> . . . any lad or grown up boy who behaves rudely to his teacher, especially if a lady teacher, must have something bad in his "make up," which had better be attended to before it is too late. . . . His conduct is also cowardly, for he takes advantage of his lady teacher that he wouldn't dare to do with a decisive man. (HB 10/1874)

Of course generalizations are not always accurate. Male teachers did not always successfully administer discipline to unruly "scholars." In 1933, Dr. Charles Shivers wrote his memories of attending Haddonfield's Grove School. His recollections are contained in the unpublished papers of Sarah Shivers Murray. Dr. Shivers wrote about effective and indecisive male schoolmasters. His memories dated back before the state ruled out corporal punishment in public schools:

> When I began my studies in this school it was taught by the late Charles Turnely, who was afterwards a florist for many years in Haddonfield. He was a mild mannered man of whom some of the older and rougher boys took advantage and by their misconduct and refusal to obey his instructions compelled him to give up his teachership. The next teacher was a man of powerful physique named Hunt. When Mr. Hunt began his duties, the same group of rough young men started a rebellion in the school. One day a younger brother of an older pupil was commanded by Mr. Hunt to come up to the platform to take his punishment. . . . the older brother arose and threw a slate at the teacher's head which missed him by a few inches. Mr. Hunt rushed down the aisle to the bigger boy and seized him by the neck; then resulted a terrific fight in which the pupil was severely punished and his younger brother was compelled to take his whipping.

Years later, New Jersey law allowed teachers to "hold every pupil accountable, in school, for any disorderly conduct on the way to or from school, or to suspend any pupil from school for good cause." (Revised Statutes of the State of New Jersey, 1874):

> . . . the use of habitual profanity or obscene language, shall constitute good cause for suspension or expulsion from school; any pupil who shall in any way cut, deface, or otherwise injure any school-house, fences, or out-buildings thereof, shall be liable to suspension and punishment, and the parents of such pupil shall be liable for damages to the amount of injury. (Revised Statutes of the State of New Jersey, 1874)

Haddon District

The township's largest school district, the Haddon District, educated children that resided in the village of Haddonfield. The one-room Grove School was the village's first and only public school until 1870. Built sometime in the first decade of the nineteenth century, the

Grove Schoolhouse, Haddonfield. Built in the early nineteenth century, the schoolhouse stood at the corner of Grove and Lake streets. After a new school was opened in Haddonfield in 1870, the one-room building became the school for African-American students. The school was in use until the early 1900s.

(Historical Society of Haddonfield Collections)

Brown Building in Haddonfield. The school opened in 1870 at the corner of Lincoln Avenue and Chestnut Street. Even before the school door's were open, the high cost of construction created controversy among Haddonfield residents. The school was torn down in the 1960s.

(Historical Society of Haddonfield Collections)

Grove School stood at the southwest corner of what is now Grove and Lake streets. With just one room, it was typical of a rural schoolhouse.

When county-wide educational reforms began to take hold in the late 1860s, the Haddon District trustees formulated plans to build a new school. After receiving voter approval, the trustees hired William Hoopes, a local carpenter, to build a structure at the corner of Chestnut Street and Lincoln Avenue. The original building contract was $14,600, a considerable sum for the village to expend. The district issued more than $17,000 in bonds to pay for the cost of the new building and other classroom necessities. The final price tag for the brown sandstone school, was nearly $20,000.

By all accounts the new school building, completed in 1870, was a magnificent edifice. George Prowell's *The History of Camden County, New Jersey*, published in 1887, described the new schoolhouse:

> . . . the beautiful stone structure . . . one of the most substantial and elegant school-houses in the State. It has four school-rooms, besides other rooms for class recitations or study purposes. (Prowell, p. 317)

The new schoolhouse, better known as the Brown Building, became a topic of controversy. Some critics charged the facility's exorbitant costs were not justifiable for the small community:

> . . . the school house $18,000 to $20,000 being out of proportion to the size of the village and the number of inhabitants. ... The taxes for the coming year will probably be very much higher then they have ever been before in this place. (WJP 7/6/1870)

The new edifice was larger and more costly than any other schoolhouse in the township. By comparison, the new Rowandtown schoolhouse built just two years later, was constructed for $2,900. Other complaints leveled at the trustees of Haddonfield's school were excessive teacher salaries and books were changed too frequently. One year after the Brown Building opened, critics kept alive the issue of extraordinary expenditures:

> . . . $20,000 school house and $1,000 teachers in small towns cannot be run without heavy taxes on inhabitants. (WJP 1/15/1871)

Upon opening, they hired four teachers to work at the Brown Building. Several years later, a fifth teacher was added to the payroll. In 1880, twelve diplomas were granted to scholars from Haddonfield's school, the largest number awarded in any of Camden County's schools. (WJP 5/5/1880)

By 1880, 390 children between the ages of five and eighteen were living in the district. About 290 children attended the village's public schools. Sixty children were enrolled in private schools, while the remaining 40 children did not go to school. Not all children living in Haddonfield were registered in the local schools. Some boarded the daily local trains to attend school in Camden or Philadelphia:

> . . . there is quite a large number of young people passing up and down the railroad daily, . . . going to school in the city. (WJP 10/11/1876)

Some children that lived outside the Haddonfield also matriculated in the Haddon District's school. Outside scholars from the Greenville District (an area in what is now Cherry Hill and Pennsauken) attended the public school in Haddonfield.

Although the *West Jersey Press* had been critical of the Haddon District's trustees decision to build such a large school, one reporter reconsidered:

> Last Wednesday evening the public school here celebrated the Christmas season along with the Sunday school in the upper room of the new school house, a building which reflect much credit on our school trustees. (WJP 1/2/1878)

When the new village school opened its doors in 1870, the Grove School became the public schoolhouse for African-Americans in the township. For many years, education of African-American children was not a high priority of the Haddon District trustees:

> For fifteen years, the board of trustees permitted the colored population of the district to go without any school. When the new school house was built, the old one was devoted to a colored school. (WJP 2/28/1872)

Mr. John A. Jackson was in charge of the "colored school" in 1874. Two years later, Henry Butler was leading classes. By way of comparison, the Grove School was antiquated when compared to the palatial Brown Building. The old one-room school had no blackboards.

During the 1870s, African-American children living in the township's other school districts did not enroll at the closest school to their homes. The African-American children that attended school and lived in the neighboring Newton and Rowandtown districts walked to the Grove School. The districts paid tuition for African-American children so they could go to school in Haddonfield.

During the era of racial segregation in schools, it is not surprising that the African-American parents opposed sending their children to classes also attended by white children. In 1868, the Camden County Superintendent, Alexander Gilmore, reported the problem facing "colored schools":

> The education of the colored children is a question of difficult solution. Applications are frequently made to me from their parents for information concerning the funds for their schools. They prefer to be separated from the whites, yet the portion of the public money which would fall to them would be wholly inadequate to the maintenance of a separate school. In some of the districts the trustees have sustained colored school a few months in the year. (ARSPS 1868, p. 757)

Rowandtown District

The township's second largest school district once covered an area that is now a good part of present-day Westmont, along with portions of Haddonfield and Collingswood. In 1870, 71 children were enrolled in the Rowandtown public school. Five children attended private schools and 74 children living in the district did not go to school.

The first schoolhouse in the Rowandtown District was a small, one-story frame structure, built about 1825. The old schoolhouse, measuring 20' x 24', sat on a one-half acre lot where today's Haddon Township municipal building is located. The schoolhouse was sided with cedar boards and a roof made of cedar shingles. The walls were lathed and plastered. Inside, some 50 pupils could fit comfortably. Two teachers worked at the small schoolhouse, the man earned $52 a month, while the woman instructor was payed $28 a month.

The schoolhouse was some 45 years old in 1870 and had deteriorated to where the county rated the condition of the building as "poor." In his 1870 report on Camden County's schools, the County Superintendent may have had Rowandtown's schoolhouse in mind when he wrote about inadequate schools throughout the county:

> There is not accommodation for more than one-half of the children between five and eighteen years of age, in the schoolhouses, and many of these schoolhouses are totally unfit for education purposes; small, low, unpainted, dilapidated, forlorn looking buildings, without any pretension to architectural proportion, the inside corresponding well with the outside, the plaster broken off the walls and ceiling in many places, panes of glass out, shutters shattered, floors uneven, desks and benches the old fashioned kind, long, high and curiously carved, the benches so high that the feet of the children cannot reach the floor, little pieces of blackboard or none at all, no maps, no charts, no cubical blocks, no globes, no anything. (ARSPS 1870, p. 115)

Rowandtown school officials were obligated to do something about their antiquated edifice. They acted by hiring William Hoopes, of Haddonfield, to build a new two-story frame schoolhouse. The trustees issued bonds to pay the builder's contract of $2,900. The old one-room school was sold and removed from the lot and a new school erected in its place.

Hoopes, a carpenter, went to work building a 28' x 36' structure completed in September 1872. The new building's ceilings were eleven feet high and each classroom had raised platforms from which instructors could oversee their classrooms. Wainscotting, three feet

The Rowandtown School. The facility was built in 1872 along Haddon Avenue in what is now Westmont. The addition in the rear was added later. The 1872-structure was removed to Center Street in the early twentieth century to make room for a new brick school.

(Courtesy of Marguritte Bennett)

in height, was placed on walls in the classrooms, cloakrooms, stairways and hallways. The builder installed slate blackboards in the classrooms and "deafening" was inserted between floors "making the ceiling impervious to sound." The school could comfortably hold 100 students. (Building Contract No. 114, 1872)

A local fire insurance agent, Jacob Rowand, referred to Hoopes's workmanship in a fire insurance survey:

> The whole wall plastered and ceiled, and well painted with three coats including the Privies, inside and out. No pain has been spared to make the building complete inside and out. (Rowand No. 357, 1872)

Mr. Brace, Superintendent of Camden County schools, wrote a report describing the new schoolhouse:

> Rowandtown school-house is a two-story frame building, thirty-six feet long by twenty-eight feet wide, with posts twenty-four feet high. It, too is furnished with the most approved modern desks, and has a plentiful supply of black-board. It is a very neat edifice. (ARSPS 1872, p. 25)

Rowandtown's school trustees also approved funds of $400 for new desks, seating, stoves, and maps. On the first floor, a bookcase was constructed extending from floor to ceiling. New books were obtained for $50 to stock the shelves of the school library.

Today, we have come to expect certain necessities in our public facilities. In 1873, the State's Superintendent of Public Schools threatened to withhold state funding if local officials did not make school outhouse acceptable:

> In consequence of continued neglect on the part of many of the districts to erect suitable outhouses, I found it necessary, during the past year to issue a circular directing County Superintendents to withhold all further payments of school moneys from such districts, until the matter received proper attention. (ARSPS 1873, p. 15)

Rowandtown's school officials were not concerned with the edict. Their new facility had an eight and one-half by eight and one-half foot privy with two sides, one each for girls and boys. Hoopes designed the privy house to appear similar to the main schoolhouse.

In 1871, trustees paid $65 tuition to the neighboring Haddon District for Rowandtown students to attend schools in Haddonfield. It is likely that some, if not all, the money was earmarked for African-American students to attend the Grove School.

Before the state increased its financial support of schools, the township's school districts received most of their funds from the township's special school tax and a poll tax. Funds received from the state made up about a third of the district's revenues. Similar to modern-day school budgets, the Rowandtown District's largest expenditures were for teachers' salaries. Another costly expenditure was to heat the school. In 1870, coal delivered by the Haddonfield firm of Willits & Evans, cost about $31.

Some fifteen years after the schoolhouse was completed, they renamed the school the Westmont School. Scholastic topics taught in the Westmont School in the mid-1880s included reading, spelling, grammar, geography, arithmetic, penmanship, bookkeeping, algebra, geometry, physiology, philosophy, history, constitution, composition, world analysis, mensuration (the process of measuring), drawing and deportment (behavior).

In many modern-day communities, quite often an election of school board members or approval of a school budget does not arouse significant voter interest. This was not so in 1874, when Rowandtown voters went to the polls. Haddonfield's newspaper, *The Haddonfield Basket*, reported on election day activities:

> There was some excitement there [Rowandtown] a few days ago on the occasion of electing a trustee for the public school. The feeling ran so high, that it was deemed advisable to have a couple of police officers on hand, but their services were not called into requisition and, we believe, nobody was hurt. There was a large turn-out, and Mr. Wm. Flinn was the successful candidate, by a large majority. The whole matter has now settled down into a state of repose, and "all is quiet along the turnpike." (HB 8/20/1874)

In the early part of the twentieth century, they moved the 1872 schoolhouse to Center Street to make room for a new brick school. The 1872 structure still stands today as a twin house at 20 and 22 Center Street.

Oak Grove District

Children that once resided in what is now parts of modern-day Audubon, Haddon Heights and Oaklyn, attended school at Baker's Corner, at the intersection of today's Kings Highway and the White Horse Pike. The district was known as the Oak Grove District.

Although a description of the frame school has not been found, judging from the age of the school and the number of students that attended, more likely than not it was a one-room building, typical of other schoolhouses of that period.

George Prowell's *The History of Camden County, New Jersey* notes the school at Baker's Corner was the second institution of learning in Camden County and dated back to the early 1700s. (p. 309) It is likely the schoolhouse that Prowell referred to did not always sit at Baker's Corner; it was nearby on the south side of Kings Highway somewhere between the White Horse Pike and the South Branch of Newton Creek in what is now Haddon Heights. The school was moved to Baker's Corner sometime between 1808 and 1839.

A former pupil of the school, William H. Nicholson, writing in his book, recalled his childhood days while attending the schoolhouse. Nicholson's home was on a neighboring property to the school in what is now Audubon. William wrote, he was "taught by Rebecca Fisher, who boarded with us. She was bright and intelligent woman and her company and instruction were a great advantage to us." (*My Ancestors*, p. 88) [See William H. Nicholson, page 182.]

In 1869, 84 school-aged children resided in the Oak Grove District, of which 37 children attended the schoolhouse at Baker's Corner. Some children attended school in the village of Mount Ephraim and others did not attend school. The trustees of the district paid the female instructor $30 a month.

In the early 1870s, county officials drew up new school districts. The township's Oak Grove district fell within the newly formed Mt. Ephraim District. Many children that formerly attended school at Baker's Corner, began walking to the Mt. Ephraim schoolhouse on the Blackwoodtown Turnpike. From all indications, the Baker's Corner schoolhouse closed its doors sometime about 1871. No longer a part of the township's educational scheme, they sold the school in 1874:

> The school trustees of Haddon Township will sell at public sale . . . on the premises of Baker's corner, the old frame building formerly occupied as a school house. The structure is in a good state of repair and a good location and will prove useful for many purposes to farmers or others. (WJP 4/15/1874)

Champion District

The Champion schoolhouse served as the place of learning for the Union District. They named the school after Samuel Champion, the one-time owner of adjoining property. During the late 1860s, the district was renamed Champion District and soon thereafter took another name, the Newton District.

The Champion schoolhouse still stands today along Collings Avenue next to the railroad tracks in West Collingswood Extension. The one-story structure was made with common bond red bricks. The builders embedded a date stone in the gable noting 1821. The main room measured 18' x 30'. Over the years, several additions were appended onto the original building. During the nineteenth century, they also referred to the school as the Union School House.

Students attending the Champion School lived on farms in areas that are now within the bounds of Collingswood, Woodlynne, Haddon Township, Gloucester Heights, Camden and Oaklyn. In 1868, school enrollment included 65 children from Haddon Township and 77 pupils from Newton Township. The school had the dubious honor of having one of the low-

Champion Schoolhouse. Built in 1821, the building stands today along Collings Avenue in West Collingswood Extension, Haddon Township. Haddon Township had four school districts in the 1870s. Children from the Champion District attended this school.

(Photo by Samuel Rhoads, 1909. Camden County Historical Society Collections)

est attendance rates among all schools in the county. During 1874, just 31 percent of enrolled students attended school throughout the year.

Even today, public school buildings often serve as voting places on election day. During the nineteenth century, residents used the township's schools for civic purposes. Citizens residing in the western part of the township would travel once a year to the Champion schoolhouse to pay their local taxes to a collector. The Newton Creek Meadow Company, an organization of landowners along Newton Creek, also utilized the classroom for their meetings.

When residents began moving into new homes in Collingswood during the early 1880s, they needed a new school. In 1883, Newton District's school trustees hired William Bozarth to build a one story 26' x 32' frame schoolhouse with a belfry along the Haddonfield Road. The site of the new school was the lot where today's Garfield School is situated. [Building Contract No. 589]

The Haddonfield School

As previously mentioned the Haddonfield School was situated at the corner of the Haddonfield Road and Lake Street. The Quaker school opened in 1782 and has survived the test of time. It is now known as the Haddonfield Friends School. The school was called several names during the 1800s, including the Haddonfield Boarding and Day School, Friends Academy and Haddonfield Friends School for Girls and Boys.

The Quaker-operated school frequently advertised in Camden's newspapers:

> Haddonfield Friends School for Boys and Girls. Branches–English, and Classical Education, Bookkeeping taught if desired, also French and German. Tuition $12 per term, 10 weeks. (WJP 8/21/1867)

In the late 1860s and 1870s, the Quaker school's superintendent was John Boadle. John's interest in education was evident when he offered evening classes at a time when such instruction was not common:

> John Boadle principal of the Haddonfield Friend School propose to give evening instruction to such young men in this town as have not the opportunity in the day time. Teach Latin, French, German, Bookkeeping. (WJP 10/14/1868)

Two separate curriculums were offered at the school. The younger students attended "primary school" classes for two years before moving onto the "second school." Courses such as reading, spelling, arithmetic and writing were taught in primary classes. Older students received instruction in arithmetic, geography, grammar, philosophy, history and drawing.

During the early 1860s, Mr. Richard Allen was in charge of the institution. Haddonfield's fire insurance agent, Jacob Rowand, insured the belongings of the school's headmaster. Allen owned "electric battery and apparatus, air pumps, mechanical-powered centrifugal apparatus and chemical apparatus." (Rowand No. 194, 1863)

The Friends school did not tolerate chronic disciplinary behavior. Newspaper advertisements were direct about students' conduct: "No student having been dismissed from another school for misconduct will be admitted." (WJP 9/19/1873) "No pupil is retained in school who will not obey its rules." (WJP 7/17/1870)

Jehu Wood, Jr., son of Isaac and Elizabeth Wood, attended the Haddonfield Friends School during the early 1860s. Jehu's walk to school was brief. His house still stands along today's Wood Lane. [See Isaac Wood, page 227.] In 1862, Jehu's parents paid $10 each quarter for tuition. The Woods incurred other school expenditures including a copy book that cost ten cents and a fifteen-cent drawing book.

The school sent a monthly report card to Jehu's parents marking their son's progress. Jehu's report in 1863, noted he was "well said 44 times, indifferent 16 times, missed 1 time." The instructor reported Jehu's penmanship was "rather careless" and had "some blots." Numeric grades documenting pupils' proficiency and progress, were also sent home to parents. The highest attainable grade, a ten, was "good." Lesser numeric grades indicated work that was "indifferent" or "poor."

Some of Jehu's classmates boarded at the Friends school. The school's brochure reassured concerned parents about oversight of their children:

> They [students] will be accompanied on their walks to the woods, and about, for games and amusement by one of the care-takers, and will not be allowed in the streets, or at the stores of the village along. Endeavors will be made to have some amusement for them when not in school or occupied with their studies, in the way of innocent games, reading, and etc. The girls will receive some instruction in the care of their rooms, clothing and etc. (Friends Academy Brochure, 1877-78)

Parents were instructed to send only the necessities with their children:

> Boarders should be furnished with a bed-blanket, towels, toilet soap, napkins, and ring, fork, umbrella, overshoes and stationery. Boys (beside the above) slippers, buttons, patches, shoebrush and blacking. (Friends Academy Brochure, 1877-78)

HADDONFIELD
BOARDING AND DAY SCHOOL,
FOR BOYS.
TERMS.
Boarders $45 per quarter, half payable in advance.
Day Scholars $10 per quarter, payable at the end of the quarter.
No Allowance for absence except on account of sickness.

Haddonfield, 4 mo. 30 1862

Isaac H Wood

To RICHARD J. ALLEN, Dr.

To 2 3/4 Quarters ~~Board and~~ Tuition of his Son Jehu $

from 9 mo 2d 1861 to 4 mo 18th 1862			27	37½
2 mo 14	2 Copy books 10c	20		
" "	Drawing book	15		
4 m 18	2 Copy books 10c	20		55
			28	12½

Recd payment in full
Richard J Allen

Tuition invoice for the Haddonfield School in 1862. Situated along Haddon Avenue in Haddonfield, the Quaker school still exist today. Jehu Wood, the student noted on the invoice, lived at his family's residence, now 201 Wood Lane.

(Wood Manuscript Collection, Historical Society of Haddonfield)

REGISTER OF RECITATIONS

AT

HADDONFIELD SCHOOL,

From 11 Mo. 1 to 11 Mo. 30 1863

WELL SAID:	43	REMARKS ON PENMANSHIP.	Some blots
INDIFFERENT:	20		
MISSED:	2	GRADE FOR INDUSTRY.	8.46
TOTAL:	65		
DAYS ABSENT:	4	GRADE FOR THE MONTH.	9.26
TIMES LATE:	0		

The highest grade given is 10. From 9 to 10 is good; from 8 to 9 is indifferent; below 8 is very poor.

The parent will please affix his or her signature.

Register of recitation of the Haddonfield School in 1863.
(Wood Manuscript Collection, Historical Society of Haddonfield)

St. John's Military Academy and St. Agnes' Hall

Another religious-affiliated institution moved to the township in 1870. The St. John's Missionary Training School of Camden moved onto a 110-acre tract owned by the school's founder, Theophilus Maxwell Reilly. The school took on a new name, St. John's Military Academy, although it was often called the College of St. John's. At various times during the 1870s, Theophilus's two brothers, William and Edward, helped out at the prep school. All three brothers were ordained Episcopal ministers from Ireland. [See Theophilus Reilly, page 223.]

The academy was southeast of the village. Its first headquarters was an old farmhouse. The school suffered a setback when fire destroyed the main facility in 1872. This catastrophe did not discourage its headmaster. Theophilus conceived plans to build a new school that would become the largest edifice in the township.

Construction began on Cottage Avenue, east of Centre Street, on the new 100-room school building. The building phase did not go without problems. Correspondence penned by Theophilus expressed regret for the ambitious building project as construction costs were more than he could manage. At one point, Theophilus planned to finish only part of the building and leave the remaining section unfinished and dormant. He may have found additional funds from the sale of some two-dozen new Camden row houses in which he had an investment. As it turned out, the large structure as originally planed was completed.

Although St. John's College had an Episcopalian affiliation, the daily routine of students was fashioned after the military. A typical day began with reveille at 6:30 A.M. The day's schedule started with breakfast followed by morning prayers, recitations, recess, recitations, dinner, recitations, evening prayers, drill, study, supper, study, and tattoo (lights out) at 9:00 in the evening.

The young cadets boarded at the new facility, as most cadets attending the school were not from the area. Many resided out of state and a good number originated from New York State. Boys under age fourteen shared a double bed with their classmate. Boys over fourteen years of age slept in a single bed. *The Daily Graphic*, a New York City newspaper, noted at St. John's College "men and boys have the advantage of securing a fist class boarding school education for less than $200 a year." (9/9/1879)

Throughout the 1870s, at least one of the Reilly brothers taught at the college. Theophilus was the Rector and instructor in biblical literature and church history. William taught cadets Hebrew, Greek, French and was Associate Rector, and Edward taught Latin. Cadets also studied arithmetic, reading, writing,

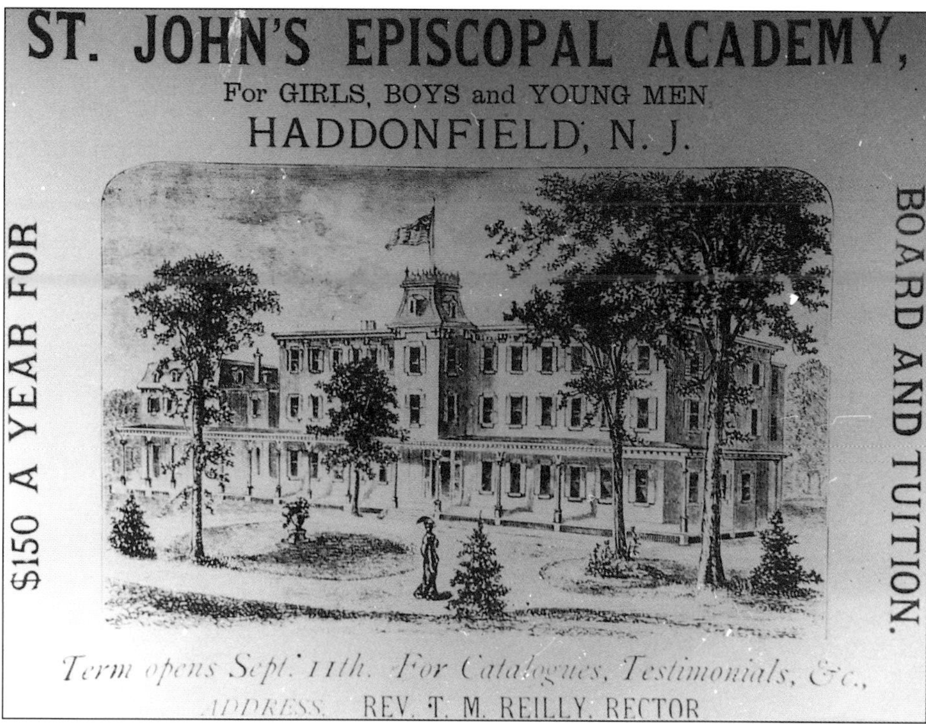

St. John's Military Academy, Haddonfield. Built in the late 1870s, the Episcopal affiliated school was situated at Cottage Avenue and Centre Street. The facility with over 100 rooms, was used as a hotel during the summer. In 1886, a fire destroyed the edifice.

(Historical Society of Haddonfield Collections)

spelling, grammar, geology, history, algebra, philosophy, bookkeeping, German, composition, music and drawing. In the 1880s, the school opened a kindergarten and a primary department to supplement its academic and collegiate departments. The Reillys also operated a school in Burlington, called Burlington College.

A cadet was expected to be on good behavior while attending school. The schoolmaster was "kind but firm" and followed military discipline. Students were expected to be prompt and attend to their duties. The school did not permit profanity, improper language and tobacco. Although ordinary clothing was worn during the week, uniforms were worn on Sundays and parade days. Cadets' military uniforms were dark blue, single-breasted coats, buttons to the throat, dark blue pants with a gold strip, black neckties and white gloves. (St. John's Military Academy Catalogue, 1886-87)

Even with the military style environment, extracurricular activities were part of the cadet's day. A brief report in the *West Jersey Press* noted a sporting event between the two schools operated by the Reillys: "Boys at St. John's College of Haddonfield played boys of Burlington College, a game of cricket." (WJP 5/14/1879)

In 1878, Theophilus opened a school for girls, named St. Agnes' Hall. The girls' school and St. John's College were situated next to each other, although it was emphasized the pupils would remain separate. A school catalogue noted "While both Schools are in the same town, yet the pupils are not allowed to associate together, nor have any communication with each other except by requests of parents, and in the presence of teachers. The only time they assemble together is on Sunday morning in the chapel." (St. John's Military Academy Catalogue, 1886-87)

On Sundays and special occasions, girls were required to dress in uniform. St. Agnes Hall's official uniform was a blue flannel suit, trimmed in red and a hat. On days other than when uniforms were worn, girls dressed in ordinary suits of everyday use.

Living at St. Agnes' Hall also took on a religious atmosphere. A catalogue from the 1880s noted:

> The supervision is that of a Christian household, each pupil being looked upon as a member of the family. Nothing is to be said or done except that which is permissible in a refined Christian home. No correspondence with, nor visits to or from outside persons, will be allowed except at the written request of parents or guardians. Regularity in rising and retiring, punctuality in chapel and dinning-hall order in room, and neatness in dress are required of all. (St. Agnes Hall Catalogue, 1886-87)

As it turned out, Theophilus was a businessman as well as an educator and theologian. He realized a prolonged vacancy in the largest building in the township was not cost effective. He took full advantage of his spacious facility, turning it into a boarding house and hotel in the summer months when cadets went home for their vacation. [See inns, page 163.]

Theophilus experienced misfortune in 1886, when fire destoyed his resort hotel/school facility.

Kindergarten and Primary Schools

Some young children, especially those living in Haddonfield, attended one of several private kindergarten schools. During the late 1870s, three women were prominent in educating young children in Haddonfield:

> The institution of the little folks of Haddonfield is well provided for, there being three Kindergarten schools there, one of them taught by Miss Hillman, who owns a fine school building there. Mrs. Kirby has charge of another, and the third one; in charge Miss Kinsman, is in Town Hall. (CDP 4/29/1879)

Miss Kinsman held classes at Town Hall, situated along the Haddonfield Road near Main Street. The importance placed on primary education was evident when the Township Committee agreed to allow Miss Kinsman to use Town Hall free of charge.

In 1868, Miss Sallie Hillman was teaching grade school in the village's public school. Several years later, this highly esteemed teacher was overseeing her own primary school and classes for girls. Sallie and her assistant, Miss Middleton, first held classes in a building on Ellis Street.

> Miss Sallie C. Hillman is about to open a school. One of the most gifted and accomplished teachers in the state. The people of Haddonfield need no longer send their daughters to the schools elsewhere—but can entrust their education to a lady whom they feel sure is fully competent. (WJP 8/30/1871)

An advertisement appeared in the *West Jersey Press*, noting the grand opening of Miss Hillman's Haddon Seminary in 1871: "Haddon Seminary—1st class school both sexes." (WJP 9/13/1871)

By 1875, Miss Hillman's school moved into Fowler's Hall at Main Street and Haddonfield Road and assumed the name Haddon Institute. The Institute's academic year included twenty-week terms, with vacations at Christmas and Easter. The range of tuition was from $12 to $20 per term. Instruction was offered to both boys and girls in branches of English, including elocution (public speaking), and drawing. Hillman charged extra tuition for classes in Latin, French, German or music.

In 1876, the works of Miss Hillman's students were displayed at the Centennial Exhibition in Philadelphia. Examples of the student's drawings, composition, penmanship, spelling, mathematics and grammar were exhibited with other educational items from around the state in the New Jersey State Building. Miss Hillman received an award for her merits during the Centennial Exhibition.

In 1878, Miss Hillman moved the Haddon Institute—Boarding Day School and Kindergarten—to Chestnut Street. A ceremony marking the dedication of the new schoolhouse included speakers, an orchestra and a reception. From a newspaper account, Miss Hillman's new school was noted as "generously supported." (WJP 4/2/1879)

Elizabeth and Mary Kirby's kindergarten school stood on Kings Highway opposite Chestnut Street. The Kirbys taught young children for almost 30 years. During its peak years, Kirby's classroom had some 50 children enrolled. The class was moved to a 20' x 20' schoolhouse behind the Kirby's home on Kings Highway, opposite Tanner Street. When "Lizzie" Kirby died in 1880, her school closed its doors.

Houses of Worship

Places of worship were very important institutions in the nineteenth century. Religion had shaped many of the nation's beliefs and values. For many, the church was not only the center of religious life, it allowed for societal interaction as well.

In the years following the Civil War, the vast majority of inhabitants of old Haddon Township were Protestants. The religious composition of the township was not unlike that of the nation. In the 1880s, eight out of ten church members in the United States were Protestants. The three largest denominational groups of Protestant Americans were Methodist, Baptist and Presbyterian.

In the early 1870s, the *West Jersey Press* published a survey of the county's churches:

> Baptist—9 edifices, 3,850; Episcopal 10 edifices, 2,500; Friends 5 edifices, 1,650; Lutheran 2 edifices 400; Methodist 19 edifices 7,300; Presbyterian 5 edifices 2,500; Roman Catholic 3 edifices 1,800. (WJP 6/4/1873)

Haddonfield was home to most churches in the township:

> The Baptists are more numerous in Haddonfield than are any other denomination of Christians except the Quakers, who have two large meetinghouses. The Presbyterians have a very handsome church near the center of the village, but the want of funds has so far prevented the members from fully completing the edifice. The Methodists have a neat church building, and the Episcopalians a cozy chapel. (WJP 9/5/1877)

It is appropriate to begin a discussion on religious institutions in old Haddon Township with the Society of Friends. In 1875 about 150 Quakers resided in Haddonfield, comprising about fifteen percent of the village's overall population. (HB 11/1875)

Almost all the original settlers of Newton Township were Quakers looking to escape religious persecution in their homeland of England. Soon after they arrived in West Jersey in the 1680s, the settlers built a meetinghouse near the Main Branch of Newton Creek at a site in today's West Collingswood Extension.

As settlement in West Jersey spread to the east, some Quakers wanted a more central location for their meeting. In 1721, a new meetinghouse was constructed by Friends on an acre of land donated by John Haddon, owner of the surrounding grounds that today comprises a large part of Haddonfield. The site of the first Haddonfield meetinghouse was near the corner of present-day Kings Highway and Haddon Avenue, where the Haddonfield Fire Company's building is located.

The central theme of Quaker worship was not a spoken sermon, but rather a silent meeting. The support and criticism that might come from a sermon, was purposively suspended so divine truth from inside the spiritual human body could emerge by silent communication or by verbal expression of a spontaneous "minister."

For much of the 1700s, the Society of Friends was the dominant religious order in both Haddonfield and throughout Newton Township. In 1760, a larger brick meetinghouse was built by the Haddonfield Meetings on the same lot as the 1721 meetinghouse.

In 1828, the Society of Friends was split into two sects, the Orthodox and Hicksites. The Hicksites followed the teachings of a New York Quaker, Elias Hicks, while the Orthodox continued to follow the precepts of George Fox, founder of Quakerism. The Haddonfield Meeting not only split into two groups with differing theological views, they physically partitioned their building to accommodate the two persuasions.

The two sects coexisted within the same meetinghouse for a quarter century. In 1851, the Orthodox Friends built a new brick meetinghouse at the corner of today's Lake Street and Friends Avenue. They built sheds and stables for horses and wagons along Lake Street. The Friends 1851 meetinghouse stands today. After they put their new building into use, the Orthodox Quakers, with legal title in their possession, demolished their former meetinghouse. This left the Hicksites without a place to meet. Wasting little time, the Hicksites purchased a lot at the corner of Ellis and Walnut streets and erected their own two-story brick meetinghouse. Wagon sheds and stables were built along the perimeter of the Hicksites' lot.

After one hundred years of separation, the two Quaker sects merged back together in 1952 and moved back to the Orthodox 1851 meetinghouse on Friends Avenue. The old Hicksites' Meetinghouse was sold to the American Stores Company. The food company moved the old Hicksite meetinghouse to another part of

Friends Meeting, Friends Avenue and Lake Street, Haddonfield. The Orthodox Quakers built the meetinghouse in 1851. The building is still used by the Friends for their meetings.

(Historical Society of Haddonfield Collections)

the tract and incorporated the structure into the center section of its new facility, the Acme Market.

Before Protestant organizations built their churches in Haddonfield, most held their initial services at the Grove School House, at Grove and Lake streets. The reason the schoolhouse doubled as a church was by decision of the original trustees of the small school. A resolution required that the school remain available for use by all religious sects. An interesting observation about the resolutions was noted by George Prowell, in his work *The History of Camden County, New Jersey*:

> . . . even if school was in session and application was made for preaching, the school should at once be dismissed. (p. 628)

In most Protestant churches, members and guests took seats in the sanctuary to sing hymns and hear readings from Scripture and sermons. Additional religious instruction and inspiration were provided in Sunday schools and prayer meetings for both adults and children. A respectable way to meet men or women was by attending worship services, Sunday School and midweek prayer meetings. In more than one instance, couples first became acquainted through church.

In 1818, members of a Baptist congregation constructed a brick meetinghouse on a lot opposite the present-day high school. In the decades that followed, the Baptist congregation grew. In 1852, the congregation built a new brown sandstone edifice at the same location with a 112-foot steeple that housed a bell. The Baptist Burial Ground was situated next to the church.

By the mid-1880s, membership in the Haddonfield Baptist Church had grown to about 400 members. The congregation purchased a lot in the center of the village and erected a new Baptist Church at 124 Kings Highway East. The church stands today at the site.

In 1843, the First Baptist Meeting built a sanctuary outside Haddonfield. The new church, a satellite of the Haddonfield Baptist Church, sat along Collings Avenue near the White Horse Pike. Most members that attended the church lived on the nearby farms. The lot of the former meetinghouse is on the west side of what is now Collings Avenue near Richey Avenue in Collingswood.

Churches in rural areas were often too small to command the services of a full-time pastor. In the early years of its existence, the First Baptist Meeting, also known as the Newton Baptist Meeting, was served by pastors that traveled from Haddonfield Baptist Church.

It is likely that the Newton Baptist Meeting disbanded about 1858. Before the church was abandoned, it was referred by a third name: the Second Baptist Church. They sold the church structure and the one-quarter-acre lot to a member of the Collings family in the 1880s.

By the late 1870s, the beginnings of a Baptist congregation had formed in Rowandtown. Several years later, the Shiloh Baptist Church of Rowandtown was formally

Baptist Church, Haddonfield. Once situated along Kings Highway across from the present-day Haddonfield Memorial High School, the church was built in 1852. Members of the church attended services at this site up until the new Baptist Church was built in a more central location in Haddonfield in the mid-1880s.

(*Daily Graphic*: New York, September 9, 1879)

Methodist Church, Haddonfield. Once situated at the corner of Grove Street and Kings Highway, the church was erected in 1854. When a new lot was purchased by the congregation in 1912, the building was sold. Several decades later the *Haddon Fortnightly* acquired the building.

(Paul W. Schopp Collections)

organized and a church was erected on a quarter-acre lot on the Haddonfield Road, at a site near the present-day Haddon Township Municipal Building. The first pastor was Thomas Wilkinson.

It was common for churches to have "church socials" and raise money for worthy causes such as paying the church mortgage, supplementing the pastor's salary, or missionary services. The *West Jersey Press* reported,

> The Baptist Sunday School at Rowandtown, held a strawberry festival last week for the purpose of raising money for an organ. (WJP 6/2/1880)

The Methodists were the second Protestant denomination to organize in Haddonfield, however, Methodist ministers were preaching in the township long before their first church was constructed. In George Prowell's work, the site of an early gathering was disclosed:

> Religious meetings were held in the open air at Rowandtown about 1797 at which Ezekiel Cooper, a Methodist of Philadelphia, preached occasionally. (p. 828)

Before they raised their church in 1835, Haddonfield's Methodist held services at the Haddonfield Baptist Church and the Grove School House. Their first structure sat along Main Street near Cooper's Creek. Today the Methodist Cemetery remains at the site of the original brick building. By 1857, the congregation had grown in numbers, and the old Methodist sanctuary could no longer accommodate its members. A new building was built on the corner of Grove Street and Kings Highway. The main portion of the Methodist Church still stands today and is home to the Haddon Fortnightly, a women's club.

In 1855, a Sunday School branch of Haddonfield's Methodist Church was established in the nearby village of Rowandtown. The congregation did not have its own house of worship until several decades later.

Sometime about 1858, the Newton Methodist Episcopal Church was built on the north side of the Haddonfield Road, near today's Wayne Terrace in Collingswood. The Newton M.E. Church was not affiliated with any other church in the township. In 1868, supporters held a "Strawberry Festival" to raise funds. Camden's *West Jersey Press* reported, "The Newton Church affords a place of worship for all the country lying round about, and the prosperity should be assured." (WJP 6/17/1868)

Sometime in the mid-1870s, the Newton M.E. Church building was turned over to the First Presbyterian Church of Camden. It was renamed Bethany Mission:

> . . . meeting at . . . the Newton M.E. Church on the Haddonfield Turnpike, formed as a mission Sunday School under the auspices of the First Presbyterian Church of the city [Camden]. The school is located in the vicinity of a number of houses, the place being known as Roseville [Collingswood]. (WJP 2/3/1875)

> Bethany Mission of the First Presbyterian Church recently established in Roseville on the Haddonfield Turnpike,

STATEMENT

of the FINANCES of

GRACE CHURCH, HADDONFIELD,

For the Year ending March 1st, 1867, made by order of the Vestry in Special Session, held February 3d, 1867.

Income.

Amount received from Pew Pents, . .	$505 00
Subscription from Nine Persons, . . .	425 00
Received from Weekly Collections, . .	115 00
	$1045 00

Expenditures.

Rector's Salary, ...	$800 00
Sexton's do.	50 00
Current Expenses, ...	158 00
	$1008 00

The Vestry, feeling that the Subscription bears unequally upon the congregation, have ordered, that the rental of the Pews, be advanced FIFTY PER CENT. to commence 1st of March, ensuing.

J. S. Coles, Sec'y.

Haddonfield, Feb. 20th, 1867.

Grace Church's statement of finance in 1867. The first Episcopal Church in Haddonfield was erected in 1842. Today's Grace Episcopal Church is on the original lot, having replaced the original structure in 1892.

(Joseph O. Cuthbert Account Book, Special Collections and University Archives, Rutgers University Libraries)

indebted to parent church for donation of a cabinet organ to be used in the mission. . . . (WJP 2/10/1875)

Although the exact date is unknown, by the late 1870s, the mission school was no longer in use. Lack of funds may have hastened the mission's downfall, although, a newspaper report offers a clue as to the church's demise. "Bethany Mission on the Haddonfield Turnpike was broke into for the fifth time." (WJP 1/27/1878)

In 1841, Haddonfield's first Episcopal Church held services at the Grove School House. By the end of the following year, Grace Episcopal Church was erected on a lot where today's church is situated at 19 Kings Highway East.

One means by which churches raised money was rental of sanctuary pews to the congregation. In 1867, about half of all Grace Church's receipts were derived from charging members rent to worship in its pews. Another way to raise cash was from member subscriptions. Although just nine members paid for subscriptions, it amounted to about 40 percent of the annual receipts of Grace Church. The remaining funds came from the collection plate. To spread the financial burden of operating Grace Church evenly among all members of the congregation, pew rental fees in 1867 increased by 50 percent. The church's financial statement showed the purpose behind the increase, "subscriptions bears unequally upon the congregation." (Statement of Finance, 2/20/1867) The rector's salary in 1867, was about 80 percent of its annual expenditures.

A new rectory was added onto the Grace Episcopal Church in 1871. In 1891, the 1842 structure was moved to the rear and a new sanctuary was raised at the site. The 1891 building stands today.

The next Protestant denomination to assemble and construct a sanctuary in Haddonfield were the Presbyterians. In 1858, worshipers, following the teachings of the Presbyterian Church, held their initial services in Town Hall and at a nearby private hall. Haddonfield's Presbyterians constructed their first church in 1874. A new church was erected in 1905 after the 1874 building was demolished. The 1905 church stands today at 26 Kings Highway.

During the 1870s, combined evangelistic services of the village's Protestant congregations often took place in outdoor venues:

> The final of a series of union meetings for religious services, was held in the beautiful grove belonging to Mr. William Mann, on last Sunday afternoon and was largely attended. Dr. Wayland from Philadelphia, presented a sermon from the words "consider the lilies. . . ." On the stand were observed Messrs. Young, Crats and Newberry respectively of the Baptist, Methodist and Presbyterian denomination, each of whom took part in exercises. The music was rendered by an impromptu choir, assisted by the congregation. (WJP 8/9/1876)

In the 1870s, many African-American inhabitants within Haddonfield that attended church did so in the nearby village of Snow Hill, now know as Lawnside. The first African-American church in Haddonfield was built in the late 1880s on Ellis Street, although the congregation existed before their building was erected. The members of Mt. Pisgah African Methodist Episcopal Church first met at the Grove School House.

Snow Hill was also the site of a Roman Catholic Church. Members of the persuasion held services in a "small frame building of a very humble appearance" built in 1859. (Prowell, p. 709) The site was chosen because it was centrally located for about 100 parishioners that resided in or near Haddonfield, Kirkwood, Blackwood and Chews Landing. The church was sponsored by St. Mary's of Gloucester City. Mass was served semi-monthly by priests that rode out from Camden and Gloucester.

The small number of Haddonfield families of the Catholic persuasion were anxious to have their own sanctuary. In 1880, a newspaper article confirmed their desires:

> The Catholics of Haddonfield are an enterprising people, and as they want a church in the borough, it is more likely that they will soon have one. (WJP 1/21/1880)

Seventeen years after the *West Jersey Press* cited the wishes of the village's Catholics, Saint Rose of Lima Church was built in what is now Haddon Heights.

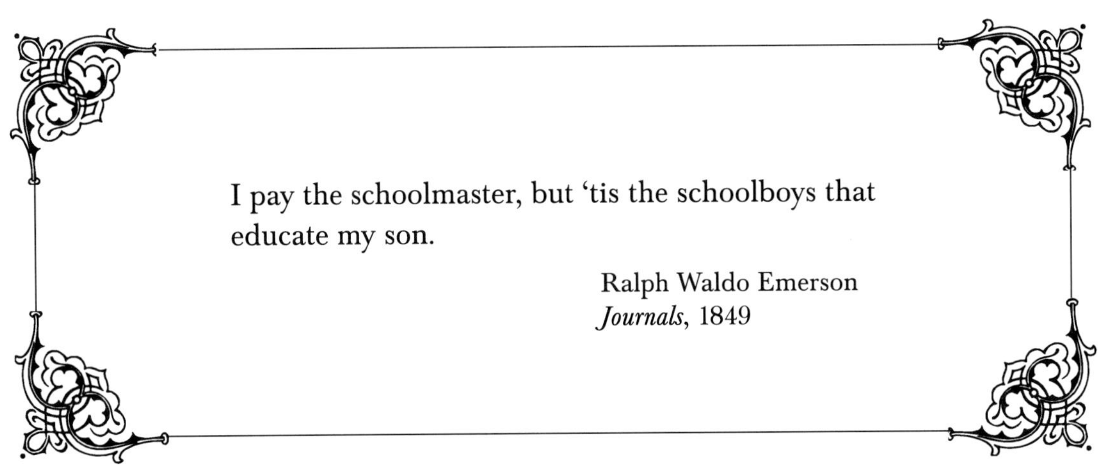

I pay the schoolmaster, but 'tis the schoolboys that educate my son.

Ralph Waldo Emerson
Journals, 1849

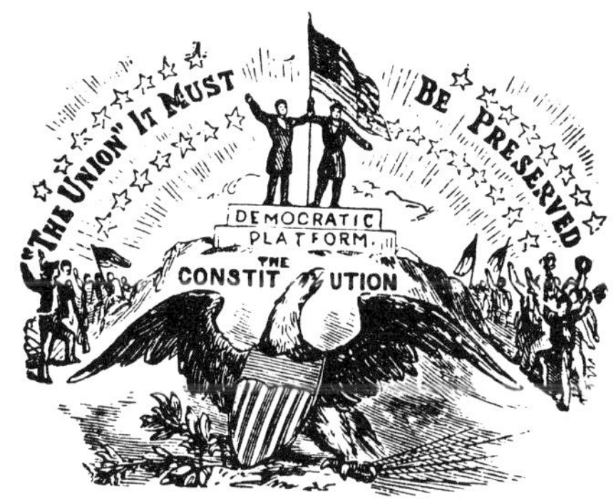

5

National and Local Issues of the Era

The Civil War

In June 1863, while Gen. Robert E. Lee's Confederate troops were marching toward the small Pennsylvania town of Gettysburg, the notion of Lee's army marching to Philadelphia was considered a genuine threat. After three days of fighting in July 1863, the Union's war effort was bolstered by pushing Lee's army out of Pennsylvania.

Had Confederate soldiers reached the city, they likely would have found military goods and materiel had been removed. While planning the defense of Philadelphia, civic leaders did not leave anything to chance. The *West Jersey Press* reported the Camden & Atlantic Railroad assisted in the region's contingent defense plans:

> ...all of the freight cars now available are employed in carrying goods for Philadelphia beyond the reach of the rebels should they succeed in visiting the city. (WJP 7/1/1863)

An anxious moment during the summer of 1863 illustrates a time when many inhabitants of the region thought the war was about to turn toward their homesteads. However, for most residents, the fighting that remained some 150 miles away did not affect their day to day routines.

The threat of losing one of the nation's largest cities to the Confederate Army was not the last incident to excite area inhabitants. A year later, the people of the Philadelphia region experienced another anxious period. During the first week of July 1864, 15,000 Confederate soldiers under the command of Jubal Early crossed the Potomac River and drove within five miles of the White House. This action forced General Grant to reposition troops in defense of the northern capital city and discourage an attack from Early's men. News of the invasion appeared in South Jersey local newspapers and spread by word of mouth. A young Newton Township farmer who resided near the village of Haddonfield wrote in his diary on July 12: "Dug a load of potatoes...took them right to town, [Camden or Philadelphia] great excitement the rebels are going to take Washington." (Jehu Wood, Jr.'s Diary)

The threat of surrendering the capital prompted President Abraham Lincoln to call for 500,000 new men to enlist in the military. Closer to home, word of the invasion galvanized support for defense of the capital. On July 12, 1864, New Jersey's governor, Joel Parker, issued a proclamation calling for new troops to enlist for 30 days. Two days later, Company A–First New Jersey Militia was mustered into the army at Camden for 30-day service. A company of some 100 men were stationed near Baltimore.

Newton Township's elected officials called many town meetings during the summer of 1864 and passed resolutions supporting the call for more men:

> Whereas–the President of the United States having called 500,000 volunteers for the military services for the aid in putting down the rebellion.
> Whereas–it becomes as loyal citizens to give all the aid in power for the support of our government. Therefore,
> Resolved–the inhabitants of Newton Township raise a sum of money exceeding $40,000 for the purpose of paying bounties to volunteers. (TM 7/28/1864)

The township's governing body was proud of the patriotic resolution. They appointed a committee of three citizens to carry a certified copy of the meeting's resolution containing the new enrollment policy to Washington, D.C.

For many young men, the decision whether to volunteer for military service or risk being drafted was a genuine dilemma. Early in the war, volunteers were likely to enlist for patriotic reasons. Earl Miers, in *New Jersey and the Civil War*, published in 1964, noted the determination of New Jersey's men to restore honor following the attack of Fort Sumter:

> Overnight New Jersey bristled with war spirit; men enlisted, bands played, Union meetings drew vast audiences, sweethearts wept, boys strutted along the streets carrying broomsticks for guns (p. x)

Just weeks after the shelling of Fort Sumter in 1861, the Washington Grays, Camden Light Artillery, and Stockton Cadets, volunteer units from Camden, assembled in response to Lincoln's call for 75,000 volunteers and marched off to put down the rebellion. The men traveled to a camp outside Trenton, then onto the nation's capital where they became part of the defense network protecting Washington from attack.

The rush to answer Lincoln's call for troops did not last. By 1863, volunteers in the North began to diminish after the realities of war became evident. Enlistment across the country was so low that Congress authorized conscription in March 1863. The War Department enforced four calls for new troops, the first in 1863 with three more drafts in 1864.

Paying bounties to enlist became a method to attract volunteers and to fill district quotas. Each congressional district was assigned a quota to fill with men between 20 and 25 years of age. Those districts that did not fill their quota of volunteers raised the remaining men by a lottery draft. A draftee had two other options. He could either hire a substitute from a pool of registered eighteen or nineteen year old men and immigrants or pay a $300 commutation fee. There was one important distinction between paying the commutation fee and hiring a substitute. A commutation fee excused a draftee from just one draft. By hiring a substitute, a draftee was exempted from all future drafts. With strong backing of the Democratic Party, the commutation fee was repealed from federal statutes in 1864. Upon enlistment or being drafted, young men were ushered into the military unless they failed the physical examination, had a mental disorder, or could show they were the sole means of family support.

Throughout August 1864, numerous war-related resolutions were offered at the weekly township meetings. They authorized bounties of $200 to be paid to volunteers and substitutes serving in the military for one year. The amount doubled for those serving three years:

> Inhabitants of the Township in the same manner as other assessments made and collected, that the monies raised at the town meeting be for the purpose of paying bounties to volunteers not exceeding $400 for a volunteer, drafted now or any person getting a substitute, as is further ordered any person refusing and neglecting to pay the sum of $10 head tax shall not receive any benefits from said money in cash if he is drafted. (TM 8/4/1864)

Draftees that avoided serving in the war by hiring substitutes or paying commutation fees included some young men whom later became prominent township citizens. On this list were Edward Bettle, Clayton French, William H. Nicholson, William P. Tatem and John Stoy. Because demand for substitutes was high and available candidates low, the "price" rose in South Jersey. Indeed, Bettle, French, Nicholson, Tatem and Stoy paid about $500 each for a substitute. During the last requisition for troops, in 1865, the minutes from a Township Committee meeting noted they had raised $10,000 from draftees to pay for their substitutes. (TC 5/8/1865)

The practice of paying money to avoid serving in the military may seem discriminatory. More affluent individuals could avoid serving, where as the man without the financial means did not have the same opportunity. The practice led to violent antidraft riots in Pennsylvania and New York City during the war.

The bounty increased as other cities and townships attempted to entice local men with higher financial incentives. Soon, the township sweetened its offer to certain draftees. The bounty was limited to white men, even though African-Americans were able to enlist in the military by 1864:

> Every white citizen drafted from Newton Township and held to the military service under the coming draft shall in addition to the $150 paid by county shall receive a township bond of $500. (TM 8/30/1864)

For some men, enlisting in the military could be a profitable venture. A young man could earn what

FORM 30.

CERTIFICATE OF NON-LIABILITY, TO BE GIVEN BY THE BOARD OF ENROLLMENT.

We, the subscribers, composing the Board of Enrollment of the First District of the State of New Jersey, provided for in section 8, Act of Congress "for enrolling and calling out the national forces," approved March 3, 1863, hereby certify that Samuel Wood, Newton Township of Camden Co county, State of N. J., having given satisfactory evidence that he is not properly subject to do military duty, as required by said act, and the act approved Feb'y 24, 1864, by reason of having furnished a substitute, is exempt from ~~all liability to military duty for the term of~~ draft during the time for w[illegible] said substitute shall not be liable to draft, not exceed the time for which said substitute has been accepted.

[illegible]

Provost Marshal, and President of Board of Enrollment.

Certificate exempting Samuel Wood from draft during the Civil War. Many young men from the township furnished substitutes, thereby exempting themselves from the draft. Samuel Wood homestead was 201 Wood Lane.

(Wood Manuscript Collection, Historical Society of Haddonfield Collections)

amounted to a year's wage upon joining the military and receiving several bounties.

Jesse Peyton, a charismatic citizen of Haddonfield, did more to advance the Union's cause than pay for a substitute. Colonel Peyton owned the "Tulip Grove Farm," in what is now Haddonfield. [See Jesse Peyton, page 223.] Soon after fighting broke in 1861, Peyton accepted the position of quartermaster in a regiment raised by a man from Peyton's native Kentucky, Colonel Young. Both Peyton and Col. Young recruited twelve companies, of which ten companies were headquartered at "Camp Peyton" near Haddonfield. It is likely the troops camped on Peyton's land. The recruits, most from Philadelphia, were known as "Young's Kentucky Cavalry."

Thirty years after the war ended, Peyton wrote *Reminiscences of the Past.* In his work, Peyton described his efforts to convince President Lincoln to supply the cavalry camped near Haddonfield:

> I had a white elephant on my hands. Here were twelve hundred men without means at their command to secure either rations, horses, or the necessary equipments for service. I went to Washington, saw Secretary Cameron, stated the condition of affairs to him, and went with him to see President Lincoln, who sent for General Meigs. It appeared as if no one could give authority for the equipping of cavalry. I told the President that the men were without the means of buying their own equipment, and that unless assistance was at once forthcoming they would have to disband. Congress was then in session, and the subject was brought to the attention of the Committee on Military Affairs. Three regiments of cavalry were authorized to be equipped,–one from New York, one from Iowa, and the so-called "Young's Kentucky Cavalry," from Pennsylvania.
>
> It was some months before the government paid the bills for provisions for the regiments, amounting to two thousand seven hundred and fifty dollars, the interest on which I had to pay personally. This was the first regiment of cavalry that reached Washington after the outbreak of war. Colonel Harlan was to have filled the position of lieutenant-colonel, but difficulties arose between him and Colonel Young, and they separated. The regiment was put under the command of Colonel (afterwards General) Averill, and was numbered the Third Pennsylvania Regiment. It distinguished itself at Salem, Virginia, where it cut the line of communication between Tennessee and Richmond. (p. 45)

Peyton opened a second recruiting office at Fourth and Walnut Streets in Philadelphia and enlisted more men from the city to join his cavalry unit. In another book penned by Peyton in 1888, entitled *Reminiscences of Philadelphia During the Past Half Century*, he wrote about the new recruits:

> The men were sent to camp Metcalf, adjoining Haddonfield, New Jersey. 445 names were on the roll when the battle of Fredricksburg, Virginia, was fought. (p. 15)

Although the Civil War battles were fought elsewhere, signs of war were present throughout New Jersey. Hospitals for Union soldiers were established in Jersey City, Newark, Beverly and Trenton. National cemeteries existed at Newark and Beverly. Throughout the war, local newspapers reported on battles and casualties. As the war raged on, subscribers of newspapers read viewpoints of opinionated politicians and partisan editorial writers on ending the conflict. Two local newspapers, the *Camden Democrat* and the *West Jersey Press*, were at opposite ends of each issue throughout the war. In his book, *New Jersey and the Civil War*, author Earl Schenck Miers noted:

> New Jersey newspapers divided sharply over whether "Mr. Lincoln's War" was a success or failure. No issue was too trivial to supply an excuse for tossing verbal brickbats. (p. 109)

In 1863, a little-known incident took place outside Haddonfield. It is likely the fracas produced the only wartime military casualty from gunfire on Newton Township's soil:

> A private in Col. Peyton's Cavalry regiment, now encamped at Haddonfield, becoming a little refractory the other day, under the influence of liquor, was shot by one of the orderlies, and was carried into camp. The ball passed through the neck. (WJP 2/11/1863)

Like most communities that sent young men into the military, the township had its share of war casualties. Included in the unpublished documents of Sarah Shivers Murray, was a paper written in 1933 by Dr. Charles Shivers, a Haddonfield physician. Shivers recalled some of those who served during the war. His account was included in a story on "The Old Grove School":

> The pupils of the Grove School where I attended included a number of older boys. Some of whom when the war broke out, enlisted in the Union army. Among them I recall Jake Dill, who was killed at the Battle of Antietam. Al Fortener was badly wounded in the hip and after his discharge from the army remained a cripple; Richard Plum was another who volunteered for the war and he was also wounded, but recovered without deformity. Richard Lippincott another older pupil, if I remember correctly, joined the Navy and was drowned in one of our Great Lakes while in Service. I think Jack Dill volunteered for service in the war and survived a number of years. There were others of my school mates who volunteered in the country's service whose names I am not able to remember. Now they are all dead but me. (Manuscript by Sarah Shivers Murray, Charles H. Shivers, M.D., 7/1/1933)

By April 1865, the tired and overwhelmed Confederate Army could no longer carry on the fight. Camden's *West Jersey Press* reported:

> When the news of the fall of Richmond reached our city there was a general display of flags from both public and private buildings. The ferry boats were tastefully decorated and everybody seemed to be brimful of patriotism. (WJP 4/5/1865)

A week later, the same newspaper reported General Lee's surrender at Appomattox, Virginia. A sample of *West Jersey Press* headlines illustrates the extraordinary nature of this:

> **The Rebellion Crushed**
> **Surrender of Lee and His Entire Army**
> **Grant Wishes to save the effusion of Blood**
> **Lee submits to Necessity and Similar Desire**
> **He Accepts General Grant's Plans**
> **Rebels Lay Down their Arms**
> **Restoration of the Union** (WJP 4/12/1865)

As the joy of victory spread across the North, the assassination of President Lincoln turned the Union triumph of arms bittersweet for many northerners, South Jersey citizens among them. Typical of the grief were the thoughts of Amelia Hopkins, a 25 year-old inhabitant of Haddonfield who recorded the tragic news in her diary:

> President Lincoln while sitting with his wife in Fords Theatre received his death wound being shot by Booth. . . . (April 14, 1865)

The next day, she observed that "The [Haddonfield] Methodist, Baptist and Episcopal churches were draped and also many of the houses." The week following Lincoln's death, Amelia wrote about the capture of Lincoln's assassin and the president's funeral procession in Washington, D.C. and Philadelphia.

Shortly after the end of the war, Camden County held a victory celebration at the grove on John Hopkins's land, near the village of Haddonfield. [See John Hopkins, page 228.] The *West Jersey Press* printed the public invitation:

> Honor to the Brave Welcome to Our Returned Soldiers Reception and Festival of the Nation's Defenders. July 4, 1865 at Haddonfield, New Jersey.
>
> All persons in the county of Camden who have served in the Army and Navy of the U.S. during the rebellion, and the widows and families of those who have fallen, are hereby cordially invited to attend as guest of the loyal citizens of the county.

> The Soldiers Reception and Festival to be held at Hopkins Woods, Haddonfield.
> The following will provide transportation to and from festival from Camden City and all townships. . . . Haddon Township–A.D. Woodruff, John E. Hopkins, Abel Clement, Joseph and Samuel Wood, J. Lewis Rowand, Charles S. Braddock, John C. Hopkins, Edward Bettle, A.W. Clement, Wm. P. Tatem, Isaac Middleton, Jacob P. Fowler, Aaron Burrough, A. P. Vandergrift, David Roe, Isaac M. Kay. (WJP 6/28/1865)

Amelia Hopkins attended the celebration held at her Uncle John's grove. Her diary entry for Tuesday July 4th noted:

> ...the soldiers of the county were over in Uncle John's woods, as there was a dinner given them also speaking by several gentlemen, a band of music and some singers. I was over in the morning also in the afternoon it all passed off quietly although there were about 4000 persons or more I suppose of course crowds besides the soldiers.

George Prowell reported 5,000 people attended the festival. Prowell's *The History of Camden County, New Jersey* noted those present were "amply fed from the bountiful tables . . ." (p. 162)

The physical war was over and the men returned home. Nevertheless, the memory of the war would remain–in the graves of those who died for the Union; in the reminiscences, gatherings and reunions of soldiers; in other Fourth of July speeches; and in the ways South Jersey adapted to the policies wrought by the war.

African-Americans

Throughout the nineteenth century, racial prejudice was woven into the fabric of American society. In the free states after the abolition of slavery in 1865, segregation of the races was common in most aspects of daily life and discrimination was openly practiced and accepted. In the years following the Civil War, the place of local African-Americans on the economic ladder changed ever so slightly. However, passage of civil rights laws provided basic rights that before did not exist, and the end of slavery in the South gave blacks and their friends hope for progress.

For a number of years before the Civil War, the underground railroad routes spread through the region by which parts of southern New Jersey became home for the slaves abandoning their southern homeland. An issue that reached a boiling point during the Civil War was the increasing population of African-Americans in the southern part of the state. During a twenty year period before the Civil War, the African-American population in southern New Jersey doubled. Some areas, especially in the extreme southern counties, attempted to halt the flow of African-Americans fleeing slavery.

In 1863, the New Jersey Legislature entertained a bill designed to stop emigration of African-Americans into New Jersey. The supporters of "The Negro Influx Bill" gave a frank explanation for the impetus of the proposed legislation:

> ...people of South Jersey required it [the bill] as by their proximity to Delaware, unless something were done, they would be completely overrun by a horde of worthless negroes! (WJP 4/11/1863)

One legislator from Camden, James Scovel, who opposed the bill, depicted the hostility experienced by many African-Americans in the region. Scovel's quote, published in the *West Jersey Press*, revealed how escaping slaves were uncovered, captured and forcibly returned to their native South:

> The houses of the negroes were ruthlessly entered by midnight by bands of kidnappers, and they were dragged from their beds, thrust into wagons and carried to the river, and from thence to slavery, without any proof that they were fugitive slaves. (WJP 1/28/1863)

Despite white fears of a "black invasion," the Negro Influx Bill failed to gather the required votes in the State's Senate chamber.

When the Civil War began, African-American males faced prejudicial government policies when they attempted to enlist in the Union Army. African-Americans were initially used militarily in a support capacity for the predominantly white armed forces. Not until the Emancipation Proclamation was issued in January 1863, were most African-Americans given the chance to enroll in the military and prove themselves on the battlefield. Even after demonstrating ability and willingness to engage the enemy, African-Americans still were not considered equal to their white counterpart. They were paid less than whites–white privates earned thirteen dollars a month, whereas a private in the U.S. Colored Troops was paid ten dollars–and they were often left to do "fatigue duty" in the camps. They were also limited in their chances to rise in the ranks.

Local government also treated the races unequally. As the casualty lists grew and the reality of war filtered through northern communities, the number of young white men volunteering for service declined. The federal government instituted a draft to fill the ranks of the military. To support the government's call for men, Camden County and local municipalities paid bonuses to draftees who went off to war. Newton Township's African-American men were not eligible for monetary incentives that local officials routinely granted to white draftees.

New Jersey was in some ways more hostile than other northern states toward Abraham Lincoln's presidential reelection bid. Indeed, it was one of only three states in which the majority of voters supported George McClellan, the unsuccessful Democratic candidate in the 1864 presidential election. All seven of the state's electoral votes went to McClellan. New Jersey's Democratic Party did not support many ideas or legislation favorable to African-American civil rights.

Racial attitudes in New Jersey were slow to change following the Civil War. First, New Jersey's Democratically controlled legislature refused to ratify the Thirteenth Amendment abolishing slavery. Shortly after that, in 1866, a Republican-controlled legislature ratified the Fourteenth Amendment, defining citizenship to include blacks and guaranteeing every citizen the right to due process and equal protection under the law. Before the amendment became law, the Democrats took control of the state legislature and rescinded the previous vote supporting the amendment. In 1870, the Fifteenth Amendment became the third piece of major civil rights law that failed ratification in the New Jersey legislature. The hotly debated amendment prohibited bans on voting based on race or color. The state's opposition to civil rights legislation did not prevent the ultimate ratification of amendments to the U.S. Constitution.

The local Republican Party's mouthpiece, Camden's *West Jersey Press*, published a letter to the editor that brings to light the uphill battle for support of the constitutional amendments even within the ranks of the party that initiated the legislation:

> Mr. Editor. Some of our Republican friends express a repugnance to negro suffrage. This is natural, and I must own it was some time before my mind sanctioned it. Prejudices often withstands reason, even in the judgment of great men. (WJP 6/19/1867)

When black enfranchisement finally became the law of the land, the headline in the Democratic Party's newspaper, the *Camden Democrat*, read: "The Fraud Consummated! The Fifteenth Amendment Illegally Forced Upon the People." The newspaper's editor lamented:

> The degradation of the white race is now complete–the Constitution a dead letter–the rights of the State no longer recognized–the house of National humiliation is upon us. (CD 4/2/1870)

The Camden County Democratic Party held fast to its position of racial segregation. The *Camden Democrat* outlined the county's Democratic platform:

1. White men only to hold office in Town, County, State, or United States.
2. No mixture of the Anglo-Saxon with African race in our public schools.
3. White men only for Juries, and all other public positions. (CD 1/7/1871)

The Democratic party bullying did not keep local blacks from exercising their newly-gained franchise and assuming an active public life. Several months after ratification of the Fifteenth Amendment, a number of "colored men" entered the political system by casting their first votes at Camden County's Republican Party meeting. According to the *West Jersey Press*, an unnamed African-American was called to serve on a county petit jury in 1871. (WJP 12/20/1871) This was a first for African-Americans within the Camden County. In the following year, African-Americans participated in the general election.

The local Republican Party stood firm in its resolve to support expansion of voting rights to African-Americans:

> Yes, the colored citizen of Snow Hill [Lawnside], and our whole county, will come forth on November 5th, and with the fidelity to the Union that was ever manifested during the war. (WJP 10/23/1872)

Despite advances in voting rights, African-Americans were not full members of local society. Segregation persisted. When Haddon Township became a municipality in 1865, African-American children did not attend public schools. The exclusions of "colored" in the public education system in Haddonfield ended in the late 1860s, when school trustees hired an African-American teacher, rented a hall, and black children began attending classes. A year later, after white children vacated the schoolhouse on Grove Street to attend a new spacious school on Chestnut Street, the antiquated one- room Grove School House became the classroom for African-American children.

In 1875, 330 African-Americans and 2,211 whites resided in old Haddon Township. About half the African-Americans that resided in the township were in Haddonfield. Many resided near the intersection of Ellis and Potter Streets. Most of the African-Americans that resided outside Haddonfield rented homes on the properties owned by their employers.

CAMDEN COUNTY.

TOWNSHIPS.	White.	Colored.	Total.
Camden, North Ward	6,579	129	6,708
" Middle Ward	6,600	85	6,685
" South Ward	6,021	671	6,692
	19,200	885	20,085
Centre	926	794	1,720
Delaware	1,457	170	1,627
Gloucester City	3,656	26	3,682
Gloucester	2,569	141	2,710
Haddon	1,706	219	1,925
Monroe	1,639	25	1,664
Newton	3,282	1,476	4,758
Stockton	1,749	632	2,381
Washington	1,532	35	1,567
Waterford	1,997	37	2,034
Winslow	2,039	14	2,053
Total	41,752	4,454	46,206

Chart of U.S. Census in 1870 for Camden County. African-Americans comprised about eleven percent of Haddon Township's population. African-Americans made up some thirty-one percent of the overall population in the portion of Newton Township that remained after Haddon Township split off.

While African-Americans made up thirteen percent of the township's population, they did not own a proportional amount of land. Of the some six thousand acres of land inside the township's borders, African-Americans only owned about a dozen acres. The largest tract, known as Saddlertown, was about five acres. By the early 1880s, some half-dozen homes stood at the site where about twenty African-Americans resided. [See Saddlertown, page 247.]

Next to Saddlertown, the Smiley family lived on a two-acre lot near present-day Briarwood Avenue. Just one dwelling stood at the site where African-American farm laborers Kit, Joshua and James Smiley and later Samuel White, resided. Kit and James Smiley had been born into slavery in Virginia. In the 1830s their lives took a turn for the better when their owner, Thomas Smiley, emancipated them. [See Smileys, page 248.]

Fusselltown was another area where African-Americans lived. The community, numbering about eighteen African-Americans in 1880, was along the White Horse Road in what is now Oaklyn. Fusselltown covered some three acres of land, having been purchased by the Fussell family in 1836. There were several homes at the site. [See Fusselltown, page 272.]

Two African-American women owned lots in the township. Mary Monroe, a homemaker, owned two dwellings situated on several acres of land in what is now Audubon. In 1880, about sixteen African-Americans were residing on this lot. [See Mary Monroe, page 189.] Phoebe Adams owned about an acre of land on the north side of what is now Haddon Avenue next to and east of Maple Avenue, in Haddon Township. [See Phoebe Adams, page 263.]

Despite civil rights legislation, the economic prospects of African-Americans in the township remained bleak. African-Americans were almost exclusively limited to farm and unskilled labor or domestic service.

The means by which the Jacobs family made financial ends meet illustrates employment of a typical African-American family in nineteenth century Haddon Township. The Jacobses rented housing from James Dobbs, owner of the nearby brickyard. The dwellings stood at the corner of what is now Lees Lane and Cuthbert Road. George and Robert Jacobs were laborers at their landlord's brickyard, but both men occasionally hired-out to nearby farmers to do odd jobs. In the early 1870s, Henry Cuthbert hired Robert to dig ditches, cut and saw trees and trim bushes around the railroad tracks that bisected Cuthbert's farm. Robert received $1.50 a day. In many instances, he took food and necessities in return for his labor.

Mrs. George Jacobs also worked on Cuthbert's farm, although he paid her just a dollar a day. When the vegetables were ready to be picked, Mrs. Jacobs received two cents for each pint of raspberries and fifteen cents for a basket of beans. Instead of her salary, Mrs. Jacobs accepted other kinds of remuneration, including meat, baskets of potatoes, pork, salted meat, cabbage and tomatoes.

Racial prejudice was commonplace throughout much of America. One common way that prejudicial attitudes were perpetuated was through negative stereotypes. For instance, prejudice against African-Americans came through reports in the newspapers' depiction of "colored" people and their assumed propensity to engage in crime. In 1874, the *Haddonfield Basket* reported a burglary of a house on Mansion Avenue, now Warwick Road. Thieves had loaded-up their wagon with tomatoes, chickens, a small cider mill and a tool chest. Although there were no witnesses, the newspaper fingered African-Americans for the crime:

> As usual with a good many people, the colored folks of Snow Hill [Lawnside] get the credit of these depredations; but it is strongly suspected by others that they come from a different directions–perhaps a worthless set of thieving tramps. Let there be a sharp look-out for them. (HB 10/17/1874)

Another display of a newspaper editor's prejudicial attitude came through a newspaper report about the referendum held in 1875, to continue a ban on the sale of liquor within the township:

> ...many of the colored people, as we are told, who voted for license two years ago, voted the other way this time, being convinced that they could make better use of their money than in spending it for that [liquor] which deprived them for the time being of their wits, and sent some of them on Saturdays at or near midnight, out of the town howling, cursing and fighting, thus "making night hideous" and themselves miserable. (HB 4/1875)

Though newspaper references to African-Americans were often unfair or unkind, there were some positive accounts in the nineteenth century press. One story, in the *Camden Daily Post*, reported on Haddonfield's social events:

> The residents of this borough are regaled during the evenings occasionally by specimens of a high order of musical arts. To be a little more explicit certain ones of the colored persuasion sing whole acres of love songs as they saunter through the streets. (CDP 4/26/1879)

Most social gatherings in the township were segregated, still there were instances where racial barriers were set aside:

> Haddonfield is quite lively of late, with entertainment of various kinds. The Jubilee Singers, lectures, and balls. At one colored ball the white element was quite noticeable. (CDP 3/17/1879)

The African-American experience in securing good jobs and exposure to educational opportunities did not change drastically during the remaining years of the nineteenth century. African-Americans continued to occupy menial jobs. Few owned their own farms. Local farmers hired most as farm hands or laborers. In the cities, black men were hired as laborers, janitors, porters, teamsters, waiters or servants. Women were predominantly employed as laundresses, dressmakers and domestic servants. Likewise, African-American school children continued to attend segregated schools physically and academically inferior to schools attended by white children.

Despite these obstacles, many African-Americans welcomed the passage in 1884 of New Jersey's first major civil rights law. The legislation guaranteed all New Jerseyans equal access to public accommodations and jury service. The law, however, was openly violated and eventually revised and weakened. African-Americans struggle for meaningful civil rights laws and parity in the nation's job market continued for many years into the next century.

Women's Issues

The era following the Civil War was a pivotal period for women. A number of important issues, including enfranchisement, were finally being debated. In 1871, the New Jersey Legislature passed a law giving men and women equal rights about their children in divorce proceedings. Before the enactment, the courts usually sided with the father. In the mid-1870s, New Jersey revised its laws enabling married women to hold property and inheritance in their name. Although they did not achieve equal footing with the opposite sex during this era, women's presence and status began to change for the better in areas of education and the workplace.

The vast majority of women in the nineteenth century stayed at home to raise children and take care of the household. The home and family were the undisputed domain of the female. Much of society believed that a woman's proper place was in the home.

For those women that worked, most did so out of necessity rather than choice. In 1870, about fifteen percent of all women in the nation over the age of sixteen were employed for wages. The majority of working women obtained positions as domestic servants. This was the case in old Haddon Township where most middle- and upper-class inhabitants had at least one domestic servant.

In industry, women occupied jobs that could be viewed as an extension of household duties. For instance, they were frequently employed to make clothing and textiles. Many of the textile factories in the nation's cities were staffed with female laborers. In nearly all instances, female employees received less wages than their male coworkers.

The U.S. Products of Industry census, taken in 1860, reveals some half dozen women in the village of Haddonfield were employed by tailors, a shoe and boot manufacturer and a butcher. Similar to wages paid to women in other parts of the country, females employed in Haddonfield's shops earned significantly less than their male coworkers. Women were most prevalent in a handful of Haddonfield dressmaker shops by the late 1870s.

Overall, those women that did enter professions became schoolteachers. Women dominated the field, while a small number of men assumed managerial roles. By 1877, female schoolteachers in Camden County numbered 149 and male instructors just 22. (CDP 3/18/1877) They paid female school teachers much less than their male counterparts. Even though the overwhelming number of teachers were women, their average monthly salaries were about 40 percent less than their male colleagues. (CDP 3/18/1877)

Women on the farm also worked, but quite often they were not paid. During harvesttime, women cooked and baked for their families, farm hands and temporary help hired to harvest crops. Women also helped with chores in the barnyard, fed poultry, milked cows and weeded vegetable gardens. Some African-American females were employed to pick vegetables and paid by the pint or basket.

Before the Civil War, only three private colleges in the country admitted women to study with men. New educational opportunities began to unfold following the war. A number of women's colleges were founded and many institutions of higher learning began to enroll females. Although the overall number of women attending medical and law schools were quite few, enrollment began to increase during the last quarter of the nineteenth century.

Though new educational opportunities were becoming available, societal views lingered about women's intellectual inferiority. For instance, the *West Jersey Press*, in a self-serving article, coaxed women to read newspapers and to become more conversant in an area once regarded as a male's intellectual domain:

> Ladies should read Newspapers It is a great mistake, in female education, to keep a young lady's time and attention devoted to only the fashionable literature of the day. If you would qualify her for conversation, you must give her something to talk about—give her education with this actually would add in transpiring events. Urge her to read the newspaper, and become familiar with the present character and improvement of our race. (WJP 7/25/1866)

During the late nineteenth century, women began to branch into other social undertakings. Women joined clubs, pursued cultural endeavors and participated in social reform. For instance, many women around the township joined the local temperance movement to end the social evils that stemmed from excessive use of alcohol.

Women were not eligible to vote in general elections during this period. The Supreme Court had concluded the framers of the Constitution intended that suffrage was not an essential right of citizenship. Enfranchisement for women was an idea that many supported in the 1870s. In Camden County, spirited debates on a woman's right to cast a ballot in general elections came to the forefront shortly after the end of the Civil War: "The Women Question A universal suffrage movement which include woman suffrage is going good." (WJP 2/2/1870)

In a distant arena, Susan B. Anthony, a veteran of other reform movements, attempted to cast a vote in the 1872 presidential elections and was fined $100. She refused to pay.

Although women could not vote in general elections, New Jersey, like many states, allowed them to cast ballots in local elections related to schools. In 1894, New Jersey's State Supreme Court declared a law unconstitutional as it applied to women voting for school trustees (school board members). After the ruling, women were allowed to vote only on the issue of school taxes. Restoring enfranchisement to women at school trustee elections ultimately required an amendment to the state constitution.

In 1875, the editor of the *Haddonfield Basket* posed the question whether women should participate in a vote to incorporate the village of Haddonfield:

> We are informed that property to the amount of $160,000 is owned by single women in Haddonfield. Should they not have a right to have a "say," when taxation or incorporation is under discussion? (HB 2/13/1875)

In a 1885 meeting of the Haddon Grange, a discussion took place on fraudulent voting in a municipal election. A female (sister) and male (brother) member of the Grange spoke their minds on the issue:

> Sister Rulon stated that this corruption would be done away with if a woman was allowed to cast her ballot. Bro. [Brother] J. Lippincott said he would be glad to see the day when women would be allowed to cast their ballots." ("Haddon Grange Beginning")

Unfortunately, the issue was not resolved in the favor of women until the twentieth century when they finally gained the right to vote.

Currency

During the nineteenth century, specie, or coined money, was the currency placed in circulation by the federal government. The U.S. Mint supplied copper, nickel, silver and gold coins. Besides denominations that still exist today, there were half-cent pieces (ceased coining in 1857), two-cent pieces, three-cent pieces, twenty-cent pieces (coined 1875 to 1878) and $2.50, $5, $10 and $20 gold pieces. The first paper money, popularly called "greenbacks," was issued by the U.S. Treasury during the Civil War. Paper money was issued in denominations of $5, $10, $20, $50, $100, $500 and $1,000.

Even though coins and paper money were used to purchase goods and services, an accurate portrayal of the nineteenth century agrarian economy must note the extended use of bartering. Exchanging goods or services was the norm in the farm district. Farm ledgers are replete with transactions where accounts were settled by exchanging farm products for goods, services and labor.

Unlike today, in the 1860s other sources of currency circulated freely. For example, state-chartered banks issued their own notes. The notes issued by several banks in Camden circulated throughout the region. After a ten percent tax was imposed by the U.S. Government in 1866 on issuance of notes by state chartered banks, it became impractical to issue bank notes. Toward the end of the Civil War, they enacted new federal laws that allowed state-chartered banks to become national banks. Many institutions took advantage of the new option, including several banks in Camden. Newly chartered national banks could issue notes that served as currency and circulated freely.

Besides coins, greenbacks and bank notes, yet another kind of currency called business certificates or shinplasters circulated in many public market places. These were paper notes of small denomination, usually issued by private companies. These types of notes circulated in Camden and the surrounding region:

> ...merchants at Camden, as well as other towns and cities issued and circulated for a time their own fractional demand notes for the purpose of encouraging trade amongst one another. But it was gradually redeemed as the national currency was supplied. (Prowell, p. 455)

At least two businesses in Haddonfield issued business certificates during the 1860s. Alfred Clement and Mickle Clement & Sons, both proprietors of general stores, issued small denomination certificates. Holders of the certificates could redeem them at the general stores and receive credit against the purchase price of goods.

A shortcoming of having many types of local currency in circulation was the likelihood of counterfeit, altered and spurious notes. According to George Wait's *New Jersey's Money*, "New Jersey had an unusually large proportion of fraudulent notes and their circulation was relatively easy." (p. 33)

During the 1870s, one of the most important monetary issues that faced the nation was how to merge the nation's currency, more specifically, what to do about the greenbacks or paper money issued by the government during the war. Hard money proponents favored a policy of withdrawing greenbacks from circulation and returning to hard currency. Inflationists, on the other hand, believed the government should issue more paper money, thereby stimulating the nation's economy and avoiding deflation that would result if a hard money policy was implemented.

In 1874, President Grant's administration followed a policy that temporarily allowed paper money to stay in circulation until further economic expansion took place. It was believed this course of action would bring on a painless return to specie payments. However, the panic of 1873, which had a devastating impact on the nation's economy, led to a renewal of discussion to inflate the paper currency supply. Two years later, the direction of the nation's money policy shifted again when Congress enacted the Specie Resumption Act that provided for a limited reduction of greenbacks and a gradual resumption of specie by 1879.

Hard money and inflationist supporters, each with their own economic scenario, were often the topic of editorial discussion. John Van Court, editor of the *Haddonfield Basket*, never held back his opinions. He favored resumption of specie payments:

> We are firmly of the opinion that we shall never get to the bottom of our financial difficulties until that much desired measure is consummated [return to specie]. Matters will then change for the better, confidence will be restored, and business done upon a firmer basis. Some weak-kneed people, with fictitious capital, may suffer, but putting resumption off indefinitely, or issuing more paper money, won't save that class of people in the end, and the longer the evil day is put off, the worse it will be for them. (HB 1/1876)

Business certificate issued by Alfred W. Clement for redemption at his Haddonfield general store. This form of currency could be redeemed by a holder and receive credit for goods at the store.

(Reprinted by permission, Newark Museum, from George Wait's *New Jersey's Money.*)

The best policy of managing the nation's currency remained a politically charged and elusive issue well into the next decade.

Local Option

In 1873, a referendum was put to Haddon Township's voters on whether liquor should continue to be sold in taverns and other public establishments. The proposal was called "the local option." The liquor question prompted as much spirited debate as any issue during that era. Newspaper reporters and editors in the area were quick to express their opinions on this divisive issue.

Haddon Township was not alone in the debate to ban the sale of liquor. Hoping to end the social evils that stemmed from drunkenness, there was a national campaign to prohibit the sale of intoxicating liquors. By 1874, the Women's Christian Temperance Union had formed with a charter ascribing to total abstinence from alcoholic beverages. After several decades, this group had 10,000 branches and a half-million members.

Shortly before inhabitants of Haddon Township voted on the local option referendum, the New Jersey legislature passed a law giving each township authority to decide whether liquor should be sold. The lawmakers provided for a fine of $50 to $100 for a first-time offender of the statute. The statute required a vote on the issue every other year. The legislation provided that:

> ...liquors shall [not] be sold at any tavern, hotel or public house of entertainment. (Acts of the 97th Legislature of the State of New Jersey, 1873.)

Before township residents voted on the referendum, local temperance organizations and their supporters positioned themselves to push their cause to ban the sale of alcohol. The Haddon Temperance Alliance, and several congregations from area churches held meetings to gain support and plan strategies for the township's first referendum:

> Baptist, Methodist and Presbyterian met to get people interested in the temperance movement to take some active measures in its favor. (WJP 4/16/1873)

In April 1873, more than 400 township inhabitants cast ballots on the liquor issue. The temperance movement carried the vote. The margin of victory was originally reported to be eighteen votes, however, they disallowed some 30 ballots because the "voters" did not reside in the township. (WJP 4/30/1873) Voting by non-residents was not the only incident on ballot day. When a "disturbance" broke out at the polls, the local Sheriff "appeared at the scene of the voting and perfect order was maintained." (WJP 4/30/1873)

The press highlighted provisions of the new ordinance:

> No liquor could be sold in any quantity large or small by the common store and taverns. The druggist may compound medicines with it and sell them. (WJP 4/23/1873)

Several months after the law took effect, the *West Jersey Press* reported, the local option law was working admirably in Haddon Township. (WJP 6/23/1873)

The unfavorable economic impact of the ordinance fell mainly on the tavern and inn owners in the township. Inns, besides offering overnight accommodations, meals and a place to board horses, also sold alcoholic beverages.

In Haddonfield, the innkeepers did not quietly comply when a profitable segment of their livelihood was suddenly banned. They struck back in a way that caused immediate concern to many. When visitors came to Haddonfield, innkeepers provided most of the available boarding for horses and carriages. To highlight their grievance, hotel owners closed their stables to the public. They not only locked up their stables, they closed their kitchens. The action inconvenienced the farmers that traveled into Haddonfield to transact their business:

> Persons having charge of hotels in Haddonfield have persistently refused to entertain man or beast, consequently people visiting our beautiful village either for business or pleasure, have found it impossible to obtain public accommodations. (WJP 2/11/1874)

> Hotels would not serve meals...no accommodation for horses, removed pump handles so they could not be used. (WJP 2/18/1874)

Commercial establishments up and down Main Street felt the intended impact of the hostlers' protest. The Haddonfield correspondent for the *West Jersey Press* reported, "Question of local option has caused nothing but turmoil and strife here." (WJP 2/18/1874) A number of store proprietors of the village found a solution to alleviate the inconvenience to their customers. Church officials in the village were persuaded to open their sheds:

> ...the church yards have been thrown open, and under the commodious sheds within them may be found an abundance of room for all teams that may arrive in town. (WJP 6/23/1873)

Although the tavern owners' method of voicing their disapproval to the local option inconvenienced many shopkeepers and visitors, the pro-temperance supporters ultimately got their way. One of Haddonfield's inns, the American Hotel, was sold in 1874 and its new owner, George Stillwell, reopened the establishment as the "American Temperance House." (WJP 5/20/1874) Business after that was conducted on temperance principles. [See inns and tavern keepers, page 162.]

Miner Rogers, the owner of another hotel, also succumbed to the inevitable. Rogers had been an ardent opponent of the local option law. He sold his hotel, tavern and livery stable situated next to the railroad tracks on the south side of Main Street. The village newspaper was not sympathetic to Roger's departure:

> Couldn't stand it. Mr. Miner Rogers, probably finding local option a little too much for him here, has "pulled up stakes," and left. His property has been bought by Mr. M. Schlect, baker, who will turn the place into a bakery and confectionery, with ice cream and other refreshments, with nothing stronger to drink, however, than mineral water. As this establishment is at the corner of Main street and the railroad, where the trains stop, it will be quite a convenience to those who may become hungry or thirsty on their way between the city and the sea.
>
> Thus two of the old prominent rum shops are put to better uses, and the sooner the town is clear of all rumsellers as a beverage and rum-drinkers the better it will be for them: for it's a mean business. (HB 7/1874)

Two years after the local option law was first enacted, the editor of Haddonfield's only newspaper described village life without rum shops:

> ...since the local option went into operation we had good order in the town—no night brawling or disturbances—a little horse racing, to be sure, occasionally, on the street on Sundays by persons perhaps from other localities, who had "fired up" before they started, and that this amusement would probably be much increased if such persons had a whiskey shop in the town to "stop" at. But we fail to see the "advantage," except to the liquor seller. (HB 2/13/1875)

The township's only inn/tavern outside Haddonfield was the Half-Way House situated on the Haddonfield Road in what is now Collingswood. [See inn and tavern keepers, page 160.] Disappointed over the results of the local option referendum, Mahlon Van Booskirk, the inn's proprietor, had his own response to the new ordinance. He ignored the law. Just months after they passed the ban on liquor, Mahlon was fined $50 for violating the provision:

> Mahlon Van Booskirk of what is known as the "Half-Way House" on the Haddonfield Turnpike was held by Justice Clement for allowing spirituous liquor to be sold on the premises in violation of local option law. (WJP 8/20/1873)

Apparently the stiff fine did not deter Mahlon. Several months later he violated the same ordinance:

> Mahlon Van Booskirk, has been fined $100 and costs for infringement of the local option law of Haddon Township. He keeps what is called the "Half-Way House." (HB 11/1874)

The local option law had to be placed on the local ballot every other year. In 1875, the township's citizens again overwhelmingly voted to continue prohibition of the sale of liquor. The tally was 243 to 168:

> When the result of the late election was announced there went up from the crowded Town Hall, three very hearty cheers, when someone exclaimed, "Who'll take a drink on that?" This was followed by a fierce farewell to the rumselling business in Haddonfield. (HB 4/1875)

John Van Court, the editor of the *Haddonfield Basket*, spoke on what he perceived to be a reason voters affirmed the referendum. The newspaper proprietor openly supported the temperance movement. Interestingly enough, Van Court ended his analysis of the local option vote with a plug for a local savings bank:

> ...it was feared that there would be a large number of "colorized" [African-American] votes brought out, and thus make the vote a close one. In this, however, the liquor folks were not as successful as it was feared they would be. And many of the colored people, as we are told, who voted for license two years ago, voted the other way this time, being convinced that they could make better use of their money than in spending it for that which deprived them for the time being of their wits, and sent some of them on Saturdays at or near midnight, out of the town howling, cursing and fighting, thus "making night hideous" and themselves miserable. They, as well as some of the whites who wasted their money in this way, now spend it in making their homes more comfortable and pleasant, or investing in the Building and Loan Association. (HB 4/1875)

A second defeat did not dampen the "liquor men's" spirits. Advocates of alcohol lobbied the state's Legislators to repeal the provision that allowed the local inhabitants the right to decide whether their township could sell liquor. The *Haddonfield Basket* announced:

> Another bill has been presented to repeal the Local Option Law of Haddon township. If this should prevail, it would be sad calamity to our town. The liquor men, it seems are leaving no stone unturned. (HB 3/1875)

The State's legislature did not scrap the local option law. With a biannual ballot required to keep the ordinance in effect, the local temperance movement remained active during the 1870s. The *Camden Daily Post* wrote in 1877, "A new lodge of "Sons and Daughters of Temperance" is likely to be formed. A bad place for whiskey that Haddonfield." (CDP 1/6/1877)

A majority of the township's voting citizens continued to favor the referendums to keep Haddon Township dry. In 1877, the vote was 347 to 39 to continue the ban on sale of liquor. (WJP 3/14/1877) The pro-temperance press touted the views of many inhabitants of Haddonfield. From their perspective, the village was a better place without liquor:

> One peculiar feature in Haddonfield is its temperance proclivities. Local option is the rule among its inhabitants, the vote on the question of liquor or no liquor being almost unanimous against its sale at the election last spring, and the people are consistently temperate. Haddonfield is not like Vineland with its drug-stores and oyster-saloons, nothing but whiskey-mills in disguise. (WJP 9/5/1877)

Two years later, in 1879, the momentum of the local temperance movement within the township was still strong. "A grand rally for local option this evening in the New Jersey Building." (CDP 3/10/1879)

In most cases, the businesses that once served liquor complied with the prohibition on alcoholic beverages. Some exceptions did not go altogether unnoticed. The pastor of the Haddonfield Methodist Church, Daniel Harris, wrote in his journal, "There is no licensed liquor selling in town, but something intoxicating is sold on the sly." (*Haddonfield United Methodist Church: A Sesquicentennial History 1829–1979*, p. 42) An article in the *West Jersey Press* suggests there may have been some instances where establishments were overlooked by the law:

> A card in a door on Main Street, "Sweet cider, three cents a glass." How does this tally with our local option law? (WJP 10/31/1878)

An interesting aspect of the debate on local option surfaced in the minutes of the Haddon Grange, a local branch of a national organization for farm families. The Haddon Grange had a good number of members that belonged to the Society of Friends. Generally, Quakers supported the ban on the sale of alcohol within the township. However, an argument came forth from the Haddon Grange that local option eliminated a personal liberty. Minutes from a Haddon Grange meeting held in the late 1880s noted:

> Resolved, that a law prohibiting the manufacturer and sale of alcoholic beverages is too restrictive of personal liberty and too sumptuary a measure for a free people. ("Haddon Grange Beginning")

Although it may have been difficult to find a place in Haddonfield to belly up to a bar, such was not so in Batesville (Cherry Hill), located just across Cooper's Creek.

> There is, just across the bridge above Evan's Mill dam, in Delaware township, an establishment under the nom-de-plume of "The Blazing Rag," where the ardent is dispensed by the quart, gallon, or barrel. The patrons of this delectable institution, as it is but a few hundred yards from our local option village, are frequently seen and heard in the streets of evenings, three sheets in the wind and the fourth fluttering. (CDP 11/19/1879)

To some extent, the 1870s' local option ordinance remains even today. In several communities that were once part of old Haddon Township, they still prohibit the sale of alcoholic beverages.

Fire Department

It was especially important in villages like Haddonfield and Rowandtown, where most buildings were made of wood, to have an effective volunteer organization capable of extinguishing fires.

Haddonfield's Friendship Fire Company was first organized in 1764. The company functioned until 1851, when it was absorbed into the Haddonfield Fire Department. Before the company had its own fire house, its equipment and apparatus were stored in sheds scattered around the village. Sometime before 1858, a "small frame fire engine and hook and ladder house" was built along the Haddonfield Turnpike next to Town Hall. (Rowand No. 122, 1859) During the 1850s, the company upgraded its firefighting equipment adding a suction engine, copper riveted hoses, hooks, chains, ladders and hose carriages.

Typically, a ringing bell summoned volunteer firefighters to a fire. They followed the pumper and hose carriage on foot or by horse. A typical four-wheel, horse-drawn, hose carriage could carry more than 800 feet of hose. Upon reaching the fire, they connected a hose from the pump to a well. Under the direction of the company engineer, volunteers worked the hand pump, drawing water to douse the fire.

In 1872, a spectacular fire at the College of St. John's on Cottage Avenue not only sent many inhabitants of Haddonfield rushing to the scene of the blaze, but it turned out to be a defining event for the village's fire department. A correspondent reported how some citizens of the village first learned of the fire:

> The alarm was communicated to the town by a colored man—Shadrach Selby—who suddenly ensuing from Centre street on horseback. yelled "*fire! fire!* College on the hill on fire." Coatless and hatless, he looked as if he had just escaped Pandemonium. Under any other circumstances he would have presented a most ludicrous appearance; but he meant "business," and the few who were in the streets at the time, knew it. Most of the citizens of the town were congregated in the churches. The effect of this alarm can be imagined. There was no panic, but the services came to a sudden termination. Everybody, both males and females, showing a strong disposition to run to the fire. Most of the contents of the building had been rescued before the arrival of the citizens. When we reached the ground we found Students Evans and Hover still in the midst of the flames, as it were, snatching from destruction whatever might yet remain of value. They had left the building but a few moments, when the pitch roof took fire, and the whole air was filled with a dense cloud of black smoke. When the atmosphere cleared, every part of the building was noticed to be in a blaze, which urged on by the fierce wind mounted to the very heavens. The flames were communicated to the trees in the adjoining grove, and the whole conspired to form the most brilliant pyrotechnical display that has every been afforded in this neighborhood. (WJP 5/1/1872)

It is unlikely that the volunteer firemen could have salvaged the structure, since the blaze had rapidly engulfed the school's wooden headquarters. In spite of this, Haddonfield's firefighters were embarrassed at what happened when the alarm was sounded. A reporter wrote:

> Acting Engineer Clement (Charles, Jr.) ran the engine out, but on looking for the hose carriage, he discovered it had but one wheel and the hose itself had been cut up and appropriated for various uses by the young sports who continually congregate in and around the engine house. The "machine" got as far as the corner of Centre and Ellis streets, where it was halted, and "the department" made a grand dash for College Hill. (WJP 5/1/72)

Everyone agreed the fire company's inability to combat the blaze brought to light an internal problem within the fire company. Township officials did what most governing bodies would have done—they formed a committee to study the matter.

One issue raised during the committee's inquiry centered on the company's antiquated fire apparatus. The condition of the equipment was perhaps the department's largest deficiency. The obvious solution was to upgrade the company's firefighting machinery. Raising the funds was another problem. To pay for new equipment, Haddon Township's governing officials authorized a new tax to be levied on all property within 1,600 yards of the intersection of Main Street and the Haddonfield Turnpike. A few months later, they raised some $900 from the assessments.

Over a period of several years, new firefighting equipment was placed in service and existing apparatus was restored to proper working order. Improvements were also made to the village water wells so that an abundant supply of water was available to extinguish fires. The editor of the *Haddonfield Basket* wrote about the changes:

> . . .and new hose has been obtained; also, a suction pump, said to be capable of drawing water from any well to the depth of thirty feet and throwing it to the top of any house of ordinary height. This pump is on wheels, and can be moved from one place to another, wherever it may be most serviceable, or where water is most plentiful.
>
> There have also been sunk more wells and cisterns, and several others needed are in contemplation. One of these cisterns, near the Town Hall, as we are informed, has a capacity of some 12,000 gallons. (HB 7/30/1874)

In 1875, no fewer than fifteen wells were scattered throughout the village where firefighters could draw abundant water. Wells were laid out about 400 feet apart to be accessible for firefighters' equipment from anywhere in the village should a fire occur. (WJP 3/31/1875)

In 1874, the fire department received permission from township officials to "place a bell in the cupola of Town Hall" (TM 3/11/1874) The bell alerted volunteer firemen of a fire. When the Borough of Haddonfield was incorporated in March 1875, the fire department was placed under the direction of the new Borough Commissioners.

By the end of the 1870s, the borough's fire apparatus would no longer fit into the small fire house. To store the equipment, they renovated the first floor of the Town Hall in 1880. Seven years later, a tower was constructed on the side of Town Hall for drying hoses and to hold a new fire bell. The fire company shared the Town Hall with other Borough departments until 1928, after which the fire company took over the entire facility. The old Town Hall was razed in 1951 to erect the fire house that stands today at 15 Haddon Avenue.

The hundreds of wooden outbuildings scattered around old Haddon Township were especially vulnerable to a carelessly tossed match, smoldering cigar butt, bolt of lightening or kerosene lamp. Large stacks of straw and hay and barns full of wheat provided fuel for an unintended spark. Rural inhabitants preached caution, safety, and fire prevention to avoid fires. Over the years, there were many instances of outbuildings in the township burning to the ground. If all else failed, fire insurance was available to lessen the financial burden of a building consumed by a blaze.

Sometimes, it took more than preventive measures or state-of-the-art fire equipment to reduce the loss from fire. When a fire destroyed several outbuildings on William Hinchman's farm, chance or good fortune, was at work: [See William Hinchman, page 225.]

> Barn and outbuildings of William Hinchman, near Haddonfield, were destroyed by fire. . . . Soon after the fire broke out the wind changed or his dwelling would have shared a similar fate. There was no insurance on the property burned. (WJP 10/9/1878)

A fire company was formed sometime before 1841 in the village of Rowandtown. Primary source documents about the village's initial firefighting organization are not available, although the minutes of an 1841 meeting of Haddonfield's Friendship Fire Company make reference to the neighboring company:

> A committee was authorized to invite the Rowandtown Fire Company to join the company. No mention is made concerning the Rowandtown Company in later minutes, and it is presumed the invitation was not accepted. (Prowell, p. 618)

It is likely that any firefighting apparatus or equipment owned by the Rowandtown company was housed in sheds of inhabitants and volunteers residing near the village. They built Westmont's first fire hall on Center Street during the first decade of the twentieth century. The Westmont Fire Company was founded during this period in time.

Outside Haddonfield and Rowandtown, many dwellings were beyond the reach of the volunteer fire companies. That is not to say the organizations did not respond to smoke spotted off in the distance. Volunteers were known to race miles to fight a fire.

Graveyards

One of the cemeteries in old Haddon Township was the Newton Burial Ground situated next to the Philadelphia & Atlantic City Railway's right-of-way in what is now the West Collingswood Extension. The cemetery was founded before 1700 as a burial ground for members of the Society of Friends. Some of the first settlers to come to West Jersey are buried at the site in unmarked graves.

George Prowell's *The History of Camden County, New Jersey*, published in 1886, offered a nineteenth century description of the graveyard. Prowell wrote the cemetery was enclosed "by a brick wall, and is overgrown by low trees and vines." (p. 650). The brick wall was taken down sometime in the 1920s.

On the northern side of the Newton Burial Ground was a small tract of land laid out as a cemetery by James Sloan in 1791. Unlike the adjoining Newton Burial Ground, decedents that did not follow Quaker teachings were permitted to be buried in this graveyard. In the nineteenth century, a low wall surrounded the Sloan Cemetery. Sloan placed a stone in the wall with the following inscription:

> Here is no distinction,
> Rich and Poor meet together,
> The Lord is maker of them all,
> By James Sloan, 1790. (Prowell, p. 650)

Soon after the Haddonfield Friends Meetinghouse was built in 1721, a lot adjoining the meeting was obtained to bury Quakers. Many early inhabitants from the vicinity of Haddonfield were interred at the Haddonfield Friends Cemetery.

The first graves at both the Newton Burial Ground and the Haddonfield Friends Cemetery were without markers. Unmarked graves were in keeping with early Quaker tradition. However, as time passed, this tradition changed and they permitted small grave-markers in

Newton Burial Ground in Haddon Township. A number of the original settlers of the region are buried at the graveyard. The cemetery is now located in West Collingswood Extension.

(Photo by S. Rhoads, 1909. Camden County Historical Society Collections)

Friends' cemetery. Even today, Quaker grave-sites are generally marked with small stones.

Samuel Nicholson, a conservative nineteenth century Quaker, was not able to accept headstones on graves-sites. Samuel's home stood next to the Haddonfield Friends Cemetery. [See Samuel Nicholson, page 221.] His actions were told in *Lost Haddonfield*:

> The story is told that Samuel Nicholson, who died in 1877, disapproved of gravestones and he would push them below ground level. Others would later come along and resurrect the grave-markers. (p. 124)

The authors of *Lost Haddonfield*, Douglas Rauschenberger and Katherine Tassini, submit that a burial ground for Newton Township's poor was set aside in 1754, next to the Haddonfield Friends Cemetery, where the less fortunate inhabitants were buried at the township's expense:

> In 1754, a 1/4-acre lot, in the glen between the Friends School and Lake Street, was purchased by Newton Township as burial land for the poor. The "Poor's Burying-Ground" later known as the "Strangers Burying Ground," was deeded to the Meeting in 1853 and was incorporated into the Friends Cemetery. (p. 124)

After some 100 years of use, Newton Township sold the "Poor's Burying Ground" in 1853 and purchased another burial site for the poor. The location of the new burial ground was along the Haddonfield and Mt. Ephraim Road near present-day Kings Highway and First Avenue in Haddon Heights. The dimensions of the acre and one-quarter lot were 125 feet along Kings Highway and about 350 feet deep.

In the 1870s, the township graveyard became a topic of controversy. Under terms agreed to when Newton and Haddon townships divided in 1865, the cemetery was to be cared for by Haddon Township, whereas Newton Township would contribute money to defray graveyard maintenance costs. In 1871, the eastern portion of Newton Township was annexed to Haddon Township and the western portion was set off to Camden. After this period, Camden, having inherited the right to use the graveyard from Newton Township, continued to send its deceased paupers to the site, but neglected to contribute money toward its upkeep:

> The latter [Haddon Township] complained that since the annexation of Newton to Camden, the latter has contributed nothing toward the support of the ground, but that the paupers of the Seventh and Eighth wards have been buried there. It was further stated that bodies were placed in very shallow graves and probing of a case in the hands of a person present, revealed the fact that some of the coffins were less than two feet below the surface. (Unidentified newspaper, 1879.)

In 1879, Haddon Township's officials took its grievance to the Camden City Council with a recommendation to settle the dispute. Haddon Township agreed to give up its claim to all unpaid cemetery costs if Camden would relinquish all claims to the ground. The following year the city's governing body accepted the terms of the township negotiators and relinquished its rights to the graveyard. Upon gaining title to the lot, the township immediately sold the "Grave-Hole" for $100 to Jacob Dodd. (TC 1880) The cemetery lot was assimilated into Dodd's adjacent farmland. In researching this matter, there was nothing uncovered suggesting the coffins buried at the site were removed. [See Jacob Dodd, page 236.]

Two church cemeteries were also within the township, both in Haddonfield. The Baptist Church Cemetery was laid out behind the original Baptist Meetinghouse sometime after 1818. The cemetery is in the area of today's 402 Kings Highway East. In keeping with the one-time Baptist tradition, the early grave sites in the cemetery were left unmarked. This tradition, similar to that of the Quakers, also changed over time. During the nineteenth century as the prosperity of members increased, so did the size of headstones and monuments in the cemetery. While the cemetery remained at the church, the sanctuary moved to a site in the center of Haddonfield in 1885.

The Methodist Cemetery is now along Kings Highway next to Lee Avenue. The cemetery's present location marks the site next to the first Methodist Church in Haddonfield. In 1857, the congregation moved into a new house of worship at the corner of Grove Street and Kings Highway.

The Bridge to Gloucester City

From the viewpoint of some nineteenth century Haddon Township farmers, maybe Gloucester City's single most important attribute was the populace's demand for market garden vegetables, farm and dairy products. For many years the Champion Bridge, on Collings Road, was the only bridge over Newton Creek to Gloucester City. On June 1, 1870, the bridge was washed away by a flood, thereby the most direct route between Haddon Township and Gloucester City was gone.

After the flood, the township's truck farmers traveled a circuitous route through Camden to market in Gloucester City. To some, the extra distance to Gloucester City's market was not worth the effort:

> ...Haddon Township farmers would prefer to dispose of their produce and do business in Gloucester City than go to Camden, but as there was no convenient way of entering Gloucester, they were obligated to go to Camden. (WJP 4/9/1879)

Unable to haul their farm products by a direct route to Gloucester City, some township farmers pressured Camden County's Freeholders to rebuild the bridge at Collings Road. In 1874, much to the surprise of citizens of Gloucester City and Haddon Township, a new site was chosen to span Newton Creek. The bridge was built at the end of a new highway called Nicholson Road.

Gloucester City's officials voiced their dissatisfaction with the site of the new bridge by delaying construction of the roadway on the west side from the bridge to fast land, a distance of some 500 feet. Without a completed roadway on the Gloucester side, passage over the marshland and into the city was impossible.

The Nicholson Road bridge was the focus of debate for five years. Many citizens of Gloucester City believed the Nicholson Road bridge was at a location that served the interest of a few:

> There was a road [Collings Road] and a bridge over Newton Creek, much used by Gloucester folks, but the tides washed the bridge away and the Freeholders built a bridge [Nicholson Road] where there is no road and the result is that neither is of any more use, than would be a wagon without a wheel or a wheel without a wagon. (CDP 9/3/1879)

> A Gloucesterian said "We did not want the new bridge for it will take us to no where, where we want to go unless it be to William Nicholson's dairy farm, for whom the sole benefit the bridge was built and new road opened. (CDP 9/3/1879) [See William C. Nicholson, page 186.]

An end to the controversy came in 1879, when a group of township farmers took matters into their own hands. They completed the road on the Gloucester City side of the creek, thereby allowing travel across the bridge and into the city:

> Freeholders built a "bob tail" bridge planted in the middle of Newton Creek, however it sat for a few years because Gloucester City would not finish it to fast land on her side. Last week Gloucester was "invaded by men, horses and carts" from Haddon Township, and before the end of the week a causeway was built to the bridge and high-ho! it was passable. (WJP 11/26/1879)

An interesting sidelight to the bridge controversy took place on the Gloucester City side of Newton Creek. Three years after the bridge at Collings Road was washed away, David S. Brown, a Gloucester businessman, created a stir when he dug cellars, laid foundations and erected walls for a number of homes directly on the former roadway leading between the then washed-out bridge and Broadway in Gloucester City. Before he could complete the dwellings, the Attorney General took Brown to court, charging the public was wronged and the new homes created a nuisance by blocking the road. Brown argued that Collings Road, at least on the Gloucester side of the creek, had not been used for three years and people could still go to Newton Creek, if they chose to, by traveling around the block where the new homes were being built. The court ruled for Brown. The public, according to the judge, was not injured by the roadway obstruction. (*The Attorney-General ex rel. Gloucester City vs. Brown and another.* The Court of Chancery, May 1873)

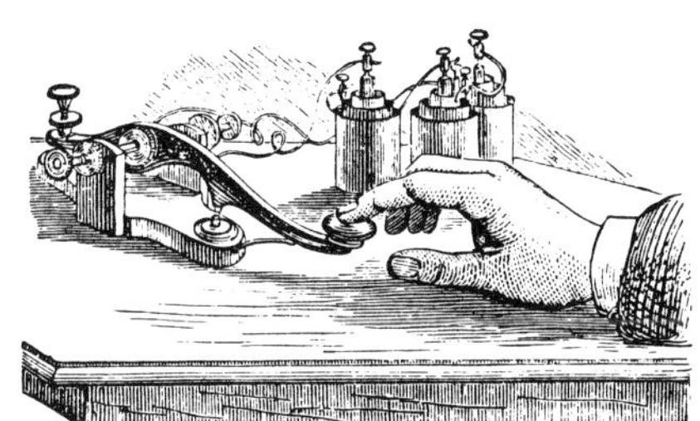

Information and Communication

Newspapers

In 1887, George Prowell observed the significance of the press in his work, *The History of Camden County, New Jersey*:

> The press in America is one of the most potent factors in the education of the masses, and its power and influence cannot be over-estimated. (p. 319)

In the 1860s, residents of old Haddon Township received their news from newspapers published in Camden. Most of the city's newspapers covered national affairs and events, although the stories were often weeks old before appearing in print. The newspapers also reported on the affairs of government in Trenton, as well as events within Camden and the surrounding county. Editorial comments and opinions were a part of most newspapers as were advertisements, legal notices and recreational or practical topics like farming and gardening. They frequently published poems in the press.

One popular Camden newspaper was the *West Jersey Press*. Published every Wednesday, patrons paid a $1.50 for a one-year subscription. More so than any other Camden newspaper of the era, the *West Jersey Press* devoted a significant portion of space to reporting events and news from the various villages throughout Camden County. "Letters from Haddonfield" contained news and reports on social events in the village. Other "Letters" published pertained to events in Berlin, Blackwoodtown (Blackwood), Merchantville, Williamstown and Gloucester City.

The *West Jersey Press* often ran articles about proprietors and local businesses. The Camden & Atlantic Railroad was frequently the subject of newspaper articles and, in all instances, reports were laudable. The railroad's right-of-way traveled across old Haddon Township, connecting Camden with Atlantic City. It is no coincidence that the *West Jersey Press* coined the nickname "Old Reliable" for the railroad. Yes, the railroad happened to advertise frequently in the weekly paper. Editorial plugs of local business were common.

Newspapers of the era were often owned by proprietors who were not reluctant to publish their opinions, particularly in the area of politics. In many instances, the partisan newspapers read like political pamphlets reporting on party activities, condemning the opposing party and urging citizens to vote for their candidate. After election day, benefits accrued to the newspaper when the publisher's party was victorious. For instance, printing contracts became a source of revenue for the paper. Similarly, contracts to publish tax lists, land sales, sheriff sales and other legal notices were more available.

The *West Jersey Press* aligned itself with the Republican Party. The paper's owner and editor, Sinnickson Chew, wrote editorials that supported the party's principles. Chew's partisan style of writing was

14-03-1677

1820—1879. Job Printing of every Description, Books & Pamphlets, Stationery, Legal Blanks, Etc. 1820—1879.

S. CHEW, Proprietor. "WEST JERSEY PRESS" Is the best Advertising Medium and has a larger circulation than any other newspaper in Camden County. $2.00 per Annum in Advance.

L. F. Camden, N. J., December 31st 1879.

Rowand Coles & Shreve Comm of the estate of Saml R. Stoy dec'd

To SINNICKSON CHEW, Dr.

Terms: N. E. Cor. Front and Market Streets.

1879 Oct	24	To printing 50 posters sale of property of Saml R. Stoy dec'd	$3.00
Nov.	26	To advertising same in West Jersey Press	7.20
			$10.20

Rec'd Payment
S. Chew

West Jersey Press invoice. The weekly newspaper was published in Camden. The paper, through its proprietor, Sinneckson Chew, was affiliated with and supported the Republican Party.

(Stoy Manuscript Collection, Historical Society of Haddonfield)

discussed in Charles Boyer's *The History of the Press in Camden County, New Jersey*:

> During the Civil War he [Chew] was bitter towards the opposition party and his scathing criticisms of the editorial policy of the "Camden Democrat" brought forth many tart and caustic paragraphs in both papers. (p.7)

The *West Jersey Press* maintained a fierce rivalry with the *Camden Democrat*, a paper loyal to the Democratic Party. The editors of the *Camden Democrat* published party policy, which was at odds with opinions expressed in the *West Jersey Press.* George Prowell wrote the *Camden Democrat* "…was never a cowardly neutral on any question. " (p. 324)

Often the two city newspapers traded editorial insults. This inflammatory and politically charged form of journalism can be illustrated by the following article that appeared in the *Camden Democrat.* The comments by the editor, Morris Hamilton, were made in response to Sinnickson Chew's previously published opinion on an amendment to the Constitution:

> Mr. Sinnickson Chew of the West Jersey Press volunteers to furnish an epitaph and not wishing to be excelled in editorial courtesy, even in so *grave* a matter, we *undertake* to

THE CAMDEN DEMOCRAT IS PUBLISHED EVERY SATURDAY At No. 96 Federal Street, Camden. TERMS: $2 PER YEAR. Having the largest circulation of any paper in Camden county it cannot be excelled as an advertising medium. All kinds of BOOK and JOB PRINTING Done Neatly, Cheaply and Promptly.

THE ONLY DEMOCRATIC PAPER IN CAMDEN COUNTY.
14-03-1676
ESTABLISHED IN 1832.

Camden, N. J. Decr 31 1879

J L Rowand J Stokes Coles John C Shreeve Com of Real Estate of Samuel R Stoy dec'd

To Wills & Semple, Dr.

To Advertising Sale of Real Estate of Samuel R Stoy dec'd — 5 wk 7.65

Rec'd Payment—
Wills & Semple
pr R J Mapes

Camden Democrat invoice. This partisan-based newspaper was associated with the Democratic Party. Fierce competition existed for many years between the *Camden Democrat* and the *West Jersey Press.*

(Stoy Manuscript Collection, Historical Society of Haddonfield)

> return the favor by submitting the following: "Here *lies* one who *s-chew-d* the Constitution and died of nigger on the brain." (*History of the Press in Camden County*, p. 24)

While the quotation highlights blunt and cutting editorial jabs of competing newspapers, it also illustrates the state of race relations during the period.

As previously mentioned, following the Civil War, the county's Democratic Party opposed the extension of basic civil rights to African-Americans. In retrospect, the Democratic Party's mouthpiece, the *Camden Democrat*, often printed insulting and racist articles.

Another popular newspaper of the era was the *The New Republic*, again a Camden weekly. They printed the first edition in 1867. Its editor and proprietor, Henry Bonsall, later went on to start another well-read paper, the *Camden Daily Post*. Although there were other Camden newspapers published during the period, their existence was, for the most part, brief.

By the mid-1870s, the *Haddonfield Basket* began its run. Initially, the owner intended the paper to be a weekly but, it turned into a monthly publication. Each issue was available for five cents, a yearly subscription could be obtained for 50 cents.

The *Haddonfield Basket* offered a mixture of national and statewide news, poems and reprinted articles from other newspapers and magazines. A general interest column entitled "Useful, Wit and Wisdom, and Miscellaneous Departments" also appeared in the village's publication.

It should be no surprise that a significant portion of the *Haddonfield Basket* pertained to news and events about its host village. Not too unlike today's local newspapers, the *Haddonfield Basket* carried announcements of marriages, deaths and events and affairs of the township's government, churches, schools, clubs, and associations. Advertising space was purchased by local shopkeepers, professionals and craftsmen.

Like most newspaper publishers of the era, the *Haddonfield Basket's* proprietor, John Van Court, held strong beliefs. One of Van Court's strongest convictions was his support of the temperance movement. When the township's populace debated the issue of whether liquor should be sold in the township, Van Court devoted many articles to advocating a ban on the sale of alcohol.

In 1876, Van Court's comments on the idea of trains passing between Haddonfield and Camden on Sundays illustrates his fervent writing style:

> Among the other matters discussed, as we understand, was the question of running a train on Sunday to the city in the morning and back in the evening...we cannot understand how any one professing to be guided by the laws and precepts of the Bible, can advocate such a measure. (HB 5/18/1876)

Unlike the editor of the *West Jersey Press*, Van Court frequently criticized the Camden & Atlantic Railroad Company. Whether the topic was insufficiently heated passenger cars or poor management decisions, he consistently chastised the railroad company. The company was not an important advertiser in Van Court's *Haddonfield Basket*.

In 1877, a weekly newspaper known as the *Asteroid* began competing with Van Court's newspaper. After just several months of competition with the new publication, the *Haddonfield Basket* closed its doors. The new publication only lasted several months longer before it, too, failed. For a brief period, in 1877, a newspaper entitled *The Letter Basket and General Advertiser* circulated about the village. Van Court in the 1880s reintroduced the *Haddonfield Basket*. Around 1880, another publication, the *Argus and Advocate*, opened an office and press room in the New Jersey Building on Haddonfield's Main Street.

Telegraph and Telephone

In the 1830s, Samuel Morse invented the telegraph. The new device flashed messages instantaneously along miles of wire. Morse's invention transformed communications in the United States.

According to Paul W. Schopp, a South Jersey historian, the Camden & Atlantic Railroad was an early convert to telegraphic communications. Schopp's published manuscript, "Wired Lightning–The Arrival of Telegraph in South Jersey," notes the railroad company's right-of-way was only partially completed in 1853 when its Board of Directors entered an agreement with a representative of the Morse System for the right to use the Morse Telegraphic System along its roadway for both company business and public accommodations. (Camden County History Journal, 9/1995) Schopp noted, "This decision...provided the population with communications that were unavailable in most other sections of America." After a decade of use, the Camden & Atlantic's Board of Directors approved a long-term lease allowing The American Telegraph Company the right to use telegraph lines along the right-of-way. American Telegraph was founded to consolidate the many local telegraphic systems into one nationwide system.

It is likely the local railroad's initial use of the telegraph system was primarily for control of train movement. By 1878, there were eleven telegraph stations

Blank No. 1.

THE WESTERN UNION TELEGRAPH COMPANY.

The rules of this Company require that all messages received for transmission, shall be written on the message blanks of the Company, under and subject to the conditions printed thereon, which conditions have been agreed to by the sender of the following message.

THOS. T. ECKERT, Gen'l Sup't, New York. WILLIAM ORTON, Pres't, O. H. PALMER, Sec'y, New York.

Dated Trenton NJ March 7 1871

Received at

To J L Rowand

Haddonfield

Bill annex

Western Union Telegraph receipt in 1871. Before invention of the telephone, the telegraph was used to instantaneously communicate messages along wire.

(Rowand Manuscript Collection, Historical Society of Haddonfield)

along the Camden & Atlantic right-of-way. During the 1870s, the Haddonfield depot had the only telegraph station within old Haddon Township. Even though no documentation exists to show public use of the local telegraph system, it is reasonable to assume inhabitants used the telegraph office at Haddonfield to transmit messages. For instance, it is likely that township residents with commercial interests in Camden or Philadelphia sent and received messages with their business associates.

In 1880, they installed another telegraph location along Camden & Atlantic's roadway to accommodate the growing community of Collingswood:

> "The railroad company has put one of the pilot houses of an old ferry boat here [Collingswood] for a telegraph station." (WJP 7/7/1880)

In the early 1870s, a new communication device, the telephone, was invented. In 1876, during a demonstration of his invention, Alexander Graham Bell transmitted his famous sentence over a telephone "Mr. Watson, come here; I want you." Later that year, Bell exhibited the new device to excited crowds at Philadelphia's Centennial Exposition. As it turned out, except possibly for electricity for light and power, no innovation rivaled the importance of the telephone.

In the year following the Centennial Exhibition, the workings of the "Bell Speaking Telephone" entertained some Camden residents. Witnesses at a demonstration of the new device envisioned ways to employ the telephone:

> They talked, read, sang, played the piano, flute and sent the ticking of a watch through their wire over 2000 feet in length. So well did the instrument operate the words were often heard by those sitting near the listener. "By this means," remarked one of those present, "friends may connect their houses at small expense, and remain at home while making calls." (WJP 10/31/1877)

Early telephone subscribers were furnished individual lines and telephones for service between two locations. Soon, however, they connected lines to a central switch board for communication among all subscribers.

The first evidence of telephone use in the area was in 1879. Samuel Willits hung a telephone wire between his lumberyard along Haddonfield's Tanner Street and his landing yard along Cooper's Creek. [See lumberyard, page 167.] Another village proprietor was also tied into Willits's telephone system:

> The telephone is daily becoming a necessity with business. S. A. Willits & Company of Haddonfield has made telephonic connection between the office and the depot in Haddonfield. It takes in R. Elmer Clement's office on the route where orders may be left. (WJP 8/13/1879)

The new device allowed simultaneous communication between two business locations; however, it was not without problems. Inclement weather could render an early telephone network useless. Less than one year after installation, the owner of the area's only telephone system, experienced an outage of service. The *West Jersey Press* reported "Telephone wire between R. E. Clement's office and lumberyard of Willits & Bacon became loaded with ice and broke down." (WJP 12/29/1879)

In 1878, the first telephone exchange in the nation opened in New Haven, Connecticut. In the following year, a telephone cable was laid under the Delaware River, connecting Philadelphia and Camden. By 1880, there was talk of stringing telephone wire between Camden and Haddonfield:

> There is some prospect of having a telephone line to Haddonfield soon. Some of the managers have signified a willingness to erect a line if the right kind of support is met. (WJP 5/5/1880)

Today, overhead telephone wires crisscrossing neighborhoods are commonplace. However, in the nineteenth century, not all citizens acquiesced to the telephone wires strung near their homes:

> There has been among some of the people of Haddonfield, some prejudice against telephone wires passing their homes. Fear...it may increase the danger of lightning. (WJP 7/28/1880)

In 1884, they strung the first telephone wire from Camden to Haddonfield. According to research contained in *Lost Haddonfield*, the first village telephone exchange was at Willard's Telephone Drug Store in 1884. Compared with modern-day computerized networks, operating the early telephone exchanges were inconvenient:

> If you wanted to make a call, Willard or one of his employees would place it and collect the money. Willard's also received telephone calls at the store and delivered messages to people's homes for a small fee. (p. 51)

In 1890, they took another important step in establishing a telephone network suitable for the public; a switchboard was installed in Haddonfield. Exploitation of the telephone continued at an exponential pace. By 1895, there were about 310,000 telephones in the country; a decade later, there were ten million.

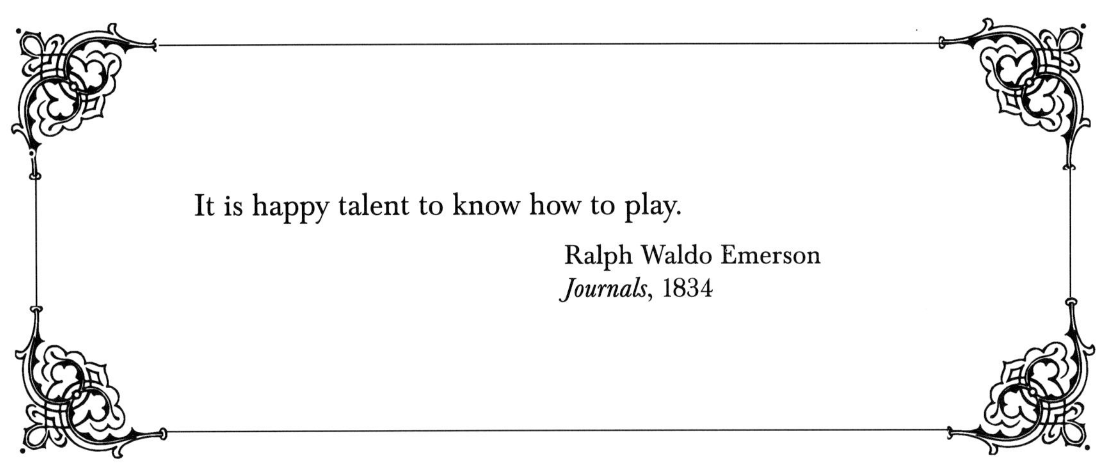

It is happy talent to know how to play.

Ralph Waldo Emerson
Journals, 1834

Life Styles and Routines

Entertainment and Leisure

In the nineteenth century it was not uncommon for laborers, shop-owners and farmhands to toil at work for ten hours a day, six days a week. Notwithstanding, there were plenty of activities to entertain the inhabitants of old Haddon Township. In an era before television, radio, computer games and movie theatres, leisure hours were consumed by sporting events, family-oriented activities, church socials and secular organizations.

One of the more popular nineteenth century pastimes was hunting and fishing. Sporting men headed for the fields when the cooler temperatures of fall arrived. Bird hunting was a popular pastime. Even before hunting season for game-birds opened, it was common to hear anxious hunters discharging their weapons in the fields throughout the township. The banks along Newton and Cooper's creeks were especially fruitful areas to hunt small game and birds:

> A gentlemen residing near the Half-Way House [Collingswood] on the Camden and Haddonfield Turnpike was gunning on the farm of Arthur Sitly located on Newton Creek between Mt. Ephriam and White Horse Road. . . . (WJP 10/29/1873)

Hunters bagged birds for sport and personal consumption; some even took the birds to Philadelphia marketplaces:

> The river shore and the creeks of this county are lined with gunners who are after reed and rail birds. Reed birds were sold in Philadelphia market last week at 60 cents per dozen. (WJP 8/8/1880)

When hunting season arrived, farmers posted caution notices on their property to keep hunters and other trespassers off. In 1870, a pigeon shooting contest was held in Haddonfield. (WJP 2/23/1870) Shooting matches were common events in the village.

Local gunning enthusiasts traveled outside the township's borders in search of game. Some boarded the Camden & Atlantic Railroad cars to travel to the woods and fields:

> For sometime now outgoing trains on our railroad will be found to contain grim-visaged men clad in corduroy and accompanied by dogs and guns . . . [traveling] to fields to hunt quail and rabbit. (WJP 11/3/1875)

Fishing the three branches of Newton Creek, Cooper's Creek, and the handful of mill ponds gave local anglers plenty of fishing options. Even today, these same waterways provide excellent fishing. The *West Jersey Press* often noted the success of local anglers:

> Sunfish of goodly size are abundant in Newton Creek this fall. (CDP 10/17/1879)

> Angling in this vicinity [Haddonfield] is becoming quite popular: at that part of Cooper's Creek which winds along

> the south eastern edge of our borough...[fishermen] peel up cat fish, an eel or perch. (NR 7/14/1877)

Not unlike today, excursions to the seashore were a popular activity for many people. In the 1870s, those in search of fresh air traveled to the ocean by railroad. If walking the Atlantic City boardwalk or bathing in the surf did not provide enough enjoyment, sporting men could join in on game and fishing excursions. William Plum, a Haddonfield resident, arranged trips to Atlantic City aboard the trains of the Camden & Atlantic Railroad. They carried Plum's advertisements in the *West Jersey Press*:

> Plum's Pleasure Excursion from Philadelphia, Camden, Haddonfield $1.00 round trip. Children under 12, 50 cents. Gunning, fishing, and other pleasures. Train leaves Cooper's Point 6:45 AM, Haddonfield 7:05 AM, arrive in Atlantic City 9:15 AM. Leave Atlantic City 6:00 PM. (WJP 9/4/1878)

Attending picnics were popular outdoor activities. Lakeside Park, in Kirkwood, was about ten miles from Haddonfield. The park, owned by the Camden & Atlantic Railroad Company, opened in the mid-1870s to bring pleasure seekers from Camden and Philadelphia. In 1877, more than 13,000 visitors entered the park between the months of May and September:

> Lakeside Park, at Kirkwood, has been improved and beautified. A large pavilion, capable of being closed against the weather, has been tastefully built, and a roomy dining saloon, kitchen, storehouse and other convenient buildings erected; large numbers of trees have been planted, gravel walks laid and levelled, and the underbrush removed. (Annual Report of Camden & Atlantic Railroad, 1877, p. 7)

Horse-racing was a prized spectator event. Some fifteen years before the Civil War, the Camden & Philadelphia Race Track stood along the White Horse Road, in what is now Oaklyn. Thousands of spectators once traveled from New York, Philadelphia and Camden to watch and bet on the horses. Newton Township's citizens, however, did not universally approve of the regional racecourse. The sport attracted many unsavory and rowdy fans that caused nearby farmers to question the desirability of a racetrack. After a half-dozen years of horse racing, the township's influential Quaker constituency lobbied state legislators and ultimately secured the passage of a statute prohibiting public horse-racing. The lawmakers' decision was aided by an accident at the racecourse where spectators were injured when the grandstand collapsed. [See Edward Bettle, page 267.]

Horse-racing within the township did not end when the racecourse ceased operating in the mid-1840s. The sport continued, however, from that point on it was now sanctioned privately. The public was often notified of the challenges in Camden's newspapers:

> On the first fair day (a good track) a race (single mile heat under saddle) will come off here between the two well-known black horses–Shakespeare rode by Jose Adams and Andy Johnson rode by C. Middleton. (WJP 3/18/1868)

The location of races varied. The turnpikes were convenient places to settle arguments over who owned the fastest horse, even though they prohibited racing on private roadways. Enforcement, however, was another matter.

Sporting enthusiasts often found a convenient time of the day to race their horses on Haddonfield's Main Street. But many inhabitants of the village frowned on horse-racing contests along the thoroughfares:

> Horse racing along main avenue [Kings Highway] of our town is out of place. Amusement occurs just at the dusk of evening. (WJP 8/23/1871)

Bicycling on the area's roadways was another popular pastime. Riders found private turnpikes offered excellent riding surfaces to pedal their bicycles. Managers of the roadways reacted to bicycling in a familiar manner.

> The [Haddonfield] turnpike authorities have issued a pronouncement against bicycles because they frighten horses and are a nuisance with or without riders. (WJP 5/12/1880)

While the operators of the turnpikes discouraged horse-racing and bicycling on their roadways, they promoted leisurely carriage touring. Of course, this activity generated tolls for the company. Philadelphia and Camden inhabitants frequently enjoyed driving their carriages in the pastoral countryside. While the toll roads were the beneficiaries of cruising along the rural highways, Camden's livery stables also benefited from the activity:

> Our smooth Turnpikes have become so attractive that they draw an immense number of vehicles from the other side [Philadelphia] for after noon drives...livery stables proprietor recoup a reasonable share of benefits occurring from their advertisement. (WJP 8/26/1868)

The modern-day "national pastime," baseball, became popular in the nineteenth century. Many learned to play baseball in army camps during the Civil War. When the soldiers returned to their homes after the war, baseball became a highly regarded sport to play and observe.

One local ballfield was situated next to present-day Lake Street in Haddonfield. Another ballfield was on the former Elizabeth Haddon Estaugh Estate, somewhere on or near the farm of Isaac Wood, just outside the village.

Haddonfield was home to a baseball club. Family and friends enjoyed watching the "Old Haddon" team (WJP 9/4/1872) or "Haddon nine" (WJP 12/9/1868) take on rival clubs from nearby villages, Camden and Philadelphia. The ball games were often high-scoring events. For example, in 1870 "Haddon best Berlin 38 to 20." (WJP 9/20/1870)

Compared with today's elaborate equipment, 1860s baseball gear was quite Spartan. For instance, the fielders played without gloves. On the other hand, nineteenth century baseball players generally played nine innings in about the same length of time as modern-day baseball games. For example, Haddonfield defeated Milford in two hours and fifteen minutes. (WJP 5/2/1866)

The Haddon's season began about April and lasted until Thanksgiving Day:

> Base Ball The season [April] for the great game is now fairly inaugurated and new clubs are springing up all over the county. (WJP 5/2/1866)

> "Haddon nine" Base Ball Club beat Marlton and Moorestown on Thanksgiving day. (WJP 12/9/1868)

Although many enjoyed watching local men play ball games, baseball was not universally loved:

> Baseball This game has so degenerated that only the most worthless and idle men and half grown boys now engaged in it. The players who came over here from Philadelphia to indulge in the game are about as degenerate a class as it is to be found anywhere in that city. (WJP 9/8/1869)

The opinionated editor of the *Haddonfield Basket*, John Van Court, was no fan of the game. While reporting on the death of a man caused by a fight in Gloucester City, Van Court equated saloons and murder with baseball. (HB 6/22/1888)

During the 1870s cricket and football were played throughout the area. Some young men in the area probably played the games, although its popularity was not confirmed in newspaper reports or any other document. One newspaper reported, "There has been talk of a Cricket Club in Haddonfield." (WJP 7/21/1880)

For the men and women who toiled in the fields to make a living, outdoor chores naturally curtailed when the winter months arrived. Although it was uncomfortable to work outdoors in harsh winter weather, there was a fondness for wintertime outdoor leisure activities. Much like today, the children of the nineteenth century had a favorite hill to sled down when snow fell. Adults, too, enjoyed similar winter activity. When snow arrived, sleighs were pulled out of the sheds and utilized for general transportation and for pleasure. In researching public documents for this project, it was observed that many township inhabitants owned sleighs.

After a winter storm, many inhabitants found adventure by hitching a horse to an open sleigh and riding in the countryside. Socializing often accompanied the activity:

> Gay Time in the County The prolonged snow of the present winter has revived some of the old-time sleighing parties in the county, and there are jolly scenes in our rural district. (WJP 1/23/1867)

> Since the recent fall of snow, the sleighing in the rural district has been very fine and largely indulged in by all classes of society. (WJP 1/22/1879)

Interestingly, even in the cold weather, the competitiveness of racing enthusiasts took hold:

> A broad, smooth and beautiful Main Street, of Haddonfield, makes a grand boulevard for sleighing, and last week, and Monday, and yesterday, it was the scene of some spirited contests of speed between the owners of noted flyers in that grand old borough and its vicinity. (WJP 12/29/1880)

Ice skating was another treasured winter event for people of all ages. The millponds of the township, especially Evans and Hopkins ponds, were choice locations to ice skate. Sometimes Newton and Cooper's creeks became frozen paths for ice skaters to glide across:

> On Saturday last a party of skaters from Camden skated to Haddonfield and returned on Cooper's Creek. The ice is said to be 20 inches thick in many places. (WJP 2/10/1875)

Jehu Wood, Jr.'s diary entries divulge some wintertime activities. When Jehu wrote in his diary in 1864 as a teenager, he lived on his parent's farm outside Haddonfield. The former Wood family's dwelling stands today at 201 Wood Lane:

> Jan. 8 Still snowing, sleighing first rate and quantities of people out.

> Jan. 11 Pa [Isaac Wood], Sam [Samuel Wood] and Unc [Jehu Wood], and I hitched the new mules to the sleigh. Went skating, very poor.

> Jan. 12 Thawed...could make first rate snow balls.

> Feb. 19 It was splendid skating on Hopkins Pond this evening and lots doing.

Winter skating scene. Ice skating on local creeks and ponds was a popular wintertime leisure activity.

(*First Lessons in Reading.* Parker & Watson's Series, A.S. Barnes & Company, NY. 1873)

Christmas, the main holiday during the winter, was a family-oriented day. Much as it is today, Santa Claus, Christmas trees, singing carols, mistletoe as well as other traditions were all part of the holiday. Between Christmas and New Year's, children enjoyed a vacation from the classroom.

Holiday shopping is entrenched in the modern-day Christmas season. Surprisingly, it is not a modern phenomenon. People participated in this endeavor many years before twentieth century shopping malls ever existed. Many local inhabitants did their shopping in Camden and Philadelphia and Haddonfield as well. In the nineteenth century, the press reported that last minute shoppers in Haddonfield were going from store to store to purchase holiday gifts:

> One evidence of the approach of Christmas may be seen in numerous bundles, packages and boxes in possession of the passengers of the railroads as they leave the city [Camden] to their county homes. (WJP 12/31/1876)

> The day before Christmas was a "full day" among our store keepers [Haddonfield] as many our people were doing unusual amount of shopping. (WJP 12/30/1879)

Much like today, homeowners decorated buildings with evergreens for the Christmas season. In the "Letter from Haddonfield" column of the *Camden Democrat*, it was reported some African-Americans gathered Christmas decorations:

> Evergreens of various sizes, shapes and prices, are on the move, and our fellow citizens of African decent, are busy. . .plunging in the woods, far and near, in search of these emblems to meet the demands of our churches, halls, and private citizens. Our Main street is covered with these mementoes of the coming holidays. (CD 12/22/1877)

In the summertime, the principal holiday was the Fourth of July. Sporting events, picnics, fireworks, parades and patriotic speeches highlighted the day. Most of the celebrations and festive events in old Haddon Township took place in Haddonfield:

> . . .firing guns, crackers, squeaks, boating and piscatorial sport on the beautiful lakelets. . . . A game of baseball. . .at grove of Samuel Reeves [Lake Street]. (WJP 7/9/1873)

> 4th of July fine display of fireworks at the residence of Wm. Mann . . . [between Hopkins Lane and Cooper's Creek.] (WJP 7/12/1871)

Independence Day was not the only time people gathered on Mann's land. People apparently enjoyed Mann's grove throughout the year:

> There is no finer grove under the sun than that of Mr. Wm. Mann, he has made a kind of public park for the beautiful Haddonfield. (NR 8/4/1877)

It is highly unlikely that Mischief Night is highlighted as a holiday on modern-day calendars. However, most people are aware of the significance of October 30.

In the nineteenth century, at least for some inhabitants, the dreaded evening came all too often. Such was the case in the 1870s, when some Haddonfield residents were treated to the annual ritual:

> "Boys will be boys," is a common saying, and is often used in such a way as to encourage them in mischief and wrong doing. Fun is one thing, mischief is another. On Hallow Eve, a parcel of big boys went through some portion of the town, opening gates, and in some cases removing them and displacing the boards in the side walk. (WJP 11/6/1878)

Reading, talking, singing or playing games around the home was a way to pleasurably pass the time away. Some people amused themselves privately by gathering around a parlor piano. Nonetheless, the public's musical activities were centered in Haddonfield.

The late twentieth century electronic entertainment mediums are in stark contrast to musical choices available in the 1870s. If someone wanted to listen to music, a live musical performance was the only option available. Musical groups played at church functions, theatre pieces, dances and group social events.

Musicians often traveled to Haddonfield to perform. Hendry Hall was one of several entertainment centers in the village. Its location was where the dwelling at 15 Potter Street is situated today. "Concert by the Camden Union at Haddonfield at Hendry Hall, Haddonfield–25 cents admission." (WJP 6/7/1865) Another popular entertainment facility was the second floor of the New Jersey Building along Main Street. [See New Jersey building, page 100.]

Audiences came from all parts of the region. For instance in 1877, three Camden & Atlantic Railroad passenger cars loaded with Camden citizens departed toward Haddonfield for an evening of entertainment:

> The entertainment given at Haddonfield last night by Frederick's Orchestra, was on the whole, successful. The Orchestra rendered several pieces excellently, "Speed Well," a waltz being well received. Mr. W. H. Muschamp did the comic song business to the satisfaction of all. Mr. Frank Carroll was loudly applauded in his ballads. Miss S. C. Hillman recited "How He Saved St. Nicholls." A comic lecture by Mr. R. Briggs . . . (CDP 1/12/1877)

Where there was music, there was often dancing. The column in the *West Jersey Press* reporting events in Haddonfield once noted:

> Amusement consist of drawing, music and conversation. Able musicians rendered the recreation of dancing all the more delightful. (WJP 1/22/1868)

Quite often musical entertainment was hired for private social gatherings. In 1874, the Odd Fellows held a picnic at a pastoral setting next to present-day Crystal Lake:

> Old Fellows Pic-Nic in Mr. John Stoy's woods. 6th Regiment Brass Band. . . . The gay groups of young ladies, the massive oaks with their overhanging foliage of green, and the sweet strains of music, formed a combination to soothe and please senses. (HB 8/1874)

A concert generally accompanied a political affair. In many instances the musical bands were affiliated with a political party:

> We take pleasure in calling the attention of political association to the Haddonfield Cornet Band. Under the leadership of Abel Clement an accomplished musician, the band has acquired a proficiency equal to the best bands in the county. It is composed entirely of loyal men who esteem it a privilege to aid the cause of Lincoln and Johnson. (WJP 8/8/1864)

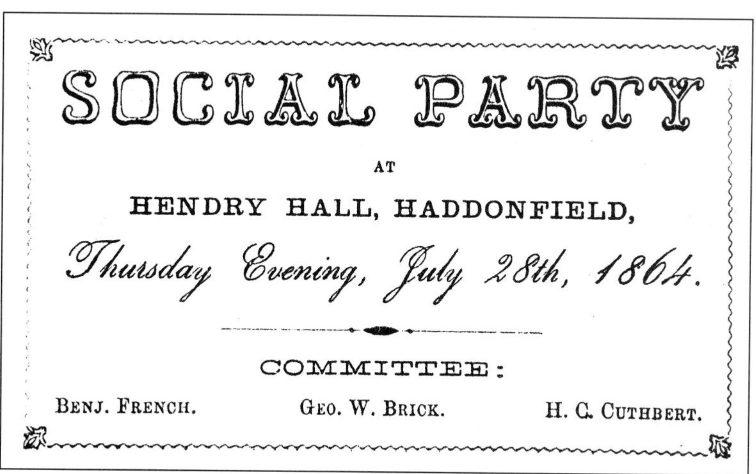
SOCIAL PARTY

AT

HENDRY HALL, HADDONFIELD,

Thursday Evening, July 28th, 1864.

COMMITTEE:

BENJ. FRENCH. GEO. W. BRICK. H. C. CUTHBERT.

Invitation to "Social Party" at Hendry Hall in 1864. The hall was once located on Potter Street in Haddonfield.

(Gloucester County Historical Society Collections)

One of the more extravagant affairs held in Haddonfield during the 1870s was the Ladies Centennial Tea Party, held in October 1874. The local women's organization used the occasion to raise money for the Philadelphia Centennial Exhibition.

Membership in a fraternal society was widespread in the late nineteenth century. These organizations often sponsored activities to entertain its members. The Grange, with chapters throughout the country, was an organization that advanced the interest of farmers and at the same time gave farm families a social outlet. A local chapter of the Grange was founded in Haddonfield in the 1870s. Besides its regularly scheduled business meetings, the organization planned social occasions, often accompanied by entertainment. The *Camden Daily Post* reported, "Haddon Grange will give musical and literary entertainment in the Jersey Building." (CDP 4/29/1879)

While churches were primarily places of worship, they were also centers for parishioner social activities:

> A social entertainment was given by the latter [Methodist Church] on New Year's Eve, to which the public was invited. (WJP 1/12/1876)

> The fist social circle of the season of the Presbyterian Church takes place ... (CDP 11/9/1879)

> The social fair and festival of the Baptist Church people in the New Jersey Building. (CDP 11/9/1879)

Church outings were commonplace:

> The Sunday School of the Methodist Church...on their annual pic-nic excursion to the woods. This is an occasion that the children always look forward to as a day of high enjoyment. (WJP 7/26/1876)

Some inhabitants sought relaxation through reading. The hub of the township's literary related activities were also in Haddonfield. They housed the only library in the township on the second floor above a store. The Haddon Library Company was a private subscription organization founded in 1803 by members of the Society of Friends. The members had decisive views on the types of books that should be placed in the library. The group prohibited books that were "vain, immoral, or corrupting tendency." (Prowell, p. 619) Therefore, popular plays, novels or romances, which an enthusiastic recreational reader might want, were not available.

In 1869, the Library Company turned its books over to an organization known as the Haddon Institute. (WJP 5/5/1869) The Institute convinced the township's officials to allow them to use a room in Town Hall as a library and reading room.

The minutes of the March 9, 1870 Town Meeting noted, "Haddon Institute...for the use of every man, women and child in the community." Even though the minutes of the Town Meeting imply all residents could use the library, only those members that paid dues were permitted to use the 1,200 volumes of books. (HB 1/1876)

A report in the *West Jersey Press* suggested the library may have struggled for lack of support by the end of the 1870s. "Charles Rhodes, President of Haddonfield Library, appeals for support of citizens of borough. . . ." (WJP 2/5/1879)

During the 1870s, citizens could purchase a wide variety of reading material. Dime novels, weekly and monthly periodicals and technical journals devoted to many topics were all available. The most popular general magazines in the era were *Harper's Weekly, Atlantic Monthly, and Scribner's Monthly.*

Mark Twain was a recognized author at that time. In 1869, the humorist published his highly-acclaimed book, *The Innocents Abroad.* The *West Jersey Press* printed an advertisement that sought local agents to distribute Twain's work:

> Agents can get Territory for Mark Twain's new book with 234 engravings. "Who has not heard of the author? Who has not laughed over his quaint sayings and queer ideas, and family succumbed to his racy stories?" (WJP 9/1/1869)

In 1878, the definitive work of Haddonfield's Judge John Clement was completed and published. Even today, the treatise entitled *Sketches of the First Emigrant Settlers in Newton Township, Gloucester County, New Jersey* remains the most important work on the early settlement in Newton Township. When it was first published, the book sold for five dollars, a hefty price for the era. (WJP 12/4/1878)

Lectures in Haddonfield were commonplace. Among the many programs on the local lecture circuit were techniques of farming, literary subjects and scientific matters. For instance, Edward D. Cope, a Haddonfield resident, presented a lecture in 1869 on a topic within his unique field of study. (WJP 5/5/1869) The widely recognized paleontologist held a prestigious position at the University of Pennsylvania. He led expeditions in search of fossils in the western territories of America. Edward Cope's home was on Main Street where the present-day Borough Hall stands.

A scholastic spelling bee provided nineteenth century amusement for both students and parents:

> "Spelling bee" Haddonfield challenged Hammonton for a spelling match. (WJP 11/13/1878)

> The "return" spelling match between Haddonfield and Hammonton. The Camden & Atlantic Railroad will furnish transportation. (WJP 1/29/1879)

If the pace of entertainment activities in the township slowed, inhabitants could readily board a Camden bound train and, if necessary, continue by ferry to Philadelphia and attend concerts, plays, lectures or other events. Something always was happening in the way of entertainment in the cities. For instance in 1872, P.T. Barnum's great traveling museum, menagerie and caravan set up its tents on a lot in Camden. Another illustration appeared in a newspaper article:

> The Darkest Night Made Bright As Day The Great Electric Light at Camden August 10, 1879. W. W. Coles Circus, Museum Menagerie 30 horsepower engine supplies electric current used to provide lumination equal to 30,000 gas jets. (WJP 7/30/1879)

Carnival shows of this type were commonplace.

Centennial

One of the truly great national events of the nineteenth century was the Centennial Exhibition held in Philadelphia. The event was open for six months during 1876. More than ten million visitors passed through the fairgrounds to visit more than 200 buildings spread over 236 acres in Fairmount Park.

Some of the fair's principal attractions were within its large buildings. These included Horticultural Hall, Memorial Hall, Machinery Hall, Agricultural Hall, Main Hall and the U.S. Government Building. The iron and glass-domed Memorial Hall still stands today in Fairmount Park. The Main Building, built as a temporary structure, was the largest building in the world at that time, covering some 21 acres.

The magnitude of the event required years of planning. A half-dozen years before the opening of the Exhibition, commissioners were appointed at the federal, state and local district levels to plan for the event. The district which included Haddon Township appointed former State Senator Edward Bettle to be commissioner. Bettle resided along the White Horse Turnpike in what is now Oaklyn. [See Edward Bettle, page 267.]

Throughout the country, each state planned for their own exhibits to be displayed at the fair. To help in financing state exhibits, women began raising money under the direction of the county and local committees. They called the fund-raising projects Centennial Teas, after the Boston Tea Party.

The ladies of Haddon and Delaware townships held a "Tea" in October 1874. The two-day gala celebrated the centennial anniversary of the Battle of Red Bank. They arranged and designated the tables at the gala by Revolutionary War events that occurred in New Jersey. Tables were labeled *Trenton, Princeton, Monmouth, Red Bank, Hancock's Bridge, Fort Lee* and *Washington's Head Quarters, Morristown.* On display were antiques and articles of historical interest. The local affair was highly successful, with almost $700 raised for the Women's New Jersey State Committee.

New Jersey's agricultural exhibit at the Centennial Exhibition, Philadelphia. Over ten million visitors attended the fair held in Fairmount Park in 1876.

(*Harper's Weekly*, December 16, 1876)

Haddonfield's local newspaper reported on the event:

> It was a complete success–the attendance large–quite a number of persons coming from the various towns, villages and abodes of the surrounding neighborhood, and some from Camden and the City, all helping swell the Haddonfield throng. The spacious audience room of the new unfinished Presbyterian church, in which the party met, was profusely decorated with the flag of the nation, and the tables presented a handsome display of flowers, cakes, etc. The room was crowded on the first evening, and well filled on the second, the audience remaining mostly upon their feet, there being but a few benches or seats, and no room for them. A very large proportion of the ladies present were dressed in ancient or Lady Washington costume, thus giving uniqueness and variety to the scene. (HB 11/1874)

Choruses were provided by the Handel and Haydn Society of Philadelphia. A Philadelphia piano company lent the "Tea" a piano. Delivery of the instrument was delayed, causing a last-minute scramble. Apparently, while transporting the piano the driver made a wrong turn when departing from the ferry and arrived at Haddonfield by the roundabout way of Woodbury.

Each state supervised the construction of its own building for the Centennial Exhibition. New Jersey's State Building was two stories high with a roof made of red clay tiles. The wood frame design included peaks, gables, porches and a tower. Inside the building were offices, reception rooms and rest areas. The building served mainly as a rest spot for New Jersey citizens attending the fair. The money raised by women at the statewide "Teas" went to furnish the building and maintain its upkeep.

In August 1876, New Jersey held an official celebration at the State Building. Thousands of visitors congregated at the building including Governor Joseph Bedle of New Jersey and Governor Hartranft of Pennsylvania. The Governors were welcomed by Edward C. Knight, head of a special reception committee composed of Philadelphia gentlemen who formerly resided in New Jersey. Mr. Knight owned several farms in old Haddon Township. Both Edward Knight and Edward Bettle spoke at the diner on New Jersey State Day:

> The Commission of the Centennial Exhibition decided that a day should be assigned to each of the thirteen original states for the special dedication of its individual property in the century past. Thursday was the first of these state days, and to New Jersey was allotted the privilege of inaugurating these series of demonstration.
>
> Large gathering of New Jersey people on the ground. About 25,000...
>
> At the Centennial depot eleven special trains arrived from New Jersey. . . . (NR 8/26/1876)

People from the southwestern part of New Jersey made day-trips to the fairgrounds. Inhabitants of old Haddon Township traveled to the Camden ferries by way of the Camden & Atlantic Railroad, carriage or by foot. Upon reaching the opposite side of the Delaware River, visitors took a horsecar to the Schuylkill River, then boarded a small steamboat to the fairgrounds. Alternatively, visitors could hire a coach or take a special train from center city. It is likely the more thrifty visitor walked from the western bank of the Delaware River to Fairmount Park.

After the Centennial Exhibition closed in November 1876, they sold many of the buildings. The New Jersey State Building was sold to Haddonfield storekeeper, Isaac Braddock. In 1949, local historian Carrie Hartel, wrote a paper entitled "The New Jersey Building." Mrs. Hartel described the site where Braddock intended to move the building on Main Street in Haddonfield. Today, this lot is 113 to 119 Kings Highway:

> There was a vacant lot on the Main Street running back to Pigtail Alley (Clement Street) that had long been an eyesore, low, full of weeds and mosquitoes, and people would throw trash there, and the sidewalk was bad, so the townspeople were glad to hear that Mr. Braddock had bought it for the Jersey Building. (p. 13)

Mr. Braddock enlisted the help of nearby farmers, who, in turn, offered their teams and drivers to go to the fairground and transport the dissembled building to Haddonfield. On a winter day, more than 30 wagons made their way to Fairmount Park to pick up the pieces of the building:

> Thirty-six loads of the New Jersey Building were taken to Haddonfield last Saturday, by a number of farmers of Haddon Township. In the evening an oyster supper given by Mr. Braddock ... (WJP 2/7/1877)
>
> The *Haddonfield Asteroid* says, "all the wood work forming the New Jersey Building has been brought from the Centennial grounds, and is laying on the lot intended for it in our borough. Mr. Braddock has teams employed every day bringing the tile roofing over. The digging of the cellar is nearly complete." (CDP 2/22/1877)

Isaac Braddock's carpenters reassembled the New Jersey Building along Main Street. For the most part it looked similar, although the "new" New Jersey Building was without some exterior features of its original design. As proud as many village inhabitants were to have the New Jersey Building, some expressed disappointment at the structure's new appearance:

New Jersey Building, Haddonfield. Following the famed Centennial Exhibition in 1876, the New Jersey Building was removed from Fairmount Park in Philadelphia to Haddonfield. The building once stood at what is now 113 to 119 Kings Highway East until it was removed in 1905.

(Historical Society of Haddonfield Collections)

> Our eyes now rest on that already historical structure, the New Jersey Building, purchased by Mr. Braddock and re-erected in Haddonfield. As an impartial chronicler, we are compelled to say that were it not for its curiously tiled roof and its corner turrets, we should fail to recognize it as the conspicuous building once standing in the Centennial grounds. Of its spacious porticos, its roomy bay windows and cosy recesses, it is shorn to fit for business purposes. It is placed flush with the street and so "cabined, cribbed, and confined" that its once fair proportions–to be seen on all sides to be admired and appreciated–is disgracefully dwarfed. (WJP 9/5/1877)

Many officials including New Jersey's Governor Bedle, attended the official grand opening. The Governor addressed the crowd, as did other speakers and an orchestra entertained the crowd.

Throughout its first decade in Haddonfield, a hardware store, fish and oyster market, barbershop, newspaper office, poolroom, and shoemaker occupied space in the building. The second floor was a large hall with a seating capacity of 500 people. In 1878, the hall was being used an average of three nights a week for entertainment by professional and amateur musicians and players. (WJP 1/9/1878) Over the years, the upper room was the site of many organizational meetings, concerts and lectures.

The New Jersey Building was not the only Centennial Exhibition edifice to find its way to southern New Jersey. Lumber from the Iowa Building was purchased by a resident in Mt. Ephraim. "The Iowa state centennial building has been purchased by one of the citizens and the timbers are being used in the construction of a commodious residence." (CDP 2/22/1877)

The Philadelphia & Atlantic City Railroad Company put to good use the Centennial's railroad assets. The railroad company's route cut through old Haddon Township. The company removed several buildings from the fair ground for use along its new roadbed, including the Board of Finance Building and the U.S. Commissioners Building. [See Railroads, page 41.] The railroad company also acquired rails from the Centennial's railway:

> The iron rails of the centennial narrow gauge railway, amounting to over 190 tons, were sold at private sale to the Philadelphia & Atlantic City Narrow Gauge Railroad, to be used in making sidings and switches. Thus will Jersey ride upon the Centennial rails and be happy? (CDP 12/7/1876)

In 1905, they again disassembled the New Jersey Building and this time its timbers were used as frame construction in new Haddonfield dwellings.

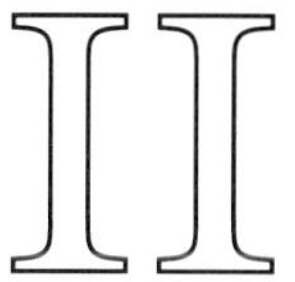

Making a Living in Old Haddon Township— Crafts, Professions and Merchants

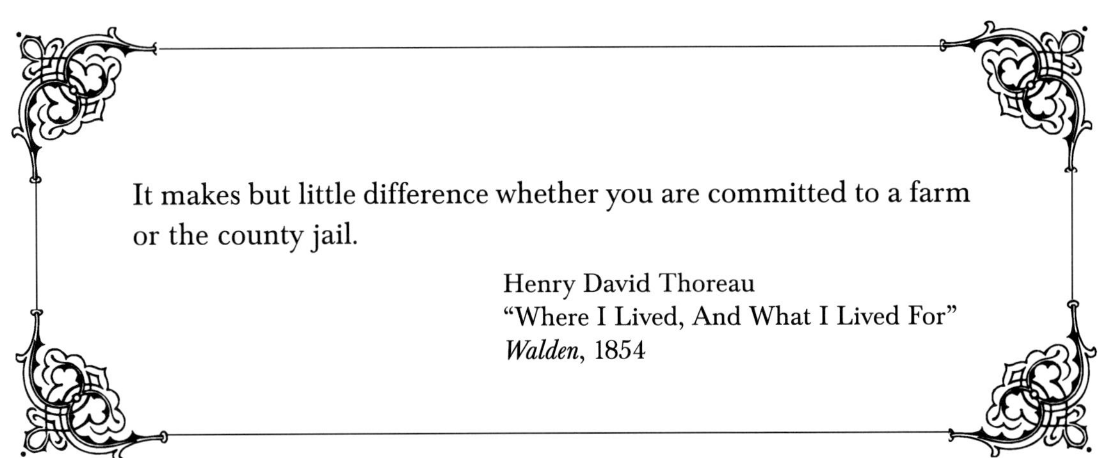

It makes but little difference whether you are committed to a farm or the county jail.

Henry David Thoreau
"Where I Lived, And What I Lived For"
Walden, 1854

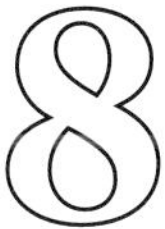

Agriculture

Introduction

In 1870, 53 percent of Americans employed worked in agriculture. The population in old Haddon Township mirrored the country's agrarian workforce. Farmers, farmhands and farm laborers were the largest category within the employed citizenry of old Haddon Township. Many other workers within the township were either directly or indirectly tied to the agricultural community.

As a whole, the farmers of old Haddon Township harvested many kinds of crops; however, only a handful were universally grown. Most farmers grew their own livestock feed. With few exceptions, all farmers raised hay, corn, wheat, and white potatoes. The cash crops for many farmers were market garden vegetables. Vegetables, known as "truck," were generally in demand at the markets of Camden and Philadelphia. Many farmers supplemented their income with the sale of livestock and dairy products. Most township farmers raised dairy cows, swine and poultry.

In 1879, there were some 69 farms in old Haddon Township. The average farm was about 68 acres. The smallest farm was twelve acres, and the largest 212 acres. About half the farms were managed by the actual landowners, with the remaining properties operated by tenant farmers. Usually, tenant farmers passed on to the landlords some of their harvest instead of cash rents.

James Lippincott, a chronicler of agricultural topics, wrote a treatise on Camden County's agricultural economy in 1864. James's work was written when he resided on a farm situated along Coles Mill Road in Haddonfield. [See James Lippincott, page 232.] Lippincott's comprehensive study entitled "Market Products of West New Jersey" was published in the 1865 *Annual Report of the Commissioner of Agriculture.* He began his treatise with a discussion on the importance of agriculture:

> The foundations of our national wealth are laid upon agriculture, manufactures, commerce, and mining. Of these agriculture is of first importance. It is that which feeds and clothes all other labor, which supplies the material to be transformed by the skill of the artist, and freights our commerce, foreign and domestic. Agricultural labor is, then, the leading and most important direct source of wealth. The skill of the mechanic may improve, the enterprise of the merchant may exchange, but the source of wealth is in the earth, and the cost and profit are alike determined by the results of agriculture. (MPWNJ, p. 249)

The U.S. Census Bureau's agricultural statistics and James Lippincott's 1864 survey of 60 Camden County farms are the two primary sources of data consulted for this project. Lippincott believed his sample of farms represented the county's entire agricultural community. Information and statistics about old Haddon Township farms were extracted from U.S. Census Bureau's agricultural data accumulated in 1870 and 1879.

Backyard gardening was one segment of the local farm economy that the Lippincott survey, and the Census Bureau statistics, did not account for. Gardening was a popular pastime of many homeowners during the nineteenth century. Amateur gardeners planted fruits and vegetables for personal consumption. The work of amateur farmers was not limited to backyard gardens. It was common for inhabitants in the villages of Rowandtown and Haddonfield to own several chickens, swine or dairy cows.

Labor on the Farm

In spite of nineteenth century technological advances made to labor-saving farming machinery, operating a farm was still quite a labor intensive feat in the post-Civil War era. Farmers hired full-time employees, or "hands" to help them. Many farmhands lived in tenant homes located on their employers' land. In many instances, landlords factored rent for living quarters into the laborers' wages.

Farmers and their helpers worked long hours. The hardest work on a farm came during the planting and harvesting months. Workers pulled up stumps, plowed, rolled and prepared the soil for young sprouts and seeds. Some crops, like corn, required cultivation during the growing period. Harvesting started with early wheat, hay or potatoes. Later, corn, grains and vegetables were brought in. During the harvest, farmers often shared employees with neighbors to help bring in the crop. Once the harvest was over, there was still work to be done. Wheat or other gains were threshed, corn husked and fields plowed up.

At harvest time, farmers hired temporary employees, known as day laborers. Often, day laborers temporarily left their regular employment to earn better wages which farmers were forced to pay at harvest time. Day laborers were generally paid piecemeal by the basket, bushel or pint of produce picked. Farmers often coaxed day laborers from the city during peak work periods:

> There is at this time plenty of work to do in the country for men, women and half-grown boys and girls. On some of the market farms in Jersey, within a circuit of from 5 to 8 miles of the Market Street ferry, large quantities of berries, for which there is always a ready market, are going to loss because the farms cannot get hands enough to pick them, Here is a demand for labor, an offer of plenty of work, almost at our door. (WJP 7/10/1867)

The wives and daughters of farmers and farmhands were also busy during the planting and harvesting season. Domestic employees were hired to work both indoors and outside. They and their female employers cooked and baked for the temporary influx of hired help. Out in the barnyard, they fed poultry, milked cows, and weeded the vegetable garden.

Caring for livestock, feeding animals, cleaning stables and walking cattle to and from pasture were some other necessary tasks. Even during the slower months on the farm, November through March, hauling manure, slaughtering animals, cutting and hauling wood, mending fences, hauling straw, shelling corn, repairing or constructing outbuildings kept men and boys busy.

David Roe had the highest farm payroll in the township. During 1879, Roe's payroll was $2,000. [See David Roe Jr., page 222.] In 1873, Henry Cuthbert paid each farm hand $16 a month for nine months during the year. Cuthbert reduced the same laborer's salary to just $10 a month for the months of January, February and March when farm duties were not as urgent. Some of Cuthbert's employees took farm products such as ham, cabbage and tomatoes instead of salary. Living quarters were also provided to farmhands by Cuthbert in return for their labor. [See Henry Cuthbert, page 254.]

Farming Implements

Many varieties of farm machinery were in use that saved labor, time and increased productivity. Two commonly used farm implements were the horse-drawn plow and harrow. The plow turned up the earth and the harrow pulverized the soil. The one- and two-row corn planters dropped kernels into the earth; cultivators, pulled by a horse between rows of corn, dug up weeds and loosened the soil; reapers cut grains and revolving rakes piled hay and grain into long rows called windrows.

During the second-half of the nineteenth century, new inventions and improvements to farm tools made farming more efficient and productive. By the 1870s, steel began to replace the iron plow. The strength of steel allowed the plow to cut the earth with greater force. The harrows, too, underwent a complete metamorphosis during the era. One significant improvement to husbandry during the last quarter of the century was the introduction of steam-powered farm equipment.

Threshing was the process where the grain or seeds were separated from the straw. In the old days, flails and other beating devices were employed to thresh grains. Another old-time technique employed horses to walk

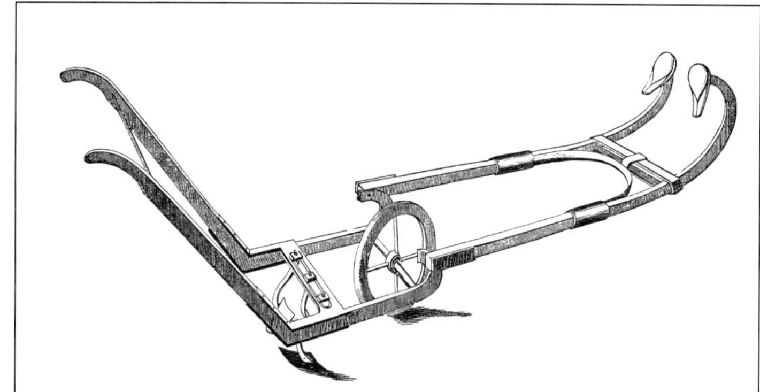

The cultivator was used to loosen the earth and destroy weeds around growing plants.

(*Annual Report of the Commissioner of Agriculture–1871*)

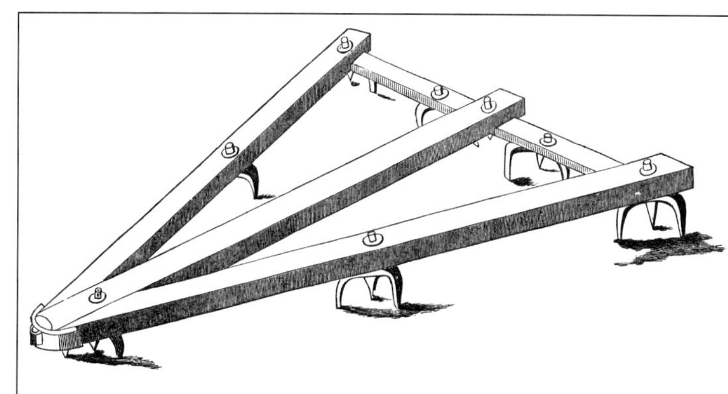

A harrow was used to break up and even off the plowed ground.

(*Annual Report of the Commissioner of Agriculture–1871*)

The plough was used for breaking up soil and cutting furrows in preparation for sowing.

(*Annual Report of the Commissioner of Agriculture–1866*)

over succeeding layers of ripe wheat piled on the barn's threshing floor to separate the seed.

Many old barns in and about old Haddon Township had threshing floors. For instance, John Sheets' barn had a threshing floor that measured 14' x 35' feet. [See John Sheets, page 187.] The usefulness of threshing floors disappeared when the threshing machine came into general use. By the 1870s, horses and steam engines were running threshing machines.

However, not all farmers enjoyed the latest in the era's technological advances. Many could not afford, nor did they want to own, the latest equipment. In some instances, farms were just too small to justify the costly expenditures. Sometimes, farmers continued to rely on manual labor, just as it had been done for centuries. Another option available to farmers was to borrow or rent a neighbor's machinery.

In 1879, the values of farm machinery on the township's farms were typically worth between $200 and $500. On the high end, they appraised David Roe's agriculture equipment at $6,000. It is not surprising that Roe's 130-acre farm was exceptionally productive. Joseph

Hollingshead's equipment was estimated to be worth about $2,000. [See Joseph Hollingshead, page 270.]

Outbuildings

Farming equipment gathered rust if left uncovered and exposed to the weather. To shelter the valuable assets, they needed an array of buildings on a farm. Animals too, required shelter during winter months of the year.

The barn was generally the largest structure on the farm. For example, one of the largest barns in the township was a 72' x 76' building on John DaCosta's farm. (Rowand No. 39, 1855) DaCosta's barn was made from the best material, an oak frame structure and cedar wood siding. [See John DaCosta, page 199.] Isaac Wood's old barn, erected in 1792, was 68' x 28'. (Rowand No. 391, 1874) It was more representative of the barns in the region. [See Isaac Wood, page 227.]

Barns were expensive to build. In 1872, Samuel French paid almost $3,000 to build a new barn on his "Pine Grove Cottage Farm." Besides the barn, Samuel paid an additional $1,320 to construct a new wagon house. [See Samuel French, page 258.]

The function of barns changed to some extent by mid-nineteenth century. For instance, threshing machines rendered the threshing floor obsolete. On the other hand, farmers were storing more feed grains and hay for their livestock than in years past. Many township farmers built a second barn to store feedstock and shelter their livestock.

Stables and storage buildings were often attached to barns. There were a variety of outbuildings in the nineteenth century. Some common structures around old Haddon Township included sheds where farmers stored machinery, wood, wagons and carriages. In many instances, sheds were open on one side. Some of the names of other outbuildings that once stood around the township included hay houses, ice houses, springhouses, carriage houses, wagon houses, poultry houses, smokehouses, tool houses, corn houses, corncribs, chicken coops, cow barns, horse barns, grain barns and milk cellars.

Fields and Fences

One of the most important tasks on the farm was preparing the earth for planting. To ensure a sufficient crop at harvesttime, the soil required adequate drainage, and deep plowing, ample fertilization and constant cultivation to keep weeds in check.

It was well-known throughout the region that Camden County farmers were adept at raising a variety of vegetables. The secret for success, however, was not the superior soil of the area. According to James Lippincott's writings, the county's soil required constant maintenance:

> Nature supplied but the crude materials of sands, and clay, and muck; the industrious and skillful farmer has wrought out the problem of existence by aid of foreign material which the neighboring city and the exhaustless "marl" beds have supplied. The soil of the district does not appear to possess the self-recuperative powers enjoyed by many regions. (MPWNJ, p. 250)

To ensure respectable crop yields, manures and fertilizers were applied by farmers to restore nutrients to the soil. The source of much of the region's manure

"Old Barn at Cuthbert Homestead." circa 1912. The Cuthbert farm was situated along the Haddonfield Turnpike, now called Haddon Avenue in today's Collingswood and Haddon Township. Joseph O. Cuthbert's residence was located on the southeast corner of what is now Haddon Avenue and Cuthbert Road.

(Paul W. Schopp Collections)

came from the stables and streets of Camden and Philadelphia. They shipped manure on sloops and flatboats to wharves and landings on Cooper's Creek where it was unloaded and hauled by laborers to the fields. Samuel French built a wharf on Cooper's Creek so that manure could be delivered to his tenant farm:

> He [French] has also, on this farm, built a large wharf, on which quantities of manure and different fertilizers for the use of his farms are landed. (WJP 9/19/1877)

Another nineteenth century soil enhancer was greensand marl. There were substantial deposits of marl throughout Camden, Burlington and Gloucester Counties, although only a few small marl beds existed in Haddon Township. One bed was at Jacob Coles's farm near Coles Mill Road. [See Jacob S. Coles, page 231.]

They used other soil improvers during the period. Guano, a expensive fertilizer, was sea bird excrement imported from Peruvian islands. Other fertilizers such as calcinated lime and gypsum, or land plaster, were also dispersed on fields.

Local railroads delivered marl and lime to points along the right-of-way. In 1866, a newspaper noted, "Farmers along the line of the Camden & Atlantic Railroad can purchase lime delivered on the cars at Cooper's Point." (WJP 4/4/1866)

Another necessary duty on the farm was to ensure excessive amounts of water did not lay on the fields. Too much water was not healthy for the crops. Farmers improved crop yields by installing systems of underdrains to remove unwanted water. Fields were excavated and ditches were filled with tile drains, stones or wood. When the soil was saturated with water, the surplus water flowed into the drains and away from the fields.

In 1866, Samuel French paid $729 for the installation of drainage tiles on his "Pine Grove Cottage Farm," situated near Rowandtown. He obtained the tiles from the nearby Dobbs Brickyard. [See Dobbs Brickyard, page 128.] In the 1870s, French installed drains on an adjacent tract known as the Creek Farm.

> ...a large well, into which over two miles of underdrains discharge their waters. From this well the water is conveyed through large terra cotta pipes into Cooper's creek. Mr. French's system of underdraining is as thorough as it well could be. No waste places or bogs are permitted about any of his farms. He has used in his different drains 125,000 tile, a considerable number of which are of the largest size manufactured, and in some instances are laid at a depth of eleven feet. (WJP 9/19/1877)

Crop rotation was another technique employed by farmers to maintain or restore soil nutrients. A farmer's arable land was usually divided into a handful of fields. After they harvested a crop, a different crop was planted in its place the next season. Farmers carefully planned periodic rotation of corn, white potatoes, wheat, and grasses over a period of years. Fields were "pastured" before being turned under by a plough and followed by a new cycle of planting.

Another important component of a well-managed farm was fencing. Most fences were installed to avert the destruction of corn by wandering cattle or to restrain one's own stock from similar destruction. Fences required frequent maintenance and were often repaired by farmhands during the winter months. More than half the township farmers incurred expenses to build and repair fences during 1879.

Truck Farming

The farms of Camden County were best known for the variety of garden vegetables or truck patches. In 1864, cabbage topped the list as the region's highest cash crop, accounting for 44 percent of the entire value of garden vegetables. Tomatoes, actually a fruit, were the second most valuable crop, comprising 28 percent of the vegetable market. Other garden vegetables grown in the region then included peas, eggplant, watermelons, squashes, beans, cucumbers, peppers, rhubarb, spinach, radishes, asparagus and sugar corn.

Preparations for spring planting began in the middle of winter. Farmers planted vegetable seeds in a mixture of manure and soil in frames or hotbeds. During the day, they exposed the beds to the sun and at night they covered them with hay or straw. In foul weather, the beds were covered by boards. Planting vegetables in a hotbed gave truck farmers an early start on the spring growing season:

> Camden County has a reputation for producing early truck not enjoyed by any other county in the state. The secret lies in hot beds and transplanting them as the season advances. (WJP 1/15/1868)

When the sprouts were ready, they moved them to the fields. Many farmers purchased young sprouts and planted them in their vegetable fields. During the 1870s, Henry Cuthbert's account book noted he obtained 2,200 sprouts from Jacob Coles.

Some farmers raised vegetables in hot houses during the wintertime:

> Camden County hot house proprietors are supplying the Philadelphia market. Salad, spinach, radish and other choicest garden luxuries. (WJP 4/9/1879)

Growing parsley in a hot box in 1896. This unidentified Haddonfield resident, like many others, grew produce in hot boxes throughout the year.
(Historical Society of Haddonfield Collections)

In 1870, the township's top vegetable producer was Stephen Collins. Vegetables worth $13,000 were harvested from the Collins's farm. [See Stephen Collins, page 236.] In the same year, David Roe's vegetables brought him $7,000. The *West Jersey Press* noted "David Roe...growing on his farm 100,000 cabbage plants. . . ." (WJP 8/23/1876)

Maybe Camden County's best known farm product was the tomato. The item was so widely grown by local agriculturalists, sometimes it was too plentiful. In 1879, a glut of tomatoes flooded the market place:

> So abundant has been the yield of tomatoes this season, they are selling for almost nothing. They have brought as low as 5 cents per basket and hundreds of baskets have been given away. Many of our truckmen have ceased to gather them and hundreds of bushels will be left in the vines to rot. (WJP 9/8/1869)

One factor contributing to the commercial success of the tomato was the coming of canning. During the 1870s, at least two commercial canning companies were operating in Camden. Abraham Anderson owned one of the largest regional canneries. In the peak summer months, Anderson's cannery bought tomatoes from the region's farmers. The *West Jersey Press* reported "The farmers in the county find a ready market for their tomatoes at Anderson's canning factory." (WJP 9/6/1871) Anderson also searched for owners of large parcels of land to grow tomatoes on a contract basis.

In the mid-1870s, Abraham Anderson formed a partnership with another Camden canning entrepreneur, Joseph Campbell. Soon after that, the company of 250 employees was processing 2,500 to 3,000 baskets of tomatoes a day during the peak season, filling 15,000 to 20,000 cans with tomato products. (WJP 8/25/75) After several years, the two men dissolved their partnership, although both Anderson and Campbell continued to operate separate canneries in Camden. It was Joseph Campbell's cannery that survived the test of time, with his company becoming the Campbell Soup Company.

The area's truck farmers prospered during the American centennial celebration in 1876. Farmers anticipated large crowds visiting the Philadelphia fairgrounds and astutely adjusted the kinds of crops they were planting:

> Very few "staples" crops will be planted in Camden County this year. The farmers pretty generally will devote their attentions and lands to trucking, in anticipation of an exigent Centennial demand. (WJP 1/19/1876)

Local truck farmers guessed right. In August 1876 a newspaper noted "The truckers reported...the Centennial has had the effect of keeping price considerably above the average." (WJP 8/9/1876)

Many variables had to come together to successfully raise crops, none of which were more important than the weather. Too much, or not enough rain had adverse effects on the size, quantity and quality of crops. When the weather did not cooperate, the local press was quick to report the impact on crops:

> ...cabbage will most likely be scarce and high-priced. The turnip crop will also be backward. But not withstanding the two long dry seasons we have had this summer, the Philadelphia market has been abundantly supplied with fruits and vegetables, very large proportion going from Jersey. (HB 9/1874)

At least in one instance, when rain was scarce, an appeal for more rain was made to a higher authority. "...prayers had been offered up in our churches for rain, as vegetation was suffering very much in the vicinity from drought." (WJP 7/19/1876)

Uncooperative weather was not the only detrimental factor. Predators of all shapes and sizes gave truck farmers fits:

> The pest (grasshoppers) are destroying the pastures in many parts of our county as well as vegetable and truck. One farmer in Haddon reports the loss of all his pasture. (WJP 9/23/1868)

> Again we advise farmers to take care of birds. They are the best protection yet discovered against bugs, beetles, worms and insects of all kinds which ravage and destroy the growing crops. Take care of birds! (WJP 8/1/1877)

Every so often a reporter wrote a tongue-in-cheek article. Once they noted the size of a common New Jersey crop:

> The mosquito crop this year has been an entire failure. In South Jersey where the crop is usually prolific there is remarkable scarcity this season. (WJP 7/28/1869)

Hay and Corn

Most all of old Haddon Township's farmers during the 1870s devoted a parcel of their farms to growing hay. A year-round ready market existed for hay as livestock feed. In earlier times, farmers mowed natural grasses on untilled and unpastured meadows. However, as the demand for the crop grew, they cultivated grasses of European origin, particularly Timothy hay and clover.

When the grass was ready to cut, mowing machines and threshers were used, although smaller hay fields were often cut by hand with scythes. After they cut the hay, it was raked and drawn to the barn. A good crop of cultivated grass could be financially rewarding to a farmer:

> Those farmers who were fortunate enough to gather a full hay crop will realize handsomely for its sale in the coming fall and winter. (WJP 7/7/1880)

Timothy hay was a popular grass grown in the region. Farmers fed the hay to their livestock.

(*Annual Report of the Commissioner of Agriculture–1881*)

Every so often the grass crop fell short of what they anticipated. When the hay crop was below par, farmers were forced to turn to corn or other root crops to feed their livestock. Several factors could contribute to a disappointing hay crop:

> The hay crop of Camden County had not been so short in ten years. Land that usually produce two tons to the acre, this season yields but two tons to seven acres. Farmer are now looking forward to corn fodder as chief support for their cattle during winter. (WJP 6/30/1875)

> Grass. . .not up to last years. The grasshoppers are charged with producing the state of this. They are terrible scrounges. (WJP 6/23/1869)

> The farmers of this county, regarding the hay crop as almost a total failure on account of drought, have already taken steps to provide food for their stock during winter by planting root crops such as millet, beets, turnips, carrots and fodder corn.
>
> Farmers who have derived a considerable source of revenue from the sale of grass report that they will have none to sell this summer. (WJP 6/2/1880)

Corn was cultivated on all but one of the 69 farms in old Haddon Township. Its popularity was attributable to its importance as feed for farm animals. Unlike wheat and hay, they did not market corn in any great quantity in the cities.

> In this locality [Haddonfield], it is necessary that the farms should produce corn; not directly for the market, but for consumption by their farm stock, a considerable amount of which is necessary for all successful farming. The production of milk, in which many of our farmers are engaged, requires considerable attention to be paid to the cultivation of corn, which is the best and cheapest food for milch cows, as the entire product of the soil can be utilized for profitable feed. The grain, when ground, is claimed by many to produce a greater flow of rich milk than anything else with the same expenditure. The stalks and leaves are very valuable, whether fed whole and dry or cut, steamed and mixed with meal, which is the customary manner of treating by many. (*New Jersey State Board of Agriculture–1879*, "Indian Corn," p. 111)

Corn stalks were cut, gathered and dried. The corn, after being husked, was placed in cribs. Corn crop yields ranged from 60 to 100 bushels per acre. In 1879, Joseph Hollingshead's 25-acre parcel was the largest corn field in the township. [See Joseph Hollingshead, page 270.]

Similar to hay, corn, too, had its natural enemies. "Grub worms have made their appearance in the

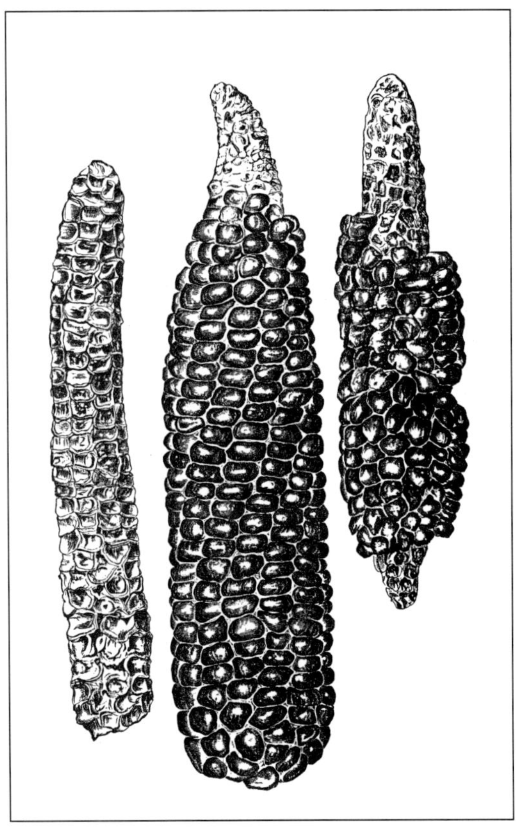

Indian corn was raised on most Haddon Township farms. The corn was grown as feed for livestock.

(*Annual Report of the Commissioner of Agriculture–1871*)

corn fields of Camden County and are doing destruction." (WJP 6/9/1875)

Grains

Wheat was grown for its kernels that were ground into flour, a staple food ingredient. Though most farmers in the township raised wheat, the region was not known for its abundant wheat crop. "Camden County has never boasted of its ability for grain growing." (WJP 8/7/1878)

The wheat harvest took place in the hottest and driest period of the year. Cutting and binding wheat was one of the toughest tasks on the farm. Even with the aid of machinery, cutting wheat was dependent on the speed and skill of workers alongside the machinery. After they cut the wheat, it was stored in the barn. During the early fall, workers threshed the wheat. In 1879, the largest wheat field in the township was on Joseph Hollingshead's farm where they took 500 bushels of wheat from his twenty-acre parcel.

Local farmers raised a variety of other grains. Generally, rye was planted as a feed crop when wheat and corn did not do well. In 1879, six township farms raised rye. William Rowles harvested 150 bushels of rye from his land. [See Martha Rowles, page 211.] Oats on the other hand, had been grown in the years before corn became the primary feedstock for horses. Richard Collings, manager of Edward Knight's property, was one of eleven township farmers that planted oats. Collings's nine-acre oat field produced 300 bushels of oats. [See Richard Collings, page 204.]

Buckwheat was not a popular crop, at least not in old Haddon Township, because it required considerable care to harvest and thresh. According to U.S. Census statistics, township farmers did not grow buckwheat, although it may have been grown in small quantities for a farmer's personal consumption. The local press noted "Buckwheat pancakes will adorn a farmers' breakfast table." (WJP 8/21/1878)

Barley was also a substitute crop for swine and poultry feed. Unlike some other grains, a ready market for barley did not always exist. For this reason, barley was raised on a small scale in the region. Apparently, it was not grown in any significant quantity in the township that warranted recording.

Root Crops

In the 1870s, the potato was a major staple food for people in many parts of the United States. On almost every township farm, they planted fields with the white potato, known as the Irish potato. Besides being a source of nutrition, the popularity of the potato was attributable to the ease of growing and storage. Irish potatoes, along with sweet potatoes, accounted for 35 percent of the market value of all crops grown in the county in 1864.

Local farmers planted a variety of potatoes. Michigan White sprouts, Dykemans and Monitors were planted early in the season. Other varieties grown locally were Buckeye, Peach Blows, Carters, Early Rose, Snow Flake and Eurikas. Although the potato was simple to grow, like all crops, unfavorable weather conditions often reduced the crop yield:

> The recent hot weather is thought to have seriously injured the potato crop in the county. The spring rain delayed the planting before the potatoes had time to mature the dry spell was at hand to check its growth. (WJP 7/8/1878)

In 1879, 29 township farmers harvested sweet potato crops. On the whole, the farmers of Camden County were not as likely to grow sweet potatoes as were farmers in Gloucester County. The reason for the disparity was sweet potatoes grew better in the sandy soil of the neighboring county.

The beet was another root crop raised as livestock feed. Beets comprised a very small percentage of all crops sold by county farmers. In 1885, Joseph Hollingshead unearthed 25 tons of mangel-wurzel beets grown on less than two acres.

Fruits

More than half the farms in the township had an apple orchard in the 1870s. Aside from the fact that apples comprised about 90 percent of the total value of the county's orchard products in 1864, they comprised a very small share of the overall crops value sold by farmers. Benjamin Lippincott's 600 apple trees yielded 250 bushels in 1879. Benjamin's fifteen-acre orchard was the largest orchard in the township. [See Benjamin Lippincott, page 237.]

According to James Lippincott, apple orchards were unprofitable. The township's agricultural specialist noted that even with constant care, a heavy apple crop occurred just once every eight or ten years. He surmised the value of other crops grown in place of apples was greater than the worth of an apple crop.

Many households in the village of Haddonfield had apple trees: "...many of the inhabitants have plenty of their own raising [apples]. The consequence is many rot upon the ground or find their way into pigpens." (WJP 8/22/1876)

New Jersey apple orchard. In the 1870s, more than half of the farms in the township had an apple orchard. (*Industries of the State of New Jersey, 1882*)

With plenty of apple orchards in the region, it is likely that many Township farmers utilized the fruit for their own use. One of the popular uses of the apple harvest was for cider, vinegar and applejack, a distilled spirit:

> The apple crop is large around, hence it will be necessary to get out the old vinegar barrels. (WJP 8/23/1876)

Peach orchards, grape vines, strawberry patches, citron, raspberry and blackberry crops were also frequently planted: "Haddonfield is well supplied with fruit of nearly all kinds in season. . . . Peaches are not so plentiful, but grapes made a good show." (WJP 8/22/1876)

In 1879, Jacob Fowler's 120-tree peach orchard spread across two acres of land. It was the largest orchard of its kind in the township on record in that year. [See Jacob Fowler, page 263.] Generally, farmers in other sections of southern New Jersey were more successful in raising peaches for commercial purposes than those in old Haddon Township.

Vineyard

Hammonton, Vineland and Egg Harbor were a few of the locations in southern New Jersey known for grape production. Old Haddon Township was not known for its grape crop. Edward Knight's vineyard was the one exception. The site of the vineyard on today's map of Collingswood would be between Haddon Avenue and Cooper River, and land between Browning Road and Crestmont Terrace. [See Edward Knight, page 205.] Richard Collings was hired to oversee the vineyard operation, known locally as the "Grape Farm."

An article entitled "A Camden Vineyard–A Visit to Edward C. Knight's Farm," appeared in an unidentified newspaper on September 18, 1880. In his column, the correspondent praised the success and wisdom of Knight. While doing so, the author penned factual details about Knight's local vineyard. The reporter noted 50 acres of Knight's farm were devoted to the culture of grapes, and each acre contained about 800 vines. The most prevalent variety of grape raised was the Concord that grew on 25,000 vines. In previous years, 100 tons of Concord grapes were picked at the farm. Other varieties of grapes grown were White Martha, Hartford, Ives' Seeding and Rentz.

When the reporter visited Knight's vineyard, farmhands picked and packed from three to five tons of grapes per day. Most laborers at the vineyard were women. The newspaper article noted women "seem to be best suited for this character of work." The correspondent described the processing of grapes. First, laborers removed a cluster of grapes from the vine. The imperfect grapes were "culled out", and "then the bunch is supported in the palm while the stem is separated from the branch by a pair of scissors." Packers carefully boxed the grapes and loaded the fruit onto wagons for shipment:

> In order to avoid unnecessary handling the grapes are placed at once in ten-pound shipping boxes. These are, with their contents, subsequently weighed at the shipping

> house, and in a few minutes are on their way to the consumers, who in many cases, receive them within twelve hours after they have been taken from the vines. (Unidentified newspaper, 9/18/80)

The reporter disclosed that Knight once entertained the idea of manufacturing wine at the vineyard. He did not follow through with his plans.

Livestock

Despite improvements to farming equipment over the course of the nineteenth century, the need for work animals on the farm was as important as ever. A typical township farmer owned a variety of livestock, none more essential than the horses and mules that pulled farming equipment across the fields. After workers harvested the crop, horses and mules pulled the market wagons destined for the outlets.

In 1875, there were 271 horses and 64 mules in old Haddon Township. (WJP 8/25/1875) According to the 1879 agricultural census, only 4 out of 69 township farms were without a horse. Some more affluent inhabitants kept special types of horses for different purposes. For instance, trotters and pacers were used to pull buggies and carriages.

About half the local farmers had the luxury of owning a mule, the more valuable beast of burden. A mule could be purchased in 1864 for about $185. The average price of a horse was $112. Mules held a number of advantages over horses. A mule was desired because of its hardiness, even temper and strength. Compared with a horse, the mule could better adapt to hot weather, was less nervous, readily accepted hard work and was less expensive to feed.

By mid-nineteenth century, a profitable market for milk and butter evolved in Camden. Before the railroads existed, the dairy farmers close to Camden had a competitive edge over other southern New Jersey farmers. Their fresh milk was readily delivered by wagon to the city's consumers. After the Camden & Atlantic Railroad was in place, the geographic monopoly once held by local farmers disappeared. For the most part, the township's farmers continued to produce a variety of dairy goods:

> The Milk Trade of South Jersey The farmers living within a radius of six to eight miles of Philadelphia enjoyed a monopoly until a few years ago.
>
> With the construction of the railroad the whole of South Jersey has been placed with the milk-supplying area.
>
> Milk is sent daily to this city [Camden] and Philadelphia from every station within the grazing districts of South Jersey, over Camden & Atlantic Railroad. Farmers wives find it much less troublesome and more profitable to dispose of their milk crop in that way than to manufacture butter, and those contiguous to

Dairy cow on Schnitzius Farm enroute to Newton Creek along Lee's Lane, Haddon Township. The Schnitzius farm was located in today's Haddon Township. Most township farms produced dairy products for market and for personal consumption.

(Courtesy of Marie Miller)

the railroad have nearly all embarked in the business. (WJP 9/11/1872)

Stock farmers have discovered it pays better to run a diary farm than fatten stock. (WJP 8/23/1876)

Local dairymen took advantage of the railroads. Township dairy farmers delivered cans filled with milk to the freight platform at Haddonfield's railroad station for shipment. The cans were unloaded at Camden's terminal, where they were sold to merchants or ferried over to Philadelphia.

Almost all farms in old Haddon Township, as well as many nonfarming households, owned dairy cows. There were 575 cows in Haddon Township in 1875. (WJP 8/25/1875)

In 1879, James DaCosta, Samuel Evans and Joseph Hollingshead operated the three largest diary farms in the township. The 30 dairy cows on James DaCosta's farm yielded 33,000 gallons of milk during 1879. [See John DaCosta, page 199.] During the same period, Samuel Evans, a tenant on William Bettle, Jr.'s land, sold 30,000 gallons of milk taken from his 30 cows. [See William Bettle, Jr., page 255.] Joseph Hollingshead was one of a few farmers to employ a full-time dairyman. In 1879, Hollingshead's 24 dairy cows provided 25,000 gallons of milk. When a quart of milk sold for 5 cents, Hollingshead's milk wagon traveled up and down the streets of Camden delivering "pure Jersey Milk." (WJP 10/26/1870)

A farmer's workday typically started before dawn. The first chore was to milk the cows. During the summer, the swarms of flies that surrounded cows made milking a dreadful task. The press reported farmers awoke "at 4 o'clock in the morning to bring in the cows from the pasture, that the milking may be done before the flies get bad." (WJP 7/29/1874) Milking in the winter time was not much better. Workers often conducted the task in close and filthy stalls.

Another important dairy product from the country households was butter. In many instances, churning cream into butter and making cheese was the responsibility of the ladies on the farm. Spring or dairy houses stood on some farms where butter and milk were stored in warmer months before delivery to the market place.

Richard Collings's thirteen dairy cows yielded enough cream to make 850 pounds of butter in 1879. The households of William Hinchman and Samuel Wood churned 625 pounds and 500 pounds of butter respectively in that same year. [See William Hinchman, page 225, Samuel Wood, page 227.]

Raising beef cattle for the market place was also profitable. In 1864, veal calves and "fattened" cattle together, comprised about 40 percent of the value of all animals sold in the county. Some of the more affluent gentlemen of the area kept purebred cattle on hand. Richard Collings's kept a "herd" of fine-blooded Alderney and short-horned Durham stock.

According to James Lippincott's research, the county's inventory of pigs and hogs represented about half the value of all animals sold at market. Hogs were a source of protein in the diet of many Americans. In 1879, 68 of the township's 69 farms raised swine. Selling piglets at market was a common means of supplementing income.

Even some nonfarm households in the area kept hog pens. Not everyone, however, thought it was a wise choice for pigs to be raised in residential neighborhoods. Although pigs were "clean" animals, their unkept pens had a peculiar odor. Apparently, many nineteenth century pig pens were not cared for. In Haddonfield and Rowandtown, the offensive odor of pens created controversy among neighbors:

The keeping of pigs in closely-built up villages, towns or cities, where the lots are small, seems to be a matter on which people are divided in opinion, as on other matters. (LBGA 6/1877)

Sheep and lambs accounted for a small percentage of all livestock sold by the county's farmers in 1864. Eleven of the township's 69 farmers raised lambs. Rebecca Collings kept a large flock of sheep on her farm. In 1879, her workers slaughtered 25 lambs and 40 sheep and sold them at market. [See Rebecca Ann Collings, page 246.] The *West Jersey Press* reported "Camden County stock raisers find no difficulty in selling their early lambs at $9.00 per head. ... Roast lamb and mint sauce are in order." (WJP 3/28/1877)

In the early nineteenth century, some farmers raised sheep for their wool. In 1879, just six of the township's 69 farmers clipped and sold sheep's wool. The most wool sheared on a township farm in 1879 was several hundred pounds. In that same year, Samuel Wood sold 33 fleeces.

One concern among sheep owners was the threat posed by stray dogs. These dogs often turned into predators, causing injury and sometimes death to sheep. The township's governing body addressed the problem by taxing dog owners. In 1867, the township collected $156 from the dog tax. The owners of sheep injured by dogs were compensated from the dog tax fund. Charles Bettle received $20 in 1868, after eight of his sheep were attacked by dogs. [See William Bettle, Sr., page 183.]

With just two exceptions, all township farmers raised poultry in 1879. Besides poultry production for personal consumption, a demand existed for both their meat and eggs at nearby markets. In 1879, Amy Nicholson owned about 200 chickens, geese, turkeys and ducks, the largest number of fowl among township farmers. [See Joseph Nicholson, page 185.] Ducks and geese were raised for their meat and eggs and for their feathery down for pillow and mattress stuffing. Samuel Wood's barnyard fowl laid 400 dozen eggs in 1879. Soon after this period, poultry husbandry changed with the introduction of the incubator.

With a henhouse on almost every farm, chickens were favorite targets of thieves. Even in the villages, chicken coops were not safe from raids:

> Two more henneries were robbed, almost a clean sweep, on Wednesday night last, right in the most thickly built up portions of our town [Haddonfield]. (HB 1/1876)

Benjamin Mann, proprietor of "Orchard Grove Poultry Yards" in Haddonfield, was of a breeder of special type of fowl. In 1877, Mann received an order from Indianapolis for a "trio of White Cochin fowls, the price being twenty-five dollars." (WJP 9/19/1877) Local farmers had little commercial interest in the sporting variety of fowl raised by Mann. The *West Jersey Press* reported:

> Mr. Benjamin Mann of Haddonfield, a large and very successful breeder of fancy fowls, placed upon the yacht "Josie R. Smith" last Thursday, a pigeon breed from an English carrier and a "Tumbler" hen. The bird was sent up at nine o'clock on Sunday morning from the breakwater, and arrived home at Haddonfield between one and two o'clock. This pigeon made good time for a half breed–and too, having no Antwerp blood in it, and never being farther away from home than Wilmington, Delaware. (WJP 9/22/1877)

Almost all animals on the farm had some purpose or function. Even dogs and cats did useful chores on the farm besides being the family pets. Dogs were kept for protection, hunting and herding cattle and sheep. Cats were helpful in keeping rats and mice in check.

As the end of the nineteenth century drew to a close, animal husbandry had become specialized. The region's comparatively small farms were no match for the large Midwestern livestock dealers. It became increasingly unprofitable for area farmers to raise animals for sale and slaughter. Thereby, the number of local farmers raising swine, cattle and sheep steadily declined. Southern New Jersey, however, had established a foothold in supplying perishable products to the region's markets. By the end of the century, the number of dairy and egg farms escalated in the region.

The Market Place

Farmers were rewarded for the risks inherent in their profession and their hard work when they sold the crops and products at market. A corespondent of the *West Jersey Press* reported on the busy season on the township's farms:

> From early dawn until long after twilight has deepened into night, the turnpikes and highways are thronged with wagons either conveying truck to the markets or returning to the farm for a new load. Long freight trains bearing vegetables, butter, eggs, fruit are swiftly flying over the rails to supply the demand of the city merchants, while the creeks and navigable streams are filled with craft of every description from large sloops to the smallest sail boats, loaded down with their burden of truck for tables of the residents of the towns. The fields too, are alive with the forms and voices of the "pickers" and farm hands, engaged in gathering the truck and preparing it for shipment to market. The number of hands employed on the different farms for this purpose reaches sometimes many hundreds. They are paid by the bushel or basket. . . .
>
> Thousands of baskets of peas and beans are taken to Philadelphia at the right season of the year, many of which are immediately shipped by water and rail to other places. Later in the season corn, tomatoes, potatoes, and other vegetable stock...as well as fruit and berries of every variety. Melons, too, are raised in large quantities and are of a rare size, and posses a rich flavor. Hay and grain, although not properly considered as truck, are grown in considerable quantities and find a ready sale at markets located in this city [Camden] or at those of Philadelphia. (WJP 7/31/1872)

Philadelphians had an endless appetite for southern New Jersey's farm products. Farmers in the region rented stalls at the city's market houses and sold their goods directly to consumers. Some farmers sold their goods on consignment through commission merchants.

Even though old Haddon Township farmers enjoyed a geographical advantage, situated just a short distance from Philadelphia, crossing the Delaware River was an unavoidable obstacle. Ferries ran day and night during the late summer so farmers could fill the demand for fresh farm products at the market place:

> Rush of wagons...the ferry boats are compelled to commence their trips shortly after midnight, and run about every one half hour until daylight. (WJP 8/19/1874)

As much as city inhabitants were the beneficiaries of South Jersey's farm products, Philadelphia's governing officials were not always accommodating to farmers. Farmers selling produce from their wagons competed with vendors at the city-owned market house stalls. In

1875, the city implemented an ordinance prohibiting farmers' wagons from standing on any street within five squares of any public or private market. In a caustic response to the ordinance, the editor of the *West Jersey Press* suggested our "Philadelphia neighbors" should be compelled to cross the river and purchase vegetables in Camden. (WJP 7/28/1875)

The Camden market was certainly more accessible to southern New Jersey farmers, although it was hardly a bustling outlet like Philadelphia. Some farmers sold their vegetables directly to Camden residents, while others sold to middlemen or consignment merchants in Camden, who, in turn, marketed the produce to consumers. Some produce that was grown locally, was even shipped from Camden's railroad depots to New York City and other places.

Many regional farmers favored unloading their produce in Camden rather than hauling it over to Philadelphia. Some farmers paid ferry fares of more than $100 a year, a considerable expense to transport their market wagons between the cities. Ideas flourished on how to organize a competitive market place in the City of Camden:

> Now our farmers are compelled to cross the river and drive their teams to the Philadelphia Hay Market, located in a distant part of the city. . . .
>
> Possibly bring hay to Camden and invite consumers over here to purchase. The Philadelphia Market can remain where it is, and we can have another here. (WJP 6/16/1869)

> Market House needed in Camden. Large majority of truckers of this section of the state forward their produce right through Camden to Philadelphia, without ever stopping to sell to dealers in Camden who are forced to go to the commission men on the other side of the river to purchase the same fruits and vegetables which were grown in fields immediately adjoining their own property. (WJP 7/30/1873)

A comparatively small outlet for southern New Jersey's farm products stood in Camden for many years. By the early 1870s, several new markets opened in Camden. First, a new hay and straw market opened in 1871 where farmers sold their field grasses on consignment. Soon thereafter, an outlet for cabbage opened. In 1876, they demolished the old dilapidated Camden market building and the Farmers & Butchers Market building was erected. The new building had 346 stalls, all of which were leased by farmers for $25 to $40 a year. The new market had a cellar where they stored fish, oysters and other perishable products. The site even had several eating outlets to accommodate hungry patrons.

The price of farm goods sold at Camden's markets were printed in Camden's newspapers. The categories included flour and grain (wheat, flour and rye), feed (corn meal, bran, corn, oats), produce (butter, eggs, ham, shoulders, potatoes, tomatoes, vegetables, apples), livestock (horses, mules, calves, sheep, lambs) and hay and straw.

Despite Camden's attempt to attract locally grown farm goods to its new market place in the 1870s, Philadelphia market houses dominated the surroundings as the principal outlet for Camden County's farm crops and other products.

Farm Organizations

In the mid-1870s, many farmers in the area were caught up in the nationwide Grange movement. The grange organizations disseminated farm-related information and provided a social outlet for farm families. The region's farmers formed an association in 1874 called the Haddon Grange. The Haddon Grange meetings were initially conducted above Alfred Clement's general store in Haddonfield. When they reassembled the New Jersey Building in Haddonfield in 1877, the Haddon Grange met in the large meeting room on the second floor.

A good portion of the Haddon Grange membership was surmised to be composed of Quaker farmers. In her paper that summarized the minutes of nineteenth century Haddon Grange meetings, Viola Garwood supported this conclusion:

> Membership largely belonged to the Society of Friends, I assume, because a resolution to disperse with the Chaplain's prayers was passed at an early meeting. ("Haddon Grange Beginning," 5/10/1947)

Grange meetings were also a forum for debate on important issues of the day. For instance, issues such as local municipal voting fraud, women's status in society, women's suffrage, improving instruction in public school and prohibition of the manufacture and sale of alcohol beverages were discussed at various meetings. The local grange gave to less fortunate citizens. The organization sent $25 in 1874 to "victims of the Louisiana Flood." The following year, the group mailed $134 "together with barrels of clothing...to suffering patrons in Kansas and Nebraska." ("Haddon Grange Beginning," 5/10/1947)

One benefit of belonging to the local grange was that members received certain privileges at Haddonfield stores and shops that did not extend to other customers: "Special prices were given to grange members by commercial firms under bonds of secrecy, but pledges were sometimes forgotten." ("Haddon Grange Beginning," 5/10/1947)

A united Camden and Gloucester counties Agricultural Society was formed in 1853. The group was associated with the New Jersey Agricultural Society. The local organization's annual fairs alternated between Haddonfield and Woodbury. Exhibitions included livestock, grain, flowers, fruits, vegetables, manufactured articles and dairy products. They also had contests:

> Ploughing matches, designed to test the performance of the various patterns and the skill of the operator, have formed a part of each exhibition. (*Report of the State Agricultural Society*, 1856, p. 25)

In 1856, Edward Bettle, Secretary of the local chapter of the Agricultural Society, described an important feature at the annual exhibitions in a letter to the New Jersey State Agricultural Society:

> ...the all-important home department, embracing the essentials of domestic economy, bread and butter, etc., and the more graceful though somewhat less indispensable evidences of the taste and skill of the ladies of the counties, have been prominent and highly creditable, and have constituted and marked and pleasing feature at each exhibition. (*Report of the State Agricultural Society*, 1856, p. 26)

Local farmers banded together during the early 1870s to create the Farmers Mutual Benefit Association of Camden County. The Farmers Mutual Benefit Association was founded because local farmers felt the New Jersey Agricultural Society ignored Camden County farmers. (WJP 1/22/1879) The group met at Town Hall in Haddonfield:

> A meeting of the Farmers Mutual Benefit Association was held in Town Hall. ... The subject of wheat growing was taken up, which drew quite lengthy, as to the kinds most profitable to grow, and best time for sowing. (WJP 10/31/1877)

The organization's main affair was its annual exhibition, where they exhibited new types of farm machinery, equipment and animals. In 1877, the "Syracuse chilled and carbonized plow" was displayed at a show. (WJP 12/12/1877) In December 1874, rabbits, pigeons, oriental birds, common fowl, ducks and geese were displayed at an exhibition at Town Hall. (WJP 12/2/1874)

Miscellaneous

Camden's Walt Whitman wrote a series of articles for the *Camden Daily Post* in 1879, entitled "A Trip Through the Wilds of New Jersey." The famous poet wrote about the sights, sounds and smell of a barnyard.

> One of my nooks is south of the barn-yard, and here I am sitting now, on a log, still basking in the sun, shielded from the wind. Near me are the cattle, feeding on corn-stalks. Occasionally a cow or the young bull (how handsome and bold he is!) scratches and munches the far end of the log on which I sit. The fresh milky odor is quite perceptible, and also the perfume of the hay from the barn. The perpetual rustle of wind round the barn gables, the grunting of the pigs, and the occasional crowing of chanticleers, are the sounds.
>
> Overall else, so vast, so clear, the marvels of the sky and light! Everyday they come, silent and spiritual–and so we seek not of them–but really what greater, what more beautiful marvels are there–or can there ever be? (CDP 1/28/1879)

Whitman's romantic portrayal of a day on the farm was in stark contrast to the hard work necessary and long hours to operate a farm.

Decline of Farms in the Region

Thomas Jefferson believed that the county's small farms were vital to a healthy national economy. As the nineteenth century passed, Jefferson's vision of a nation of small independent farmers gradually became obsolete. It became more difficult to make a living in agriculture in old Haddon Township as well as the surrounding region. William H. Nicholson wrote in his book on the difficulty of a farmer's livelihood at the end of the century. He wrote, "Farming in New Jersey was then [1866] a good business. Time, however, afterwards changed in this respect. ..." (p. 106) [See William H. Nicholson, page 182.]

Nicholson was alluding to a number of factors that had changed the face of the region's one-time agricultural economy. As the twentieth century approached, it became more difficult to operate a profitable farm. One reason resulted from developments in agricultural technology. Although new machinery increased production, the purchase price also increased a farmer's debts. To pay these debts, farmers eluded diversification and specialized in cash crops. Specialization, in turn, made the farmers more dependent upon crop prices that, in many cases, was dictated by middlemen. Many farmers experienced financial losses because of the new agricultural environment. Farmers that lacked the wherewithal to adapt to the new market place left the profession.

Making a living on a farm was also hard work and, often, the labor and risk were not worth the rewards. Some farmers left the countryside to seek employment in Philadelphia and Camden, where manufacturing jobs were abundant.

Finally, by the end of the century, new housing developments began to appear throughout the township. As enthusiasm for a suburban lifestyle grew, land became more valuable to the developer than for the crops that could be grown. Farmland eventually disappeared, as did the professional farmer.

The Wood Diaries

Isaac and Elizabeth Wood lived on their 130-acre farm on the outskirts of the village of Haddonfield. The couple's dwelling stands at 201 Wood Lane. They raised seven children. [See Isaac Wood, page 227.]

From the perspective of modern-day history enthusiasts, it is fortunate Samuel and Jehu Wood, Jr. and their mother, Elizabeth, kept journals. Reading the Wood chronicles, one senses the seasonal rhythm of living and working on a nineteenth century farm. In each season, farmers toiled at seemingly unending tasks. Hard work alone did not guarantee a successful harvest; farmers' good fortunes were also dependent on favorable weather. The importance of weather in the daily lives of local farmers is apparent throughout the journals.

The following selected entries illustrate the lives of these members of the Wood family:

Jehu Wood, Jr.

Jehu Wood, Jr. was a teenager when he recorded notes in his diary in 1864. Jehu's diary portrays the personal routine on a farm.

Jan. 6 Thermometer 11. Finished filling Sam Abbott's ice house and put two loads in our own.

8 Still snowing, sleighing first rate and quantities of people out. The bull hooked Higgins this morning pretty bad.

11 Pa [Isaac Wood], Sam [Samuel Wood], and Unc [Jehu Wood] and I hitched the new mules to the sleigh. Went skating, very poor.

25 Had the new mules to the plow the first time.

Feb. 19 It was splendid skating on Hopkins Pond this evening and lots doing.

22 Went to town and had a good time, the streets were crowded with people. Lots of troops in the parade today, quantities of ice in River.

26 Had to stay home [from school] to help thrash.

Mar. 12 Planted our first potatoes today. I had to go away to find turkeys; didn't find them though.

17 Splendid clear day for Quarterly Meeting and there were a good many. I have been to Haddonfield four times today.

24 Last Wednesday we sent 5 lambs to the Ferry got $5 and a half a head.

Apr. 6 Clear for once, just like spring, Jim was here tarring the fence.

21 Planted early corn and beans today.

23 ...went to the mill. When I came home planted cucumbers and squash and weeded the strawberry bed. It was awful hot.

29 Staid home from school to plant corn.

May 2 Sam went to Camden with some lambs and a calf. Planted watermelons and citrons.

11 We have planted about 10,000 sweet potato plants, got ready to plant broom corn.

13 Planted late beets, set out some cabbage plants. The men were harrowing potatoes and peas, some putting up fence.

19 Pa first thing this morning went hunting eggplants. We planted about 300, also a few pumpkins.

20 Sam, Unc, and I replanted Unc's carrots. Washed the sheep then planted 150 eggplants and 10 or 15 rows of pumpkins.

22 Had a splendid rain last night, crops look well generally. Last Thursday Sam and I had a race with a three minute horse and beat him scandalous. The man blows about his being a three minute horse.

24 Sam and I ran the steam engine faster at noon than she was ever run before. Worked in the garden.

25 Replanted Sam's carrots this morning.

26 Billy Tomlinson took a calf from here, weighed 236 lbs. $18.88.

27 Hard rain yesterday and all night, men at work letting water off in all the fields.

28 Pa went to town, Pat McGuirk here shearing sheep.

29 Had strawberries for supper Friday and tonight.

31 Unc and Pa went to town with the wool there was 60 lbs. and we got $45.45 for it. I

went in to swim for the first time this season.

June 2 Sam and I went to I. Shivers and got 100 cabbage plants.

9 I took Poll down to the blacksmith shop to have her shoes taken off. Pa and Ma have gone to Redmans for tea.

10 Went to the Sanitary Fair today and went through all the departments. Had a splendid time and did not get home until 11 o'clock. The Horticultural Department was splendid when it was lighted up.

15 Sam and Pa set out a few tomatoes this morning, we set out a lot this evening.

16 I rode Jenny over to the P.O. and Sam took the mowing machine to J.E. Bates [blacksmith]. Sam and I had a race down and up the lane twice.

17 Had 20 pea pickers, picked 54 baskets. Sam took them down [to market] this afternoon.

18 I went to Camden with Pa and took a load of straw.

20 We hauled in 6 loads of hay this afternoon. 3 we unloaded and 3 we did not.

26 Awful hot here today 100 for 3 or 4 hours. Awful hard blow at 5 o'clock.

July 1 Set out our cabbage plants, then Unc's. Finished planting tomatoes that Unc brought from S.G. Collins [Stephen Collins].

4 All hands went to cutting wheat and cut all day and nearly finished the big field, and quit early because it is the Fourth. Joe and I had to go to Tompkins to get 3 qts. of ice cream, had a good time and a good ear.

7 Helped Ma make ice cream and sponge cake, the aunties were up here to dinner and supper.

12 Dug load of potatoes and Sam took them right down to town, great excitement the rebels are going to take Washington.

Aug. 5 Cutting corn, picking tomatoes, and eggplants, 107 qts. blackberries, Sam took them down to town we had two loads.

26 We thrashed all the morning and got about 60 bushels of wheat. In the afternoon I went to Steve Collins and got two kittens.

Sept. 1 We cut clover seed yesterday. I took the light wagon to the shop to be mended.

3 Pa and Ma came home from Atlantic [Atlantic City].

7 Put up corn and picked eggplants and digging potatoes.

8 Pa and I took down 4 calves and got over $80 for them and got back by 9 o'clock...went to Bills to help raise a crib house. Unc and I stayed to supper.

In the fall of 1864, Jehu began attending Polytechnical College in Philadelphia. From that period on, Jehu's diary was filled with entries about school courses and homework assignments.

Samuel Wood

Jehu Wood's brother, Samuel, was 26 years old when he kept a diary of his daily activities in 1871. At that time, Samuel had assumed the lion's share of responsibility for operating the family farm. Years later, after his mother and father passed away, Samuel Wood inherited the family farm.

Jan. 2 Teams hauling marl working around the house. Uncle [Jehu Wood] hauling from the landing.

3 Teams hauling from marl holes.

5 Sent down load produce [Produce was sent to market quite frequently during the winter months.] Ma [Elizabeth Wood] at the sewing circle at James Lippincotts.

18 Killed heifer. Finished hauling marl from Lippincott's. Was down at Bettles before dinner.

19 Salted meat. Hauled load compost from Camden.

20 Sent down load produce. Trimming trees. Hauling.

21 Cutting wood.

22 Was out sleighing before dinner.

23 Was at lecture in Methodist Church

27 Sleighing around. Took up the hams.

28 Had Jennie shod. Hung the hams in smoke house.

29 Was at meeting. Snowed about 2 inches in morning. Was out sleighing after tea with K. Mr. and Mrs. Bettle spent the evening at Haddon.

Feb. 1 Threshed.

2 Cleaning up wheat.

3 Threshed. Working at the wheat.
6 Cleaning harness.
11 Took 41 bushels of wheat to Jos. G. Evans and Co. [grist mill]
20 Killed turkeys.
Apr. 10 Working my blackberries, put one-half ton of Pacific guano on them. Made a hot bed after dinner.
28 Raked the front lawn.
May 1 Planting corn in the big field.
2 Finishing planting corn. Working at the blackberries.
4 Rained all day. Sheared the sheep before dinner.
5 George H. Hopkins gave me a check for $30 for 10 young pigs. Trimming box.
8 Paid Richard Clement three dollars for set of harrow teeth. Hauled load compost from Pea Shore.
11 Pa [Isaac Wood] and Uncle went to Atlantic. Harrowing and marking for tomatoes.
12 Getting ready for tomatoes, set out 1000.
13 Working at the fence along the swamp. [Throughout the summer months, the Woods made numerous trips to the market to deliver produce.]
29 Built fence across the wheat field.
July 13 Picked 450 qts. of blackberries. Pa went to Atlantic.
Aug. 23 Put cap on barn. Putting up lightning rods.
29 Unloading boat at Landing [on Cooper's Creek].
Sept. 23 Spreading compost on wheat ground.
Oct. 14 Finished getting out peachblows and sowed the place with rye.
Nov. 2 Husking.
21 Bought a pair of young mules.
Dec. 11 Killed hogs. 15 weighted 4614 lbs.
15 Finished filling ice house.

Elizabeth Wood

Elizabeth Wood kept a diary during 1878. During the year, her husband, Isaac, was losing his health. The following year, he died at the age of 86. Besides the frequent references to her husband's health, Elizabeth often commented on the weather as well as ongoing efforts on the farm. Elizabeth passed away in 1880.

Jan. 12 Uncle [Jehu Wood] better, Samuel [Wood] took him for a ride.
25 Samuel had the Sociable here, they had a very pleasant evening.
31 Made scrapple.
Feb. 21 Killed a beef.
Mar. 26 Made candles.
Apr. 2 Sowed celery seed.
3 Planted out apple trees, set out early cabbage.
13 Tommy cleaned out the hen house.
May 19 Uncle picked the first strawberries.
June 24 Clear, got in 24 loads of hay. Pa [Isaac Wood] went to the City to the doctor.
28 Began to cut the large field of wheat.
Aug. 7 Preserved plums.
22 Made Pepper sauce. Antoinette Hopkins called.
23 Pa did not come down stairs today.
Sept. 28 Made the first fire in the sitting room. Pa upstairs 4 weeks today.
Oct. 1 Finished putting in the wheat.
9 Finished putting up sweet potatoes. Dr. Kline here to see Pa. Not very encouraging.
16 Jehu Wood Jr. was married this morning to Annie Thomas. Pa not well enough to be present.
23 Commenced raining and blowing in the night, destroyed a great many trees, houses and fences.
Nov. 28 Thanksgiving Day not well enough to go downstairs. Sent for Dr. Levis. Uncle got a pound of tea.
Dec. 2 Samuel killed pigs.
3 Made sausage.
11 Uncle Jehu went to Cape May a gunning.
25 No company. Christmas Pa very poorly.
31 Clear and cold an elegant winter's day. The men here with their machine threshing out wheat.

Industry and Shopkeepers

Introduction

During the early development of old Haddon Township, proprietors of small industries played an important role in the local economy. Most of the small industries were in the villages of Haddonfield and Rowandtown. Several mills were scattered around the remaining parts of the township near waterpower, the region's most important natural resource.

Many trades, manufacturing technologies and processes used at the time of the Civil War, had been developed and carried over from the previous century. However, concentrated industrialization took place throughout America during the three decades following the war. By the time the Industrial Revolution had ended, locally manufactured products such as flour, lumber, carpets, clothing, shoes, bricks, wagons, tools and nails, were being mass-produced at much lower costs in the nation's cities, where abundant cheap labor and new technologies were employed.

Once essential to the agrarian economy, one by one the mills and shops disappeared from the local scene. Gone, too, were the craftsmen, tools, apparatuses and processes that were familiar to most nineteenth century citizens. The routine workings of a gristmill, wheelwright and blacksmith's shop, tannery, harnessmaker's business and other small cottage industries probably unfamiliar to most people, are revisited in this chapter. Several topics related to the township's industries are also thrashed out, including nineteenth century photography, funerals, the unpopular tax on liquor and men's and women's fashion.

Albumenized Paper Mill

One unique business venture in the area was David Morgan's photographic paper mill situated along Cooper's Creek. Morgan's former home, now known as the Hopkins House, is in Haddon Township along South Park Drive. [See David Morgan, page 260.]

David was trained in college as a chemist. His scientific background, combined with entrepreneurial skills, enabled David to become one of a few photographic paper manufacturers in the Philadelphia region. Morgan was a pioneer in the development of the albumen process of making photographic paper. The process employed the clear egg white from eggs, called albumen, as an adhesive to bond light-sensitive chemicals to the surface of paper. Photographers used the paper made by Morgan.

During the last 30 years of the nineteenth century, two factors in photographic technology created a great demand for albumen paper. First was the invention of the stereograph. The stereograph viewer provided a three-dimensional view of a photograph. Albumen paper was the paper of choice for use in a stereograph viewer because of its smooth surface and ability to pro-

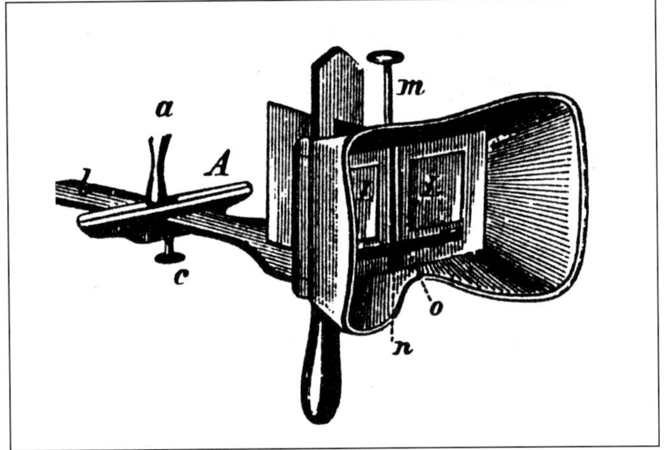

A nineteenth century stereograph viewer. The viewer offered three-dimensional view of photographs. Albumen paper was the paper of choice used in stereograph viewers.

(*The Albumen & Salted Paper Book*, by James Reilly)

vide fine photographic detail. The second and perhaps the largest reason for the increased demand of albumen paper was the emergence of cheap portraitures. During the era, small photographs mounted on cards, called card d'visite, became popular in all segments of society. Photographs of family members, faraway places, famous people, great works of art, and advertising material were all reproduced on albumen paper.

Shortly after purchasing his 78-acre farm in 1866, Morgan began to produce photographic paper. In 1870, Morgan floated some 50 reams of paper in the albumen solution. (One ream is 500 sheets of paper) During that year, his receipts from the sale of photographic paper was $2,000. Initially, Morgan worked by himself during the three months he devoted to making albumen paper. David oversaw the operation of his farm and sold his photographic paper during down time throughout the year. By 1880, the business had grown considerably. He employed eight workers throughout the year to manufacture his photographic paper.

The albumen process used thousands of eggs purchased from nearby farmers. In 1870, the entire paper coating process was done by hand; a decade later, David had incorporated a small steam engine into the production process.

To obtain the desired results, the albumen process required raw paper stock made from mineral-free water. Unfortunately, the special paper was not obtainable anywhere in the United States. Morgan imported his paper stock from Rives, France. Rives was one of just a few places in the world where mineral-free mountain lake water was used to make photographic paper stock.

The process of producing albumen-coated photographic paper required several steps. Albumen was first beaten to a foam and allowed to settle. The homogenous liquid was mixed with silver nitrate, forming a light sensitive insoluble silver albumen solution. Each sheet of raw paper stock was floated by hand and sometimes floated twice in the silver albumen solution so that a glossier finish could be obtained. The homogenous liquid formed an even layer on the paper and they hung it to dry on racks. When it was dry, the paper was "calendered" by a rolling process to make the coated paper more flexible.

The other segment of Morgan's business was selling the inventory. In the 1870s, the centers for manufacturers of albumen paper in the United States were Philadelphia, Rochester and New York City. Morgan opened a store at 832 Market Street in Philadelphia to sell his photographic paper. In 1880 his receipts from the sale of albumen paper had grown to $21,000.

In *The History of Camden County, New Jersey,* published in 1886, George Prowell wrote about David Morgan's paper mill:

> About twenty years since, David U. Morgan ventured in a new enterprise of manufacture, and established himself in Haddon Township about one mile from Cuthbert's Station on the line of the Camden and Atlantic Railroad in the preparation of the finer qualities of paper for use by photographers, which has developed into a success. He imports from France the quality of paper needed, and by a chemical preparation of albumen, known to himself, produces a material popular among the class of artists. His reputation for this kind of goods is extensive, and he had, while residing in Philadelphia, made a series of experiments which culminated in the business now pursued by him. (p. 653)

George Prowell's observations could not have been more accurate. Upon David's death in 1889, his wife and several former employees tried to duplicate David's

An advertisement for David Morgan's photographic paper. Morgan used eggs to bind light-sensitive chemicals to paper.
(*The Albumen & Salted Paper Book*, by James Reilly)

secret formula for making the albumen solution; however, they were unsuccessful and they dissolved the business.

Blacksmiths, Wheelwrights and Coachmakers

During this age, most transportation was still dependent on horses and mules to pull farm wagons, delivery carts, carriages and buggies. Before mass-produced horse-drawn vehicles came to be, local blacksmiths and wheelwrights made practically all wagons, carts and carriages. A nineteenth century community would have a hard time functioning without a blacksmith or wheelwright. The wheelwrights and blacksmiths in the township worked in the villages of Rowandtown and Haddonfield.

The duties of a blacksmith and wheelwright often overlapped. Blacksmiths' tasks typically included shoeing horses, making or repairing tools, kitchen utensils, household hardware, farming tools, wagon and carriage hardware, metal tires and sharpening plows and other farming equipment. By strict definition, a wheelwright was a maker of wheels. In most instances, they were skilled carpenters. Wheelwrights in and about the township were coach-builders and repairmen capable of fixing all kinds of farming implements or horse-drawn vehicles. The basic materials used by wheelwrights and coachmakers were lumber, hardware, varnish, oils, spokes, hubs and trimmings.

A typical one-forge blacksmith shop required at least two workers. Usually an apprentice blacksmith or laborer did the strenuous work around the shop. A good portion of a blacksmith's workday was spent over a hot forge. Stone coal (anthracite coal) or charcoal was used to heat the iron until it became malleable. Steel made from iron was used to form cutting tools. The bellows fanned the fire that heated iron for the blacksmith to beat into shape. Although steam power could move bellows, old Haddon Township smiths pumped their bellows by hand.

Generally, wheelwrights and blacksmiths ran their shops with the help of a journeyman or young apprentice. Craftsmen were trained in the traditional apprentice system in which young men worked for a master wheelwright or blacksmith to learn the trade. In carriagemaking, the apprentice learned the skills of a blacksmith as well as body making, finishing, painting, stitching, trimming, varnishing and wheelwrighting. Some wheelwrights did the necessary ironwork on vehicles, while others sent the "ironing" to a blacksmith.

The small village of Rowandtown was the site of about a half-dozen wheelwright and blacksmith shops, all of them situated along the Haddonfield Turnpike

Wheelwright shops in the township were along what is now Haddon Avenue in Westmont and in Haddonfield. Wheelwrights made and repaired all types of horse-drawn vehicles. They also repaired farming implements and other household items.

(*First Lessons in Reading*, Parker & Watson's Series. A.S. Barnes & Company, NY 1873)

(Haddon Avenue). David Albertson's blacksmith shop once stood on the south side of the turnpike, near what is now West Albertson Avenue. David, a master blacksmith, employed two apprentices, Espen Ashton age 22, and his 16 year-old brother, Thompson Ashton. Both boys lived at the site of the shop. [See David Albertson, page 261.]

In 1860, Albertson derived most his income from the twenty wagons "ironed" at the shop. It is possible the shop made the iron hardware for wagons assembled across the road at Thomas Albertson's wheelwright shop. Shoeing horses and general repairs were other types of work done at David Albertson's shop.

When the time came to repair his wagons and farm tools, George Lee, a local farmer, distributed the work to several Rowandtown blacksmiths. Notes contained in Lee's estate papers reveal David Albertson sharpened harrow teeth, hooped cart and wagon wheels, and banded hubs for Lee. [See George Lee, page 208.]

Kimber Clement's blacksmith shop was on the southwest corner of the Haddonfield Turnpike and Stoy's Mill Road, now known as Crystal Lake Avenue. Clement's shop was in operation before 1850. A significant portion of the patronage at Clement's shop, at least in 1860, came from hooping. This task involved placing a circular band of medal or wood around a wheel, cask or barrel. Clement's blacksmith shop was also a popular place for inhabitants to take their horses for shoes. In 1860, he shod 150 horses at the shop.

George Lee also took broken items to Kimber Clement for repair. During the early 1860s, the master blacksmith charged Lee for mending a tea kettle lid, replacing a set of potato harrow teeth, mending a mowing machine, putting a blade on a scythe, mending a knife, fork, shovel, plow, cart, chain and raker and hooping a barrel and bucket.

Kimber passed away in 1869. The administrator of his estate placed an announcement in the newspaper listing the assets of the blacksmith shop:

> Blacksmith tools and stock—two forges, two bellows, two anvils, and blocks, a large lot of tongs, two vices, punches, files, screw plates, taps and other smith tools of great variety. About 600 pounds of horse shoes, about 25 pounds horse shoe nails, about 100 pounds screw bolts assorted sizes, about 600 pounds new iron and steel assorted, about two and one-half tons of old iron. (WJP 12/1/1869)

After they laid Kimber to rest, Richard Clement became proprietor of the business. During 1870, Richard and his two employees used 400 pounds of iron and 100 pounds of steel to shoe horses and make and repair items. After just several years as proprietor, Richard sold his business:

> ...blacksmith shop with two forges, shoeing shed and coal shed attached, a well established...business. (WJP 3/5/1873)

In 1870, Joseph Engle's wheelwright shop was at the corner of the Haddonfield Turnpike and Stoy's Mill

Road, next to Clement's blacksmith shop. A typical day at Engle's shop included repairing, welding, painting and replacing trimmings on wagons and carriages. Engle was 64 years-old at this time.

After Joseph died in 1875, they took an inventory of his coach building tools and materials. The contents of the shop included:

> . . .seven planers, five drawing knives, whipsaws, trimming tools, oak clamps, sixty-six large spokes, sixty-three small spokes, shaft, patterns, four hubs, carriage pole, five iron clamps, turning lathe, lot of chains, wheel bench and blocks, set of carriage wheels, old carriage body, new carriage body, a market wagon, block and rope, fifty foot of poplar boards, vice, shop carriage bench, plains, saws, eight augers, files, two lots of hair for trimming purposes, seven and one-half yards of curtain material and oak planks. (Inv. E-172, 1875)

Although it has not been documented, it is likely Russell Williams acquired Engle's assets. In any case, Williams was a proprietor of a wheelwright/blacksmith establishment in Rowandtown during the late 1870s. During that period, William fixed wagon wheels, shafts and springs and farm tools.

Thomas Albertson's wheelwright shop was at the junction of the Haddonfield Turnpike and Willis Lane, now Cooper Street. In 1860, the master wheelwright employed two craftsmen, a coach trimmer and an eighteen year-old apprentice wheelwright. In that same year, Albertson assembled twenty wagons, applied paint and trimmings and sold them at an average price of $125 per vehicle. The eight carts assembled by the wheelwright sold for about $40 apiece. The U.S. Census Bureau's data on local industry reveals Albertson's shop did "other work" which probably included general repair work. George Lee's estate paid Albertson a dollar for the acquisition of two plough handles and $2.50 for replacing a cart body. [See Thomas Albertson, page 260.]

By 1880, it is probable that Charles Haines had obtained ownership of Thomas Albertson's business. The carriage builder hired two employees that labored ten hours a day, in return for wages of $1.50. One of Haines's employees was Joseph Collings, a carriage-maker and wheelwright. Collings later became a very successful carriage builder in Camden.

Henry Cuthbert's account ledger shows that "C.M. Haines wheelwright and blacksmith" accepted payment in kind. Cuthbert paid Haines with crops, hay and potatoes, and allowed Haines's three cows to graze on his land. The same farm ledger noted the Haines Brothers repaired Cuthbert's shovel handle, worked on a wagon body, placed new hooping on the wagon wheels and replaced a bolt and two nuts on a wagon. Haines also fixed the shoes of Cuthbert's two horses "Nell" and "Jim." [See Henry Cuthbert, page 254.]

One might expect to find a higher concentration of blacksmith and wheelwright shops in the township's most populated village, Haddonfield–and there were. Samuel Matlack's blacksmith shop was at the intersection of Potter and Ellis streets. About two-thirds of his business came from general repair work. During 1870, Matlack and his apprentice blacksmith used five tons of iron and steel to make wagon parts. Ten years later, Samuel Matlack's operation employed two laborers, one of which was a child. The employees' workday at Matlack's shop was not unlike most businesses of the era, with helpers laboring ten hours a day.

At the junction of Haddon Avenue and Mechanic Street stood Joseph Bates's blacksmith shop. In his younger years, Bates had been a carriage-builder. By the 1870s, most of his work came from fixing horse-drawn vehicles. Sometime about 1873, Joseph retired and George Tule took over as proprietor. Tule had previously been an apprentice blacksmith under Bates's direction.

The hectic times of the year for blacksmiths were the winter months, when snow and ice laid on the roadways. During the cold weather, a blacksmith sharpened the shoes of horses for better traction on the slippery roads.

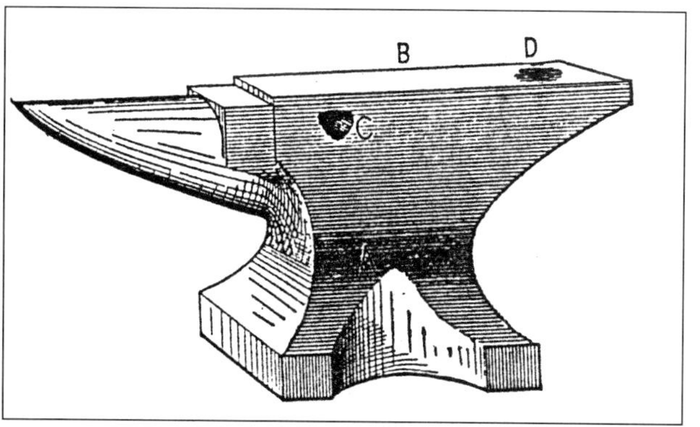

An anvil was an important component in blacksmith shops. Like wheelwrights, nineteenth century blacksmiths worked in shops along the main thoroughfares in the township. One of the more important tasks of the local blacksmiths was shoeing horses.

(*Practical Blacksmithing*, by M.T. Richardson)

The *Camden Daily Post* took note of the busy wintertime business at Tule's shop: "George Tule, the blacksmith, shod and roughed 218 horses and mules the first week of sleety driving." (CDP 1/6/1877) In 1882, Tule boasted of having the largest horseshoeing concern in Camden County. (*Industries of New Jersey Part II*)

Besides fixing wagons, mowers and reapers, Tule branched out and began producing carriages and wagons in the late 1870s:

> George Tule...running a blacksmith shop in Haddonfield for about six years, is now adding to it a frame building 34' x 45', two stories, will carry on wheelwright business. Mr. Tule has had in his blacksmith shop six men, and has now employed one more smith and a wood-worker. (WJP 8/27/1879)

> Wagons, Carriages and Sleighs–manufacturer and repair as well as all wheelwright and blacksmith work. Horseshoeing. (WJP 12/31/1879)

Tule's fourteen employees earned $1.50 a day in 1882. His shop had several departments. The blacksmith shop measured 30' x 32'; the wheelwright shop 30' x 60'; the finishing and paint shops were on the second floor. A wood shed measured 32' x 40'. The company specialized in building light and heavy farm wagons and buggies.

William McKnight's wheelwright shop was situated at the corner of Matlack Street and Parkham's Alley, now Mechanic and Clement streets. In 1860, McKnight, along with four employees, assembled twenty wagons and sold them for an average price of $125. One employee was a fifteen year-old apprentice wheelwright. Like most apprentices, the young man lived in his master's household. The 1870, census takers listed McKnight's profession as a coach trimmer. The shop was sold in 1875 after McKnight passed away.

James Webster's coach-building business stood near the intersection of Ellis and Potter streets. Webster commenced business in Haddonfield sometime before 1850. In 1860, a wagon or carriage assembled by James, and his two helpers, sold for about $150.

When Isaac Wood needed the services of a wheelwright, he called on James Webster. In one year, Webster painted Wood's wagon, furnished a new curtain for a carriage, mended a curtain, replaced spokes and felloes (the iron of a wheel supported by spokes), and replaced wagon tongues. [See Isaac Wood, page 227]

During the era covered by this project, other blacksmiths and wheelwrights were open for business in Haddonfield including William Tomlinson, Daniel Fortiner, Thomas Williams and his son Charles, Mark Bareford, Richard Elwell, and the partnership of Weinman & Collings.

The undertakings of blacksmiths and wheelwrights continued to be in demand while horse-drawn vehicles remained in use. Repairing vehicles, farm equipment and shoeing horses were especially important tasks in the agricultural region. As the nineteenth century progressed, a growing demand for horse-drawn vehicles stimulated productivity. The factory and its efficient production system were able to meet the increased demand and soon dominated manufacturing. Although local wheelwrights continued to make carriages and wagons until the end of the century, by the 1870s mass-produced carriages were widely available and more affordable. It became increasingly difficult for the small owner-operated shops to meet a level of production required by customers at a competitive price. The country had passed into an age where the village carriage-maker was no longer needed and the craft faded away.

Brickyards

Neither Philadelphia nor southern New Jersey had a shortage of brickyards during the nineteenth century. All over the Delaware Valley, clay was plentiful and there was an abundance of wood to fuel kilns. In 1858, they estimated 50 brickyards existed within the city limits of Philadelphia. Across the Delaware River, most brickmakers in and near Camden accommodated builders with stock for brick homes.

Two brickmaking establishments operated in old Haddon Township during the 1870s. James Dobbs was proprietor of a yard that stood along Mill Road, now Cuthbert Road, in Haddon Township. Dobbs Brickyard also manufactured drainage tiles. The other brick manufacturer was situated on the banks of the North Branch of Newton Creek, at a site along what is now Mt. Ephraim Avenue in Camden. During the 1870s, the yard was named after its proprietors, Stone & Deno.

The Dobbs Brickyard was situated on the northern side of Cuthbert Road, between Lees Lane and the Main Branch of Newton Creek. The yard's original proprietors, James and Samuel Dobbs, came from England. The brothers learned their profession from their father, who was a brickmaker in their native land. When the brothers arrived in American, they formed a brickmaking business. The Dobbs family ran other brickyards in the region.

Most of the workers at the Dobbs's yard were African-Americans. In 1870, seven African-Americans were working at the yard, including fourteen year-old

Peter Jacobs and George Whoely, age 80. The labor demands in a brickyard required both semiskilled and unskilled workers. Piecework was a customary method by which employees were compensated. Dobbs's employees, however, were paid by the day. For a ten-hour day, skilled mechanics received $1.50 a day, and they paid unskilled laborers $1.20. Bricks were made during five months of the year, with the yard idle during the remaining months. Many of Dobbs's laborers lived on or near the brickyard premise. Two helpers of African-American decent, George and Robert Jacobs, resided in tenant homes on Dobbs's property.

Other than the clay, brick manufacturers required little in the way of raw materials. Red brick clay was found in various parts of southern New Jersey. Although Dobbs found some clay elsewhere, he also excavated the raw material from his own pits. The Dobbs Brickyard pits or clay banks were situated near Newton Creek. After clay was extracted from the earth and dried, the first labor-intensive step in making bricks was grinding the clay to a powder. Tempering involved mixing the powder with water thoroughly so that it was neither soft nor hard, but suitable for molding into the shape of a brick. Usually, they employed unskilled laborers to mix clay, although horses could be used to turn an apparatus known as a tempering or pug wheel, that churned the clay. Later, they used steam-power in the tempering process to rotate the mixing apparatus.

After the clay was tempered, employees placed clay into brick-shaped molds. Workers removed the raw, unfired bricks from the molds and placed them in drying sheds where they were exposed to the air and sun. The dried bricks were then placed in kilns and fired to become hard bricks. After many centuries of making bricks by hand, brickmaking machines powered by steam engines eventually replaced the technique of molding bricks by hand.

An interesting fact about American bricks was that they varied in size from one manufacturer to the next. Builders used several types of bricks. Dobbs's brickmaking operation made salmon bricks (common red-orange color bricks); pressed bricks (better grade, smooth, rich-color bricks); hard bricks (lesser grade semi-fired bricks); and pavers (long and thin bricks).

Wood was the other ingredient needed to manufacture bricks. It was common to burn several hundred cords of wood in the kilns during a season of making bricks. In 1850, five kilns were in use at the yard.

By 1870, Dobbs was using a ten-horsepower steam engine to operate a brickmaking machine, or possibly to turn the tempering apparatus. A brickmaking technique known as the stiff-mud process was employed at the site. The method used clay tempered with less than the usual amount of water so that it was stiffer. The stiff clay was forced through the rectangular die of a brickmaking machine, then cut by a wire into bricks of proper size. In 1880, a stiff-mud machine made 200,000 common bricks at the site.

Manufacturing drainage tiles was a large segment of Dobbs's overall operation and may have accounted for more sales than bricks. Dobbs's business went by another name, The Union Steam Tile Works. In 1871, they

Manufacture of brick by the stiff-mud process. The process was used at Dobbs Brickyard. Clay was forced through a die and cut into bricks.
(*Geological Survey of New Jersey, The Clays & Clay Industry of New Jersey*, by Henrick Ries and Henry Kummel)

Haddonfield, N. J., Mar 25 1870

UNION
Steam Tile Works,
TERMS:
Thirty-days credit will be given to responsible parties and lawful interest after that date.

Mr Camden County

Bought of JAMES C. DOBBS,
WHOLESALE AND RETAIL DEALER IN
BRICK AND DRAIN TILE,
Near Haddonfield, New J

Feb	5	500 hard brick @ $10	$ 5 00

Received Payment of C. Glover
James C. Dobbs

An invoice from James C. Dobbs Brickyard. This brickyard was situated along Cuthbert Road at the Main Branch of Newton Creek in Haddon Township.

(Gloucester County Historical Society Collections)

made 250,000 tiles for customers. (WJP 1/4/1871) A newspaper article even suggested Dobbs's tiles were exported to other regions:

> The Union Steam Tile Work near Haddonfield is turning out large quantities of superior tile. The tiles from this works are popular at home and abroad, 150,000 having been sold already this season. (WJP 5/12/1880)

Farmers were frequent customers at Dobbs's yard, as they could improve the productivity of their fields by installing a system of underdrains to remove water. In this process, fields were excavated and tiles laid to drain the unwanted water. Most agricultural underground drain tiles were two to ten inches in diameter and came in sections of one to two feet in length. Drainage tiles were either molded flat and bent around a form to the proper shape or made into a curved form by mechanically pressing clay through a die to obtain the proper shape and form.

In 1866, Samuel French, an owner of several farms in the township, hired Samson Dobbs to dig trenches and lay drainage tiles in the fields of his "Pine Grove Cottage Farm." In this era before the backhoe was in use, they called workers that dug the trenches, ditchers. [See Samuel French, page 258.]

After many years in the brickmaking business, James Dobbs's interest turned to farming. He pursued his agricultural interest on an adjacent field situated on Cuthbert Road. [See James Dobbs, page 256.] By the early 1870s, Samuel Dobbs's sons, James C. and Samson Dobbs, were probably in charge of the brickwork. In 1875, the cofounder of the brickyard died:

> James Dobbs age 69 years died. Mr. Dobbs was an Englishman by birth and came to this country when a boy. Manufacturer of brick and tile "It is claimed that to him belongs the credit of making the first tile in the country used for the purpose of underdraining." (WJP 5/26/1875)

The J.C. Dobbs Brick and Tile Yard carried on business at the same site for three-quarters of a century until it closed in the early 1900s.

Sometime in the 1840s, Peter Stetzer organized a brickmaking yard along the eastern side of the Mt. Ephraim Turnpike where the road crossed the North Branch of Newton Creek. In 1850, Stetzer's brickwork was a busy place. Peter's kilns consumed 540 cords of wood, purchased for $2,160. Clay cost $450 for the year. Workers also dug clay at the site of the brickyard. Fifteen helpers were employed during the seven months of the year the yard's kilns were baking bricks. Unlike Dobbs's yard where both bricks and drainage tiles were made, Stetzer's operation only manufactured bricks. Workers molded bricks by hand at the yard, although Stetzer and his laborers were aided by horses when mixing the clay.

It is likely Stetzer was proprietor until the time of his death in 1863, after which John Stone and James Deno took control of the brickyard. Stone was a well-known builder in Camden. Deno's expertise was in manufacturing bricks.

Both Stone and Deno capitalized on the growth and development in Camden to support their yard. Brick row homes, typical housing stock, were being built throughout the city. A Camden City ordinance enacted in 1853, prohibited erection of wooden buildings. After they enacted the law, new buildings were constructed of bricks, stone or iron. Stone and Deno supplied builders of brick homes mainly in South Camden:

> James Deno...is prepared to supply contractors and builders with brick in large or small quantities. (WJP 2/23/1870)

In 1878, Newton Creek overflowed its banks and almost put an end to the brickyard:

> The old brick yard on the Mt. Ephraim Turnpike first started more than 30 years ago by Peter Stetzer and lately operated by Stone & Deno, has been closed. The flood of October 23, destroyed 170,000 green [unburned] brick for the above firm, who refuse to continue to manufacture because the owner of the property refuses to locate the yard at higher ground. (WJP 1/15/1879)

Contrary to what they reported in the newspaper, brickmaking at the site continued after the flood. In the summer of 1879, a newspaper reported the brickyard made two million bricks during the season. (WJP 6/4/1879) Unfortunately, James Deno did not live to fully enjoy any profits earned in that year. He passed away during the latter months of 1879. The exact date the yard ceased producing bricks is unknown.

During America's industrial era the brickmaking industry changed. Machines powered by steam gradually replaced yards where bricks were made by hand. As the twentieth century approached, the larger yards dominated brick manufacturing because they took advantage of modern methods and machine power for handling material. The small companies, finding it difficult to compete with larger, more efficient, brickyards, slowly disappeared.

Cabinetmakers, Coffinmakers and Undertakers

Although carpenters, joiners and cabinetmakers all worked with wood, the craft of the latter required more exacting skills. Cabinetmakers made and repaired household furniture such as tables, stands, bureaus, sideboards, desks, bookcases, sofas and bedsteads. They made furniture from both hard and soft woods. A cabinetmaker used hand tools such as hammers, saws, augers, chisels, specialized planes, gouges, files and brace and bits to make and repair furniture.

In the nineteenth century, wooden coffins were often purchased from cabinetmakers. Assembling coffins was a natural product for the woodworker. The two cabinetmakers in Haddonfield during the 1870s also made coffins and eventually assumed the role of undertakers.

William Githens called himself as a "joiner," a similar profession to a cabinetmaker. Githens's house was situated at 21 Potter Street. In the 1820s, his products included wooden clock cases. He worked with cherry, mahogany and walnut and fabricated various styles of these cases.

As time passed, U.S. Census Bureau statistics suggest Githens supported himself primarily from the sale of coffins. In 1870, Githens utilized a thousand board feet of white pine and eight hundred board feet of walnut when constructing coffins and making, repairing and refinishing household furniture. By the end of the 1870s, William's son, Charles Githens was in charge of his father's cabinetmaking shop. Charles emulated in his father as a coffinmaker and took on the additional duties of an undertaker.

Samuel Burrough, Sr. worked out of his cabinet shop at 37 Kings Highway in Haddonfield. In 1870, about 90 percent of Burrough's earnings were from fabricating

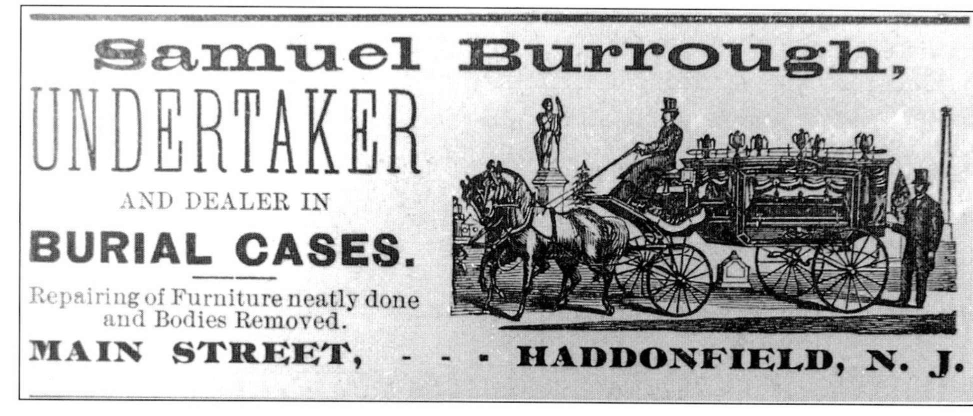

Samuel Burrough was an undertaker and cabinetmaker along Main Street in the village of Haddonfield.

(*New Jersey State Gazetteer & Business Directory*, 1882-1883)

coffins. Samuel kept ready-made coffins on hand for funerals. As an undertaker, Burrough took charge of corpses and temporarily kept them in an ice box at his shop. Burrough transported the remains in his large black, horse-drawn, hearse. It was common to travel many miles to transport bodies to family burial plots or churchyard cemeteries.

Waiting in the wings to carry on his father's cabinetmaking and funeral business was young Samuel Burrough. After his father passed away in 1870, Samuel continued in the business of repairing furniture, although assembling coffins and performing the duties of an undertaker made up the largest portion of his income. Usually, the local woodworker assembled plain coffins. For people of moderate means, most coffins of the post-Civil War era were made of pine.

Unlike today's funeral customs, most nineteenth century funeral ceremonies were held in the home of the deceased's family. Neighbors sometimes helped a family prepare and "lay out" the corpse. Very few families chose to embalm bodies before the 1880s. While on view in the parlor, the corpse generally rested on a wooden board placed between two chairs. Blocks of ice were placed under the board and around the body to preserve the corpse until after the viewing. During the era, undertakers began to take on more of a noticeable roles in preparing bodies for funerals and making arrangements for burials.

In 1871, Henry Kendig, an undertaker from Paulsboro, New Jersey, recorded his services in an account book. It is likely that similar services were done by the two cabinetmakers/undertakers in Haddonfield. Representative services and Kendig's prices for a funeral included a walnut coffin $18, lining and pillow $3.40, shroud $10, case stained $12, putting on ice $4, attendance of funeral $8 and digging grave $3.50. Other charges could include ribbons 25 cents; shirt, draws, stockings $3.60; and collar and handkerchief $1.25.

Cidermakers and Cooper

Apple orchards were common on many farms in southern New Jersey. Throughout the eighteenth and nineteenth centuries, farmers frequently made their own cider by pressing the fruit. Before the sale of alcoholic beverages were outlawed in 1873 within Haddon Township, apple brandy, or applejack may have been the drink of choice. They served the popular beverage at taverns, inns and other shops within the township.

Peter Weinnmann's distillery sat next to the South Branch of Newton Creek where it flowed under the Camden & Blackwoodtown Turnpike in West Collingswood Heights. His products included cider, apple brandy, wines and vinegar. During four months in 1870, Weinnmann turned 1,000 bushels of apples into 1,000 gallons of cider and 1,000 gallons of vinegar. [See Peter Weinnmann, page 264.]

The distilling process employed by Weinnmann had been in use by people to make vinegar and distilled spirits for hundreds of years. The recipe for apple brandy began with ground up apples placed in a hand-operated cider press where pressure forced out the apple juice. Although the liquid squeezed from the fruit was the primary product, the solid waste residue was fed to horses, hogs and cattle. The juice was allowed to ferment naturally. After fermentation, the hard cider contained about six to ten percent alcohol. Wine could be made from the hard cider by filtering and aging. Weinnmann also fermented the juice obtained from purchased grapes to produce wine.

Weinnmann heated fermented cider in his two cooper stills. Alcoholic vapor formed and passed through a long tube, known as a worm. Cold water condensed the vapor into a distillate containing 50 to 75 percent alcohol. Distillate with a high content of alcohol came out first; the alcoholic strength declined as the process continued. Distillate with low alcoholic content, known as "low wine," was returned to the still for redistilling. The average yield of apple brandy for each 100 gallons of fermented cider was about ten gallons. The distilled spirit aged in barrels for up to two years. Peter also used blackberries and cherries to make liquor by the same process.

Vinegar was another product made by distillers. It was used in households as a preservative and in condiments. Cider vinegar was obtained by distilling the juice from apples beyond the alcohol state.

During the Civil War, the federal excise tax on distilled spirits was as high as $2.00 a gallon. Because the rate encouraged distillers to evade their tax obligations, the tax was reduced to 50 cents a gallon in 1868. By 1875, Congress had raised the tax by an additional 40 cents a gallon. Many distillers continued to evade their federal tax responsibilities that made enforcement of the law a difficult task for revenue collectors. In his book *The Second Oldest Profession–An Informal History of Moonshining in America*, Jeff Carr noted the difficult job of enforcing compliance of the liquor tax laws:

> The bands of revenue agents operating during any of these years [1875 to 1880] were pitifully small for the task at hand and the almost boundless geographical territory they were expected to police. Even with authority to organize posses and call upon other federal agents, marshals, and deputy marshals, the number of seizures made, compared to violators in existence, was slight. (p. 37)

In his book, Carr provides extracts of reports issued in 1880 by the Commissioner of Internal Revenue. The Commissioner's comments suggest the lives of federal employees were placed in jeopardy upon seizing stills:

> ...during the last four years and four months, 4,061 illicit distilleries have been seized, 7,339 persons have been arrested for illicit distilling, 26 officers and employees have been killed and 57 wounded, in the enforcement of the internal-revenue laws. (p. 38)

Local Internal Revenue Collectors attempted to encourage compliance with excise tax laws on liquor by publicizing the number of legal distilleries in a district. For instance, the *West Jersey Press* printed data on the distilleries that complied with the law: "27 apple brandy distillers in full operation in the First Revenue District." (WJP 8/7/1878)

In 1871, Peter Weinnmann's stills, liquid inventory and containers were seized by federal agents. The impetus for confiscation is not known with absolute certainty; however it is likely he was not complying with federal excise tax laws. Fortunately, the local Federal Marshal's office did not incur any casualties upon seizing Peter Weinnmann's distillery. With authority to sell seized property, the government agents placed an advertisement in a Camden newspaper. The first public sale of Weinnmann's assets was to take place in November 1871, although it is likely it did not happen. A second public sale was advertisement about six months later:

> U.S. Marshal Public Sale of Distillery of Peter Weinnmann on the road leading from Camden to Mt. Ephraim about 3 miles from Camden. 60 gallons of low wine, 64 casks of vinegar, 14 hogshead of mash, 60 empty hogshead, 2 copper stills, worms and worm tub, 2 large cedar vats, 25 iron-bound puncheons, 26 empty barrels, 5 beer kegs...cider press, 2 large mash tubs. (WJP 11/22/1871)

> Public Sale U.S. Marshal on premise known as the Distillery of Peter Weinnmann. 14 hogshead containing 800 gallons of mash, cask containing Blackberries, keg low wine, keg wild cherry, 2 copper stills, 1200 gallon vat, 22 iron-bound casks, 36 empty hogshead...and two presses. (WJP 5/29/1872)

Not too long after his distillery was confiscated and sold, Peter sold his land and moved from the township.

Difficult times fell upon the township's hard cider drinkers in 1873, when they banned the sale of liquor in the township. [See local option, page 79.] While the only distillery in old Haddon Township had been shut down by federal agents, distillers in neighboring communities continued to make apple cider. One nearby distillery in Batesville manufactured apple cider for local consumers. Joseph Peacock's distillery was situated outside Haddonfield in what is now Cherry Hill.

Making apple cider, brandy, wine and vinegar was not Peter Weinnmann's primary occupation. In 1870, the U.S. Census Bureau noted Peter's occupation as a cooper. Weinnmann's still operated just four months during the year. The remaining months he made barrels. In years past, Peter had worked as a cooper in Haddonfield. Coopering was the art of making wooden containers out of staves and hoops. Weinnmann's two professions were quite compatible. It is probable that Peter made the containers he used to hold his liquid stock.

The various types of nineteenth century containers differed in the volume of liquid they were able to hold. For example, a typical barrel held between 31 and 42 gallons; a keg held 5 to 10 gallons; a hogshead 63 gallons. A cask was a general term that referred to any size container.

Peter was a skilled craftsman, known as a wet cooper, that made barrels to hold liquids. A wet barrel had to be leak-proof and durable. Oak wood was used to make a barrel water tight. A dry cooper made barrels to hold nonliquid products. The techniques employed to make a dry barrel was less exacting because the containers did not have to be water tight. For centuries the techniques and tools of coopering did not change. By the last quarter of the nineteenth century, skilled coopers became scarce after barrelmaking machinery replaced the handmade method.

Isaac Prine was one of the township's more industrious entrepreneurs. He was an overseer of a sawmill, proprietor of a retail ice business and a cidermaker. Prine's cider mill was on or near his two-acre lot along the eastern side of Cuthbert Road near what is now Stokes Avenue in Haddon Township. [See sawmill, page 143, ice farming, page 163.]

It is unclear whether Prine's cidermaking operation produced nonalcoholic apple cider or whether he distilled and fermented his liquid stock. Though the sale of spirituous liquors in Haddon Township was against the law beginning in 1873, its possible that Prine peddled distilled products outside the township's border.

Although it is not known for sure what kind of machinery Prine used, a steam engine provided the source the power. The *Camden County Courier* reported "A two story steam cider mill was just completed by Isaac Prime [sic]." (7/31/1880)

Cidermaking machinery was not overly sophisticated. A grinder with steel grate knives was used to cut apples into a fine consistent pulp. One type of apple grinder, powered by a two horse steam engine, could grind more than 100 bushels of apples per hour. Prine may have employed a steam-powered cider press in which a lever and screw-press placed continuous pressure to squeeze out the clear juice. Some cider presses could yield more than 60 barrels of cider a day.

During the mid-1870s, Prine's drink was a favorite among visitors at the Centennial Exhibition in Philadelphia:

> During the Centennial Exposition in 1876, Prime [sic] also had a cider mill at a lower portion of the lake and this drink became famous among the thousands of visitors who attended the World's Fair. (*Tri-City Sun* 6/11/1925)

Gristmills

Wheat flour was a staple commodity in America. It is likely most of the old Haddon Township inhabitants secured the "staff of life" from local millers. Following the Civil War, Newton, Mt. Ephraim and Haddonfield mills were grinding flour and feed for the residents of the surrounding countryside. A fourth gristmill, the Haddon Mill, once stood near the village of Haddonfield on John Hopkins's land. Hopkins Pond provided the waterpower for the mill until it ceased operating sometime in the early 1860s. [See John Hopkins, page 228.]

The Newton Gristmill operated for almost 100 years, commencing in 1802. The mill was on the eastern side of Cuthbert Road opposite Merrick Avenue. Although it was known throughout the area as the Newton Mill, over its existence it was also referred to by the name of its many proprietors. In 1860, John C. Hopkins was in charge of the Newton Mill. During this period, Joseph Webster was also working at the site.

Hiram Smith acquired the mill, dwelling and six acres of land from Hopkins in 1866. Soon thereafter, Smith and his family moved from Camden to Haddon Township. [See Hiram Smith, page 257.] In 1870, the mill processed 50 bushels of grain a day and operated throughout the entire year. In 1871, a Camden newspaper reported Newton Mill was "running steadily night and day." (WJP 7/12/1871) Smith's main product was flour, although he also ground rye and oats into livestock feed and corn into corn meal.

The source of power for Newton Mill was the Main Branch of Newton Creek. A dam about 500 feet from the mill created a pond. Sometimes dams were made from logs with planks secured over them. They built some dams from rocks laid dry or with mortar, or bolted with iron bars. Throughout the years, the pond took the name of the respective mill owners. Smith's millpond was about 1,000 feet in length and 200 feet wide. By the late 1880s, it was known as Cuthbert Lake. Although the millpond is no longer there, the creek still winds through the former pond basin.

Water flowed over the dam through a racegate, and entered a raceway. Water that did not enter the raceway traveled over the dam at the wastegate, where it contin-

Cuthbert Mill along Cuthbert Road in Haddon Township was also known as the Newton Mill. The mill commenced grinding grain in 1802 and continued to do so for some 100 years.

(Historical Society of Haddonfield Collections)

ued to flow downstream. Once water was channeled through the 500-foot raceway, the vertical drop to the Newton Mill waterwheel was fourteen feet. The force and weight of the water turned the waterwheel. The water then returned to the stream in a tail race.

An interesting piece of the mill's past took place sometime about 1848. Amos Taylor, owner of the mill, wanted to increase water in his millpond. To accomplish this, Taylor planned to pipe additional water from another stream, across a neighboring farm to his mill pond. The nearby unnamed stream flowed into the Main Branch of Newton Creek. Taylor's scheme required pipes or trunks to pass across a neighbor's land to get the water to the mill pond. His neighbor collected ten dollars a year rent and was permitted to let livestock drink from the trunk.

The four-foot wide wooden water wheel used at Newton Mill was an overshot wheel. The overshot wheel was the most efficient of the three types of vertical water wheels. It turned by the water falling on the paddles, or buckets, from above. The Newton Mill's water wheel was rated at ten horse power.

Despite its efficiency, overshot wooden water wheels were often out of balance when they turned. Exposure to the sun and water caused shrinking and swelling, resulting in loose parts and leaky buckets. In cold weather, ice formed on water wheels and inhibited their operation. In the second half of the nineteenth century, iron water wheels and turbines began replacing the old wooden water wheels.

A wooden gearing system took the power from the rotating water wheel and turned the millstones. Grain poured into a hopper and fell through a hole in the upper millstone. Flour was ground by a "run of stone," that is, a pair of millstones, both of which were furrowed, or grooved. The grooves of the stones cracked the outer husk of grain and the flat areas pulverized the husks and kernels into flour. The runner, or upper stone, had grooves cut on the bottom and the lower or bed-stone had patterns cut on the top. The grooves served as channels through which ground flour or meal escaped and provided a path for hot air created by friction during grinding to escape. Millstones required proper balancing; otherwise, the product could be ruined, stones damaged, or unnecessary friction could ignite a fire.

The last step in grinding grain occurred when the flour dropped from the millstones into a box and then traveled into a bolting chest, a device for separating the flour into different grades.

It was not uncommon for the mill operation to shut down during periods of extreme weather conditions. Water could not flow through the racegate when the millpond was frozen or when the pond's water level was too low during periods of dry weather:

> The milling business in all parts of South Jersey had been seriously interfered with by the drought. The water in the mill ponds has been so low the mills could not be run more than half the time. (WJP 8/7/1872)

Often, local mills were equipped with an alternative source of power. A boiler, fueled by coal or wood, produced steam used to run a small engine. Belts connected the engine with the mill gears. A steam engine rated at 45 horse power was available to run Newton Mill when needed.

The possibility of fire was foremost on the minds of gristmill proprietors. A danger during the grinding process was the volatile combination of flour dust and air. All that was needed was an overheated bearing or careless employee to ignite the explosive wheat dust. Hiram Smith had at least one close call:

> Last Wednesday evening a conflagration occurred in the Newton Mill belonging to Mr. Hiram Smith located near Haddonfield. The fire had its origin in the igniting of flour which was falling from the bolting apparatus, and the bolting cloths themselves were soon in a blaze. The flames were extinguished, however before any serious damage was done. (WJP 11/27/1872)

Farmers often delivered grain to the miller and the goods were returned as ground flour or feed. Millers usually agreed to keep a portion of the product as a fee for his services. New Jersey statutes allowed a miller to extract a "toll" of one-tenth part of a bushel out of every bushel of grain that he ground. In other instances, the miller and farmer settled their accounts by bartering. In 1873, Henry Cuthbert traded peppers, potatoes, apples and straw with Hiram Smith in return for flour and corn meal. [See Henry Cuthbert, page 254.]

Smith's customers were also outside the farm district of old Haddon Township. An article in the *West Jersey Press* suggested patronage of Newton Mill's products came from throughout Camden County:

> The flour manufacturer by Mr. Hiram Smith at his Newton Mill is deservedly popular with residents of Camden county throughout which Mr. Smith has a large patronage. The mills are running at their full capacity nearly all the time, and the proprietor has frequently to bring into requisition both the water and steam power with which it is provided. The sale of the Newton Mill's flour is greatly increased by the gentlemanly and accommodating

> driver he employs, Mr. Charles Clement, who is well known to almost every one in the county. (WJP 1/10/1872)

From newspaper accounts, Smith did not have the best of years in 1872. First a period of dry weather reduced the pond's water level, thereby decreasing the flow of water to the mill. Then a fire almost destroyed the facility, and at year's end, yet another setback:

> At the Chestnut Street crossing of the West Jersey Railroad yesterday morning, the uptrain from Cape May ran over a flour wagon belonging to Mr. Hiram Smith of the Newton Mill, totaling demolishing the vehicle and destroying about 600 hundred weight of flour. (WJP 12/25/1872)

Eventually, Hiram's delivery route grew to such an extent, he established a permanent presence in Camden. In 1874, Smith began selling "flour, meal or stuff..." at his new store:

> To my Patrons, Friends and others of the City of Camden: Hiram Smith in order to more promptly fulfill orders established an office and depot at Northwest corner of 5th and Benson Streets. (WJP 5/20/1874)

By 1880, Smith had disposed of his interest in Newton Mill and a new proprietor, Charles Vennell, was in charge. U.S. Census Bureau data on the region's manufacturing concerns reveals Vennell hired five employees to work in the mill.

In the 1890s, Joseph Schnitzius, a nearby farmer, managed the mill. The letterhead on Schnitzius' business stationary read "Manufacturer of and dealer in flour, feed and grain." The mill ceased operating sometime about 1906.

Glover Eastlack's mill, generally known as the Mount Ephraim Mill, was situated along the South Branch of Newton Creek at Haddon Lake in Audubon. [See Glover Eastlack, page 189.] The mill stood several hundred feet from King's Highway. The Mt. Ephraim Mill took its name from the nearby Centre Township village. Eastlack obtained the mill and an adjacent 26 acres of land in 1869.

It is likely that a mill in the area began operating sometime in the mid-eighteenth century. In years before Eastlack's proprietorship, the mill was familiar to local inhabitants by a name of former owners including Albertson's Gristmill and Hugg's Mill.

A dam next to Kings Highway created the millpond that backed up several hundred feet to the south and east of the road. Today, a stream still runs through the former pond site.

Flour was the predominant product; however, oats, corn and rye were also ground into feed for livestock. In comparison to the Newton Mill, the Mt. Ephraim Mill was a smaller operation. It had a capacity of 25 bushels of grain a day. The vertical fall of the water between the dam and the water wheel generated just 5 horsepower of energy, half the horsepower generated by the falling water at Newton Mill.

In the early 1870s, Julius Ochme and Joseph Richyards were living and working at the mill. It is likely these two men were the last millers as the gristmill ceased operating sometime in the mid-1870s.

The Haddonfield Mill, also known as Evans Mill, was along Cooper's Creek in Delaware Township (Cherry Hill). Even though the mill was physically outside the township, it was important to the residents of Haddonfield and the nearby vicinity. Before 1780, the mill was on the Haddonfield side of the creek. It is believed a gristmill stood on or near this site from as early as 1696. A dam built in 1779, formed the millpond known today as Evans Pond. The Evans family purchased the mill in the early 1800s. In 1854, after Josiah B. Evans inherited the mill from his father, the operation became known as Josiah B. Evans & Company.

While fire was always a concern for millers, another hazard was heavy rains or flooding. Josiah Evans lost his life because of a flood. In *The Early Grist and Flouring Mill of New Jersey*, the peril was illustrated:

> Josiah B. Evans, of Haddonfield, died in 1868 as a result of strains while struggling with the gates of the millpond during a heavy flood. Walter Wills Evans has described the flood warning system that was in use. The Evans mill, like others, was on a stream already dammed by mills higher up. The nearest, at Kirkwood, had a weak dam which often gave way during spring thaws and heavy rains. When the Kirkwood dam gave evidence of bursting someone hurried on horseback to the Evans mill and warned them promptly so that the floodgates could be opened. Many millers had to be alert in sudden storms and during flood times in order to avoid damage. (p. 85)

The dam at Evans Pond failed again in 1885 shortly after a cloudburst. The *Camden County Courier* reported "Evans Mill pond at Haddonfield burst on Monday morning owning to the heavy rain." (2/21/1885)

Following Evans's death in 1868, his son Joseph G. Evans inherited ownership of the mill. In that same year, William Myers leased the mill and took charge of its operation:

> Josiah Evans Flour Mill leased by Wm. R. Myers. Pays rent of $1,700 year and required three large teams to carry his wares to market. (WJP 1/22/1868)

> Wm. R. Myers proprietor of "The Haddonfield Mills" an experienced and skillful miller, boasts of his ability to

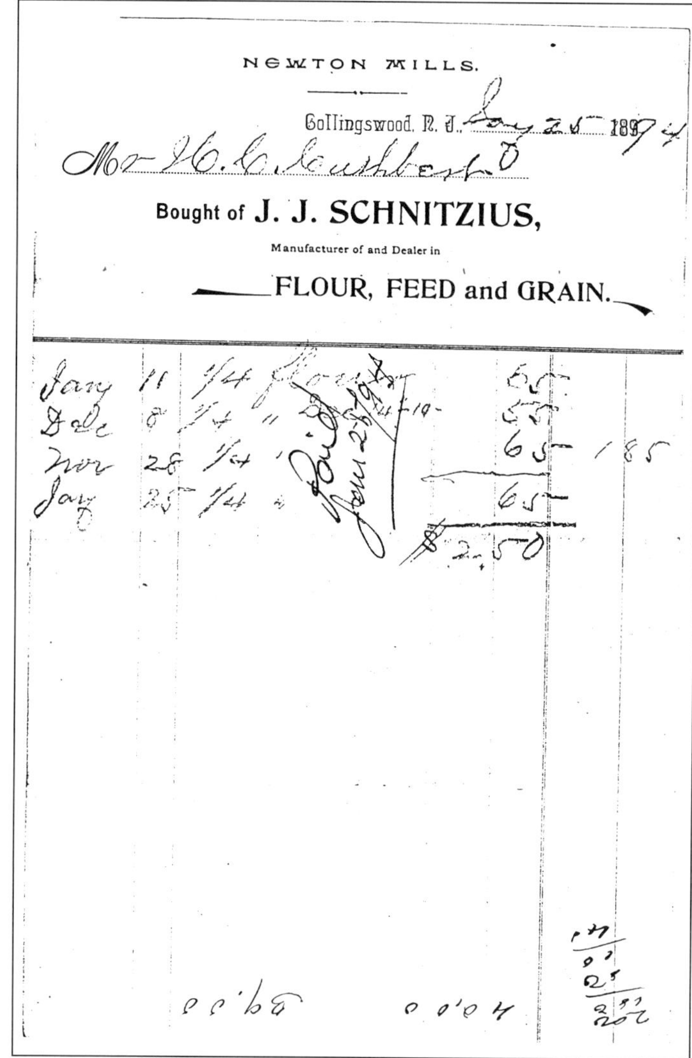

NEWTON MILLS.

Collingswood, N. J., ... 189

Bought of J. J. SCHNITZIUS,

Manufacturer of and Dealer in

FLOUR, FEED and GRAIN.

Invoice from Joseph. J. Schnitzius, the last proprietor of Newton Mill. The mill ceased operating about 1906.

(J. O. Cuthbert Manuscript Collection, Historical Society of Haddonfield)

> supply a genuine article of the "staff of life." (WJP 5/19/1869)

It is likely William Myers supplied flour to many residents in the Haddonfield area as well as patrons in Camden:

> Haddonfield Mill, Wm. R. Myers Proprietor Flour and Feed. Supplied in large and small quantities to parties of Camden. (WJP 5/26/1869)

Myers's tenure at the mill was brief. In 1870, at 26, he sold his assets. Joseph Evans resumed oversight of the mill after Myers vacated the business:

> At residence at Haddonfield Mills W.R. Myers. Stock and farming utensils…one light mill wagon. 150 bushels ground rye. (WJP 3/16/1870)

In 1870, the mill's two water wheels had the ability to grind 45 bushels of grain a day. The water descending from Evans Pond generated 25 horse power. Joseph modernized the mill in 1872, by installing a new turbine in place of the water wheel. Turbines were more efficient than the water wheel, providing more horsepower:

> J.G. Evans & Co. proprietor of the Haddonfield Flouring Mill have just placed a new turbine wheel in their mill, which gives them greatly increased facilities for accommodating the public. (WJP 8/7/1872)

By the 1880s, two turbines were in use. In 1882, they converted the old grist mill into a more efficient roller mill with a capacity of 75 barrels of flour a day. Just before the beginning of the twentieth century, Evans Mill ceased production.

Evans Grist Mill in Delaware Township. The mill used the water from Evans Pond to power its operation. Flour ground at the mill was sold throughout the region.

(Historical Society of Haddonfield Collections)

The local gristmills began as small operations, offering the rural inhabitants a time- and labor-saving service of grinding grain. The demand for flour increased as the population grew. By the turn of the twentieth century, newly developed sources of energy enabled larger sophisticated rolling mills to make flour with greater speed and efficiency. The local mills disappeared as more dependable manufacturing techniques became available to serve the growing urban population with an ever-increasing amount of flour.

Harnessmaker

The harnessmaker was called upon to supply bridles and harnesses for horses and mules. These articles were absolute necessities to anyone that relied on animals for transportation or to pull farm implements across the field for cultivation.

At least two harnessmakers worked in old Haddon Township during the 1870s. Isaac Vandergrift's shop was in the village of Haddonfield, while the other harnessmaker, Mr. Dieter, carried on his trade in Rowandtown.

For the most part, harnessmakers secured their raw materials from curriers. It would not be beyond sound reasoning to surmise Vandergrift purchased leather from James White, a tanner/currier on Tanner Street. [See tanner, page 145.] When purchasing material, an experienced harnessmaker identified good quality leather with the appropriate weight and strength for the kinds of harnesses designed to be made, and the particular parts for which they intended it. Heavier weight leather straps were used for harnesses that would be under greater tension.

After the proper weight was selected, workers cut and soaked the leather. Some harnesses were custom-made and the horses were measured for size and form so the straps would fit properly. When it was necessary to splice articles together, the harnessmaker used an awl to make holes for stitching. Needles and strong thread joined leather goods so the lines of the pattern and stitches were of uniform length. Some articles required hardware, such as buckles, that had to be fitted into the harness.

Depending on its intended use, there were dozens of types of harnesses that could be crafted by a harnessmaker. Several more common types included cart harness, mule harness, single harness, double road harness and team harness. Other leather products that harnessmakers frequently made were coach, wagon and riding bridles, halters, reins, straps, and collars.

Isaac Vandergrift began making leather goods for horses sometime before 1850. He was still in business some 30 years later at his shop on Main Street. His year-round operation employed several helpers. Most of the work was done by hand or with the aid of simple machinery such as a leather-press. In 1870, he purchased 50 tanned hides and turned them into single and sets of harnesses. George Vandergrift was a saddler in his father's shop.

Vandergrift's saddlery and harness shop also crafted items out of patent leather. Hides destined to become patent leather were tanned, dressed, varnished, dried and finished to a smooth glazed leather. In 1870, they used eighty square feet of patent leather at Vandergrift's shop. An important part of Vandergrift's business was repairing harnesses. Whether it was restitching, restoring a buckle, or splicing a strap, harnessmakers restored strength, form and pliability to a customer's leather goods.

Mr. Dieter, the township's other harnessmaker, worked in Rowandtown. The exact location of Dieter's shop is unknown, although it was probably close to one of the wheelwright or blacksmith shops along the Haddonfield Turnpike.

Manufacturer of Jewelry Cases

One of the more peculiar enterprises in old Haddon Township stood along the western side of Warwick Road where it intersects Mountwell Avenue. In 1880, Julius Smith was in charge of a company that manufactured jewelry cases. Demand for Smith's product in the township was not overwhelming. All his clients were in New York City.

In 1880, the business employed four male and two female workers and two children. The more experienced and skilled workers were paid $2.00 a day, semi-skilled laborers received a $1.25 a day. An 1882 publication, entitled *Industries of New Jersey*, showed Smith started making his product sometime about 1877:

> The building occupied is a neat two-story frame structure of forty-five feet square and is fitted with the best approved modern machinery, which is operated by a steam engine. Twelve experienced hands find constant employment in all the departments of the factory. Morocco and velvet cases and boxes of every shape and size are made and all the products of the factory are shipped to New York. (p. 382)

Watch and Clock Repairman

During the second half of the nineteenth century, pocket watches were popular and often prized family heirlooms. Passing a gold pocket watch on to a son or close relative was carefully attended to when planning for the division of one's assets at death. Provisions in wills for transferring gold or silver pocket watches to the next generation were common.

By the 1850s, the nation's clock factories were producing affordable clocks with interchangeable parts. Watches, on the other hand, were still handmade by watchmakers. This changed by the end of the Civil War, after which American watchmaking became industrialized and watches, too, were being made in factories. Although watches were being produced en masse by the late nineteenth century, they were still expensive. In the 1870s, broken watches and clocks were not discarded as many low cost timepieces are today. A good timepiece was worthy of repair.

In 1870, William Cowrd repaired watches and clocks during six months of the year from his Haddonfield home. In an era before digital watches and battery-powered timepieces and electric clocks, the movement in a watch or clock had to be kept immaculate to function properly. Nineteenth century watch repairmen like Cowrd often used small brushes to clean the movements. They also used interchangeable parts and small watchmaking tools to repair timepieces.

Pottery Works

The first pottery works in Haddonfield began making earthenware vessels in 1805. Eleven years later, in 1816, Richard Snowden, Sr. took over the concern and his family operated the pottery works for the next 65 years. Snowden's pottery works was at 50 Potter Street. Richard, Sr. passed away in 1868, after which his son, Richard, Jr., assumed control of the family business.

During the Snowden tenure at the pottery works, common household earthenware vessels such as bowls, jugs, dishes, jars and pitchers were manufactured. In 1860, 40 tons of clay were molded into 30,000 vessels by Snowden and his workers. The proprietors also crafted stoneware. A slight difference existed between the two types of pottery. Earthenware vessels had a rougher surface whereas stoneware, because they heated it at higher temperatures, had a glassy texture and appearance. Earthenware was red from the iron in the clay.

The process of manufacturing earthenware vessels included throwing, turning, pressing, burning, painting, pointing and glazing. Snowden's process relied on horse power to grind clay. The horse was attached to a barrel-shaped apparatus called a pug mill. The shaft of the pug mill turned as the horse circled the machinery. Attached to the shaft were short extending blades that rotated while water and dry clay were consolidated into a smooth elastic mix. Sand was added to the clay mix to ensure the pottery did not crack and to provide texture and strength.

Once properly mixed, the clay was placed on a lathe and turned into the shape of the desired vessels. Sarah Crawford Hillman described the shaping process of Snowden's pottery in her work, entitled *Historical Sketch of Potter Street in Haddonfield, New Jersey*:

> Many recall the lathe which was a machine consisting of a framework, bearing an adjustable center, between which a

The Snowden Pottery in Haddonfield. The former pottery building is now 50 Potter Street. The pottery commenced making earthenware goods in 1805 and continued for about 100 years.
(Haddonfield Library Collections)

cutting tool is thrust against the work, shaping or turning it down, usually to some circular form. (p. 4)

The molded clay vessels were placed in kilns and baked into finished products. The temperature in a kiln usually exceeded 1,000 degrees Fahrenheit. When making stoneware, the temperature in the kilns was several hundred degrees higher than what was normally required to burn earthenware. In 1860, Snowden consumed about 30 cords of wood to keep the kilns fired.

When Richard Snowden, Jr. died in 1883, an inventory of his property revealed the value of his earthenware stock was $850. Raw materials at the pottery included twelve loads of clay worth twelve dollars and eight cords of wood appraised at $40. (Inv. G-288)

Following Snowden's death, the pottery works continued to operate under the direction of an employee. Toward the end of the nineteenth century, they sold the many products made at the pottery works in John Wanamaker's department store in Philadelphia. Stoneware products then included butter pots, jars, jugs, pitchers, water coolers, and vases. The red earthenware articles made at the Haddonfield pottery were bean pots, pie plates, hanging plants, flower pots, garden vases and stove-pipe collars. In 1904, the business moved to another location in Haddonfield and continued in its endeavor well into the twentieth century.

Paint Works

In 1880, two paint manufacturers operated in old Haddon Township. Before John Willits opened his own paint works in Haddonfield, he was a founding partner of the Crystal Lake Paint Works. His partner, James Flinn, had been employed at John Lucas's Paint Works in Gibbsboro for some eighteen years prior to formation of the partnership. The union of the two entrepreneurs was a natural fit: Willits possessed skills in marketing and sales, while James Flinn's expertise was in paint manufacturing. The partnership formed in 1874 after Flinn and Willits paid $5,000 to John Stoy for some six acres of land. The paint works' tract sat across the street from Crystal Lake along Stoy's Mill Road, now Crystal Lake Avenue. For over a half-century a sawmill had existed on the same lot. [See sawmill, page 143.]

The partners hired a carpenter from Haddonfield to construct a two-story 28' x 65' frame building. Upon completion of the main factory building in 1875, they installed the necessary machinery and the company proceeded to produce paint. To be closer to his work, Flinn moved his family into a house next to the factory. [See James Flinn, page 252.]

The paint works, also called the Westmont Paint Works, manufactured dry and ready-mixed lead and zinc color paints and varnish. Even before they made the first gallon of paint at Crystal Lake Paint Works, the partnership was dedicated to manufacturing a specialty color, green. Flinn developed a formula for green paint that he believed was the best money could buy. An announcement that appeared in the newspaper noted, "Messr. Flinn and Willits will make the manufacturer of green a speciality, and claim that their green is best in the U.S." (WJP 11/1/1874) Future newspaper advertisements were no less bold. "The standard green has great body and fineness of texture, durability of color, brilliancy, beauty and tint." (WJP 7/7/1875) Besides green paint, other colors were mixed at the Rowandtown site.

John Willits's tenure in the business did not last long. A year after the works began making paint, Willits, apparently for reasons of ill health, transferred his partnership interest to Flinn. In return, James assumed Willits's share of the balance on the outstanding mortgage of the plant.

By 1880, Flinn had invested some $50,000 into the company. He employed seven helpers at the Crystal Lake Paint Works. Flinn paid his skilled mechanics $1.50 a day, while ordinary laborers earned a dollar during their workday.

The Rowandtown site was chosen because of its proximity to water. On the opposite side of Stoy's Mill Road was Crystal Lake, a source of power for the paint work's machinery. The vertical drop from the lake to the creek below was sixteen feet. When the paint works was in operation, water entered through the dam and into two turbines measuring two feet in diameter. The turbines revolved 100 times a minute turning gears, shafts and belts connected to grinding and mixing machines. A twenty horsepower steam engine was also used to run the machinery.

In the nineteenth century, workers made paint in several steps. A base of linseed oil, white lead, zinc oxide and silicate of magnesia, was prepared in a large drum with the help of large mixing blades. A color-tinted pigment, previously mixed, was added to the base along with thinners. The mixture was stirred until a uniform consistency was attained. They stored the completed product in tanks, until placed in tin cans, which were they then labeled, packed and shipped.

Several buildings at Flinn's paint works had large smoke stacks. These stacks carried off the smoke and fumes generated from varnish ovens. Manufacturing varnish began by cooking gum from natural plant products, such as rosin and copal in large kettles with linseed oil and spirits of turpentine or alcohol. After the product was cooked, the varnish was cooled, thinned and filtered before being canned or combined with ready-mixed paints.

The paint work's buildings and the towering smoke stacks were in stark contrast to an otherwise small cluster of homes and diminutive shops in the village of

Varnish oven building at James Flinn Paint Works in Westmont. The business, located at Crystal Lake Avenue and Crystal Lake, manufactured paint and varnish. The business moved to Camden in the early 1900s.

("Notes on W.S. Clement Paint Company," Camden County Historical Society)

Willits & Bacon Paint Works along Tanner Street in Haddonfield. The paint works manufactured colored paints and varnish. (*Daily Graphic*: New York, September 9, 1879)

Rowandtown. The *Haddonfield Basket* depicted Flinn's plant as "quite a conspicuous appearance from the [Camden & Atlantic] railroad. (HB 5/1875)

Although the railroad right-of-way bisected Flinn's lot, he made the most from the situation. He placed a large billboard next to the tracks, visible to the thousands of passengers that rode past the paint works. In 1880, the *West Jersey Press* reported Flinn's sign had been repainted and "now presents a fine appearance to the passersby on the Old Reliable Railroad." (WJP 4/20/1880)

In 1878, Flinn set up in a store at 124 North Fourth Street in Philadelphia to sell his products. Misfortune occurred several months later when fire destroyed the store and its contents. They reported the damage to be $15,000. (WJP 3/27/1878) Flinn reacted quickly to the setback. Within several weeks, he reopened a new store a block away at 127 North Third Street.

The liquid waste from the paint manufacturing process was most likely dumped into the creek. The byproducts from lead and zinc paint were, at a minimum, annoying to Isaac Prine, an ice farmer downstream from the paint works. The quality of Prine's ice, taken less than a mile from Flinn's plant, eventually caused Prine to seek a new location for harvesting ice. [See ice farm, page 163.]

James Flinn's sons worked alongside their father and eventually inherited the business. In 1904, W.S. Clement obtained the James Flinn Paint and Varnish Company from the Flinn family. Clement continued making paint in Westmont for several more years, then moved the concern to Van Hook Street in Camden where it still operates today.

By 1877, Flinn's former partner, John Gill Willits, had regained his health and opened the Haddonfield Paint Works next to Samuel A. Willits's lumber yard on Tanner Street, near today's Euclid Avenue. The Haddonfield Paint Works manufactured lead and zinc colored paint and varnish. Willits shared the duties of his new concern with a Mr. Brown. Unlike Flinn's Rowandtown plant, the Haddonfield works did not have water to power its machinery. They ground and mixed paint with the aid of a fifteen horsepower steam engine.

The pace of residential home building in Haddonfield had picked up during the 1870s. One could assume that Willits, with an expertise in marketing and selling, recognized a chance to profit from selling his paints in the village. In addition to the local market, the firm sold its output in Philadelphia. The Willits Safety Oil Company, 111 North Fourth Street, was the primary outlet for the paint products manufactured in Haddonfield.

Willits's labeled some of his paint products with a parochial identity:

> White Lead Color and Varnish Work Manufacturer of "Cottage" Ready-Mixed Paints, Haddon French Green, Haddon Iron Brown, Golden Shield Prime Lead. (WJP 4/9/1879)

> Some specialties in their manufacture in the color line have acquired a high reputation in the market such as "Haddon Iron Brown" the "Golden Shield" and "Old

King" white lead. The latter by their peculiar process will not chalk crack nor peel off like lead. . . . (*The Daily Graphic*, 9/9/1879)

It is likely the firm's sales were promising for the first few years. In 1880, a new addition, measuring 23' x 27', was built onto the Haddonfield paint shop. The owners invested a considerable sum of capital into the business. By 1880, $50,000 had been invested. In the mid-1880s, the company was sold to A.W. Wright. The new owner continued to manufacture paint at the site.

Sawmill

From the time when European emigrants first settled in America, a great demand for wood existed. Wood was the raw material used in building houses, tools, bridges, furniture, wagons and boats. Fortunately, this country was rich with this natural resource. Local sawmills, similar to John Stoy's, operated throughout the county fulfilling the demand for lumber.

Stoy's sawmill was well-known throughout old Haddon Township. It came into existence in the early 1800s. The mill was on the western side of Crystal Lake Avenue, along the northern bank of the stream that formed the Main Branch of Newton Creek. John Stoy inherited the sawmill from his father, James. The Stoy family owned farmland along Stoy's Mill Road. John Stoy's family once lived in a dwelling that stands today at 330 Westmont Avenue. [See John Stoy, page 251.]

At one time, up and down sawmills were in use to cut most of the wood. This type of waterpowered sawmill derived its name from the motion of the saw blade. The up and down sawmills were eventually replaced by the more efficient circular sawmills sometime around the 1840s. During John Stoy's years as proprietor of the township's only sawmill, he used circular saw blades.

Waterpower for the sawmill came from a pond known as Crystal Lake. Part of the old millpond still exists near where today's Haddon Township swimming pool and recreational area are situated.

Sawmills relied on a water wheel to harness waterpower. When the saw blade was engaged, it was powered by a series of gears, wheels and belts connected to the water wheel. A drawback of the wooden water wheel was it required frequent repairs due to weathering. As time advanced, more durable and efficient metal turbines gradually replaced the old wooden water wheels.

John Stoy's records show the sawmill operated part-time. Stoy's principal occupation was farming and his records reveal the mill was dormant during the harvest period of June to September. Even during the peak periods, sawing was not done on a steady basis.

Some more common types of wood cut at the mill were hickory, walnut, pine, locust, popular, chestnut, oak, and apple. During the early 1860s, Joseph Cuthbert, obtained 30 locust posts from Stoy for 8 cents apiece. Another local farmer, Isaac Hinchman, hired Stoy to cut boards. John Dialogue purchased posts and planks at the mill. Other wood products cut at the mill included lumber for framing houses, fencing, shelving for farmers' wagons and tile boards.

In 1864, Stoy leased his mill to Isaac Prine. During the next six years, Prine was in charge of the mill and responsible for its upkeep. [See Isaac Prine, page 257.]

During his tenure, Prine used various size saw blades to cut lumber. The largest circular saw blade employed was 32 inches in diameter, the smallest was 8 inches across. An advertisement in the *West Jersey Press* revealed the types of tools and equipment employed by Prine:

> ...two large benches suitable for sawing cord wood, crosscut saw, one dozen circular saws...one six inch belt seventy-two feet long, a lot of small belts, log wagon, cant hook, hand saws, augers, chisels, planes, axes, hammer, files, and work bench with vice and wedges. (WJP 4/6/1870)

In 1870, an inventory of wood at the mill included boards cut for a wheelwright. It is likely that Prine cut the wood for one of Rowandtown's wheelwrights to erect wagons and carts.

In 1870, Isaac sold his tools, machinery and stock at the sawmill and pursued other commercial ventures like ice farming and cidermaking. [See ice farming, page 163, cidermaking, page 132.] John Stoy resumed oversight of the saw mill, even though work was sporadic. One of Stoy's new vendors was the Willits Lumber Yard in Haddonfield. In April 1872, the last of the lumber rolled through the mill. Several months later, Stoy sold the sawmill and some six acres to James Flinn and John Willits, two entrepreneurs in the paint manufacturing business. [See paint works, page 140.]

Shoemakers

Much like today, boots and shoes were articles of high utility in past centuries. The village of Haddonfield had over a half dozen shoemaker shops in 1870 where they assembled footwear.

During the nineteenth century, boots were a popular footwear for men and boys. Farmers and laborers often wore heavy-soled shoes. A popular footwear for women and girls were gaiters. The ankle-high shoes were fastened with lacings or buttons up the side.

The process of making shoes and boots started with securing the appropriate leather and trimmings. It is probable that some township shoemakers secured their raw materials from James White, a tanner/currier in Haddonfield. [See tanner, page 145.] The thickest of leather, made from the hides of cattle and horses, was used for shoe soles. The thinner hides taken from calves, goat or sheep, called upper leather, were used for the upper part of shoes.

Shoemakers first cut the leather to fit a style and size. Leather was fitted around hand carved foot molds called lasts corresponding to different size feet. During this era, there were no half sizes and widths were simply slim and wide. Sometimes, there was no distinction between a left and right shoe. Shoes and boots were shaped and assembled on work benches with tools of the trade including knives, awls, pincers and hammers. Some shops added rudimentary automation to an otherwise manual process. Most shoemakers in the township worked with boot turner and crimping machines. They stitched the parts of the upper shoe together, trimmed, tacked and sewed to the bottom of the sole leather. After a heel was added, the shoe was trimmed and polished.

The busiest shoemaker in the township was Daniel Garret. For many years, Garrett's cobbler shop stood near 247 Kings Highway East. Garrett, along with several helpers, made 624 pairs of men's and women's shoes in 1870.

While Garret may have been the most active shoemaker in Haddonfield, other shoe tradesmen earned a living in the village during the 1870s. Thomas Harrison and his son Thomas, Jr. operated a shoe repair shop in Haddonfield. In that same year, another Haddonfield shoemaker, Peter Hudon, made 54 pairs of men's shoes and 12 pairs of women's shoes. In 1870, Ralph Borton and his son Benjamin ran a footwear shop in the village. In addition to making shoes for men and women, Borton's business was heavily dependent on steady repair work.

Simeon Bond's shop employed 52 hides of sole and upper leather to craft shoes and boots in 1870. Bond's "Old Established Boot and Shoe Store" was at the corner of Tanner and Main Street. (HB 1/1875) Bond's advertisement appeared in the *Haddonfield Basket*:

> A general assortment of men's, women's, boy's, and Misses' Boots and Shoes. Measured work made to order. Repairing done in a neat and substantial manner. (HB 1/1875)

Another boot and shoe concern was owned by Elmer Clement and Joseph Clement. In 1876, Elmer transferred his interest in the business to his partner and went on to become a Realtor and insurance agent:

> Owning to the multiplicity of duties connected with his office and real estate agency, Squire R.E. Clement retires from the firm Jos. S. & R.E. Clement, and has disposed of interest to Joseph S., who will continue the boot and shoe business at the old stand on Main street, where he keeps a variety of goods suitable for men, women and children, including India rubber wear, at the lowest cash price. (WJP 10/18/1876)

At least one shoemaker in the township practiced his trade outside Haddonfield. The exact location of Thomas McMannus's shop is not known, although it was likely in Rowandtown. McMannus and a helper specialized in assembling women's shoes. In 1870, the two shoemakers assembled 218 pairs of ladies' footwear. During the early 1860s, Charles and Samuel Clement made boots and shoes from a shop in the village of Rowandtown.

The role of village shoemaker slowly changed following the Civil War. The shoemaker's handcrafted products could no longer compete with the less expensive machine-crafted factory shoes. Many shoe craftsmen were squeezed out of business. Other shoemakers became merchants, purchasing ready-made shoes to sell in their shops while continuing to do custom shoemaking and repairs.

Tailor, Dressmaker and Milliner

Generally, men in rural areas dressed in plain clothing. Pants, shirts and jackets were made of heavy fabrics like cotton, canvas or denim. Loose-fitting vests were popular for work or dress and pants were held up with suspenders. Businessmen and professionals usually wore suits. Suit-pants had baggy tube legs and coats had broad shoulders and wide sleeves.

Several larger Philadelphia department stores, including Strawbridge & Clothier and Wanamaker Brothers, reached out to rural shoppers. The *Haddonfield Basket* ran apparel advertisements for the center city stores. Many township citizens routinely journeyed to Philadelphia and purchased apparel, although not all residents were persuaded to shop in the city. Some chose to buy their clothing in Camden, while others shopped in Haddonfield.

Nineteenth century tailors specialized in making custom-fit mens pants, vests and coats. A tailor's task began with measuring and fitting a customer, then they cut the selected cloth to conform with the measurements. Before sewing machines came into general use, all clothing was stitched by hand. By the 1860s, local tailors and their apprentices were using sewing machines powered by foot treadles. Once completed, the garment was pressed to give the product a neat appearance.

Haddonfield had several tailor shops in 1870. Charles Lippincott's shop cut 1,700 yards of cloth to make 200 pairs of pants, 200 vests and 100 coats. The average price charged by Lippincott was ten dollars for a coat, three dollars for a vest and five dollars for a pair of pants. Muslin, a fine thin cotton cloth, was frequently used in Lippincott's suits. In that same year, Joseph Wilson's men's shop produced 100 coats, 300 pants and 300 vests.

Making men's clothing was just one of several types of employment where females worked side by side with their male counterparts. In the cities, female factory workers assembled most of the ready-made clothing. In Haddonfield, women were likewise employed by tailors to make custom-fit clothing. The U.S. Census Bureau's 1860 statistics reveal tailors and shoemakers were the two trades that frequently employed women in old Haddon Township. Equal pay between the sexes was nonexistent. Charles Lippincott's female helper earned an average of $15 a month. Male apprentices were paid $30. It is unclear whether the disparity in wages was partially or wholly attributable to the number of hours worked or the type of duties performed. Rennels Fowler's tailor shop employed three females and two male helpers. Rennels Flower shared the same building with Charles Lippincott.

Women around the countryside generally wore plain floor-length dresses made of calico, gingham or linsey woolsey. Women's formal attire would typically be a hooped skirt trimmed with fringe, lace, braid or ribbon. Dainty boots or shoes were often hidden by wide spread long skirts.

One common aspect of the local dressmaking profession in the early 1880s was the proprietors were all women. Unfortunately, government census takers did not accumulate information or statistics about local dressmakers. An 1882 Haddonfield directory listed Annie Fry, Latitia Gibbs, Sarah Mayers, Elizabeth Van Culin and Harriet Tule as Haddonfield dressmakers.

Before the development of the sewing-machine in the 1840s, every stitch in every article of clothing made, every sheet, or quilt, was sewn by hand. By the 1870s, widespread use of machines had a dramatic affect on dressmaking in America. Besides reducing the time and drudgery of making garments, styles and fashions, too, changed with prevalent use of sewing-machines. Trimmings and drapery were used to shape dresses in the 1870s. Machines allowed dressmakers to use "flounces, frills, pleating, and ruching" when fashioning apparels. (*Costume in Detail*, p. 228)

Even though there was no shortage of tailors and dressmakers in Haddonfield, women frequently made their own clothing and sewed garments for other members of the household. Needles, buttons, thread and fabric were available at the millinery or general stores.

It is unclear whether Miss Edwards's millinery shop in Haddonfield sold hats, notions, or both. A milliner made, trimmed, repaired or sold bonnets and hats for ladies and children. However, the nineteenth century Haddonfield millinery may have also specialized in the sale of ribbon, laces and notions.

Tanner and Currier

In 1828, Samuel Allen became proprietor of a tannery in Haddonfield. His tannery was on a six-acre tract of land between what is now 30 and 74 Tanner Street. He ran the business until James White took over sometime before the Civil War. Allen kept his interest in the tanyard real estate.

A tanner made leather from the hides and skins of animals. There was a distinction between the two kinds of leather products. Hides were taken from large animals such as cattle and horses, while skins were taken from smaller animals like calves, goats and sheep.

A tanner often procured his hides and skins from nearby farmers and butchers. For instance, Samuel Wood, a township farmer, sold lamb and sheep skins to White. In 1870, White obtained about 200 hides and the same number of skins and converted them into leather products. He employed one helper during the six-month period that the tannery operated. A decade earlier, the tannery converted some 1,000 hides and skins into leather goods.

The process of changing hides and skin into leather varied depending on the nature of the leather and the uses to which they applied it. They often made hides into shoe sole leather and coverings for carriages. Generally, thick hides were converted by a process that employed soaking and removing the hair before they bathed them in a solution containing tannin. The process of transforming hides into leather could take many months.

One of the more popular sources of tannin was oak bark. Oak had an advantage over other tannin substitutes such as spruce, hemlock and chestnut because oak was cheap and had better tanning qualities that made the leather tougher and more pliable. White consumed 50 cords of oak to secure enough bark necessary for his operation in 1870. White hooked up a horse to a small apparatus called a bark mill that ground the bark. Afterwards, they mixed the bark with water to form what was called ooze. The hides and skins were laid between layers of ooze and allowed to set, so the change to leather could take place.

Skins were often made into light or thin leather, much of which was used in making harnesses. The process of tanning skins was different in detail than making hides. Processing skins, however, did not require as much time and effort.

A small creek, known as Hopkins Mill Branch, ran across White's tannery and continued onto Hopkins Pond. Waste was dumped during the tanning process into the run and floated downstream into the pond. The refuse flowing down stream from the site was likely a source of a pungent odor.

Carrie Nicholson Hartel, a local historian, wrote *The Tanyard and Its Owners*, published by the Historical Society of Haddonfield. In her work, she devoted a portion to the era of James White's proprietorship. Hartel's source of information was from a longtime Haddonfield resident, J. Lewis Rowand.

According to Rowand, the first steps in White's tanning process was to place hides in a pit by the creek and cover them with lime until the hair, surplus flesh and fat were loosened. Next,

> A man wearing a leather apron that covered him from neck to feet would lift, with heavy iron hooks, a hide from the pit and place it on a rounded wooded block, two or three feet long, probably a piece of buttonwood tree split in half. Then sitting on the ground he scraped, with an instrument like a carpenter's draw knife, all this hair and lime and flesh from the skin. It was a messy smelly job.
>
> After this process the hides were ready to be tanned. But first the tan bark had to be ground.
>
> As there is not hemlock near here, it was, no doubt, oak bark that was used, cut in the spring when the sap is beginning to run. It was brought in big wagons and unloaded at the barn which stood along the street. A bark mill, like a huge coffee mill, ground the bark after it was broken into small pieces, by being held against the rim of the iron bowl of the mill and hit with a wooded mallet. A rod went up from the center of this bowl and an arm extended from that to which was hitched a horse who walked around the mill.
>
> The vats, in rows, were at the side of the house, near where Wilkins Avenue is now. They were six feet deep and a little longer than a hide, lined with heavy planks, and one end partitioned off in such a manner as to allow the water to filter through into the small compartment, which held a pump. A hide was put in a vat and covered with tan-bark, another hide and more bark until the vat was full, and then water from the well was pumped into it. The vats were connected by troughs; when the water in the last vat became dark it was pumped out into the ditch and water from the next vat was pumped in and so on until the first vat was reached, then that was filled up with fresh water. When all the tanning qualities were out of the bark the vats were cleaned out and fresh bark put in.
>
> Along the street was a worm fence, the hides were hung on that to dry, and in the workshop were marble tables on which they were finished. . . . (*A Tanyard and Its Owners*, p. 13)

Once hides and skins were converted into leather, a currier dressed the leather. As was the case with James White, the duties of a tanner and currier were often done by the same individual.

A currier's mode of dressing the different kinds of leather varied. Dressing involved soaking, shaving, scouring and scraping the leather. White made firm, hard leather for shoe soles. Another product, known as upper leather, was produced by White and sold to harnessmakers. Upper leather was made to be pliable and tough.

A currier applied tanners' oil to one side of the skin and the other side was blacked with lampblack and tanner's oil. White dressed his leather on a marble table in his workshop. He consumed or used 200 gallons of tanner's oil in 1870. In that same year, White's finished leather goods brought in more than $3,500.

By 1875, White's tannery was idle. Several years later, they tore down what remained of the old tannery:

> The old tanyard property at Haddonfield has fallen by will into possession of A.W. Clement, who is making improvements. The building, with the exception of the dwelling are being torn away and the premises put in order generally. (WJP 10/29/1879)

Tinsmith

The tinsmith probably made more articles used in daily life than any other craftsman. Tin was used in the manufacture of a great variety of nineteenth century household items and farm devices. In the household, tinware was used mainly in the kitchen. Utensils and cooking-ware were generally made of tinplate and tin lanterns were a common nineteenth century device. Because tin was inexpensive, malleable and light, it was ideal for making toys. Tinsmiths made children's buckets, teapots, utensils, boxes and doll house furniture out of tinplate.

A tinsmith's raw material was tinplate, commonly called tin. Tinplate was a combination of tin and iron. They coated sheets of iron at the foundry with tin producing the final product. Iron gave the material its strength. For the most part, American tinsmiths worked with tinplate imported from England during the 1800s.

In 1860, Daniel Wright made some 1,000 pieces of tinware. Several journeymen worked alongside Wright at the shop. During the 1870s, Wright moved his tin shop onto Main Street in an area opposite Tanner Street. Wright sold his tin pieces at an unidentified "5 cent store" in 1880. (WJP 4/28/1880) The same newspaper divulged that Wright contemplated opening his own "five cent counter in connection with his tin shop." (WJP 4/28/1880)

The hand tools used by tinsmith Daniel Wright were the same kinds of tools used by tinsmiths in centuries past: wooden mallets, tin shears or snips, various size chisels, crimpers, rollers, seamers, and a soldering iron. Working on a wooden bench, tinsmiths used a charcoal brazier to heat the soldering iron and melt the solder to join the pieces of metal. Craftsman cut objects from handmade patterns and often decorated articles with designs punched and pierced into the metal. Some tinware pieces were painted.

One of Wright's tin products aided farmers. Wright assembled a device that permitted guano, a fertilizer produced from bird droppings, to fall to the ground without being blown about by the wind:

> D.D. Wright the tinman, makes a contrivance for the purpose of putting guano, phosphate etc., by hand for corn etc., when the wind blows, without scattering. It will have its value in "backache" on a windy day. (WJP 4/14/1880)

Wood- and coal-burning stoves were displayed and sold at Wright's shop. It was common for nineteenth century tinsmiths to sell and install stoves. Cooking and heating stoves were becoming standard household appliances at this time. In 1868, the township hired Wright to install a stovepipe in Town Hall. He received $4.70 for his effort.

A significant portion of Wright's earnings came from another business–roofing. Wright advertised in the *Haddonfield Basket* "Tin and Sheet Iron Worker–All Kinds of Metallic Roofing." (HB 8/1874) Tin roofs were made of tin and lead coated iron sheets. Tin roofs were popular because they were durable, weatherproof, lightweight, maintenance-free and easily installed. [See roofers, page 152.]

Weaver Shop

Clayton Brown, a master weaver, worked out of his weaving shop next to his dwelling on Hopkins Mill Road. Today, Brown's home still stands at 419 Maple Avenue in Haddon Township. [See Clayton Brown, page 258.]

Carpeting became a common household item in the second-half of the nineteenth century. Brown's expertise was in making rag rugs. This type of carpeting was made from worn-out garments, bedding and household furnishings that were no longer large or strong enough to be used for any other purpose. The rags were stitched together and converted into long strips. The strips were given new strength by weaving them into a practical, durable floor covering. Besides being affordable, rag rugs added warmth to the room and were easy to clean.

Rag rugs were predominately woven on hand-operated looms. The size of Brown's two hand-operated carpet looms is not known, although most handmade rag carpets were 39 inches wide. Weavers made larger rugs on looms that could weave single piece carpets nine, twelve and fifteen foot wide. In 1850, U.S. Census Bureau data showed Clayton employed help in producing 6,000 yards of woven carpeting.

The knowledge needed to make rag rugs was not overly complicated. One could learn to use a hand-operated loom and weave rag carpets in a week or less. That is not to say that fancy patterns and color combinations were easily achieved in weaving rag carpets. Colors and patterns were limited only by one's imagination. A rug could be constructed from random multicolored rags used in the weft (the cross-threads in the loom) to sophisticated plaids, carefully planned with color warp (the lengthwise threads in a loom).

The township's only carpet factory ceased fabricating carpets sometime in 1869, after Clayton Brown passed away. The executors of Brown's estate placed an announcement in the *West Jersey Press*, notifying customers to claim their carpet. At the time of his death, Brown had about 300 yards of rag carpeting on hand:

> There is a number of rolls of new rag carpet on hand belonging to different persons, some of which has remained for two years. All such persons are hereby notified to call and pay for the weaving of said carpet and take the same away before the day of sale, or it will be sold to pay expenses. (WJP 8/25/1869)

Soon thereafter, the executors of Brown's estate sold the weaver shop looms and other assets.

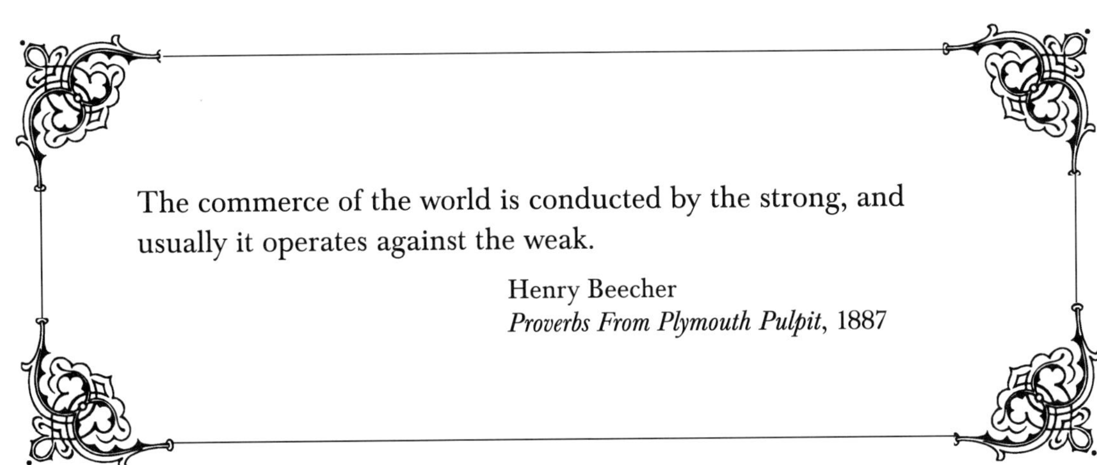

The commerce of the world is conducted by the strong, and usually it operates against the weak.

Henry Beecher
Proverbs From Plymouth Pulpit, 1887

10

Tradesmen, Storekeepers, Professions and Other Workers

Introduction

In the late 1700s, the village of Haddonfield became the center of commerce in the region. During the two decades following the Civil War, residential development and population growth created new commercial opportunities within the village. The number and variety of stores, shops, businesses and professional workers continued to grow as the nineteenth century drew to a close. To this day, Haddonfield remains a prosperous borough with its thriving commercial district along Kings Highway. This tree-lined highway of commerce, with its brick edifices, has endured, perpetuating the ambiance of the former country village.

Aside from several gristmills, blacksmith and wheelwright shops in the township, only a few stores and proprietors of non-farm businesses operated outside Haddonfield. What follows is a representative cross-section of merchants, proprietors and professionals, and their contributions to the community during the 1870s.

It is not the intention of the writer to identify or portray every shopkeeper or businessman who worked within the township during the era. There are a number of trades and professions that are not part of this study.

General Stores and Hardware Stores

The half dozen or so general stores in the township were an integral part of the local agrarian economy. Farmers and village inhabitants relied on general stores for their groceries, drygoods, tools, kitchen utensil, sewing notions and hardware. Likewise, the proprietors were dependent on the rural inhabitants for their patronage and as a source to acquire foodstuffs for resale.

The inside of a typical small village general store was crowded with goods hanging from the walls and ceiling. In some stores, long counters separated customers from the walls, shelves and drawers loaded with merchandise. Working behind a counter, storekeepers and clerks waited on customers. Because some articles arrived in bulk, it was not unusual to have barrels, kegs or bins situated throughout in the store. Clerks weighed products on scales while the customer looked on. Some stores, like Alfred Clement's general store in Haddonfield, delivered merchandise to patrons by wagon.

Alfred W. Clement learned retailing at his father's Haddonfield store. In 1859, Alfred opened his own general store at the corner of Ellis and Main Streets, now 200 Kings Highway East. Fifteen years later, Alfred admitted one of his clerks, Theodore Giffin, as a partner. The store, Clement & Giffin, prospered during the 1870s, employing over a half dozen clerks to wait on customers and ship goods. During this period, having outgrown their one-story building, Clement & Giffin added two floors to the building. The third floor, called Clement Hall, was used for public lectures, concerts and

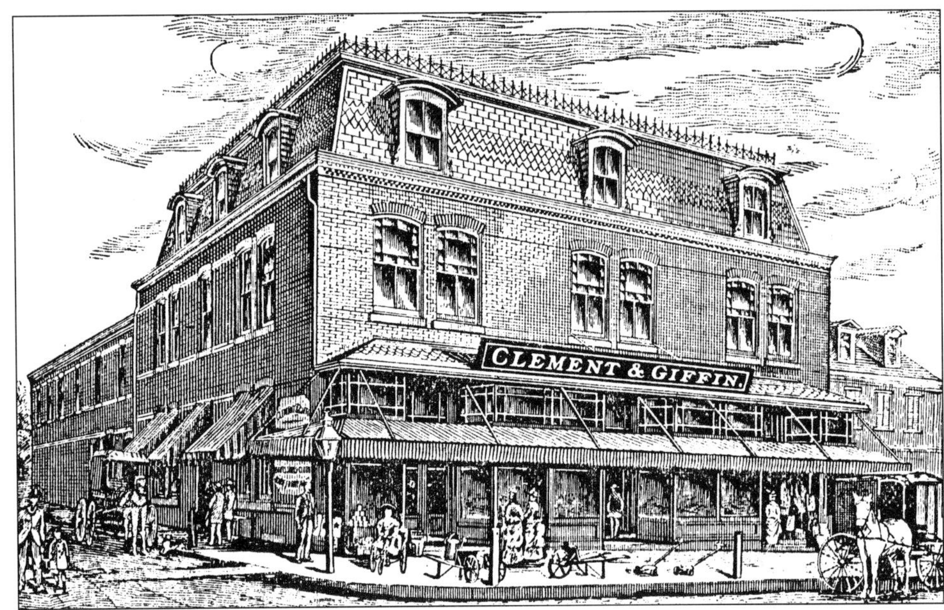

Clement & Giffin general store in Haddonfield. Built in the mid-1880s on the west side of Ellis Street at Kings Highway, the new building replaced the old general store located on the opposite side of Ellis Street.

(*Historical and Industrial View of Camden, New Jersey*, Commercial Publishing Co., NY. 1890)

meetings. Some years later, the general store moved to a new location across the street.

The Clement & Giffin general store sold many types of items including drygoods, groceries, boots and shoes, crockery, glass, tin, hardware and notions. The store owners were also agents for several large dealers of agricultural implements. The annual sales at the store was about $55,000 in the early 1880s.

Long before neon signs existed, the front and sides of a building served as billboards for advertisements of store wares and services. "Farming Implements" was painted in large lettering between the second and third floors of Clement & Giffin's store. Other advertisements scrolled on their building noted "Harrisons' Town and Country Ready Mixed Paints for Sale Here." The public was greeted with signs reading "Seed Peas" and "Hot Bed Glass." In the front window, they displayed other goods for sale, such as lanterns. Farm tools such as shovels and rakes rested against the building and other merchandise was piled on the store's front porch.

Alfred Clement's store also served as the township's post office. It was common throughout the country for a storekeeper in rural parts to serve as Postmaster. "A.W. Clement–Postmaster and head of the firm Clement & Giffin the principal storekeeper in town." (WJP 1/8/1878) [See postmaster, page 172.]

Benjamin F. Fowler's general store operated on Main Street at the corner of the Haddonfield Road, 149-151 Kings Highway East. Fowler was a former clerk at Alfred Clement's store. Aaron C. Clement's drygoods and grocery store was also in Haddonfield at the corner of Potter Street and Kings Highway. The outside cover of the Clement & Company customer account book reveals a list of the store's specialty, grocery products:

> Dealers in Fine Groceries. Flours of all grades. Selected Teas, Pure Coffee and Spices, Butter and Cheese from the best Dairies, Foreign and Domestic Fruits, Canned Fruits and Vegetables, and a full variety of other goods usually kept in a first class store. Goods promptly delivered free of expense. (Wood Family Manuscript)

Before Rennels Fowler opened a store in Haddonfield, he was a tailor. Fowler's general store was near the corner of Friends Avenue and Kings Highway. When Fowler died in 1877, they took an inventory of his stock and merchandise. A list of store contents highlights the variety of goods on hand. Grocery items included casks and kegs of vinegar, sacks of salt, sugar, nutmeg, tea, cornstarch, soda and baking powder and flour. Other goods and merchandise such as feed, coal oil, oil cans, measurers, cheese boxes, lamp chimneys, candles, glass jars, vest patterns, shoe strings, thread, shirts, linen handkerchiefs and white and black cotton spools were available at Fowler's store. The store even sold books to patrons. (Inv. E-566, 1877)

George H. Clement sold "Imported and Domestic Groceries, fruits and vegetables" as well as fresh meats and salted oysters at his store. George's motto, "With us it is Quality not Quantity." (LBGA 6/77) George Clement's store was attached to the American House hotel, now 233 Kings Highway. The store, known then as the Ark, was later demolished when the Indian King Tavern was restored.

William H. Clement's store stood at the corner of Main Street near the Camden & Atlantic Railroad's right-of-way. An advertisement in the *Haddonfield Basket* noted: "Dealer in Coal, Wood, Flour and Feed, Kindling Wood, Lime, Hair, Plaster, Cement, Drain Pipe, Chimney Tops, etc." (HB 11/17/1874)

David Middleton's general store, opened at its Main Street location sometime in the 1860s, just west of the railroad tracks, at 4 Kings Highway West. The 1870 U.S. Census Bureau noted David's occupation as a "flour, feed and coal dealer."

A certain amount of trust existed between merchants and their customers. Because most store owners sold goods on credit, it was inevitable that some outstanding accounts could not be collected. When it came time for customers with outstanding debts to settle with Benjamin Fowler's estate, about $100 of the $600 amount due was judged to be uncollectible. Storekeepers often pursued deadbeats within the legal system. It was common to sign judgements against non-paying customers.

Besides extending credit, bartering was a common way to pay for items. Some farmers exchanged farm products or feed for store merchandise. Isaac Wood was a creditworthy customer at Clement & Company's store. Throughout 1877, the Wood family procured grocery items including sugar, lemons, coffee, bread, molasses, crackers, rice, salt, starch, pepper and bread at the store. The Wood's grocery bill for the year came to $73.68. During the year, the Woods most likely exchanged farm products in return for credit of $59.25. On January 1, 1878, Isaac paid the balance due, $14.43, in cash. [See Isaac Wood, page 227.]

For many years, a general store operated in Rowandtown under the proprietorship of Dayton Duval. The site of the store was probably along the Haddonfield Road near the intersection of Stoy's Mill Road, or Crystal Lake Avenue. By 1878, Richard Clement was the "grocer" in Rowandtown. (WJP 1/2/1878)

In 1882, J. Stokes Collings recognized an opportunity for a general store to serve inhabitants moving into new homes near the Camden & Atlantic Railroad's Collings Station. Collings opened a store at the intersection of Collings and Haddonfield roads. After a half dozen years of operation, the vicinity near Collings's store incorporated as the Borough of Collingswood.

As the population of Haddonfield, Westmont and Collingswood grew, general stores began to face competition from a variety of specialty stores. As more specialty stores opened, the general store's role lessened as the rural township's dominate retail outlet. Specialty stores, better at accommodating the specific retail needs and desires of customers, soon became commonplace.

Butcher, Baker and Confectionery

Various kinds of meats served with potatoes were popular entrees of Americans' diets. Likewise, bread, made from wheat flour, was a staple food. In the rural parts of the country, they usually made bread and other baked goods at the home while they often procured meat from livestock raised on the farm. In cities and villages, butcher and bakery shops provided a variety of foods for consumption.

The half dozen or so meat markets in Haddonfield were an indication of the popularity of fresh meat at a time before refrigeration. During the 1870s, Charles Smith, Samuel Albertson, William and Samuel Tomlinson, Isaac Ellis and Theodore Margerum operated butcher shops in the village. Beef, veal, pork, sausage and mutton were the the primary stock at a meat cutter's store.

Butchers purchased their products from cattle dealers and farmers. After they slaughtered an animal, butchers stripped the hide, cleaned out inside the carcass and carved it into quarters with knives, saws and broad iron cleavers. Dressed meats were often hung in the butcher's store so that patrons could inspect the product. It was a common practice for meat cutters to deliver orders to the homes of their customers. Before electric refrigeration, butchers required ice to keep their meat from spoiling.

Data gathered in 1850, notes Charles Smith carved and sold 36,000 pounds of beef taken from 60 slaughtered cattle. Smith dropped 136 calves for their veal and 50 sheep providing 2,500 pounds of mutton for the dinner tables of local residents. By the end of the 1870s, Charles Smith had laid down his butcher cleaver and taken up buying and selling cattle and horses. [See horse trader, page 159.]

The workings of Isaac Ellis's butcher shop were chronicled by a Haddonfield resident, Sarah Shivers Murray:

> Isaac Ellis made the lard, sausage and scrapple, and sold chops, roasts, etc., but at the beginning [1850s] no other meat. Lard was made in a copper kettle; meat for sausage was ground by hand in a small hand machine and stuffed with a wooden potato masher which had been made by hand. The pork was purchased from farmers in the vicinity of Haddonfield. For many years, Isaac Ellis served the

> Deaf and Dumb Asylum in Philadelphia. He drove over with his sausage scrapple, lard and pork meat twice a week. (Sarah Shivers Murray Manuscript–Isaac Ellis)

Samuel P. Hunt's butcher store in Haddonfield advertised in the local newspaper, the *Letter Basket and General Advertiser*:

> Samuel P. Hunt's Central Meat Market 145 East Main Street. Beef, Mutton, Lamb, Veal and Pork. Also Pork Tenderloins, Sweet Breads, Calves' Liver, Butter, Eggs and Poultry imported German Sauer Kraut, Mush, Scrapple and Lard. Orders Solicited and Promptly Delivered. (LBGA 6/1877)

Theodore Margerum & Brothers store stood along Haddonfield's Main Street. Fresh and salted meats, butter, eggs and lard were sold here. In the 1880s, the concern had three wagons making deliveries to patrons living as far away as five miles.

After 1875, a transformation in the meat industry came about from the domination by Midwestern stock yards and meat-packing plants. Before this period, spoilage was the chief obstacle facing shipment of fresh meat. By the end of the decade, efficient refrigerator railroad cars had solved the dilemma. Although the local slaughtering rapidly declined in importance with the rise of the western meat-packing industry, a market for home-killed meat continued to some degree in small towns.

During the 1870s, two German brothers began baking and selling bread, cakes and pies in Haddonfield. Martin Schlecht opened a bakery in the early 1870s at 222 Kings Highway East. Soon afterwards, in 1874, Martin's brother Jacob acquired the Railroad Hotel and converted it to a bakery and confectionery shop. Jacob carried on as overseer of an existing stable and livery at the same site for commuters riding the Camden & Atlantic Railroad. Some may believe a stable and bakery are an unusual complement of businesses. They are probably right, at least from a modern-day perspective. The former bakery/stable is now 4 Kings Highway East.

Jacob Rowand's fire insurance survey notes that Schlecht's "bake house" was a separate dwelling measuring 12'x 15'. (Rowand No. 344, 1872) Always mindful of risks or sources of a fire, Rowand noted:

> ...nothing manufactured on premise except bread and cakes. The oven stands outside building, is heated with anthracite coal and is well guarded in every practice, there being less danger from fire than a common cook stove. The floor above the oven being of bricks. (Rowand No. 344, 1872)

The Schlecht brothers encouraged and accommodated both walk-in and mail order patronage:

> Schlecht Brothers. Terms cash. Mail orders solicited. Bread, pie, and Fancy Cake Bakery, Ice Cream. Large and small orders promptly attended to. (LBGA 6/1877)

Besides baked goods and ice cream, they sold and sweets at Schlecht's store. Items typically sold at a confectionery were candies, cakes, ice cream and soda water. Another confectionery stood along Main Street. George Stillwell, the proprietor of the American Temperance House, opened a confectionery at the site that is now known as the Indian King Tavern. In 1877, Rowand wrote in his insurance ledgers that Stillwell's establishment, besides being a hotel and stable, was also "an ice cream factory and confectionery." (Rowand No. 471, 1877)

Carpenter, Masonry, Roofer, Painter, Paperhanger

The woodworking industry experienced the Industrial Revolution following the Civil War. For the first time, factory machines made windows and doors in standard size, ready-to-install, building components. The new technology in the factory changed the nature of the carpenter's craft and almost eliminated it as a separate and distinct skill.

Lower wages were another factor that changed the building trades at this time. Because many woodworking skills once required to build homes became obsolete, the overall skill level of carpenters declined, resulting in lower wages. They hired workers with lesser skills to erect buildings.

Another significant change affecting carpenters and the home building industry was the introduction of the balloon frame construction technique. Before the new method was widely employed, skilled craftsmen were hired to raise homes made of thick beams joined by mortise, tenon and wooden pegs or handmade nails. Balloon frame construction used two-by-four lumber for studs, joined to the framing by machine-made nails. Lightweight plates, joists and rafters made from thin lumber added to the new construction method.

In the decades before the Civil War, many homes, especially the more prominent dwellings, were of traditional architectural design. For example, Edward Bettle's mansion and William Bettle, Jr.'s home were constructed in a Greek Revival style. [See Edward Bettle, page 267, see William Bettle, Jr., page 255.]

Samuel Hinchman's house exhibited Gothic Revival architectural features. [See Samuel M. Hinchman, page 246.] Following the 1860s, often, the new building techniques and declining craftsmanship in carpentry, coupled with changing values in many cases, resulted in a mix of interior and exterior home styles.

A typical middle-class wood frame two-story house built in the 1870s generally had three sets of rooms. The public rooms included the parlor, family room and dining room. Private rooms, usually on the second floor, included chambers, or bedrooms, and perhaps a bathroom. In many instances, they used attics as bedrooms. Finally, the working areas of the house included the kitchen, pantry and cellar.

One of the more notable carpenters in old Haddon Township was William Hoopes. William was responsible for building many buildings, dwellings and outbuildings in area. One of Hoopes larger assignments commenced in 1869 when local school trustees hired him to oversee construction of the new Haddonfield school at Chestnut and Haddon streets (Lincoln Avenue). Upon completion, the Haddonfield school was a magnificent edifice for a small rural village. [See schools, page 54.]

Having successfully completed the Haddonfield school project, trustees of the Rowandtown school district employed Hoopes in 1872 to build a new school along the Haddonfield Road. The site of this project is now the lot where the Municipal Building is in Westmont. His task included excavating, grading, building foundation walls, erecting privies, framing, building stud partitions, roofing, installing windows, doorways and doors, plastering, wainscotting, painting, glazing, installing hardware, digging a water well and installing a pump.

When building plans for the Haddonfield school called for a brown sandstone exterior, William Hoopes subcontracted with Elwood Braddock to do the work. Braddock, of Haddonfield, was a stone mason. Besides building brick and stone edifices, masons also constructed foundations for buildings. Wood frame homes also required the services of a mason to build brick chimneys or fireplaces. Bricklayers in old Haddon Township did not have to travel too far to purchase their stock. The township was home to two brick manufacturers in the 1870s.

Elwood learned his stone and masonry skills while he served as an apprentice in Burlington. He practiced his trade in New York City, Atlantic City and as far away as Iowa before moving back to New Jersey and settling down in Haddonfield. Besides laying the masonry for Haddonfield's school, Braddock helped in construction of the Baptist Church as well as other buildings in Haddonfield.

Although masonry was his primary occupation, Elwood was also a "pioneer in cranberry culture in New Jersey." (WJP 9/6/1871) He owned cranberry bogs in Burlington and Atlantic Counties.

Before asphalt roofing shingles came into existence, roofs consisted of metal, slate or wood. Tin and slate met the basic requirements for a good roof: durability, fireproof and watertight. They constructed many modest dwellings in old Haddon Township with wood shingle roofs. Wooden roofs were common in rural areas. Farmers were quite adept at placing wood shingles on their outbuildings. Most shingle roofs built before 1850s were made of hand-split shingles of cedar, oak, or pine. During the second half of the nineteenth century, milled shingles replaced handmade shingles.

Daniel Wright, a Haddonfield tinsmith, also made a living constructing and repairing roofs in and around the township. [See tinsmith, page 146.] Wright's services were advertised in a local newspaper: "Tin and Sheet Iron Works. All Kind of Metallic Roofing." (HB 8/74) One of Daniel's more sizable jobs took place in 1882, when he constructed the roof on another Haddonfield school called the White Building, put up next to the 1870 school.

Another type of laborer associated with home building was the painter. A number of painters lived in the township including John Allen and his sons. In the 1870s, some painters still mixed their own paints, though ready-mixed colored paints were available. The nearby Haddonfield Paint Works sold ready-mixed paints including two popular colors, Haddon French Green and Haddon Iron Brown. [See paint works, page 142.]

The interior walls of homes were often finished with paint or wallpaper. Some home owners employed paperhangers to hang wallpaper. Walter Wayne, a Haddonfield paperhanger, was one of several township men that specialized installing wallpaper. Many types of wallpaper were available in the 1870s. Printed wallpaper designs were popular as well as historical subjects and events, panoramic views of well-known towns, cities and subjects of mythology and literature.

Collector of Internal Revenue

On July 1, 1862, President Lincoln signed into law what was then the most sweeping revenue producing legislation in the nation's history. The measure was

Collector's Office,

1st District, State of N. Jersey,

Div. No. 9 Camden, May, 1869.

Mr. Isaac H. Wood
Haddonfield

To The United States, Dr.

(FOR INTERNAL REVENUE.)

	RATE.	AMOUNT TAX.	
Tax on Income for the year 1868. Amount, $200	5 PER CENT.	10	00
Tax on the following articles, for the year ending March 1, 1869:			
Billiard Tables, kept for private use			
Carriages			
Plate, 14 oz.			70
Gold Watches			

Amount of Tax . . . . $

Penalty . . . . . 5 per cent. . . .

Total $10.70

Received Payment, Wm. P. Tatem, Collector.

Tax receipt issued by William Tatem, Internal Revenue Collector, in 1869. The receipt issued to Isaac Wood, a Haddon Township farmer, for payment of excise taxes.

(Wood Manuscript Collection, Historical Society of Haddonfield)

enacted to pay for the cost of the Civil War. The Office of the Commissioner of Internal Revenue was created and revenue collection offices were opened around the country. Before, the nation supported itself on internal excise taxes tariffs, and land sales. The nation's first income tax was levied at a rate of three percent on annual incomes more than $600, but less than $10,000, and a tax of five percent on any income more than $10,000.

In addition to taxes on income, citizens were also liable for excise taxes. Annual taxes were collected on articles considered to be luxury items such as carriages, pleasure yachts, pianos, organs or parlor musical instruments, billiard tables, gold watches and silver plate.

In the mid-1860s, William P. Tatem was Collector of Revenue for the New Jersey First District. William resided on a farm near the Haddonfield Turnpike in what is now Collingswood. [See William Tatem, page 211.] His house still stands at 829 Maple Avenue. Tatem was politically connected, having served as Camden County's Tax Collector, Sheriff and Clerk before being elected to the New Jersey Senate in 1860.

A federal tax collector's job was a political appointment. Often, tax collectors were political allies who were not qualified for the job. After appointment, they exerted political influence and were often the recipients of favoritism and bribes. While many tax collectors were not the most popular public servants, Tatem was appreciated, if by no one else, than by the editor of Camden's *West Jersey Press*:

> The government neither has nor can it have a more faithful and honest officer than Mr. Tatem, and we are proud of the fact. (WJP 7/18/1877)

During the era when the income tax was first introduced, citizens were unaccustomed to the idea of paying a direct tax, especially on income. This made Tatem's job unpopular. An article in the *West Jersey Press* offered a glimpse of the public's acceptance and compliance with the laws:

> Probably no law was ever enacted the provision of which were so utterly disregarded or evaded, as the one imposing tax on income. (WJP 7/21/1869)

Tax collectors worked from lists of taxpayers prepared by the District Tax Assessor. Within twenty days of receiving his annual lists from the assessor, Tatem gave notice to taxpayers through the placement of newspaper advertisements and notices posted in public places. Notification informed the public that taxes were due and payable on income and on certain personal property:

> Internal Revenue Notice Report income whether more or less than $600. Also number of carriages, gold watches, pianos, organs or parlor musical instruments, yachts, gold and silver plates and billiard tables. (WJP 4/25/1866)

The citizens of the district paid their annual tax payments at the collector's office at the Camden Court House. Tatem, and his three deputies were responsible for collecting taxes in Camden, Gloucester and Cumberland Counties. Collectors had a financial incentive to collect as much tax as possible. Their compensation was based on commissions from the first $400,000 of taxes collected.

Some receipts issued to local citizens have survived and are now stored at several historical societies. An 1869 tax receipt divulges Tatem collected $10.70 of taxes from Isaac Wood. Mr. Wood's income tax was computed on his 1868 earnings of $200 and an excise tax of 70 cents on the Wood family silver plates.

The income tax system began to unravel shortly after the Civil War ended. In 1867, Congress abandoned the progressive income tax rates and shortly afterwards, cut the income tax rate. The income tax system was abandoned altogether in 1872. Some 41 years later, Congress again enacted the Federal income tax.

One of the more formidable tasks of the tax collector was to enforce compliance with excise taxes due on liquor and tobacco. Federal excise taxes applied to manufacturers of stills and makers, wholesalers, retailers, dealers and peddlers of liquor, beer and tobacco. In 1865, taxes on spirits were as high as $2 per proof gallon.

In the region's newspapers, Tatem fulfilled his annual responsibility of reminding entrepreneurs of their tax obligation. "Special Tax—all dealers in liquor and tobacco required to purchase a stamp. Wm. P. Tatem Collector—Internal Revenue 1st District." (WJP 7/7/1873) Tatem periodically released information on voluntary compliance in the district. For instance, 44 distillers in the district manufactured 64,003 gallons of applejack during the month of October 1876. (WJP 11/22/1876) In 1878, 27 brandy distillers were in full operation in the district. (WJP 8/7/1878) Presumably these operations complied with tax laws. It is unlikely Tatem's statistics included every still operator in the area. Evading taxes, especially by "liquor-men" was commonplace.

If a taxpayer failed to pay the excise tax, the collector had full authority to seize and sell his assets. An 1867 newspaper reported an incident that took place on a craft floating on the Delaware River:

> Three men on board and a still in full operation, and rendering forth fragrant perfumes from "mash" in various stages of fermentation; besides several barrels of "the pure stuff, ready for the "Rogue's market;" manufactured from Molasses; ...miserable stuff, which if drank to excess is capable of filling more Lunatic Asylums in a given time, than any other concoction on record. The mate and crew were immediately escorted to comfortable quarters in Sheriff Sharp's Palace.... (WJP 9/25/1867)

Another instance of internal revenue law enforcement occurred in 1874. The innkeeper at the Railroad Hotel on Main Street in Haddonfield neglected to pay federal taxes on his retail liquor operation. The hotel's owner, Minor Rogers, was cited for neglecting to acquire a federal revenue stamp:

> Minor Rogers...charged with exercising a business of retail dealer of liquor without paying special tax of Internal Revenue. (WJP 3/4/1874)

Minor's problems did not end with the Collector of Internal Revenue. During this era, the sale of liquor within the township was prohibited by a local ordinance. Mr. Rogers vehemently opposed the township ordinance and continued to serve liquor. Besides Mr. Tatem's enforcement of the federal tax laws, local authorities fined Minor for selling liquor in violation of the township ordinance. [See local option, page 79.]

Conveyancer, Surveyor and Real Estate Agent

In the 1870s, conveyancers drew up the appropriate legal documents whenever real estate was transferred, conveyed or assigned. They were quite common in rural areas like old Haddon Township, where attorneys were scarce. During the 1870s, John Clement, Jacob Rowand, John Lewis Rowand and Charles Rhoads were conveyancers with offices in Haddonfield.

In 1880, the fee typically charged by local conveyancers was $1.50 for drawing a common deed or mortgage and 50 cents for drawing a bond. A conveyancer's duties also included representing the seller upon the sale of property. When property was sold, a conveyancer received one percent of the sale price for real estate and three percent for personal property or wooded lots.

Surveyors laid out and divided land, settled boundaries, and surveyed and marked land. In many cases, conveyancers also surveyed the land they were transferring. In those instances, training in the techniques of surveying was necessary. Jacob and John Rowand and John Clement were experienced and skilled surveyors. In 1880, the going rate for surveying in southern New Jersey was $5 per day and an equal daily amount for preparing maps and calculations.

Deeds, maps and surveys prepared during the era were done so using English units of measurement. The length of property lines, roads, etc. were delineated in chains (66 feet), rods (16 1/2 feet) and links (7.92 inches). A surveyor carried a chain to take linear measurements when surveying a tract of land. The chain had 100 iron or steel links connected measuring 66 feet (4 rods) in length. The steel tape eventually replaced the surveyor's chain. With a surveyor's chain and iron pegs, two men could measure the linear distance of property lines. The angles between adjacent boundaries were measured using a theodolite or surveying compass. Once they knew a tract's dimensions and angles, a surveyor could calculate its area. Surveyors placed their identifying marks or blazes on a tree along the property line. The Surveyor's Association of West New Jersey assigned an identifying blaze to each of its members.

By 1870, having reached the age of 71, Jacob Rowand's days as a surveyor were for the most part behind him. One of Rowand's more notable professional accomplishments was his surveys in the early 1850s of the barrier island that became Atlantic City.

Jacob's son, John Lewis Rowand, followed in his father's footsteps as a surveyor and conveyancer. John was also trained as an engineer. One of John's assignments was to improve Haddonfield streets soon after the borough incorporated:

> J. Lewis Rowand, an experienced civil engineer, has been employed to make, and is now at work fixing the gravel of the streets, sidewalks, etc. (WJP 5/12/1875)

John Clement may have been the most prolific surveyor in the township at that period. Today, John Clement's drawings, surveys and maps are valuable references for historical research. Many of his documents are housed at the Historical Society of Pennsylvania. [See lawyers, page 166.]

Elmer Clement, a Haddonfield boot and shoemaker, recognized a niche in real estate related services. In 1876, Elmer Clement sold his interest in a shoemaking concern and opened a real estate office on Ellis Street. He may have been the first individual in the village to take on the job title of real estate agent. Over time, real estate agents and attorneys absorbed the work once performed by conveyancers. Elmer, also known as Squire Clement, served as the township's Justice of the Peace.

A real estate specialist familiar with the local market of selling and renting property found plenty of clients. It was estimated in 1875 that about ten percent of the people that resided in Haddonfield's 300 homes were boarders. (HB 1/14/1875) Advertisements published in the *Haddonfield Basket* revealed the importance of a rental property's proximity to the Camden & Atlantic Railroad depot:

> To Rent or For Sale R. Elmer Clement, Real Estate Agent.
>
> A 3 story brick house, containing 11 rooms, situated on Main Street, Haddonfield, NJ about 6 minutes walk from the R.R. depot, in good repair. Rent $325 per annum. Vacant.
>
> A French roof house, 9 rooms, with bath, on Chestnut street, Haddonfield , Rent, $25 per month. 4 minutes from depot.
>
> A double front frame dwelling, on Main st., Haddonfield, at $18 per month. 2 minutes from depot.
>
> A Good house and barn, with 7 acres of land, on the C. [Camden] and H. [Haddonfield] turnpike road near Stonetown at or near White Horse road, on C. and Atl. Railroad [Camden & Atlantic]. Rent $15 per month.
>
> A six-roomed new house on Potter street, 10 minutes from depot. Rent, $10.50 per month. (HB 11/1875)

In the late 1860s, the village of Haddonfield witnessed a "flood tide of progress and development." (WJP 4/22/1868) The *Haddonfield Basket* reported, "eighty houses are said to have been erected in Haddonfield within the last eight years." (HB 7/30/1874) A handful of Haddonfield entrepreneurs were building, selling and renting homes during the 1870s. One developer of a large area of land in Haddonfield, William Massey, was a corporate officer of the Camden & Atlantic Railroad Company. Samuel A. Willits, proprietor of a Haddonfield lumber and coal yard, was also active in real estate ventures within the village.

Domestic Servants and Farm Laborers

During the era covered by this book, domestic service amounted to half of all the nation's female employment. One in every eight American families employed domestic help in 1870. It was common for a township household to have employed an African-American or white female domestic servant. Servants often lived in the same house with their employers and were an integral part of households.

Domestic servants did many household chores, besides helping in the care of their employers' children.

Making beds, emptying chamber pots, washing dishes, preparing meals, purchasing groceries, washing clothes, ironing, sewing, cleaning, dusting and baking were some duties of the domestic servants. A servant hired by a family in the rural parts of the township often ventured outside to feed chickens, milk cows and hoe gardens.

In 1870, Joseph Cuthbert employed three domestic servants. [See Joseph Cuthbert, page 254.] John DaCosta, a retired merchant and railroad executive, hired five domestic servants to live and work at his premises along the White Horse Road. [See John DaCosta, page 199.] John Sheets, a lumber merchant, had two domestic servants and a nurse to help care for his seven children. [See John Sheets, page 187.] Jacob Rowand, a Haddonfield conveyancer, had a nineteen year old female domestic helper at his home. Edward D. Cope, a highly regarded naturalist, employed a domestic servant and a waiter at his Haddonfield residence.

Along with domestic servants, farm laborers were another prevalent class of worker in the rural township. Farm laborers provided the human muscle that fueled the local agricultural economy. Hired-help did many farm-related chores including planting, harvesting, driving farm goods and produce to market and construction and repair of outbuildings and fences. Most farm owners employed full-time helpers and assistants to do the day-to-day farm chores. Often, farm laborers and their families resided in tenant dwellings on their employers' premises. Additional help on the farm was hired seasonally, for instance at harvest time.

Drug Stores

In the 1870s, Charles Braddock, Sr.'s pharmacy stood at 201-203 Kings Highway East. An advertisement appeared in the *Haddonfield Basket* in 1874 that noted the various articles available at Braddock's drug store:

> Dealer in Drugs, Medicines, Chemicals, Toilet and Fancy Articles, Patent Medicines, Brushes, Soaps, Perfumery. Prescriptions Carefully Compounded at all Hours Day or Night. A complete assortment of Hardware always on Hand. (HB 8/1874)

Charles operated the drug/hardware store for 25 years until 1878, when he turned the concern over to his brother Isaac and his son Charles, Jr. The new proprietors were both graduates of Philadelphia College of Pharmacy. Charles, Sr. did not retire from the business world. He opened a hardware store across the street.

Flitcraft's West End Pharmacy opened in Haddonfield sometime in the early 1870s. An advertisement in *The Letter Basket and General Advertiser* noted:

> Here's the Rub. For all the aches and pains rub with Flitcraft's Green Oil" the Magic Pain Extractor. 25 cents the bottle at Flitcraft's West End Pharmacy." (LBGA 6/1877)

Sometime about 1874, another pharmacist opened a drug store in the village. Mr. F.M. Tilton attended the Philadelphia College of Pharmacy and, upon graduating, moved to Haddonfield:

> A fine laboratory is in the rear where Mr. Tilton makes up from the finest line of medicines and prescriptions, and manufactures Crystal Pepsine, Saccharated Pepsine, his leading specialty of dyspepsia mixture, and the

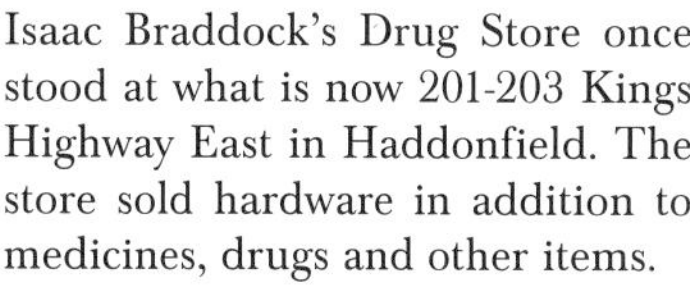

Isaac Braddock's Drug Store once stood at what is now 201-203 Kings Highway East in Haddonfield. The store sold hardware in addition to medicines, drugs and other items.

(*Daily Graphic*: New York, September 9, 1879)

manufacture of all fluids, extracts and chemicals, a line of chemicals being made and shipped to Philadelphia. The stock carried bears a representative value of $1,200 and is made up of the fullest and finest line of drugs and medicines and mixtures and horse powders for diseases of pink eye and epizooty. (*Industries of New Jersey*, p. 382)

Competition for the pharmacist during this era came from physicians. It was common for doctors to mix their own prescriptions for their patients. Another source of medicines was home remedies. They often published recipes and concoctions for illness and aches in newspapers for readers to assimilate:

"...the infusion of one ounce of roasted coffee daily will diminish the waste" going on in the body "by one-fourth," and Dr. Christison adds that tea has the same property. (HB 1/1876)

To Cure Cough Take one handful each of herb hoarhound, catnip, tansey, hyssop, hops, and grated horse radish; boil them in one gallon of water till reduced to one half; strain, and add one oz. of elecampane and three pints of molasses; boil till reduced to three quarts; dissolve one oz. gum camphor in one pint best brandy, and add when cold. Take a wineglass full at morning, or when the cough is bad. (HB 3/1876)

Rheumatism Take the yolk of one egg, three table spoonfuls of vinegar, six of water, and two of turpentine; put them in a glass bottle, shake well; bathe cold a few times. (HB 3/1876)

The best remedy for bleeding at the nose, as given by Dr. Gleson in one of his lectures, is a vigorous motion of the jaws, as if in the act of mastication. In the case of a child, a wad of paper should be placed in the mouth, and the child instructed to chew it hard. ... This remedy is the motion of the jaws that stops the flow of blood. (HB 3/1876)

Fire Insurance Agents

Fire insurance offered policyholders financial protection in case of destruction of property by fire. In Haddonfield, Jacob Rowand was an agent for the Mercer County Mutual Fire Insurance Company. Jacob sold fire insurance coverage to many shop and home owners both within and outside old Haddon Township. Rowand also made a living as a surveyor and conveyancer. [See conveyancer and surveyor, page 155.]

Before fire insurance coverage was accepted by the insurance company, Rowand carefully evaluated and surveyed the applicant's property. Rowand noted in his ledger the location, size, age and type of construction of all structures on the property, including outbuildings. Mercer County Mutual Fire Insurance Company reserved the lowest fire insurance rates for the best risks. In 1880, the premium for a ten-year policy on a brick or stone house, covered with a slate or metal roof was three percent of its fair market value. For a wood roof dwelling, the rate of insurance increased to four and one half cents per hundred dollars of value. Frame dwellings, covered with wood, cost the insured a premium as high as five percent of market value. The rates for insuring agricultural implements, products and stock housed in frame barns and outbuildings were five to seven cents per hundred dollars of market value.

Joseph B. Tatem insured the dwelling and outbuildings situated on his farm on Collings Road in 1857. His house is now known as the Collings-Knight House in Collingswood. [See Edward Collings, page 202.] Rowand surveyed Tatem's property and prepared the fire insurance paperwork. The ten-year premium on the two-story house and other wood frame outbuildings, including the corn house, barn, grain and hay barns,

Mercer County Mutual Fire Insurance Company letterhead. Jacob Rowand of Haddonfield, was an agent for the fire insurance company. The company insured many dwellings in the region that acquired policies from Jacob Rowand. (Historical Society of Haddonfield Collections)

brick smoke house, and one and one-half story tenant house was $84.

The highest insurable risks were public stabling and livery stables. Premium rates for a ten-year policy ran as high as fifteen-percent of the structure's value. Carpenters, wheelwrights, cabinetmakers' shops and small shops were charged premiums rates between ten and fourteen-percent of market value. The Mercer County fire insurance company refused to underwrite risks where fires were known to occur frequently. For instance, the company did not underwrite insurance on small buildings where machinery was operated by water or steam-power, nor did the company accept risks from mills, factories, large summer boarding houses, or any building with a steam engine in or connected to it.

When Rowand recorded descriptions of the insured structures, he probably had no idea his surveys would later be used for purposes other than fire insurance records. The surveys have survived and are housed in the Historical Society of Haddonfield. Rowand's description of local dwellings, shops, churches, schools, are a one-of-a-kind primary source of information for local history enthusiasts.

Several other Haddonfield proprietors also sold fire insurance. Samuel Willits, a lumber, coal and hardware proprietor sold insurance from his office. Willits represented four fire insurance companies. [See lumberyards, page 168.] Alfred Clement operated Haddonfield's largest general store. An early version of one-stop shopping came close to being realized when, from his general store, Clement began selling fire insurance coverage for two insurance companies. [See general stores, page 149.] Clement was an agent for the Millville Fire and Marine Mutual Insurance Company.

Several other insurance agents resided in Haddonfield. Samuel Shererd sold marine insurance. John Scott, a Rowandtown resident in 1870, sold life insurance.

Horse and Cattle Traders

Although the railroad made its mark on passenger transportation during the second half of the nineteenth century, local travel was still dependent on horses and mules. These types of animals were both valuable nineteenth century assets. They were used for dragging farming implements across the fields, lugging fertilizer from the wharves to the fields and hauling farm products to the marketplace. The vast majority of farmers in old Haddon Township owned at least one horse. A horse, on average, was worth about $125 in the 1870s. In most instances, a mule commanded a better price than a horse.

During the 1870s, George D. Stuart of Haddonfield, having previously tried farm life, abandoned the plough and became a dealer in horses and cattle. George found it necessary, and profitable, to periodically venture out west to select and bring back animals to Haddonfield for sale to the public:

> Mr. Geo. D. Stuart, our townsman, is in Ohio, looking for horses suitable for our market. (HB 1/1876)

> Public Sale of Horses Will be sold at the American House, Haddonfield. Seventeen head of horses just arrived from the west. Geo. D. Stewart. [sic] For family, business and general use. (WJP 2/2/1876)

The stables at inns and taverns were typically the sites where horse sales took place. Upon selling his stock, Stuart ventured out west looking for more horses:

> George Stuart...whom there is no better judge of the merits of horses in Camden County, is now in the west securing a drove of good breed, which he will dispose of immediately upon his return to this section. (WJP 4/5/1876)

The *West Jersey Press*, Camden's probusiness newspaper, seldom missed an opportunity to comment on Stuart's whereabouts: "George D. Stuart of Haddonfield started west on Monday and will return with a drove of superior western horses. ..." (WJP3/6/1878) Deacon Stuart, as he was known to his neighbors on Potter Street, also acquired cows: "George Stewart [sic] brought a lot of fresh milch cows from the west." (WJP 6/2/80) Nearby farmers and butchers were the primary beneficiaries of a cattle dealer's inventory.

The other Haddonfield horse trader, Charles Smith, had once owned a "meat shop" in the village. (WJP 8/19/1868) [See butchers, page 151.] Sometime during the 1870s, Charles opened a livery stable. The site of his stable was along Mechanic Street. The inn was once at what is now 125 to 129 Kings Highway East: "Charles Smith opened a first class livery stable...the place of business the Haddonfield House. He deals in stock mules and horses." (WJP 12/18/1878) The concern traded as C.H. Smith Sale and Exchange Stables. Guests at the inn and visitors in the village often boarded their horses at the site. Smith's livery service was similar to a modern-day automobile rental company. He made horses available for hire by the hour or day.

Charles Smith also traveled vast distances out west to obtain his stock. In January 1880, the *West Jersey Press* reported Smith returned with a "string of 37 horses and mules." (WJP 1/28/1880)

Ideally, horses could be divided into two classes: those used for work and those kept for pleasure. Work-horses included farm-horses and team-horses employed in the transportation of goods or moving heavy and bulky articles. Pleasure horses included race-horses, trotters, private gentlemen's saddle and carriage horses. In actuality, many horses were "general purpose" animals, that is mixed-breed horses of fair to good quality and used for anything and everything, as their name inferred.

The age of a horse was an important component of its value in the marketplace. Unscrupulous dealers attempted to hide the age of horses by doctoring the animals' teeth, a good indicator of its true age. Older horses had longer and more protruding teeth. Filing down teeth could make a horse appear younger. Whether deserved or not, the reputation often associated with a modern-day used car salesman, may have been spawned in the era of the horse traders. An advertisement for a manual entitled "How to Tell the Age of a Horse" noted:

> The importance of knowing how to tell the age of a horse by an examination of his teeth, cannot be over-estimated by those who have occasion to BUY HORSES. Such knowledge is valuable alike to the FARMER, MERCHANT and MECHANIC, and may often save many dollars to its possessor. By a study of this book, all may learn in a short time to become experts. Engravings are given showing the shape of the teeth from the age of two-and-a-half years up to twenty years. The TRICKS of horse traders who "Doctor-Up" the teeth of OLD HORSES to make them LOOK YOUNG, and thus deceive purchasers, are fully EXPOSED ... (*Practical Blacksmithing* [advertisement])

Mules were more desirable as work animals on the farm. A mule was particularly useful as a beast of burden because of their stamina, tough skin, strong hooves and surefootedness.

Most farmers in the area raised cattle, a few kept special breeds. Charles H. Shinn raised thoroughbred Alderney cattle. Shinn, once a proprietor of a lumber-yard on Potter Street, resided at the corner of Main and Grove Streets. His cattle were frequently the topic of newspaper reports. The *West Jersey Press* noted "Mr. Shinn has obtained national reputation" (WJP 1/15/1869) for his cattle:

> C.H. Shinn Alderney Cattle at Public Sale—sale at residence at Haddonfield about 50 head of choice pure bred Alderneys, among them are many fine cows, some excellent stock, bulls, and promising yearlings, of both sexes. Bred by Shinn. (WJP 6/2/1869)

Alexander Cooper's farm was situated outside Haddonfield in Delaware Township (Cherry Hill). In 1878, Cooper housed 25 head of cattle, valued at $1,500, in a large cattle shed. Cooper sold his cattle in Haddonfield:

> Alexander Cooper of Haddonfield has been noted for the fine cattle he fattens. Last week he sold 32 head to John Welsh of this city [Camden], which averaged 1,450 pounds each. (CDP 11/18/1879)

Inn and Tavern Keepers

In the 1870s, a wayfarer traveling through old Haddon Township in need of lodging could find a room at one of four inns in the village of Haddonfield. If a traveler's itinerary took him along the Haddonfield Road, he might choose to stay about two and one-half miles outside Haddonfield at a hotel called the Half-Way House.

Nineteenth century inns and taverns in old Haddon Township were quite plain in comparison to the present-day hotel accommodations. In the past, guests at a local inn would sometimes share a room with another guest. By today's standards, the typical chamber was much smaller. Hospice guests, besides renting a place to sleep, at a minimum expected a nearby shed or stable for their horse and a place to purchase a hot meal or drink. New Jersey's laws required certain accommodations:

> ...every innholder and tavern-keeper shall have and keep in his or her house, at least two good feather beds for guests, with good and sufficient bedclothes for the same, and provide and keep good, wholesome and sufficient diet for travelers, and stabling and provender of hay and grain for four horses more than his or her own stock. (Rev. 1877, p. 488) (*Compiled Statutes of the State of New Jersey,* "Intoxicating Liquors" 1911 p. 2894)

The Half-Way House, also known as the Union Hotel, was an inn and tavern at Haddon and Lincoln Avenues in Collingswood. The inn was a welcomed rest stop for weary teamsters, and a spot where the local citizenry could gather for conversation. The hotel was a three-story frame structure with porches off each of the first two floors where guest could sit and overlook the turnpike. Unlike the inns in Haddonfield, farmland surrounded the Half-Way House in all directions.

Shortly after the end of the Civil War, Mr. L.D. Wood was proprietor of the Half-Way House. From the few documents that survived, it appears Wood attracted a sporting clientele to his establishment. Even though the authorities prohibited horse-racing on the turnpike, it did not stop Wood from encouraging matches. One need not stretch their imagination to envision patrons' placing bets at the tavern before the start of the race:

> A spirited trot took place on the Haddonfield Turnpike on Saturday afternoon between a horse belonging to Mr. Chas. Caffrey of this city [Camden] and one belonging to L.D. Wood, proprietor of the Half-Way House. A large concourse of sporting men assembled to witness the sport. The race was won by Mr. Caffrey, times not given. (WJP 6/23/1869)

In 1869, Mahlon Van Booskirk purchased the hostelry from Wood. Mahlon's legacy as an innkeeper may have been his indifference to a local ordinance. In 1873, the citizens of the township voted to ban the sale of alcohol in the township. The ordinance was known as the local option law. [See local option, page 79.] As one might imagine, the law was not well received by the township's tavern owners. Several months after the voters approved the law, Mahlon found himself in front of a judge answering charges that he violated the municipal law. The judge found Van Booskirk guilty and fined him $50 for the indiscretion. [See Mahlon Van Booskirk, page 212.] After paying the fine, it is unlikely that Mahlon converted his tavern into a tea room. Less than a year later, they cited him a second time for violating the township's antiliquor law.

According to an 1878 fire insurance survey, Van Booskirk finally saw the errors of his ways and complied with the local ordinance. Notes contained in the survey state, "This building was formerly kept as a public tavern, but under our local option, no tavern has been allowed or kept in Haddon Township for the last 5 years." (Rowand No. 499, 1878) Rowand's survey also reveals the hotel was no longer open to public. On the other hand, another contemporaneous document conflicts with Rowand's 1878 survey, suggesting Mahlon may have revived his tavern. An inventory of Van Booskirk's belongings notes the existence of a bar. In addition, the contents in his cellar could lead one to conclude Mahlon was up to his old tricks. Mahlon's stock in his cellar included wine, cider and vinegar, all at various stages of fermentation. The listing noted 180 grape boxes, 100 truck baskets, 30 cider cloths, 50 vinegar barrels, 182 vinegar hogsheads, 74 wine barrels, four wine hogsheads, seven demijohns, four wine kegs, many old iron staves and old lumber and barrels. An accounting of the liquid stock included 18,936 gallons of old vinegar, 23,000 gallons of new vinegar, 912 gallons of new cider, 710 gallons new wine and 2,482 gallons of old wine. (Inv. I-181, 1888)

Teamsters, businessmen and travelers took their meals and rented rooms in Haddonfield, the township's hub of commercial activity. For those visitors that arrived in the village on the Camden & Atlantic Railroad, accommodations were just a short distance from the station. The Railroad Hotel stood east of the tracks on the south side of Kings Highway. The inn was

The American House in Haddonfield. Better known as the Indian King Tavern, the building is now 233 Kings Highway East. Soon after a local ordinance prohibited the sale of liquor in the township, the proprietor renamed the hotel the American Temperance House.

(*Genealogy of the Descendants of Thomas French*, by Howard French)

at 4 Kings Highway East. In the early 1870s, its proprietor, Minor Rogers, operated the inn and a tavern, stable and livery. Rogers was an ardent opponent of the movement to ban the sale of liquor. When township voters approved the local option referendum in 1873, Rogers and several other tavern owner in Haddonfield joined to fight the enactment. Their efforts fell short. In 1874, a baker from Germany acquired the old Railroad Hotel from Rogers and opened a bakery and confectionery. [See baker, page 151.]

The Indian King Tavern was once the principal hotel in the village. In the 1860s, the edifice was known as the American House. The inn/tavern was a three-story brick structure. A two-story frame addition was attached to the back of the building. (Rowand No. 471, 1877) The historic landmark, at 233 Kings Highway, was purchased by the State of New Jersey in early 1900s because of its association with the State legislature during colonial times.

The American House was once known by another name:

> ...the "Old Tavern House" had been kept as an old fashioned inn with its fine old parlor, bar-room and great kitchen on the first floor. Its dining room, back of the bar room, was of moderate size: its ball, or assembly room at the east end of the second floor was reached by a wide reversing and easy ascending stairway from a spacious hall which ran through, bisecting the building. The bedrooms were on the second and third floors ("History of the Old Tavern House in Haddonfield, New Jersey"–Dr. Stevenson)

The hotel was named by a former owner:

> Between the years 1850 and 1855, the political party known as the Native American, came into prominence in New Jersey. John K. Roberts, the owner of the tavern at that time took an active part in the affairs of the new party. ... It was during this period that Mr. Roberts in his enthusiasm for his party selected the name "American House" for the sign. ("History of the Old Tavern House in Haddonfield, New Jersey," Dr. Stevenson)

The American House closed its doors following the township's ban on selling liquor. George Stillwell acquired the establishment in 1874 and reopened the tavern for business, "conducted on temperance principles." (WJP 5/20/1874) The editor of the *Haddonfield Basket*, John Van Court, never passed on a chance to extol the virtues of the "dry" hotel:

> About a year ago, Mr. Stillwell took the old American Hotel, changed it into a Temperance House, and runs it as such, with accommodations for man and horse, and with all the appointments of a well-conducted village hotel, as we believe, and as Mr. Stillwell informs us, except rum. (HB 2/13/1875)

In 1877, an "ice cream factory" was also operating at Stillwell's "American Temperance House." (Rowand No. 471, 1877) The *Haddonfield Basket* noted:

> The American House, now kept as a Temperance Hotel and ice cream saloon, by Mr. Stillwell, is as we are informed, doing a successful business, and travellers and others, are well and pleasantly accommodated, without being compelled to enter a filthy bar-room and having their olfactories regaled with bad whiskey, and their ears saluted very often with the ribaldry and blasphemy of "toddied" humans. (HB 7/1874)

Another well-known tavern in the village was the Haddonfield House, situated along the Main Street. The three-story brick structure still stands at the corner of Kings Highway East and Mechanic Street, now 125-129 Kings Highway East. Its beginning dates to 1777, when Edward Gibbs built the structure and opened a tavern. Solomon Matlack was proprietor of the establishment in the 1860s. During the mid-1870s, Aaron Smith was in charge.

The building had a two-story frame addition attached to the back. A bar was on the building's first floor along with a reading, sitting and dining rooms. Five bedrooms were on the second floor, while the third floor had seven chambers. A local fire insurance agent, Jacob Rowand, noted in an 1876 survey, the building was "used as a public house, but is unoccupied present." (Rowand No. 65, 1876) Situated behind the building were stables, a wagon shed and granary barn.

Unlike the other taverns in the township, the press did not report any incidents at the Haddonfield House when the local option was first introduced. The only newspaper reference to the hotel was a report of an unfortunate incident:

> Suicide Joseph B. Albertson aged about 35 years, while under a fit of delirium tremors, jumped from the second-story window of Matlack's Hotel,...and broke his neck. He was a single man. (WJP 8/24/1864)

At the corner of Potter and Main streets stood the Haddon House. The hotel officially opened in the late 1870s. Its owner William C. Shinn, had previously housed boarders in his dwelling before converting it into a hotel. Shinn added the Victorian features to the building that stands at 300 Kings Highway East. In 1875, Shinn advertised in the *Haddonfield Basket*:

> A large well-arranged Boarding House, Furnished, 25 rooms, and Cottage adjacent, 11 rooms. Also, two

The Haddon House is now at the corner of Potter Street, 300 Kings Highway East in Haddonfield. One of four hotels in the village, the Haddon House opened in the late 1870s.

(Haddonfield Library Collections)

> Cottages, 11 rooms each. Apply by letter, for interview. . . . (HB 11/1875)

William Shinn was a highly regarded citizen, due in part to his wartime record. He served as a Captain in the Twenty-Fourth New Jersey Volunteers before being discharged when he lost sight in one eye at the Battle of Fredricksburg. He returned home to work in his coal-shipping business. Shinn also represented the district in the State Legislature. After Shinn's death in 1879, the building was sold to Thomas Baxindine, who, with his family, kept the hotel well into the twentieth century.

It was not uncommon in the nineteenth century for city residents to escape from their urban environment and venture into the countryside. The proprietors of the Haddon House set out to attract patrons from Camden and Philadelphia. An announcement in the *Camden Daily Post* emphasized "summering in Haddonfield:"

> This eligible and delightful resort for a "Summering in Haddonfield," formerly under the control of Capt. Wm. C. Shinn and whose opening at an earlier period in the season was delayed owing to the lamented death of its proprietor, is now open for the season, and presents unsurpassed attractions for those who desire at a moderate outlay to secure the cool comforts of a country residence within a few minutes of the heart of the city. (CDP 6/18/1879)

The Maxwellton Park House was another local resort that catered to city dwellers desirous of fleeing the oppressive heat and humidity of summer. The hotel stood at Cottage Avenue, east of Centre Street. Built in the early 1870s, the 100-room building was the largest edifice in the township. In the mid-1880s, a room could be rented for $15 a week and $2.50 per day; children and servants were half-price. Despite its primary purpose as a school and dormitory for St. John's Academy, it took on a dual role soon after being placed into service. [See schools, page 60.] The hotel opened when they dismissed the cadets of St. John's Academy for the summer. Utilizing an otherwise idle building in the summer made good business sense.

The founder of the military school and hotel was Theophilius Reilly, an Episcopal minister, educator and businessman. [See Theophilius Reilly, page 223.]

An advertisement highlighted the hotel's pastoral location:

> Maxwellton Park House and annex contain over one hundred rooms, and are delightfully situated on eminences overlooking the surrounding country. They are supplied with pure water for bath and other uses, by hydraulic power, from extensive springs one-eighth of a mile distant. This water is said to be very invigorating to the system, and to be especially beneficial in the case of kidney and liver troubles.
>
> The grounds contain one hundred and ten acres, seventy of which are farming and pasture lands, the remainder being lawns, woods, ravines, and small watercourses.
>
> The table will be first-class. Milk, fruit and vegetables will be supplied fresh daily from the farm. (Unidentified advertisement–Historical Society of Haddonfield)

An unfortunate event took place in 1886. The school/hotel was destroyed by fire.

Ice Farming

Before refrigeration, many rural inhabitants gathered ice during the winter months from creeks, streams and ponds. Packed correctly in an ice house, ice could last throughout the summer. Camden's *West Jersey Press*, when referring to ice houses, reported "no country residence is considered complete without one" and most farms in the county had "a commodious ice house." (WJP 12/18/1878)

Some rural inhabitants, as well as those in the cities and villages, did not own an ice house. They relied on local dealers for delivery of this commodity for their wooden iceboxes.

Purchasing ice had not always been routine for the general population. In the city, inhabitants routinely visited the local market to purchase perishable food products. Over time, people wanted to keep food fresh and on hand, thereby demand for ice increased. Camden ice dealers once delivered eight pounds of ice a day to a house for a price of 65 cents per week. (WJP 6/29/1864)

> Ice...no longer regarded as an article of luxury but a necessity of life and travel. To our milkmen and butcher, in public and private homes. (WJP 12/31/1862)

> Ice grows more and more in demand every summer, and it has become one of the most profitable crops that can be raised. (WJP 12/23/1863)

> ...nothing is more essential to the comfort of the human race during hot summer months than ice. (WJP 7/24/1872)

Isaac Prine was an ice farmer and dealer that served many customers in and about old Haddon Township. Prine, a Rowandtown resident, had his hand in several other business ventures. While he operated his ice company, known as Cold Spring Ice Company, Prine operated a sawmill on Stoy's Mill Road. The two professions were compatible. While the sawmill was inactive during the summer months, Prine's ice delivery business was at its peak. Prine also operated a cider mill. [See Isaac Prine, page 257.]

The huge demand for ice in the summer created an opportunity for ice dealers to earn large profits. Prine's first ice route was in Haddonfield:

> Cold Spring Ice Mr. Isaac Prine, proprietor of the Cold Spring Ice Company intends to supply the citizens of Haddonfield, the coming summer with pure spring water ice. (WJP 5/27/1868)

> Spring Water Ice Inform the citizens of Haddonfield and vicinity that he [Isaac Prine] is again prepared to supply them with pure Spring Water Ice. Orders received by George Stillwell or David D. Middleton, or by driver. (WJP 6/2/1869)

Prine secured a good portion of his inventory of ice from a nearby millpond. The pond, utilized by the Newton Grist Mill, was in Haddon Township between Stokes and Albertson avenues. Isaac acquired two acres of land adjacent to the pond in 1872. Prine's dwelling stands today at 308 Cuthbert Road.

Not too long after he ventured into dealing ice, Isaac took on a partner, William House, and extended his door-to-door ice route into Camden. In 1869, the partnership supplemented its inventory with ice shipped on coastal schooners from New England:

Isaac Prine and his ice wagon. Prine took ice from Cuthbert Lake, a mill pond that once existed near Cuthbert Road. He delivered his product year round to customers throughout Haddon Township.

(James Duff Collection, Camden County Historical Society)

> Boston Ice The subscribers have made arrangements for an ample supply of Boston Ice which they are prepared to serve the citizens of Camden at their dwellings in large or small quantities. Office No. 1218 South Second St. Camden. William House and Isaac Prine. (WJP 6/2/1869)

Needless to say that it was important for the outside temperature to cooperate when harvesting ice. In 1869, a mild winter resulted in the "failure of the ice crop." (WJP 12/29/1869) More than once, warm winter weather prevented Prine from harvesting a sufficient amount of ice:

> Isaac Prine who serves Haddonfield with ice during the warm weather did not harvest any ice during the "cold snap" last week, as it was too thin to be handled profitable by him. He will get his supply of ice elsewhere unless he has an opportunity to cut later in the season. (WJP 2/18/1880)

When the winter temperatures were favorable, ice farmers filled their storehouses, as did the area farmers. The local newspapers kept pace with the weather; the *West Jersey Press* reported "farms filling ice houses from frozen ponds and streams while cold weather lasts. . . ." (WJP 1/21/1874)

The *Camden Democrat* reported the impact of ice harvesting on prices charged by local dealers:

> Most farmers have stored away a quantity for private use. Already ice has fallen. Last year forty cents per 100 pounds. At present twenty-five cents. (CD 1/17/1877)

Generally, a farmer cut ice when it was between ten and twelve inches deep, but sometimes settled for thinner ice. Ice farmers could use various techniques to improve their yields. For instance, before they gathered ice, greater thickness could be accomplished by piercing the ice field with a bar or auger to allow water to force itself to the surface and form a new frozen layer of ice. When the ice was sufficiently thick, any snow was removed by means of a shovel or by a horse and scraper. Ice farmers scored the ice into rectangular patterns called cakes. Often, cakes of ice taken from the larger bodies of water were cut with plows pulled by horses. Use of an ice plow was not confined to larger ice fields that could bear the weight of a horse. Plows could be readily attached to a light cable or rope and operated from the bank by a horse. They also cut ice with saws worked by hand.

An account published in the *Camden Democrat*, revealed the method of harvesting ice from a pond in Kirkwood, a site less than ten miles from Haddon Township. Although the operation in Kirkwood was more extensive than Prine's ice farm, the technique employed to cut ice may have been similar:

> Ice cut by plows, first length wise then crosswise, the blocks being square from ten to eighteen inches thick. After the blocks are cut it is floated to and through a channel under the hoisting machine, which raises it to the ice house windows where workmen are engaged in carefully storing it away. The plows are worked by horse power, fifty men are employed all winter in cutting, hoisting and stacking ice, these men being mostly farmers or their sons living near Kirkwood . . . (CDP 1/17/1877)

They filled the Kirkwood ice house with blocks of ice that they floated to the storehouse. Prine may have loaded his ice onto a sled or wagon and hauled it to the nearby ice house.

Prine's ice house, once situated off Cuthbert Road next to the pond, probably existed on the lot before Prine's ownership. In 1875, a Haddonfield newspaper reported on the building's dimensions:

> Isaac Prine has a large ice house in the neighborhood of Haddonfield measuring length sixty-five feet, width thirty-seven feet, height twenty feet and capable of holding 900 tons. (HB 2/13/1875)

By 1879, patronage along Prine's ice route had increased to where three ice houses were necessary to store the annual harvest. His success apparently continued into the 1880s when he added onto his ice storage facilities:

> Isaac Prine, who supplies Haddonfield with ice, has his three houses filled with 3,000 tons, twelve inches thickness. This is from a pure spring water pond. (WJP 11/15/1879)

> Isaac Prine, who supplies Haddonfield, with ice is building large additions to his ice houses at Cuthbert's road. (WJP 6/23/1882)

Ice, being a perishable commodity, had to be stored in layers and spaced as closely as possible. They filled in space between ice cakes with crushed ice or snow, to cause the whole mass to freeze into a solid block. It was also common to spread sawdust or wood shavings on the ice for insulation and to absorb moisture. Coincidentally, Prine had an ample supply of sawdust and wood shavings from the nearby sawmill.

In 1883, Isaac secured a new location to harvest ice. He leased eight acres of meadow land along Browning Road near Cooper's Creek, on a lot that is now within Collingswood's borders. In the 1880s, the land was part of Edward Knight's "Grape Farm." [See Edward Knight, page 205.] The 1883 lease with Knight noted that Prine's purpose for renting the land was to till and farm an ice pond. Prine had

Knight's permission to build an ice house, office and stables at the site. A clause in the lease agreement may be a clue to the possible demise of Prine's former ice field near Cuthbert Road.

James Flinn's Crystal Lake Paint Works stood a quarter-mile upstream from Prine's Westmont ice farm. It is highly probable the Flinn factory discharged waste from the production of lead-based paints into the creek. The pollution found its way downstream into Prine's ice field and may have put an end to ice farming on the millpond. [See paint works, page 140.]

To prevent such a occurrence from happening again, Prine proceeded cautiously before agreeing to rent the Browning Road ice field from Edward Knight. Knowing that Knight owned land on both sides of the lot he was about to rent, Prine inserted a clause into the agreement that required Knight to refrain from the "use of any paints or chemicals" on neighboring lands "so as not to affect the purity of the water and thereby affecting the quality of the ice." (Camden County Clerk's Office, 108-168)

Law Enforcement Officers, Lawyers and the Courts

Old Haddon Township's inhabitants were not served by a full-time police department when the municipality was formed in 1865. The township's primary law enforcement officers were the Constable and two Justices of the Peace, both part-time elected positions.

A Constable had similar responsibilities of a modern-day police officer. Among their duties were serving warrants and keeping the peace, which included apprehending disorderly persons, drunkards, paupers and thieves. They had authority to arrest persons suspected of committing crimes. The township's first Constable, James Middleton, was a farmer. Middleton received $25 in compensation for his first full year of service. James also served as the township's first Overseer of the Poor.

The first Justices of the Peace elected in Haddon Township were Charles Redman and Samuel Tomlinson. A Justice of the Peace was comparable to today's municipal judge. Besides possessing many of the same powers as a Constable, New Jersey's statutes granted a Justice of the Peace full power to conserve the peace by using force, imprisonment and punishment. Among their responsibilities, a Justice of the Peace "solemnized" marriages, heard tenant and landlord complaints, delivered tax warrants to Constables for serving to tax delinquents, tried cases of petty larceny (less than $20) and oversaw the keeping of bastard children.

Training in legal rules and proceedings was not a necessity or requirement to serve as a Justice of the Peace. For instance, Elmer Clement was a Haddonfield shoemaker and real estate agent when he was elected Justice of the Peace in the mid-1870s. Jacob P. Fowler, known as Squire Fowler, was a proprietor of a hardware store when he was elected to the post.

Enforcing the law and administering justice was not always popular duties. Justice Fowler upheld local ordinances, even when it went against public opinion:

> The action of Justice Fowler in his recent movement towards more strict enforcement of the Sunday law meets with much disapproval in certain quarters. It is said by some that if the barber shops, segar stores, etc. are closed, the proprietors will retaliate by taking action against milkmen and others. (WJP 5/8/1879)

> Justice Fowler of Haddonfield, has given the barbers notice that if they shave tomorrow [Sunday] he will fine them, and it is understood that they will not shave. (CDP 5/17/1879)

Certainly, most cases heard by a Justice of the Peace were routine and uneventful. One trial, heard by Justice Fowler in 1879, caught the interest of the village's citizens:

> The staid citizens of Haddonfield are greatly excited over a bastardy case. . . . The defendant is Paul Paullin, a highly respected citizen and businessman of the borough, and the alleged victim Catharine Castello, a prepossessing girl of 17 years, who at that date of the transgression was a domestic in the defendant's family. The respectability of Mr. Paullin has excited very general interest, and the matter is the universal theme. The trial came off yesterday before Justice Fowler and...a jury of twelve men. J. Eugene Troth, Esq., appeared for the township and P.S. Scovel, Esq. for defendant, At nine o'clock last night the case was given to the jury, who after being out all night, at ten o'clock this morning, agreed to disagree and were discharged. (CDP 1/4/1879)

Today, municipalities rely on full-time police and other law enforcement officials to pursue criminals and investigate crimes. When called upon, old Haddon Township's Constable and Justices of the Peace did their best to locate, apprehend, convict and punish thieves. Theft of livestock was a troubling problem to the farmer. In the 1870s, local farmers joined to protect their property and assist the township's law enforcement officials. They formed the Mt. Ephraim and Haddonfield Mutual Pursuing and Detective Company.

The group carried on in an informal manner until they incorporated in 1899. The Articles of Incorporation noted the organization's purpose:

> ...detection, apprehension, arrest and prosecution of thieves, tramps, marauders and other depredators on the persons and property of the members. ... (Certificate of Incorporation, 1899)

The company's bylaws gave additional powers to the organization's members:

> In addition to detecting and arresting thieves and the recovery of stolen property, this association may attend to ferreting out incendiaries and suppressing outrages of any kind against the peace of the community. ... (Certificate of Incorporation, 1899)

The bylaws of the company noted "Any white male person sixteen years of age and over, of good moral character, residing within seven miles of Haddonfield (exclusive of incorporated cities), may become a member." The annual membership fee was $1.

They referred to the organization's "detectives" as pursuers. Tracking down horse and cattle thieves and escorting them to a hearing with the nearest Justice of the Peace was the primary duty of a pursuer. If found guilty, the culprits were sentenced to serve a prison term in the Camden County Jail. The pursuing company survived long after the old Haddon Township's farms disappeared. In 1964, the organization still had 125 members.

Civil and criminal judicial proceedings of a more serious nature were generally heard in county or state courts. They tried criminal cases in Inferior Court of Common Pleas, Court of Oyer and Terminer, Court of General Quarters Session of the Peace, and Court of Common Pleas; they heard civil cases in Court of Chancery and the Circuit Court. Hearings regarding wills, estates and custody cases were heard in The Orphans Court and Prerogative Court. The judicial system established by the state's Constitution of 1844 remained in place until the 1948 Constitution, after which the judicial network was revised into its present form.

Probably the best known old Haddon Township citizen that worked in the judiciary system was John Clement of Haddonfield. Judge Clement served on the New Jersey State Court of Errors and Appeals in Trenton. In addition to his duties on the bench, John Clement was also a surveyor and conveyancer. [See surveyors, page 155.]

One of Judge Clement's professional accomplishments took place when he served on a three-member commission that examined the state's prison system in 1877. Judge Clement's assignment was explained in the *West Jersey Press*:

> Judge Clement, of Haddonfield, has been appointed by Governor Bedle, a member of the board of commissioners to report on the present prison system of the State, and to suggest plans for improvement. (WJP 9/26/1877)

Judge Clement's most lasting work was his historical writing. While sitting on the bench and in surveying, Clement had access to deeds and other state records from which he reconstructed the early history of Newton Township. The history of the first Newton Township settlers was the product of John Clement's research. The culmination of Judge Clement's historical work was his classic volume *Sketches of the First Emigrant Settlers Newton Township, Old Gloucester County, West New Jersey*, published in 1877. Clement also consulted with George Prowell and wrote portions of Prowell's treatise, *The History of Camden County, New Jersey*, printed in 1887.

In the 1870s, it is probable the volume of legal work in Haddonfield could not sustain a legal practitioner on a full-time basis. At least one lawyer, James Young, resided in Haddonfield in 1870, although it is not known where he practiced. The vast majority of attorneys during this era were practicing law in the cities. Most Haddon Township citizens probably traveled to Camden to seek legal help. Some Camden lawyers advertised their services in Haddonfield's local newspaper, the *Haddonfield Basket*. During the 1880s, several attorneys were practicing law in Haddonfield.

For the most part, attorneys survived on paperwork and litigation provided by the transfer and purchase of real estate, mortgages, sales and claims jumping. Another source of a lawyer's billing was collecting debts. In the 1870s, it was common for a conveyancer to prepare legal documents necessary to transfer real estate. The duties of the conveyancer would later become a service generally associated with an attorney.

Although 31 law schools operated across America in 1870, many lawyers had acquired their legal education as apprentices. The education requirements for the bar were not very high. Generally, a couple of years studying law under the direction of a law judge or practicing attorney enabled a young man with sufficient knowledge of law to pass the state bar examinations. Much like the medical field, men dominated the law profession. Changes within this male-dominated profession were slow.

The local legal community took a step forward in 1881 with the founding of the Camden County Bar

Samuel A. Willits & Company Lumberyard in Haddonfield. Situated at Euclid Avenue and Tanner Street, customers purchased lumber, coal, hardware, building materials and gardening implements.

(Historical Society of Haddonfield Collections)

Association. The new organization promoted, encouraged and studied law and the administration of justice.

Lumberyards

There were two lumber and coal yards in old Haddon Township. Samuel A. Willits of Haddonfield, owned both yards. One of the Willits's yards was on five acres of land along Cooper's Creek near the Haddon Township/Haddonfield border. Samuel's other lumberyard was in Haddonfield at Tanner Street and Euclid Avenue. Willits inherited both lumberyards from his father. During the 1860s, the business operated under the partnership name of Willits & Evans. Joseph Evans was related to Samuel's wife, Abigail. Evans, eventually disposed of his interest in the partnership.

For a good portion of the nineteenth century, the Landing Yard or Coles Landing site along Cooper's Creek was a terminal for receiving lumber and coal. It was here that patrons could purchase lumber and coal that had been brought down the Lehigh River to the Delaware River, up Cooper's Creek and unloaded. Willits stored a good share of his lumber at the Landing.

Many homes in the area were heated with coal stoves or furnaces. Customers could purchase Lehigh Coal at either yard to heat their homes and to use in stoves for cooking. Patrons were enticed to purchase lumber and coal at Coles Landing with reduced prices. "Lumber—$1.00 per board feet and coal $1.00 per ton cheaper at the Landing Yard." (WJP 1/5/1870) A special type of fuel, blacksmiths' coal, was also stocked at the yards.

The Landing Yard had a handful of buildings within its boundaries. The yard's one story office was just 8' x 12'. Several tenant homes and out buildings were also on the property. In 1870, William Wilmon, an employee of the lumber company, and his wife and eight children, resided at one dwelling on the premise.

The other Willits site, known as the Haddonfield Lumber Yard and Coal Depot, was in Haddonfield. In addition to coal and lumber, the Haddonfield site offered customers a wide selection of building materials, hardware and gardening items. During the 1870s, Willits stocked several types of fertilizers including a popular soil enhancer, Guano. Building products kept in stock were fence wire, nails, molding, doors, shutters, blinds, cord and kindling wood. In the winter of 1878, they stocked 10,000 cedar rails at the yard. (WJP 1/2/1878) Construction stock was a significant segment of Willits's inventory. Stock at the yard included:

> Hemlock joists, cedar and cypress shingles, yellow and white pine flooring, cedar and white pine siding, cedar boat boards.
>
> General variety of lumber used for building. Cedar, white pine, spruce, white oak posts, and fencing boards. Building hardware, paints, oils, glass, putty, Kaighn's Plough Points and Shares. (WJP 3/21/1866)

During this era, Haddonfield was a growing village and the local carpenters were beneficiaries of the building boom. It is likely that the Willits lumberyard was a busy place. Willits himself jumped into the construction business. In 1874, Willits built five new homes on Tanner Street. (WJP 8/19/1874)

For many years, wagons transported lumber from the Cooper's Creek yard to the other Willits site. By 1881, a railroad siding connected the Haddonfield yard to the adjacent Camden & Atlantic Railroad right-of-way. Afterwards, coal, lumber and bulk supplies arrived at the yard by railroad car. Six employees worked at the yard in the early 1880s.

An obvious risk that lumberyard proprietors faced was the threat of a fire. An accident with a lantern or mishap caused by a discarded cigar could destroy a yard. Deliberate attempts to set a fire was also a concern:

> An attempt was made. . .to fire the lumber yard of Saml. A. Willits, of this place; but fortunately failed. A pile of shavings was found under one of the sheds partially consumed. (HB 9/15/1875)

Fire insurance coverage on a lumberyard was a necessary business reality. An 1875 fire insurance survey shows the Haddonfield yard had three lumber sheds. The office and storeroom were a one-story structure with dimensions of 18' x 32'. The dimensions of the lumber sheds were 92' x 20', 39' x 20' and 20' x 16'. A tenant house and barn were also situated at the yard. (Rowand No. 418, 1875)

Samuel Willits's business interest were diverse. He was a builder, lumber merchant and an agent for four fire insurance companies. By the early 1880s, Samuel was selling fire insurance policies to his patrons.

Willits had the distinction of being the first businessman in the township to make use of the telephone. Workers strung telephone wires from Willits's Cooper's Creek office to his lumberyard in Haddonfield. [See telephone, page 89.] The lumberyard stood at the Tanner Street site for some 100 years until the 1960s.

Medical Profession

The majority of the physicians in Camden County practiced in Camden during the 1870s; four doctors practiced medicine in Haddonfield. Many physicians chose to practice medicine in Camden, where travel was not an obstacle. The disproportionate number of physicians in Camden came about in part because people in rural parts lived miles from town and travel consumed physicians' time going to and from patients' dwellings.

Haddonfield, N. J., 187

To S. A. WILLITS & CO., Dr.

—DEALERS IN—

Lumber, Wood, Coal and Hardware,

TERMS—Cash for Coal and Wood. Interest added if not paid within 30 days. Orders dropped in Box at R. E. Clement's Office will receive prompt attention.

An invoice from Samuel A. Willits & Company. In addition to his Haddonfield location, Willits also owned a yard along Cooper's Creek near today's Coles Mill Road.

(Stoy Manuscript Collection, Historical Society of Haddonfield)

The average doctor worked long days. In the cities, physicians had office hours, and visited patients in their homes. Outside the cities, most small town doctors traveled by buggy or horseback to administer to the sick. Overall, a doctor was rewarded for his long hours with a generous income. Rural doctors often accepted in-kind payment for their services.

Compared with modern-day standards, in the 1870s, doctors worked with primitive instruments such as scalpels, forceps and probes. Practical medical instruments such as thermometers and stethoscopes were just beginning to find general acceptance. Medical knowledge was also in a state of infancy. The cause of many diseases was not generally known nor were ways to prevent their spread.

Besides the usual colds, fevers, accidents and internal disorders, mid-nineteenth century Americans experienced epidemics. For instance, in the late 1860s, epidemics of cholera, typhoid fever, typhus, scarlet fever and smallpox troubled Philadelphians. During the mid-1860s, an outbreak of cholera killed 900 citizens. In Camden, concerned physicians took measures to keep the cholera epidemic in check. Some doctors studied what was thought to be the root cause of disease. A report cited deplorable conditions in Camden as a source of medical problems:

> Upon inspection they found Camden to be as filthy as any city of its size in the Union. The drainage was superficial and imperfect; garbage and coal ashes were thrown into the streets, but few of which were paved; the cesspools, shallow in depth, were in many places overflowing upon the ground and pig sties had been allowed to be erected in the yards of the poorer classes. (Prowell, p. 257)

The report prompted Camden's elected officials to enact new ordinances to change unhealthy conditions, but not before 30 citizens died because of cholera. Outside the city's limits in Newton Township, 25 African-Americans died from the disease.

The movement to monitor and improve public health received a boost in 1880 when the Legislature of New Jersey passed an act requiring each city, borough and township to form a Board of Health. Haddon Township's Board of Health comprised the township committee, the Tax Assessor and the Township Physician.

Initially all the doctors that practiced medicine in old Haddon Township resided in Haddonfield. Benjamin Whitall Blackwood began practicing medicine in the village in 1828, the same year he graduated from the University of Pennsylvania. Dr. Blackwood was known throughout the township in another capacity. He served as the school superintendent for Newton Township in 1864. He retired from medicine in the mid-1860s.

Dr. Blackwood was trained as a homeopathic doctor. Homeopathy was a form of medical practice in which the doctor administered remedies that caused a reaction in a person that was similar to the symptom of the illness. The philosophy is in marked contrast to modern-day conventional medical practices. During much of the nineteenth century, homeopathic doctors were viewed with disdain by regular medical physicians and were not welcomed in their medical society.

Napoleon Bonaparte Jennings graduated from Jefferson Medical College of Philadelphia in 1856 and began practicing medicine in Haddonfield. Jennings practiced for some 30 years in the village. During Dr. Jennings's years as a physician, he gained the admiration of many inhabitants. He served as Haddon Township's first Township Physician. Sarah Shivers Murray, a chronicler of nineteenth century Haddonfield history, disclosed Jennings's routine before the era of the automobile, ambulances and hospitals:

> In all the years Dr. Jennings spent among the people here until he was worn out, he literally gave his life for the people who were suffering. He was never too tired to drive ten or more miles to see and render aid to the sick or dying, no matter what the state of the roads might be, or whether it rained, snowed or was scorching hot. (Sarah Shivers Murray Manuscript–Dr. Napoleon Jennings)

During the 1870s, other doctors hung their shingles in Haddonfield. Dr. Theodore Williams practiced homeopathic medicine in Philadelphia before relocating to Haddonfield. His son, Franklin Williams, followed his father and practiced medicine in the village as a specialist in internal medicine and chronic diseases. Dr. Jonathan Comfort, a medical doctor, was administering medicine in the village in 1870. Charles Hendry Shivers, a native of Haddonfield, attended the University of Lewisburgh, in Pennsylvania. Like his one-time medical mentor Dr. Jennings, Shivers also nurtured a large practice in the area.

Dr. John Hobensack, a Rowandtown resident, practiced psychiatry at the Hobensack Institute at 206 North Second Street, Philadelphia. [See John Hobensack, page 262.] Patients from the city and Camden received treatment at Hobensack's psychiatric institute. During the 1870s, he advertised quite frequently in Camden's newspapers. An advertisement, in the *Camden Democrat*, claimed:

> J.N. Hobensack 231 patients last month, all diseases of a private nature and the suffers of the wrong treatment of quacks;. . .
>
> Also young men suffering from disease which cause pimples on the face, fear of friends, melancholy habits, loss of ambition and memory, down-cast looks, insanity. . . . (CD 1/15/70)

The institute also had a mail order department. Inquiring individuals could write to the Institute to obtain a copy of "Wisdom in a Nutshell." Subscribers, requesting Hobensack's words of wisdom, had to enclose a three-cent stamp to cover mailing costs.

It is likely that Rowandtown's first practicing physician was Dr. Edgar Sharp. In 1881, this homeopathic doctor set up his practice in the community that had recently been renamed Westmont.

Although the number of medical schools throughout the country was growing during the second-half of the nineteenth century, one "medical college" with a Haddonfield address had no students, professors, books or classrooms. Remarkably, the "students" that paid "tuition" received medical diplomas.

The diploma mill scheme was masterminded by Dr. John Buchanan, a professor of medicine at a Philadelphia medical college. Dr. Buchanan formed a fictitious medical school called the American University of Philadelphia. Soon Buchanan expanded the number of his "medical schools" in Philadelphia, then Haddonfield and even Charlestown, West Virginia. Buchanan's "schools" offered medical diplomas, many of which were sold overseas in foreign countries.

Dr. Buchanan's scheme took hold because New Jersey's vague laws allowed graduates of any medical school chartered in any state to practice medicine in New Jersey by simply having a copy of his diploma recorded with the County Clerk and making a payment of five dollars.

The location of the college "campus" was a post office box at Alfred Clement's general store. Buchanan owned a farm several miles from Haddonfield in Centre Township. For some ten years, the diabolical professor sold medical diplomas granted by the mythical University of Medicine and Surgery of Haddonfield, New Jersey.

Buchanan's scheme began to unravel in Germany, of all places, after a person, suspicious of the school's credentials, checked it against a list of approved colleges. After some investigation, they indicted Buchanan in U.S. District Court in Philadelphia for using the mails for fraudulent purposes. The day following the indictment, the honorable doctor, while crossing the Delaware River on a ferry, jumped over the side into the river. The ferrymen searched for Buchanan's body, but had no success. The elusive doctor turned up several months later in Canada. Law enforcement officials successfully enticed him to cross the border into Michigan. Buchanan was arrested and later tried and convicted. He served ten months in prison and was fined $500.

It was of great concern to legitimate physicians, and the state's lawmakers, that diploma mills like Buchanan's could so easily place the public's well-being in jeopardy. Many years later, Dr. William Snape, a physician and local history buff, researched the incident and wrote "The Rise and Fall of John Buchanan "M.D." Dr. Snape recounted the extent of deception among Camden County's practicing physicians:

> In 1880 just before the "diploma mills" were closed down there were 85 graduates of acceptable schools. There were nine persons practicing without license and nine practicing with unacceptable diplomas, or eighteen in toto. Thus seventeen percent of the practitioners of Camden County, generally regarded by the public as physicians, were practicing under a cloud. (p. 18)

The legal loopholes that encouraged issuance of phony diplomas were tightened in 1890 when the Legislature created a licensing body, the State Board of Medical Examiners.

The first semblance of a hospital in the vicinity opened its doors in Camden during 1867. The dispensary contained twelve cots on the second floor, a pharmacy and examination office on the first floor. Two years after it opened, they sold the beds because of financial woes.

The three-story Cooper Hospital was completed in 1877 at a cost of $94,753. However, the Camden hospital stood dormant for ten years. Not until 1887 was there enough money to open the front doors, operate the facility and provide free care for all patients who needed it, which was a strict requirement of the hospital's benefactor, the Cooper family.

In the 1870s, senior citizens could still recall a time when extracting teeth was once a service performed by a barber. Eventually a medical specialty evolved. During the second-half of the nineteenth century, there was extensive progress in the dentistry profession.

By the late 1870s, slightly decayed teeth were being filled with improved dental instruments. Pulling an ailing tooth was common, although it was less traumatic if the patient was anesthetized. The *New Republic,* a Camden newspaper, printed an advertisement about the new dental procedure: "Nitrous oxide gas—for painless extraction of teeth." (NR 8/8/1876) Sometimes, with no remedies, people just suffered when they had an aching tooth. The unpublished diary of Amelia Hopkins notes in 1865, "...my teeth commenced to ache me from taking cold in them...sick with them in bed." (Wood Papers, 1865)

A dentist that practiced early-on in Haddonfield, Dr. Francis Tomlin, did so part-time. In 1877, the Philadelphia dentist practiced three days a week at his Haddonfield office and three days in Philadelphia.

Post Office, Postmaster and Express Service

The first post office in the township was established in Haddonfield about 1800. During most of the nineteenth century, a post office was housed at various locations in the village including several general stores, a harnessmaker's shop and a tavern. When stagecoaches passed through Haddonfield, the mail arrived at irregular intervals. By 1824, the village mail came on a regular schedule, twice a week, carried by coach between Camden and Haddonfield.

When the railroads arrived on the scene, transporting mail from city to city was greatly improved in the United States. By the early 1860s, the nation's railroads were the dominant means by which mail was moved. The railroad offered fast delivery and more direct service to many centers of population. They could serve the smallest villages on a railroad's right-of-way, even if trains did not stop there.

After the Federal Government began paying the railroads to transport and handle the mails, almost all the mail destined for Haddonfield arrived by way of the Camden & Atlantic Railroad. The village's postmaster picked up the mail at the train depot in a wagon. Outgoing mail was hauled from the post office to Haddonfield's train depot and loaded onto a mail car. Route agents worked inside the mail cars sorting mail while the train moved along. In 1877, the railroads used five mail cars to pick up and deliver mail along the line between Camden and Atlantic City.

Alfred Clement, Haddonfield's postmaster for almost a quarter of a century, was appointed by the Lincoln Administration. Except for a six-month interval where Jacob Fowler was politically appointed as postmaster, Clement served continually until 1885. During the 1870s, the township post office was in Alfred Clement's general store. [See general stores, page 149.] Clement devoted the back of his general store to functions related to mail handling. (WJP 11/27/1878) The post office in Haddonfield serviced an area outside the township's boundaries including parts of Delaware Township. The nearby villages of Mt. Ephraim and Ellisburg had their own post offices during the 1870s.

Unlike modern-day postal employees, nineteenth century mail handlers and postmasters received their job through political patronage. Usually, the local postmaster was expected to donate a part of his pay to the local party at election time. The partisan newspapers of the era were quick to lash out at the opposing party when the spoils of governing did not go the way of their party.

> Jacob P. Fowler appointed postmaster at Haddonfield. Alfred W. Clement removed. Mr. Clement's only crime is his firm adherence to the doctrine of the Union Party. He received his appointment from Abe Lincoln and is displaced because he believes in the great principles for which Lincoln was murdered. (WJP 8/15/1866)

By the end of the Civil War, the framework of the modern-day postal service was in place. Congress had eliminated distance as a factor in determining postage rates. Three cents was the standard rate for carrying a letter from one end of the country to the other. In 1874, the penny postal card was adopted by the U.S. Post Office.

Compared to their urban counterparts, rural inhabitants did not fare so well in the early days of the postal delivery system. For most of the nineteenth century, free mail delivery to rural inhabitants was nonexistent. By way of comparison, the largest cities in the nation began receiving free mail delivery in the early 1860s. Wayne Fuller, author of *The American Mail–Enlarger of the Common Life*, wrote, "compared to the cities, the rural mail service was a poor country cousin. No letter carrier in uniform brought the mail to the farmer's gate each day." (p. 75)

Farmers generally picked up their mail at their small local post offices, usually within a store or shop, once or twice a week. Trips to pick up the mail could be a time-consuming venture for an otherwise busy farmer. On the other hand, some rural inhabitants enjoyed the trips to the post office. Sometime about the mid-1860s, John Whitall, a retired glassworks entrepreneur, purchased a farm and used it as a family retreat. [See John Whitall, page 248.] According to Whitall's daughter, Hannah Whitall Smith, riding into Haddonfield to pick up the mail was a memorable experience of her childhood. In her work, *John M. Whitall, the story of his life*, Smith wrote of her fond memories of growing up in the rural countryside:

> ...and there were endless joys to be found in the daily drives to the village of Haddonfield, about a mile and a half off, to get the mail, and to do the family errands. (p. 273)

The rural mail system, although poor and time-consuming, was all inhabitants living outside the cities had ever known. All this changed in 1893, when they implemented Rural Free Delivery.

Equally as important as the U.S. Mail and more important to the nation's economy, were the services of express companies. Express companies forwarded goods for merchant and manufacturing concerns by railroad, vessel or wagon service. They were the equivalent of today's package delivery services. The larger companies of the era included the Adams Express Company, United States Express Company and Wells, Fargo & Company.

During the Civil War, express companies offered the only means of communication between soldiers and their families. Even the government shipped its securities and money by express because it was safer than the mail. At one point, express companies took on the nation's mail system by undertaking letter carrying. Even though the public supported the venture, it met opposition from the government and was ultimately abandoned.

In addition to forwarding packages and freight, express companies offered other services. For example, they collected money upon delivery and turned it over to the shipper. They also introduced the express money order system that allowed a safe means to transmit money to any locality. Express wagons, carrying packages to and from customers, were common sights in cities and villages.

The railroad companies were major beneficiaries of the express business. They used special train cars for transportation of express packages between cities. The Camden & Atlantic Railroad Company's annual receipts from express service were more than $23,000 in 1872. By way of comparison, the same railroad received just $3,000 from the U.S. Government for transporting mail along its roadway.

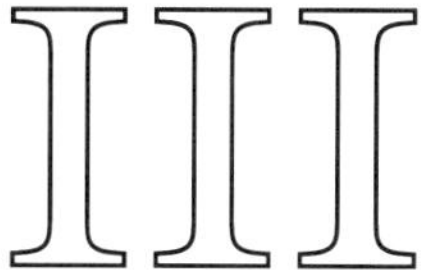

The Unfolding

of Old Haddon Township

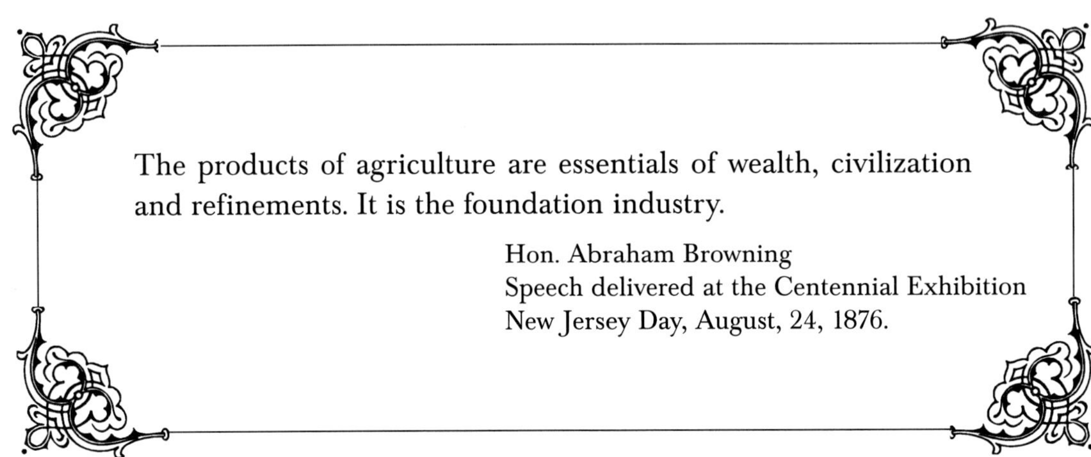

The products of agriculture are essentials of wealth, civilization and refinements. It is the foundation industry.

Hon. Abraham Browning
Speech delivered at the Centennial Exhibition
New Jersey Day, August, 24, 1876.

Introduction

Over many years, transformation of the nineteenth century landscape is the most noticeable change to have occurred in the region.

The terrain surrounding the villages of Rowandtown and Haddonfield in the nineteenth century, was planted with cornstalks, grain, hay, potatoes and vegetables. Farms were separated by fences, rows of trees, underbrush, creeks or narrow dirt lanes. Sheep, cows and horses once grazed on meadows, pastures and untilled fields. On most farms, barns and other outbuildings were clustered around the main dwelling. Horse-drawn vehicles traveled along tree-lined lanes connecting homesteads with public roadways.

Today, the same land is predominately residential neighborhoods. The boroughs that evolved from old Haddon Township now blend into one another. Only with the help of a map can one determine where the boundary of one borough ends and another begins. Homes were once few and far between along old turnpikes and country lanes. Now, these same roads are lined with single family homes, apartment complexes, office buildings or rows of stores.

Many would agree that it is inevitable the old lifestyles give way to new realities and that the topography surrenders its timeless natural assets. The farmland of the township is gone, as are most of the outbuildings and old dwellings. However, some structural and topographical facets of the nineteenth century still exist here and there within the suburban neighborhoods. It is the intent of this section to view what once existed in the township. Through a better understanding of the nineteenth century geographical characteristics of the region, the reader can better visualize and appreciate the appearance of old Haddon Township. By knowing what once existed, one can better understand and assess the changes that took place over time in the area.

The following chapters examine the 1870s topography that unfolded into today's municipalities and biographical accounts of the farmers, tenants or landowners associated with the township. Approximately 100 tracts of land and more than 130 people are examined in this segment. Anecdotal reports, narrative sketches, agricultural data, newspaper items and facts gathered from public records help create a portrait of the farms and individuals who were vital forces within the nineteenth century township.

Lippincotts, Hinchmans, Hopkins, Collings, Glovers and Nicholsons were all established families of the township making a living off the land in the 1870s. These families were direct descendants of settlers that came to America in the late seventeenth and early eighteenth century. Old Haddon Township was home to a number of successful industrialists and merchants including Samuel French, John Whitall, John DaCosta and John Dialogue. Although he did not reside in New Jersey, Edward Knight, a wealthy Philadelphia businessman, owned more land in the township than anyone else. Dozens of other citizens, including successful politicians, merchants, dairy farmers, a writer and poet, a Civil War hero, former slaves, proprietors of mills and cottage industry shops, and absentee landlords provide accounts from all walks of life that captures the scope of people that lived in old Haddon Township.

A few notes of caution are in order. To help readers envision the nineteenth century geographic scheme to modern times, the chapters are named for the municipalities that ultimately evolved out of old Haddon Township. (Several farms were conveyed to Gloucester City and Camden.) Keep in mind that before 1875, no boroughs existed. Except, perhaps, for the Borough of Haddonfield, the notion of discrete boroughs in the township had not yet been contemplated.

Descriptions of nineteenth century property lines are presented within the context of modern-day streets. Many references are approximations and are only meant to put the reader in the general vicinity. For the most part, the streets used to frame the location of lots did not exist in the 1870s. Furthermore, the owners of the hundreds of small lots in the village of Haddonfield were not traced. All maps in this section were drawn by Denise Fox based on the map of Haddon Township in *Atlas of Philadelphia and its Environs* (G.M. Hopkins Company).

Finally, if biographical information on an inhabitant is lacking, in most cases it has not been found. This is especially true for many farmers. The daily routine of these ordinary men was occupied with everyday chores of running the farm. However, they are no less important to the region's social history.

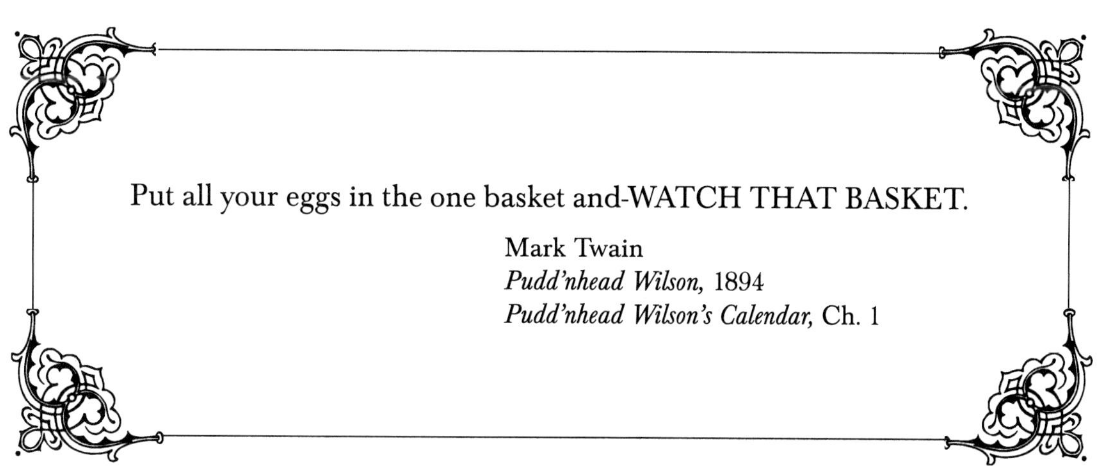

Put all your eggs in the one basket and-WATCH THAT BASKET.

Mark Twain
Pudd'nhead Wilson, 1894
Pudd'nhead Wilson's Calendar, Ch. 1

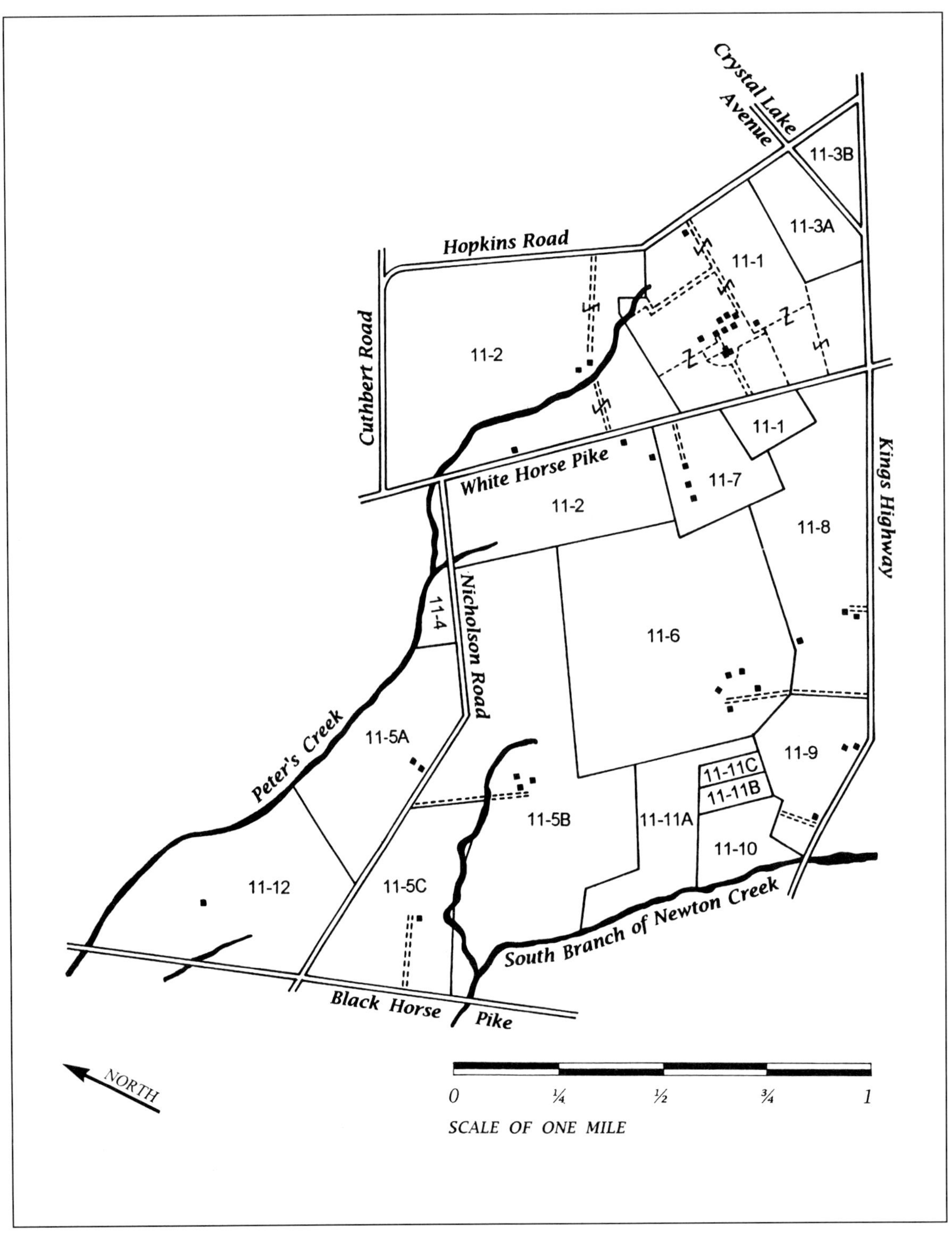

Map of the area that became Audubon and Audubon Park, 1877.

11

Audubon and Audubon Park

11-1 William H. Nicholson

This 108-acre farm extended between Hopkins Road (Hopkins Avenue) and the White Horse Pike and between East Pine Street and Kings Highway. Nicholson's tract also included a small lot on the western side of the White Horse Pike near Spruce Street.

11-2 William Bettle, Sr.

This 205-acre farm covered an area from Hopkins Avenue (Hopkins Road) to the White Horse Pike and between Cuthbert Road and East Pine Street. His real estate holdings also included land along the western side of the White Horse Pike extending to the vicinity of Virginia Avenue and between Nicholson Road and near Oak Street.

11-3 Hannah Ann Hinchman / Samuel M. Hinchman / Rebecca Ann Collings

Lot A Hanna Ann Hinchman's 22 acres of land was next to where Hopkins and Crystal Lake avenues intersect near Park Place.

Lot B Samuel Hinchman and Rebecca Collings's triangle-shaped fourteen-acre lot was within the area where Kings Highway intersects Hopkins Avenue, Hopkins Avenue crosses Crystal Lake Avenue, and Crystal Lake Avenue meets Kings Highway.

11-4 William Bettle, Jr.

Bettle's lot now straddles the Audubon/Oaklyn municipal boundary. The tract was between Nicholson Road and West Cedar Avenue and between the White Horse Pike and where Wyoming Avenue meets Nicholson Road.

11-5 John Cook / Mary Carson / Joseph Nicholson / William C. Nicholson

Lot A Ownership of John Cook's lot passed to Mary Carson, Joseph Nicholson and William C. Nicholson. The tract's 52 acres were between Peter's Creek and Nicholson Road and between Audubon Park, along the north side of Nicholson Road to opposite Wyoming Avenue.

Lot B Joseph Nicholson's odd-shaped tract encompassed the area between Virginia Avenue and the South Branch of Newton Creek, and between Nicholson Road and the area of Audubon Avenue.

Lot C William Nicholson inherited a 56-acre farm where the Audubon Shopping Center is situated.

11-6 John H. Dialogue

This 125-acre tract was between the vicinity of Virginia and Edgewood avenues and between Audubon Avenue and Walnut Street.

11-7 John A.J. Sheet

The boundaries of this 63-acre lot were between Oak and Spruce streets and between Third Avenue extending to the White Horse Pike.

11-8 Jeremiah Willits, Jr.

This 70-acre tract was along Kings Highway between the White Horse Pike and Edgewood Avenue. The farm extended from Kings Highway to the vicinity of Walnut Street.

11-9 Joseph Ewen

The borders of the farm were between Edgewood Avenue to near the South Branch of Newton Creek and Kings

Highway to the area of Walnut Street. At one-time, Ewen owned 82 acres of land in the township.

11-10 Glover Eastlack

The 26 acres of land was along the South Branch of Newton Creek, now Haddon Lake. The tract's borders were between Edgewood Avenue to Haddon Lake and near Graisbury Avenue to West Pine Street.

11-11 John T. Glover, The Howells and Mary Monroe

Lot A John Glover's 20-acre tract was between the vicinity of Edgewood Avenue and the South Branch of Newton Creek and between an area near Graisbury Avenue to Maple Avenue.

Lot B The Howell's small tract was near Hampshire and Mansion avenues.

Lot C The several acres of land owned by Mary Monroe were at the end of Mansion Avenue, near the athletic fields of Audubon High School.

11-12 Joseph Eldridge

The boundaries of this 101-acre farm were the same as those of Audubon Park.

During the 1870s, the area within old Haddon Township now known as Audubon and Audubon Park consisted of about a dozen farms plus a handful of smaller tracts.

11-1 William H. Nicholson

Born in 1827, William Hopkins Nicholson grew up on his family's 108-acre farm called "The Linden." Both his parents were members of the Society of Friends. William's mother, Rebecca Hopkins Nicholson, passed away when William was just ten years-old. Before departing, she arranged for her cousin Beulah to "take an interest in her children, and use her influence to have them brought up plainly and consistently as Friends." (*My Ancestors*, p. 89) Within two years after Rebecca passed on, William's father, Samuel Nicholson, married Beulah and the family moved to her house in Haddonfield, 65 Haddon Avenue. [See Samuel Nicholson, page 221.] "The Linden" was rented to tenant farmers.

William moved back to "The Linden" in 1855 after his marriage to Sarah Whitall. The couple temporarily resided in the old dwelling while a new spacious home was constructed. The Nicholsons' new dwelling was midway between Yale and Vassar roads where the streets intersect with Amherst Road. The couple's new home was a handsome three-story dwelling surrounded by outbuildings.

Much of what is known about the Nicholson family and "The Linden" can be traced to William's writing on his family's past:

> My parents started housekeeping at Linden, where my father had dwelt since infancy. . . . The house they dwelt in was plain, but very comfortable. A part of it still exists, moved a short distance from the old spot, to give place to that built for me to occupy after my marriage, in 1855. A hall, parlor, sitting-room, kitchen, two bedrooms and an enclosed shed, made up the first story, while the second contained four bedrooms and above these was an unfinished attic. A piazza was back of the house and under it an ice vault approached through the cellar. An open porch with seats stood before the hall-door in front. It may be here observed, that the chamber where I and all my sisters were born, and in which my mother died, is contained in that part of the house now tenanted by my farmer.
>
> The accompanying buildings at that date were, first, what we called the "old shop" a hip-roofed tenement near by, which had been the home of some earlier inhabitant; a smoke-house, carriage house and crib-house; a horse-barn and a grain barn; a cow barn and shedding; a wood-shed, a pig-pen and a cider-press. Before the house stood a range of tall Lombardy poplars, and the front lane was shaded by an avenue of cherry-trees. A fine old paper mulberry and two locust-trees, an ash, and many fine pear-trees stood near at hand. It was a pleasant home. (*My Ancestors*, p. 80)

A lane from the White Horse Pike approached the farmhouse in the direction and vicinity of Yale Road. The lane traveled past the dwelling and outbuildings and exited where Cornell Avenue meets Hopkins Avenue. Near this intersection, a tenant house once stood on Nicholson's land.

After a number of years, William and Sarah's family grew with the addition of John, Rebecca, Margaret and William, Jr. In keeping the house, Sarah Nicholson had ample help provided by domestic servants, a cook, and, for a period, a seamstress. Farm laborers also resided on the property. William was a cousin of William C. Nicholson, a farmer who resided

William H. Nicholson's dwelling in Audubon. The house once stood between Vassar and Yale roads, near Amherst Road. The house stood on a 108-acre farm called "The Linden."

(*My Ancestors*, William H. Nicholson)

on the west side of the White Horse Road. [See William C. Nicholson, page 186.]

In 1864, William's in-laws, the Whitalls of Philadelphia, acquired a tract near to "The Linden," known as "The Cedars," in Haddon Township. The Whitalls used the tract as a summer retreat. [See John Whitall, page 248.] In 1879, Sarah Nicholson's sister, Hannah Whitall Smith wrote a book about her father, John Whitall. It is likely that William Nicholson was influenced to chronicle his own family history by his sister-in-law's publication written some twenty years earlier.

In 1869, a career change proved to be a wise decision for William:

> Farming in New Jersey was then a good business. Times, however, afterwards changed in this respect, and I was fortunate in 1869, in accepting a request to enter the counting-house of Whitall, Tatum & Co., and eventually in becoming a member of the firm of that prosperous house. (*My Ancestors*, p. 106)

John Whitall, William's father-in-law, was the owner of Whitall, Tatum & Company, on Race Street in Philadelphia. The firm was a highly successful manufacturer of molded glass vials and bottles. The Nicholsons moved the family to Tenth and Arch streets in Philadelphia where it was more convenient for William to travel to work. "The Linden" became the Nicholson's summer home.

In 1879, James Peters, a tenant farmer, worked the fields at Nicholson's farm. The tenant paid his rent with a share of the harvest. A good portion of the farm was grasslands, filled with hay.

By the late 1880s, Nicholson's farm was near a new stop along the right-of-way of the Philadelphia & Atlantic City Railway known as Orston. The stop was where Chestnut Street intersects the railroad tracks in Audubon.

At the time of his death in 1908, William had garnered considerable wealth. His son John and son-in-law Joseph Rhoads inherited the family's farm. They tore down Nicholson's house during the course of residential development in the twentieth century.

11-2 William Bettle, Sr.

William Bettle, Sr. did not reside on his farm; rather, he lived in Philadelphia. His son Charles, a 27 year-old bachelor, was in charge of the farm in 1870. William, Sr. was the uncle of township resident Edward Bettle and father of William Bettle, Jr. Together the Bettle family members owned all the land along the eastern side of the White Horse Pike from the Main Branch of Newton Creek, in Oaklyn, to East Pine Street in Audubon. [See Edward Bettle, page 267, William Bettle, Jr., page 255.]

There were at least four dwellings on Bettle's land. The main dwelling was near Haviland Avenue between Graisbury and East Pine streets. Outbuildings stood behind the dwelling near Davis Avenue. A lane lead from the White Horse Pike to Bettle's house and continued onto Brick Kiln Road, later renamed Hopkins

Road. A second house, probably used by tenants, was along the turnpike near East Merchant Street.

Two houses were positioned on Bettle's lot, on the west side of the White Horse Pike near Graisbury Avenue. Part of the lot was wooded.

The beginning of Peter's Creek bisected Bettle's farm. The creek, also known as Money Run, originated on the neighboring Nicholson farm and traveled past Bettle's dwelling, across the farm, and passed under the White Horse Pike just west of Nicholson Road.

A valuable asset of a farmer was his livestock. In 1870, William Bettle, Jr. assigned two mules worth $450 and six horses to Charles Bettle. In addition, Charles was assigned eight cows, a bull, a calf, 41 pigs, 12 hogs, and 50 chickens. Charles also took possession of a Rockaway carriage, a York carriage, two carts, a sleigh, a farm wagon and a large market wagon. (Camden County Surrogate, Assignment Book A, p.12)

By 1879, oversight of the farm was given to James Anderson, a tenant farmer. Anderson tilled some 140 acres of Bettle's farm, raising crops commonly grown on most township farms.

11-3 Hannah Ann Hinchman / Samuel M. Hinchman / Rebecca Ann Collings

Several unimproved lots situated on the eastern side of the White Horse Pike fell within what became Audubon's borders. Hannah Ann Hinchman's lot contained 22 acres. Samuel M. Hinchman was Hannah Ann's appointed guardian, they had judged her a "lunatic." (Camden County Clerk's Office, 152-419)

The other fourteen-acre lot was owned by Samuel Hinchman and later came into the possession of Rebecca Collings. In 1863, they divided it into small lots and they offered the standing timber for sale. The *West Jersey Press* advertised that "oak and pine of handsome growth" covered the tract. The owners estimated between ten to fifteen cords of wood could be gathered on each acre. The newspaper noted the timber was "suitable for market wood or family use." (WJP 9/23/1863) [See Samuel M. Hinchman, page 246.]

11-4 William Bettle, Jr.

Bettle's lot, bisected by Peter's Creek, was west of the turnpike. Today, part of the lot is within Audubon. William Bettle, Jr.'s homestead was on the eastern side of the White Horse Turnpike, now known as the Bettlewood section of Haddon Township. [See William Bettle, Jr., page 255.]

11-5 John Cook / Mary Carson / Joseph Nicholson / William C. Nicholson

In 1865, John and Caroline Cook owned 52 acres of farmland on the north side of Nicholson Road. The Cook family resided in the region going back to the

William C. Nicholson's residence in Audubon. The house once stood next to Nicholson Road, opposite Ward Avenue. William Nicholson and his father Joseph Nicholson, owed some 245 acres of land in what is now Audubon.

(Courtesy of Joseph Hartel)

early 1820s. John and his wife Caroline, and their son Samuel, lived on the premises along with domestic servants and farm laborers.

The Cook house was on the north side of Nicholson Road, opposite where Ward Avenue meets Nicholson Road. Today, the Holy Maternity Church Rectory now stands next to the site of the original dwelling. In 1873, the house and outbuildings were offered for sale:

> Two and one-half storied frame dwelling home with three rooms on first floor, five on the second floor, two wells of good water, one at the house one at the barn. All necessary out buildings in good repair. (WJP 2/5/1873)

In the same newspaper advertisement, they described the farm, "in good state of cultivation, suitable for grain, grass or truck."

Samuel Cook eventually inherited the family farm. His father John, however, had reservations about his son's motives when it came to preserving the timber growing on the lot. John Cook inserted a covenant on Samuel's inheritance of the farm. If the trees were cut down or destroyed, John's will provided that the farm would pass from Samuel to John's grandson:

> ...in the case my said son should cut down sell and destroy any of the green and thrifty timber growing on said farm, his estate therein shall cease and determine that said farm should thereupon be vested in John Cook grandson, son of Samuel A. Cook. (Will, B-741)

In 1867, Mary Carson, age 40, purchased the Cook farm and assigned it to Isaac Carson. Carson held title to the property for several years. Besides selling the tract, they acquired an adjacent ten acres situated on the north side of Peter's Creek in Oaklyn.

In 1873, Joseph Nicholson, a neighbor, purchased Carson's land for his son, William Cooper Nicholson. After William married Anna Clement in 1875, the couple moved into the house on Nicholson Road and began to make renovations to the dwelling. William and Joseph were related to William Nicholson, the owner of a farm along the White Horse Road. [See William H. Nicholson, page 182.]

Over a period of many years, Joseph Nicholson amassed a substantial amount of real estate by obtaining several contiguous farms including the neighboring Carson farm. Together, Joseph and his son William owned 245 contiguous acres of land in Audubon.

Joseph Nicholson lived his entire life in a farmhouse which today stands at 528 West Merchant Street in Audubon. The dwelling, built in the eighteenth century, was where Joseph, his wife Sarah, and their son William and daughter Elizabeth resided.

A lane traveled from Nicholson Road, in the area of Brittin Avenue, toward Joseph Nicholson's house. The lane hooked between Nicholson's house and his barn. The road crossed over a small run that once flowed into the South Branch of Newton Creek. The creek, once known as Dennis Creek, took its name from Thomas Dennis, a seventeenth century land owner of land along the creek.

After Sarah's death in 1866, Joseph married Amy Haines. They had a son, George. After a long life, Joseph developed cancer and died in 1880. In his will he

Joseph Nicholson. Joseph resided in the dwelling now known as 528 West Merchant Street in Audubon. Joseph, a life-long farmer, passed away in 1880.

(Courtesy of Joseph Hartel)

John H. Dialogue. The Dialogues lived in what is now 355 Mansion Avenue. John owned an iron shipyard along the Delaware River in Camden.
(*The History of Camden County, New Jersey*, by George Prowell, 1886)

left Amy all the household goods and $8,000 to be invested in bonds and mortgages. His oldest son William inherited the deed to the farm where his wife and he resided on the northern side of Nicholson Road. Joseph's daughter, Elizabeth, and his minor son George, inherited their father's homestead farm. Joseph's legacy to his children included the rights to rentals and all crops, farming tools and livestock including an old blind mare. (Will, G-331)

Amy Haines Nicholson continued to reside on the tract and assumed oversight of the farm after her husband's death. Apparently the occupational title of "farmer" was once reserved for men. According to the U.S. Census Bureau in 1880, they noted Amy's profession as "carries on farm." Her livestock included some 200 chickens which produced 125 dozen eggs. Amy died in 1891.

William Nicholson, like his father Joseph, was a farmer. He planted the same types of crops grow throughout the township, although by the late 1870s the Nicholson farm was best known for its dairy products. William inherited an adjoining 56-acre farm from his grandfather, John Kaighn. This tract, where the Audubon Shopping Center is situated, had a tenant dwelling toward the center of the property. A lane traveled between the house and the Blackwoodtown & Camden Turnpike, now the Black Horse Pike.

Joseph Hartel was a grandson of William Nicholson. In a 1991 interview at his Haddonfield home, Mr. Hartel recalled that when his grandfather married Anna Elizabeth Clement, William was "read out of meeting" because she was not a Quaker. Mr. Hartel recalled that not only was his grandmother a Presbyterian, she was a "piano-playing Presbyterian."

According to Mr. Hartel, his grandmother Anna Nicholson found rural life to be very difficult, and she longed for her former life-style. She was raised in Haddonfield where her father Alfred Clement owned a general store. In 1887, William, Anna and their children moved from their farm to East Cottage Street in Haddonfield while they were building their new house. The following year, they moved into their new dwelling on Union Street, now called 45 West End Avenue in Haddonfield. William gave up the hard life of tilling the soil and became superintendent of the West Haddonfield Land Company.

Although he had moved into a village, William did not totally disengage from the agrarian life-style. At the time of his death in 1896, he still owned farming implements, a cow and calf and twenty chickens. Anna Nicholson passed away in 1956, two months short of her 100th birthday. Based on her longevity, the decision to move off the farm to Haddonfield was a wise one.

11-6 John H. Dialogue

In 1861, John H. Dialogue purchased a 125-acre farm known as the "Cedarcroft Farm." In 1870, John and his wife Mary had a son and three daughters. A domestic servant lived in Dialogue's household. The tenant farmer who resided on Dialogue's farm for many years, Charles Stafford, tilled the soil during the 1870s.

The Dialogues' brick house stands today at 355 Mansion Avenue. Several barns and outbuildings once surrounded the dwelling. A roadway, known as Sutvan's Lane, once traveled to the dwelling from Kings Highway. Although Sutvan's Lane still appears on some current road maps, the lane itself is now difficult to find. Sutvan's Lane intersects Edgewood Avenue near Kings Highway and travels diagonally meeting Chestnut Street at Cedarcroft Avenue.

Dialogue's farm adjoined land owned by John Sheets. Dialogue and Sheets were also business neighbors along the Delaware River at Kaighns Point in Camden. It was Sheets's business partner, John Norcross, that sold the 125-acre farm to the Dialogues.

John Dialogue, born in Philadelphia in 1828, was the son of the inventor and manufacturer of the riveted leather hose used by fire fighters. John, trained as a mechanic, opened a business in Camden repairing locomotives for the Camden and Amboy Railroad Company and steamers for several ferry companies. As work increased, a successful shipbuilding and repair operation evolved.

In 1858, Dialogue acquired 18 acres of land at Kaighns Point and built a foundry, forges and machine and boiler shops for the construction of vessels and engines. In the mid-1860s, his company merged with a company owned by Randolph Wood. They named the new firm Wood, Dialogue and Company. The company specialized in building and repairing vessels. The concern built ice boats for the City of Philadelphia and tug boats. It also did work for the U.S. Government. The shipyard built several steamships for the predecessor of the United States Coast Guard. One of the company's more memorable assignments was done in 1876 on the United States frigate "Constitution." The historic vessel underwent repair and refurbishing at the yard over a six month period:

> "Old Ironsides" This historical vessel, having been rebuilt by Wood, Dialogue & Co., is now at their yard, in this city, and visitors desiring to go aboard are permitted to do so. (CDP 10/9/1876)

After John's partner, Randolph Wood, committed suicide, the focus of the operation shifted. The shipyard became known for constructing iron tugboats. The concern took on a new name, River Iron Company, and manufactured and sold tugboats in both domestic and foreign cities.

In 1866, it is likely that John Dialogue wanted a more direct route to take to his business in Camden. He entered into an agreement with his neighbor, Joseph Nicholson, to build a private road leading over Nicholson's land and meeting Nicholson Road opposite where the Holy Maternity Church Rectory now stands. The lane was sixteen and one-half feet wide (one rod). Dialogue agreed to build fencing along the lane to "keep cattle from escaping" from his neighbor's farm. The agreement with Nicholson granted Dialogue permission to erect a gate at one or both ends of the road. (Agreement, 2/6/1866, Historical Society of Haddonfield.)

In 1874, Dialogue sold the farm to his partner and moved to Camden. John took on civic responsibilities in his new city; he was elected to the Camden City Board of Education and to City Council. He ran unsuccessfully for the New Jersey Senate. John died in 1898 at the age of 70. By 1877, Horatio Wood was the owner of the farm.

11-7 John A.J. Sheets

Next to the Dialogue property was a 63-acre farm owned by John and Rachael Sheets. The Sheets moved onto their farm in 1862, having lived in Camden and Philadelphia before that time. By 1870, John, Rachael and their seven children were living under the same roof with two domestic servants, a nurse and a gardener.

John Sheets was born in Williamsport, Pennsylvania in 1828. At the age of eighteen, John was employed at a sawmill along the Susquehanna River. It was here John befriended John Norcross. The two subsequently joined to form a wholesale and retail lumber concern along the Delaware River at Kaighns Point in Camden. The company's main product was wholesale timber and milled lumber. After a number of years on Camden's waterfront, the proprietors moved across the river to a wharf in Philadelphia.

The Sheets house once stood near what is now the intersection of Chestnut Street and West Atlantic Avenue. An 1858 fire insurance survey depicted the two-story brick structure's physical features. The dwelling had a slate roof, a "piazza" [veranda] and a side portico. The first floor had a parlor, sitting room, open hall and stairway with balusters and mahogany railings and newels. There were three chambers on the second floor and two bedrooms in the finished attic. (Rowand No. 185, 1862)

In 1864, Sheets built a two-story addition onto the dwelling. The first floor had a kitchen, the second floor, a bathroom and bedroom. At this time indoor plumbing was new. The bathroom had "...fixtures for raising water from the cistern to the bathroom." (Rowand No. 210, 1864)

Sheets's barn had stalls for six horses, a 14' x 35' threshing floor and bays to store hay. Other outbuildings stood on the tract including an eight-stall cow house, corncrib, wagon and storage sheds for wood and John's tools. The Sheets's ice house was used for cold storage and storing ice.

In 1872, the family moved to a new spacious stone house in Haddonfield. The new house was situated at the intersection of Chews Landing Road and Kings Highway. By all accounts, the house was a first rate dwelling, reportedly costing $30,000 to build and furnish. (WJP 9/18/1872). This amount was a considerable sum for a house then. They tastefully furnished the interior with a piano, library, and marble tables. Outside the house, John kept livestock on the premise including several cows, heifers and chickens. (Inv. I-61, 1888)

The Sheets's farm remained in the family for a number of years following their departure to Haddonfield. The property was occupied by Charles Osmond, a tenant farmer. Osmond utilized 53 acres on the farm. The remaining ten acres were wooded. In 1878, Sheets "country house" was put up for sale. The newspaper advertised that the twelve room brick mansion had "all the conveniences except gas." (WJP 2/13/1878) They sold the farm just about the time the Philadelphia and Atlantic City Railway Company built its right-of-way across the property.

John became an active citizen in Haddonfield. He served as a Borough Commissioner and Director of both the First National Bank of Camden and the Haddonfield Mutual Loan Association. During the summer months, the Sheets traveled to their cottage on Ocean Beach in Monmouth County. John continued to work in his lumber business up until the time he passed away in 1888.

11-8 Jeremiah Willits, Jr.

Jeremiah Willits, Jr.'s brick house was situated along Kings Highway in an area of Washington Terrace, between Cedarcroft and Wyoming avenues. Jeremiah's grandfather farmed on the tract as far back as the 1830s. In 1861, Jeremiah, wife Henrietta and their three children moved out of the township. Charles Willits, of Centre Township, acted as Jeremiah's agent after the owners vacated the farm.

Another house, most likely inhabited by farm laborers, stood on the tract's northern boundary near Chestnut Street. A third dwelling stood on the lot at the intersection of the White Horse Pike and Kings Highway.

William Sutvan rented the Willits's farm for many years. Sutvan resided on the lot with his wife Hannah and three children. Sutvan Lane formed the farm's western boundary with the neighboring property owned by Joseph Ewen. This thoroughfare led to John Dialogue's mansion. On today's map, Sutvan's Lane would run from Edgewood Avenue, near Kings Highway, to the vicinity of Chestnut Street near Cedarcroft Avenue.

"Sutvan Farm." William Sutvan, a tenant farmer, lived in the house surrounded by trees on the right side of the photograph. The house once stood near what is now Elm Avenue and Kings Highway. Sutvan's farm was situated along Kings Highway in what is now Audubon. The farm was owned by Jeremiah Willits, Jr.

(Audubon Historical Society Collections)

11-9 Joseph Ewen

The tract on the opposite side of Sutvan Lane was the homestead where Joseph Ewen, his wife Sybrilla and their six children lived. Although Ewen's land extended along both sides of Kings Highway, their dwelling was on the larger northern portion of land in Audubon. Ewen's property situated on the southern side of Kings Highway, was near Keswick, Sylvan and Thirteenth avenues in Haddon Heights.

Joseph, with the assistance of his three oldest sons and four laborers, worked the land. The Ewens' dwelling was located along Kings Highway, opposite Thirteenth Avenue. The barn, sheds and stables were behind the house near Washington Terrace. A second house was built on the property sometime during or after the Civil War. This house is 623 Kings Highway. The dwelling's flat roof exemplifies the Italianate Revival style of design.

A lane cut across the northern part of Ewen's tract in the vicinity of Hampshire Avenue and traveled toward two tracts of land near Audubon High School's athletic fields.

Roaming dogs were a nuisance to farmers because of the threat they posed to sheep. A local ordinance required owners of dogs to purchase dog licenses so that funds were available to compensate owners of sheep killed by dogs. The 1866 minutes the Township Committee meetings noted they reimbursed Joseph Ewen six dollars for sheep killed by stray dogs.

In 1881, the Ewens sold their farm to a nearby farmer, Jacob Dodd.

11-10 Glover Eastlack

Glover Eastlack operated a gristmill, known as Mt. Ephraim Mill, that once stood on his 26 acres. The mill, having been in existence since the mid-1700s, had been known by the names of the previous owners including Albertson's Mill and Hugg's Mill. Eastlack's mill received its power from a water wheel driven from the overflow of a millpond on the south side of Kings Highway in Haddon Heights. The mill's capacity was 35 bushels of grain a day. Eastlack operated the mill by himself, producing flour, feed, corn meal and oatmeal. Flour, however, was the main source of income for the mill owner. [See grist mills, page 136.]

By the early 1870s, Julius Ochme and Joseph Richyards were living and working at the mill. It is likely they were the last proprietors at the mill as the operations halted sometime in the mid-1870s.

11-11 John T. Glover, The Howells and Mary Monroe

John T. Glover owned twenty acres of woodland in what is now Audubon. John resided on the other side of Kings Highway in today's Haddon Heights. [See John T. Glover, page 238.]

The Howells owned a small tract near the Audubon High School's athletic fields. The property was also heavily wooded. The Howells lived in the village of Mt. Ephraim. They also owned several other small lots in old Haddon Township.

Mary Monroe and her family lived on several acres of land at the end of Mansion Avenue, near the athletic fields of Audubon High School. There were at least two dwellings on the lot. Mary, a 50 year-old African-American, was keeping house for three other family members in 1870. Nearby farmers employed male occupants of the house to work in the fields as laborers.

In 1870, Esther Monroe was living in the dwelling next to Mary's house. Ten years later, James Farmer, an African-American farm laborer, and his family were residing next to the Monroes. The property remained under African-American ownership until well into the twentieth century.

11-12 Joseph Eldridge

Joseph Eldridge acquired the 101-acre Albertson farm in 1866. The farm's boundaries were the same as those of Audubon Park. Joseph and his wife Susan had a large family, although at the time they obtained the farm, some of their ten children were grown and living elsewhere. Eldridge had previously resided on the Ridgway farm situated on the opposite side of Peter's Creek in Oaklyn. The Eldridge's two and one-half story brick mansion was located in the vicinity of Goldfinch and Eagle roads.

Two years after he purchased the farm, Joseph passed away. His wife Susan continued to live on the property with her four daughters. Joseph left all his farm products, implements and stock to his family, including four horses; "Lady", "Harry", "Lizzy" and "George." (Inv., C-406, 1868)

In 1868, the Eldridge barn was filled with feed for livestock that included ten tons of clover hay, fifteen tons of mixed hay, 200 bushels of wheat, thirty bushels of oats, fourteen tons of timothy hay, straw and wheat. They planted the fields with 80 rows of turnips, fourteen acres of corn, four acres of cabbage, sweet potatoes and late and early white potatoes. About 138 cords of firewood were stacked at the farm. (Inv., C-406)

Before James Eldridge moved onto his parents' farm to till the land, he resided on E.C. Knight's farm along Collings Road in what is now Collingswood. James raised a variety of livestock on the family farm including five horses, nine cows, thirty-nine sheep, twenty-one cattle, ten swine and thirty barnyard poultry. Like most township farmers, James raised hay and other feedstock for his animals.

In 1879, five acres of the farm was woodland. A small run surfaced on Eldridge's farm, near Kennedy Drive, traveled under the Black Horse Pike, crossed the adjoining Logan farm, where it emptied into the Main Branch of Newton Creek.

After James's mother died in 1878, they put up the farm for sale. An advertisement contained a description of the farm:

> ...high state of cultivation well adapted for raising grain and grass. Improvement–2 and one-half story brick mansion, 3 large barns, crib house, ice house, and other out-buildings, two wells, one at the house the other at the barn. Apple orchard with cherry and other fruit trees. The farm is also admirable adopted for dairy purposes and in the hands of an experienced dairyman, could be made to yield a handsome profit. (WJP 10/16/1878)

Despite attempts to sell the property, the farm remained in the Eldridge family. James's brother, Joseph C., assumed oversight of the farm in the 1880s.

Boroughs of Audubon and Audubon Park

The first large-scale residential development was initiated by Charles Schnitzler and William Heaney, partners in the Linden Homestead and Building Association. The development was west of the railroad's right-of-way to Fourth Avenue, and between Oak and Cherry streets.

Shortly after that, in 1894, John Logan, a retired employee of Standard Oil Company and Oscar Stager of the Reading Railroad, organized a land development company upon acquiring William Bettle's 60 acres of land on the western side of the White Horse Turnpike. Some five years later, H.D. LeCato purchased Bettle's land lying east of the turnpike. The new owners set into motion development of residential housing. Soon, passenger trains stopped to pick up commuters along the Philadelphia & Atlantic City Railroad right-of-way and trolley service extended through the area. In March 1905, 1,060 acres of land were incorporated into the newly-created Borough of Audubon. Encompassed within the Borough of Audubon's original 1905 borders were some 100 acres that were ceded to the Borough of Audubon Park in 1947.

Audubon Park remained farmland until the Second World War. In 1941, President Franklin D. Roosevelt recognized a need for adequate housing for industrial workers employed in the nation's expanding defense programs. The Federal Works Agency, a branch of the U.S. Government, financed the construction of some 500 housing units, contained in 184 buildings, in what was called Audubon Village. Shipbuilding workers, the original inhabitants of the units, did not buy or rent their homes. They purchased stock from the Federal Government in a mutual home company that owned the project.

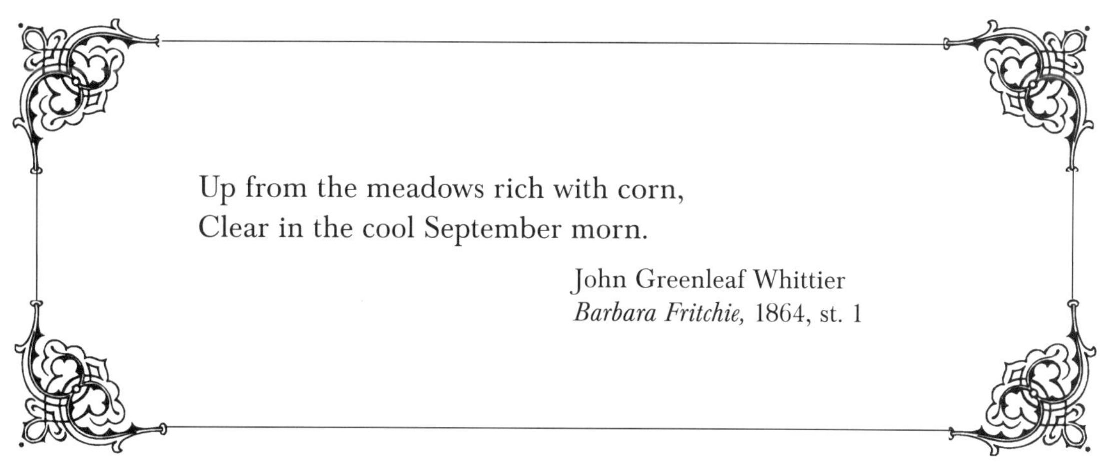

Up from the meadows rich with corn,
Clear in the cool September morn.

John Greenleaf Whittier
Barbara Fritchie, 1864, st. 1

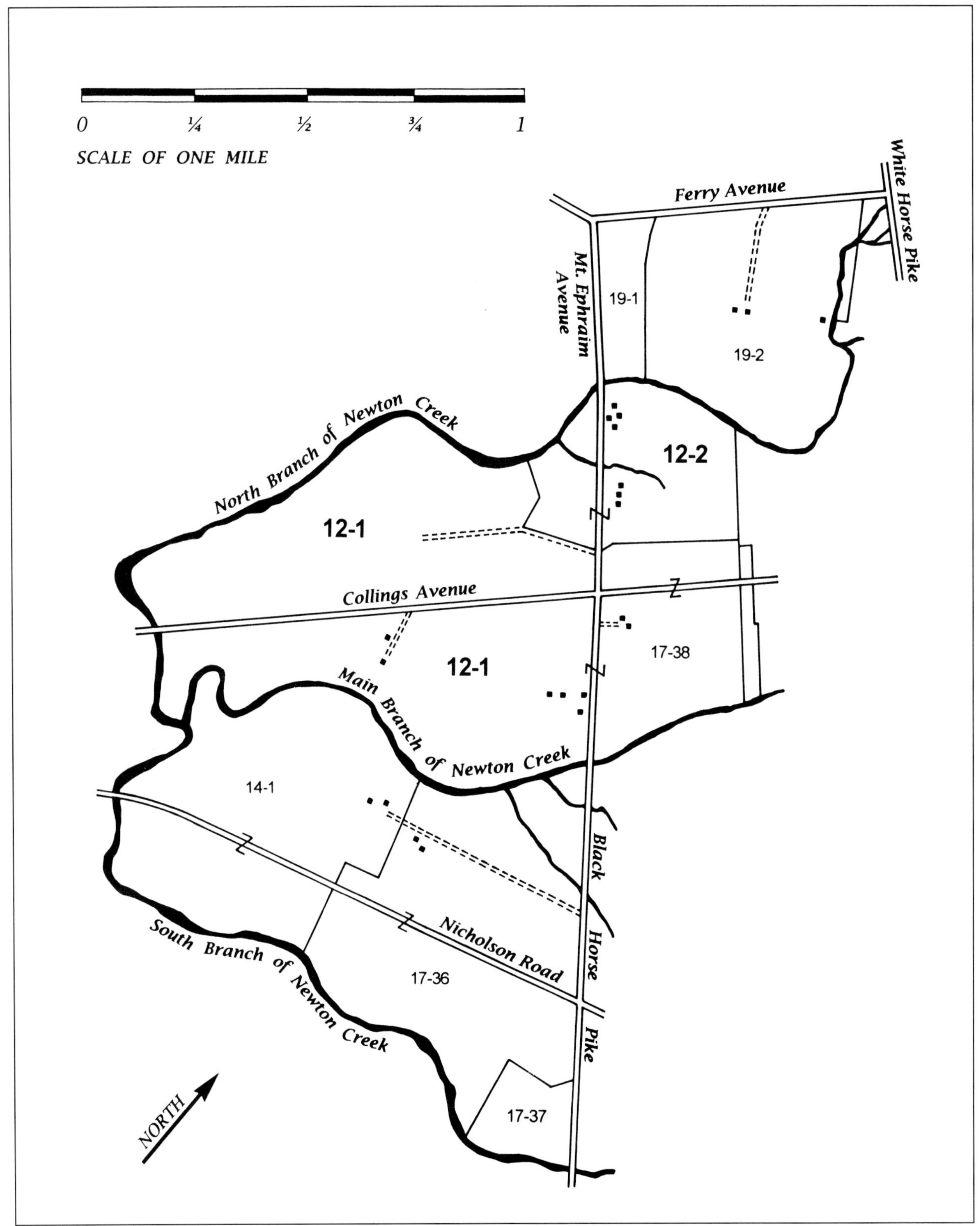

Map of the area that became part of Camden, including Fairview, West Collingswood Extension (Haddon Township), Gloucester Heights (Gloucester City), West Collingswood Heights (Haddon Township) and Woodlynne, 1877.

12

Camden (Fairview)

12-1 Estate of Samuel Champion
The Champion Estate's four farms comprised 434 acres, including the Fairview section of Camden. The Estate owned most of the land west of Mt. Ephraim Avenue, between the Main Branch and the North Branch of Newton Creek. The neighboring farm, owned by the heirs of Edward Smith, owned part of the land on the southwest quadrant where the North Branch of Newton Creek crosses under Mt. Ephraim Avenue. The Champion Estate also owned what now is Haddon Township's West Collingswood Extension. The lot is between Mt. Ephraim Avenue and Collingswood's border and from the Main Branch of Newton Creek to near Grant Avenue.

12-2 Estate of Edward Smith
This 68-acre lot was positioned predominantly on the eastern side of Mt. Ephraim Avenue to Collingswood's border, and between West Collingswood Extension and Woodlynne. A small portion of the estate extended to the west side of Mt. Ephraim Avenue, between Fairview and the North Branch of Newton Creek.

During the 1870s, the heirs of the two estates held title to land along the western edge of old Haddon Township. The Estate of Samuel Champion owned four separate farms. Three of the farms became part of the City of Camden, while the fourth, now known as West Collingswood Extension, remained in Haddon Township. The second estate, administered by the heirs of Edward Smith, was, for the most part, farmland; however, a brickyard stood on a small portion of the property.

12-1 Estate of Samuel Champion

The heirs of Samuel Champion were overseers of four adjoining farms that comprised more than 430 acres. Together the farms made up the largest contiguous tract in old Haddon Township. Throughout the 1860s and 1870s, many tenant farmers lived on the four Champion farms and worked in the fields. Hay, wheat, corn, potatoes and market garden vegetables were raised on the Champion farms.

Samuel Champion resided on the tract during the first half of the nineteenth century. His wife, Elizabeth, was a direct descendent of Robert Zane, one of the original Newton colonists. Samuel, Elizabeth and their children lived on a lot known as the "Mineral Springs Farm." Champion obtained the 78-acre lot in 1825. The farm was between the vicinity of Mt. Ephraim/Black Horse Pike and New Hampshire Avenue and between the Main Branch of Newton Creek and Collings Avenue. A small portion of the tract was situated on the northwest corner of the intersection of Collings and Mt.

Samuel Champion's house in Fairview. The brick dwelling was once near the Main Branch of Newton Creek and the Black Horse Pike in today's Camden. The Estate of Samuel Champion held some 430 acres of farmland in Haddon Township.

(Camden County Historical Society Collections)

Ephraim avenues. Some years later, Samuel added fifteen adjoining acres to his homestead farm, east of what is now New Hampshire Avenue. Champion's brick house and outbuildings were situated on the west side of Black Horse Pike near the Main Branch of Newton Creek.

Throughout the nineteenth century, many people drank bottled water taken from springs that they credited with having medicinal qualities. Visitors from Philadelphia and Camden traveled to the outlying countryside to fill their jugs and bottles at these springs. The "Mineral Springs Farm" was once a watering place known as Sloan's Mineral Springs. In 1814, James Sloan built a building to sell spring water to travelers passing along the road that is now Mt. Ephraim Avenue/Black Horse Pike. An advertisement placed in a Philadelphia newspaper entitled *Poulson's American Daily Advertiser* on June 24, 1814 noted that Sloan:

> ...has erected a spacious and commodious building for the accommodation of families or individuals in the vicinity of his Mineral Springs, ...

Many years later, the author of a book on the history of bottled spring water described the site:

> The house is situated on a rising eminence, surrounded by a country which is healthful, fertile, and highly pleasing to the eye. From the mineral contents of the water, which are iron, sulphurated hydrogen, and some saline matter, it has been found useful in dispeptic complaints and general debility. (*They Took to the Waters*, p. 102)

Champion once owned a brickyard in the 1830s on the White Horse Road. Besides bricks, the concern sold tiles and pipes for "under draining." The brickyard was on "Clover Hill Farm," now a part of Oaklyn.

The area that is now Haddon Township's West Collingswood Extension was the second farm acquired by Champion in 1826. The 79-acre lot was called the "Cedar Grove Farm." A brick house stood on the lot near the intersection of Mt. Ephraim and Eldridge avenues. Route 130, which cuts through Camden and the West Collingswood Extension, did not exist in the nineteenth century.

Adjoining the "Cedar Grove Farm" were two narrow lots along Collings Road. The Old Newton Grave Yard, on the south side of Collings Road, is the site where the families of the first settlers of the area were buried. On the north side of Collings Road was the Champion School. Both landmarks still exist in West Collingswood Extension. [See graveyards, page 83, education, page 57.]

Samuel Champion played an important role in the early history of the Champion School. The school was built in 1821 by the Newton Union School Society. After they built the school, title to the school property came into question. Samuel resolved the problem by obtaining the deed from the former owners. The inhabitants of Newton Township elected four trustees, who raised money to pay Champion. Then they transferred the deed to the school to the trustees.

In 1832, Champion again added to his farmland by acquiring the 100-acre "Ashland Farm." The lot was between Collings Avenue, and the Main Branch of Newton Creek, and between New Hampshire Avenue and where Merrimac Street intersects Collings Avenue. The tract extended on the north side of Collings Avenue to Common Road, and between Hartford and Sumter roads.

A farmhouse once stood on the lot next to Collings Road near what is now Malandra Hall. The dwelling, built in the eighteenth century, stood until a fire destroyed it in 1974. The house was the supposed birth place of Elizabeth Griscom Ross, better known as Betsy Ross.

Champion purchased his fourth farm, some 162 acres, in 1843 from a neighbor, John Campbell. The lot, known as the "Willow Grove Farm," included a section of Fairview north of Common Road, to the North Branch of Newton Creek. The farm was west of Sumter Road including the area of Routes 76 and 676 and the Walt Whitman Bridge entrance/exit ramps. A house once stood on the lot to the north of Collings Road near the Main Branch of Newton Creek.

Samuel died in 1847, leaving the land to his six daughters. He had acquired property in the village of Haddonfield, and other locations in southern New Jersey. Eventually, Champion's last surviving daughter, Rebecca Cooper, inherited the property in the township. When Rebecca passed away in 1884, her heirs sold the 434-acre tract to the Champion Land Company.

12-2 Estate of Edward Smith

The tract of land belonging to the Estate of Edward Smith was predominantly on the eastern side of Mt. Ephraim Avenue. The one-time owner of the lot, Edward Smith, resided on the 68-acre tract until his death in the 1850s. The lot was generally known as "Brick Yard Farm," named for an adjoining brickyard.

Smith's outbuildings and brick farmhouse were on the eastern side of the Camden & Blackwoodtown Turnpike located midway between Collings Road and the North Branch of Newton Creek. After Smith passed away, tenant farmers occupied the farm. In 1880, corn was the crop of choice, although other grains and grasses were grown.

A small stream emerged on Smith's lot, crossed Mt. Ephraim Avenue and onto the Champion Estate for a short distance before flowing into the North Branch of Newton Creek. The run was known as Sloan's Mineral Spring.

One tenant farmer on the Smith Estate lot was the grandfather of Charles Whiley, formerly of Collingswood. The Whiley family moved onto the farm sometime in the 1880s and remained there for some 40 years. In a 1992 interview, Charles Whiley recalled when his grandfather told stories about Gypsies traveling through the area. Grandfather Whiley allowed the travelers to pull their wagons off the road near Newton Creek and camp on the farm. The children from the surrounding countryside were curious about the "guests" and wanted to witness them firsthand. Their mothers on the other hand, were fearful for their children's welfare due to a common belief that Gypsies, given the opportunity, would kidnap unsuspecting children. It was not until the Gypsies passed through the area did the mothers of the area feel relieved.

During the 1840s, Edward Smith was building brick row homes in South Camden. It is fitting that Smith would have an association with a brickyard. For many years, Peter Stetzer's brickyard operated on part of Smith's land, along the eastern side of what is now Mt. Ephraim Avenue at the North Branch of Newton Creek. Stetzer's proprietorship commenced in the 1840s and lasted until his death in 1863.

Early on, the yard did a substantial business. In the 1850s, fifteen workers were manufacturing bricks seven months of the year at the site. After Stetzer passed on, John Stone and James Deno took over the operation. At that period in time, most of their customers were builders raising homes in the southern part of Camden. In 1879, the brickyard closed after the creek overflowed its banks and flooded the premise. They reopened it for just a short period when James Deno died. The business ceased operating in the 1880s. [See brickyards, page 130.]

City of Camden

Construction of Yorkship Village, later renamed Fairview, began in 1918 when the U.S. Shipping Board's Emergency Fleet Corporation recognized a need to house shipyard workers. The new community required sewer lines, water pipes, fire hydrants, and police and fire protection all of which Haddon Township was unwilling or unable to provide. Camden, better able to furnish the services to the new village, extended its borders in 1918 to include most of the former Champion Estate and all of the former Smith Estate. The former Champion Estate's "Cedar Grove Farm," was not ceded to Camden but remained part of Haddon Township. It is now known as West Collingswood Extension.

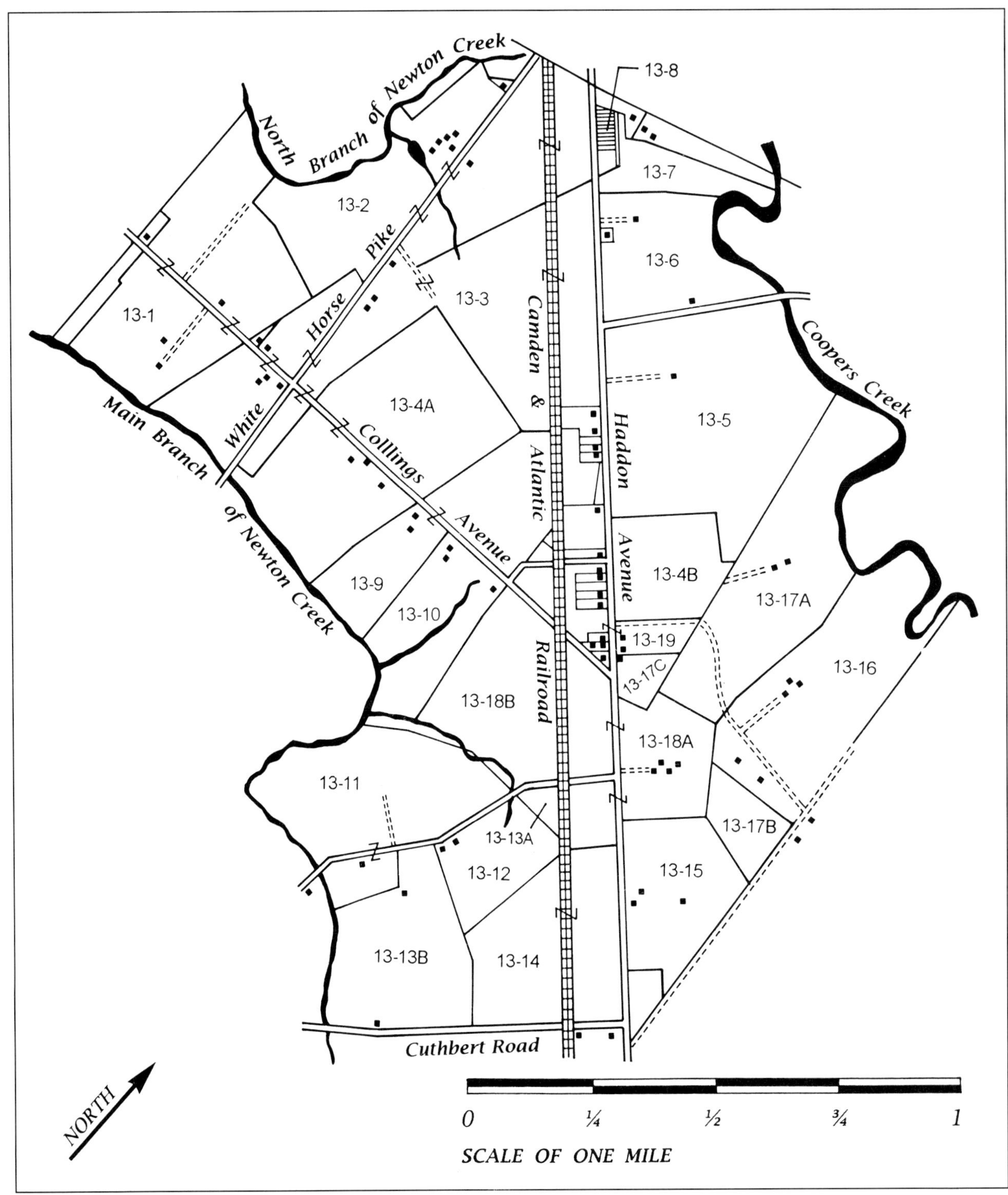

Map of the area that became Collingswood, 1877.

13

Collingswood

13-1 John Campbell

This 98-acre farm was between Cattell Avenue and the vicinity of West Collingswood Extension, and from the Main Branch of Newton Creek to the vicinity of Harrison Avenue.

13-2 John C. DaCosta

This tract borders on the west side of the White Horse Pike near Harrison Avenue, to Collingswood's border with Woodlynne and Camden. DaCosta's land, on the east side of the pike, would approximate Jessamine Avenue to the borough's municipal border with Camden, and between the White Horse Pike and Haddon Avenue. DaCosta's lot was 106 acres.

13-3 Samuel H. French

Most of this 140-acre tract was on the north side of Collings Road and east of the White Horse Pike. The area was between the White Horse Pike and near Franklin Avenue, and between Collings Avenue and Harrison Avenue. The borders also extended from near the intersection of Harrison and Franklin avenues to Haddon Avenue. Along Haddon Avenue its borders were between the area of West Summerfield Avenue and near Route 130.

French's tract, on the southeast quarter of Collings Avenue and the White Horse Pike, was a narrow strip of land near the pike that extended to near the Main Branch of Newton Creek. French's land on the southwestern quadrant of Collings Avenue and White Horse Pike was between an area near Catell and Richey avenues to the White Horse Pike and between the Main Branch of Newton Creek to Collings Avenue. The area on the northwest quadrant of Collings Avenue and the White Horse Pike was between the vicinity of what became Richey Avenue and the White Horse Pike, and between Collings Avenue to near Harrison Avenue.

13-4 Edward Z. Collings / Edward C. Knight / Richard T. Collings

Lot A Collings Road cut across the 96-acre tract. A large part of the tract is Knight Park. The tract's perimeter would be between the Main Branch of Newton Creek and an area in Knight Park, and between Franklin Avenue and Harrison Avenue to the eastern property line of Collingswood High School.

Edward Knight acquired a number of farms totaling 178 acres of land on the northeast side of Haddon Avenue.

Lot B The first of these lots was a 30-acre farm located between the vicinity of Crestmont and Woodlawn avenues and between Haddon Avenue and near Highland Avenue. A description of Knight's other lots follow.

13-5 Robert Wood / Edward C. Knight

This 106-acre tract was along Haddon Avenue between Browning Road and Crestmont Terrace. The farm extended from Haddon Avenue to Cooper's Creek.

13-6 James Stevenson / Edward C. Knight

The perimeter of this 40-acre lot was between Haddon Avenue and Cooper River, and between Browning Road and the area near East Narbeth Terrace.

13-7 Peter Wagner

The seven acres were between Stonetown and Cooper's Creek.

13-8 Stonetown

A number of small lots along Haddon Avenue, where it intersects Route 130, made up Stonetown.

13-9 Jacob Collings / Thomas S. Collings / Joseph Z. Collings

This tract's boundaries, south of Collings Road, were between the Main Branch of Newton Creek and Collings Road, and between Collingswood High School and Colford Avenue. The farm, north of Collings Road, included a good portion of present-day Knight Park and land between Park Avenue and the PATCO High Speed Line. The farm encompassed 60 acres.

13-10 Anna Maria Collings / Joseph S. Collings / Robert McLaughlin

The perimeter of this 40-acre tract was between the vicinity of Colford Avenue and the area of Bettlewood and Park avenues, and between Newton Creek and Collings Avenue.

13-11 George Lee / William Jones

The 68-acre property included the area within Collingswood, south of the intersection of Lees and Park avenues, including near Stokes, Linwood, Belmont, Merrick, Mansion, Chelsea, Ventnor avenues and Newton Park Drive, between Merrick Avenue and Lees Lane.

13-12 Charles B. F. O'Neil / Thomas P. Hanbest

This tract's property lines would cut diagonally across current streets and blocks. This 25-acre property was between Lees Lane and a point near Conard Avenue. The land extended between the PATCO High Speed Line's right-of-way to an area near Linwood Avenue. The majority, if not all of the land, fell within what became Collingswood.

13-13 John Schnitzius

Lot A The small lot was on the southeastern quadrant of the intersection of the PATCO High Speed Line's right-of-way and Lees Avenue.

Lot B Schnitzius also owned a 69-acre farm situated between the Main Branch of Newton Creek in the locality of the Collingswood/Haddon Township border, and between Lees Lane and Cuthbert Road. In 1888, the municipal border near Linwood and Stokes avenues was set when they created Collingswood. Most of the tract fell within Haddon Township. The boundary was moved every so slightly in 1953 to its present location.

13-14 Joseph O. Cuthbert, Sr. / Henry Cuthbert

This 110-acre farm was on the south side of Haddon Avenue between Conard and Albertson avenues. Roughly half the farm was in Collingswood, the other portion in Haddon Township. Cuthbert's real estate holdings included a small wooded lot along the north side of the Haddon Avenue. Today this small lot would be between Strawbridge and Penn avenues.

13-15 Amos Willis, Sr. / William Bozorth

This 42-acre farm was on the northeastern side of Haddon Avenue between the area of Penn and Fern avenues. This tract's borders extended from Haddon Avenue to the vicinity of the intersection of Lawnside and Homestead avenues. The lot's eastern boundary was Burr's Lane, now a border separating Haddon Township and Collingswood.

13-16 James DaCosta

This tract's borders were between the Cooper River and near Lincoln Avenue, and between the area of Cedar Avenue and Collingswood's eastern border with Haddon Township. The farm contained 68 acres of land.

13-17 Martha Rowles

Lot A The boundaries of this 70-acre farm were between Cedar Avenue and west to a line that would cut diagonally across Woodlawn Terrace, Harvard, Knight, East Madison Avenue and Crestmont Terrace, then meet Cooper's Creek.

Lot B Rowles owned an eighteen-acre tract situated along the Haddon Township/Collingswood border, between the vicinity of Lawnside and New Jersey avenues in Collingswood.

Lot C Martha also owned a small lot along Haddon Avenue opposite Collings Avenue.

13-18 William P. Tatem

Lot A The 40-acre farm was on the northeastern side of the Haddon Avenue, between what is now Washington and Fern avenues. Its borders extended between Haddon Avenue and a line that crossed diagonally over New Jersey, Fern and Lawnside avenues. Tatem's land on the southwestern side of Haddon Avenue was between Stiles and Collings avenues and between Haddon Avenue and the PATCO High Speed Line tracks.

Lot B Tatem's other 40-acre lot was south of the PATCO High Speed Line's right-of-way to Linwood Avenue, between Collings Avenue and near Lees Avenue.

13-19 Mahlon Van Booskirk

This eighteen-acre lot was between Woodlawn and Lincoln avenues and between Haddon Avenue and an area near Autumn Avenue. Van Booskirk also owned land on the opposite side of Haddon Avenue.

"Thackara House" located in Collingswood. Today the house is at 912 Eldridge Avenue. The house, built in 1754, took the name of its builder, Thomas Thackara.

(Camden County Historical Society Collections)

In the early 1870s, about a dozen dwellings and an inn or tavern stood along Haddonfield Turnpike near the center of Collingswood. On the turnpike, at the township's border with Camden, stood about a dozen homes in a community known as Stonetown. The remaining area, soon to be incorporated as Collingswood, was farmland.

13-1 John Campbell

For many years John Campbell owned 98 acres of land in West Collingswood. He acquired the farm in 1839 when he was 39. It was here that John and his wife Mary raised their four children. John retired from farming early in the second half of the nineteenth century and moved off the tract. The land was then rented to tenant farmers.

The Campbell house still stands at 912 Eldridge Avenue. The structure is frequently called the "Thackara House," named after the dwelling's builder in 1754. A lane once lead from Collings Road to Campbell's brick dwelling at a point between Comely and Taylor avenues. Many years later, Collingswood's historian George Palmer described the dwelling:

> This early house displays the characteristic simplicity of 18th century vernacular houses. Noteworthy features include the symmetrical arrangement of window on the facade, the Flemish Bond brick pattern, the husband's and wife's initials and construction date set into the brickwork at the gable end, and the large chimneys. ("Collingswood Centennial Walking and Auto Tour of 1987")

George Newkirk was a tenant farmer who lived and worked on the Campbell farm during 1870s. The *West Jersey Press* reported Newkirk was an "old Salem County boy." The same article revealed Newkirk did most of the chores on the farm without hired help: "Forty acres, Mr. Newkirk does nearly the whole work himself except during hay time and harvest." (WJP 9/18/1872) Newkirk also raised turkeys. Other tenant farmers that worked the land were George and Isaac Stratton.

After John Campbell died in 1882, his children inherited his land. Five years later, they conveyed the deed to Edward Knight. Knight planned to turn the fields into residential building lots. Soon thereafter, home construction began in West Collingswood.

13-2 John C. DaCosta

The White Horse Turnpike divided John C. DaCosta's 106-acre farm into two sections. DaCosta's dwelling and outbuildings sat along the west side of White Horse Pike, where the road now intersects Route 130. John DaCosta and his wife Hannah lived in the large house with their five children. Edward DeHaven, a relative of the family, and his seven children also resided on the farm. Edward was a Captain in the United States Navy. Tenant farmers and farm hands also lived and worked on the property. DaCosta's financial means was quite evident. He employed five domestic servants to help on the premise.

The three-story brick dwelling was 52' x 28' with an attached one-story brick kitchen. A 6' x 37' shed was affixed to the back of the house. The front of the house faced south and had a portico along its entire length supported by six turned wood columns. On the first floor, the parlor and dining rooms each had two fireplaces. A center hall and a stairway led to the second and third floors where there were four rooms on both floors. (Rowand No. 39, 1855)

Near the house stood a large barn that measured 72' x 76'. Another smaller barn, 38' x 26', stood nearby. Jacob Rowand wrote on his fire insurance survey that the barns were "built of the best material, oak frame, cedar wood, cedar siding, and oak studs." Other outbuildings on the premise included a hay house, cow stables, and grain "barrics." [sic] (Rowand No. 39, 1855)

A small creek originated on DaCosta's lot on the east side of the White Horse Pike, crossed under the road near the dwelling and emptied into the North Branch of Newton Creek. A dam formed a small pond along the run, near Richey Avenue. Some years after ownership passed from the DaCosta family, the lot took on the name "Lake View."

DaCosta achieved considerable success in business before retiring to become a gentlemen farmer. John started as a merchant with an office on North Front Street, in Philadelphia. His firm did a considerable amount of overseas trading, particularly with East India. In 1850, *Dun & Bradstreet* noted DaCosta was "considerably wealthy" and "largely engaged in business in Philadelphia." John's wealth allowed him to invest in other businesses: one was a southern New Jersey venture. John was a founder of the Camden & Atlantic Railroad Company. Beginning in the early 1850s, the company planned the resort town of Atlantic City so excursionists could visit the sandy beaches during the summer. DaCosta, along with several other incorporators, officers and directors of the company are generally credited with founding Atlantic City. [See railroads, page 35.]

Being a railroad executive had its advantages. Though the surrounding countryside was farmland, the Camden & Atlantic Railroad placed a train stop next to DaCosta's farm. The White Horse Station stood near where the present PATCO High Speed Line Ferry Avenue Station stands.

Shortly before John died in 1875, the family moved back to Philadelphia. When John passed away at the age of 75, *The Haddonfield Basket* wrote, "He was largely interested in the Camden & Atlantic Railroad and the Cooper's Point Ferry. The ferryboats had their flags at half mast, and the engines on the road were draped in black on the day of the funeral." (HB 4/1875) The *Philadelphia Inquirer* wrote that DaCosta held large amounts of stock in the Camden & Atlantic Railroad and "some valuable farm lands on the White Horse Turnpike in Camden County." (3/26/1875) John was interred at Philadelphia's Christ Church burying ground at Fifth and Arch streets. After John passed away, the Camden & Atlantic Railroad Company paid tribute to one of its founders. The company acquired a Baldwin locomotive steam engine for its line and named it the "J.C. DaCosta."

After DaCosta's passing, the farm was conveyed to his son, James DaCosta. James resided along Cooper's Creek, before moving to his parent's farm. [See James DaCosta, page 210.] The focus of James's pursuits was raising thoroughbred cattle. By the end of the 1880s, most of the farm was purchased by Edward Knight's Collingswood Land Company.

13-3 Samuel H. French

Samuel Harrison French purchased the 140-acre "White Mansion Farm" from his younger brother Clayton in 1865 for $42,438. The tract's dimensions extended over all four quadrants at the intersection of Collings Avenue and the White Horse Pike.

The French mansion is now 315 White Horse Pike. The structure, now known as "Dungarvan," is presently owned by The Excelsior Scottish Rite Temple. This dwelling, built sometime around 1850, was designed with Greek Revival and Italianate architectural features. After purchasing the "White Mansion Farm," Samuel wasted little time making improvements. A new roof was placed on the mansion and a new tenant house and stone and brick cow house were constructed.

Born in 1816, Samuel grew up in Mullica Hill and Swedesboro. As a young man he moved to Salem, Ohio where he met his wife Angelina. During their marriage, the couple raised five children. In 1852, the French family returned to Philadelphia where Samuel and his brother Clayton established the manufacturing branch of French & Richards. The firm was a wholesale dealer in drugs and a manufacturer of paints and oils, cement and building materials. Samuel's expertise was in the manufacturing side of the business. Clayton's skills were centered in selling the products.

Even though he was a Quaker, Samuel, unlike other Friends, took a stance during the Civil War. Samuel's son Howard French, noted in his book *Genealogy of the Descendants of Thomas French*, that his father,

Samuel H. French's house in Collingswood. The house today is 315 White Horse Pike. Samuel's farmstead, known as "White Mansion Farm," spread over some 140 acres. Samuel French was a wealthy businessman.

(*Genealogy of the Descendants of Thomas French*, by Howard French)

> ...furnished substitutes for himself—though he was beyond the age limit—two sons and two business associates and especially cared for the families of those in his employ who enlisted, duplicating the bounty paid by State, county and city. (p. 257)

In 1865, fire destroyed the French, Richards & Company seven-story warehouse at Tenth and Market Streets [Philadelphia], and resulted in damages of some $300,000. On the morning after the blaze, Samuel was crossing the Delaware River on a ferry traveling to work when news of the catastrophic fire reached him. His response illustrated Samuel's calm and reflective personality. His son wrote that Samuel, upon hearing the news, said, "That's too bad." (p. 255)

In 1883, Samuel and Clayton dissolved their partnership. Samuel continued to operate a paint works plant at Fourth and Callowhill Streets under a new organization called Samuel H. French & Company. Samuel's sons, Howard and William, soon became partners in the new concern. Later, the firm opened a paint works in City of Camden.

Samuel's brother Clayton continued in the endeavor of making and selling drugs at the Tenth and Market streets location. The firm's other partner was William Richards, Clayton's brother-in-law. Many years later, French, Richards & Company evolved into the Philadelphia-based international pharmaceutical firm Smith, Kline & French.

Samuel French's commercial success enabled him to make many real estate investments. He acquired three farms totaling about 195 acres in the Westmont section of Haddon Township. The "Creek Farm," "Pine Grove Farm" and "Osler Farm" were situated between Cooper's Creek and the Haddonfield Turnpike. [See Samuel French, page 258.] His land holdings were not limited to old Haddon Township. He owned some 30 city blocks of undeveloped property along Camden's Federal Street and land in Pennsylvania, Maryland and as far away as Texas.

As a gentlemen farmer, Samuel had an interest in husbandry. The *West Jersey Press* reported:

> Samuel French, at his country seat on the White Horse Turnpike has a fine herd of imported Jerseys. Valued at $500 to $700 each they are the gentlest creatures of cow kind, and their milk is nearly all cream. (WJP 8/24/1879)

An interesting feature of the "White Mansion Farm" is revealed in Howard French's *Genealogy of the Descendants of Thomas French*:

> As a fitting and lasting tribute to the one hundredth anniversary of the birth of the nation, Mr. French planted, in the spring of 1876, one thousand shade trees along the roads surrounding his summer home in Camden county, New Jersey. Most of these trees have grown to large size, and now [1913] add much to the beauty of the neighborhood and the comfort of the inhabitants of that very populous locality. (p. 261)

The rural countryside provided a welcome relief from the fast-paced city life. The French homestead offered all that was considered wholesome in the countryside. However, even inhabitants of the farm district were not untouched by crime:

> Early in the evening of Wednesday last the residence of Mr. French, of the firm of "French, Richards & Company" 10th and Market Street, Philadelphia, who resides on the White Horse Road about a mile from Camden, was entered and robbed of several valuables. Mrs. French was at home sitting in the drawing room downstairs. She heard someone open the hall door and go downstairs but supposed the person to be one of the family, not an intruder. There is no trace of the bold thief. (CDP 11/24/1876)

Farmers rented the arable land on the French homestead. A tenant house sat on the southwest corner of the White Horse Pike and Collings Avenue. Two barns and a wagon house stood next to the dwelling along the southern edge of Collings Avenue. The Haines brothers lived and worked on the property:

> Joshua Haines who with his brother "works" the farm of Samuel H. French. The Haines have already sent to market ten thousand baskets of truck of different kind. . .22 cows the milk of which goes to Philadelphia. While the farm in grain, grasses and other produce is quite sufficient to maintain a large stable of horses and other stock. (WJP 9/18/1872)

In 1877, Franklin Haines's wheat field was on the western side of the turnpike.

Two other buildings were situated near the Haines dwelling. A toll house for the White Horse Turnpike Company stood on the turnpike at Collings Road. [See tollgate keepers, page 30.] The other structure was the Newton Baptist Church. This small church, built in 1843, sat along the north edge of Collings Avenue near Richey Avenue. The congregation heard sermons from the pastor of the Haddonfield Baptist Church. [See houses of worship, page 64.]

In the 1880s, another successful Philadelphia businessman, Edward Knight was buying up land around the township. French sold his farm to Knight in 1886 and moved back to Philadelphia where he stayed until his death in 1895. Soon after that, Knight transferred the tract to his corporation, the Collingswood Land Company.

13-4 Edward Z. Collings / Edward C. Knight / Richard T. Collings

Members of the Collings family owned most of the land along Collings Road, to the east of White Horse Turnpike. Collectively, the farms were known as "Garden Farms."

Edward Z. Collings III owned a 96-acre farm. The former Collings dwelling is one of Collingswood's historic homes, the Collings-Knight House. The house, built by Edward's father sometime between 1824 and 1827, was constructed in the federal style. A fire insurance survey prepared in 1857, describes the house and outbuildings. The two-story brick house was 22' x 28'. On the first floor, two parlors and an open stair-bay leads to three bedrooms on the second floor. Two dormers on the front and one off the back provided adequate height on the third floor for additional living space. The first floor of a two-story brick addition attached to the main structure served as a dining room; the second floor was a large bedroom. Another wood frame addi-

Collings-Knight House in Collingswood. Today the house is at Browning Road and Collings Avenue. In this photograph of the front of the house, Collings Avenue travels between the dwelling and the fence. The two-story brick building, once situated on some 96 acres of farmland, was home to Edward Z. Collings and Richard T. Collings.

(Collingswood Library Collection)

Sutler's chit used to purchase goods from Edward Z. Collings during the Civil War. Collings followed the troops during their campaigns selling them foodstuff and provisions. Edward once lived at the Collings-Knight house on Collings Avenue in Collingswood.

(Camden County Historical Society Collections)

tion served as a kitchen with a box stairway leading to the second floor. (Rowand No. 84, 1857)

The outbuildings included a 40' x 30' frame barn, a 27' x 37' grain barn, a hay barn and a brick smoke house. Nearby, along Collings Road, stood a story and one-half frame tenant house.

Edward Collings was born on the homestead in 1837. He was a descendant of Robert Zane, an original settler of Newton Township. Elizabeth, Edward's mother, became a widow before her son's birth. By 1850, Elizabeth and her second husband, Joseph B. Tatem, were living at the homestead with Edward, William P. Tatem and William Tatem, Jr.

Edward attended the nearby Champion School before going onto boarding school and finally completing his studies in Bridgeton. Following his formal education, Edward taught school for a brief period, then acquired a fruit farm in Salem County.

During the Civil War, Edward was a sutler for the 99th Pennsylvania Regiment. Sutlers followed soldiers from camp to camp selling provisions and supplementing soldiers diets with all kinds of foodstuff and sundry items like pipes, chewing tobacco, cigars, stationery, socks, underwear and books. After he secured his military storekeepers commission, he took boatloads of provisions to other sutlers at the front. According to George Prowell's *The History of Camden County, New Jersey*, Mr. Collings made a "handsome profit" in his wartime capacity. (p. 395)

When the Civil War was drawing to a close, Edward returned to his Newton Township property and resumed farming. Collings specialized in raising peach trees and strawberry and blackberry plants. He soon became immersed in the political arena and, with his neighbor Edward Bettle, ran on the Republican ticket in the 1866 for state office. Both candidates' campaigns were successful, Collings was elected to the New Jersey Assembly, while Bettle became the district's State Senator. [See Edward Bettle, page 267.]

During the late 1860s, the farm was rented to a tenant farmer, James Eldridge. Some years later, James moved to a farm in Audubon Park. In 1868, Collings sold the farm to his cousin Edward Knight for $19,000. The farm was the first of nine properties purchased by Knight in Newton and Haddon townships.

Edward Collings looked elsewhere for business opportunities after selling his farm:

> Hon. Edward Z. Collings of Haddonfield has sold his property in this State and designs removing to Omaha, on the Pacific Railroad, with the view of making that place his future residence. (WJP 5/13/1868)

Edward's two sons also moved to Nebraska and engaged in cattle-raising with their father. Edward's stay out west turned out to be temporary. He moved back east and purchased a dairy farm in Montgomery County, Pennsylvania. Years later, he operated a profitable cranberry farm in southern New Jersey. By the late 1880s, Edward and Susan, having raised five children, were living in Camden.

Edward Collings Knight was born in Newton Township in 1813 and spent time during his youth living on the Collings farm. His professional career began in a country store at Kaighns Point, Camden. By 1846, he was the principal partner of E.C. Knight & Company. In 1849, Knight's firm was active trading goods between Philadelphia and California. The firm specialized in wholesale groceries, importing and sugar refining. During the 1870s, his company's main business was refining sugar at its two large facilities along the Delaware River. The company also imported sugar and molasses from Cuba and tea from China.

Edward Knight's commercial accomplishments were unmatched by any other person associated with old

Haddon Township during the nineteenth century. During his career, Knight held many executive positions outside his own company. He was president of the Luzerne Coal and Iron Company, the Coastwise Steamship Company and the Central Railroad of New Jersey; director of Southwark Bank, The Bank of Commerce, the Corn Exchange Bank, Girard Life Insurance and Annuity Trust Company, Pennsylvania Railroad, Lackawanna & Bloomsburg Railroad, North Pennsylvania Railroad, Trenton Railroad and West Jersey Railroad; and, trustee of the Philadelphia City Ice Boats. One company he headed invented the sleeper railroad car. They later sold the patent to this invention to the Pullman Company. While affiliated with the Pennsylvania Railroad, one of Knight's endeavors was the American Steamship Company. This maritime line linked the Philadelphia trading community with Europe. Knight was also active in real estate development at New Jersey's seaside resort of Cape May.

Over a period of several decades, Knight became the largest landholder in old Haddon Township, acquiring about 725 acres. His initial venture into local real estate came in 1868 when he obtained the Edward Z. Collings farm. Knight is remembered today for his generous gift of Knight Park, to the Collingswood citizens in 1893. George Palmer, a Collingswood historian, wrote that Knight had specific plans for his land:

> His mother's family was a descendant from Robert Zane who first settled on 375 acres of this land in 1682. For thirty years Knight nurtured a dream of reassembling the original Zane tract for development. ("Collingswood Centennial Walking and Automobile Tour of 1987.")

Knight's intent for accumulating old Haddon Township land related to his entrepreneurial instincts rather than nostalgia for the family's homestead.

During the 1870s, Knight acquired some 178 acres of farmland on the east side of Haddon Avenue. One of these farms, a 30-acre tract, was rented to a tenant farmer. No buildings stood on the lot. Knight acquired two other lots along Haddonfield Road from James Stevenson and Robert Wood. [See James Stevenson, page 206, Robert Wood, page 205.]

Knight may have purchased land along Haddon Avenue in anticipation of a railroad right-of-way. After his involvement with the Pennsylvania Railroad ended, Knight became associated with affiliates of the Philadelphia & Reading Railroad. An early 1880s survey was prepared for the P&R Railroad on which a right-of-way ran parallel to and about 300 feet east of the Haddonfield Turnpike. The survey reveals the railline would have traveled from Camden across Collingswood, Westmont, Haddonfield and on to Atco. Had it been built, the line would have provided head-on competition for the Camden & Atlantic Railroad, located on the other side of the turnpike.

It was acceptable in the nineteenth century for officers and directors like Knight to use private information to gather up land along a proposed route from unknowing landowners. Once they finalized the plans to build a railroad, the executive insiders would sell the land to the railroad company at a handsome profit.

Richard T. Collings was the third individual during this era to have an association with the Collings-Knight House and surrounding farmland. He was born in a brick dwelling that stood, until 1862, at the corner of

Edward C. Knight. Knight, born in Newton Township, became a successful Philadelphia businessman. By the 1880s, Knight was the largest landholder in Haddon Township, owning some 725 acres of land.

(*The History of Camden County, New Jersey*, by George Prowell, 1886)

the White Horse Pike and Collings Avenue. His parents, Isaac Z. and Rachael Ann Collings, moved the family to Camden in 1853. Four years later, the Collingses moved to Maryland, along the Elk River. Richard returned in 1876 and moved onto Edward Knight's farm and took up residency at the Collings-Knight House. Richard and Edward were cousins.

An article from an unidentified 1880 Camden newspaper described the "Home Farm" where Richard Collings resided:

> It comprises nearly one hundred acres, and is devoted to grain and grass growing and stock raising. The buildings include a spacious brick mansion house erected years ago in that substantial and large-hearted style characteristic of our fathers. The barns and out-buildings are complete in all their appointments and of ample proportions. ("A Camden Vineyard. A Visit to Edward C. Knight's Farm." 9/18/1880 "Historical Clippings Relative to Camden, NJ. John Carney, Camden County Historical Society)

Once settled on the farm, Collings became the general manager and superintendent of all Knight's Haddon Township properties. He raised horses, cows, sheep and poultry on his farm, although the fine-blooded cattle brought most attention. The cattle were known as "E.C. Knight's Collingswood Herd." It seems the stock was a favorite subject of Camden newspaper correspondents. The Republican newspaper, the *West Jersey Press*, covered the herd's whereabouts at fairs and exhibits. It was good business for the newspaper to mention Edward Knight's name in as many articles as possible:

> R.T. Collings on the farm of E.C. Knight situated on Collings road near station...sale: Alderney & short horned Durham stock, 17 head of cattle, 30 head of sheep and lambs, young ewes, buck lamb, sows, one Chester white boar. Also 500 gallons, pure cider vinegar in good barrels. (WJP 5/22/1878)

> E.C. Knight, Esq. of Philadelphia raises on his farm near Haddonfield some of the finest blooded stock in the country. He makes frequent sales of his stock. (WJP 6/25/1879)

> Mr. R.T. Collings manager of Edward C. Knight farms exhibits six animals at Mt. Holly last week. (WJP 10/8/1879)

> Mr. Knight has bred upon these premises some unusually fine stock, among which we may mention the celebrated short-horn Durham bull Centennial. This animal was calved at the Exhibition Grounds in Philadelphia in 1876. ... He is now at the Pennsylvania State Agricultural Fair, where he has attracted considerable attention. For condition, size and symmetry of form, there are few three year-olds that can view with him. ("A Camden Vineyard—A Visit to Edward C. Knight's Farm." 9/18/1880 "Historical Clippings Relative to Camden, NJ" John Carney, Camden County Historical Society.)

Both Richard and his cousin Edward Knight had similar plans for Collingswood. In 1886, Richard purchased William Tatem's 40-acre lot near Collings Avenue and the Camden & Atlantic Railroad tracks. Collings's efforts shifted to selling residential building lots in what was the first large-scale real estate venture in the township outside Haddonfield. Favorable publicity continued to follow Richard; his real estate exploits were the topic of many newspaper reports. Besides his own real estate project, Richard managed Knight's Collingswood Land Company. In the late 1880s, the company subdivided several farms in what became West Collingswood and sold building lots.

The *West Jersey Press* reported an incident that may have contributed to Richard's decision some years later to venture off the farm:

> Richard T. Collings...serious accident while superintending the killing of some turkeys. A knife which was cutting the turkey's throats slipped and entered his wrist severing arteries. He recovered. (WJP 12/24/1879)

Before Collingswood's inhabitants voted to form a separate borough in 1888, Richard served as Chairman of the Haddon Township Committee and Constable. With the emergence of Collingswood, he served as President of the Borough Commissioners in 1888. Over the next twenty years he stayed active in Borough affairs serving as Secretary, Treasurer, and Mayor. Richard could rightfully be called the "Father of Collingswood."

Richard Collings may best be remembered for gathering support to build and finance a bridge between Camden and Philadelphia. He served on the Interstate Bridge and Tunnel Commission and the New Jersey and Pennsylvania Joint Bridge Commission. Collings was aided in convincing the New Jersey Legislature to authorize preliminary planning for a bridge, although he did not live to see a bridge span the Delaware River. He died in the summer of 1920, a half-dozen years before the structure was completed.

13-5 Robert Wood / Edward C. Knight

Robert Wood of Philadelphia, acquired his 106-acre Newton Township farm in 1869. A renter occupied a house that stood near Palmer and Maple avenues. Many years later, the dwelling became the clubhouse for the Camden County Country Club.

The "Grape Farm" house in Collingswood. The dwelling once stood in the vicinity of Palmer and Maple avenues. The farm on which the house stood had the largest vineyard in the township.

(Camden County Historical Society Collections)

John Barton held title to the property for many years. In 1863, Barton's heirs placed the property up for sale:

> Farm and tract of land Haddonfield and Camden Turnpike and Browning Road and Creek. Barton Farm land heir of John Barton deceased and others, containing 106 acres. Two story frame dwelling house with the necessary out-buildings. The high land is well adapted to the raising of truck or market vegetables and the tide meadow on the creek is good bottom and well adapted to grass.
>
> The nearness of this property to the City, with its ready access by turnpike or tide water, renders it valuable as an investment, having a water front well adapted as a location for factories. (WJP 3/11/1863)

When Robert Wood obtained the tract, building a factory was not what he had in mind. Robert turned the property into a vineyard:

> "Allenwood Farm" on Haddonfield Turnpike, Robert Woods Proprietor. Theo. Brown, Foreman. Grape vines for sale: 250 Concord, 1000 Creveling, 4 years old, 1200 Concord, 150 Creveling, 250 Ives 2 years old, 300 Martha, 300 Alvey, 300 Hartford, 300 Rentz, 1 year old. Also 5000 Philadelphia Raspberry Canes and 5000 Kittantinny Blackberry Canes. Apply at farm. Robert Woods–2101 Spring Garden Street, Philadelphia. (CD 12/10/1870)

In 1872, they gathered about 100,000 pounds of grapes during the growing season. The following year Camden's *West Jersey Press* reported:

> Allenwood Grapery. Robert Wood Proprietor of celebrated Allenwood Grapery occupies sixty acres. Known for Concord, the Ives, the Rentz and the Matha. Cost of planting and preparing land is great. Wood earns a handsome profit. Sells in Philadelphia in 20 pound baskets and then shipped to different parts of the U.S. Also cultivates peaches and pears. (WJP 9/17/1873)

In 1874, the vineyard produced 2,100 gallons of wine, and sold 100 tons of the grapes. Sweet potatoes were the predominant crop grown where grape vines had not been planted.

Wood's vineyard lot was sandwiched between two farms owned by Edward Knight. In 1876, the "Allenwood Grapery" was conveyed to Knight. Thereafter, the farm, renamed the "Knight Vineyard," operated under Richard Collings's direction. [See vineyards, page 114.]

13-6 James Stevenson / Edward C. Knight

In 1876, Edward Knight acquired a 40-acre farm from James Stevenson of Philadelphia for $12,000. Stevenson had previously purchased the deed from the Estate of John Kaighn. Isaac Parker, a tenant farmer, resided at one of the two dwellings on the tract. One house stood along the turnpike near East Narbeth Terrace. The other dwelling stood near Browning Road in the vicinity of Maple Avenue. A lane once traveled across the lot between the turnpike and a wharf built out into the mud-flats of Cooper's Creek.

13-7 Peter Wagner

Peter Wagner farmed seven acres of land behind the Stonetown homes. In 1870, the only crops harvested on Peter's land were peas and beans. Wagner's ten cows produced 7,000 gallons of milk, providing another source of income.

13-8 Stonetown

Sometime during the 1850s, some one-dozen twin homes were built along the Haddonfield Road. The former dwellings were at the intersection of Haddon Avenue and Route 130. [See Stonetown, page 14.]

13-9 Jacob Collings / Thomas S. Collings / Joseph Z. Collings

Jacob S. Collings and his son Thomas, owned 60 acres of farmland along Collings Avenue. Jacob inherited the tract from his father Joseph. A wood frame dwelling sat on the lot along Collings Avenue where Collingswood High School is situated today.

Jacob Collings was a founder and partner in a carriage building factory on North Front Street in Camden. The business started making large frame carriages in 1829, employing workers skilled in woodworking, smithwork, painting, trimming and finishing carriages. The company's sales room was located in a warehouse at Sixth and Arch streets in Philadelphia. After Jacob turned the business over to his two sons, Thomas S. and Joseph Z. in 1862, the company traded as Collings Brothers. Joseph eventually acquired his brother's interest in the firm and the operation again was renamed, this time to the Collings Carriage Company. Joseph and his wife Emily lived at Sixth and Cooper streets in Camden.

In the mid-1860s, Jacob married Rebecca Ann Hinchman. It was the second marriage for both. Rebecca's first husband, Samuel Hinchman, passed away in 1866. [See Samuel Hinchman, page 246.] The couple resided in both Camden and Haddonfield until Jacob passed away in 1873. After Jacob passed away, the property on Collings Road was conveyed to his son Joseph. In 1865, Thomas Collings resided on the lot.

By the mid-1870s, Charles Latcham was a tenant farmer on the property. Charles's livelihood, like all farmers, was dependent on the weather. When the weather was favorable, crops were abundant. Sometimes the elements turned violent. A newspaper reported a near disaster for the Latcham family:

> The barn of Charles Latcham on the farm of Joseph Z. Collings, on the road from Haddonfield to Gloucester, [Collings Avenue] was struck by lightening on Friday. . . . Two new milch cows were instantly killed and the end of the building was torn out. Mr. Latcham and his hired man were knocked down and stunned. (WJP 8/18/1875)

In 1879, Joseph Eldridge was renting the farm. Soon after this period, Eldridge inherited a farm in today's Audubon Park. The Collings's property was eventually sold to Edward Knight.

13-10 Anna Maria Collings / Joseph S. Collings / Robert McLaughlin

Anna Maria Collings and her husband, Joseph C. Collings occupied the site inherited from Joseph's father. Joseph's brother, Jacob, was the owner of the neighboring tract. Anna Maria was daughter of long-time Newton Township resident, Jacob Stokes. Anna Maria and Joseph raised fourteen children. Following her husband's death in 1854, Anna Maria took over the task of managing the farm and outlived her husband by many years. She died at 92.

Anna Maria Collings's dwelling was several hundred feet off Collings Avenue near Maple Lane. This three-story brick dwelling is believed to have been built in the early part of the nineteenth century. A photograph, taken in the early 1900s, shows two large verandas on the front and side of the house. A small creek traveled across the tract and emerged near Collings Road, then flowed to the Main Branch of Newton Creek. The run is still to be found between Lakeview Drive and Collings Avenue.

Having inherited a considerable amount of land near their homestead tract, Joseph and Anna Maria were parties to many real estate transactions during their lifetimes. In the 1850s, 35 years before Richard T. Collings started selling-off building lots in Collingswood, Anna Maria and Joseph were selling lots of less than an acre of land along Haddon Avenue. Collings also sold William Tatem about 40 acres of real estate situated next to the Camden & Atlantic Railroad's right-of way. Richard Collings acquired the lot in the 1880s and initiated large-scale residential development in Collingswood.

In 1868, one of Collings's children, Joseph Stokes Collings, was probably living on the family homestead tract. An advertisement in a local newspaper noted a sale of farm products:

Anna Maria Collings's home in Collingswood. The dwelling once stood along Collings Avenue near Maple Lane. This photograph taken in the early 1900s.

(Paul W. Schopp Collections)

> Public Sale at the residence of subscriber on Collings road, near Union Hotel in Haddon Township. Stock and farming implements. 75 bushels of white peachblow potatoes, 150 bushels of corn. J. Stokes Collings (WJP 11/25/1868)

In 1882, Joseph Stokes Collings opened a general store at the southwest corner of Collings and Haddonfield roads. The store became the first Collingswood Post Office.

The tract was sold to Robert McLaughlin for $8,000 in 1878. Robert, a native of Ireland, moved from Philadelphia to the farm with his wife Mary, five sons, a daughter and an Irish servant. The first year of operating the farm, Robert raised corn, oats, wheat, potatoes, sweet potatoes and hay. Some five years later, he sold the land to Edward Knight for $12,500.

13-11 George Lee / William Jones

George Lee's 68-acre farm bordered along a road named after him, Lees Lane. The old road connected Haddon Avenue with Mill Road, now Cuthbert Road. The Lee house still stands today at 615/617 Lees Avenue. The old home is better known as the Stokes-Lee House. The Stokes family lived in the house before the Lees. The house, believed to have been built in 1761, was originally much smaller. By the mid-1800s, a handful of large outbuildings stood near the dwelling including two barns where they stored grain and hay, two large hay houses and a crib house for storing corn. A lane once traveled from Lees Lane to the farmhouse. The same lane traveled to the other side of Lees Lane, toward the Schnitzius farm house, situated near Merrick Avenue. [See John Schnitzius, page 257.]

George and Martha Lee were both born around 1800. George acquired the farm in 1828. He once operated a tannery on the farm. In the early 1860s, three of the Lee children, a domestic servant, a farm laborer and tenant farmer were living at the homestead.

According to an account written in the 1890s, George Lee was one of the first farmers to deliver milk in Camden:

> The milk supply of Camden, was...derived from a solitary dairy owned by one George Lee, whose farm was somewhere between Haddonfield and Camden, and was brought to town by his wife in an old fashioned Jersey wagon of the Bolster variety. I [Joseph Jones] remember seeing it on its daily trips, and hearing the sound peculiar to that description of vehicle as it jogged along the road going to and fro. I do not mean to say that this dairy furnished all the milk used in the place, for many of the inhabitants had cows of their own, which enabled them to supply others beside their own families, but, so far as I know, there was no one else who made a business of bring milk into town from the country. I would suggest that such a source of supply of this indispensable article should be contrasted with the array of milk cans now daily delivered by railroad and distributed not only to the citizens of Camden, but to Philadelphia as well. (*Camden History*, edited by Charles Boyer. *Early Recollections of Camden and the Adjoining County by An Old Citizen*, Vol. 1, No. 10, 11, 12. p. 18)

Lee's personal property at the time of his death included bonds, household items, farming tools, 46 pounds of ham, 133 pounds of shoulders and 25 pounds of new hen feathers. (Inv. C-283, 1866) The estate's executor paid an eight-dollar bill for medical attendance by Dr. Shivers of Haddonfield. Lee's funeral, handled

A Magic Fountain

Indeed is that which through its waters cures
Bright's and other Diseases of the Kidneys,
Dyspepsia, Rheumatism, Dropsy, etc.,
and this is what the celebrated

KALIUM SPRING WATER
(Registered)

Will do. Do not take our word for it, but send for
pamphlet containing the voluntary
testimonials of those who
have tried it.
Remember, all you have to do is to drink
FREELY of a pure, delightful water,
without taste or smell.
IT IS CHEAP and ABSOLUTELY EFFECTIVE.
Orders by mail promptly attended to.
3 Miles on the Camden and Atlantic Railroad.
Address WILLIAM JONES,
(at the Spring), Collingswood, N. J.
N. B.—Recollect, we have no agent; wagon in
town every day.

William Jones's Kalium Springs Spring Water advertisement. Jones lived at what is now 615/617 Lees Avenue. William bottled spring water taken from his farm and sold it to customers in the region.

(Camden Daily Courier, July 29, 1886)

by Roberts & Sons, cost $103. Even a fishmonger, Henry Finger, filed a claim with the executor for $30.98 to cover the cost of seafood consumed by the Lees. When they sold the Lee farm, the estate distributed the proceeds to the four Lee children, one of which was daughter Mary Stoy, wife of Aaron Stoy. [See Aaron Stoy, page 247.]

William Jones obtained the farm in 1871. William, born in England, was 40 when he moved onto the property and continued with the chores of running a farm. In 1880, William and Mary had two children. Like the previous owner of the property, Jones, too, operated a dairy farm here.

Shortly after William acquired the Lee farm, he developed a kidney ailment. His symptoms disappeared after a period of drinking spring water from behind his house. Convinced the water had healing qualities, he had the spring water tested by a chemist employed at Edward Knight's Company. The test results supported William's suspicions and, with the endorsement of a medical doctor, Dr. Harry Shivers of Haddonfield, Jones began selling the spring water. The registered name given to his product was "Kalium Spring Water."

Jones sold his spring water from a wagon to residents in Camden and Philadelphia. Customers could also order the spring water through the mail. Jones advertised quite frequently in Camden's newspapers. The *Camden Daily Courier* reported the mineral springs of William Jones were "achieving great success" because of its medicinal qualities. (11/20/1885)

Modern-day marketing executives would find it difficult to conjure up a more direct sales pitch than that used by Jones. The *Camden Daily Courier* printed an advertisement: "A Magic Fountain, For the Positive Cure, Cheap as Dirt, Take Heed and Beware of Frauds." (11/18/1886)

By the 1890s, several ongoing real estate projects were transforming Collingswood farm land into a residential community. Having delivered on one idea, Jones attempted to parlay his success into a real estate venture. William developed plans to sell shares of stock in a company that would own and operate an amusement facility and real estate company. Jones forecasted some 10,000 people daily would flock to Collingswood on rail lines from Camden and Philadelphia. The amusement park was to be built on his grounds along Newton Creek. His plan called for a 60-room hotel, restaurant and lake boats. Jones also envisioned selling building lots and cottages to interested takers. An important feature of Jones's idea was the sale of Kalium Spring Water to thirsty amusement park patrons. A modern-day investor might be interested to know Jones's idea of inducing people to purchase capital stock also included an offer of $10 worth of free Kalium Spring Water for the subscribers of the first 1,000 shares of stock.

As a side note, Jones's plan for promoting the amusement park with his marque product, Kalium Spring Water, was not the last time such an idea was hatched. One hundred years later, Busch Gardens, a successful amusement park in Virginia, was built with similar mar-

strategy in mind. The park is associated with the parent company's main product, beer.

Jones's grandiose idea never materialized, although he sold some building lots from his tract. William died in 1910 in Collingswood.

13-12 Charles B. F. O'Neil / Thomas P. Hanbest

Charles B. French O'Neil resided on 25 acres of land situated on the eastern side of Lees Lane. At least two houses were on the tract, both were east of Lees Lane in the vicinity of Linwood Avenue. During the mid-1860s, Charles, a lawyer, resided one home. By 1867, he had moved from the township. The minutes of a Township Committee meeting noted Charles absconded without satisfying his local tax obligation.

Toward the late 1860s, Thomas P. Hanbest took title to the tract. Unlike the former owner, Hanbest never resided on the property. In the 1870s, Thomas and James Wilkinson were residing on the tract. A decade later, Thomas Wilkinson served as pastor of the Shiloh Baptist Church of Rowandtown. The census-taker listed James as a bookkeeper.

Henry Samuels, a tenant farmer from England, his wife Caroline and two sons, daughter-in-law and two grandsons were also living at this location in the 1870s. Henry worked the land growing hay, corn, oats and potatoes. By 1878, Thomas Hanbest had passed away and his estate held the title to the farm.

13-13 John Schnitzius

The majority of the John Schnitzius farm was along the Main Branch of Newton Creek in what is now Haddon Township. Part of the farm, near Dill and Linwood avenues, is now within Collingswood. John also owned a small lot near the intersection of the Camden & Atlantic Railroad right-of-way and Lees Avenue. [See John Schnitzius, page 252.]

13-14 Joseph O. Cuthbert, Sr. / Henry Cuthbert

Joseph Ogden Cuthbert, Sr. owned 100 acres on the south side of the Haddonfield Turnpike. Joseph's house was on the southeast quadrant at the intersection of Haddon Avenue and Cuthbert Road in today's Haddon Township. [See Joseph Cuthbert, page 249.]

13-15 Amos Willis, Sr. / William Bozorth

Amos Willis, Sr. was 83 in 1865, his wife Elizabeth was 77. The Willises lived in a two-story frame dwelling that stood near Homestead Avenue, between Maple and Oriental avenues. There were two tenant houses on the lot, both along the turnpike.

After retiring from farming in the late 1860s, Willis employed farm laborers to work on his 42-acre farm. Amos and Elizabeth raised five children, of which two sons, Edwin and Amos, Jr., lived nearby. Edwin resided near Crystal Lake, while Amos lived along Cooper's Creek near Rowandtown, now called Westmont. The elderly Amos Willis moved in with his son, Edwin, where he stayed for the remaining years of his life. [See Amos Willis, page 257, Edwin Willis, page 247.]

In 1870, the property was placed on the market. A newspaper advertisement noted the farm was "adaptive to the growth of grain, grass, vegetables and fruit." (WJP 12/7/1870) The lot's location was ideal, being just one block away from the Camden & Atlantic Railroad. The same advertisement noted "quick access by rail to Philadelphia."

In 1871, William Bozorth acquired the farm. Bozorth made a living farming. In 1879, he had the distinction of owning more swine than any other farmer in the township.

13-16 James DaCosta

In 1867, James DaCosta, 21, purchased a 68-acre tract from his father, John DaCosta. [See John DaCosta, page] There were at least two homes on the property in the 1870s. One was along a lane now called Lincoln Avenue, near Center Street. The second house was in the vicinity of Woodlawn Avenue and Center Street. The lane ran past the two dwellings and turned to the east at the tract's eastern border, known as Burr's Lane. Burr's Lane traveled from the vicinity of Cooper's Creek to near the intersection of Haddon Avenue and Cuthbert Road. Burr's Lane became the Collingswood/Haddon Township boundary.

In the late 1870s, James moved to his father's farm on the White Horse Pike. Tenant farmers moved onto James's old farm. The renters ranked first in harvest of peas and beans among all farms in old Haddon Township. Not too long after he moved off the farm, James sold the property to William Tatem, owner of an adjoining lot.

13-17 Martha Rowles

A map drawn in 1877 reveals Martha Rowles's 70-acre farm was known as "Locust Grove." Martha inherited all her property from her father, William McElhaney, who died in 1856. From the Haddonfield Turnpike, one approached the Rowles's property on a lane that became Woodlawn Avenue. Rowles's farmhouse was in the area of Knight and Highland avenues. The house had three bedrooms, a dining room, parlor, sitting room and kitchen. In the late 1800s, the dwelling became known as the "Pest House" when smallpox victims were quarantined there.

In 1871, Chalkley Parker was living at the Rowles's farm. Seventeen years later, Parker became Collingswood's first mayor. By the end of the 1870s, Martha's son, William, was farming the lot. Rye was the principal crop, grown on roughly half the tract's arable land in 1879.

After her father passed away, Martha inherited several nearby lots. One eighteen-acre tract, situated along Burr's Lane, had standing timber in the 1870s. Martha also inherited three houses built on a five-acre lot along the Haddonfield Road, between East Collings and Lincoln avenues.

13-18 William P. Tatem

William P. Tatem owned a 40-acre farm along the Haddonfield Turnpike. William and his wife Achsan lived in a dwelling at Frazer and Maple avenues, now 829 Maple Avenue. The date-stone embedded in the gable of the structure dated 1854, although an earlier portion of the house was probably completed by 1850, the same year William acquired the farm. The three-story brick dwelling had a front and side portico with a frame leanto kitchen shed attached to it. The roof was Susquehanna slate. They built the front of the house with a better quality pressed brick, and the sides and rear were constructed with stretcher bricks. There were three rooms on the first floor, four chambers on both the second and third floors. The barn had six stables, a hay loft and bay. (Rowand No. 85, 1857)

In 1860, William, his wife, their three children, a domestic servant, a farm laborer, and William Fortiner, a brick mason, were living on the farm. Another tenant, Samuel Tatem a Deputy Sheriff of the County, was also residing on the premise.

William Tatem was well known around the region. During his adolescent years, William resided in the "Collings-Knight House." In 1849 he was the county's tax collector; in the following year he taught children at the Champion School. He was elected Sheriff of Camden County in 1853 and County Clerk in 1860. The highest elected office Tatem held was State Senator from 1860 to 1864.

Shortly after the Civil War, William was appointed Collector of Internal Revenue for the First Congressional District. His political connections within the township, county and state, were instrumental in securing and holding onto the federal appointment. As tax collector, William was responsible for collecting federal income taxes and monies from the sale of revenue stamps. He carried on his duties as tax collector for some twenty years. [See Collector of Internal Revenue, page 153.]

William kept his hand in farming even while collecting taxes. He grew sweet potatoes, wheat and hay for his livestock. In an agricultural region, many farmers put up fences to delineate property lines and prevent their livestock from wandering. The *West Jersey Press* reported an incident that occurred on a cold winter evening on Tatem's tract:

> Three tramps named Henry Allen, John Dill and George Hall, encamped near the farm of Judge Wm. P. Tatem in Haddon Township, on Monday night, but feeling cold they tore down part of the fencing and built fire therewith. (WJP 12/29/1878)

Another incident involving Tatem's livestock, illustrates the hazards of owning a farm near railroad tracks:

> Judge Tatem of the county was the loser of 2 cows struck by an express train of Camden & Atlantic Railroad. The train was 20 minutes behind time, but the man who was driving the animals did not know it and it was while attempting to cross the track that the cows were killed. (WJP 9/22/1880)

When the Collingswood historian, George Palmer, researched the Borough's formative years, he concluded that in 1885, William Tatem became one of the first to sell building lots on the eastern side of the Haddonfield Road in an area along Lincoln Avenue. Other builders and real estate people followed Tatem's lead. Tatem owned other real estate throughout the township. During the 1870s, he teamed up with several investors and acquired land in Rowandtown and along Warwick Road in Haddonfield.

In the early 1870s, Tatem purchased an adjacent 40-acre lot situated on the southern side of the Camden & Atlantic Railroad's right-of-way, and between Collings Avenue to the vicinity of Lees Avenue. In the mid-1880s,

"Old Half-Way House," once situated at the corner of Haddon and Woodlawn avenues in Collingswood. The three-story building was the only inn/tavern within the township outside the village of Haddonfield.

(Collingswood Library Collections)

Richard Collings obtained the tract and turned it into Collingswood's first large-scale residential building venture, erecting many fine homes.

13-19 Mahlon Van Booskirk

In 1869, Mahlon Van Booskirk took possession of the Half-Way House, an inn or tavern at the corner of Haddon and Woodlawn avenues. In the 1870s, the innkeeper also owned the small seven-acre wooded tract on the opposite side of the Haddonfield Turnpike.

A fire insurance survey reveals the Half-Way House was built about 1828. The 1878 survey noted the building had been "much enlarged and improved within the past 20 years." The house was a frame three-story structure with a front veranda extending two stories high. A leanto kitchen and shed were attached to the back of the hotel. (Rowand No. 499, 1878)

Real estate tax records from the early 1870s, show five guests resided at Van Booskirk's inn. Even though he was a hotelkeeper, Mahlon also kept a garden on the premises.

Mahlon promoted his establishment with festive events:

> We see it stated that Mahlon Booskirk's woods at Collings station on the Haddonfield Turnpike about a mile this side of Rowandtown, is to be the scene of a grand "ox roast" on the 10th of September. (WJP 8/28/1872)

In 1873, the year the township passed an ordinance prohibiting the sale of liquor, Mahlon's troubles began. Just months after the law was enacted, Mahlon was fined $50 for serving liquor at his tavern. Less than a year later, he was fined again, $100, for violating the law. [See local option, page 79.]

In 1878, fire insurance agent Jacob Rowand of Haddonfield, penned "This building was formerly kept as a public tavern, but under local option law, no tavern has been allowed or kept in Haddon Township for the last 5 years." (Rowand No. 499, 1878) [See inn and tavern keepers, page 160.]

Borough of Collingswood

In the late 1880s, Richard Collings and his Collingswood Real Estate Company subdivided a former farm and new homes began to appear on some nine newly-marked blocks between Atlantic and Linwood avenues and from Collings Avenue to the area of Lees Avenue. Edward Knight's Collingswood Land Company was subdividing land in West Collingswood during the same period. The projects marked the beginning of large-scale residential development that coincided with incorporation of the locality. The new Borough was on its way to becoming a suburb.

On May 22, 1888, a majority of the township inhabitants, living within some 1,257 acres, voted to organize their community into the Borough Commission of Collingswood. Despite minor alterations in 1953, the Borough's original 1888 borders are almost identical to its modern-day boundaries.

Collingswood has the distinction of being one of the few communities that was incorporated twice. In 1911, the New Jersey Legislature found it necessary to reincorporate the Borough after the County Clerk was unable to find the original 1888 referendum results.

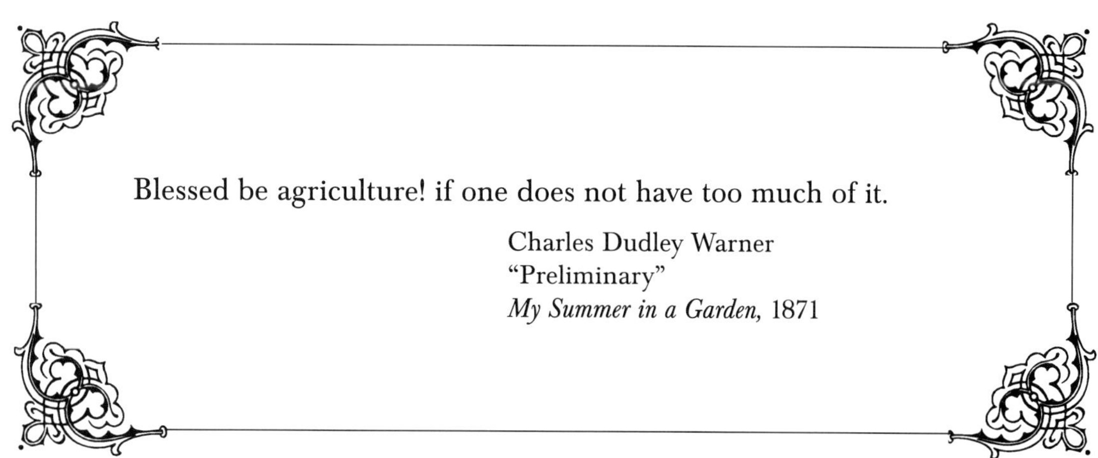

Blessed be agriculture! if one does not have too much of it.

Charles Dudley Warner
"Preliminary"
My Summer in a Garden, 1871

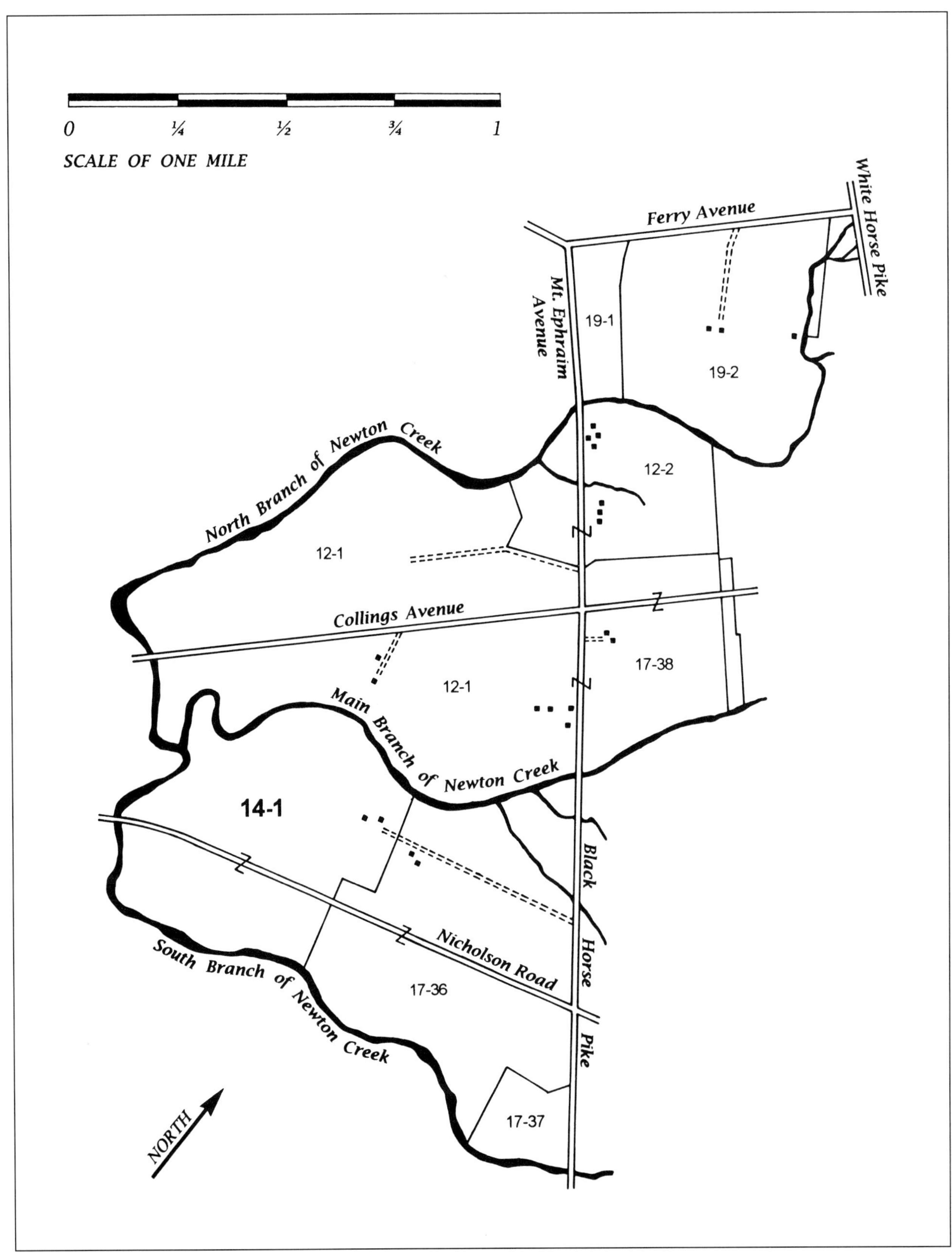

Map of the area that became part of Gloucester City (Gloucester Heights), West Collingswood Extension (Haddon Township), Camden, including Fairview, West Collingswood Heights (Haddon Township) and Woodlynne, 1877.

14

Gloucester City

14-1 David Henry Estate

The heirs of David Henry held the deed to a 183-acre farm in an area they now call Gloucester Heights. Henry's dwelling was near the banks of the Main Branch of Newton Creek in the area of Lehigh and Yale avenues. The house was a two-story frame structure measuring 20' x 30' with a two-story brick structure attached to it. The brick structure was the original house built in the early 1700s. Next to the house stood two barns and a wagon house.

In 1853, a new barn was constructed on the farm. The plans for the 25' x 50' structure, now held by the Camden County Historical Society, called for four horse stalls, a threshing floor and a hay bay. The contract price was $175.

David Henry farmed his land until his death in 1853. David's wife Matilda and her sons continued to live and work on the farm until sometime in the early 1860s, when they rented the farm to a tenant farmer.

For many years, a private lane jutted in a western direction from the Black Horse Pike, near Bellevue and Berwick avenues, past the dwelling on a neighboring farm and continued another quarter-mile ending at Henry's residence. In the mid-1860s, the Henry lot was split into two parts when Nicholson Road was extended west of the Black Horse Pike to Newton Creek.

In George Prowell's *The History of Camden County, New Jersey* he noted a deer park once existed on the property. A ditch and bank surrounded the park. It is likely the park was used for hunting. The park's perimeter was still visible in the post-Civil War era. Prowell's work also pointed out that a race course once stood at the site. (p. 648)

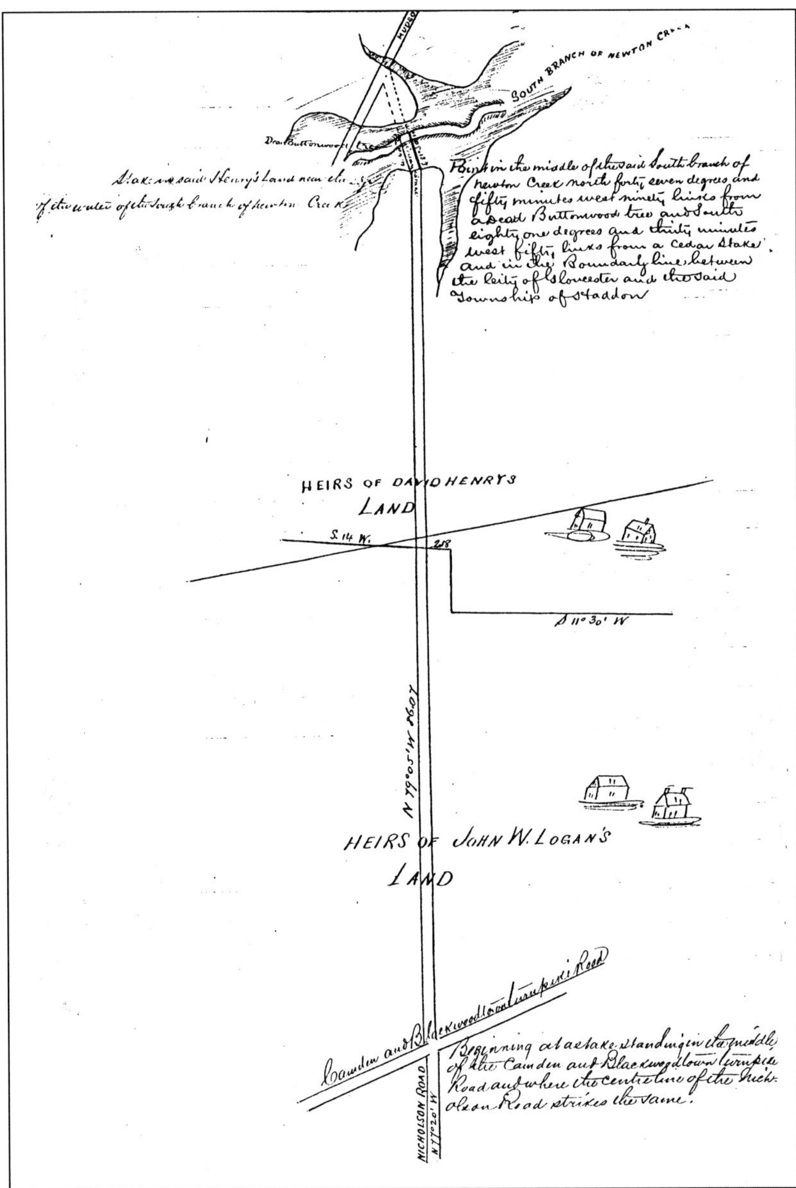

John Clement's survey of Gloucester City. In the mid-1860s, Nicholson Road was extended from the Black Horse Pike to Newton Creek across from Gloucester City. The road traveled over two farms that today comprise West Collingswood Heights and Gloucester Heights.

(Camden County Historical Society Collections)

The trustees of the Henry Estate attempted to sell the farm in 1863. The *West Jersey Press* described the property as containing 50 acres of meadow land and the balance of "upland adapted to either grain, grasses, truck or dairy purposes. A good apple orchard on the premises and considerable quantity of timber." (WJP 6/13/1863)

Ownership of the farm did not change hands at that time. William Smith, a tenant farmer, his wife Margaret and their three daughters moved onto the Henry's land and remained there until the 1870s. Smith maintained one of the largest cornfields in the township. Joseph Avis rented the farm after Smith moved.

Gloucester Heights

The lot owned by the Henry Estate, and two neighboring farms that would later form West Collingswood Heights, became geographically isolated from the township when the Boroughs of Audubon and Oaklyn were formed in 1905. The Henry Estate was merged into neighboring Gloucester City in 1927.

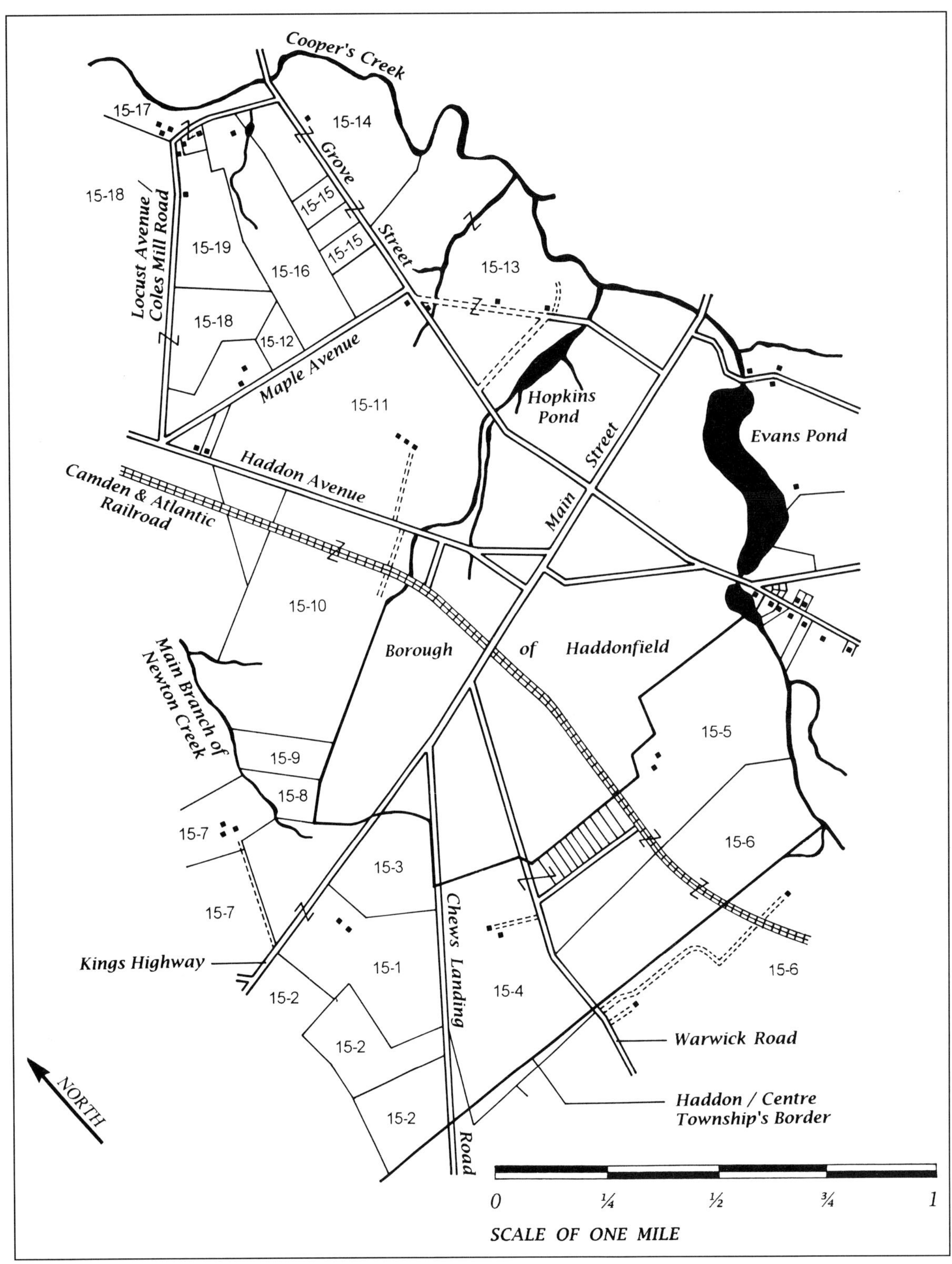

Map of the area that became Haddonfield, 1877.

Haddonfield

15-1 Nathan Lippincott

This 70-acre farm, on the southern side of Kings Highway, was between Hinchman Avenue and the Borough's border with Haddon Heights, and between Kings Highway and Chews Landing Road. Nathan's land on the northern side of Kings Highway extended from an area near Redman Avenue to Kings Highway and between North Drive and Avondale Avenue.

15-2 Charles L. Willits, Benjamin Cooper and the Hinchmans

The Haddonfield and Haddon Heights border now crosses what were three lots situated between Kings Highway and Chews Landing Road.

15-3 Samuel Nicholson

Nicholson owned a twenty-acre lot situated at the southwest corner of Kings Highway and Chews Landing Road.

15-4 Estate of David Roe, Sr. / David Roe, Jr.

The largest section of the 115-acre farm was between Chews Landing and Warwick roads and from approximately Mountwell Avenue to Oak Avenue and Chestnut Street. A small portion of the farm extended into neighboring Centre Township.

The Estate also held the deed to a narrow piece of land between Warwick Road and the PATCO High Speed Line right-of-way near West Summit and Mountwell avenues.

15-5 Jesse Peyton / Theophilus Reilly

This 100-acre lot was situated between the PATCO High Speed Line and Cooper River and between the area near Lakeview Avenue to Mountwell Park. Peyton's lot extended to the western side of the railroad tracts near Lafayette Avenue.

15-6 John Gill, Jr.

The portion of the 242-acre farm within Hadden Township was located between Warwick Road and Cooper River and between Jefferson Avenue and Gill Road. The PATCO High Speed Line bisects the tract as did the Newton Township/Centre Township boundary.

15-7 William C. Hinchman

Today's Haddon Township/Haddonfield border traverses Hinchman's homestead. The 74 acres were along the eastern edge of Crystal Lake Avenue from Mt. Vernon to Hopkins avenues. It would include today's Redman, Homestead, East Greenman, Greenman, Birchal avenues, North Drive, Bewley Road and Barberry Lane.

15-8 Rebecca Ann Collings

Collings held title to a small lot in what is now Haddonfield. The lot is in the vicinity of Barberry Lane and Redman Avenue.

15-9 Nathaniel T. Clement

This sixteen-acre tract would be situated along both sides of Avondale Avenue, between Kings Highway and the Haddonfield and Haddon Township border.

15-10 John E. Redman

The 114-acre tract was between Haddon Avenue and the vicinity of Peyton Avenue, and between Euclid Avenue and the Haddonfield and Haddon Township boundary near Elm Avenue.

15-11 Isaac H. Wood / Samuel Wood
The perimeter of this 130-acre farm was along Maple Avenue to Grove Street, south along Grove Street to a line near Hopkins Avenue, along this border to Haddon Avenue, then along Haddon Avenue to the vicinity of Princeton Avenue, returning to Maple Avenue.

15-12 Jehu Wood
This seven-acre lot was on the north side of Maple Avenue in the area of Ardmore Avenue.

15-13 John E. Hopkins
The 120-acre farm was between the vicinity of Grove Street to the Cooper River, and between Hopkins Pond and Beechwood Avenue.

15-14 Joseph C. Stoy
The boundaries of this 58-acre property abutted the eastern side of Grove Street. This lot was near Beechwood Avenue and north to Cooper River, and between Grove Street and east to Cooper River. Stoy's domain also included a smaller tract west of Grove Street, between the area of Cedar Avenue and Grove Street and from the vicinity of Redwood Avenue to Cooper River.

15-15 William Goldy
Goldy's two tracts were near Redwood and Farwood avenues along Grove Street.

15-16 Samuel R. Stoy
The 39-acre tract was between Maple Avenue and north to Cooper River and between the area of Cedar Avenue and Ardmore Avenue.

15-17 Samuel A. Willits
Willits owned a small lot where Coles Mill Road turns east toward Grove Street in Haddonfield.

15-18 Jacob S. Coles
The boundaries of this 70-acre farm went between Coles Mill Road and north to near Oneida Avenue and between the vicinity of Virginia Avenue to Cooper River. Jacob owned an adjacent tract on the south side of Coles Mill Road in the vicinity of Melrose and East Emerald avenues.

15-19 James S. Lippincott / Robert Frazer / Owen Stockton
The 31-acre lot extended east from Coles Mill Road about 1,000 feet and between the vicinity of Melrose Avenue to near Cooper River.

15-1 Nathan Lippincott

Nathan and Mary Lippincott owned about 70 acres of land along both sides of Kings Highway. Their wood-frame dwelling was near Hinchman and Loucroft avenues. Several generations of Lippincotts farmed in the area. Nathan, born in Centre Township in 1826, was raised in a Quaker household. He attended a common school and became a farmer. Nathan's brothers, Joseph and Benjamin, lived on a nearby farm. Nathan eventually inherited Joseph's 135-acre farm in Haddon Heights. [See Joseph & Benjamin Lippincott, page 239.]

Mary Lippincott also grew up in Newton Township in a family of devout Quakers. Her father was Joseph M. Hinchman. Mary's brothers, William, Samuel, and Isaac lived in the township. [See William Hinchman, page 225, Samuel Hinchman, page 246, Isaac Hinchman, page 246.] She married Nathan in 1854, but the couple had no children.

During the period he was an active farmer, one of Nathan's civic chores was keeping the nearby roads passable and in good repair. When Haddonfield incorporated as a borough, Lippincott's experience in road-way maintenance may have helped him secure a position as a Commissioner of Streets. One of Lippincott's first recommendations was to pass an ordinance requiring sidewalks to be placed before many Haddonfield properties.

The Lippincotts were one of the more financially secure couples in the township. When Nathan retired from farming, he and his wife moved a short distance to the village of Haddonfield and into a new house situated next to the Camden & Atlantic Railroad. "Nathan Lippincott's handsome residence on the corner of Main street and the railroad, Haddonfield, is approaching completion. It will be ready for occupancy in a short time." (WJP 4/5/1876)

The farm became part of the Borough of Haddonfield in 1904.

15-2 Charles L. Willits, Benjamin Cooper and the Hinchmans

Three lots were situated along what later became the Haddonfield and Haddon Heights municipal boundary. Included in the chapter on Haddon Heights are discussions of the landholders and their properties. [See Charles Willits, Benjamin Cooper & the Hinchmans, page 237.]

Most of the area that comprised the three lots joined Haddonfield in 1904, although the boundary between Haddon Heights and Haddonfield was moved in 1947 and 1951.

15-3 Samuel Nicholson

In 1870, at 77, Samuel Nicholson was a well-respected citizen around the township. Samuel resided at 65 Haddon Avenue in Haddonfield. He owned several lots in the township, including a twenty-acre field situated between Main Street and Chews Landing Road. Samuel's son, William inherited the tract in the mid-1880s. In 1904, the tract united with Haddonfield.

Samuel was a descendant of a family that arrived in Salem, New Jersey in 1675. His family raised him on a farm known as "The Linden" in Audubon. Samuel's main occupation was farming. As a young man, his farm along the White Horse Pike was known for the fruit trees raised and sold to other farmers. Eventually, Samuel's son, William, moved to "The Linden" and worked the land. [See William H. Nicholson, page 182.]

In 1826, Samuel married Rebecca Hopkins of Haddonfield. Her father, William Estaugh Hopkins, owned "Birdwood Farm" and a grist mill, both situated next to Hopkins Pond. Rebecca and Samuel had five children that were reared in the Quaker tradition. Samuel was active in the Friends Meeting, serving as an Elder and Overseer. Samuel's son, William, wrote about his parents in a book published privately in 1897 entitled *My Ancestors*:

> Until after their marriage, my father and mother dressed in the fashionable habits of the day. My father was fond of music and practised on the flute. But a change came, which is unfolded in the following relation by my father: ...I gave up music, convinced that it was not right, and destroyed my instrument and books, and changed my dress to that of a Friend. Soon after Rebecca changed hers also, without any solicitation from me, feeling the responsibility of training up a family of children in the way they should go. (p. 83)

Rebecca died at 34. Samuel remarried in 1839 to his wife's cousin, Beulah Hopkins. They moved the family from "The Linden" to her house at 65 Haddon Avenue in Haddonfield. Beulah's lot was situated between Lake Street and near Euclid Avenue. At his new home along the Haddonfield Road, Samuel kept horses and cows in the barn and raised swine and poultry on the premise.

Although Quakers embraced an unpretentious life style, many, including Samuel, were shrewd businessmen. First and foremost, Samuel had been a successful farmer. Good fortune in this area allowed him to invest in stocks issued by the Pennsylvania Railroad, Haddonfield & Camden Turnpike Company and the National State Bank of Camden. He held private bonds and mortgages and owned land on which valuable cedar trees grew. Nicholson owned the triangular shaped lot opposite his personal residence where the Haddonfield Library is located. During his life time,

Samuel Nicholson's residence, now located at 65 Haddon Avenue in Haddonfield. The dwelling was built in 1799.

(*My Ancestors*, William H. Nicholson)

Samuel was also a surveyor and acted as trustee and guardian of estates.

In *My Ancestors*, William Nicholson reflected on his father's life:

> Keeping an interest in the affairs of the day, my father valued his morning paper. He did his duty as a citizen by always voting. He lived under the administration of twenty-two Presidents: first that of Washington, and lastly that of Cleveland. He was first qualified to vote when James Monroe was elected, and probably voted the Republican ticket. Afterwards he was a Federalist, then a Whig, again a Republican, and finally a Prohibitionist, voting with that party, for its presidential candidate in 1884, then in his ninety-first year. Very early, my father was a strong temperance man, and when it was common to give ardent spirits to harvest hands, he stopped that practice and satisfied his men with increased wages. The result proved highly satisfactory, securing a more speedy harvest, and better health to the men, a fact soon conceded by the men themselves.
>
> My father's habits were regular and methodical. Most of his life he retired at nine in the evening, and rose at five in the morning. After his toilet, in later life, he always fed his fowls before breakfast. He kept a model vegetable garden, which afforded him a field for exercise and pleasant occupation. He did not hesitate to harness his horse even when above the age of eighty. It was while detaching one from his carriage, in 1875, that he met a serious accident. The animal, starting suddenly, threw him under foot, spraining his ankle, and otherwise injuring him, so that he had to be brought to the house and carried up stairs. He however, soon recovered his usual activity, and in 1876 in his eighty-third year, visited the Centennial Exposition in Philadelphia, and showed a vigor which surprised me. (p. 106)

Samuel's second wife Beulah died in 1863. The elderly Nicholson had gained an upright status in the community for his various avocations, religious convictions and longevity. He passed away in the mid-1880s. Among his assets that he left to William were a silver hunting case watch, buffalo robe, surveyors compass and mathematical instruments.

15-4 Estate of David Roe, Sr. / David Roe, Jr.

In 1865, the heirs of David Roe, Sr. owned about 115 acres of land. David, Sr. and his wife Rebecca had four children. David moved to Haddonfield in the early 1820s and opened a merchant store. Eventually his interests lead him to the field of agricultural. The Roes lived in a house on the southeast corner of Snow Hill Road, now Warwick Road, and Kings Highway. Their house, 32 Kings Highway West, still stands today. Another house stood on the property in the vicinity of Jefferson Avenue.

One of Roe's legacies was his ardent opposition toward consumption of liquor. In George Prowell's work, *The History of Camden County, New Jersey*, Roe's personal campaign and contribution to the temperance movement was noted:

> He became an active opponent of the sale and use of intoxicating liquors, and at time when such sentiments had but few advocates, and were generally unpopular. In no way discouraged, he pressed his opinions on this question on all proper occasions; and, as it was shown that his precepts were no more observable than his example, and controlled by a disinterested and moral motive, everyone admired his consistency, if they did not accept his practice. The use of liquors among his workmen was not allowed, and even during harvest he adhered to the rule, and at last convinced those employed by him that its use was not beneficial. His conversion to this belief was due to a careful and thorough study of the subject, and, as an evidence of his strong conviction of the harm caused by the use of liquor, it is known that he destroyed a large quantity he had in his store, believing that it would be wrong to return it to those from whom he obtained it as to sell it himself. (p. 616)

Following David, Sr.'s death, his son David, Jr. assumed the chores on the farm. In 1870, David, Jr., his wife Ella, their five children, domestic servants and farm laborers resided at the farm. David went on to become one of the township's more financially successful farmers. During 1879, his earnings from the sale of farm products were the highest among all township farmers:

> David Roe, a farmer residing near Haddonfield, has growing on his farm 100,000 cabbage plants all or nearly all in an excellent state of forwardness. (WJP 8/23/1876)

> David Roe of Haddonfield was awarded $50 for the best five acres of wheat by the State Agricultural Society. (WJP 1/28/1880)

Like most township farmers, David also raised poultry. He was a member of the Philadelphia Poultry Associates and sold his fowl in Philadelphia and New York marketplaces. They portrayed David in the press as having a keen interest in a certain type of bird:

> Mr. David Roe devoted much time and spared no expense in procuring and breeding the aforesaid "Brahmas". … Besides being among the very best table fowls we know of, they are superior layers of large eggs.

Mr. Roe has had a ready sale at high figures of all his surplus stock in the vicinity, in Philadelphia and New York. (WJP 4/8/1868)

The Roe family owned a lot along Chews Landing Road and a triangular shaped lot situated on the southwest side of Chews Landing Road and Kings Highway within the 1875 Borough of Haddonfield. Most of the Roe farm was ceded to Haddonfield in 1904.

15-5 Jesse Peyton / Theophilus Reilly

Jesse Peyton was the owner of the 110-acre "Tulip Grove Farm." At one time, Peyton's property was the site of an amusement park known as the "Pleasuring Ground." In Julia Gill's 1922 work, "A Brief History of Mountwell," she described the park and identified its former owners, many of whom were affiliated with the Camden and Atlantic Railroad Company:

For a few years tenants occupied the staunch old home, and on March 23, 1854, John Gill 4th sold the property, 130 acres and the home, to the following persons: Walter D. Bell, William W. Fleming, Samuel Richards, all of Philadelphia, and William Coffin of Newton Township, who formed the organization known as the Haddonfield Land and Improvement Company. Later a Pleasuring Ground was carried on there by Jesse Peyton and Charles Shinn. This place occupied about twelve acres. It was enclosed by a fine, high fence of close, wide boards with pointed tops. Visitors paid an entrance fee and found inside a one-story house about 75' x 25', covered over, for enjoyment and shelter in stormy weather, while for sunny days there was a long open platform for dancing down near the stream. There was also a short race course, and a place for rifle shooting. The men who composed the Haddonfield Land and Improvement Company entertained the hope of building up a town on their tract, and they laid off a place for a railroad station. But their project failed of success. (p. 7)

Peyton was a charismatic individual. He was born in Kentucky in 1815 and as a young man, moved to Philadelphia and opened a dry goods business. Jesse moved to Haddonfield in 1854. During the Civil War, he was instrumental in forming two calvary regiments. His township land was headquarters for more than a thousand young recruits from Pennsylvania. Both regiments temporarily camped at "Camp Peyton" until their assignments were issued. [See Civil War, page 69.]

In the 1930s, Sarah Shivers Murray wrote a short biography about Jesse Peyton:

During the Civil War he secured a camp site adjacent to the town, at which newly enlisted troops were equipped and drilled preparatory to being sent to the front. (Unpublished manuscript–Historical Society of Haddonfield)

Colonel Jesse Peyton was a supporter of the arts. He was aided in bringing lectures, musicals and entertainment to the village where he resided with his wife Jennie and three children. Sarah Murray wrote:

Colonel Peyton was a born promoter. In our then simple village he busied himself with securing oil lamps at the street corners. With the erection of a public hall on Potter St. ... in which hall he arranged concerts by Gilmores' band (then the most famous band in the U.S.), and by Star singers. ... In the Fall of 1886, in a lively political campaign he brought to Haddonfield all the important marching clubs of Phila., for an old fashioned torchlight parade. Some ten thousand men were in line, and there were not streets enough in those days to receive them all. He helped much to promote the Centennial Exposition of 1876. ... (Unpublished manuscript–Historical Society of Haddonfield)

In the late 1860s, Henry Simons acquired the property from Peyton. Shortly after that, the farm was awarded to Henry Allen in a legal matter. Less than a half-year later, the *West Jersey Press* reported:

Rev. T.M. Riley, [sic] an Episcopal clergyman, has bought the Gill property [Peyton's lot] in Haddonfield and intends erecting a large school for girls and boys up on the same. The farm contains about 100 acres. (WJP 7/13/1870)

Theophilus Maxwell Reilly's travels took a circuitous route before settling in old Haddon Township. Theophilus and his younger brother William were born in Ireland in the 1830s. They were ordained as ministers in their homeland and subsequently moved to the United States preaching in Wisconsin and Nevada before moving to Camden. Theophilus was the Rector of St. John's Church in Camden from 1861 to 1870.

The Reillys opened St. John's Academy near Haddonfield in 1871. The press reported, "...[The] Episcopal Seminary in course of construction occupies "The Pleasure Grounds." (WJP 8/2/1871) The school set up its headquarters in an old dwelling built by Francis Collins, an original settler of the area. Shortly after opening, fire destroyed the main building. When the ashes cooled, Reilly announced his intention to reconstruct the "College of St. John's." (WJP 7/31/1872)

The new 100-room schoolhouse was the largest building in the township. The building stood at what is now Cottage Avenue east of Centre Street. Once completed, the school became a military academy. In the mid-1880s, about two thirds of the cadets were from the state of New York. In 1878, a sister school for girls, called St. Agnes Hall, opened at the site. [See education, page 60.]

Theophilus was also a businessman. He speculated in real estate, having built at least two-dozen brick row homes on Benson, Hamilton, Washington and West streets and Broadway in Camden. He also used the Academy's main building as a boarding house and hotel during the summer months after the students returned to their homes. Reilly charged vacationers and travelers $15.00 per week and $2.50 per day at the "Maxwellton Park House.' Children and servants paid half-price. [See inns, page 163.]

In 1886, Reilly experienced another setback–the school/hotel burned to the ground. Not one to quit, Reilly again regrouped and kept the school open. Not until Theophilus died in 1907, did the school close its doors for good.

In 1904, Reilly's tract was incorporated into the Borough of Haddonfield.

15-6 John Gill, Jr.

The Gill family owned two large farms during the 1860s. Only a part of the 242-acre lot, known as the "Haddon Farm," was in Haddon Township. The other 300-acre property, situated entirely within Centre Township, was incorporated into the Borough of Tavistock in 1921. The Gill family worked the land in the area going back as far as 1728. John, Sr. gave his son the 242-acre farm in 1863.

Like his ancestors, John, Jr. was a farmer. Off the farm, he also served as a Director of the National State Bank of Camden, an institution his father headed for many years as President.

John Gill, Jr.'s homestead was situated just over the township border in Centre Township where a house at 613 Warwick Road stands. The three-story dwelling measured 42' x 30'. They built a veranda off the front and rear of the house and side porticos. A lane leading from Warwick Road to Gill's home, continued toward Cooper's Creek passing several tenant dwellings on the way. An 1869 fire insurance survey described Gill's dwelling:

> Situated on the East side of the public road leading from Haddonfield to Snowhill. Built in 1853, a superior building in every respect. Used as a Mansion or private residence and occupied by the Insured, being on his farm: Stands more than eight-rods (more than 132 feet) from any other building: No manufacturing in or near the building. Description: Built of the best material and well furnished and papered. Brick paned throughout. 4 flues, or chimneys but no fireplaces. Roof tin–first floor of the main building is divided into parlor, sitting room, dining room and hall 8 feet wide–open stairway to 3rd story–2nd & 3nd stories

John Gill Sr's. dwelling in Haddonfield. Today this building is at 343 Kings Highway East and now home to the Historical Society of Haddonfield. The Gill family also owned a large farm on the Haddon and Centre townships border, now in Haddonfield.

(*Daily Graphic*: New York, September 9, 1879)

have 4 chambers and hall. The kitchen has one chimney, one room on the first-floor and two chambers on the second. (Rowand No. 307, 1869)

Fire destroyed the Gill dwelling in 1974.

John, Sr's. large house, now called "Greenfield Hall," was situated on eighteen acres along Main Street in Haddonfield. Today, the Gill dwelling is 343 Kings Highway East, home of the Historical Society of Haddonfield.

The portion of the farm that was in Haddon Township did not join the Borough of Haddonfield until 1904. The Centre Township portion of the farm was ceded to Haddonfield in 1926.

15-7 William C. Hinchman

William Collins Hinchman was born on this tract in 1834. In 1865, the township's tax ledger notes William owned 194 acres. Three years later, he paid taxes on just 74 acres of land. For whatever reasons, William and other Hinchman family members that lived nearby transferred land between each other.

The Hinchman family also owned a 22-acre lot in today's Hadden Heights. Tax records show that William Hinchman was the owner, although a map drawn in 1877 suggest Joseph H. Hinchman held the deed to the lot.

William, like his two brothers, Isaac and Samuel Hinchman, was a farmer. [See Isaac Hinchman and Samuel Hinchman, page 246.] Their sister, Mary, lived with her husband, Nathan Lippincott, on an adjacent farm. [See Nathan Lippincott, page 220.] In 1863, William married Mary Jane Bewley of Philadelphia. The couple had four boys, although only two survived to reach adulthood.

William's former house stood near Hinchman and Homestead avenues. The dwelling, built around 1758, lasted into the twentieth century. Before they tore it down, it was a clubhouse for a golf club, the Haddonfield Country Club. A lane traveled from Kings Highway to the farm house in the vicinity of the roadbed that is now North Drive. A small pond once existed on the Hinchman farm near Lansdowne Avenue. The creek that emerged on the property formed a small pond. The run was the source of the Main Branch of Newton Creek.

It is likely the Hinchmans were not convinced of the benefits of insuring real estate from financial loss due to fire. In 1878, the *West Jersey Press* reported fire destroyed William's uninsured barns and outbuildings. The newspaper noted, "Soon after the fire broke out the wind changed or his dwelling would have shared a similar fate." (WJP 10/9/1878) Within three weeks, William built a new barn. One wonders whether William

Hinchman's dam on William C. Hinchman's farm in Haddonfield. The small pond was near the source of the Main Branch of Newton Creek. Today the site of the former pond is near Lansdowne Avenue in Haddonfield.

(Historical Society of Haddonfield Collections)

changed his mind and acquired fire insurance on his new structure?

After Mary died, William remarried in 1886. Twelve years later, he was struck and killed by a trolley car in Westmont.

Most of what was Hinchman's tract was incorporated into Haddonfield in 1904, although a small segment joined the Borough in 1941. The remaining segment of the old Hinchman farm that was not ceded to the Borough of Haddonfield, remained in Haddon Township.

15-8 Rebecca Ann Collings

Rebecca Ann Collings's small lot was just outside the 1875 Borough of Haddonfield. Rebecca Ann owned a larger farm in what is now Haddon Township. The lot joined the Borough in 1904. [See Rebecca Ann Collings, page 246.]

15-9 Nathaniel T. Clement

Nathaniel Clement owned a narrow sixteen-acre unimproved lot. When Haddonfield incorporated as a borough in 1875, about half the lot fell within the Borough's jurisdiction. The borough line crossed Clement's lot, in the area where Redman Avenue intersects Avondale Avenue. The portion of the tract that did not fall within Haddonfield in 1875, was annexed to the Borough in 1904.

In 1870, Nathaniel was 67 years old. The retired farmer operated a business in Philadelphia. Nathaniel, or "Tiley" as he was known to his friends, resided in the village of Haddonfield with his wife Mary. The couple's comparatively large village property on the southern side of Main Street, was to the east and near the Camden & Atlantic Railroad. At the time of his death in 1890, Nathaniel was one of the oldest inhabitants in the borough.

15-10 John E. Redman

John E. Redman's farm had 114 acres of land. Like many farms that surrounded the village of Haddonfield, the Redman farm passed through several generations of the family. John's farmhouse, built in 1834, still stands today at 140 Westmont Avenue. The Camden & Atlantic Railroad was near the Redman dwelling.

The dwelling cost $3,500 to build. Upon entering the front door, a center hallway stood between two parlors, each measured 18' x 20'. An 18' x 22' sitting room and a 18' x 13' a washroom were also on the first floor. The water pump was situated just outside the back door. An 1835 fire insurance survey noted the cellar windows were finished "with glass lights and wired on the outside to keep rats out." (Franklin Fire Insurance Company of Philadelphia, Policy No. 1101)

Approaching Redman's dwelling from Haddonfield Road, one turned onto a lane that went by the eastern side of the house. A second lane that went in a similar direction to today's Westmont Avenue, traveled past the house and onto the outbuildings. On the western side of the house was Redman's garden. The same lane passed the barns, hay house, crib and other outbuildings situated some 240 feet from the dwelling. (Franklin Fire Insurance Company of Philadelphia, Policy No. 1101)

John Redman, born in Haddonfield, attended school at the nearby Friends School and later at an academy near Burlington, New Jersey. Following his formal education, he became a farmer. Upon retiring, John's avocation turned to literary pursuits. He wrote poetry and published a small volume of his work entitled "Miscellaneous Poems." His poems covered topics including depiction of local landmarks such as "The Old Mill." One sonnet, titled "Women," praised man's "most precious gift." Ironically, John was a life-long bachelor. Sarah Shivers Murray's unpublished manuscript was written in the 1930s. One of her short biographies was about John Redman:

> John E. Redman lived as a bachelor with a bachelor brother and maiden sister. . . . John Redman was born with a poetic vision and pressure to write. A Volume of his Poems was printed, and from time to time he would print newly written poems on separate sheets of paper and distribute them to his friends. In his youth he was said to resemble Lord Byran, and he was proud of his noticed resemblance.

Redman's farm stood on the outskirts of the village of Haddonfield. When residential development was on the rise in the 1860s, John recognized what the future held in store for his family's farm. He advertised a private sale of 75 acres of land in 1867. John was unsuccessful in finding buyers:

> . . .valuable farmland and building lots. . .fronting on Haddonfield and Camden Turnpike. . .very desirable location for building sites or farming purposes, being well watered and divided into fields of desirable size. (WJP 12/4/1867)

A small pond once existed behind Redman's dwelling in the vicinity of Linden and Estaugh avenues. The small creek that led from the pond in the direction of Estaugh Avenue emptied into another creek and formed Crystal Lake.

The Redman farm was the site of the largest wooded area in old Haddon Township. In 1879, Redman's Woods covered about 30 acres in the vicinity of Peyton and West End avenues. John also kept an apple orchard of some 200 trees near Elm, Westmont and Linden avenues. The farm was incorporated into Haddonfield in 1904.

15-11 Isaac H. Wood / Samuel Wood

Isaac Wood's house stands at 201 Wood Lane, built on the former site of John and Elizabeth Haddon Estaugh's dwelling. Elizabeth Estaugh, an early settler in the region, owned a large tract of land that comprised much of Haddonfield. The Woods built the Tuscan villa, Italinate style structure in 1842, soon after the old Estaugh residence home burned down.

A fire insurance survey of the Wood's dwelling notes the first floor had three rooms, the second and third floors each had four chambers. An open stairway with mahogany rails and newels went from the first to third floors. An extended two-story brick kitchen and two chambers were attached to the main structure. Next to the mansion stood hay and grain houses, along with barns and other outbuildings, all of which they had whitewashed. The oldest barn, built in 1792, was 65' x 28'. (Rowand No. 391, 1874)

Isaac Wood was raised on a farm along Cooper's Creek in Delaware Township (Cherry Hill). He married Elizabeth Cooper in 1831 and together they raised seven children. Isaac and his brother, Jehu jointly owned a 160-acre farm on the Marlton Turnpike, now called Route 70, in Delaware Township. Today, the tract is part of Garden State Park.

The lane to Wood's home traveled from the Haddonfield Road along a path near Merion Avenue and continued past the house and onto Stoy's Landing Road, now Grove Street. Yews planted many years earlier by John and Elizabeth Estaugh grew in the yard. In the era following the Civil War, several tenant houses stood on Wood's land. One dwelling stood at the corner of Maple Avenue and Grove Street. Another dwelling was on Grove Street near Rhoads Avenue. Wood's 100-tree apple orchard was near Hawthorne Avenue and Wood Lane.

In 1947, local historian Carrie Nicholson Hartel wrote about the farm in her paper entitled "Estaugh Plantation–Wood Farm." Hartel used farm account ledgers and several diaries in describing life on the Wood farm:

> ...there was always building going on; a new shed at the homestead or a tenant house or repairs, and fences. There seems no end to lumber bills. (p. 34)

When Isaac and Elizabeth's sons were old enough, they put them to work on the farm. Diaries kept by the Wood children reflect the endless chores on the farm. The boys drove a team of horses to deliver grain and corn to the local mill. Hauling compost, marl and other fertilizers were familiar chores for the boys. In 1866, 100 loads of dung were delivered by boat to a wharf on Cooper's Creek and hauled to the Wood farm. In that same year, they purchased 70 tons of marl and 320 bushels of lime. The Woods also purchased ash from the other side of the Delaware River and transported it to the farm. [See Wood diaries, page 120.]

Carrie Hartel's work on the Wood family reveals that despite all the work on the farm, the Wood boys found time for fun:

> A story the Wood grandchildren loved to hear was about the young Wood boys hitching up mules or horses to the snowplow scrapers and making paths through the snow to the farm buildings, and down the lane and over to neighbor Redman's to make their path. They were always rewarded with pie or doughnuts. ("Estaugh Plantation–Wood Farm," p. 55)

The Wood diaries show the various types of crops grown on the farm. The records show Mercer potatoes, Valentine beans, stringless beans, Prussian blue peas, beets, flat and Dutch turnips, cucumbers, corn, sweet potatoes and oats were grown on the farm. In 1860, Isaac rented an "In and Out" stall for $20 a year from the City of Philadelphia's Department of Market Houses. Products from this township farm were sold in the rented stall.

Isaac Wood lived during an era when significant changes came quite frequently to the art of farming. Isaac, however, had learned his profession in an earlier era. Carrie Hartel noted some of Isaac's sources of agricultural tips:

> One of Isaac Wood's books was the "American Farm Book" being a practical Treatise on soils, manures, drainage, irrigation, grasses, roots, fruits, etc., published 1854. It is a small compact book which gives information on everything from soil analysis to how to build a barn or pig pen. There had been many changes in farming methods in half a century; his father had planted by the moon. "Potatoes, early apricots, in the old of the moon of March. Early beans–the new of the moon soon in April." However, he no doubt used his father's book "The Gentleman Farrier's Repository of Elegant and approved Remedies for the Diseases of Horses", published 1775.

Mr. Wood also owned "The Farmer's Land Measurer or Pocket Companion," 1843. ("Estaugh Plantation–Wood Farm," p. 37)

Isaac's son, Samuel, assumed responsibility over the farm even before his father passed away in 1879. Elizabeth Wood died seventeen months after her husband. Samuel eventually inherited his parent's farm along with the livestock, equipment and farming tools. Samuel lived at the Wood Lane house until he died from injuries sustained when a bus collided with his horse-drawn buggy in 1929. The Wood farm was incorporated into the Borough of Haddonfield in 1904.

15-12 Jehu Wood

Jehu Wood owned a seven-acre lot next to his brother Isaac's farm. Like his brother, Jehu too was a farmer. He resided with Isaac's family. When Jehu passed away in 1882, Isaac and Elizabeth Wood's children became beneficiaries of their Uncle's estate. Jehu's heirs received stocks in railroad and canal companies, horses, carriages, farming implements, their grandfather's desk and an eight-day clock. The tract was united into Haddonfield in 1904.

15-13 John E. Hopkins

John Estaugh Hopkins's 120 acres was next to Hopkins Pond. Hopkins's dwelling, known as "Birdwood," stands at 519 Hopkins Lane. John's grandfather, William Hopkins, built the house in 1794. Three tenant dwellings stood on the Hopkins farm. One house exists today at 413 Birdwood Avenue. Two other dwellings stood along Grove Street. John also owned a small lot of land on the northwest corner of Grove Street and Maple Avenue.

John, a lifelong farmer, was born in 1810. He and his wife Antoinette had three children. The Hopkins family presence in Newton Township dated from the early 1700s. The family was heirs to Elizabeth Haddon Estaugh's estate.

Present-day Hopkins Lane, between Kings Highway and Grove Street, existed during John Hopkins era. At one-time, the lane also continued straight past "Birdwood," intersecting Grove Street near Maple Avenue.

Two creeks crossed Hopkins's property and emptied into Cooper's Creek. One stream, called Hopkins Mill Branch, emptied into Hopkins Pond, while the other crossed under Grove Street near Rhoads Avenue and flowed to Cooper's Creek. This run is known as Birdwood Branch.

The Hopkins family once operated the Haddon Mill. The grist mill commenced operations near the end of the eighteenth century. The mill sat next to Cooper's Creek at a point east of "Birdwood." The location of the mill was ideal; water from Hopkins Pond fell vertically some twenty feet to Cooper's Creek. By the 1860s, the millstones had ceased grinding grain. Maps drawn many years after the mill was dormant still noted the location of the old gristmill ruins.

William H. Nicholson, a nephew of John Hopkins, shared his childhood memories of the mill in *My Ancestors*:

> After his marriage, my grandfather William Estaugh Hopkins, lived in the house built for him on Cooper's Creek near Haddonfield, in which George H. Hopkins now lives. His possessions were a large farm and some woodland, and a grain-and grist-mill run by water-power, which stood not far from the house. This mill within my recollection was in active operation, and in its day did a profitable business. The location of the house looking over the clear and beautiful mill-pond with its skirting and large forest trees, yet exhibits attractions which must have always been a delight. At first, the mill was supplied with the wings of a windmill, to be used in case of a scarcity of water. As these proved to be unnecessary, they were taken down. The old mill, when I was a boy was in charge of my genial uncle, Griffith Hopkins, and a visit to it was to me a special treat. (p. 79)

During his lifetime, John Hopkins had the distinction of being associated with several memorable incidents. One event took place after the Civil War had ended. On July 4, 1865, Hopkins hosted Camden County's victory celebration at his grove. The *West Jersey Press* informed readers the event was a "Welcome to Our Returned Soldiers–Reception and Festival of the Nation's Defenders." (WJP 6/28/1865) Some 5,000 citizens attended the gala.

The other uncommon event that took place on Hopkins's property occurred when the most complete dinosaur skeleton found to that date in America was discovered along the banks of a ravine near Maple Avenue. When John was still a young man, workers unearthed large bones while digging in a marl pit. They later identified the find as dinosaur bones. Some twenty years later, in 1858, William Park Foulke, a paleontologist, became aware of the bones and was granted permission to dig on Hopkins's tract. Foulke uncovered other bones that they subsequently assembled and placed on display at Philadelphia's Academy of Natural Science. It is noteworthy that Foulke's team never found the dinosaur's head. Foulke's find proved it was possible to find and reconstruct dinosaur bones. The remains of the

Hadrosaurus foulkii, to this day, are part of the Academy's permanent collection.

Hopkins's tract was one of a few farms in old Haddon Township where they excavated marl. Farmers spread the greenish clay on their fields to enrich the soil. Marl was a mixture of clays, carbonates of calcium and magnesium and remnants of shells. Digging marl was generally done by removing the top soil and digging pits to get to the marl. In George Cook's *Geology of New Jersey*, published in 1868, it notes Hopkins's marl had been used with some success as a fertilizer. Marl dug from Hopkins's farm was on exhibit at the Centennial Exhibition in Philadelphia in 1876. They displayed the marl, along with other New Jersey farm products, at the New Jersey State Building.

By the late 1860s, Hopkins had retired from farming and his son George assumed the daily chores. In 1868, George entered a business venture with Collins, Alderson and Company, a Philadelphia seed dealer. According to the local press, the company was the "most extensive dealer in seed and seed grower in Philadelphia." (WJP 3/17/1869) The concern was known for selling "quality seed to farmer and gardener of both amateur and professional agriculturalist." (WJP 10/14/1868) Seeds, along with and other products, were sold through the company catalog.

After some time had passed, the joint venture with Collins, Alderson and Company ended. However, George had learned well from his association with the dealer. He started selling his own seed products to local farmers. In 1875, he placed an advertisement in the *West Jersey Press* "Seed Potatoes–Snow Flake–The potato is very productive and superior quality." (WJP 2/20/1875) Hopkins's land came under Haddonfield's jurisdiction in 1904.

15-14 Joseph C. Stoy

Joseph Stoy's 58-acre farm adjoined Stoy's Landing Road, now Grove Street. Built in 1837, his two-story dwelling was along the east side of the road, in the neighborhood of Pardee Lane. Two barns stood on the tract, both made of oak, boarded in white pine, with cedar shingle roofs. One barn, 43' x 24', had a threshing floor, and stalls for ten horses and three cows. The smaller of the barns, situated about 130 feet from Joseph's residence, also had a threshing floor and stables for seven cows. A wagon house, cow stalls, corn house, milk cellar, smokehouse and chicken coops were also scattered about Stoy's lot. (Rowand No. 336, 1871, & No. 460, 1877)

The Stoy family owned and occupied the farm for many years. Joseph was 61 years old in 1870, and his wife Amelia was thirteen years younger. The couple raised two daughters and a son.

During a four year period, the Stoys experienced a

Joseph Stoy's residence was once situated along the east side of Grove Street, near Pardee Lane in present-day Haddonfield. The dwelling was built in 1837.

(Historical Society of Haddonfield Collections)

string of unfortunate events. The first occurred in January 1871, when fire destroyed one of their barns, causing $1,700 loss in property including the destruction of a large quantity of hay. Stoy was not adequately insured. The proceeds from the insurance company were only $200. The local insurance underwriter wrote in his insurance ledgers, "J.C. Stoy had his barn with contents, destroyed by fire yesterday...suppose to be set on fire by some evil disposed person, at present unknown." (Rowand No. 331, 1871) Six months later, fire reduced to rubble Joseph's wood shed and smokehouse. Several years passed and another fire broke out on the farm. The *Haddonfield Basket* reported "A new dwelling house belonging to Joseph C. Stoy...was destroyed by fire, valued at $5,000. No insurance." (HB 9/15/1875) An arsonist was suspected of setting the tenant dwelling ablaze. Lastly, more bad luck occurred during the string of fires:

> The chicken thieves still continue to make great havoc among the poultry of our farms. A few nights ago Joseph C. Stoy had his hen house roost robbed of about 50 fine chickens. (WJP 2/7/1872)

Besides farming, Joseph also cut and sold lumber. His family was in the lumber business going back to the early nineteenth century. Timber, much of it cut from their land in Delaware Township, was hauled to Stoy's Landing on Cooper's Creek and shipped to Camden and Philadelphia. The *West Jersey Press* reported "Joseph C. Stoy recently purchased a tract of timber. ..." Joseph proceeded to cut and haul "oaken giants" from the Delaware Township lot. (WJP 1/2/1878) When Joseph died in 1882, an inventory of his implements included a log wagon, chains, lumber stored in several places, hewn lumber, rails and white planks. (Inv. G-156, 1882)

An important agricultural commodity was received at Stoy's Landing. Boats loaded with manure from Philadelphia's stables and streets floated up Cooper's Creek and were unloaded at the landing. In 1882, Joseph had $400 worth of manure piled-up on "field numbers one, three, upper field, east of the house, in the farm, in the barn yard, on the road and east of the house." (Inv. G-156, 1882) The farm remained part of Haddon Township until it was ceded it to the Borough of Haddonfield in 1943.

15-15 William Goldy

William Goldy owned two small tracts of land consisting of eight acres along the south side of Stoy's Landing Road between John Hopkins's farm and Joseph Stoy's land. There were no improvements on the lots. During the mid-1860s, Goldy also owned a lot and shop in the village of Haddonfield. He was not a resident of the township at that period. By the end of the 1870s, Goldy owned two small lots next to the Baptist Burial Ground along Main Street.

The 1904 Haddonfield/Haddon Township municipal line was fixed near or across the lots. The borough boundary with Haddon Township was relocated in 1943.

15-16 Samuel R. Stoy

Samuel Stoy, a farmer, lived with his wife Mary Ann and their three children in a house built sometime before 1845 by James Stoy, Samuel's brother. Samuel inherited most of his 39-acre farm from his father, Phillip. Stoy's house was a two-story structure situated on top of a hill overlooking Cooper's Creek. A good portion of Stoy's former house was torn down in the mid-twentieth century; however, a part of the old structure was apparently incorporated into what is now 600 Coles Mill Road, near Jobel Drive. In the cellar of the structure, the original fire place foundations, joists and floor boards, once a part of Samuel's Stoy's house, may still be found.

A stream originated on Samuel's property and formed a pond before merging with Cooper's Creek. The pond is still visible today, adjacent to Coles Mill Road near Grove Street.

Samuel's other real estate holdings included an interest in timber land in Delaware Township near Merchantville. Closer to home, along the road between Haddonfield Road and Cooper's Creek, Samuel owned a house and lot that were leased to tenants. The lot was on Locust Avenue.

After Samuel passed away in 1879, his son Samuel, Jr. acquired the interest in the farm. The portion of the lot near Maple Avenue was incorporated into Haddonfield in 1904. The remaining area of Stoy's former land merged into the Borough of Haddonfield in 1943.

15-17 Samuel A. Willits

Samuel Abbott Willits's two tracts were situated along Coles Mill Road. The "Landing Yard" tract was the site of one Willits lumber and coal yard. Today the former landing is in Haddon Township. Several dwellings stood on Samuel's second lot, next to the "Landing Yard" in today's Haddonfield. The small lot and surrounding farms joined Haddonfield in 1943.

Samuel and Abigail Willits resided at 49 Grove Street

in the village of Haddonfield. The couple had five children. Both parents were born in 1843 and brought up in Quaker households. Several generations of the Willits family lived in the region. One side of Samuel's family, the Abbotts, were operators of Abbott's Dairies, a well-known dairy in the region for many years. Abigail's family owned and operated Evans mill, a gristmill situated outside Haddonfield in Delaware Township, now Cherry Hill. [See gristmills, page 136.]

Samuel followed in his father's footsteps as a lumber merchant. For many years, the family's lumberyards were in Haddonfield. Besides his site at Cooper's Creek, Willits operated a lumber and coal yard at Tanner Street and Euclid Avenue. [See lumberyards, page 168.]

Willits's lot, along with other nearby farms, were incorporated into Haddonfield in 1943.

15-18 Jacob S. Coles

Although most of Jacob Stokes Coles's 70 acres of land was within the boundaries of today's Westmont, his dwelling was situated along Coles Mill Road in Haddonfield. The house where Jacob, his wife Hannah, and their two children resided stands at 523 Coles Mill Road. Jacob, born in 1820, inherited the farm from his father, Josiah Coles.

Jacob's father owned the landing situated along Cooper's Creek known as Coles Landing. Years later, Samuel Willits's coal and lumber business used the landing. The former landing would be where the Haddon Township/Haddonfield border intersects Cooper River.

The road that passed in front of the dwelling took the name of the Coles family. Before the Delaware River Railroad & Bridge Company's tracks bisected the road, Coles Landing Road traveled between the Haddonfield Road and Coles Landing. Today, the old road's roadbed is Locust Avenue and Coles Mill Road.

Jacob Coles's farm had 51 acres of arable land, with the remaining 19 acres wooded. Jacob planted crops familiar to most farmers in the area. He also maintained one hundred apple trees on five acres of soil. A township farmer, Henry Cuthbert, noted in his account ledger that Coles sold potato sprouts. Jacob also sold nursery products including garden plants and evergreen bushes. Jacob stored his grain and hay in a 20' x 30' barn along with his agricultural tools and implements.

Before refrigeration, farmers harvested ice during the winter months from nearby ponds and stored it in ice houses. The *West Jersey Press* reported "the dam upon the farm of Jacob S. Coles of Haddon Township was broken by the storm last week. Mr. Coles succeeding in filling his ice house the day before the break." (WJP 1/9/1878)

Despite his agricultural chores, Jacob found time to serve as treasurer of both the county and state agricultural boards. These organizations were formed to advance the interest of farmers. He also served as a trustee for the Rowandtown school. In 1890, Jacob passed away; Hannah Coles outlived her husband by seven years.

A part of the farm was joined to Haddonfield in 1943. The section of the farm that was not ceded to Haddonfield remained in Haddon Township.

Jacob S. Coles's residence in Haddonfield. The house is at 523 Coles Mill Road. When the Coles resided here, the lane in front of the dwelling was known as Coles Landing Road named after an adjacent landing on Cooper's Creek.

(Photo by Samuel Rhoads, 1909, Camden County Historical Society Collections)

15-19 James S. Lippincott / Robert Frazer / Owen Stockton

James S. Lippincott's home stood opposite the Jacob Coles home along the eastern side of Coles Landing Road. Lippincott's frame Tuscan villa style house, now 540 Coles Mill Road, stood on a 31-acre lot. The barn on the tract was 40' x 20' and a tenant house stood nearby.

Before James had retired from farming, he became a devotee of literary projects. With a background in both agriculture and writing, James wrote a 46-page article entitled "Market Products of West New Jersey" published by the U.S. Department of Agriculture in the *Report of the Commissioner of Agriculture for the Year 1865.* The treatise analyzed the many products grown in this part of the state. The work was a thorough analysis of crop yields, reports on livestock, farmers' profits and other agricultural statistics. It was utilized extensively in this project. Lippincott penned other articles for the U.S. Department of Agriculture. Some topics included studies on grape vines, geography of plants, fruit regions of the Northern United States, and a study on atmospheric humidity.

Although he was widely respected for his knowledge in the agricultural area, Lippincott wrote and edited works on other topics. George Prowell's *The History of Camden County, New Jersey*, noted that James:

> ...edited an American Edition of "Chambers' Encyclopedia," and did much work on "Lippincott's Biographical Dictionary."

He was a close observer of the weather, and his notes of climatic changes and influences are valuable additions to that branch of knowledge. His industry and perseverance are shown in the general and exhaustive index he made of the *Friends*, a religious journal, and devoted to the interests of that society, extending through forty volumes. (p. 335)

James Lippincott married twice, but did not have children. He died in 1885 at 65.

In the early 1870s, Lippincott sold his farm to Robert Frazer. A detailed description of Frazer's two-story "Mansion" was contained in an 1875 fire insurance survey. The house, built around 1850, was sided with cedar boards and covered with a tin roof:

> All plastered and ceiling and well painted inside and out. Panel doors and window shutters below and venetian shutters to the 2nd story window above. The first story is divided as follows–parlors, sitting room, dining room, hall 4 and one-half feet wide and kitchen. In the hall, open stair with mahogany newels and hand rails with curled maple balusters to 2nd story. Box stairs in the dining room. Warmed by a furnace in the cellar with flues for warm air and gas. 6 chambers on the 2nd story with hall and passage ways. Cupboards in all the rooms except the parlor. (Rowand No. 431, 1875)

In the mid-1870s, Frazer sold the farm to Owen and Mary Stockton. The Stocktons continued to farm the land. The Borough of Haddonfield acquired the farm along with other neighboring lots in 1943.

Borough of Haddonfield

During the 1870s, over half the township's citizens lived in the village of Haddonfield. Notwithstanding this fact, village inhabitants could not garner the support of residents in outlying rural regions of the township to endorse installation of street lights, sidewalks and improvements along Main Street. They resolved their dilemma in March 1875, when the village incorporated. The borough's 1875 boundaries included an area of several blocks to each side of Main Street and between what is now Chews Landing Road and Cooper River. [See village of Haddonfield, page 6.]

Today's Borough of Haddonfield encompasses a much larger area than the 1875 borough. The dozen or so farms in the township surrounding the 1875 incorporated-village were ceded to the Borough in 1904 and 1943. One of the borough's boundaries with Haddon Township was relocated in 1941, another border with Haddon Heights, was reset in 1947 and 1951.

His brow is wet with honest sweat,
He earns whate'er he can,
And looks the whole world in the face,
For he owes not any man.

Henry Wadsworth Longfellow
"The Village Blacksmith," 1839, 2

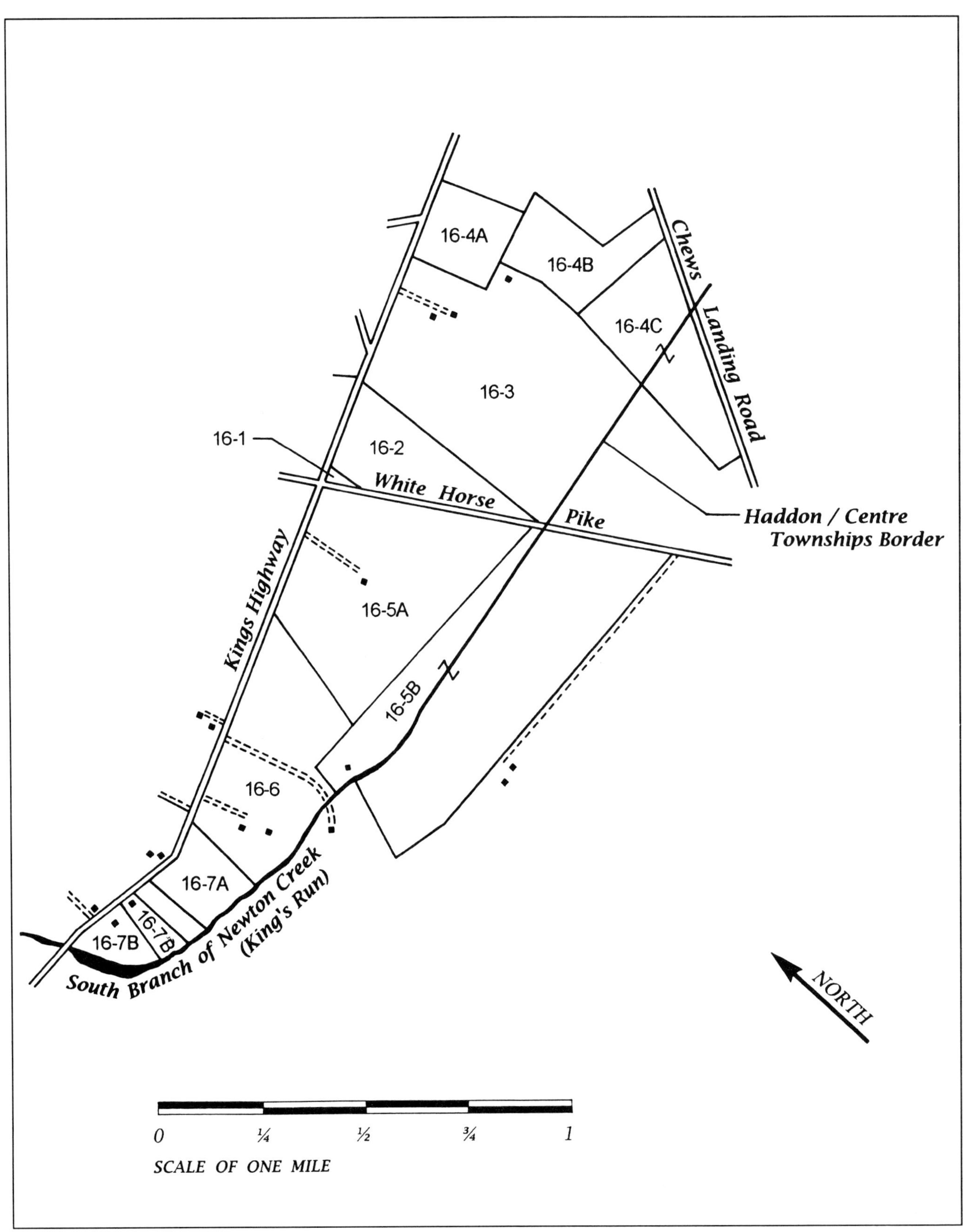

Map of the area that became part of Haddon Heights, 1877.

16

Haddon Heights

16-1 Schoolhouse at Baker's Corner

A schoolhouse stood on a small lot at the northeast corner of the White Horse Pike and Kings Highway.

16-2 Maria Glover

The perimeter of this 30-acre lot ran at an angle from near Third Avenue, at Kings Highway, to the vicinity where Garden Street crosses the White Horse Pike, then to Kings Highway and back to the vicinity of Third Avenue.

16-3 Stephen Collins / James Redman / Jacob Dodd

This 100-acre farm situated between the vicinity of First to Third avenues and between Kings Highway and Garden Street.

16-4 The Hinchmans, Charles L. Willits and Benjamin Cooper

The Haddonfield and Haddon Heights border now crosses what were three lots situated between Kings Highway and Chews Landing Road.

Lot A The Hinchman's 22-acre lot was near Kings Highway to Station Avenue and the area between First Avenue and opposite where North Drive intersects Kings Highway.

Lot B Charles Willits's 21-acre lot was near Crest Avenue between Chews Landing Road and Station Avenue.

Lot C Benjamin Cooper's 37 acres was along the western side of Chews Landing Road near First and Second avenues.

16-5 Benjamin Lippincott and Joseph Lippincott

Lot A Benjamin's 81-acre tract was between the White Horse Pike and the vicinity of Ninth Avenue and, along the White Horse Pike, between Kings Highway and the former Haddon and Centre townships' boundary, near Garden Street. The boundary of this lot ran at an angle from the White Horse Pike, near Garden Street, toward the Camden County Park.

Lot B The perimeter of Benjamin and Joseph's 109-acre tract, in Haddon Township, was along a line beginning near Glover Avenue, at North Park, then angling across Station Avenue to the White Horse Pike, near Garden Street. The Centre Township portion of the lot was between the township boundary and a line that ran at an angle from Prospect Ridge Boulevard at Bellmawr Avenue to the White Horse Pike opposite of East High Street. Most of this 109 acres was within Centre Township.

16-6 John T. Glover

This 70-acre tract was between Kings Highway and Kings Run leading to the South Branch of Newton Creek, and between Ninth Avenue extending opposite the juncture where Edgewood Avenue and Kings Highway meet.

16-7 Joseph Ewen, the Howells and Joseph Baker

The small lots were between John Glover's farm and where King's Run meandered under Kings Highway.

Lot A Ewen's lot was between the area opposite where Edgewood Avenue and Kings Highway meet and Thirteenth Avenue, and Kings Highway to the South Branch of Newton Creek.

Lots B Today this location would be between Thirteenth Avenue and the South Branch of Newton Creek, and Kings Highway and the creek. Joseph Baker's lot was next to where the South Branch of Newton Creek crosses under Kings Highway.

The 1865 boundary separating Haddon and Centre townships crossed the White Horse Pike near Garden Street. Heading east, the township line crossed Chews Landing Road, near Crest Avenue, and continued through what is now Haddonfield to Cooper's Creek. On the western side of White Horse Pike, the township boundary was near Garden Street and extended in a westerly direction toward Station Avenue to what today is a county park and along the small stream known as King's Run. The border between the two townships continued along the South Branch of Newton Creek.

16-1 Schoolhouse at Baker's Corner

A small schoolhouse once stood on the southeast corner of the White Horse Pike and Kings Highway. The intersection was once known as Baker's Corner. The one-room school, built in the early 1800s, functioned as a public school for Newton Township, then Haddon Township.

In 1874, the township school trustees offered the "old frame building formerly occupied as a school house" for sale. A correspondent reported that the school was "in a good state of repair...and will prove useful for many purposes to farmers or others." (WJP 4/15/1874) They removed the building from the lot shortly thereafter. [See education, page 57.]

16-2 Maria Glover

Maria Glover's 30-acre lot sat next to Baker's corner. There were no dwellings on the lot and it is likely the land was leased to a farmer. Maria gained possession of the lot in 1858 from her father, James Glover. At one time, valuable timber on the lot was a source of income for its owner. In 1839, James Glover divided the tract into half-acre lots and auctioned the standing timber. Most of the trees were gone when Maria came into possession of the real estate.

In 1860, Maria resided with her brother Ridgeway Glover, a nearby farmer. Shortly after this period, Ridgeway sold his 62-acre farm to John Sheets. [John Sheets, page 187.] Maria's other brother, John T. Glover, also lived on a nearby farm. [See John T. Glover, page 238.] Maria never married and died in 1877 at the age of 43.

16-3 Stephen Collins / James Redman / Jacob Dodd

Stephen Collins's house still stands today at 7 First Avenue. The three-story frame dwelling had front and back verandas. A two-story addition and a leanto shed kitchen were attached to the main structure. The various outbuildings surrounding the house included two barns, a cow barn, a chicken house, a corncrib, a two-story carriage house and open carriage and wagon sheds. The lot was 100 acres. Its location is at the high point of a gradual incline that begins near Haddonfield. They once called the rise Collins Hill. It is likely that a tenant dwelling stood on Collins's tract at 200 Station Avenue. The frame building may have existed as early as 1850. Collins employed several domestic servants to help with house chores.

In 1870, Collins's cash crops were market garden produce. He also sold sprouts to other farmers. Jehu Wood, a township farmer, purchased tomato sprouts from Collins for transplant. Stephen was an active member of an association of farmers and fruit growers that looked out for the interests and concerns of local farmers.

In 1874, Collins advertised in a local newspaper, "Wanted an active industrious man to take the farm on shares, or for rent another season." (WJP 7/29/1874) Soon after that, James Redman acquired the farm and Stephen moved into a new house in Haddonfield. Collins subsequently moved to Philadelphia then returned to Haddonfield in the late 1880s.

James Redman's ownership was brief, lasting a couple of years. Isaac Kay, of Haddonfield, came into possession of the property through a sheriff's sale. Then in 1877, Jacob F. Dodd, a farmer from Delaware Township, acquired the tract. Dodd was the beneficiary of several favorable newspaper accounts. Jacob was probably a loyal Republican as the partisan *West Jersey Press* praised Dodd as, "one of the most successful as well as enterprising of Haddonfield farmers." (WJP 1/19/1880) A month later, the same Camden paper noted Dodd, "whose farm lies on Collins Hill has some of the finest watermelon in the vicinity." (WJP 8/14/1880) In the same report, it was revealed the watermelons taken from Dodd's four-acre patch, weighted 65 to 70 pounds a piece.

Dodd's farm adjoined the old Newton Township Burial Ground. The burial lot was located along Kings Highway near First Avenue. The dimensions of the graveyard lot were 125 feet along Kings Highway and 350 feet deep. [See graveyards, page 84.] Although the burial ground was physically in old Haddon Township, title to the municipal lot was in dispute during the 1870s. After township negotiators forged a settlement and resolved the quarrel over legal title, the lot was sold to Dodd for $100. A newspaper article reported on the reason the township sold the lot:

> It is said that outsiders have been using the township burying ground to an unwarranted extent for depositing their dead, and this is the reason why it has been ordered sold. (WJP 3/24/1880)

In the early 1880s, Dodd acquired a second farm along the Mt. Ephraim & Haddonfield Road in Audubon.

16-4 The Hinchmans, Charles L. Willits and Benjamin Cooper

Three lots were once situated along the Haddon Heights/Haddonfield boundary line between Kings Highway and Chews Landing Road. It is likely that the lots were without dwellings.

The first lot, some 22 acres, was owned by a member of the Hinchman family. The tax assessment ledgers suggest William Hinchman paid taxes on the lot, although an 1877 map of the area infers Joseph H. Hinchman owned the lot. [See William Hinchman, page 225.]

Charles Willits held the deed to a 21-acre lot. Willits owned a larger tract of land on the White Horse Pike within Haddon Heights and Barrington. Charles resided at the intersection of the White Horse and Clement's Bridge roads in Centre Township. He also owned property in Philadelphia and a summer residence in Atlantic City. Charles was the uncle of Samuel A. Willits, a lumber merchant in Haddonfield. [See lumberyard, page 168.]

Although Charles Willits accumulated considerable wealth during his life time, he maintained his Quaker beliefs and principles. He displayed his generosity through a bequeath provided in his will of $10,000 to the Philadelphia Friends Meeting to disperse "among the colored people of the southern states of the United States and. . .the Colony of Liberia so that religion and morality may be promoted." (Will, I-84)

Benjamin Cooper, of Centre Township, owned the 37-acre lot adjoining Willits's land. Cooper was a blacksmith. The former boundary between Haddon Township and Centre Township cut across Cooper's lot. About half the lot fell within the 1870s Haddon Township.

16-5 Benjamin Lippincott and Joseph Lippincott

Benjamin and Joseph Lippincott, together and individually, owned more than 300 acres of land in Haddon and Centre townships. The brothers were well-to-do farmers. A third brother, Nathan, owned a nearby farm. [See Nathan Lippincott, page 220.]

Benjamin Lippincott's 81-acre farm was on the southwestern quadrant of the intersection of White Horse Pike and Kings Highway. Lippincott's dwelling was at the southwest corner of Seventh Avenue and Green Street. Benjamin's father, Abraham built the house. One approached the dwelling from Kings Highway along a lane that ran parallel to the Philadelphia & Atlantic City Railway's right-of-way.

The Lippincotts were descendants of settlers that came to America in the seventeenth century. When Benjamin took up farming, he was following the footsteps of past generations of farmers in his family. Benjamin married Pricilla Nicholson of Mt. Ephraim in 1849 and both adhered to Quaker beliefs. The household was composed of their children, Benjamin A., Sarah and Mary; a domestic servant, and Benjamin's brother, Joseph.

The large number of cows on the farm provided milk in such quantity that Lippincott's herd was one of the largest producers of dairy products in the township. The farm had the distinction of also having the largest apple orchard in the entire township in 1879. The 600 trees yielded more than 250 bushels of apples. Apples The apple were not the sole crop cultivated on the farm. Corn, wheat and potatoes were also planted.

At the time of Benjamin's death in 1892, his safe contained more than $53,000 in stocks and bonds, a considerable sum at that period. Besides his farm,

Benjamin's real estate holdings included several rental properties in Camden. Young Benjamin inherited his father's farm and eventually turned the tract into a residential real estate development.

In 1863, Benjamin and his brother Joseph acquired James Hurley's 109-acre farm. Situated partly in Haddon and Centre Townships, the tract was between Benjamin's 81-acre Haddon Township farm and Joseph's 135-acre Centre Township farm. Most of the lot was in Centre Township.

When the Lippincott brothers acquired the Hurley farm, about 70 acres was cultivated with grass and grain. The farm had a large apple orchard and other fruit trees. In 1879, William Hatcher was a tenant farmer residing on the lot.

The Hurley farmhouse was on Haddon Township soil at 1019 North Park Avenue. Today, part of the house is believed to be one of the oldest private residences in Camden County, built about 1700. In the 1860s, the two-story brick house had four rooms on each floor and a frame kitchen addition. One structure on the property was a springhouse "with a never failing spring. . . ." Supplementing the dependable spring was "a pump of excellent water" near the dwelling. (WJP 2/4/1863) Other outbuildings included a barn, hay house, wagon house and corn shed. An advertisement announcing a public sale at the house stated the 109 acres were "well fenced." (WJP 2/4/1863)

At one time, a lane traveled from Kings Highway, near Glover and Eleventh avenues, crossed John Glover's land, then divided into two lanes. One lane traveled toward the old Hurley dwelling, the other leg headed to a neighboring farm in Centre Township.

In 1870, Joseph Lippincott resided with Benjamin's family. At that time, Joseph had retired from farming. Without a spouse or children, when Joseph died, his brother's children were named beneficiaries of the estate. His nieces, Sarah and Mary, inherited all of Joseph's household goods, bedding and books. His nephew Benjamin fared better—he inherited his uncle's 135-acre Centre Township farm.

16-6 John T. Glover

John T. Glover's dwelling stands at 1212 Sylvan Avenue. Some believe part of the dwelling may have been constructed in the early 1700s. The original house consisted of one-room on the first floor, now situated on the northeastern side of the house. The room measured about 20' x 15'. It is possible that sometime before 1800, the rooms on the western side of the structure were added, including a center hallway. It is likely that sometime in the mid-1800s, the design of the original roof was changed and raised to its present form and a new addition was attached to the southern side of the dwelling. At that time, the Gothic Revival features were probably added to the house.

John, his wife Anna and their two children, two domestic servants and several farm laborers resided on the 70-acre farm. The Glover family tilled the soil in the area for many generations. John's brother Ridgeway, and sister Maria lived nearby. [See Maria Glover, page 236.]

The lane leading from Kings Highway to Glover's dwelling is now Thornolden Avenue. A second lane, beginning in the area of Glover and Eleventh avenues,

"Hurley House." Today the old farmhouse, now 1019 North Park Avenue, Haddon Heights, is one of oldest private dwellings in the region. James Hurley's house and farm was purchased by Benjamin and Joseph Hinchman in 1863. A tenant farmer lived and worked the 109-acre Hinchman farm.

(Haddon Heights Library Collections)

Fulling mill on John T. Glover's farm in Haddon Heights. The mill was along the South Branch of Newton Creek in what is now part of the county park. Glover's nearby house is present-day 1212 Sylvan Avenue. The mill was in operation until about 1840.

(Haddon Heights Library Collections)

at Kings Highway, crossed the lot and headed onto Joseph and Benjamin Lippincott's neighboring lot and continued toward a farm on the other side of the creek in Centre Township.

At one time, Glover's tract was the site of a fulling mill. The Glover fulling mill is thought to have been built by John's ancestors, sometime around 1740. When woolen fabric came off a loom, it was soiled with grease or oils. The fuller placed cloth in a vat of water containing a caustic substance like animal urine or a silicate earthy matter called fullers' earth. A water wheel on one end was connected by a shaft, gears, cams, and belts to a hammer that continually hit and turned the cloth. The process cleaned and shrunk the cloth. During the operation, the fibers of the weave worked themselves free from the thread and filled the space between the treads. After the cloth reached the desired consistency, it was pressed and sheared so that the surface was evened. Glover's fulling mill also dyed cloth for customers.

The mill was destroyed by fire in 1821; it was subsequently rebuilt and in use until about 1840. The mill was torn down about 1917. A small portion of the mill's stone foundation still exists along the banks of the creek that wanders through the Camden County Park.

A small dam blocked the King's Run, creating a pond that provided waterpower for Glover's fulling mill. The dam, situated next to the mill, formed a pond that backed up about 700 feet to the east. Although the fulling mill was not in use in the 1870s, the dam and mill pond existed during John Glover's lifetime.

Glover raised crops that were prevalent on all farms in the region. In 1880, John was one of several township farmers that sold cordwood. At this time, most of the woodlands in the township had been cleared. John's real estate included a lot on the opposite side of Kings Highway, next to the South Branch of Newton Creek in Audubon. It is likely Glover's timber was cut from his lot in Audubon.

16-7 Joseph Ewen, the Howells and Joseph Baker

Several lots were situated between John Glover's farm and where King's Run went beneath Kings Highway. Joseph Ewen owned one lot. His homestead was on the opposite side of Kings Highway in Audubon. [See Joseph Ewen, page 189.]

Two dwellings stood on two small lots along Kings Highway between Joseph Ewen's property and King's Run. The Howell family of Centre Township, owned one of the homes. Joseph Baker, a plasterer, owned the neighboring home. Baker lived at the site along with his wife and six children.

The southern border of Baker's lot was a millpond. The pond was the source of waterpower for the Mt. Ephraim Mill. [See gristmills, page 136.] The pond, once known as Hugg's Millpond, extended a quarter-mile to the south of a dam built near Kings Highway.

The gristmill was on the other side of Kings Highway in Audubon. The creek still flows through the site of the former mill pond.

Borough of Haddon Heights

Benjamin A. Lippincott is credited with being the first to attempt residential development in Haddon Heights. In the 1890s, building lots were laid out by Lippincott in an area between Fourth through Eighth avenues and Kings Highway to High Street.

One of Benjamin's more astute ideas was persuading the management of the Philadelphia & Reading Railroad to build a passenger station in the center of his development. Commuters rode trains to work. Soon thereafter, Benjamin aided in forming the borough. It was only fitting that Lippincott serve as the borough's first mayor when Haddon Heights was incorporated in 1904 from portions of Haddon and Centre townships. The borough's boundary with Haddonfield was relocated in 1947 and 1951.

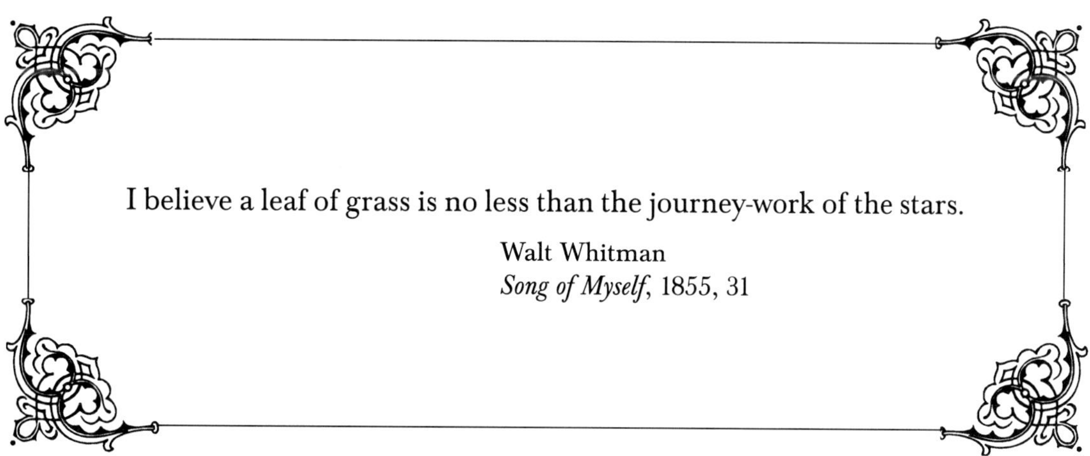

I believe a leaf of grass is no less than the journey-work of the stars.

Walt Whitman
Song of Myself, 1855, 31

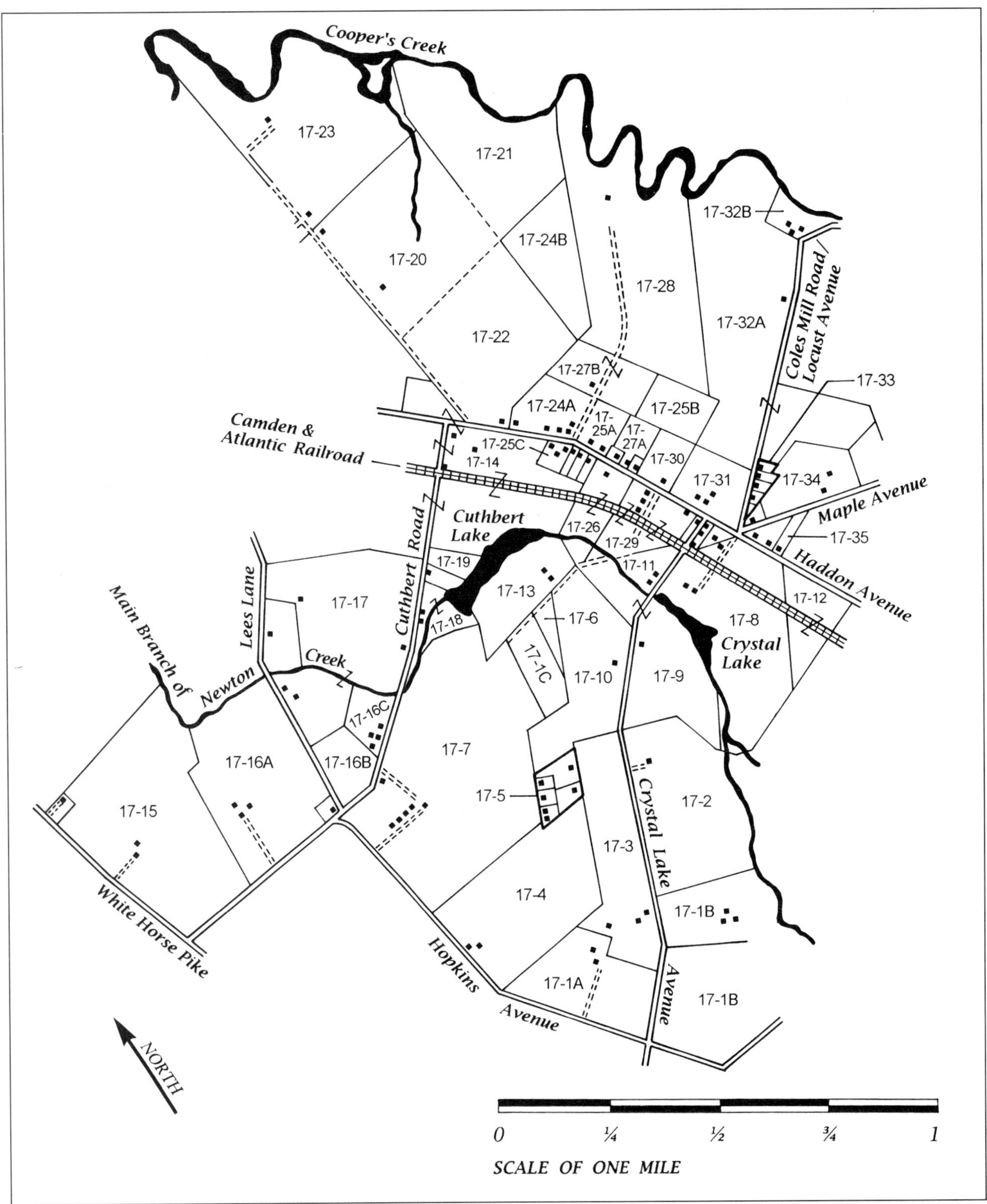

Map of the area that became Haddon Township, 1877. (See page 192 for Collingswood Extension and West Collingswood Heights.)

17

Haddon Township

17-1 Samuel M. Hinchman / Rebecca Ann Collings / William C. Hinchman

Lot A The portion of Samuel Hinchman's tract that is now in Haddon Township was along Hopkins Road (Hopkins Avenue), between Crystal Lake and Mt. Vernon avenues, and from Austermuhl Avenue to Hopkins Road.

Lot B Today's Haddon Township/Haddonfield border traverses William Hinchman's homestead. The 74 acres were along the eastern edge of Crystal Lake Avenue from Mt. Vernon Avenue to Hopkins Road. It would include today's Redman, Homestead, East and West Greenman and Birchal avenues, North Drive, Bewley Road and Barberry Lane.

Lot C Rebecca Ann Collings inherited Samuel Hinchman's land. Collings also owned ten acres of land near Fern and Ivywood avenues in Haddon Township.

17-2 Isaac E. Hinchman

The area of this 57-acre farm, on the eastern side of Crystal Lake Avenue, was between Mount Vernon Avenue and the opposite side where MacArthur Boulevard intersects Crystal Lake Avenue. The property extended between Crystal Lake Avenue and the creek that flowed into Crystal Lake.

17-3 Daniel Middleton / Sarah Hunt

The borders of this 42-acre farm were between MacArthur Boulevard and the vicinity of Homestead Avenue. The farm's boundary extended west from Crystal Lake about one block.

17-4 Susan Hampton / Rhoda Hampton

This 60-acre farm was between Mt.Vernon Avenue and opposite Graisbury Avenue, and between Hopkins Road and Austermuhl Avenue.

17-5 Saddlertown

This area was near MacArthur Boulevard, and included Rhoads and Beechwood avenues and First and Second streets.

17-6 The Smiley Family

The two-acre tract was near what is now James Stoy School on Briarwood Avenue.

17-7 John M. Whitall

This 114-acre tract was on the southern side of Cuthbert Road and east of Hopkins Road. MacArthur Boulevard crosses through Whitall's tract. The lot would include most of what is now the Haddon Township High School and Pope Paul VI High School complexes and the Westmont Plaza shopping center.

17-8 John Stoy

The boundary of this 69-acre farm, would be between Haddon Avenue and Crystal Lake and from Crystal Lake Avenue to the township border with Haddonfield.

17-9 Edwin and Elizabeth Stoy Willis

The perimeter of this 38-acre lot ran from Crystal Lake along Crystal Lake Avenue to a location opposite MacArthur Boulevard and continued east to a branch of Newton Creek, along the branch to Crystal Lake and Crystal Lake Avenue. The couple's smaller lot was situated on the western side of Crystal Lake Avenue. The lot was between the area of West Park Boulevard and the creek, and between Crystal Lake Avenue to the vicinity where Briarwood Avenue intersects Park Boulevard.

17-10 Aaron Stoy

This 42-acre lot was on the western side of Crystal Lake Avenue in an area between West Park Boulevard and MacArthur Boulevard, and between the area of Briarwood and Crestwood avenues to Crystal Lake Avenue.

17-11 James Flinn

The six-acre lot was on the northern side of Crystal Lake Avenue between the PATCO High Speed Line and the creek west of Crystal Lake.

17-12 Samuel M. Reeves

This nine-acre triangular-shaped lot was along the southwestern side of Haddon Avenue between the area of Hazel Avenue to the Haddon Township/ Haddonfield municipal boundary.

17-13 Hannah Webster / Samuel Webster

This 30-acre tract was situated on the western side of the stream that emptied into the Main Branch of Newton Creek. Webster's tract included the area of Buckner, Bradley and Memorial avenues.

17-14 Joseph O. Cuthbert, Sr. / Henry Cuthbert

This 110-acre tract formed the southwestern side of Haddon Avenue, between Albertson and Conard avenues. The lot's southern boundary ran along the Main Branch of Newton Creek, and crossed Cuthbert Road to Stokes and Linwood avenues. Cuthbert's lot on the northeast side of the Haddon Avenue was in Collingswood, between Cuthbert Boulevard and Penn Avenue.

17-15 William Bettle, Jr.

Bettle's 92 acres was on the northeastern side of the White Horse Pike, between East Clinton Avenue and Cuthbert Road, and between the White Horse Pike, and east for several blocks. Today the area is known as the Bettlewood section.

17-16 James Dobbs / James C. Dobbs / Anthony Heck

Lot A Dobbs's 74-acre farm was situated along the northern side of Cuthbert Road. The farm was made up of three sections, the largest portion was on the Haddon Township side of Cuthbert Road, between Lees Lane and where Haviland Avenue meets Cuthbert Road. This lot extended between Cuthbert Road and the Main Branch of Newton Creek. The area is now known as Heather Glen.

Lot B Dobbs's other lot was at the intersection of Lees Lane and Cuthbert Road. The lot was between Lees Lane and opposite where MacArthur Boulevard meets Cuthbert Road. Dobbs's lot extended toward Newton Creek some 800 feet from Cuthbert Road.

Lot C Dobbs's brickyard lot was between Newton Creek and an area opposite where MacArthur Boulevard meets Cuthbert Road. The lot extended about 800 feet from Cuthbert Road.

17-17 John Schnitzius

This 69-acre Schnitzius farm was divided into two sections. The largest section, was between the Haddon Township/Collingswood border in the area of Linwood Avenue, to the Main Branch of Newton Creek and between Cuthbert Road, west to Lees Lane.

Schnitzius's other tract of land was on the southeastern quadrant, where Lees Lane crossed Newton Creek. The lot is within today's county park.

17-18 Hiram Smith

This narrow six-acre lot extended along Cuthbert Road between the area opposite where Linwood Avenue meets Cuthbert Road to the Main Branch of Newton Creek. The tract's other dimensions were between Cuthbert Road and an area just to the east of the creek bank.

17-19 Isaac Prine

This two-acre lot was on the eastern side of Cuthbert Road in the vicinity of Stokes Avenue.

17-20 Samuel H. French

Had Cuthbert Road extended to the north side of Haddon Avenue in the nineteenth century, it would have cut through the 75-acre "Pine Grove Farm." On the west side of Cuthbert Boulevard, the farm included all or parts of Haddon Township's Addison, Penn, Linden, Lawnside, New Jersey and Emerald avenues. On the east side of Cuthbert Boulevard, the farm included areas to the north and south of Emerald Avenue including portions of Addison and Bradford avenues.

17-21 Arthur Powell / Samuel H. French

This 60-acre "Creek Farm" encompassed an area on the east side of Cuthbert Boulevard. The tract's approximate area at Cooper's Creek was in between Cuthbert Boulevard and east to the vicinity of Edgewood Avenue and from the creek to the section of Stratford Avenue between Emerald and Geneva avenues. A small portion of the farm, near Cooper's Creek, may have extended west of Cuthbert Boulevard.

17-22 Joseph Osler / Samuel H. French

Along Haddon Avenue, Osler's 43-acre tract was between Albertson and Strawbridge avenues. The "Osler Farm" dimensions, on the east side of Cuthbert Boulevard, would include portions of Strawbridge, Stratford, Cambridge, Emerald and Oriental avenues. The tract encompassed a small area on the western side of Cuthbert Boulevard, near Oriental and Addison avenues.

17-23 Anthony Woodward / David U. Morgan

This farm's 78 acres would be between the Haddon Township/Collingswood boundary and Cooper River and from the area near Haddon Township's New Jersey Avenue to Cooper River. The area is now known as the Bluebird section.

17-24 Thomas Albertson

Lot A This eight-acre lot was between Cooper Street and near Albertson Avenue and between Haddon and Virginia avenues.

Lot B Albertson also owned a triangular shaped nineteen acre lot with a perimeter along Emerald and Stratford avenues to Alton Avenue, and along a line cutting across Utica, Elgin and Melrose avenues and back to Emerald Avenue, just west of Cooper Street, and returning to near Stratford Avenue.

17-25 David Albertson

Albertson owned three lots comprising 23 acres.

Lot A One lot was between Cooper Street and near Reeve Avenue, and between Haddon and Virginia avenues.

Lot B A second tract was between an area near Emerald and Melrose avenues and Virginia Avenue, and between the area of Reeve Avenue and Center Street.

Lot C The third lot, on the southwestern side of Haddon Avenue, was between Walnut and Albertson avenues. This tract extended from Haddon Avenue to Lindisfarne Avenue.

17-26 Briggs Kay

This lot contained some seventeen acres and was situated between Haddon Avenue and a stream that emptied into Newton Creek and between the area of Chestnut and Wynnewood avenues to West Walnut Avenue. A small part of the tract was on the southern side of the creek.

17-27 Samuel A. Reeve

Lot A The smaller tract was between Haddon Avenue and near Virginia Avenue and between the vicinity of Reeve Avenue and near Center Street.

Lot B The other tract was between the area of Virginia and Melrose avenues and about one block to each side of Cooper Street. Reeve owned two lots containing a total of seventeen acres.

17-28 Amos Willis, Jr.

This 100-acre lot was between the vicinity of Emerald and Melrose avenues and Cooper River, and extended two blocks to the east and one block to the west of Cooper Street.

17-29 John N. Hobensack

The twenty acres were at the southwest quadrant of the intersection of Haddon and Crystal Lake avenues. The lot was between the vicinity of Chestnut and Wynnewood avenues and near Crystal Lake Avenue. The tract's southern border went from the area where the PATCO High Speed Line met Crystal Lake Avenue, to a point near the intersection of Park and Chestnut avenues.

17-30 Thomas W. Wilkinson

The nine acres, along Haddon Avenue, went about 200 feet to each side of Center Street and between the vicinity of Virginia and Haddon avenues.

17-31 Jacob P. Fowler

The thirteen acres of land were between Maple Avenue and midway between Crystal Lake Avenue and Center Street. The lot extended from Haddon Avenue to Virginia Avenue.

17-32 Jacob S. Coles, Samuel A. Willits

Lot A The boundaries of Coles's 70-acre farm went between Coles Mill Road and north to Oneida Avenue, and between the vicinity of Virginia Avenue and Cooper River. Jacob owned an adjacent tract on the south side of Coles Mill Road near Melrose and E. Emerald avenues.

Lot B Samuel Willits owned five acres of land along Cooper's Creek, known as the "Landing Yard," in Haddon Township next to the municipal boundary with Haddonfield.

17-33 Lots along Coles Landing Road

A handful of narrow lots situated on the eastern side of Locust Avenue.

17-34 Clayton Brown / John Macaulay

This twenty-acre tract was situated along Haddon Township's side of Maple Avenue. The odd-shaped lot was between Marne and Elm avenues. The lot reached north from Maple Avenue to near East Emerald Avenue.

17-35 Phoebe Adams

This one-acre lot was on the northern side of the Haddon Avenue, just east of Maple Avenue.

17-36 John W. Logan Estate

(See page 192 for 1877 map.)

This 212-acre farm made up most of today's West Collingswood Heights. The other tract making up what is now West Collingswood Heights, was the neighboring Weinnmann/Doughten lot along the Black Horse Pike.

17-37 Peter Weinnmann / William Doughten

(See page 192 for 1877 map.)

The 23-acre lot included the vicinity of Main Avenue, Thomasina Avenue and Park Drive in West Collingswood Heights. The lot was along the Black Horse Pike at the South Branch of Newton Creek.

17-38 Estate of Samuel C. Champion

(See page 192 for 1877 map.)

This 79-acre "Cedar Grove Farm" was between Black Horse Pike/Mt. Ephraim Avenue and the Newton Burial Ground and from the Main Branch of Newton Creek to near Grant Avenue. The tract is now West Collingswood Extension.

The Hinchmans

The first Hinchmans emigrated to Newton Township in the late seventeenth century. The heirs to the original hundreds of acres included Isaac E. Hinchman, William C. Hinchman and Samuel M. Hinchman. Today, Hinchmans land is in Audubon, Haddon Heights, Haddonfield and Haddon Township. The 1870s tax assessment ledgers attribute most of the Hinchman's township land holdings to these individuals. Recorded deeds and maps show that other Hinchmans, including Charles, Hannah Ann and Joseph H., also owned land in the same area of the township.

17-1 Samuel M. Hinchman / Rebecca Ann Collings / William C. Hinchman

Samuel Mickle Hinchman owned land within the borders of Haddon Township and Audubon. In 1860 Samuel, his wife Rebecca Ann, son Joseph, two domestic servants and farm hands resided on the farm. The Hinchman dwelling stands at 401 Austermuhl Avenue. As far back as 1834, a dwelling existed at this site. It is likely the house was remodeled sometime after the 1850s with Gothic Revival architectural features.

The outbuildings on the homestead tract once included two barns, crib and sheep houses, a stable, and two wagon sheds. A "front drive," or lane, approached the Hinchman house from Hopkins Road. The "back drive" went from the house to Crystal Lake Avenue.

Samuel Hinchman's primary occupation was farming, although he was an active citizen in the community. He served on the first Township Committee when the newly formed township was set off from Newton Township in 1865. Before that time, he was an influential Newton Township citizen, having represented the people as a freeholder.

Samuel died in January 1866. His wife Rebecca Ann moved into the village of Haddonfield and the farm was rented to tenant farmers. Samuel and Rebecca Ann's only son, Joseph, died in 1871 at 22. Rebecca Ann, now age 54, remarried to Jacob Collings. It was also Jacob's second marriage. The couple resided in Camden and the village of Haddonfield. [See Jacob Collings, page 207; Rebecca Ann Collings, page 246.]

In 1879, Stokes Sutvan worked and occupied Rebecca Ann Collings's farm. Sutvan paid his rent with half the profits earned from the harvest. Rebecca Ann maintained an interest in ownership of the livestock on her farm. Sutvan grew hay, wheat, corn, potatoes, sweet potatoes and apples.

William C. Hinchman's dwelling stood near Hinchman and Homestead avenues in Haddonfield. Today's Haddon Township/Haddonfield municipal boundary crosses the farm. [See William C. Hinchman, page 225.]

Most of what was William Hinchman's tract was incorporated into Haddonfield in 1904, although a small segment joined the Borough in 1941. The remaining segment of the old Hinchman farm that was not ceded to the Borough of Haddonfield, remained in Haddon Township.

17-2 Isaac E. Hinchman

In 1865, Isaac Ellis Hinchman owned 57 acres of land along the east side of Crystal Lake Avenue. A sizeable portion of the tract is now athletic fields owned by Haddon Township Board of Education. Isaac's wood-frame house was near the Rohrer Tower high rise residential building at 300 Crystal Lake Avenue. During the twentieth century, the Hinchman farmhouse became a tavern; fire destroyed it in the early 1960s.

In 1858, at age 30, Isaac married Eunice Eastlack of Camden. The couple had three children, Walter, Clarence and Samuel. Domestic servants and farm laborers also resided on Isaac's farm. In 1879, the Hinchman farm had the second largest apple orchard in the township. Three hundred trees were spread over ten acres of land.

One of the more interesting historical facts about Isaac's land is its association with Thomas Githens's plastering mill. The mill was situated along the creek that, years later, became the eastern boundary of the Hinchman property. During Thomas Githens's lifetime, a pond provided the waterpower to pulverize lime rock into fertilizer plaster. Githens operated the mill until his death in 1826.

17-3 Daniel Middleton / Sarah Hunt

In 1865, Daniel Middleton lived on and worked a 42-acre farm along the west side of Crystal Lake Avenue. The Middleton house stood along Crystal Lake Avenue near Redman Avenue. The frame dwelling's dimensions were 28' x 28'. The house had two rooms on the first floor, four rooms on the second floor and a room in the finished attic. A barn stood near the house. (Rowand No. 502, 1879)

Daniel's wife, Sarah Hinchman Middleton, and daughter, Sarah, moved into Haddonfield sometime in the 1870s. When David passed away in 1879, his daughter Sarah Hunt took possession of the farm. Sarah

Rhoda Hampton's dwelling, now 807 Avondale Avenue in Haddon Township. The front of the home is along Hopkins Road. The Hamptons owned a 60-acre farm in the township.
(Courtesy of Rita Masters)

leased the farm to Samson Dobbs in 1879. Dobbs also worked at his family's brickmaking business on Cuthbert Road. [See brickyard, page 128.] Dobbs was also an experienced farmer, having previously farmed land in Delaware Township.

17-4 Susan Hampton / Rhoda Hampton

The Hamptons lived on a 60-acre farm situated on the east side of Hopkins Road. The former Hampton dwelling still stands today at 807 Avondale Avenue along Hopkins Road. It is possible this Greek Revival style home was built as early as the 1830s. A barn once stood behind the dwelling at the intersection of Breslin and Avondale avenues.

Susan Hampton was 75 in 1865. Her daughter Rhoda Ann Hampton was 41. Domestic servants and farm laborers also resided on the lot. Besides their Haddon Township property, the Hamptons owned farms in Stockton and Delaware townships. In 1870, the Hamptons leased the Haddon Township farm to James Anderson. James, born in Ireland, lived and worked on the farm with his wife and four children. In 1879, William Haines was renting the tract. At that time, four acres of woodland still existed on the property. Haines was one of a few local farmers that dealt in sheepskin. He sold 23 fleeces in 1879.

It was considered prudent in the nineteenth century to provide for the distribution of one's assets upon death. When Susan Hampton died in 1870, her heirlooms including a gold watch, a lot of foreign coins, a dozen tablespoons, six cows, nine shoats (young pigs), the grain in the ground, and hay, grain and potatoes were passed onto her daughter. (Inv. C-539, 1870)

17-5 Saddlertown

African-Americans comprised about ten percent of old Haddon Township's population. Outside of the village Haddonfield, the largest concentration of African-Americans resided in Saddlertown. To this day, the area is known by the same name. The community of some five acres was nestled between several larger farms.

As early as 1842, Joshua Saddler, an African-American, owned five acres in Saddlertown. Some years later, Joshua transferred part of his land to John and Joseph Saddler. Following the end of the Civil War, Joshua divided his remaining real estate into six lots and passed them onto his children Henrietta Bryant, Melissa Mott, Hannah Ann Coly and sons William and Joseph.

Some of Joshua Saddler's lots were heavily wooded. Even after he was gone, Joshua provided for the protection of the timber by inserting a restriction on his heirs that "in no instance to commit waste, by cutting the timber growing thereon, . . ." (Will G-261, 1868)

In 1858, Joseph Saddler sold fifteen hundredths of an acre to Jefferson Fisher of Saddlertown. Fisher later increased the area of his property to a half-acre.

Haddonfield insurance agent Jacob Rowand wrote a fire insurance policy covering Fisher's Saddlertown home. The dwelling's front part, was a two-story frame structure built in 1851 measuring 18' x 12'. A two-story frame addition was attached to the structure in 1878. A kitchen was housed in the back. The house was plastered, painted and in good repair. Rowand's survey showed a one-story frame outbuilding also stood on Fisher's lot filled with potatoes, coal and wood. A dwelling on the neighboring lot was similar in size to Fisher's house. (Rowand No. 518, 1879)

Other African-Americans that resided in Saddlertown homes included Charles Faucett, Charles and Robert Hankinson and William Smith. The Faucetts later moved to another African-American community, Snow Hill, now known as Lawnside.

Most African-American men in the township were either farm laborers or day laborers. Thomas Jefferson Fisher was a farm laborer on Henry Cuthbert's farm. Elias Fisher worked on the William Hinchman farm. William Saddler was an exception, He worked outside the agricultural region. He was a steward on the railroad, a job traditionally reserved for African-American men. The African-American women residing in Saddlertown were employed as domestic servants, or worked at home raising their children. [See African-Americans, page 73.]

17-6 The Smiley Family

In close proximity to Saddlertown was a two-acre tract owned by the Smiley family. During the 1860s and 1870s, Christopher, Kit, Joshua and James Smiley were the owners of record. Kit and James Smiley came from Virginia where they were born into slavery. In the 1830s, their lives took a turn for the better when their owner, Thomas Smiley, emancipated them. Thomas Smiley's last will and testament read:

> I do hereby emancipate and set free my negro man Jim and negro woman Amy and give them one hundred dollars to be equally divided between them. I do hereby emancipate and set free my negro man Kit and woman Judith with their future increase as I give them their children now born, to wit, Alfred, Charlotte, Mary and Amy until the said children arrive to the age of twenty one years at which age the said children and their increase to be set free. (Camden County Clerk's Office, Misc. Records Book #1, p. 124)

The Virginia slave owner's will contained a second benevolent clause. His estate paid the former slaves expenses to move:

> I do hereby authorize my executor to pay the expenses of my negroes emigrating to where they may think proper to enjoy their freedom.

In the mid-1870s, another African-American, Samuel Moore, alias Samuel White, purchased the lot from Christopher Smiley.

17-7 John M. Whitall

The Whitalls's permanent home was in Philadelphia, thought the family kept a summer residence in Atlantic City. They sold the seashore house and summer vacations were after that spent at their new country retreat in Haddon Township. John and Mary Whitall acquired "The Cedars" in 1864 from Samuel Merrick. It is likely

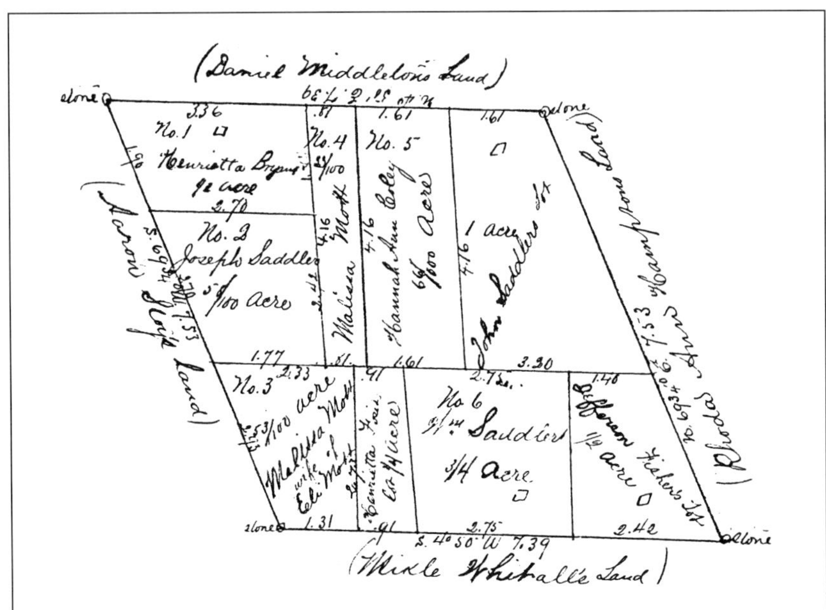

Saddlertown lots in Haddon Township as contained in Joshua Saddler's will. The five-acre site near MacArthur Boulevard was home to a number of African-American families. Most of the residents of Saddlertown worked on neighboring farms.

(Camden County Surrogate's Office, Wills, Book G-261)

John Whitall's summer retreat in Haddon Township. The home once stood on the present-day shopping center lot between MacArthur Boulevard and Hopkins Road. The buildings roof tower offered a view of the surrounding countryside.

(Courtesy of Robert and Bernadette Mehmet)

the Whitalls were first made aware of the availability of the 114-acre farm through their son-in-law, William H. Nicholson. William, a resident of a nearby farm, was born and raised in Newton Township. [See William H. Nicholson, page 182.] The Whitalls's summer house was in the area of the Westmont Plaza shopping center near MacArthur Boulevard.

One of the dwelling's unique features was its roof tower. The location of the house on a hill allowed for a splendid view of the surrounding countryside, especially from the window of the roof tower. The house was large as evidenced by a sale announcement after Whitall's death:

> The farm and country seat known as "The Cedars" belonging to the estate of John M. Whitall. 15 minute walk from the railroad station...16 rooms, neatly furnished, ground well shaded 4 to 5 acres, including a large vegetable and fruit garden. 10 room tenant house, ice house, carriage house, and stables. (WJP 6/23/1880)

Two lanes led in different directions from the dwelling. One lane went to Hopkins Road, the other lane traveled to Mill Road, now called Cuthbert Road. At least one tenant house stood on Whitall's land along Cuthbert Road, near the intersection of MacArthur Boulevard. Whitall's property had one of the largest wooded areas that remained in the township. Twenty-seven acres of woodland stood in the vicinity of the Van Sciver School and the Haddon Township High School.

In 1816, young John Whitall emulated his father and became a sailor and trader in foreign markets. John became the captain of several boats including the *New Jersey*, which sailed four times loaded with cargo to Canton, China from Philadelphia between 1824 and 1828. Whitall's days at sea ended in 1829 when he was 30. Soon thereafter, John became a merchant in Philadelphia; however, this venture ended in failure. Many years later, after he recovered from financial ruin, John paid off the long past-due debts incurred when he was a merchant. Because of the attention he gave to fiscal responsibility, he became known as "The Honest Quaker Merchant." (*Newsletter of the Philadelphia Maritime Museum–Winter 1984-1985*)

Whitall's wealth came from a glass manufacturing business that began operating in 1836. The Whitall, Tatem & Company grew to become one of the largest producers of glass in the country. The offices were at 410 Race Street in Philadelphia and in New York City. Glass manufacturing was carried out in several Millville plants and finished glassware was shipped by rail and water. The company owned sloops, schooners and

1880.

WHITALL, TATUM & CO.

GLASS MANUFACTURERS,

Druggists', Chemists' and Perfumers'

GLASSWARE.

DRUGGISTS' SUNDRIES.

No. 410 Race Street,	46 & 48 Barclay Street,
P. O. Box 2712,	P. O. Box 3814,
PHILADELPHIA.	NEW YORK.

1880.

Letterhead of Whitall, Tatem & Company. The company's offices were in Philadelphia, although its glassware manufacturing operation was in Millville.

(Whitall, Tatem & Company, Glassware Collection, 1880, in private collection)

steamboats that carried their products to stores for sale and distribution.

Having retired from his commercial pursuits, Whitall was not ready to take up the rigorous duties of farming. He leased most of his township land to a tenant farmer. His daughter wrote about her father's acquisition of "The Cedars" and his thoughts about profiting from the farmland:

> Our dear father especially enjoyed it all, and always felt that it was a most successful purchase, although he never found it very profitable in a pecuniary point of view. The farm was a source of almost constant outlay, but upon each fresh evidence of this he would console himself with a joke he had greatly enjoyed out of a magazine article on the deceitfulness of farming as a money-making business. In one of his letters he says concerning it:
>
> > "My having a farm, is like the man who had an elephant given to him, and did not know what to do with it. Only I have leased mine to a good farmer, who is to give me half of the produce. James says it will take all the profits of my glass business to pay my farm losses! Hope he may be mistaken." (*John M. Whitall–the story of his life*, p.274)

John Whitall's financial good fortunes allowed him to purchase his summer retreat. Hannah Whitall Smith, in her book about her father, offers a description of the summer vacations at the family's country seat. Hannah's childhood memories of walking along Newton Creek, visiting Crystal Lake and Newton Mill Pond and gathering the mail at the Haddonfield post office document memorable days of her childhood during the 1870s:

> "The Cedars" was from this time [1864] the summer home of our parents until our father's death [1877], and the summer resort of children and grandchildren in large parties for weeks at time. A bowling alley on the lawn was altered into a little cottage for the accommodation of the children. Our father named it "The Barracks," and there my sister Mary and I spent many happy summers of free and easy housekeeping together. It was a great delight to us all to gather thus every summer at the home of our beloved parents; and "to go to the Cedars," became the crowning point in the year to the grand-children, as one after another grew old enough to enjoy it. The place contained over one hundred acres, besides the house and private grounds, and was a genuine Jersey farm, with its orchard, and watermelon patch, and hay fields, and corn-fields, with cows to milk and horses to ride to pasture, and farm wagons starting off to market at two o'clock in the night, and all the untold delights of farm life, which were ever fresh pleasures to children from the city. There was a beautiful piece of woods down at the end of a shady lane, with a stream running through it, and two ponds large enough to sail a boat on; and there were endless joys to be found in the daily drives to the village of Haddonfield, about a mile and a half off, to get the mail, and to do the family errands. . . . I do not believe there were ever happier children anywhere, than roamed the lawn, and woods, and fields of "The Cedars" during all those lovely family summers. The meeting together of the cousins from all their various homes was of itself most delightful, and the

sources of enjoyment in boating, swimming, blackberrying, riding on horseback, driving, climbing trees, building dams, paddling, going to the mill, and picnicking in the woods, were almost endless. (p. 273)

Like many believers of Quaker principles, the Whitalls were humanitarians. John founded the St. Mary's Colored School in Philadelphia in 1862. The school's mission was to provide "religious instruction of the adult colored people." (The Starr Centre, *History of a Street*, p. 15) During the Civil War era, many of the school's 150 to 200 adult students were "contrabands" that migrated from southern states. Whitall was superintendent of the school for fourteen years.

John Whitall passed away in 1877, his wife Mary died in 1880. Following Mary's passing, the family sold the house and farm.

The Stoys

In 1828, James Stoy purchased more than 150 acres of land known as the "Crystal Lake Plantation." The tract surrounded a millpond called Crystal Lake. Stoy's land was situated on both sides of what is now Crystal Lake Avenue. Following James's death in 1842, his land was divided among his three children. John Stoy received the largest tract, some 69 acres, including the Stoy family homestead. Elizabeth Stoy and her brother, Aaron Stoy, each inherited 42 and one-half acres of land from their father's estate.

17-8 John Stoy

John, wife Rebecca, and their six children lived in a house now known as 330 Westmont Avenue. The two sections of the dwelling were completed at different times. The larger wing was built in 1793, and the smaller portion was finished in 1836.

Crystal Lake once provided waterpower for Stoy's sawmill, situated just west of Crystal Lake Avenue along the north side of the creek. It is not clear when the mill was built; however, it was in existence in 1813. James Stoy operated the mill long before his son, John, took over. The mill turned out wooden truck shelving for farmers' market wagons, boards for wheelwrights, and lumber for construction of homes, outbuildings and fencing.

John Stoy leased the sawmill to Isaac Prine during the 1860s. Prine later abandoned the sawmill in the early 1870s. In 1874, James Flinn and John Willits acquired a half-dozen acres of real estate including the sawmill. The partners turned the site into a paint works. [See sawmill, page 143, paint works, page 140.]

Two lanes originated from Stoy's home. One lane led from the home to the sawmill. The other lane ran from the dwelling, over the railroad tracks, and joined the Haddonfield Road. The roadbed for the former lane is near Stoy Avenue.

During the post Civil War era, John Stoy became very active in the affairs of the township. A *Courier-Post* reporter interviewed John Stoy's son, Walter in 1953. Walter claimed his father originated a petition that the New Jersey Legislature considered when it divided Haddon Township from Newton Township in 1865. Walter also noted his father headed the Township Committee for more than 40 years. Walter, 91 when the interview took place, also stated his father served on the school board for 40 years. Walter's memory was accurate. While researching this book, John Stoy's name appeared many times in the minutes of township meetings. The label "father of Haddon Township" could easily apply to John Stoy.

In 1950, the *Newark Star Ledger* published an interesting story, as told by Walter Stoy, to author and columnist Henry C. Beck. Walter asserted that he was one of a small number of residents of the area that spoke positively about the aging poet from Camden, Walt Whitman. It was Walter's recollection that township citizens did not welcome the poet as "odd talkes" circulated about Whitman. Walter Stoy explained why they thought Whitman was odd:

> As far as I could find out, white-haired and bearded Walt had a peculiar habit of divesting himself of most of his clothing come a warm summer afternoon and thereupon walking off to the nearest swimming hole. If anyone had asked him, I suppose he would have replied that he owned no bathing suit, even of the kind that was acceptable then. (*Newark Star Ledger* 4/16/1950)

Stoy remembered when Walt Whitman came to the family's farm and asked to borrow a rowboat. He recalled Whitman rowing on Crystal Lake:

> He [Whitman] said he had come out on the toll-road [Haddonfield Turnpike] and he wanted to think quietly, on the water. We found him a boat and he rowed out in the shade of some willows. Maybe he did a little fishing, I don't know. All I know was that when he rowed in, he wanted to pay and we wouldn't take anything. My father and I knew who he was, of course, and we were glad if the old mill pond gave him some inspiration. (*Newark Star Ledger* 4/16/1950)

Walter Stoy's encounters with Whitman were accurate. Whitman's own day book corroborates Walter Stoy's recollections.

Other citizens around the township also enjoyed the pastoral setting of Crystal Lake and adjacent woods. For instance, the Morning Star Lodge of Haddonfield held a "pic-nic" in John Stoy's woods in the summer of 1874:

> . . .wagon-loads of ladies and gentlemen began to arrive on the ground. . . .
>
> At 10:30 A.M. the "6th Regiment Brass Band" made its appearance. . . . The table was groaning under a load of substantials and delicacies.
>
> The gay group of young ladies, the massive oaks with their overhanging foliage of green, and sweet strains of music, found a combination to soothe and please the senses. (HB 8/20/1874)

Walt Whitman, members of the Morning Star Lodge, and other responsible citizens were welcomed at Crystal Lake, while certain other visitors were not. The *West Jersey Press* reported on John Stoy's method of responding to a common nuisance of the era–tramps. He built a nineteenth century version of a home security system:

> The farmers and the rural population generally have been put to their wits end to protect themselves from these marauders, and several ingenious inventions have been the result, but none of them excel that adopted by Mr. John Stoy of Haddon Township. Mr. Stoy has provided himself with a large bell which he had mounted upon a pole 25 feet high. The bell is rung by the women of the house whenever they are in danger from assault from tramps, and the farm hands are warned, upon hearing the bell, to leave their work and proceed to the house at once. (WJP 9/17/1879)

John Stoy died in 1905. The title to his farm was transferred to the Westmont Realty Company in which the Stoy family owned all the stock. The farm, like many others in the early 1900s was destined for residential development. The original plans for development called for more than 230 building lots laid out on the farm.

17-9 Edwin and Elizabeth Stoy Willis

In 1870, Elizabeth Stoy Willis and her husband, Edwin, resided on the 42-acre property inherited from Elizabeth's father, James Stoy. Their land included two lots along both sides of Crystal Lake Avenue. Two-story garden-style apartment buildings (Haddon Hills) now occupy the former site of the Willis house. The dwelling and outbuildings were situated along the eastern side of Crystal Lake Avenue near West Park Boulevard. It is likely their home was built about the period Elizabeth and Edwin were married in the late 1860s. A tenant house sat near the Willis dwelling.

Amos Willis, Sr., Edwin's father, also resided on the tract. The elderly Willis moved in with his son and daughter-in-law, having previously lived on a farm in Collingswood. [See Amos Willis, Sr., page 210.] Isaac Prine, an ice dealer, lived at the site in 1870. Prine also operated the Stoy sawmill along Crystal Lake. [See Isaac Prine, page 257.]

Although Edwin's efforts were primarily devoted to running the farm, he assumed other duties in the newly-formed township. In 1865, he was appointed the Overseer of Highways for his district. Weather and wear and tear from wagons, carts and carriages could quickly erode the surface of a road. Edwin hired work crews to keep the roads in good condition.

17-10 Aaron Stoy

Aaron and Mary Stoy's dwelling stood along Crystal Lake Avenue, near Patton Avenue. Aaron built his house opposite the home of his sister Elizabeth and brother-in-law Edwin Willis on a lot of about 42 acres. Aaron's wife Mary was the daughter of George Lee, a township farmer. [See George Lee, page 208.] The Stoy's employed a domestic servant to help with the house chores and farm laborers to work in the fields.

In 1870, Aaron and Mary lived with their son Harry along with James Stoy, Aaron's brother. A note made by the census enumerator in 1870 stated James Stoy's profession as "nothing." More likely than not, James, a grown man, was retarded and not employable. James was passed over in favor of his brothers and sister when their father divided the family plantation.

17-11 James Flinn

In 1874, John Stoy sold some six acres of land on the northern side of Crystal Lake Avenue to James Flinn and John Gill Willits. The new owners transformed the premise into a paint works. James, his wife and their seven children and two nephews lived next to the factory. Flinn employed several family members in the business.

Flinn was well-versed in the manufacturing process of making paint. He worked eighteen years at John Lucas's paint manufacturing firm in Gibbsboro. John Willits's expertise was in sales. By mid-1875, a new two-story building was erected along Crystal Lake Avenue for the mixing of paint. The company used the water-power from Crystal Lake to turn the paint grinding and mixing machinery. The firm's signature product, the color "superior green," was sold from a store in Philadelphia. [See paint works, page 140.]

17-12 Samuel M. Reeves

Samuel M. Reeves had a nine-acre tract, situated between John Stoy and John Redman's farms, known as the "Grass Lots." The site had no dwellings. The Camden & Atlantic Railroad bisected the tract. Reeves resided in Haddonfield at 232 Kings Highway. He owned several other properties in Haddonfield. The largest was next to the Friends Meeting House between Lake Street and Willits Avenue.

Before retiring, Samuel's main occupation was farming. During his lifetime, he accumulated considerable wealth. At the time of his death in 1886, a significant amount of Reeves's assets were invested in stocks and bonds including hundreds of securities issued by railroad companies, banks and local turnpike companies. Samuel invested in local companies, including the Haddonfield & Camden Turnpike Company, Haddonfield Hay Scales Company and Haddonfield Building Association.

Samuel died at age 95. An unidentified newspaper article carried a report about Samuel's death and the passing of three other prominent Haddonfield citizens, Joseph Kay, Samuel Nicholson and John Gill. All four gentlemen died within a two-year period. These elderly men, whose association with Haddonfield went back to the 1790s, held a special status in the minds of the local citizenry in the 1880s:

> ...Haddonfield loses her four oldest businessmen and excellent citizens. It is a strange fact that with the past two years all the residents between 90 to 100 years, in this place have died. Mr. Reeves being the oldest and the last. ... (Unidentified newspaper, 1886–Historical Society of Haddonfield)

17-13 Hannah Webster / Samuel Webster

Hannah Webster lived with her sister Sarah Ann Webster on a farm of some 30 acres of land. The Webster dwelling is now 205 Memorial Avenue and the home's Gothic Revival architectural features suggest it was built in the 1840s or 1850s. At least two barns were situated near the dwelling.

While Hannah was "keeping house" in the 1860s, tenant farmers worked the land. By 1870, the farm was under the direction of Samuel Webster, Hannah's 27 year-old nephew. In 1880, Samuel, his wife Emma, three sons, Aunt Sarah Ann and a servant were all residing on the farm.

Webster's lane ran from Webster's homestead to Haddon Avenue. The lane also provided access to two neighboring lots owned by Samuel Hinchman and Rebecca Ann Collings. Part of the lane, on the north side of the creek, became the roadbed for Glenwood Avenue.

Samuel Webster's residence in Haddon Township. The house is now 205 Memorial Avenue. The Webster dwelling stood on some 30 acres of farmland. The Webster family owned and operated the nearby Newton Gristmill for many years during the nineteenth century.

(Courtesy of Robert and Bernadette Mehmet)

Joseph O. Cuthbert's residence in Haddon Township. The house once stood at the southeast corner of Haddon Avenue and Cuthbert Road. The Cuthbert family moved to their New Jersey home in 1850.
(Courtesy of Marguritte Bennett)

In the early 1800s, the Webster family operated the Newton Mill, known then as Webster & Sons Mill. The stream next to the lot had been dammed to form a pond and provided waterpower for the gristmill. The pond extended from Cuthbert Road to near Albertson Avenue. In the 1850s, a canal crossed Webster's farm, joining the millpond with another small unnamed branch of Newton Creek. It is likely the canal diverted additional water to the pond, increasing waterpower at the mill. [See gristmills, page 134.]

17-14 Joseph O. Cuthbert, Sr. / Henry Cuthbert

Joseph Ogden Cuthbert's 110-acre farm was along Haddon Avenue in Haddon Township and Collingswood. The Cuthbert Mansion once stood at the southeast corner of the turnpike and Cuthbert Road. The house was built in the mid-1700s and razed in the twentieth century. Joseph's real estate holdings also included a small wooded lot situated along the north side of the Haddonfield Turnpike.

Joseph Cuthbert was born in Philadelphia during the year 1800. After serving an apprenticeship as a currier, he purchased a farm in West Philadelphia. In 1823, he married twenty year-old Elizabeth Coles. Joseph and Elizabeth moved to their Newton Township farm in 1850, where he took up farming. The Cuthbert's raised four children. When Joseph retired from farming in the late 1860s, his son Joseph, Jr. assumed the duties on the farm. In 1872, Joseph Jr. sold his livestock and farming utensils and his younger brother Henry took over operation of the farm.

The Camden & Atlantic Railroad traveled across the Cuthbert tract. Not far from the Cuthbert's mansion, at Cuthbert Road, was a railroad stop called Cuthbert Station. Records from the post-Civil War era reveal Henry Cuthbert used the railroad to transport farm products.

Bartering was common in the farming community. Henry Cuthbert's farm ledger is replete with entries showing bartering transactions during the 1870s. For instance, Henry Morgan, a helper on the farm, received his earnings by taking a pair of boots, three plugs of tobacco, gloves, and a housing allowance. Cuthbert paid farm hand George Jacobs with roast meat, a basket of potatoes, pork, salt meat and tomatoes. Joseph Johnson was compensated for his tasks of chopping wood, digging wells, cutting rails and working the fields, with a housing allowance of $2 a month. Henry Cuthbert also paid Johnson with corn, hay and the use of his wagon.

Henry Cuthbert purchased cornmeal, flour and other merchandise from his neighbor, Hiram Smith. Smith's gristmill, also known as the Newton Mill, was next to the Cuthbert's tract. Cuthbert paid his debts to Smith with produce from his garden: potatoes, apples, straw and stacks of hay. Isaac Prine, an ice farmer and cidermaker, once rented a cider house from Cuthbert. Prine paid his rent with cider and ice.

Charles Haines was a wheelwright with a shop along the Haddonfield Turnpike. Charles repaired Cuthbert's wagons, placed new hoops on wheels, and fitted horseshoes on "Nell" and "Jim." Henry paid the wheelwrights with hay, potatoes and livestock. In the late 1870s, Henry was buying his bread and baked goods from John Rehfus, a Camden baker. The baker's bills were paid with potatoes, corn, hay and hens. Cuthbert also boarded the baker's horses.

A list of Cuthbert's household articles provides a glimpse of Joseph, Sr. and Elizabeth's decorative tastes. Hung on the walls in their mansion were pictures that depicted the "Capital at Washington," a "Shipwreck," and "Pike County Falls." Portraits of "Washington" and the "Madonna" were suspended from the wall in the house with an engraving of the "Last Days of Webster." (Inv. H-458, 1887) Joseph, Sr., must have admired the great spokesman of the time, Daniel Webster. An entry in Cuthbert's farm journal on October 24, 1852 confirmed the admiration he had for Webster: "Daniel Webster–Secretary of State died."

Elizabeth Cuthbert passed away in 1873, while her husband outlived her by fourteen years. Following Joseph, Sr.'s death in 1887, the family heirlooms were distributed among family members. Joseph Ogden Cuthbert III inherited a share of stock in the Philadelphia Library Company that his grandfather held for 70 years. Joseph, Sr. also passed on books, manuscripts, silverware, old relics and objects of curiosity to his children and grandchildren. Besides his township property, Joseph's heirs received property in Delaware Township (Cherry Hill) and real estate at Forty-Ninth and Market streets in Philadelphia.

The Haddon Township/Collingswood boundary was initially fixed in 1888 when Collingswood was incorporated. Cuthbert's land was next to the boundary line. The Collingswood/Haddon Township boundary near Stokes, Linwood and Penn avenues was relocated in 1953.

17-15 William Bettle, Jr.

In 1865, William Bettle, Jr. owned 92 acres of land that now comprises most of the Bettlewood section in Haddon Township. In 1870, William and Mary Bettle lived with their two daughters and son in the Greek Revival style house that stands today at 9 East Holly Avenue. Built about 1847, the dwelling measured 44' x 34'. The walls above ground were built with "good Jersey Brick laid in mortar" and the front wall is "Philadelphia pressed brick." The cellar was made of Pennsylvania stone. There were three rooms on the dwelling's first floor, and a kitchen and a wash room. The second story had six chambers and a "wash-house." The third floor had five rooms. A piazza went along the side of the house and around to the back. A three-story addition extended from the back of the home. The roof was "lead tin" and the dwelling was "warmed" by a large cast-iron furnace with nine openings into as many rooms. They built a one-story woodshed off the wash house. The barn measured 60' x 40'. The first floor had six horse stalls and thirteen cow stalls. (The Franklin Fire Insurance Company of Philadelphia No. 8484, 1847)

The farm was one of three properties along the White Horse Road owned by a Bettle family member. William, Jr.'s cousin, Edward Bettle, lived in a similar style mansion near East Bettlewood Avenue. Their uncle William Bettle, Sr. owned more than 200 acres of land along the White Horse Road. [See Edward Bettle, page 267, William Bettle, Sr., page 183.]

A second home on William Bettle's land has also endured in time. It stands at 2 East Clinton Avenue. Before the neighboring row of stores were erected along the White Horse Pike in the twentieth century, the dwelling's front faced the White Horse Road. The house, designed with Gothic Revival architectural features, was probably built in the 1850s. Several other tenant dwellings stood on Bettle's land along Cuthbert Road.

William Bettle, Jr. also owned a lot on the western side of the White Horse Turnpike. A tenant house stood by the turnpike near what is now Capitol Avenue. The lot, bisected by a stream known as Money Run or Peter's Creek, became incorporated into Oaklyn and Audubon boroughs.

A few years before the Bettles moved onto the farm, the Camden and Philadelphia Race Course was on this site. In the mid-1840s, Philadelphia horse-racing fans took the ferry to New Jersey and traveled several miles into the countryside to watch the popular sport. It is likely the track was laid out between East Bettlewood to East Holly avenues.

William Bettle, Jr. was born into a Philadelphia Quaker family in 1830. Some twenty years later, he moved to Newton Township and took up farming. Several of the township's largest dairy farms were along the White Horse Pike. One was the Bettle farm. After William retired from farming, Samuel Evans, a tenant farmer, operated the dairy farm. In 1879, Evan's dairy cows produced 30,000 gallons of milk.

Bettle was active in the county's Republican Party. His cousin Edward Bettle was a prominent member of the party and an influential State Senator. In 1897, the Governor of New Jersey appointed William, Jr. Commissioner of Banking and Insurance. He also served as a director of several South Jersey railroad companies affiliated with the Pennsylvania Railroad.

The *West Jersey Press*, a newspaper associated with the Republican Party, frequently reported on the whereabouts of party loyalists. William and his family were inclined to spend hot summer months in the mountains:

> William Bettle, Jr. is living quietly in Stroudsburg, Pa. He rented a house for the summer, has his horses and carriage with him, has brought a cow and is living in clover. Mr. B. went to Stroudsburg, to give his family the benefit of the pure mountain air of that region. (WJP 8/1/1877)

One reporter noted the Bettles had returned home after spending the summer in the White Mountains. (WJP 9/15/1880) Upon retiring, Bettle continued to travel.

Both Mary and William gave unselfishly to the humanitarian needs of Camden. For more than a decade, the couple served on the Board of Trustees and Managers of The West Jersey Orphanage for Colored Children. Founded in 1874, the orphanage housed, schooled and trained poor African-American children.

17-16 James Dobbs / James C. Dobbs / Anthony Heck

James Dobbs owned 74 acres of land along the northern side of Cuthbert Road. The lane at Cuthbert Road to Dobbs's brick dwelling and surrounding outbuildings was opposite the area of Davis Avenue to the vicinity of Heather Road and Park Avenue.

James and his brother Samuel Dobbs, Jr., were proprietors of Dobbs Brickyard, on Mill Road (Cuthbert Road) near the Main Branch of Newton Creek. (See brickyards, page 128.] Both men learned brickmaking from their father while still in their native land—England. James arrived in America in 1827. In 1840, he renounced allegiance to "Victoria Queen of the United Kingdom of Great Britain and Ireland" and became a naturalized citizen of the United States. (Gloucester County Inferior Court of Common Pleas, 10/12/1840)

As the years passed, James devoted less time to making bricks and tile, and increased his pursuit of agricultural interests. His wife Isabella and their son Joseph were living on the farm in 1860. At that period, Joseph was helping his father run the farm. By 1871, James' nephew, James C. Dobbs, was overseeing the family's brickyard and clay pits.

A least one tenant house existed on the northwest corner of Cuthbert Road and Lees Lane. Two African-American employees of the nearby brickyard, George and Robert Jacobs, resided at the site. A small stream once traveled across Dobbs's farm and emptied into the Main Branch of Newton Creek. The run has since been eliminated and several Heather Glen homes now stand where the stream bed was once located.

In 1874, James Dobbs sold the largest portion of his farm, some 61 acres, to Anthony Heck of Philadelphia for $9,800. Heck's land is now Heather Glen. The brickyard and a small half-acre lot at the northwest corner of Cuthbert Road and Lees Lane, were not part of the transfer. In 1879, Anthony Heck was farming on his lot.

Dobbs passed away in 1875:

> James Dobbs, age 69 years died. Mr. Dobbs was an Englishman by birth and came to this country when a boy. ... It is claimed that to him belongs the credit of making the first tile in this country used for the purpose of underdraining. (WJP 5/26/1875)

The Heck lot had an interesting historical connection to the early period of Newton Township. A tavern/inn stood near Newton Creek and Lees Lane in the early 1700s. Atmore's Inn was a stop on a stagecoach road from Philadelphia to Egg Harbor. Atmores Road, later renamed Lees Lane, was once a segment of this stagecoach route.

John Clement's *Sketches of the First Emigrant Settlers Newton Township, Old Gloucester County, West New Jersey*, published in 1877, described Atmore's old tavern along Lees Lane:

> On the south side of Newton creek and near the end of Atmore's dam, not many years since, stood a small antiquated house, built partly of brick and partly of frame, one and a half stories high, with hipped roof, small windows and low, narrow doors. In early times this was kept as a tavern, and stood beside the public road leading from Philadelphia to the seashore. (p. 163)

Clement described the era when the inn was an important meeting place for inhabitants of the countryside:

> About the year 1773, Thomas [Atmore] died, and his son Caleb took possession, and by this name it has been known among the people of later times. The situation being near the middle of the township, it was a suitable place for business meetings, and there the politicians of that day "most did congregate," to discuss the affairs of he colony. Here, for many years the few inhabitants elected the various officers to carry on the machinery of their little municipality, and, here, personal rivalry and political prejudice cropped out, just as in these days of ambition and greed for office. Before the days of mails, this was the place where news from city or county could be gathered, and whence correspondence could be forwarded to various parts of Gloucester and Salem counties by the few travelers going to and from their several homes. The name of the inn has passed into oblivion. (p. 164)

17-17 John Schnitzius

In 1859, John and Catherine Schnitzius moved from Bridgeboro, New Jersey to Newton Township. Five years later, Joseph C. Dill sold his 69-acre farm to the couple for $8,000. The Schnitzius house was situated near 924 Merrick Avenue. The house, built about 1825, was described in a fire insurance survey as "sound, principally oak and in good condition. . . ." (Rowand No. 16, 1855) The dimensions of the barn near the house, was 26' x 36'. It had three stalls, a granary and a hay bay. Other outbuildings surrounding the dwelling included a corncrib and cow shed. (Rowand No. 16, 1855) A lane once led from the house to Lees Lane. The path of the former lane fell between present Mansion and Merrick avenues.

John and Catherine Schnitzius had eight children. The two oldest children, Joseph and Mary, were born in the family's native land, Prussia. The remaining children: Matilda, Catherine, Agnes, Henry, John, Jr. and Anthony were born in America.

The granddaughter of John and Catherine Schnitzius, Marie Miller, was over 90 when she reflected in 1991 about growing up on the family farm. Although she was born some six years after her grandmother died, Mrs. Miller recalled many stories about the family matriarch. According Marie, her grandmother Catherine, "cracked the whip around the farm." "Catherine was the first one up in the morning and every day she woke up the farm help. Mrs. Miller described Catherine as a thrifty individual. This trait enabled the family to acquire several neighboring farms, including Anthony Heck's 61-acre farm, Thomas Hanbest's 25-acre tract and the Newton Mill lot.

Mrs. Miller remembered a routine that most certainly dated to a time when her grandparents owned the farm. She recalled when young boys, with the assistance of dogs, would herd cows to bathe in Newton Creek near "Boogie's Bridge," now Lees Lane Bridge. On warm days, the boys did not sit idly by while the cows cooled off; they too swam in the creek. After the respite, the boys rounded-up the cows and returned to Lees Lane.

Mrs. Miller pointed out that before her grandfather's death, John had been sick for a considerable period. In 1880, the census-taker noted John was "insane." John passed away in the late 1880s, while Catherine died in 1895 from typhoid fever caught during an epidemic. One week later, her youngest son Anthony became a victim of the disease.

The family also owned two tenant homes facing Lees Lane on the south side of Newton Creek. The Schnitzius family owned a tract in what is now Collingswood. This small triangular lot is now the southwest quadrant of Lees Avenue and the right-of-way of the PATCO High Speed Line.

By 1879, Joseph Schnitzius, was overseeing his parent's farm. Some years later, Joseph purchased and operated the Newton Mill. In 1888, the border separating Collingswood and Haddon Township was established near the area of Linwood and Stokes avenues. The border was relocated in 1953 to its present location.

17-18 Hiram Smith

At 48, Hiram Smith of Camden acquired six acres from John C. Hopkins along the eastern side of Cuthbert Road. Upon acquiring the lot in 1865, Smith became the proprietor of Newton Mill. Smith's wife and four children moved from their city residence to Haddon Township. The building that housed the gristmill was along Cuthbert Road opposite Merrick Avenue. The old gristmill's beginnings dated to the early 1800s. The Smith dwelling sat several hundred feet north of the gristmill. [See gristmill, page 134.]

A miller's main task was to grind wheat into flour, rye into feed, corn into cornmeal, or pulverize any other variety of grain for customers. For a brief period, Smith was the miller; however, as business grew, Charles Vennel worked at the mill while Smith assumed the duties of selling his product.

Smith's customers were both farmers and city residents. For instance, Smith's neighbor, Henry Cuthbert, was a regular at the mill. The Cuthbert farm ledger noted that Smith accepted peppers, potatoes, apples and straw as payment in exchanged for flour and cornmeal. Flour from the Newton Mill was delivered to Camden on Smith's wagon. Eventually, he opened a store in the city.

By the mid-1870s, the Smith family had returned to Camden, taking up residency next to their flour store. Less than a decade later, Joseph Schnitzius, a former neighbor in Haddon Township, purchased and operated the mill until 1906.

17-19 Isaac Prine

In 1872, Isaac Prine acquired a dwelling situated on two acres. The building still stands at 308 Cuthbert Road. Although its exterior appearance has changed, a part of the original structure remains within its walls. An old photograph taken before remodeling shows the original structure had Greek Revival architectural features.

Isaac farmed and marketed ice. Ike, as he was called by those that knew him, hauled ice from the neighboring millpond and stowed it in his ice house. Prine's ice house was 65' x 37' feet and 20' high. The ice house was enlarged in 1879 to hold 3,000 tons of ice cut from the "pure spring water pond." (WJP 6/2/1869) The pond, about 1,000 feet long and 200 feet wide, provided water power for the Newton Mill. Today, the remnants of the pond bottom can be seen between the areas of Stokes and Albertson avenues. A stream still travels through the site of the former millpond where Prine harvested ice for customers in Haddonfield and Camden. [See ice farming, page 164.]

Ice was not the only product Isaac sold. According to a reporter's story written in 1925, Prine's apple cider was delicious:

> During the Centennial Exposition in 1876, Prime [sic] also had a cider mill at a lower portion of the lake and this drink became famous among the thousands of visitors who attended the World's Fair. (*Tri-City Sun* 6/11/1925) [See cidermaking, page 132.]

Besides his ice and cidermaking business, Prine was once the operator of the Stoy sawmill at Crystal Lake. He rented the mill from John Stoy for $200 a year. In 1870, the sawmill ceased operating and the stock, fixtures, machinery and lumber were sold. [See sawmill, page 143.]

17-20 Samuel H. French

During the post Civil War era, Samuel H. French owned more than 300 acres of real estate in old Haddon Township. His homestead was a 140-acre farm along the White Horse Pike in Collingswood. [See Samuel French, page 200.]

Fueled by his successful business interests, Samuel made substantial investments in real estate. Over ten years, French acquired the "Pine Grove Farm," "Osler Farm," and "Creek Farm." The three tenant farms, totaling 195 acres, were situated near Rowandtown. Samuel's real estate holdings went beyond the township; he held title to land in Camden, Pennsylvania, Maryland and Texas.

French's first real estate venture near Rowandtown came in 1863, when he purchased John Chamberlain's 75-acre lot known as "Pine Grove Farm." During the late 1860s, Edwin Shoemaker, a tenant farmer, lived in a dwelling that has survived the test of time. The house, known then as the "Pine Cottage," is now 217 East Linden Avenue. Shoemaker harvested more sweet potatoes than any other township farmer. In 1879, more than 700 bushels of the popular crop were harvested on the farm.

Substantial improvements and additions were made around the tract after French took possession. They installed new glass in the windows of the "Pine Cottage." Painters, paperhangers and tilers were hired to spruce up the dwelling. The barn was repaired and a new water trough and shed were constructed. In 1872, expenditures more than $5,000 were made to build a new barn, wagon house and install new fencing. During the same year, over $2,000 worth of fruit trees and grape vines were acquired and planted on the tract. (Samuel French's Account Ledgers)

Burrwood Lane, also called French's Lane, was one property line of the "Pine Grove Farm." The lane went between David Morgan's dwelling on Cooper's Creek, and intersected with Haddon Avenue near Strawbridge Avenue. Morgan's home is now the Hopkins House on South Park Drive in Haddon Township. When Collingswood incorporated in 1888, Burrwood Lane became the dividing line with Haddon Township.

17-21 Arthur Powell / Samuel H. French

In the early 1870s, Arthur Powell, who resided on Market Street in Gloucester City on a 94-acre farm, owned the 60-acre "Creek Farm" near Rowandtown. [Gloucester City's Powell Street was named for him.] In 1865, William Anderson rented the lot from Powell. Anderson's former dwelling was not far from Cooper's Creek, near the area where Bradford Avenue meets South Park Drive.

When Haddon Township split off from Newton Township in 1865, the municipalities did not settle on a definitive boundary in the area of Cooper's Creek. Township Commissioners hired Jacob Rowand of Haddonfield to survey the land between Haddon Avenue and Cooper's Creek. Rowand's survey revealed that Powell's land was just 22 inches inside Haddon Township's boundary.

The *West Jersey Press* advertised a sale of standing timber on Powell's land in 1864:

> Timber land standing on about 10 acres of land, situated on my farm, in the Township of Newton, adjoining the farm owned by Samuel A. Reeve and near Cooper's Creek about one half mile from Rowandtown. The timber consist of Black & White Oak, Maple, Spruce, Pine, and will cut 12 to 25 cords per acre. To be divided into small lots. (WJP 11/30/1864)

Depending on which direction one was traveling, two routes approached the lot. Coming from Camden, a lane intersected Haddon Avenue, near Lincoln Avenue in Collingswood, and cut across several farms to Burrwood Lane, the present-day Haddon Township and Collingswood border. Another lane, off of Burrwood Lane ran past the "Pine Cottage," on the "Pine Grove Farm," and onto Powell's "Creek Farm."

A second lane ran from the farm to the Haddon Avenue. It traversed the perimeter of the "Osler Farm," along land owned by Thomas Albertson and crossed Samuel Reeve's lot where it joined Willis Lane, the present Cooper Street. A part of the lane can still be viewed today between the homes of Emerald and Melrose avenues, west of Cooper Street.

In the early 1870s, title to Powell's farm passed onto John Hobensack and Thomas Albertson. Shortly after that, the farm was conveyed to Samuel French. In 1876, French acquired more than a thousand trees to plant on his old Haddon Township farms. He planted the trees to commemorate the centennial anniversary of the nation:

> [French] has planted on his different farms in this county, eleven hundred and sixty additional trees, exclusive of a number of fruit trees. (WJP 9/19/1877)

French spared no expense when it came to properly draining rain off his land. Attention to this matter attracted publicity. The *West Jersey Press* described the large drainage ditch on French's farm that emptied into Cooper's Creek. French used tiles made at Dobbs Brick Yard to drain his farms:

> The lane connecting his "Pine Grove" and "Creek" farms crosses a ravine, about twenty feet in width. The embankment or roadway is 120 feet in width at the base and 40 feet at the top. In the valley just below this causeway, is a large well, into which over two miles of underdrains discharge their waters. From this well the water is conveyed through large terra cotta pipes into Cooper's creek. Mr. French's system of underdraining is as thorough as it well could be. No waste places or bogs are permitted about any of his farms. He has used in his different drains, 125,000 tile, a considerable number of which are of the largest size manufactured, and in some instances are laid at a depth of eleven feet. (WJP 9/19/1877)

A good portion of the "Creek Farm" along the banks of Cooper's Creek was marsh land when French acquired the property. Samuel hired workers to reclaim a sizeable portion from the tidal creek and turn it into productive meadow land. French also had a wharf erected along Cooper's Creek so fertilizer could be shipped to his farms from Philadelphia:

> On the "Creek Farm," which he [French] recently purchased from the late Dr. Hobensack, he has, by means of a substantial bank reclaimed a large tract of excellent meadow abandoned years ago to the tides, and the yield of grass thereon this season is simply immense. (WJP 9/19/1877)
>
> He [French] has also, on this farm, built a large wharf, on which quantities of manure and different fertilizers for the use of his farms are landed. (WJP 9/19/1877)

17-22 Joseph Osler / Samuel H. French

The 43-acre lot known as the "Osler Farm" was home to Joseph Osler for many years. The Osler dwelling stood along the turnpike, near the location of the Westmont Theater building, between Stratford and Albertson avenues. The oldest wing of the house was built in 1816. One wing was 15' x 26', the other section was 16' x 24'. The first floor had a "dwelling room, parlor and kitchen." A box stairway lead to the four chambers on the second floor and the attic had two bedrooms. Inside Osler's house was "lathed and plastered throughout and painted." A frame leanto kitchen and an open shed was attached to the back of the house. (Rowand No. 64, 1856)

The outbuildings, situated behind the house, included a 40' x 22' barn with four stables and a hayloft, a hay and grain barn, a hay and corn barn, a cow house with birthing stalls, a crib and wagon house and a wagon shed. Lightning rods were built on all the structures. (Rowand No. 64, 1856)

Joseph Osler decided to sell the farm and other possessions in 1863:

> Stock and farming utensils. Two horses, eleven milch cows, two bulls, five fat hogs, one breeding cow, wagon, cart, plough...also a good watch dog.
>
> Household goods. Carpet, clock, table, chairs...
>
> Forty-three and one-quarter acres divided into six tillages, the soil is of excellent quality for grain or grass and in good state of cultivation. The buildings are in good condition, ample and commodious. (WJP 10/28/1863)

In 1865, Samuel French acquired the lot and leased it to a tenant farmer. Joseph Osler, his wife Hannah, and their four children moved from their rural habitat into City of Camden.

Soon after he took title to the lot, French invested $1,300 to install drainage tiles throughout the farm. He used the drain tiles, acquired at Dobbs Brick Yard, to move excess water away from the fields. In 1879, George Kirk, a farmer, was renting the lot.

17-23 Anthony Woodward / David U. Morgan

In 1859, Anthony Woodward of Philadelphia and his family moved onto their 78-acre Newton Township farm. Anthony and his two sons worked the land. Woodward's house, along South Park Drive at Shady Lane, is the Hopkins House. The building is one of the oldest structures in the area. Ebenezer Hopkins built the two-story brick western half of the house in 1737. The original eastern section was also brick; however, it no longer exists, having been demolished in 1925. Today's eastern half, built in 1939 by the Work Projects Administration, resembles the original structure.

A kitchen, parlor and back room were on the first floor of Woodward's dwelling. The kitchen, 21' x 21', was situated on the eastern side of the house. The parlor on the western side measured 22' x 32'. A back room and the parlor each had a fireplace. A shed was attached to the house on the eastern side and wrapped halfway around the back of the structure. A water pump was underneath the shed's roof. A porch overlooking Cooper's Creek came off the back of the house. (Franklin Fire Insurance Company of Philadelphia, No. 1101)

Passage between Woodward's dwelling and Haddon Avenue was along Burrwood Lane. The lane began at the turnpike, near Strawbridge Avenue, and traveled toward Cooper River, near the Hopkins House. Shady Lane was once the path that lead between the dwelling and Burrwood Lane.

In 1849, a proposal was made to extend Collings Road onto the other side of the Haddonfield Turnpike toward Cooper's Creek and over to the road going between Camden and Marlton, known now as Marlton Pike or Route 70. Although it was not built, plans showed a road about 31 feet to the west of the Woodward's dwelling.

When Haddon Township ceded from Newton Township in 1865, Collings Road became the boundary. The dividing line of the land to the north and east of Collings Avenue, between Haddon Avenue and Cooper's Creek, was not specifically defined. Several months after the township was formed, officials hired a surveyor to mark the boundary in the area between the Haddonfield Turnpike and Cooper's Creek. As it turned out, the Woodward Farm, first thought to have been within the new township, was actually in Newton Township. The farm remained part of Newton Township until 1871, when it joined Haddon Township.

In 1866, David U. Morgan acquired the property and moved from Pennsylvania onto the farm with his wife Anna and their four children. David's cousin, Samuel French, was a township resident and probably introduced the Morgans to the area.

It is believed that Clayton French, Samuel's brother, wanted Morgan to work at the Philadelphia firm of French, Richards & Company, but David was moving toward a different career. Morgan entered an interesting and unique profession after graduating from the Philadelphia College of Pharmacy. Although a chemist by trade, David became a manufacturer of albumen-covered photographic paper.

Morgan's albumen paper business opened shortly after he moved to his New Jersey farm. His process used the clear white of eggs, called albumen, to bind light-sensitive chemicals to the paper's surface. The process required many eggs. Morgan secured his ingredients from local farmers. [See albumemized paper mill, page 123]

David juggled two professions during his stay in the area. Not only did he manufacture photographic paper, he also supervised the operation of the farm, which had 50 acres of arable ground. David advertised the sale of his harvest in a Camden newspaper: "For sale–Five tons of good Meadow Hay at $20/ton. Apply at D.U. Morgan." (WJP 9/18/1872)

In the late 1870s, James Pidgeon was a tenant farmer on Morgan's land. Pidgeon lived in a tenant house built near the intersection where Burrwood Lane met another lane that later became known as Lincoln Avenue.

Pidgeon rented part of Morgan's land to grow and harvest his own crops. In 1878, James Pidgeon boasted of being "champion" among sweet potatoes growers. The *West Jersey Press* noted Pidgeon claimed to have harvested the largest crop ever grown in the area during August. The newspaper also commented that a few local farmers disputed Pidgeon's claim. (WJP 8/4/1878)

One of the more unusual apparatuses on the Morgan farm was the windmill that once stood near his dwelling. An 1883 survey, prepared for a proposed railroad right-of-way near the Haddonfield Turnpike, showed a windmill situated to the east of Morgan's house. Morgan may have employed the windmill in the albumen paper process.

In December 1886, the Morgan family moved back to Pennsylvania. Following David's death in 1889, his wife and several former workers tried, but failed, to keep the photographic paper business going. The heirs of Morgan owned the farm until 1922.

17-24 Thomas Albertson

Thomas Albertson's wheelwright shop was on the northwest side of Willis Lane (Cooper Street) and the

Haddonfield Turnpike. The lot was about eight acres. In 1860, Thomas, his wife Elizabeth and their daughter resided next to the shop. Albertson's apprentice wheelwrights also lived on the site. Albertson employed wheelwrights and coach-trimmers to repair and build wagons, carts and fix farm tools. [See wheelwrights, page 125.]

For several years, Albertson held title to the adjacent "Creek Farm," situated along Cooper's Creek. The lot was eventually transferred to Samuel French.

Albertson also owned a nineteen-acre tract of land next to the "Creek Farm." The lane, between Emerald and Melrose avenues, was once a boundary for his tract and allowed passage from the adjoining "Creek Farm" to Willis Lane and Haddon Avenue. There were no dwellings on the lot.

Sometime in the late 1860s, Albertson retired from his trade and took up farming. By late 1870s, at 59, he withdrew from farming.

17-25 David Albertson

David Albertson's three Rowandtown lots totaled 23 acres. Several buildings stood on Albertson's lot along the northern side of Haddon Avenue. No dwellings existed on another lot situated between the area Emerald and Melrose Avenues and Virginia Avenue, and between Reeves Avenue and Center Street. The third lot, along the south side of the turnpike near Albertson Avenue, was the site of David's blacksmith shop. Albertson's shop repaired carriages and wagons, shod horses, sharpened farming utensils, and hooped wheels. [See blacksmiths, page 125.]

David lived with his wife Mary and two daughters, Esphen Ashton, a blacksmith and Thompson Ashton, an apprentice blacksmith. Although David's primary profession was blacksmithing, he also tilled the soil on his tracts. Walter French, Albertson's son-in-law, probably took care of some farm chores. By 1880, David had retired. He continued to reside in his Rowandtown home until his death in 1885.

17-26 Briggs Kay

Briggs and Maria Kay's seventeen-acre tract was on the southern side of Haddon Avenue. Maria, Briggs's second wife, and the couple's four children and a servant resided in a house that stood along the turnpike at what is now West Walnut and Chestnut avenues.

Kay, a farmer, was 55 in 1865. Though his Rowandtown tract was a comparatively small farm, Kay planted crops typically grown in this area including, hay, wheat, corn, potatoes, and sweet potatoes. He also owned a 235-acre farm in Delaware Township.

17-27 Samuel A. Reeve

Samuel A. Reeve's two lots totaled seventeen acres of land. Reeve's house, erected in 1838, was a hip roof, two-story structure that measured 33' x 28'. The house stands at 5 Reeves Avenue and was constructed by joining two smaller existing homes. A leanto kitchen and a bath house were attached to the dwelling. The homestead was about 100 feet west of the Rowandtown School. (Rowand No. 48, 1955)

A fire insurance survey described the interior of Reeve's homestead. The first floor had a parlor, setting room, a wide hall with vestibules and open stair bay with mahogany balusters up to the second floor. The walls in the parlor were coated with gilt paper. The hall and setting room were decorated with ordinary glazed paper. The vestibules were "handsomely papered." The upstairs had four chambers and the attic had three furnished bed rooms. Reeve's 22' x 35' barn had a large shed attached to it. The barn was built in 1839. A wagon house and an open wagon shed stood next to the barn. (Rowand No. 48, 1855)

In 1870, Samuel was 57. Also residing in the Reeve household were his wife Lilpah, their son Edward and his wife Mary. Samuel spent most of his life farming. On his land he raised livestock and grew market garden produce, wheat, corn, potatoes, sweet potatoes, and hay.

Reeve was one of about a dozen citizens elected to a municipal position when the township became a separate political entity in 1865. He was the township's first Tax Collector. He also served as a trustee for Rowandtown's only school.

Cooper Street bisected Samuel's other lot. The old lane, known then as Willis Lane, ran from the Haddonfield Road and passed over the lot and onto Amos Willis, Jr.'s house along Cooper's Creek. A tenant house stood along the lane. Today the house is 103 1/2 Cooper Street. Older residents familiar with the house may recall the country store that operated out of the dwelling in the early twentieth century.

17-28 Amos Willis, Jr.

Amos Willis, Jr.'s tract contained 72 acres of arable land, nineteen acres of unimproved land and nine acres of woodland. The dwelling on this farm was near Cooper's Creek in the vicinity of Cooper Street and Stratford Avenue. The house and outbuildings stood at the end of Willis Lane. The lane, from Haddon Avenue, ran across two lots and onto the Willis property. The lane eventually became the location of Cooper Street. Several small stream branches met near the border of the Willis lot at the end of Toledo Avenue. The main stream, known as Dick's Hole, flowed from that point into Cooper's Creek.

A tenant dwelling stood on the lot along Willis Lane at 209 Cooper Street. It is likely the dwelling was built sometime in the late 1870s, or early 1880s.

In 1870, Amos attempted to sell his land. The published advertisement divulged the following information about the farm:

> Valuable Farm on Cooper Creek, Haddon Township 100 acres of valuable land in a high state of cultivation. The land is well adapted to the growth of grain or grass. Dwelling house, three good barns, two wagon houses, spring house and other outbuildings. (WJP 2/23/1870)

They did not sell the farm and the Willis family remained at the site. In the early 1870s, Amos continued to work his land. Amos's wife Mary and their sons and daughter lived on the property. Amos's father, Amos Willis, Sr. and brother Edwin Willis lived near by. [See Edwin Willis, page 252.]

17-29 John N. Hobensack

Dr. John N. Hobensack owned twenty acres of land on the southwest corner of Haddon and Crystal Lake avenues. The Hobensacks's dwelling, built about 1835, was at the southwest corner of Glenwood and Haddon Avenues. The two-story, five bedroom frame dwelling faced the turnpike and measured 28' x 28'. A veranda extended across the front of the house and a two-story addition was attached to the back of the dwelling. The Hobensacks's outbuildings included a one-story summer kitchen, a brick tool house, barn, carriage house and a wagon shed attached to a cow house.

In 1870, at the age of 50, John and his wife Lucilla and their son and daughter resided in the dwelling. Two farm laborers and two African-American domestic servants also lived on the property. The family also owned a home in Philadelphia.

One of the older lanes in Rowandtown crossed Hobensack's tract. The path, called Webster's Lane, went from Haddon Avenue, across the railroad tracks, turned west, passed over the creek, and headed in a direction toward the lot owned by the Webster family. [See Hannah Webster, page 253.] A part of the lane, at Haddon Avenue, became Glenwood Avenue.

During their years in Rowandtown, the Hobensacks were active in the real estate market. In 1869, John purchased the nearby 58-acre "Creek Farm" along Cooper's Creek and leased it to a tenant farmer. Four years later, the property was sold to Samuel French. By the late 1870s, several tenant homes stood on Hobensack's lot along Haddon Avenue. One rental dwelling had been removed from its former site and hauled down the turnpike from Haddonfield:

> Dr. Hobensack of Rowandtown, created a sensation hear the other day by removing with the aid of eight horses, a house from Haddonfield to Rowandtown. (WJP 2/17/1875)

As active as John was in the local real estate market, it was not his primary means of support. John and his son James practiced medicine at the Hobensack Institute, at 206 North Second Street in Philadelphia. Today, we would probably categorize their medical speciality as psychiatry. For many years, the Hobensacks regularly publicized their business in Camden's newspapers. An advertisement claimed:

> Dr. J.N. Hobensack and Dr. J.B. Hobensack, son, graduates of best medical university for last thirty years. Those inflected with habits which destroy both mind and body and send thousands to insane asylums and premature deaths, call and be saved. (WJP 10/31/1878)

Most of their patients were from Philadelphia, although some traveled from the Camden area for diagnosis and treatment. [See medical profession, page 168.]

In the late 1880s, a part of Hobensack's Rowandtown tract was subdivided into building lots and houses were soon built.

17-30 Thomas W. Wilkinson

In 1873, Thomas Wilkinson purchased a nine-acre lot along Haddon Avenue for $4,300 from Floyd and Rebecca Archer of the City of Brooklyn (New York). In 1871, Thomas and his brother James, were living on the Hanbest farm in Collingswood. [See Thomas Hanbest, page 210.] Had the dwelling on Wilkinson's lot survived, it would be on Haddon Avenue along the east side of Center Street. By the mid-1880s, a lane evolved on Wilkinson's lot that is now Center Street.

Thomas Wilkinson went on to become the first pastor of The Shiloh Baptist Church of Rowandtown. They built the sanctuary on the lot soon after the religious society's governing body organized in 1883. The former church was just east of Haddon Township's Municipal Building.

17-31 Jacob P. Fowler

Jacob P. Fowler's thirteen acres were along Haddon Avenue. Before moving to this Rowandtown farm in the mid-1870s, Jacob his wife Mary and their three sons lived in Haddonfield. Fowler's dwelling is situated near the northwest corner of Crystal Lake and Haddon avenues at 225 Haddon Avenue. The two-story frame Federal-style house with a two-story addition, was built about 1809. In 1875, Fowler built a barn that measured 40' x 30'. Other outbuildings on the farm included a leanto shed, a two-story grain and store house and wood, poultry, cow and wagon houses. (Rowand No. 421, 1875)

Jacob made his living as a hardware merchant in Haddonfield. For a brief period he served as Postmaster for the village. Judging from the number of times he was a party to real estate transactions, it is likely Fowler dealt in real estate as a source of income. By 1890, the year Jacob died, his land holdings included lots along both sides of Haddonfield Road near Crystal Lake Avenue. Squire Fowler, as local inhabitants knew him, was also a Justice of the Peace.

In 1879, Charles Latchum was renting Fowler's land. His crops included hay, corn, wheat, potatoes and apples. With its 120 peach trees, the lot had the largest peach orchard in the township.

17-32 Jacob S. Coles, Samuel A. Willits

Although most of Jacob Stokes Coles's 70 acres of land was within the boundaries of modern-day Haddon Township, his dwelling, 523 Coles Mill Road, is within present-day Haddonfield. Part of the farm was joined to Haddonfield in 1943. The section of the farm that was not ceded to Haddonfield remained in Haddon Township. [See Jacob Coles, page 231.] Today, the senior citizen housing complex occupies the site.

Samuel Willits's lumber and coal yard along Cooper's Creek, known as the "Landing Yard," was at a site in today's Haddon Township. Samuel's second lot was next to the Cooper's Creek lumberyard in what is now Haddonfield. Samuel resided along Grove Street in the village of Haddonfield. (See Samuel A. Willits, page 230.]

17-33 Lots along Coles Landing Road

During the 1870s, there were several small lots on Locust Avenue. Before the railroad bisected the thoroughfare, Locust Avenue and Coles Mill Road were connected. The road was known as Coles Landing Road. James Stoy, Samuel Stoy, Elis Bates, Joseph Webster and the estate of William McElhaney owned the rental properties. Two of the dwellings still stand at 30 and 33 Locust Avenue. These dwellings may date to the 1840s.

17-34 Clayton Brown / John Macaulay

In 1860, Clayton and his wife Sarah and their two sons Charles and Samuel, resided in a house that stands at 419 Maple Avenue. The lot contained twenty acres. Clayton was a master weaver. He made rag rugs in a shop next to his home. Rag rugs were a practical and durable floor covering made from worn out garments, bedding and household furnishings. The rags were given a second life after they were made into rugs. [See weaver shop, page 147.]

When Brown passed away in 1869, his two carpet looms were sold along with his weaving fixtures. Brown's patrons were placed on notice to claim some 300 yards of rugs that remained in the shop at the time of his death. Clayton also planted crops on his lot. Advertisements show how Brown used his land:

> Comfortable frame two story dwelling house, barn, weaver shop, apples, peaches, cherries and other fruit trees in abundance and bearing condition. Five minute walk to station Camden & Atlantic Railroad. (WJP 7/28/1869)

> One brown mare, two cows, two hogs, chickens, carriage, wagon, 225 rails, posts, lot of manure, six acres Indian corn, round and sweet potatoes in the ground, wheat, rye, oats, pumpkins, cabbage, apples, pears on the trees. (WJP 8/26/1869)

Clayton's heirs sold the homestead to a Camden resident who, shortly after that, sold the real estate to Philadelphian John Macaulay. The tract's new owner made his living off the land. In 1879, Macaulay was one of the few township farmers that did not grow hay. Corn and potatoes were the crops of choice.

17-35 Phoebe Adams

Phoebe Adams's one-acre lot was situated along the north side of the Haddonfield Turnpike. Phoebe was one of just a handful of African-American women in the township to hold land title. Her dwelling was also home to Joseph and James Adams, Rachael Furney, and Rosa Scott.

West Collingswood Heights

17-36 John W. Logan Estate

The 212-acre property held by the Estate of John W. Logan was a working farm going back as far as 1767. The Logan farm comprised most of West Collingswood Heights. An 1866, survey prepared for the heirs of John Logan, showed the farm consisted of 165 acres of fertile land, eleven acres of woodland and 36 acres of meadowland.

The location of the dwelling was near Hillside Avenue, east of Route 130. The house, built in 1827, was a two-story wood frame dwelling measuring 39' x 22' with an attached leanto kitchen. The layout of the first floor revealed a center hall between two rooms, the second floor had four chambers. (Rowand No. 128, 1859)

The farm had two barns, one of which was built in 1767. The old barn had twenty cow stalls, six horse stalls, and a bay and loft for storing hay. The other barn had a 15' x 30' threshing floor used to store hay and grain. Other outbuildings included a 36' x 8' poultry house, a 6' x 6' smokehouse, a 20' x 40' crib house, and a wagon house. (Rowand No. 128, 1859)

Little biographical information exists on the Logan family. John Logan inherited the land from his father, Zachery. Neither Mrs. Logan nor any of her direct heirs lived in the township during the era of this project.

John Logan's heirs attempted to sell the farm in 1866. A newspaper advertisement described some features on the farm:

> ... 165 acres of arable farm land in the very highest state of cultivation. ... The whole farm is well fenced and in perfect order. This farm is one of the most productive in the county. It has been farmed for many years by Joseph Sheppard, who can be found at the farm. To either farmer or capitalist it presents an investment of most desirable land. The farm produced net last year over $3,700 clear of all expenses. (WJP 8/15/1866)

Joseph Sheppard, a farmer, and his wife Sarah and three daughters were tenants on the farm for at least twenty years. Like many farms in the area, the Sheppards owned cows that grazed on the meadow grasses. His cows yielded 7,300 gallons of milk in 1870. Sheppard's farm was second in the township in production of milk. A large number of apple trees as well as cherry trees once grew on the property.

As it turned out, the overseers of the farm had good foresight to insure the buildings in case of fire. In 1871, a fire destroyed a barn. Mrs. Logan hired William Hoopes, a Haddonfield carpenter, to build a new barn. The $1,800 contract called for the rebuilt barn to be at "the same site occupied by the barn recently destroyed by fire and was 32 feet wide and 80 feet in length." Hoopes built the foundation with "good sound building stone laid not less than twelve inches below the surface of the ground and extended eighteen inches above the surface of the ground and eighteen inches in thickness at any point." The barn's foundation walls were topped out with hard bricks. The floor of the wooden superstructure was two inches of seasoned yellow pine. There were twenty "sleepers" for horses and cows. (Building Contract–Camden County Historical Society, June 1871)

In the 1870s, the Sheppards were victims of two burglaries. In one incident, as reported in the *West Jersey Press*, the Sheppard's house was broken into "by prying the shutter from one of the windows." The thieves walked off with silverware, clothing and a table cloth. (WJP 8/9/1871) As luck would have it, the family was "robbed" again in 1872. This time the culprits helped themselves to a silver hunting case (a watch), pocketbook containing $10 and a revolver. (WJP 11/13/1872) It may be mere coincidence, two months after the second break-in, the Sheppards sold their household goods and farming utensils and moved.

17-37 Peter Weinnmann / William Doughten

Peter Weinnmann, previously of Haddonfield, acquired his 23 acres sometime in the 1860s. By the mid-1870s, two dwellings stood along the Black Horse Pike near the South Branch of Newton Creek. Peter, his wife Amelia and three daughters resided in one dwelling, while a tenant farmer lived in the other home.

Soon after the Weinnmann's moved to their property, Peter put together a distillery. His assets included two copper stills, two cider presses and a 1,200 gallon vat. Peter turned apples, grapes and other fruits into cider, vinegar, wine and applejack. The distillery process was a seasonal business, lasting just four months of the year. Peter's other trade was a cooper, fabricating wooden containers out of staves and hoops. The two crafts were compatible, since his casks and barrels held the finished goods that came from the stills and cidermaking operation. [See cidermaker and cooper, page 132.]

Weinnmann's distillery ran afoul of the law in 1871. It is probable that Peter "forgot" to pay the federal excise tax on his liquid products and stills. U.S. Marshals seized all of the stock and contents at the distillery and subsequently sold them. Few assets remained after the government agents were through; they even confiscated his livestock.

Weinnmann was also neglectful when it came to paying his township taxes. Over a period of years, the township issued several tax warrants to collect Weinnmann's local taxes. Finally, the township's tax collector gave up trying to collect Peter's delinquent taxes and he judged the obligation to be uncollectible.

Not too long after his equipment and stock were confiscated and sold, Weinnmann sold the tract to William Doughten. Doughten owned other properties in the township, including lots in Haddonfield. Doughten was proprietor of several lumberyards along the Delaware River and a planing mill in Camden.

William Wood, a tenant farmer, rented most of the arable land on the lot from Weinnmann, then Doughten. Wood lived on the property and cultivated a variety of crops. In the 1880s, Wood acquired the tract.

West Collingswood Extension 17-38 Estate of Samuel C. Champion

Today's West Collingswood Extension was once a 79-acre lot known as "Cedar Grove Farm." The lot was one of four farms owned by the heirs of Samuel Champion. The Champion Estate's property encompassed all of present-day Fairview and other adjacent parts of Camden. [See Camden (Fairview), page 193.]

Haddon Township

During the era when large-scale residential development took hold on the township's farms, many suburban homeowners believed their interest were best served if their developments came under independent municipal jurisdictions. Political autonomy gave new homeowners a greater degree of control over their new communities. Beginning with Haddonfield in 1875, newly incorporated boroughs annexed Haddon Township land. The area now comprising Haddon Township is what remains from the 1871 township, minus what was ceded to Audubon, Audubon Park, Camden, Collingswood, Gloucester Heights, Haddonfield, Haddon Heights, Oaklyn and Woodlynne.

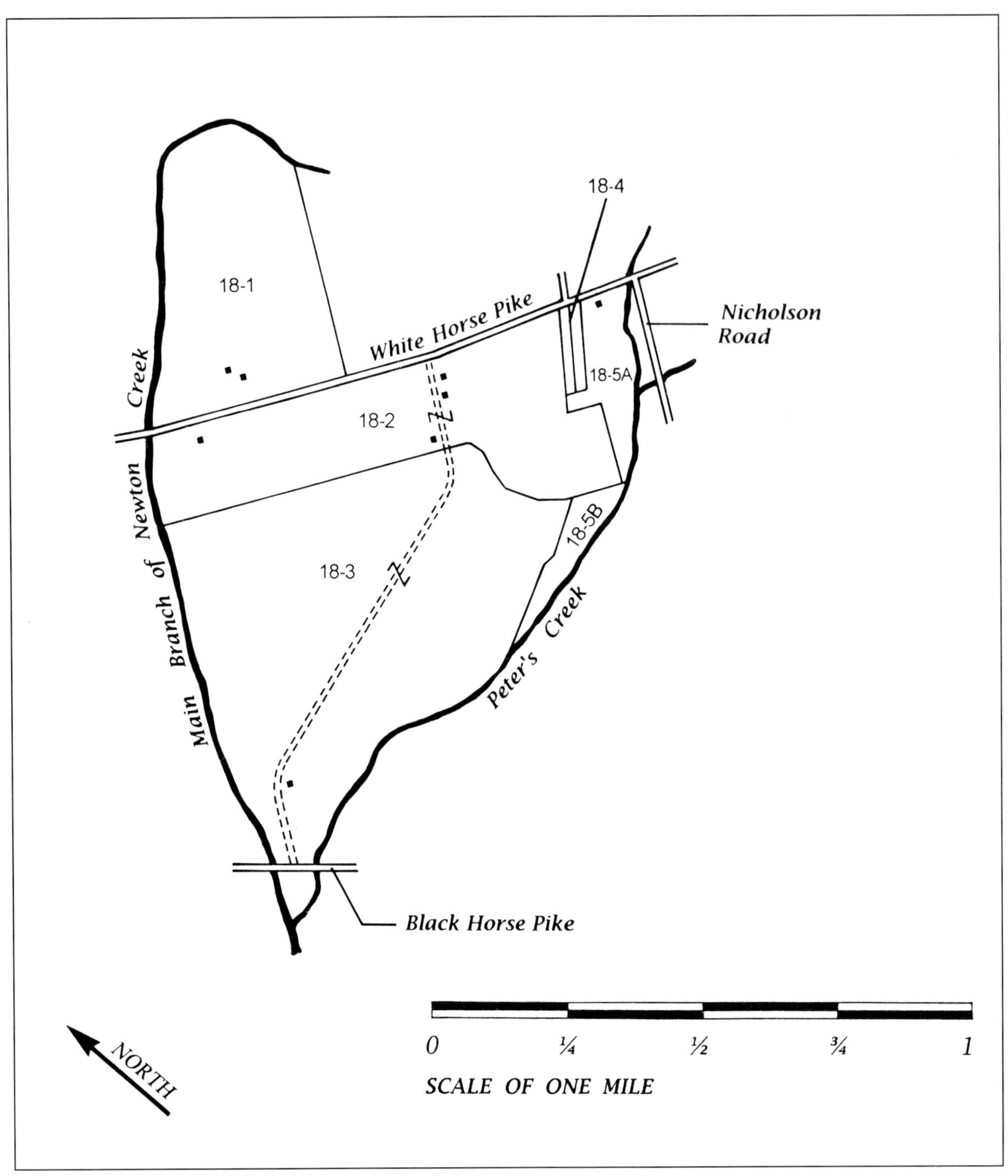

Map of the area that became Oaklyn, 1877.

18

Oaklyn

18-1 Edward Bettle
The perimeter of this 100-acre farm was the White Horse Pike, the Main Branch of Newton Creek and East Clinton Avenue. This lot is now the entire part of Oaklyn east of the White Horse Pike.

18-2 Joseph C. Hollingshead
The property boundaries were between the White Horse Pike and the vicinity of Newton Avenue and between the Main Branch of Newton Creek to West Cedar Avenue. The lot was 95 acres.

18-3 Jeremiah Ridgway
This 180-acre farm included all land between the vicinity of Newton Avenue and west to Peter's Creek and between the Main Branch of Newton Creek and Audubon.

18-4 Fusselltown
The narrow lots called Fusselltown were opposite Cuthbert Road along the White Horse Pike.

18-5 William Bettle, Jr. and William C. Nicholson
Lot A Bettle's lot now straddles the Oaklyn/Audubon municipal boundary. The lot was between West Cedar Avenue to Nicholson Road and between the White Horse Pike and where Wyoming Avenue meets Nicholson Road.

Lot B Nicholson's land, in Oaklyn, was between the area of Spruce and Maple avenues and Peter's Creek.

18-1 Edward Bettle

Edward and Martha Bettle owned 100 acres of land that encompassed Oaklyn's eastern side of town. The Bettles resided in a three-story mansion that stands between East Bettlewood and East Beechwood avenues. The Oaklyn Baptist Church now owns the building. The Edward Bettle mansion was built about the same time and was similar in appearance to Edward's cousin William Bettle, Jr.'s mansion at 9 East Holly Avenue. [See William Bettle, Jr., page 255.]

They built the three-story brick house in 1847, which measured 44' x 34'. The structure was originally designed in a Greek revival style. Its original dimensions and appearance were described in a fire insurance survey prepared in the mid-1800s. The south side of the house had a veranda with a roof held up by four wrought iron columns. A portico extended over the

Oaklyn Baptist Church Sunday School. Formerly home of Edward Bettle. The three-story dwelling, built in 1847, is now situated between East Bettlewood and East Beechwood avenues in Oaklyn. Edward Bettle was a farmer, businessman, politician and legislator.

(Photo by Dennis Raible, 1998)

front door supported by two fluted columns. A self-supporting portico was hung over the back entry. On the north side of the house, an enclosed vestibule led to the dining room. Attached to the house was a small weatherboard shed that enclosed an artesian well. A kitchen and wash house were attached to the back of the dwelling. (Franklin Fire Insurance Company of Philadelphia. Survey 8484, 1847)

Before municipal water service existed, most township farmers raised well water with outdoor pumps. The Bettles, on the other hand, had an early system of indoor plumbing. On the roof of the mansion sat a 2,500 gallon tank or cistern that supplied the household with fresh water.

Born in Pennsylvania in 1828, Edward came from a family of Quaker merchants. Before becoming a public servant, Edward was a farmer. In 1860, he cultivated crops commonly raised by most Newton Township farmers. Domestic servants as well as farm laborers also lived on the premises.

Edward was well known throughout the political landscape as evidenced by his appointment to chair the first "Town Meeting of the Inhabitants of Township of Haddon," held on March 8, 1865. For several years, Bettle occupied a highly visible position in state government. In 1866, he received the nomination at the county's Republican Union Convention to be a candidate for the New Jersey State Senate. The Republican party's mouthpiece, the *West Jersey Press*, noted that Bettle was, "practically and classically educated, he is one of the most successful agriculturalists and businessmen in the county. . . ." (WJP 10/3/1866) Edward's neighbor, Edward Collings also ran as a Republican candidate for the State Assembly. Both candidates were successful in their election bids for state office. [See Edward Collings, page 202.] The citizens of the district returned Bettle to the State Senate in the next election for office. His colleagues in the Senate voted Bettle President of the State's upper house, a position he held for one year.

Bettle was not without political "baggage." While serving in the Senate, he was involved in an incident of "alleged complicity with the Erie Railway Company" in matters before the governing body. (WJP 8/23/1871) Other newspapers, especially those publishing the Democratic Party's point of view, may have made political hay of the incident.

Edward's political connections led to business opportunities. In 1869, he was an incorporator of the Philadelphia and Camden Bridge Company. This New Jersey corporation was authorized to sell stock in a company that held the rights to build a bridge across the Delaware River. The bridge never materialized and the company's right to span the river expired. A bridge connecting the two cities was not completed until over a half-century later.

During the years Bettle served in the New Jersey Senate, he also served as a director of the National State Bank of Camden and New Jersey Trust & Savings

Deposit Company. He was also active in important charitable causes of the day. He was a manager in the Soup House of Philadelphia and the Frankford Insane Asylum. Bettle served as first Vice President of The West Jersey Orphanage for African-American children. Located in Camden, the orphanage provided a home for destitute "colored" children of the county. He was also a member of the State Board of Assessors and Chairman of New Jersey's World's Fair Commission.

The *Manual of the Legislature* for 1872 provides a biography of the Senate President:

> He [Bettle] is of an old wealthy Quaker family, his ancestors coming over with William Penn, and their descendants for many generations being merchants in Philadelphia. The grandfather and uncle of the Senator are prominent ministers in the Society of Friends. Senator Bettle studied medicine at Jefferson college, but not with a view of practicing it as a profession and has never done so. He then traveled to Europe and on the Continent, making a journey up the Nile and penetrating far into the interior of Egypt. In 1860, Mr. Bettle was a delegate to the convention that nominated Lincoln and was Acting Secretary of the Chicago Convention of 1860, preparing with two other delegates, the printed report of the Proceedings. ... He has been frequently urged to accept the nomination for Congress in the First District, but has uniformly declined.

In 1871, Edward decided to step down from his legislative duties. They praised him in newspapers across the state. The *West Jersey Press* carried excerpts from other New Jersey newspapers. One excerpt from the *New Brunswick Fredonian* stated:

> Hon. Edward Bettle, the President of the New Jersey Senate, has fairly earned the reputation of being one of the best Legislative presiding officers ever known in New Jersey. (WJP 4/19/1871)

Several months after retiring from the Senate, Bettle refused to consent to have his name placed in nomination for Governor at the Republican State Convention. The *West Jersey Press* reported that, "with the nomination of Mr. Bettle, the Republican Party of New Jersey would have ample assurance of success." (WJP (8/23/1871) Bettle remained active in the party after leaving his elected position. In 1877, he was President of the Republican State Convention.

State officials in 1879 called on Edward to investigate prison labor. The problem, as argued by some entrepreneurs, was products made in state prisons unfairly competed with goods made outside the prison walls at a higher cost. A State Commission headed by Bettle was established to make recommendations to the New Jersey Assembly. Bettle and his commission proposed to diversify products made by inmates, thereby no single item of output from the prisons would dominate the marketplace and products made outside the penitentiaries would not suffer adverse consequences.

A tragic time for the family occurred in 1876 when the Bettle's only child died. Condolences arrived from all over:

> The many friends of ex-Senator Bettle, including the Republican press of the State, have united in extending to him their sympathies at the loss of his only child, a daughter sixteen years old. (WJP 11/1/1876)

The Bettles sold their farm and moved to Camden during the later stages of their lives. Like many affluent residents of the era, the Bettles vacationed at their "cottage" in Atlantic City. Edward died at his vacation home in 1894.

Even though the Camden and Philadelphia Race Course was in existence several decades before the era considered by this study, nonetheless it had an association with the Bettle property. Before the Bettle family moved to Newton Township, William Johnson held title to the land along White Horse Pike in Oaklyn and Haddon Township. Johnson and four investors from Virginia erected a one mile gravel track, grandstands, stables and a hotel. A high wooden fence circled the entire track. The hotel, which was built to accommodate race crowds, had frontage along the White Horse Pike. Its location was near the site where Edward Bettle's residence was built years later.

The track was a popular spot for Philadelphia race fans. Many came by ferry across the Delaware River from Philadelphia and continued onto the grandstands. One can only imagine the contrast in life-styles of the Quaker farmers of pastoral Newton Township and some boisterous racetrack patrons.

Farmers from around the countryside were not the only group opposed to the racecourse. Many Camden residents were likewise against the horse track because of the unsavory clientele. On days when the track was closed because of inclement weather, some of the race crowds congregated in Camden. In *A Gentlemen of Much Promise The Diary of Isaac Mickle*, the Camden diarist lamented in 1841, " Our town was lively enough with gamblers, jockies and other knaves, from nine o'clock this morning till night." (p. 171)

The rowdy element attending the complex presented a problem for Newton Township farmers. In William H. Nicholson's book entitled *My Ancestors*, the author recalled when his father, Samuel Nicholson, took up the cause for the local citizenry in opposing racecourses in

New Jersey. At that period in time, Samuel lived on a farm along the White Horse Road in Audubon. [See Samuel Nicholson, page 221.] Samuel Nicholson's argument carried the day:

> In 1846, the Camden and Philadelphia Race Course, situated on the present side of Bettlewood, was in active operation, and a great source of public demoralization. My father, and a number of prominent citizens, were anxious to rid the country of this vicious influence. I remember going with him to a public indignation meeting, held at the Court House, in Woodbury, called to take measures for the suppression of this evil. Immediate action to this end was desired of the legislature, but was prevented by the sporting fraternity. Before long, however the serious injury to many persons by the breaking down of a part of the grand stand, during the great race between Fashion and Peytona, prepared the way for legislative action, and my father embracing the opportunity, went alone to Trenton, while the legislature was in session, and obtaining the interest of Richard Stafford, the Democratic Senator representing the county, secured the enactment against public horse-racing which stood upon the statute book for many years. A son of the Senator told me that his father was offered $20,000, not to press the bill, but resisted the temptation. (p. 93)

Shortly after horse-racing ended and the local track was closed, Samuel Bettle acquired the land in 1847 and razed the racecourse buildings. He divided and bequeathed his landholdings to his grandsons, Edward and William, Jr. Sometime about 1847, Edward moved onto his new homestead and returned the land to agricultural use.

18-2 Joseph C. Hollingshead

Joseph and Abigail Hollingshead purchased their 95-acre farm in 1865. Hollingshead's wood frame house was just off the White Horse Pike between West Oakland and West Holly avenues. A barn, corncrib, carriage house and several other outbuildings surrounded the house. The tract had a tenant house along the White Horse Pike near the Main Branch of Newton Creek.

A lane once came off the White Horse Road, ran past the Hollingshead house, and continued west onto the adjacent Ridgway farm to the Black Horse Pike. A segment of the route was similar, if not the same, as Kendall Boulevard. The Philadelphia & Atlantic City Railway laid their tracks across the Hollingshead property in 1877. Ten years later, local trains stopped at a small depot called Oakland Station, in the proximity of West Oakland Avenue.

Hollingshead was 42 in 1870, and his wife, Abigail was 36. At this period in time the couple's son Edward, daughter Mary, domestic servants, farm laborers and a dairyman resided on the farm.

Joseph was a dairy farmer. His farm was one of the top three milk producers among the old Haddon Township farms. He delivered his "pure Jersey Milk" in the morning to patrons along his milk route throughout Camden. The *West Jersey Press* reported that Hollingshead "added a new and tastefully built wagon in order to meet the demands of his constantly multiplying customers." (WJP 10/26/1870) Like most dairies in the region, feed for the livestock was grown right on the farm. Hollingshead's property also contained 125 apple trees.

In 1880, Hollingshead entered politics and was elected County Clerk. He was no stranger to the affairs and workings of the township. He served on the Township Committee for many years besides being an Overseer of Highways. Farmers, including Hollingshead, had an interest in ensuring the roads were in good condition. Their wagons passed over the roads when bringing farm products to market. For many years, Joseph was responsible for the upkeep of Collings and Nicholson roads.

18-3 Jeremiah Ridgway

Jeremiah Ridgway's 180-acre lot was actually two separate farms, each with a dwelling. A brick house was in the vicinity of the Manor area of Oaklyn. The other house was near the intersection of Kendall Boulevard and Ridgeway Avenue.

In the 1860s, several tenant farmers lived and tilled the soil on both Ridgway farms. Joseph Eldridge once resided here. He would later acquire the farm across Peter's Creek in Audubon Park. [See Joseph Eldridge, page 189.] Other tenants who resided on the Ridgway farm during the era included, Horace Haines, William Horner and Arthur Sitley. George Ward, a tenant farmer, worked the land situated near Peter's Creek in 1879. In addition to growing crops common to the region, Ward raised grapes on three acres of land. Some 300 pounds of the fruit were picked in 1879.

The Ridgway family attempted to sell the farm in 1874. Centre Township's Charles Willits acted for the absentee owners. An advertisement in the *West Jersey Press* noted the farm's "soil is particularly adapted to the growing of grass and at present in a high state of cultivation." (6/10/1874) The property was described as having some 25 acres of woodland of "first growth white oak." The one-time wooded area was west of the railroad tracks

Pumpkin patch in Oaklyn. Although not entirely free from doubt, the location of this farm was probably on the west side of the White Horse Pike.

(Camden County Historical Society Collections)

near West Holly and West Park avenues. The tract had about 25 acres of marsh and meadowland along Peter's Creek and the Main Branch of Newton Creek.

Jeremiah Ridgway, born in 1804, was raised in New Jersey. About 1840, he and his wife Sarah Anne and family moved from New Jersey to Michigan City, Indiana and opened a general store. Two years later they moved to LaPorte County, Indiana. Shortly before the Civil War, they packed their belongings and, with their three children, traveled by railroad to St. Joseph, Missouri. From here they pushed on by stage coach to California, eventually settling in Santa Rosa where they stayed for the next 25 years. In the later stages of his life, the pioneer of America's West, Ridgway returned to LaPorte County. Upon his death in 1885, the *Indianapolis News* reported:

> Jeremiah Ridgway died yesterday morning from lung trouble, aged 83 years. He was one of the early settlers of the county but for the past twenty-five years resided in California where he accumulated much wealth. He returned a few months ago to make the county his home and contemplated the erection of some large business buildings when spring opened. (*Indianapolis News* 2/21/1885)

Following Jeremiah's death, his Haddon Township land passed to his children, Jeremiah, Jr., Judith Ann, and Joseph.

Jeremiah, Jr., also lead an adventurous life. He was born in Newton Township in 1835 and moved with his family to Indiana. At the age of nineteen, Jeremiah followed his parents to California. His obituary, published in an unidentified LaPorte newspaper in 1921, documented Jeremiah's exploits:

> Following a short illness, Jeremiah Ridgway, 85 years old, one of the best known men of this community, passed away in his home. ... Mr. Ridgway was one of LaPorte's pioneers, having come here at an early date with his father's family, then leaving for other lands and finally returning after many years of wandering to make his home in LaPorte, where the last years of his life were spent. A career took him from coast to coast he having been born near Camden, New Jersey, was fraught with many interesting experiences.
>
> Jeremiah Ridgway came to Michigan City first with his parents from New Jersey, landing there in 1840. For two years the father ran a general store there and then moved to LaPorte. After several years in the city the family decided to go to California, that country at that time offering many advantages to the eastern man, so the father, mother and sister left by railroad, going as far as St. Joseph Mo., on the old Hannibal & St. Joseph railway, probably the first railroad to cross any of the states west of the Mississippi river, and from there they took stage coaches to the far west.
>
> But Jeremiah, Jr., with John Ball, (a close friend) had engaged themselves to the drovers to assist in driving 400 cattle and a band of horses to the far western state. It took eight months to make the journey and many thrilling experiences were encountered enroute. ... After the trip had been completed Mr. Ridgway became a professional drover and was known in the far west as the "boy drover."
>
> In 1861 Mr. Ridgway left the far west and came a large part of [the] way back to New York City by boat. He entered a law school in Albany, where he studied that

> course for two years. In 1865 he went back to California where he practiced law for several years. He married in 1874 to Miss Frances Dysard in Santa Rosa, California. On the death of his father in 1885 he returned to LaPorte with his wife, where they have lived ever since.
>
> Mr. Ridgway inherited considerable property in the east. A large amount of property also came to him through his family. . . .
>
> He was a pure blooded Quaker in belief, according to his widow and had strong convictions in many ideas. (Unidentified newspaper, 1/10/1921, LaPorte County Historical Society)

By 1886 Jeremiah Ridgway, Jr., had acquired the interests of his brother and sister in the Haddon Township property. The land remained in his possession until his death in 1921.

18-4 Fusselltown

The vicinity along the west side of the White Horse Pike positioned between Joseph Hollingshead's farm and land owned by William Bettle, Jr. assumed the name Fusselltown, named after an African-American family. The Fussell family acquired the property in 1836. Despite its name, the "town" comprised several narrow lots that extended west from the White Horse Pike. When they built the Philadelphia & Atlantic City Railway in 1877, the tracks traveled through the Fusselltown lots.

James and Rebecca Fussell owned one and one-half acres in Fusselltown. In 1880, the couple's four daughters and two sons were residing at home. Charles and Lucinda Fussell and their children, John and Robert, lived on a neighboring lot. Tax assessment ledgers reveal both James and Charles had previously resided in Saddlertown, a nearby African-American community.

Many nineteenth century African-American males were farm laborers. James and Charles Fussell were no exception. James was employed at Cuthbert's farm, situated along the Haddonfield Turnpike at Cuthbert Road.

Several families living under the same roof was not uncommon during this period. Although there were just three dwellings in Fusselltown, several African-American families lived here. Joshua Barnard and Josiah Hinson, both farm laborers, as well as Anna Fussell, a domestic servant lived in Fusselltown. For many years, Isaac and Hannah Hinson lived here. Isaac was a preacher and owner of property in a section of Camden known as Centerville.

18-5 William Bettle, Jr. and William C. Nicholson

William Bettle, Jr. resided on the eastern side of the White Horse Turnpike, on a farm in the Bettlewood section of Haddon Township. Bettle owned another tract of land west of the turnpike through which the stream that formed Peter's Creek passed. A part of the tract was in Oaklyn. [See William Bettle, Jr., page 255.]

The vast majority of William C. Nicholson's land was in what is now Audubon, although he owned a small area near Oaklyn's Spruce and Maple avenues. [See William C. Nicholson, page 186.]

Borough of Oaklyn

Sometime about 1890, Joseph Hollingshead, followed the lead of several other landholders in old Haddon Township and subdivided most of his farm into building lots. Hollingshead's project took the name "Oakland the Beautiful." In 1905, the Borough of Oaklyn was established. Over the next quarter of a century, the owners of the one-time Bettle and Ridgway farms succumbed to lucrative offers of residential real estate developers.

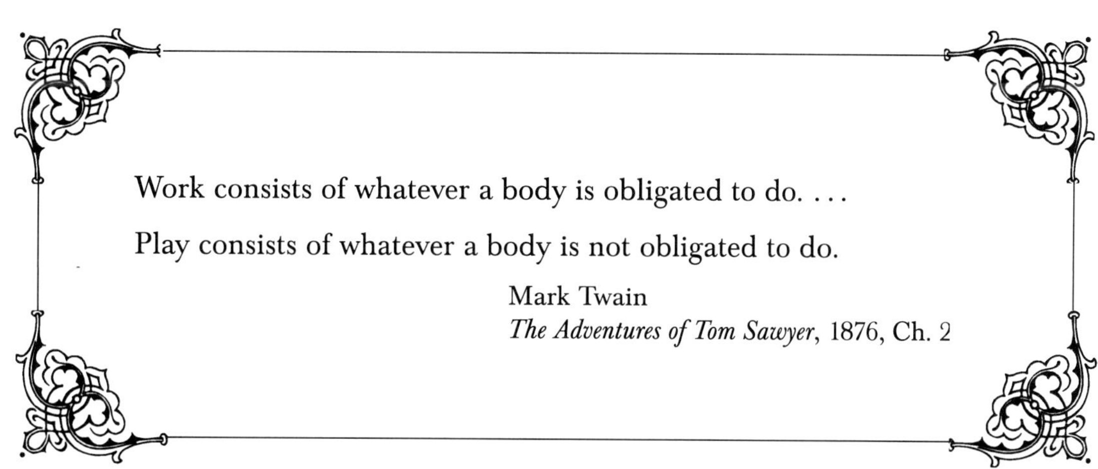

Work consists of whatever a body is obligated to do. . . .
Play consists of whatever a body is not obligated to do.

Mark Twain
The Adventures of Tom Sawyer, 1876, Ch. 2

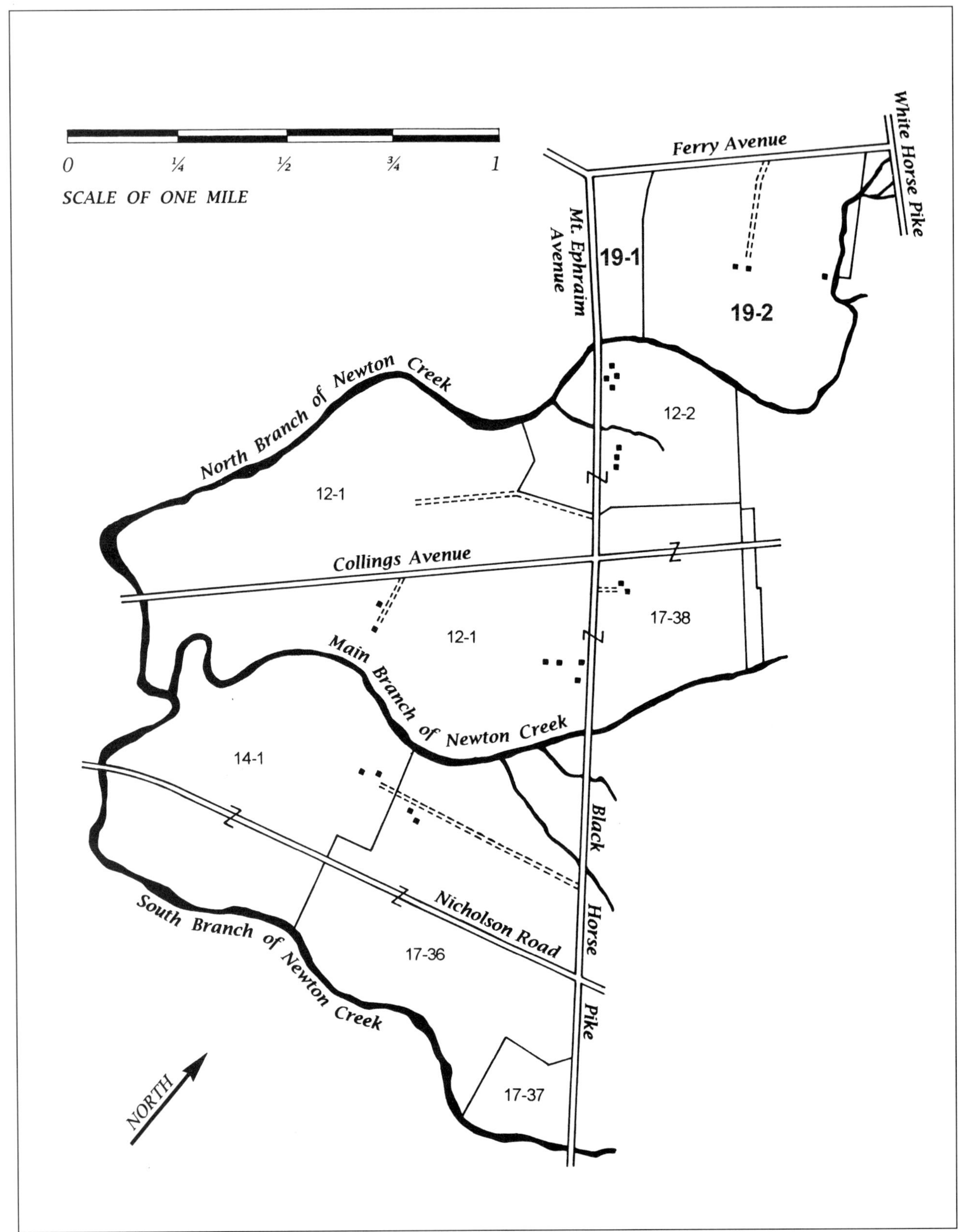

Map of the area that became Woodlynne, West Collingswood Extension (Haddon Township), Gloucester Heights (Gloucester City), West Collingswood Heights (Haddon Township), and Camden, including Fairview.

19

Woodlynne

19-1 Marmaduke Cope

Marmaduke Cope's small piece of real estate was along Mt. Ephraim Avenue. There were no improvements on the lot. Cope owned a much larger tract on the west side of Mt. Ephraim Avenue in Camden. Marmaduke also owned hundreds of acres of land in other parts of the city. He inherited much of his real estate from his mother Margaret Cope, a descendant of the Cooper family.

19-2 Joseph B. Cooper / Charles Cooper

Joseph and Hannah Cooper resided on a 112-acre farm that encompasses most of Woodlynne Borough. Joseph's ancestors were the original settlers of Camden.

The Coopers's brick house stood at the center of the farm. Built about 1818, the large mansion was where the Woodlynne municipal building stands on Cooper Avenue. The old farmhouse was demolished in the early 1970s. A lane ran from Ferry Road to the dwelling in the same vicinity and direction as Cooper Avenue.

Located next to the mansion were a number outbuildings. Cooper's barn measured 24' x 40'. A large hay house, stored with hay and grain, had been added to the barn. A corncrib and wagon house stood nearby. (Rowand No. 42, 1855) The farm was known for its dairy products.

During the first-half of the nineteenth century, private turnpike companies took over many roadways across the state, including the White Horse Road. The turnpike company roadway passed next to the Cooper farm. Farmers like Joseph Cooper, had a vested interest

Charles Cooper's dwelling in Woodlynne. Once located on Cooper Avenue, the building was used by borough officials during the twentieth century. It was demolished in the 1970s.

(Camden County Historical Society Collections)

in the existence of good roadways so they could get their products to market. Good roads also increased the value of nearby farms. For these reasons, farmers residing near the toll roads invested in stock and participated in the management of the turnpike companies. Joseph Cooper was an original incorporator of the White Horse Turnpike Company.

Sometime in the early 1860s, Joseph and Hannah moved onto an adjoining three-acre lot at the corner of Ferry Avenue and White Horse Pike. Their son, Charles, moved into the mansion and assumed responsibility for operating the farm. Joseph Cooper passed away in 1862. When they divided the last vestige of land in Newton Township between Camden and Haddon Township in 1871, the Cooper farm fell within the borders of Haddon Township.

During Charles tenure, dairy products continued to be the primary focus of the farm. The farm had the distinction of being the largest dairy farm in Newton and Haddon townships. In 1870, Charles sold 9,500 gallons of milk. Like most diary farms, Charles raised the feed for his cows. Sometime in the 1870s, Charles decided to rent most of his farmland to Henry and William Lovell. By the end of the decade, Charles Kelley was renting about 80 acres. Cooper shared in Kelley's harvest in stead of cash rent. A tenant house stood at a site near what is now Cypress and Woodlynne avenues.

Near the vicinity of Linden and Elm avenues was a wooded area in the 1870s. The source of North Branch of Newton Creek once emerged near Ferry Avenue and the White Horse Pike.

In 1877, the *West Jersey Press* featured Charles's homestead in an article entitled "A Peep into a Rural Home":

> The residence of Mr. Charles M. Cooper, on Ferry road, between the Mount Ephraim and White Horse turnpikes, in the extreme southern part of this city, is one of the most attractive rural homes to be met with anywhere. The house faces a lawn studded with trees and lined on its sides with a row of beautiful cypress trees, and at the rear end of this lawn is the yard enclosing the mansion house, within which, and fronting the house, is the largest Thyoides Cypress in Camden county, measuring fifteen feet in circumference, and planted by one of Mr. Cooper's ancestors in 1607.[date incorrect] This yard contains a number of other trees of different species, planted by Mr. Cooper in his youthful days. To the left of the building is another yard, handsomely laid out with flower beds and walks. Within the enclosure there is a small ravine, of romantic appearance, and here the largest white oak known of anywhere, rises in the majesty, towering far above the surrounding trees, and measuring, around the butt, twenty-one feet. It is a striking reminder of the famous "Charter Oak," as represented in the pictures given in our school histories. Near this is another attraction, consisting of a circle of trees planted by Mr. Cooper about twenty years ago, which is entered by an opening of four feet. Upon entering this enclosure one finds himself entirely secluded from outside view, with the "blue canopy heaven" overhead. A lovers' treat forsooth! The scene is really very charming, and the visitor is wont

to seat himself upon one of the *tete a tetes*, and thus undisturbed, enjoy the "thick-coming fancies." Leaving this retreat, the visitor passes through the side portico of the house, at the west end of which is that old familiar painting which hung for so many years over the entrance to the upper slip at the foot of Market street, Philadelphia. This painting represents the slip, with the old "Fish House" in the back ground and those who were in the habit of frequenting that place in the days of yore. It also gives a view of the Delaware river, with the steam ferry boats, "William Ray" [William Wray] and "Philadelphia," plying from shore to shore. Then there is a representation of the Camden shore, with here and there a house in sight. This painting is made upon mahogany boards and was painted by Woodside, in 1832. One other object is worthy of mention, and that is a rustic stand for flower pots. Several years ago a gentlemen from Bridesburg, Pa., while visiting the premises, carelessly twisted two young shoots together, and sometime afterwards it was noticed that they were growing together. The wood now forms a flower stand as curious as many other freaks of nature. (WJP 9/12/1877)

Borough of Woodlynne

The Cooper farm passed from the family in 1892 after Charles moved into Camden. Three years later, an amusement park was built and opened to the public, called Woodlynne Park. By the late 1890s, building lots and dwellings began to spread across the former dairy farm. Following the turn of the century, municipal improvements demanded by new home owners were such that the community incorporated as a borough in 1901. The former Cooper mansion stood in the middle of the new community. Before they razed it, the borough used the old mansion as a fire station, police headquarters and municipal offices.

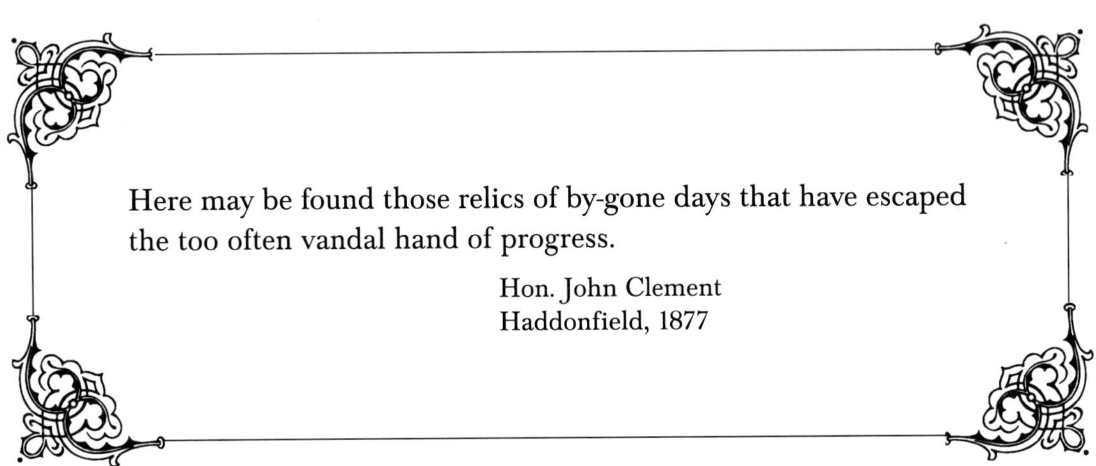

Here may be found those relics of by-gone days that have escaped the too often vandal hand of progress.

Hon. John Clement
Haddonfield, 1877

20

The Suburbs

A dramatic expansion in American agriculture took place between 1870 and 1900. During this period, the number of farms, acres of farmland and value of farm property doubled in size. A good portion of expansion within agriculture was quickened by the new technologies developed during the years of the Industrial Revolution. Part of the expansion was due to the opening of the Great Plains, the last agricultural frontier in the United States.

While the nation's farms doubled in numbers and acreage, the urban population in American increased threefold. In 1870, there were 25 cites in the country with a population exceeding 50,000; thirty years later there were 78 such places. Farmers, marketing their agricultural products, profited from the increasing populous.

Despite enlargement of agriculture in the country as a whole, farming was on the downswing in old Haddon Township. Productivity increased on local farms with the coming of new agricultural techniques and employment of more efficient farm machinery. However, the number of farms in the township declined as the twentieth century approached. Increasingly, landowners were more inclined to turn their fields and pastures into building lots for residential development.

The village of Haddonfield was the first area of old Haddon Township to experience sustained residential development following the Civil War. Later, in the 1880s, large-scale subdivision of land and subsequent building in Collingswood took place. The other municipalities highlighted in this project soon followed Haddonfield and Collingswood.

Old Haddon Township's transformation from an agrarian community to suburbia was not an isolated phenomenon. Other rural municipalities in the Philadelphia and Camden region experienced a similar progression. For that matter, formation of new suburbs was taking place throughout America in the late nineteenth century.

Many factors influenced suburban growth. Arguably the most influential factor contributing to suburbanization came with the unprecedented expansion of railroad service in the United States between 1865 and 1900. Routes radiated out from cities and short commuter runs were scheduled from downtown to nearby villages and the countryside. The steam railroad connected what had formerly been geographically isolated villages to the urban centers. By the end of the nineteenth century, another important transportation innovation, the trolley, linked outlying neighborhoods with center city.

The commuter was an important variable in the development of the suburbs of Philadelphia and Camden. Locally, they constructed a number of passenger stations in old Haddon Township along the two right-of-ways that extended between Camden and Atlantic City. The railroad facilities at Collingswood, Westmont, Haddonfield, West Collingswood, Oaklyn, Audubon and Haddon Heights became the geographical focus of new residential neighborhoods. By the turn of the century or shortly afterwards, trolley lines ran through most of the incorporated communities that had departed from old Haddon Township.

Other variables influenced suburban growth. They included an abundance of comparatively cheap land; high workers' wages compared to elsewhere in the world; middle class aspirations to own single family dwellings; balloon-frame construction that created affordable homes for the working person; and the establishment of services and an infrastructure such as roads, sewers, street lighting, storm sewers, schools and police and fire protection.

Another element contributed to the movement out to the suburbs. As cities grew larger, many families became discontented with the urban environment. Promoters of the new railroad suburbs encouraged families to experience a natural wholesome life style outside the city. Many people identified with the rural way of life. Gardens, shrubbery, and in some instances, facilities for a cow and a few chickens connected suburban living with the agrarian ideal.

Author Margaret Marsh wrote that the middle-class suburban ideal emerged from an agrarian belief. In *Suburban Lives*, published in 1990, She states,

> ...the suburban ideal offered a spatial equivalent for the agrarian community. Ownership of a suburban house did not make a man a farmer, but it bought him closer to nature than an urban townhouse did, and it recognized the political importance of property ownership. (p. xiii)

Though local promoters and developers boasted a new suburban life-style, in reality, the new way of life remained intertwined with urban centers. The burgeoning economic activity in Philadelphia and Camden, where most of the jobs were, sustained the livelihoods of most residents in the new communities formed from old Haddon Township. In Robert Fishman's 1987 publication, *Bourgeois Utopias*, he studied the interdependent relationship of city and suburb. A suburb was:

> ...a natural world of greenery and family life that appeared to be wholly separate from the great city yet was in fact wholly dependent on it. (p. 134)

As even more people moved outside the cities, the perceived advantages and attractions of the suburbs came into question to some that were lured from their urban habitats. The new suburbs did not bring universal joy. Kenneth Jackson wrote in *Crabgrass Frontier*:

> A more common criticism of the burgeoning peripheral subdivisions was that their very popularity undermined the results incoming families hoped to achieve. Privacy and solitude disappeared as the populace streamed outward, blighting the rural charm that had lured them in the first place. The environment they found was never quite as open or as isolated as theorists had wished. (p. 136)

In any event, one observable fact that is not debatable—suburbanization forever altered the pastoral countryside of old Haddon Township and brought the era of agriculture in the region to an end. The rural way of life that existed for two centuries in the area gradually disappeared.

Bibliography

Bibliography

Many sources have been used to gather information for this project. Some are repeated throughout the text. Those sources used frequently are listed here with the respective chapter numbers listed in the brackets following the citation. All other references are arranged by chapter.

By listing the sources in this fashion, the author hopes to provide the reader with proper citation with a minimum of clutter and confusion.

Manuscripts

Farr, William. "Waterways of Camden County." Manuscript in process, Mt. Holly, NJ. **[3, 9, 11, 12, 15, 17, 18, 19]**

Haddonfield, NJ. The Historical Society of Haddonfield. J. L. Rowand Fire Insurance Surveys. Surveys 1851 to 1879 consulted. **[1, 3, 4, 5, 8, 9, 10, 11, 15, 16, 17, 19]**

Government Documents

Haddon Township, NJ. "Minutes of Township Committee Meetings." Minutes 1865 to 1901 consulted. **[1, 3, 4, 5, 9, 10, 18]**

Haddon Township, NJ. "Minutes of Town Meetings." Minutes 1864 to 1881 consulted. **[1, 3, 4, 5, 9, 10, 18]**

Haddon Township, NJ. "Tax Assessment Ledgers." Ledgers 1865 to 1878 consulted. **[1, 2, 3, 4, 5, 9, 11, 12, 13, 14, 15, 16, 17, 18, 19]**

U.S. Department of Agriculture. *Report of the Commissioner of Agriculture for the year 1865.* "Market Products of West New Jersey." Washington, D.C.: Government Printing Office. 1866. **[3, 8, 15]**

U.S. Department of Commerce. Bureau of the Census. *Nonpopulation Schedules on Production of Agriculture, New Jersey, Camden County, Newton Township–1860, 1870.* **[8, 11, 12, 13, 14, 15, 16, 17, 18, 19]**

U.S. Department of Commerce. Bureau of the Census. *Nonpopulation Schedules on Production of Agriculture, New Jersey, Camden County, Haddon Township–1870, 1880.* **[8, 11, 12, 13, 14, 15, 16, 17, 18, 19]**

U.S. Department of Commerce. Bureau of the Census. *Nonpopulation Schedules on Products of Industry, New Jersey, Camden County, Newton Township–1850, 1860, 1870.* **[1, 3, 5, 9, 10, 11, 12, 13, 15, 17]**

U.S. Department of Commerce. Bureau of the Census. *Nonpopulation Schedules on Products of Industry, New Jersey, Camden County, Haddon Township–1870, 1880.* **[1, 3, 5, 9, 10, 11, 12, 13, 15, 17]**

U.S. Department of Commerce. Bureau of the Census. *Population Schedules, Seventh and Eighth Census of the United States, New Jersey, Camden County, Newton Township–1860, 1870.* **[1, 2, 3, 5, 9, 10, 11, 12, 13, 14, 15, 16, 17, 18, 19]**

U.S. Department of Commerce. Bureau of the Census. *Population Schedules, Eighth and Ninth Census of the United, States, New Jersey, Camden County Haddon*

Township–1870, 1880. **[1, 2, 3, 5, 9, 10, 11, 12, 13, 14, 15, 16, 17, 18, 19]**

Maps

Atlas of Philadelphia and its Environs—Haddon Township, Plate No. 34 and 35. Philadelphia, PA: G.M. Hopkins Company. 1877. **[1, 3, 4, 9, 10, 11, 12, 13, 14, 15, 16, 17, 18, 19]**

Atlas of Philadelphia and its Environs—Borough of Haddonfield, Plate No. 33. Philadelphia, PA: G.M. Hopkins Company. 1877. **[1, 3, 9, 10, 15]**

Atlas of The Vicinity of Camden, New Jersey. Philadelphia, PA: G.M. Hopkins Company. 1907. **[1, 3, 11, 12, 13, 14, 15, 16, 17, 18, 19]**

Map of Camden and Vicinity. Philadelphia, PA: G.Wm. Baist. 1887. (Camden County Historical Society, M83.90.676) **[1, 3, 9, 11, 12, 13, 14, 15, 16, 17, 18, 19]**

Map of Camden County, NJ. New York, NY: G.H. Walker. 1877. (Camden County Historical Society, M83.90.598) **[1, 3, 9, 11, 12, 13, 14, 15, 16, 17, 18, 19]**

Map of the Vicinity of Philadelphia. Original survey by D.J. Lake and S.N. Beers. Philadelphia, PA: C.K. Stone, A. Pomeroy. 1860. (Camden County Historical Society, M83.90.572) **[1, 3, 4, 9, 11, 12, 13, 14, 15, 16, 17, 18, 19]**

Plan of the Township of Union and Newton of Camden County. Original survey of J.C. Sidney. Philadelphia, PA: Richard Clark. 1850. (Collingswood Library) **[1, 3, 4, 9, 11, 12, 13, 14, 15, 16, 17, 18, 19]**

The City of Camden, NJ and Camden County. Philadelphia, PA: R.J. Barnes and Lloyd Vanderveer. 1856. (Camden County Historical Society, M83.90.746) **[1, 3, 9, 10, 11, 12, 13, 14, 15, 16, 17, 18, 19]**

Printed Sources

Clement, John. *Sketches of the First Emigrants Settlers Newton Township, Old Gloucester County, West New Jersey.* Camden, NJ. 1877. **[1, 9, 13, 15, 16, 17]**

Lane, Wheaton, L. *From Indian Trail to Iron Horse.* Princeton, NJ: Princeton University Press. 1939. **[1, 2, 3, 9]**

Prowell, George. *The History of Camden County, New Jersey.* Philadelphia, PA: L.J. Richards and Co. 1886. **[1, 2, 3, 4, 5, 6, 8, 9, 10, 11, 13, 15, 17, 18]**

Rauschenberger, Douglas and Tassini, Katherine Mansfield. *Lost Haddonfield.* Haddonfield, NJ: The Historical Society of Haddonfield. 1989. **[1, 3, 4, 5, 6, 9, 10, 11, 15, 17]**

Sutherland, Daniel E. *The Expansion of Everyday Life 1860–1876.* New York: Harper and Row. 1989. **[Preface, 5, 6, 7, 8, 9, 10]**

Newspapers

Camden (NJ) Daily Post. October 1875 to December 1881. Newspapers consulted 1876, 1877, 1879. **[1, 2, 3, 4, 5, 6, 7, 8, 9, 10, 11, 13, 15, 16, 17, 18]**

Camden (NJ) Democrat. November 1846 to June 1908. Newspapers consulted 1870, 1871 (January and February), September 18, 1877, December 22, 1877, October 4, 1879. **[1, 2, 3, 4, 5, 6, 7, 8, 9, 10, 11, 13, 15, 16, 17, 18]**

Camden (NJ) New Republic. November 1867 to 1879. Newspapers consulted 1876 to 1878. **[1, 2, 3, 4, 5, 6, 7, 8, 9, 10, 11, 13, 15, 16, 17, 18]**

Camden (NJ) West Jersey Press. April 1860 to December 1940. Newspapers consulted 1862 to 1880. **[1, 2, 3, 4, 5, 6, 7, 8, 9, 10, 11, 12, 13, 14, 15, 16, 17, 18, 19]**

Haddonfield (NJ) Basket. July 1874 to June 1876. **[1, 2, 3, 4, 5, 6, 7, 8, 9, 10, 11, 13, 15, 16, 17, 18]**

1 The Municipal Landscape

Manuscripts

Philadelphia, PA. Historical Society of Pennsylvania. Clement Papers. Minutes of Newton Township's Annual Meetings.

Government Documents

Camden County, NJ. Clerk's Office. Deed Books: Jacob Dodd, 100-651.

New Jersey. *Acts of the Eight-Ninth Legislature of the State of New Jersey.* An act to incorporate Haddonfield. (p. 334-339). Newark, NJ: Newark Printing and Publishing Company. 1865.

New Jersey. *Acts of the Eight-Ninth Legislature of the State of New Jersey.* An act to create the township of Haddon out of the township of Newton. (p. 119-120). Newark, NJ: Newark Printing and Publishing Company. 1865.

New Jersey. *Acts of the Ninetieth Legislature of the State of New Jersey.* An act to authorize owners of real estate in the village of Haddonfield to improve sidewalks in the public streets. (p. 479-482). Paterson, NJ: Criswell and Wurts. 1866.

New Jersey. *Acts of the Ninety-Fifth Legislature of the State of New Jersey.* An act to set off a part of the township of Newton and annex the same to the township of

Haddon. (p. 387-389). Morristown, NJ: Vance and Stiles. 1871.

New Jersey. *Acts of the Ninety-Fifth Legislature of the State of New Jersey.* An act to amend the charter of the city of Camden. (p. 210-214). Morristown, NJ: Vance and Stiles. 1871.

New Jersey. *Acts of the Ninety-Eighth Legislature of the State of Jersey.* An act to prevent Horses, Cattle, Sheep and Swine from running at large in the township of Haddon. (p. 404-405). Paterson, NJ: Chriswell and Wurts. 1874.

New Jersey. *Acts of the Ninety-Ninth Legislature of the State of New Jersey.* An act to incorporate the Borough of Haddonfield. (p. 334-339). Trenton, NJ: Naar, Day and Naar. 1875.

New Jersey. *Acts of the One Hundred and Second Legislature of the State of New Jersey.* An act to set off a part of the Eighth ward in the city of Camden and annex to the township of Haddon. (p. 577-579). Elizabeth, NJ: Drake and Cook. 1878.

New Jersey. Department of State. Division of Archives and Management. New Jersey State Census. Haddon Township, 1875. (microform)

Printed Sources

Beers, F.W. *State Atlas of New Jersey.* New York, NY: Beers, Comstock and Cline. 1872.

Dorwart, Jeffery M. and Mackey, Philip English. *Camden County, New Jersey 1616–1976 A Narrative.* Camden, NJ: Camden County Cultural and Heritage Commission. 1976.

Effross, Harris, I. *County Governing Bodies in New Jersey.* New Brunswick, NJ: Rutgers University Press, 1975.

Elmer, Lucius Q.C. *A Digest of the Laws on New Jersey.* 4th ed. 1709-1868 John T. Nixon. Trenton, NJ: Martin R. Dennis and Company. 1868.

Gordon, Thomas F. *A Gazetteer of the State of New Jersey.* Trenton, NJ: Daniel Fenton. 1834.

Ingram, Dr. Harry A. "Audubon and the Surrounding Areas." 1987. Camden County Historical Society.

Snyder, John P. *The Story of New Jersey's Civil Boundaries 1606-1968.* Trenton, NJ: Bureau of Geography and Topography. 1969.

Newspapers

Camden (NJ) Courier-Post. (Camden, NJ). January 27, 1953.

Haddonfield (NJ) The Basket. November 8, 1889.

Woodbury (NJ) Constitution. December 26, 1883.

2 Nearby Cities and Villages

Printed Sources

Beers, F.W. *State Atlas of New Jersey.* New York, NY: Beers, Comstock and Cline. 1872.

Weigley, Russell F., Ed. *Philadelphia–A 300 Year History.* New York: W.W. Norton and Company. 1982.

3 Routes and Modes of Transportation

Manuscripts

Camden, NJ. Camden County Historical Society. "Historical Clippings Relative to Camden, NJ." assembled by John Carney. Original survey "Bettlewood and Vicinity" by Bettlewood Land Co., Camden, NJ. No date. Survey of Nicholson Road 1866, by Johm Clement.

Collingswood, NJ. Collingswood Library. Samuel French Account Book.

Haddonfield, NJ. The Historical Society of Haddonfield. Hinchman Papers. Stoy Papers. Wood Papers. Jehu Wood Diary.

Philadelphia, PA. The Historical Society of Pennsylvania. John Clement Papers. Map of Land owned by Benjamin and Joseph Lippincott, 1877 (No. 23).

Philadelphia, PA. Free Library of Philadelphia. Sanborn Fire Insurance Map, Westmont. (microform) Sandborn Map and Publishing Co. Ltd. 1919.

Riverton, NJ. Paul W. Schopp Collection. Survey of proposed Railroad Right-of-Way by H.C. Smith. August, 1883.

Trenton, NJ. New Jersey State Archives. "Camden and Atlantic Railroad Company Annual Statements." Statements 1872 to 1883 consulted.

Woodbury, NJ. Gloucester County Historical Society. Newton Creek Meadow Company. (Vertical file)

Government Documents

Camden County, NJ. Clerk's Office. Deed Books: William Mann, 65-236. William Coffin, 65-415.

Camden County, NJ Surrogate's Office. Inventory of: Joseph C. Collings, B-707. Joseph Nicholson, F-379. David Roe, B-739. Samuel M. Reeve, H-307. Samuel A. Willits, J-204. Jacob S. Collings, D-424. John A. J. Sheets, I-61. Charles H. Shinn, D-1. Joseph C. Stoy, G-156.

Camden County, NJ Surrogate's Office. Assignment Book: Charles Bettle, A-12.

New Jersey. *Revised Statutes of the State of New Jersey passed 1874.* Roads. (p. 732, 733). Trenton, NJ: Printed by order of Governor. 1874.

New Jersey. *Acts of the Sixty-Third Legislature of the State of New Jersey.* An act to incorporate the Haddonfield and Camden Turnpike Company. (p. 172-181). Camden, NJ: P.J. Gray. 1839.

New Jersey. *Acts of the Ninety-First Legislature of the State of New Jersey.* An act to enable owners and possessors of meadow and marsh laying on Newton Creek to make and maintain a bank and dam. (p. 880-882). Paterson, NJ: Chriswell and Wurts. 1867.

New Jersey. *Acts of the Ninety-Sixth Legislature of the State of New Jersey.* A act to restore and improve the navigation of Newton Creek. (p. 915). Trenton, NJ: Naar, Day and Naar. 1872.

U.S. Congress. Letter from the Secretary of War. 47th Congress, 1st Session. Senate. Ex. Doc. No. 141. 1882.

U.S. Department of Agriculture. *Report of the Commissioner of Agriculture for the year 1866.* "Country Roads." Washington, D.C.: Government Printing Office. 1867.

U.S. Department of Agriculture. *Report of the Commissioner of Agriculture for the year 1868.* "Country Roads and Road Laws." Washington, D.C.: Government Printing Office. 1869.

U.S. *Report U.S. Engineer Surveys of New Jersey Waterways.* "Preliminary Examination of Cooper River, NJ." 11 January 1911.

U.S. *Report U.S. Engineer Surveys of New Jersey Waterways.* 52d U.S. House of Representatives, 2nd session, Ex. Doc. No. 81. 1892. 53rd U.S. House of Representatives, 3rd session, Ex. Doc. No. 176, 1895. 63rd U. S. House of Representatives, 1st session, Doc. No. 134. DATE

Printed Sources

Boyer, Charles S. *Annals of Camden–Old Ferries Camden, New Jersey.* Annals of Camden No. 3. Camden, NJ: Camden County Historical Society. 1921.

Boyer, Charles S. *Rambles Through Old Highways and Byways of West Jersey.* Camden, NJ: Camden County Historical Society. 1967.

Boyer, Charles S. *The Span of a Century–The Chronicle History of the City of Camden 1828–1928.* Centennial Anniversary Committee. 1928.

Butler, Frank. *Book of the Boardwalk.* Atlantic City, NJ: Haines and Co. 1952.

Cook, George W. and Coxey, William J. *Atlantic City Railroad–The Royal Route to the Sea.* Oaklyn, NJ: West Jersey Chapter National Railway Historical Society. 1980.

Fishman, Robert. *Bourgeois Utopias–The Rise and Fall of Suburbia.* New York, NY: Basic Books, Inc. 1987.

Gladulich, Richard M. *By Rail to the Boardwalk.* Glendale, CA: Trans-Anglo Books. 1986.

Gloucester County Historical Society. *Bulletin of the Gloucester County Historical Society. Vol. 8. No. 3.* (p. 9). Woodbury, NJ. March 1962.

Hillman, Sarah Crawford. *Historical Sketch of Potter Street in Haddonfield, New Jersey.* Haddonfield, NJ: Haddon Gazette Press. 1910.

Mackey, Philip English, Ed. *A Gentleman of Much Promise: The Diary of Isaac Mickle 1837-1845.* Philadelphia, PA: University of Pennsylvania Press. 1977.

Meyer, Henry W. *Memories of the Buggy Days.* Cincinnati, OH: Brinker, Inc. 1965.

Morgan, John D.F. *Rambles Through Old Highways and Byways of West Jersey.* Camden, NJ: Camden County Historical Society. 1967.

19th Century American Carriages. Stony Brook, NY: The Museums at Stony Brook. 1987.

Palmer, George. "A Collingswood Centennial Walking Tour—1985." Collingswood, NJ: Collings-Knight Homestead Committee, Collingswood Library.

Rhoads, Catherine E. *Memories of My Youth.* Haddonfield, NJ. 1925 Reprinted by Haddonfield Historical Society Publications, Second Series No. 1. 1967.

Richardson, M.T. Compiled and Edited. *Practical Blacksmithing.* New York, NY: Weathervane Books. 1978.

Rittenhouse, Jack D. *American Horse-Drawn Vehicles.* New York, NY: Bonanza Books. 1968.

Schmidt, Hubert G. *Agriculture in New Jersey–A Three Hundred-Year History.* New Brunswick, NJ: Rutgers University Press. 1973.

Seabold, Kimberly R. *From Marsh to Farm–The Landscape Transformation of Coastal New Jersey.* National Park Service. Washington, D.C.: U.S. Department of the Interior. 1992.

Tatem, Marion Pennypacker. *Haddonfield: Its Life with Railroads 1854-1976.* Haddonfield, NJ: Historical Society of Haddonfield. 2nd Series No. 2. 1979.

Towe, Charles L. *History of the Camden and Atlantic Railroad and Associated Railroads 1852-1897.* Bulletin No. 73. Boston, MA: The Railway and Locomotive Historical Society, Inc. Baker Library, Harvard Business School. 1948.

Newspapers

Camden (NJ) Courier-Post. January 27, 1953.

Haddonfield (NJ) Letter Basket and General Advertiser. June 1877

Newark (NJ) Star Ledger. Henry Beck. April 16, 1950.

4 Education and Houses of Worship

Manuscripts

Camden, NJ. Camden County Historical Society. Building Contracts: Haddon School District, A-243. Rowandtown School, No. 114. Collingswood School, No. 589. Gloucester Township School Register 1870-1871.

Collingswood, NJ. Whiley, Charles. Private research.

Haddonfield, NJ. The Historical Society of Haddonfield. "Catalogue of St. Agnes' Hall and St. John's Military Academy (Episcopal Schools) Haddonfield, NJ 1886-1887. Friends Academy Brochure, 1877-1878. The "Old Grove School," Sarah Shivers Murray Papers. Reilly Papers. Hinchman Papers. Ameilia Hopkins Diary.

New Brunswick, NJ. Rutgers University Library. Joseph O. Cuthbert Farm Journal. Statement of Finances of Grace Church, Haddonfield. March 1867.

Philadelphia, PA. Free Library of Philadelphia. Sanborn Fire Insurance Map–Westmont. (microform) Sandborn Map and Publishing Co. Ltd. 1887.

Woodbury, NJ. Gloucester County Historical Society. Survey for James Glover's Woodlands (A-304). 1839.

Government Documents

Camden County, NJ. Clerk's Office. Deed Books: Trustees of the First Baptist Meeting, 11-351.

New Jersey. *Revised Statutes of the State of New Jersey passed 1874.* Schools. (p. 772-777). Trenton, NJ: Printed by Order of Governor. 1874.

New Jersey. *Annual Report of the Superintendent of Public Schools of the State of New Jersey.* 1864 to 1875 consulted.

Maps

A Plan of the City of Philadelphia and Environs. Survey by John Hills in the Summers of 1801, 1802, 1803, 1804, 1805, 1806, 1807. Philadelphia, PA: William Kneass. 1808 (Camden County Historical Society, M83.90.714)

Printed Sources

Finkelstein, Barbara. *Governing the Young–Teacher Behavior in Popular Primary Schools in Nineteenth-Century United States.* Philadelphia, PA: The Falmer Press. 1989.

Griffiths, Thomas S. *A History of Baptist in New Jersey.* Hightstown, NJ: Bar Press Publishing. 1904.

The History Book Committee. *This is Haddonfield.* Haddonfield, NJ: The Historical Society of Haddonfield. 1963.

Hoogenboom, Ari and Olive. *The Guilded Age.* Englewood Cliffs, NJ: Prentice Hall, Inc. 1967.

Levy, Barry. *Quakers and the American Family–British Settlement in the Delaware Valley.* New York, NY: Oxford University Press, Inc. 1988.

New Jersey State Literacy Union. *The Northern Monthly Vol. 1 No. 6.* "The New School Law." Newark, NJ: M.R. Dennis and Co. 1867.

Nicholson, William H. *My Ancestors.* Philadelphia, PA: Austin C. Leeds. 1897.

Publication Committee. *Collingswood–The First One Hundred Years 1888-1988.* Collingswood, NJ: 1988.

Thomas, Dorothy Kille. Ed. *Haddonfield United Methodist Church: A Sesquicentennial History 1829-1979.* Compiled by the Archives and History Committee of the Church. Haddonfield, NJ. 1979.

Weigley, Russell F., Ed. *Philadelphia–A 300 Year History.* New York, NY: W.W. Norton and Co. 1982.

Newspapers

New York, Daily Graphic. September 9, 1879.

5 National and Local Issues of the Era

Manuscripts

Camden, NJ. Camden County Historical Society. Survey of James Stoy land, Jacob Rowand. (M83.90.260). 1861. Unidentified Newspaper Article "Pauper Graveyard." February, March 1879.

Haddonfield, NJ. The Historical Society of Haddonfield. Amelia Hopkins Diary. Notes by Mr. and Mrs. Haydock on conversations with Walter Stoy, 1945, Stoy Papers. Wood Papers, Jehu Wood

Diary. "The Old Grove School," Sarah Shivers Murray Papers. Henry Cuthbert's Account Book.

Woodbury, NJ. Gloucester County Historical Society. Survey of Isaac Wood's land, (A-260). 1839. "Haddon Grange's Beginning," Viola E. Garwood. 1947.

Government Documents

Camden County, NJ. Clerk's Office. Deed Books: Joseph Stokely, 117-11, 117-13. Christopher Smiley, 93-224. Jefferson Fisher, 32-99. Josiah Hinson, 58-225. James Fussell, 58-225, 54-128, 107-308, 88-656. Joshua Saddler, X-395. Charles Fussell, 107-250, 109-321, 98-334.

Camden County, NJ. Surrogate's Office. Inventory of: Charles Faucett, R-116. Rebecca Fussell, P-145. Benjamin Pearce, T-470. William Monroe, A-373.

Camden County, NJ. Surrogate's Office. Will of: Isaac Hinson, H-459. Rebecca Fussell, GG-35. Charles Faucett, NN-1. Joshua Saddler, G-261. Julia Smiley, F-96. Anna Fisher, 54-100. Benjamin Pearce, YY-423. Phoebe Adams, ZZ-469. Samuel Monroe, UU-168.

Camden County, NJ. Surrogate's Office. Miscellaneous Records Book: Thomas Smilley, Book #1, p. 124.

New Jersey. *Acts of the Ninety-Seventh Legislature of the State of New Jersey.* An act to regulate the Sale of Malt, Vinous and Spirituous Liquor in the township of Haddon. (p. 620, 621). Morristown, NJ: Vance and Stiles. 1873.

New Jersey. *New Jersey Equity Reports, No. 24. Reports of Cases Argued and Determined in The Court of Chancery, The Prerogative Court, and, on Appeal, in The Court of Errors and Appeals of the State of New Jersey. Vol IX.* The Attorney-General v. Brown. Trenton, NJ: MacCrellish and Quigley. 1897.

Printed Sources

Devine, Robert, Breen T.H., Fredrickson, George, Williams, R. Hal. *America Past and Present.* Glenview, IL: Foresman and Company. 1987.

Foster, John Y. *New Jersey and the Rebellion.* Newark, NJ: Published by the Authority of the State. 1868.

House of Collectibles, Inc. *The Official Blackbook Price Guide of United State Coins.* Orlando, Florida. 1980.

McGoldrick, Neal and Crocco, Margaret. *Reclaiming Lost Ground: The Struggle for Woman Suffrage in New Jersey.* McGoldrick and Crocco. 1993.

McPherson, James M. *Battle Cry Freedom.* New York: Oxford University Press. 1988.

Miers, Earl Schenck. *New Jersey and the Civil War.* Princeton, NJ: D. Van Nostrand Company, Inc. 1964.

New Jersey Historical Commission. *An Outline of Black History in New Jersey.* Trenton, NJ: Department of State. 1983.

Peyton, Jesse E. *Reminiscences of Philadelphia During the Past Half Century.* Haddonfield, NJ. 1888.

Peyton, Jesse E. *Reminiscences of the Past.* Philadelphia, PA: J.B. Lippincott Company. 1895.

Thomas, Dorothy Kille. Ed. *Haddonfield United Methodist Church: A Sesquicentennial History 1829–1979.* Compiled by the Archives and History Committee of the Church. 1979.

Trescott, Paul B. *Financing American Enterprise–The Story of Commercial Banking.* New York: Harper and Row. 1963.

Vinovskis, Maria A. Ed. *Towards A Special History of the American Civil War.* New York: Cambridge University Press. 1990.

Wait, George W. *New Jersey's Money.* Newark, NJ: The Newark Museum. 1976.

Weigley, Russell F., Ed. *Philadelphia–A 300 Year History.* New York: W.W. Norton and Company. 1982.

Wright, Giles R. *Afro-Americans in New Jersey–A Short History.* Trenton, NJ: New Jersey Historical Commission, Department of State. 1988.

6 Information and Communication

Manuscripts

Trenton, NJ. New Jersey State Archives. "Camden and Atlantic Railroad Company Annual Statements." 1872 to 1883 consulted.

Printed Sources

Boyer, Charles S. *History of the Press in Camden County, New Jersey.* Camden, NJ: West Jersey Press. 1921.

Boyer, Charles S. *The Span of a Century–The Chronicle History of the City of Camden 1828–1928.* Camden, NJ: Centennial Anniversary Committee. 1927.

Devine, Robert, Breen T.H., Fredrickson, George, Williams, R. Hal. *America Past and Present.* Glenview, IL. Foresman and Company. 1987.

Industries of New Jersey–Part II. New York: Historical Publishers Company. 1882.

Schopp, Paul W. *Camden County History Journal.* "Wired Lightning–The Arrival of the Telegraph in South

Jersey." Camden, NJ: Camden County Historical Society. September 1995.

7 Life Styles and Routines

Manuscripts

Haddonfield, NJ. The Historical Society of Haddonfield. Jehu, Jr., Samuel, and Elizabeth Wood Diaries. Wood Papers.

Trenton, NJ. New Jersey State Archives. "Camden and Atlantic Railroad Company Annual Statements." 1872 to 1883 consulted.

Printed Sources

Hartel, Carrie E. Nicholson. "The New Jersey Building." 1949. Haddonfield, NJ: Historical Society Publications. 1975.

Weigley, Russell F., Ed. *Philadelphia–A 300 Year History.* New York: W.W. Norton and Company. 1982.

8 Agriculture

Manuscripts

Camden, NJ. Camden County Historical Society. "Historical Clippings Relative to Camden, NJ." Assembled by John Carney.

Collingswood, NJ. Collingswood Library. Samuel French Account Book.

Haddonfield, NJ. The Historical Society of Haddonfield. Henry Cuthbert's Account Book. Wood Papers and Diaries.

Woodbury, NJ. Gloucester County Historical Society. "Haddon Grange Beginning" Viola E. Garwood. 1947.

Government Documents

Camden County, NJ. Surrogate's Office. Inventory of: Joseph Hollingshead, Q-62. William H. Nicholson, P-56. William C. Nicholson, K-363.

New Jersey. *Annual Report New Jersey State Board of Agriculture.* 1879 and 1880 consulted.

New Jersey. *Report of the State Agricultural Society of New Jersey.* 1856 and 1857 consulted.

Printed Sources

Encyclopedia Americana. "Mules," Danbury, CT: Grolier Inc. 1994.

Jones, Joseph. *Early Recollection of Camden and the Adjoining County by an Old Citizen. Camden History Vol. 1 No. 10, 11, 12.* Reprinted by West Jersey Press. Edited by Charles Boyer. Camden County Historical Society. 1935.

Nicholson, William H. *My Ancestors.* Philadelphia, PA: Austin C. Leeds. 1897.

Schmidt, Hubert G. *Agriculture in New Jersey–A Three-Hundred-Year History.* New Brunswick, NJ: Rutgers University Press. 1973.

Wigginton, Eliot, Ed. *Foxfire 3.* "Animal Care." Garden City, NY: Anchor Books. 1975.

9 Industry and Shopkeepers

Manuscripts

Camden, NJ. Camden County Historical Society. Bolger, William. *The Lucas Paint Works–A Historical and Architectural Record* Two Volumes. 1982. Unidentified Newspaper "Pauper Graveyards." February and March 1879. Directory of Haddon Township 1895, Tribune Publishing Company. Building Contract: James Flinn and John Willits and Wm. Hoopes and Sons, #249. Notes on W.S. Clement Paint Company, Interview by William Leap. 1983.

Greenville, DE. The Hagley Library. *Dunn and Bradstreet–1850.* (microform)

Haddonfield, NJ. The Historical Society of Haddonfield. "Charles Lippincott," Sarah Shivers Murray Papers. Henry Cuthbert's Account Book. Estate of George Lee Papers, Rowand Papers. Stoy Papers. Wood Papers and Diaries.

Philadelphia, PA. Free Library of Philadelphia. Sanborn Fire Insurance Map–Haddonfield. Sanborn Map and Publishing Co. Ltd. 1887.

Woodbury, NJ. Gloucester County Historical Society. Agreement- Diversion of Water to Mill Pond, Sharpless-Taylor. 1848. Account Book and Burial Records of Henry C. Kendig, Paulsboro, NJ.

Interviews

Morgan, Elizabeth. Interviewed by the author. Haddon Township, NJ. January 1988.

Government Documents

Camden, NJ. *Acts of Incorporation of the City of Camden, and the Supplements Thereto; Together with the Ordinances of the City Council.* "To prohibit the erection of wooden buildings within the limits of the City of Camden, February 24, 1853." Camden, NJ: J.H. Jones and Company. 1857.

Camden County, NJ. Clerk's Office. Deed Books: James Flinn, 78-555, 81-36, 110-167.

Camden County, NJ. Surrogate's Office. Inventory of: David Albertson, H-51, I-374. Joseph Bates, M-344. Thomas Williams, N-377. Samuel Matlack, M-361. Kimber Clement, C-521. William McKnight, D-256. Joseph Engle, E-172. Samuel Burroughs, D-50. Richard Snowden, G-288.

Camden County, NJ. Surrogate's Office. Will of: Thomas Williams, CC-339. William McKnight, D-462. Joseph Engle, E-488. Samuel Burroughs, D-189. William C. Githens, G-216. Richard Snowden H-395.

New Jersey. *Compiled Statutes of New Jersey. Volume 3.* "Mills and Mill-Dams." (p. 3396-3399). Newark, NJ: Soney and Sage. 1911.

New Jersey. *Geological Survey of New Jersey. Volume III.* "Report of Water-Supply." Trenton, NJ: The John L. Murphy Publishing Company. 1894.

Printed Sources

Arbor, Marilyn. *Tools and Trades of America's Past.* Doylestown, PA: The Mercer Collection, The Bucks County Historical Society. 1981.

Boyd, William H. (Compiler) *Boyd's General Directory of Camden, New Jersey.* Philadelphia, PA: William H. Boyd, Directory Publisher. 1860.

Boyer, Charles S. *Old Mills of Camden County.* Camden, NJ: Camden County Historical Society. 1962.

Bradfield, Nancy. *Costume in Detail.* Boston, MA: Plays Inc. 1983.

Carr, Jess. *The Second Oldest Profession–An Informal History of Moonshining in America.* Englewood Cliffs, NJ: Prentice-Hall Inc. 1972.

Coffin, Margaret. *The History and Folklore of American County Tinware 1700-1900.* New York: Galahad Books. 1968.

Davis, Charles Thomas. *A Practical Treatise on the Manufacture of Bricks, Tiles, Terra-Cotta Etc.* Philadelphia, PA: Henry Carey Baird and Co. 1884.

Drost, William, E. *Clocks and Watches of New Jersey.* Elizabeth, NJ: Engineering Publishers. 1966.

Fitz-Gerald, W.N. *The Harness Makers' Illustrated Manual.* NY: 1875. Reprint ed. Croton-on-Hudson, NY: North River Press, Inc. 1977.

Hartel, Carrie E. Nicholson. *The Tanyard and Its Owners.* Publication No. 1. Haddonfield, NJ: Haddonfield Historical Society. 1922.

Hazen, Edward. *The Panorama of Professions and Trades.* Philadelphia, PA: Uriah Hunt. 1836.

Hillman, Sarah Crawford. *Historical Sketch of Potter Street in Haddonfield, New Jersey.* Haddonfield, NJ: Haddon Gazette Press. 1910.

Industries of New Jersey–Part II. NY: Historical Publishing Company. 1882.

New Jersey State Gazetteer and Business Directory 1882-1883 Vol. 1. Philadelphia, PA: R.E. Polk Company. 1882.

N. and G. Taylor Company. (Paul W. Schopp Collection.) *Selling Arguments for Tin Roofing.* Philadelphia PA: N.and G. Taylor Company. 1911.

19th Century American Carriages. Stony Brook, NY: The Museum of Stony Brook. 1987.

Reilly, James. *The Albumen and Salted Paper Book.* Rochester, NY: Light Impressions Corporation. 1980.

Richardson, M.T. *Practical Blacksmithing.* New York: Weathervane Books. 1978.

Ries, Heinrick, and Kummel, Henry B. *Geological Survey of New Jersey. The Clays and Clay Industry of New Jersey Final Report Vol. VI.* Trenton, NJ: MacCrellish and Quigley. 1904.

Von Rosensteil, Helen. *American Rugs and Carpets from the Seventeenth Century to Modern Times.* New York: William Morrow and Company. 1978.

Weiss, Harry B. and Grace. *Early Brickmaking in New Jersey.* Trenton, NJ: New Jersey Agricultural Society. 1966.

Weiss, Harry, and Sim, Robert. *The Early Grist and Flouring Mill of New Jersey.* Trenton, NJ: New Jersey Agricultural Society. 1956.

Weiss, Harry and Grace. *The Early Sawmills of New Jersey.* Trenton, NJ: New Jersey Agricultural Society. 1968.

Weiss, Harry B. *The History of Applejack.* Trenton, NJ: New Jersey Agricultural Society. 1954.

Weiss, Harry B. and Kemble, Howard R. *They Took to the Waters.* Trenton, NJ. The Past Times Press. 1962.

Newspapers

Camden County (NJ) Courier. July 31, 1880

New York, Daily Graphic. September 9, 1879.

Haddonfield, Collingswood, Westmont (NJ) Tri-City Sun. June 11, 1925.

10 Tradesmen, Storekeepers, Professions and Other Workers

Manuscripts

Camden, NJ. Camden County Historical Society. Building Contracts: Rowandtown School House, No. 114. Haddon School District, No. A-243. The Haddon District, No. 617. *Articles of Incorporation and By-Laws of the Mount Ephraim and Haddonfield Mutual Pursing Company.*

Haddonfield, NJ. The Historical Society of Haddonfield. Wood Papers. Hinchman Papers. Henry Cuthbert's Account Book. Sarah Shivers Murray Papers. "History of the Old Tavern House in Haddonfield," John R. Stevenson A.M.M., M.D. 1906.

Trenton, NJ New Jersey State Archives. "Camden and Atlantic Railroad Company Annual Statements." 1872 to 1883 consulted.

Government Documents

Camden County, NJ. Clerk's Office. Deed Books: Edward C. Knight, 108-168.

Camden County, NJ. Surrogate's Office. Inventory of Rennels Fowler, E-566.

New Jersey. *Statutes of the State of New Jersey–1847.* An act concerning inns and taverns. (p. 581). Trenton, NJ: Phillips and Boswell. 1847.

U.S. Department of Treasury. Internal Revenue Service. *IRService Doc No. 6862.* 1987.

U.S. Department of Treasury. *Report of the Commissioner of Internal Revenue, Year Ended June 30, 1863.* Washington, D.C.: Government Printing Office. 1864.

Printed Sources

Arbor, Marilyn. *Tools and Trades of America's Past.* Doylestown, PA: The Mercer Collection, The Bucks County Historical Society. 1981.

Beers, F.W. *State Atlas of New Jersey.* New York, NY: Beers, Comstock and CLine. 1872.

Biographical Review Volume XIX–Camden and Burlington Counties, New Jersey. Boston, MA: Biographical Review Publishing Co. 1897.

Brody, David. *The Butcher Workmen–A Study of Unionization.* Cambridge, MA: Harvard University Press. 1964.

Carr, Jess. *The Second Oldest Profession–An Informal History of Moonshining in America.* Englewood Cliffs, NJ: Prentice-Hall Inc. 1972.

Christie, Robert A. *Empire In Wood–A History of the Carpenters' Union.* Ithaca, NY: Cornell University. 1956.

Corbett, L.C. *Ice Houses.* U.S. Department of Agriculture–Farmers Bulletin 475. Washington, D.C.: Government Printing Office. 1917.

Depew, Chauncey M. *One Hundred Years of American Commerce.* NY: Greenwood Press. 1968.

Devine, Robert, Breen T.H., Fredrickson, George, Williams, R. Hal. *America Past and Present.* Glenview, IL. Foresman and Company. 1987.

Encyclopedia Americana. "Mules." Canbury, CT: Grolier Inc. 1994.

Fuller, Wayne E. *The American Mail–Enlarger of the Common Life.* Chicago, IL: The University of Chicago Press. 1972.

Hazen, Edward. *The Panorama of Professions and Trades.* Philadelphia, PA: Uriah Hunt. 1836.

Keasbey, Edward Q. *The Courts and Lawyers of New Jersey, 1661-1912.* NY: Lewis Historical Publishing Company. 1912.

Kirk, Margaret O. *The Story of Cooper Hospital.* Camden, NJ: Cooper Hospital/University Medical Center. 1987.

New Jersey State Gazetteer and Business Directory 1882-1883. Vol. Philadelphia, PA: R.E. Polk Company. 1882.

Hillman, Sarah Crawford. *Historical Sketch of Potter Street in Haddonfield, New Jersey.* Haddonfield, NJ: Haddon Gazette Press. 1910.

Industries of New Jersey–Part II. NY: Historical Publishing Company. 1882.

Museums at Stony Brook. *19th Century American Carriages.* Stony Brook, NY: The Museums at Stony Brook. 1987.

Proceedings, Constitution, By-Laws, List of Members of the Surveyors' Association of West New Jersey. Camden, NJ: S. Chew, Printer. 1880.

Richardson, M.T. Ed. *Practical Blacksmithing.* NY: Weathervane Books. 1978.

Scheele, Carl H. *A Short History of the Mail Service.* Washington, D.C.: Smithsonian Institution Press. 1970.

Schmidt, Hubert G. *Agriculture in New Jersey–A Three-Hundred-Year History.* New Brunswick, NJ: Rutgers University Press. 1973.

[Smith, Hanna Whitall.] *John M. Whitall, the story of his life.* Philadelphia, PA: N.P. 1879.

Snape, William J. M.D. *The Rise and Fall of John Buchanan "M.D"* Bulletin Vol. 6, No. 1. Camden, NJ: Camden County Historical Society. December, 1970.

Wigginton, Eliot, Ed. *Foxfire 4.* "Horse Trading." Garden City, NY: Anchor Books. 1977.

Newspapers

Haddonfield (NJ) Letter Basket and General Advertiser June 1877.

Philadelphia Bulletin. "Pursuing Company Still in Business Catching Thieves After 94 Years." (Clipping at Camden County Historical Society). circa 1964.

11 Audubon and Audubon Park

Manuscript Collections

Camden, NJ. Camden County Historical Society. "History of Audubon Park" (Vertical File). No Date. Survey of Ridgeway Glover's "Dillworth Tract," Edward H. Saunders, 1856. (M83.110.3.415).

Haddonfield, NJ. The Historical Society of Haddonfield. "Private road across J. Nicholson's farm for John Dialogue." Abstract of Title to Horatio Wood's farm.

Philadelphia, PA. Historical Society of Pennsylvania. Clement Papers. Map of Joseph Nicholson's land, John Clement. 1874.

Woodbury, NJ. Gloucester County Historical Society. Survey of John Cook's Farm by J. Rowand, (B-66). 1858.

Interviews

Fox, Edward. Interviewed by the author. Collingswood, NJ. October 1991.

Hartell, Joseph. Interviewed by the author. Haddonfield, NJ. July 1991.

Government Documents

Camden, County, NJ. Clerk's Office. Deed Books: Joseph Howell, 124-311. Joseph Ewen, 103-238. Joseph Eldridge, 93-653.

Camden County, NJ. Surrogate's Office: Assignment Book: Mary Carson, A-43. Charles Bettle, A-15.

Camden County, NJ. Surrogate's Office: Inventory of: William H. Nicholson, P-56. William C. Nicholson, K-363. John Cook, B-654. Joseph Ewen, G-253. Jacob F. Dodd, H-292. Joseph Nicholson, F-379. John A.J. Sheets, I-61. Joseph Eldridge, C-406, C-406. James Eldridge, H-331.

Camden County, NJ. Surrogate's Office: Will of: William Bettle, J-341. William H. Nicholson, GG-453. John Cook, B-741. Joseph Ewen, H-362. Joseph Nicholson, G-331. John Kaighn, D-395. Joseph Eldridge, C-477.

New Jersey. *Acts of the One Hundred and Twenty-Fifty Legislature of the State of New Jersey.* A act to incorporate the borough of Audubon. (p. 47-48). Paterson, NJ: News Printing Company. 1905.

Printed Sources

Audubon Celebration Committee and The Audubon Tercentenary Committee. *Audubon–Celebration of the New Jersey Tercentenary 1664-1964.* Audubon, NJ. 1964.

Boyer, Charles S. *Old Mills of Camden County.* Camden, NJ: Camden County Historical Society. 1962.

Fiftieth Anniversary 1905–1955. Audubon, NJ. 1955.

Gopsill's Sons, Publishers. *Philadelphia City Directory for 1887.* Philadelphia, PA: Gopsill's Son, Publishers. 1887.

Kogan, Kenneth. *New Jersey History, Vol. 108 No. 1 and 2.* New "John H. Dialogue–Shipbuilding Pioneer on the Delaware River." 1990.

Nicholson, William H. *My Ancestors.* Philadelphia, PA: Austin C. Leeds. 1897.

Newspapers

Camden (NJ) Courier-Post. December 13, 1941.

12 Camden (Fairview)

Manuscripts

Camden, NJ. Camden County Historical Society. *Fairview–Camden's Best Kept Secret* by L.H. Schuldiner. (Typescript Report). 1981.

Collingswood, NJ. Whiley, Charles. Private Research. "Minutes of the Haddonfield Monthly Meeting–December 12, 1831."

Interviews

Whiley, Charles. Interviewed by the author. Collingswood, NJ. November 7, 1992.

Government Documents

Camden, County, NJ. Clerk's Office. Deed Book: Samuel C. Cooper, 138-2.

Camden County, NJ. Surrogate's Office: Inventory of Samuel C. Champion, A-112.

Camden County, NJ. Surrogate's Office: Will of: Peter Stutzer, C-142. Joseph Shoemaker, AA-55.

Printed Sources

Boyer, Charles S. *Rambles Through Old Highways and Byways of West Jersey.* Camden, NJ: Camden County Historical Society. 1967.

Timmins, Dr. William D. and Robert Yarring, W. *Betsy Ross–the Griscom Legacy.* Salem, NJ: Salem County Cultural and Heritage Commission. 1983.

Weiss, Harry and Grace. *Early Brickmaking in New Jersey.* Trenton, NJ: New Jersey Agricultural Society. 1966.

Weiss, Harry B. and Kemble, Howard R. *They Took to the Waters.* Trenton, NJ: The Past Times Press. 1962.

13 Collingswood

Manuscripts

Camden, NJ. Camden County Historical Society. "Historical Clippings Relative to Camden, NJ." Assembled by John Carney.

Collingswood, NJ. Collingswood Library. George Palmer Papers. The Manor House of Collingswood, NJ. N.D. Untitled newspaper article, February 16, 1892. Samuel French Account Ledger.

Greenville, DE. The Hagley Library. *Dun and Bradstreet–1850.* (microform)

Philadelphia, PA. Historical Society of Pennsylvania. Franklin Fire Insurance Company of Philadelphia. Survey No. 21437, John DaCosta.

Riverton, NJ. Paul W. Schopp Collection. Survey of proposed Railroad Right-of-Way. H.C. Smith. August 1883.

Woodbury, NJ. Gloucester County Historical Society. Survey of Samuel French Farm, 1865 (C-14).

Government Documents

Camden County, NJ. Clerk's Office. Deed Books: 85-122. 58-417. 60-54. 75-497. 51-103. 50-349. 81-351. 37-384. 68-480. 54-257. 75-501. 45-196. 50-349. 54-386. 85-487. 108-168. Anna Marie Collings, R-539, T-570, N-281, 49-257, 60-54, 58-417, 75-497, T-570. Edward Z. Collings, 54-386. John DaCosta, 50-349. Robert McLaughlin, 90-355, 111-56. John Campbell, 129-122, 129-578, 87-326. Jacob S. Collings, 91-483. William P. Tatem, 65-518. James DaCosta, 81-351. Edward C. Knight, 54-386, 85-487. Nathan Clement, L-296. Joseph B. Tatem, R-490, R-539, K-79, V-260. Robert Wood, 68-480, 37-384. Isaac Prine, 108-168. Samuel H. French, 45-196. Mahlon Van Booskirk, 54-257.

Camden County, NJ. Surrogate's Office. Inventory of: Joseph B. Cooper, C-48. Joseph C. Collings, B-707. Jacob S. Collings, D-424. James Dobbs, E-165. George Lee, C-283. William McIlhaney, B-826. Amos Willis, Sr., F-54. Mahlon Van Booskirk, I-181. Joseph B. Tatem, G-175. William Fortiner, C-346. John Kaighn, D-196. Samuel Tatem, I-457. George Stratton, K-274.

Camden County, NJ. Surrogate's Office. Will of: Joseph B. Cooper, C-84. Joseph C. Collings, B-705. Joseph S. Collings, E-211. James Dobbs, E-480. John C. DaCosta, I-470. Joseph A. Collings, TT-189. Joseph S. Collings, HH-225. William McIlhaney, B-876. William P. Tatem, S-329. Amos Willis, Sr. F-427. Peter Wagner, 56-207. Joseph B. Tatem G-175. William Jones, II-381. John Kaighn, D-395. Charles Whiley, 69-478. Chalkey Parker, EE-154.

New Jersey. *Acts of the One Hundred and Thirty-Fifth Legislature of the State of New Jersey.* A act to ratify, confirm the incorporation of Collingswood and to fix the boundaries and corporate name. (p. 41, 42). Paterson, NJ: News Printing Company. 1911.

New Jersey. *Acts of the One Hundred and Forty-Eighth Legislature of the State of New Jersey.* A act to annex the township of Haddon, a portion of Collingswood. (p. 376-377). Trenton, NJ: MacCrellish and Quigley. 1924.

New Jersey. *Acts of the One Hundred and Seventy-Sixth Legislature of the State of New Jersey.* A act to relocate, fix and establish the boundary line between Collingswood and the township of Haddon. (p. 1399-1403). Trenton, NJ: MacCrellish and Quigley. 1953.

U.S. Department of Agriculture. *Report to Commissioner of Agriculture for the year 1866.* "Wine Making and Vine Culture. Washington, D.C.: Government Printing Office. 1867.

Printed Sources

Bicentennial Committee. *The Collingswood Bicentennial Book.* Collingswood, NJ. 1976.

The Biographical Encyclopedia of New Jersey of the 19th Century. Philadelphia, PA: Galaxy Publishing Company. 1877.

Biographical Review Vol. XIX Camden and Burlington Counties, New Jersey. Boston Biographical Review Publishing Company. 1897.

Boyer, Charles S. Morgan, John, Ed. *Rambles Through Old Highways and Byways of West Jersey.* Camden, NJ: Camden County Historical Society. 1967.

Butler, Frank. *Book of the Boardwalk.* Atlantic City, NJ: Haines and Company. 1952.

Cohen's Philadelphia City Directory of 1860. Philadelphia, PA: Hamelin and Company. 1860.

French, Howard B. *Genealogy of the Descendants of Thomas French.* Philadelphia, PA. 1913.

Jones, Joseph. Edited by Charles Boyer. *Early Recollections of Camden and the Adjoining County by An Old Citizen. Camden History Vol. 1 No. 10, 11, 12.* Camden, NJ: Reprinted by West Jersey Press. 1935.

Palmer, George A. "A Collingswood Centennial Walking Tour for 1985. Collingswood, NJ: Collings-Knight Homestead Committee, Collingswood Library. 1985. "A Collingswood Centennial Walking Tour for 1986." Collingswood, NJ: Collings-Knight Homestead Committee, Collingswood Library. 1986. "A Collingswood Centennial Walking and Automobile Tour for 1987." Collingswood, NJ: Collings-Knight Homestead Committee, Collingswood Library. 1987. "A Collingswood Centennial Walking and Automobile Tour for 1988." Collingswood, NJ: Collings-Knight Homestead Committee, Collingswood Library. 1988.

Publication Committee. *Collingswood–The First One Hundred Years 1888-1988.* Collingswood, NJ: Centennial Committee. 1988.

Smith, Edward Y. "Dungarvan" The Excelsior Scottish Rite Temple West Collingswood, New Jersey." Paper presented before Triple Tau Council No. 54, A.M.D. April 1, 1986.

Towle, Charles L. "History of the Camden and Atlantic Railroad 1852—1897." Bulletin No. 73. Boston, MA: The Railway and Locomotive Historical Society, Inc. Harvard Business School. 1948.

Weiss, Harry B. and Kemble, Howard R. *They Took to the Water.* Trenton, NJ: The Part Time Press. 1962.

Newspapers

Philadelphia Inquirer. March 26, 1875.

Philadelphia Public Ledger. March 24, 1875.

14 Gloucester City

Manuscripts

Camden, NJ. Camden County Historical Society. Building Contract, Matilda Henry, 1853. Survey of John Logan's land, John Clement. 1866.

Government Documents

New Jersey. *Acts of the One Hundred and Fifty-First Legislature of the State of New Jersey.* A act to annex a portion of township of Haddon, to the city of Gloucester. (p. 463-468). Trenton, NJ: MacCrellish and Quigley. 1927.

15 Haddonfield

Manuscripts

Camden, NJ. Camden County Historical Society. Building Contracts: T. M. Reilly, No. 431. Jehu Wood, Jr., No. 349. Survey of John Gill's land, J. Rowand, (#154). 1863.

Haddonfield, NJ. The Historical Society of Haddonfield. Henry Cuthbert Account Book. The Reilly Papers. The Wood Papers. Map of Joseph M. Hinchman's land, Samuel Nicholson. Hinchman Papers. Sarah Shivers Murray Papers. Amelia Hopkins Diary.

Philadelphia, PA. Historical Society of Pennsylvania. Clement Papers. Map of Cooper Road, John Clement, N.D (No. 4). The Franklin Fire Insurance Company of Philadelphia. Survey 1101, Thomas Redman.

Interviews

Fox, Edward. Interviewed by the author. Collingswood, NJ. October, 1991.

Government Documents

Camden County, NJ. Clerk's Office. Deed Books: 57-323. 54-536. 67-599. 67-603. 67-605. 65-236. Nathan Lippincott, 41-226, 41-214. William C. Hinchman, 154-419. William Coffin, 54-536. William Massey, 54-536, 67-599, 67-603, 67-605, 57-323. William Mann, 65-236. Aaron C. Clement, 47-593.

Camden County, NJ. Surrogate's Office. Inventory of: Samuel Allen, F-303. John Gill, H-41. William C. Hinchman, L-377. Joseph Lippincott, K-12. James S. Lippincott, H-114. Samuel Nicholson, H-58. Josiah Evans, C-513. Jesse Peyton, L-47. David Roe, Sr., B-804. Theophilus Reilly, O-269. John E. Redman, N-40. Charles H. Shinn, D-1. Joseph C. Stoy, G-156. Issac Wood, F-171. Jehu Wood, G-215. William S. Doughten, G-87. Aaron C. Clement, I-324. Joseph Stokley, E-314.

Camden County, NJ. Surrogate's Office. Will of: Samuel Allen, G-172. John Gill, I-291. William C. Hinchman, U-362. John E. Hopkins, I-281. Nathan Lippincott, EE-428. Joseph Lippincott, Q-86.

Samuel Nicholson, I-370. William Massey, N-143. Josiah B. Evans, D-68. Jesse Peyton, T-221. David Roe, Sr., B-804. Theophilus Reilly, EE-340. Isaac Wood, Jehu Wood, H-319. Aaron C. Clement, L-470. Joseph Stokley, F-112.

New Jersey. *Acts of the One Hundred and Twenty-Seventh Legislature of the State of New Jersey.* A act to annex a portion of the township of Haddon to the Borough of Haddonfield. (p. 55-57). Trenton, NJ: MacCrellish and Quigley. 1904.

New Jersey. *Acts of the One Hundred and Fiftieth Legislature of the State of New Jersey.* A act annexing to the borough of Haddonfield, a part of Centre township. (p. 140-141). Trenton, NJ: MacCrellish and Quigley. 1926.

New Jersey. *Acts of the One Hundred and Sixty-Fifth Legislature of the State of New Jersey.* A act to annex the borough of Haddonfield, a part of township of Haddon. (p. 921-922). Trenton, NJ: MacCrellish and Quigley. 1941.

New Jersey. *Acts of the One Hundred and Seventy-First Legislature of the State of New Jersey.* A act to relocate, fix and establish the boundary line between the borough of Haddonfield and the borough of Haddon Heights. (p. 1100-1103). Trenton, NJ: MacCrellish and Quigley. 1947.

New Jersey. *Acts of the One Hundred and Seventy-Fifth Legislature of the State of New Jersey.* A act to relocate, fix and establish the boundary line between the borough of Haddonfield and the borough of Haddon Heights. (p. 705-707). Trenton, NJ: MacCrellish and Quigley. 1951.

Printed Sources

Biographical Review Vol. XIX Camden and Burlington Counties, New Jersey. Boston Biographical Review Publishing Company. 1897.

Cook, George H. *Geology of New Jersey.* Printed at the Daily Advertiser Office 1868.

Evaul, Philip. *The Hinchman Line.* Newland NC.

Gill, Julia B. *A Brief History of Mountwell.* Haddonfield, NJ: Haddonfield Historical Society. 1922.

Hartel, Carrie E. Nicholson. *Estaugh Plantation–Wood Farm.* Haddonfield, NJ: Haddonfield Historical Society. 1947.

Hartel, Carrie E. Nicholson. *The Original Papers of Carrie E. Nicholson Hartel–The New Jersey Building.* Haddonfield, NJ: The Historical Society of Haddonfield. 1975.

Hartel, Carrie E. Nicholson. *The Tanyard and its Owners.* Haddonfield, NJ: Haddonfield Historical Society. 1922.

Nicholson, William H. *My Ancestors.* Philadelphia, PA: Press of Austin C. Leeds. 1897.

Peyton, Jesse E. *Reminiscences of the Past.* Philadelphia, PA: J.B. Lippincott. 1895.

Peyton, Jesse E. *Reminiscences of Philadelphia During the Past Half Century.* Haddonfield, NJ. 1888.

Vermeule, C.C. *Geological Survey of New Jersey. Report on Water-Supply Vol. III.* The Final Report of the State Geologist. Trenton, NJ: The John L. Murphy Publishing Company. 1894.

Weiss, Harry and Sim, Robert. *The Early Grist and Flour Mill of New Jersey.* Trenton, NJ: New Jersey Agricultural Society. 1956.

Willits, Alfred C. *Ancestors and Descendants of James and Ann Willits of Little Egg Harbor, NJ.* Homesburg, Philadelphia, PA. 1898

16 Haddon Heights

Manuscripts

Camden, NJ. Camden County Historical Society. Survey of Ridgeway Glover's "Dillworth Tract," Edward H. Saunders, 1856. (M83.110.3.415)

Haddonfield, NJ. The Historical Society of Haddonfield. Jehu Wood, Jr. Diary 1864.

Philadelphia, PA. Historical Society of Pennsylvania. John Clement Papers. Survey of Benjamin and Joseph Lippincott's land, 1877 (No. 23).

Woodbury, NJ. Gloucester County Historical Society. Survey of James Glover's Woodlands. (A-304). 1839.

Interviews

Fox, Edward. Interviewed by the author. Collingswood, NJ. October 1991, November 1997.

Leap, William. Interviewed by the author. Haddon Heights, NJ. November 1997

Government Documents

Camden County, NJ. Clerk's Office. Deed Books: 31-586. 31-588. Benjamin Cooper, L-387. Robert Roe, L-343, 103-238. Jacob F. Dodd, 100-651, 88-237. Stephen G. Collins, 88-129. Maria Glover, 31-588. John Glover, 31-586, 36-582. Joseph B. Howell, 124-311. Benjamin D. Cooper, L-397, E-506.

Camden County, NJ. Surrogate's Office. Inventory of: Maria Glover, E-513. Benjamin Lippincott, J-277.

Joseph Lippincott, K-12. Robert Roe, C-75. Benjamin D. Cooper, G-303. Charles L. Willits, G-404. James H. Redman, L-43.

Camden County, NJ. Surrogate's Office. Will of: Joseph Lippincott, Q-86. Robert Roe, C-107. Charles L. Willits, I-84.

New Jersey. *Acts of the One Hundred and Twenty-Eighth Legislature of the State of New Jersey.* A act to incorporate the borough of Haddon Heights. (p. 29, 30). Trenton, NJ: MacCrellish and Quigley. 1904.

New Jersey. *Acts of the One Hundred and Seventy-First Legislature of the State of New Jersey.* A act to relocate, fix and establish the boundary line between the borough of Haddonfield and the borough of Haddon Heights. (p. 1100-1103). Trenton, NJ: MacCrellish and Quigley. 1947.

New Jersey. *Acts of the One Hundred and Seventy-Fifth Legislature of the State of New Jersey.* A act to relocate, fix and establish the boundary line between the borough of Haddonfield and the borough of Haddon Heights. (p. 705-707). Trenton, NJ: MacCrellish and Quigley. 1951.

Printed Sources

Borough of Haddon Heights. *An Historic Guide Through Haddon Heights.* Haddon Heights, NJ. 1992.

Biographical Review Vol. XIX Camden and Burlington Counties, New Jersey. Boston Biographical Review Publishing Company. 1897.

Boyer, Charles S. *Old Mills of Camden County.* Camden, NJ: Camden County Historical Society. 1962.

Haddon Heights Historical Society. *Haddon Heights Remembered.* Haddon Heights, NJ. 1990.

Heston, Alfred M., Ed. *South Jersey–A History 1664-1924.* NY: Lewis Historical Publishing Company, Inc. 1924.

Weiss, Harry B. and Ziegler, Grace M. *The Early Fulling Mills of New Jersey.* Trenton, NJ: New Jersey Agricultural Society. 1957.

Zimiles, Martha and Murray. *Early American Mills.* New York: Clarkson N. Potter, Inc. 1973.

17 Haddon Township

Manuscripts

Camden, NJ. Camden County Historical Society. Survey of Stoy Plantation, John Clement, 1813. (M83.90.268). Survey for Heirs of James Stoy, Jacob Rowand, 1861. (M83.90.260). Survey of John Logan's land, 1874, Building Contract, E. Logan, 1871. Survey of Nicholson Road 1866 by John Clement.

Collingswood, NJ. Collingswood Library. Deed of George Lee and Samuel Congers 1848. Samuel French Account Ledger.

Haddonfield, NJ. The Historical Society of Haddonfield. Henry Cuthbert Account Book. Map of Joseph M. Hinchman's land, Samuel Nicholson. Hinchman Papers. Stoy Papers. Unidentified newspaper, obituary of Samuel Reeves. 1886.

New Brunswick, NJ. Rutgers University, Alexander Library. Joseph O. Cuthbert Farm Journal 1840 to 1873.

Philadelphia, PA. Historical Society of Pennsylvania. John Clement Papers: Survey of James Dobb's Farm. (No. 29). 1868/1874. The Franklin Fire Insurance Company of Philadelphia: Survey 8484, William Bettle, Jr. Survey 1127, William Hacker.

Riverton, NJ. Paul W. Schopp Collection. Survey of proposed Railroad by Right-of-Way by H.C. Smith. August, 1883.

Woodbury, NJ. Gloucester County Historical Society. Survey of John A. Cook's farm, J. Rowand, (B-66), 1858. James Dobbs Petition to Inferior Court of Common Pleas, 1840.

Interviews

Fox, Edward. Interviewed by the author. Collingswood, NJ. October 1991.

Masters, Rita. Interviewed by the author. Haddon Township, NJ. March 1997.

Miller, Marie. Interviewed by the author. Haddon Township, NJ. January 1991.

Government Documents

Camden County, NJ. Clerk's Office. Deed Books: 60-698. 123-309. 37-381. 57-401. 47-187. 78-555. 81-36. 110-167. 71-225. 108-168. James and Kit Smiley, Miscellaneous Records Book #1, (p. 124-126). Samuel M. Hinchman, N-486, 42-102, 60-19, 21, 154-419. Daniel Middleton, 96-23, 96-537. Dayton Duval, J-257. John Morris, U-284. Paul Sand, 38-486, 71-187. Thomas Albertson, Q-359, T-576, 28-43, 96-630. David Albertson, Q-359, 28-43. John Macauley, 72-504. Anthony Heck, 76-84, 56-496. Thomas W. Wilkinson, 85-144. Aaron Stoy, 37-381. Joseph Cuthbert, 60-698. Isaac Prine, 71-225, 108-168. James Flinn, 78-555, 81-36, 110-167. Thomas Albertson, 57-401, 96-630. John Hobensack, 57-401, 47-187. Samuel H. French, 57-401.

Camden County, NJ. Surrogate's Office. Inventory of: David Albertson, H-51. Clayton Brown, C-457. Joseph O. Cuthbert, H-458. James Dobbs, E-165. Jacob Fowler, I-471. Samuel M. Hinchman, C-314. Joseph M. Hinchman, D-162. Susan Hampton, C-539. Isaac Hinchman, M-422. Briggs Kay, L-116. Daniel Middleton, A-159. Samuel M. Reeve, H-307. Samuel A. Reeve, L-359. Aaron Stoy, K-92. James Stoy, I-490. Edwin Willis, O-263. Hannah Webster, D-413. Rebecca Ann Collings, H-400. Isaac Prine, N-33, E-91. Joseph Sheppard, E-491.

Camden County, NJ. Surrogate's Office. Will of: William Bettle, Jr., BB-378. David Albertson, I-374. Clayton Brown, D-12. Joseph O. Cuthbert, K-213. James Dobbs, E-480. Jacob Fowler, M-233. Isaac Hinchman, AA-181. Briggs Kay, L-15. Joseph Osler, C-332. Samuel M. Reeve, J-262. Samuel A. Reeve, V-117. Joseph Schnitzius, K-318. Edwin Willis, FF-33. Hannah Webster, E-182. Samuel H. Webster, JJ-14. John M. Whitall, F-439. Rebecca Ann Collings, J-351. Paul Sands, Z-91. Joseph Sheppard, F-206. Joshua Saddler, G-261.

New Jersey. *State of New Jersey Legislative Manual.* 1898 and 1903 consulted. Trenton, NJ: T.F. Fitzgerald Legislative Reports.

New Jersey. *Acts of the One Hundred and Twenty-Eighth Legislature of the State of New Jersey.* A act to annex a portion of the township of Haddon to the Borough of Haddonfield. (p. 55-57). Trenton, NJ: MacCrellish and Quigley. 1904.

New Jersey. *Acts of the One Hundred and Forth-Eighth Legislature of the State of New Jersey.* A act to annex the township of Haddon, a portion of Collingswood. (p. 376-377). Trenton, NJ: MacCrellish and Quigley. 1924.

New Jersey. *Acts of the One Hundred and Fifty-First Legislature of the State of New Jersey.* A act to annex a portion of township of Haddon, to the city of Gloucester. (p. 463-468). Trenton, NJ: MacCrellish and Quigley. 1927.

New Jersey. *Acts of the One Hundred and Sixty-Fifth Legislature of the State of New Jersey.* A act to annex the borough of Haddonfield, a part of township of Haddon. (p. 921-922). Trenton, NJ: MacCrellish and Quigley. 1941.

New Jersey. *Additional Acts of the One Hundred and Seventy-Sixth Legislature of the State of New Jersey. Vol. 2.* An act to relocate, fix and establish the boundary line between Collingswood and the township of Haddon. (p. 1399-1403). Trenton, NJ: MacCrellish and Quigley. 1953.

Printed Sources

American Historical Catalog Collection. *Whitall, Tatem and Company 1880.* Princeton, NJ: The Pyne Press. 1971.

Biographical Review Vol. XIX Camden and Burlington Counties, New Jersey. Boston Biographical Review Publishing Company. 1897.

Boyer, Charles S. *Old Mills of Camden County.* Camden, NJ: Camden County Historical Society. 1962.

Philadelphia City Directory for 1887. Philadelphia, PA: Gopsill's Sons, Publishers. 1887.

Philadelphia Maritime Museum. *Newsletter of the Philadelphia Maritime Museum–Winter 1984-1985.* Philadelphia. PA.

Ries, Heinrich and Kummel, Henry B. *The Clays and Clay Industry of New Jersey Vol. VI.* Trenton, NJ: MacCrellish and Quigley. 1904.

[Smith, Hannah Whitall]. *John M. Whitall, the story of his life.* Philadelphia, PA: NP. 1879.

The Starr Centre. *History of a Street.* Philadelphia PA: The Starr Centre. January 1901.

Vermeule, C.C. *Geological Survey of New Jersey. Report on Water-Supply Vol. III.* The Final Report of the State Geologist. Trenton, NJ: The John L. Murphy Publishing Company. 1894.

Von Rosensteil, Helene. *American Rugs and Carpet.* New York: William Morrow and Company. 1978.

Whitall, Tatem & Company, Glassware Collection, 1880. Private collection.

White, William Ed. *Walt Whitman Daybooks and Notebooks 1876 to 1891.* New York: New York University Press. 1978.

Newspapers

Camden (NJ) Courier-Post. January 27, 1953. November 28, 1962.

Haddonfield, Collingswood, Westmont (NJ) Tri-City Sun. June 11, 1925.

Newark (NJ) Star Ledger Henry Beck. April 16, 1950.

18 Oaklyn

Manuscripts

Camden, NJ. Camden County Historical Society. Unidentified newspaper clipping, Oaklyn vertical file.

Philadelphia, PA. Historical Society of Pennsylvania. The Franklin Fire Insurance Company of Philadelphia. Survey 8484, Edward Bettle.

LaPorte, IN. LaPorte County Historical Society. Unidentified newspaper. Jeremiah Ridgway obituary, January 10, 1921.

Interviews

Fox, Edward. Interviewed by the author. Collingswood, NJ. October 1991.

Government Documents

Camden County, NJ. Clerk's Office. Deed Books: Jeremiah Ridgway, U-600, 138-71, 495-2.

Camden County, NJ. Surrogate's Office. Inventory of: Joseph Hollingshead, JJ-142.

Camden County, NJ. Surrogate's Office. Will of: Edward Bettle, Q-322. Joseph Hollingshead, Q-62.

New Jersey. *Manual of the Legislature–Ninety-Sixth Legislative Session–State of New Jersey.* Compiled by F.L. Lundy. Newark, NJ: Martin R. Dennis and Company. 1872.

New Jersey. *Acts of the One Hundred and Twenty-Ninth Legislature of the State of New Jersey.* A act to incorporate the borough of Oaklyn. (p. 45-47). Paterson, NJ: News Printing Company. 1905.

Printed Sources

Boyer, Charles S. *Rambles Through Old Highways and Byways of West Jersey.* Camden, NJ: Camden County Historical Society. 1967.

Brick, Gertrude N. and Ridgway, Thurman. *Ridgways U.S.A.* Baltimore, MD: Gateway Press, Inc. 1980.

Mackey, Philip English, Ed. *A Gentleman of Much Promise: The Diary of Isaac Mickle 1837-1845.* Philadelphia, PA.: University of Pennsylvania Press. 1977.

Nicholson, William H. *My Ancestors.* Philadelphia, PA: Austin C. Leeds. 1897.

Heston, Alfred M., Ed. *South Jersey–A History 1664-1924.* New York: Lewis Historical Publishing Company, Inc. 1924.

Newspapers

Indianapolis News. February 21, 1885.

19 Woodlynne

Government Documents

Camden, County, NJ. Surrogate's Office. Deed Books: Inventory of: Charles M. Cooper, M-215. Joseph B. Cooper, C-48. John Kaighn, D-196.

Camden, County, NJ. Surrogate's Office. Will of: Charles M. Cooper, Y-157. Joseph B. Cooper, C-84. John Kaighn, D-395.

New Jersey. *State of New Jersey Legislative Manual* (1898 and 1903). Trenton, NJ: T.F. Fitzgerald Legislative Reports.

New Jersey. *Acts of the One Hundred and Twenty-Fifth Legislature of the State of New Jersey.* A act to incorporate the borough of Wood-Lynne. (p. 93-94). Trenton, NJ: MacCrellish and Quigley. 1901.

Printed Sources

Boyer, Charles S. *Rambles Through Old Highways and Byways of West Jersey.* Camden, NJ: Camden County Historical Society. 1967.

50 Years–The Borough of Woodlynne. Golden Jubilee Program. Woodlynne, NJ. 1951.

20 The Suburbs

Printed Sources

Danbon, David B. *Born in the Country–A History of Rural America.* Baltimore, MD: The Johns Hopkins University Press. 1995.

Fishman, Robert. *Bourgeois Utopias–The Rise and Fall of Suburbia.* New York, NY: Basic Books, Inc., Publishers. 1987.

Jackson, Kenneth T. *Crabgrass Frontier–The Suburbanization of the United States.* New York, NY: Oxford University Press. 1985.

Marsh, Margaret. *Suburban Lives.* New Brunswick, NJ: Rutgers University Press. 1990.

Index

D

E

F

G

H

I

N

S

Y

Z